readings
for reflective
teaching

in schools

2nd edition

Available and forthcoming titles in the *Reflective Teaching* series

Series Editors: Andrew Pollard and Amy Pollard

Reflective Teaching in Schools (4th edition), Andrew Pollard et al.

Reflective Teaching in Further and Adult Education (3rd edition), Yvonne Hillier

Forthcoming titles

Reflective Teaching in Early Education, Jennifer Colwell et al.

Readings for Reflective Teaching in Early Education, edited by Jennifer Colwell and Andrew Pollard

Reflective Teaching in Higher Education, Paul Ashwin et al.

Reflective Teaching in Further, Adult and Vocational Education, Margaret Gregson, Yvonne Hillier et al.

readings for reflective teaching

in schools

2nd edition

Edited by Andrew Pollard

Bloomsbury Academic
An imprint of Bloomsbury Publishing Plc

BLOOMSBURY
LONDON · OXFORD · NEW YORK · NEW DELHI · SYDNEY

Bloomsbury Academic
An imprint of Bloomsbury Publishing Plc

50 Bedford Square
London
WC1B 3DP
UK

1385 Broadway
New York
NY 10018
USA

www.bloomsbury.com

BLOOMSBURY and the Diana logo are trademarks of Bloomsbury Publishing Plc

First published 2014
Reprinted by Bloomsbury Academic 2015 (twice)

British Library Cataloguing-in-Publication Data
A catalogue record for this book is available from the British Library.

ISBN: HB: 978-1-4725-0656-6
PB: 978-1-4725-0974-1
ePDF: 978-1-4725-1252-9
ePUB: 978-1-4725-0911-6

Library of Congress Cataloging-in-Publication Data
A catalog record for this book is available from the Library of Congress.

Series: Reflective Teaching

Typeset by Fakenham Prepress Solutions, Fakenham, Norfolk NR21 8NN
Printed and bound in Great Britain

Contents

Part two Creating conditions for learning

Part three Teaching for learning

Part five Deepening understanding

Acknowledgements

The most important issue which editors face is, 'What should be included?'. I have worried away at this for several years, and imposed on a large number of people in exploring possible selections for various chapters.

I've had a great deal of advice from colleagues in Scotland, Wales, Northern Ireland and England who participated in consultation meetings or completed a questionnaire on the content of this volume. I learned too from an all-Ireland teacher education (SCOTENS) event. Additionally, particular thanks go to the Editorial Board for the *Reflective Teaching for Schools* textbook, who offered advice on many selections. They are: Kristine Black-Hawkins, Gabrielle Cliff Hodges, Pete Dudley, Mary James, Holly Linklater, Sue Swaffield, Mandy Swann, Fay Turner, Paul Warwick, Mark Winterbottom and Mary Anne Wolpert (all Cambridge). Editors of other textbooks in the Reflective Teaching series also commented helpfully on the selection – Paul Ashwin (Lancaster), Jen Colwell (Brighton), Yvonne Hillier (Brighton) and Maggie Gregson (Sunderland).

My thanks go also to former colleagues in three Yorkshire schools and at Oxford Polytechnic, University of the West of England, University of Bristol, University of Cambridge and at the Institute of Education, University of London, who have significantly influenced my understanding of teaching and learning over the years. They too may find that echoes in this book.

The administrative complexity of preparing the manuscript and obtaining permissions has been very considerable. This was helped along by Becky Plant and Chris Ellingham. I am also extremely grateful to Frances Arnold, Ally Baker, Kasia Figiel, Rosie Pattinson and their colleagues at Bloomsbury for their contributions and advice on many occasions.

We would of course like to thank all the publishers, editors and other publishers' representatives, both in the UK and overseas, who were kind enough to grant permission for material to be reprinted. Some provided exceptional levels of support in respect of multiple readings and in this respect we acknowledge the generosity of IOE Press, Routledge, SAGE and Bloomsbury. A listing of permissions for the reproduction of extracts is formally provided at the end of the book. Attempts to trace permission holders have been sustained, though a very few cases remain where replies to our enquiries have not yet been received. Any enquiries on such matters should be sent, in the first instance, to the Permissions Manager at Bloomsbury Academic.

Finally, we would like to thank all the authors whose work features in this book – and apologise to the many other researchers and educationists whose high quality material does not! Some, of course, may be delighted to have escaped, for word-length constraints have occasionally forced detailed editing. I offer sincere apologies if any authors feel that their work has suffered in that process.

Having reviewed a wide range of publications for possible inclusion in this book, we remain enormously impressed by the richness of research and thinking which is available to teachers, mentors and trainee teachers. The collection can be seen as a representation of the work of several generations of educational researchers – though, even with so many readings, it has not been possible to include all the excellent material which is available. In a sense though, the book remains a collective product and I would like to pay tribute to the many academic colleagues and educationalists who remain obsessed enough to keep on trying to describe, analyse and understand education in so many diverse ways.

Andrew Pollard
June 2013

A note on citation

If wishing to quote from a reading within this book in coursework or for a publication, you will need to cite your source. Using the Harvard Convention and drawing only on this text, you should provide a bibliography containing details of the *original* source. These are provided in the introduction to each reading. You should then put: 'Cited in Pollard, A. (ed.) (2014) *Readings for Reflective Teaching in Schools.* London: Bloomsbury.

If you are building a substantial case around any reading, you are strongly recommended to go back to the original source and to check your argument against the full text. Sources will be available through the libraries of most colleges and universities with teacher education provision, and many are accessible online. If using hardcopy, you should then cite the full text only, with the specific page numbers of any material that you quote. If using an on-line resource, you should cite page numbers as appropriate and the date on which the site was accessed.

Preface

This book is part of a set of professional resources. It links directly to a textbook, *Reflective Teaching in Schools*, and to a website, *reflectiveteaching.co.uk*. They are part of a series with explicit provision for early years, schools, further, adult and higher education.

For primary and secondary schools, we offer three fully integrated and complementary sources of materials:

- *Reflective Teaching in Schools* (4th edition) (the core book for school-based professional development)
- *Readings for Reflective Teaching in Schools* (2nd edition) (a portable library with 112 readings linked to the core book)
- *reflectiveteaching.co.uk* (a website for supplementary material, updated 'Notes for Further Reading', 'Reflective Activities', links, downloads, etc.)

Reflective Teaching in Schools considers a very wide range of professionally relevant topics, presents key issues and research insights, suggests 'Reflective Activities' for classroom work, and offers notes for selected 'Key Readings'. The text is used to support professional development by many schools, universities and training consortia, and has become a central textbook supporting school-based practice for initial teacher education courses across the UK and beyond. Secondary and primary specialists from the University of Cambridge have developed the 2014 version to support, in particular, teacher education in England, Wales, Scotland, Northern Ireland and the Republic of Ireland.

Readings for Reflective Teaching in Schools, the present book, has been extensively updated since earlier versions. Whilst some classic papers remain, most of the 112 readings are new. Material from important recent research has been added, drawing internationally as well as reflecting the unique character of the countries of the UK and Ireland. The balance of the book has been adjusted to reflect current issues and concerns in education – and to support a wide range of school–university partnership arrangements.

reflectiveteaching.co.uk is a website supplementing the two books. For example, there are materials on mentoring which will be particularly helpful for school-based teacher education, and also on how to design and carry out teacher research and classroom enquiry as part of professional development. The web enables the Editorial Board to update material regularly. This is particularly relevant for 'Notes for Further Reading', a more extensive and current source of suggestions than is possible in a printed book. There is also a compendium of terms and additional 'Reflective Activities', download facilities for diagrams and supplementary resources of various kinds. The section on 'Deepening Expertise' offers access to more advanced features, including a framework linking research evidence to powerful concepts for the analysis of classroom practice.

Three major aims have guided the production of *Readings for Reflective Teaching in Schools*.

First, it is intended as a resource for busy teachers, mentors and trainee teachers in primary and secondary education who appreciate the value of educational thinking and research, and who wish to have easy access to key parts of important publications. There are illustrative readings from the UK and Ireland, but the issues are of relevance anywhere.

Second, the book provides an opportunity to 'showcase' some of the excellent educational research from across the world which, in recent years, has been accumulating clear messages about high quality teaching and learning. Readers may then wish to consult the full accounts in the original sources, each of which is carefully referenced.

Finally, these materials provide a unique resource for professional development activities and for initial teacher education courses. The structure of the three sources is identical, so that the chapters map across from one book to the other and to the web. Thus, whether used in classroom activities, private study, mentoring conversations, workshops, staff meetings, seminars or research projects, the materials should be easily accessible.

Reflective activity is of vital importance to the teaching profession:

- It underpins professional judgement and its use for worthwhile educational purposes;
- It provides a vehicle for learning and professional renewal – and thus for promoting the independence and integrity of teachers;
- Above all, it is a means to the improvement of teaching, the enhancement of learning and the steady growth in standards of performance for both schools and national education systems.

We hope that you will find these materials helpful in your professional work and as you seek personal fulfilment as a teacher.

Andrew Pollard
Bristol, Cambridge, London, June 2013

part one

Becoming a reflective professional

Identity

Who are we and what do we stand for?

1

The readings in this chapter assert the significance of values, perspectives and identities of both teachers and pupils. We see how social expectations and contemporary change impacts on these roles, but also how they are enacted in deeply personal ways. For both 'teacher' and 'pupil', we thus need to understand each person and the roles which they enact.

On ourselves as teachers, Gu (1.1) reviews some contemporary studies of teacher careers and the ways in which professional commitment is sustained. Swann et al. (1.4), together with Jones (1.5), challenge us to consider the basic assumptions which we make about children and young people as learners – a theme which recurs through the book.

On pupils, Pollard and Filer (1.2) suggest how children and young people exercise their agency and develop 'learner identities' as a product of their experiences in school, playground, home and online. Rudduck and Flutter (1.3) build on this with more detailed consideration of the benefits of consulting pupils and engaging them fully in classroom life.

The final reading, from Feinstein et al. (1.6) paints a 'big picture' of how circumstances shape experience and of the 'wider benefits' of learning for later life.

The parallel chapter of *Reflective Teaching in Schools* is structured in a similar way. 'Knowing ourselves as teachers' suggests ways of thinking about personal values and the ways in which they influence teaching. The second part is on 'knowing children as pupils'. This reviews the educational literature on pupil cultures and offers activities for investigating student perspectives and experiences of schooling. The chapter concludes with suggestions for 'Key Readings'.

reflectiveteaching.co.uk offers 'Notes for Further Reading' on these issues, as well as additional 'Reflective Activities', resources and suggestions for 'Deepening Expertise'.

Reading 1.1

Being a teacher in times of change
Qing Gu

How do people become effective teachers?

Qing Gu outlines some of the challenges facing teachers in contemporary societies. In particular she points out the way in which teachers are positioned as mediators between society's past, present and future – as realised in a very wide range of expectations. And yet teachers are simply people who occupy a particular role on behalf of society.

To meet these challenges, teachers need a robust sense of personal identity and a commitment to professional development and reflective practice – and these must be sustained throughout their career. And even so, it is often the case that a strong sense of moral purpose generates personal and emotional challenges. (For further insights into these issues and to teacher career, see Day et al., 2007).

How confident do you feel as a person in the role of a teacher?

Edited from: Gu, Q. (2007) *Teacher Development: Knowledge and Context*. London: Continuum, 7–12.

Current changes in the global and local context pose profound implications for the teaching profession:

> An education system needs to serve the needs of society. When that society is undergoing profound and accelerating change, then particular pressures emerge for improvement in the alignment between the education system and these changing societal needs. The teaching profession is a key mediating agency for society as it endeavours to cope with social change and upheaval. *(Coolahan, 2002: 9)*

Teachers thus play a mediating role in bridging the past, the present and the future, the traditions and the innovations, the old and the new. Hargreaves (2003: 15) describes teachers as catalysts of successful knowledge societies who 'must be able to build special knowledge of professionalism'. This new professionalism means that teachers may not have the autonomy to teach in the way they wished, that they have to learn to teach in way they were not taught, and that they need to build and develop a capacity for change and risk (Hargreaves, 2003; see also Robertson, 1996, 1997).

Teachers' knowledge, values and beliefs are subjected to constant re-examination and testing by the process of change in modern society.

For these reasons, continuing professional learning and development has become a necessary condition for teachers to sustain commitment and maintain effectiveness. OECD (2005: 14) calls to transform teaching into a knowledge-rich profession:

> Research on the characteristic of effective professional development indicates that

teachers need to be active agents in analysing their own practice in the light of professional standards and their own students' progress in the light of standards for student learning.

Teachers' professional identities – the way teachers perceive themselves as professionals in the classroom, the school, the community and the society – are undergoing profound change. In between the tensions embedded in the context where teachers work and live are their struggles to negotiate their understanding of what it means to be a teacher and their endeavours to 'integrate his various statuses and roles, as well as his diverse experiences, into a coherent image of self' (Epstein, 1978: 101). Castells (2004: 6–7) defines identity as people's source of meaning and experience. He distinguishes identities from roles:

> Roles ... are defined by norms structured by the institutions and organizations of society. Their relative weight influencing people's behaviour depends upon negotiations and arrangements between individuals and these institutions and organizations. Identities are sources of meaning for the actors themselves, and by themselves, constructed through a process of individuation ... In simple terms, identities organize the meaning, while roles organize the functions. I define *meaning* as the symbolic identification by a social actor of the purpose of her/his action. I also propose the idea that, *in the network society*, ... for most social actors, meaning is organized around a primary identity (that is an identity that frames the others), which is self-sustaining across time and space.

However, teachers' roles are an indispensable part of their professional identities. Teachers play a variety of roles within the classroom: an authority, facilitator, parent, friend, judge and counsellor. Their strong sense of moral purpose and the immense satisfaction derives from the academic and personal progress of their students and makes a major contribution to the teacher's professional outlook. Outside the classroom, a teacher may also have additional managerial responsibilities. These managerial roles often give teachers a broader view of the education system, and help to promote the quality of their teaching in the classroom. In their national study of 300 teachers, Day et al. (2006, 2007) found that teachers' identity is a composite construct consisting of interactions between personal, professional and situated factors. Teachers' personal lives influence, positively or negatively, the construction of teachers' professional identities. For example, a teaching family background, being a parent, and taking on active roles in the local community may all affect how teachers view the part they play in the classroom; marriage breakdown, ill health and increased family commitments can, on the other hand, become sources of tensions 'as the individual's sense of identity could become out of step' (Day et al., 2006: 149).

In contrast to many other professions, teaching is emotionally attached and value-laden. Teachers' intense feelings in the job are not 'merely intrapersonal, psychological phenomena' (Kelchtermans, 2005: 996):

> Emotions are understood as experiences that result from teachers' embeddedness in and interactions with their professional environment. They are treated as meaningful experiences, revealing teachers' sense making and showing what is *at stake* for them ...

In other words, a teacher's emotions are contextually embedded and highly rationalised with their values, beliefs and philosophies of education. They are inextricably bound up with their *moral purposes* and their ability to achieve those purposes (Hargreaves 1998). Hargreaves reminds us that for teachers, students are an 'emotional filter'. The OECD's Ro study on attracting and retaining effective teachers also suggests that seeing children achieve remains a major, intrinsic source of teachers' job satisfaction and fulfilment. Roles for teachers are not merely associated with functions, duties and responsibilities. They are filled with positive emotions:

> Good teaching is charged with positive emotion. It is not just a matter of knowing one's subject, being efficient, having the correct competences, or learning all the right techniques. Good teachers are not just well-oiled machines. They are emotional, passionate beings who connect with their students and fill their work and their classes with pleasure, creativity, challenges and joy. *(Hargreaves 1998: 835)*

For many teachers their jobs consist of far more than fulfilling routine requirements that are externally imposed upon them. Numerous studies suggest that this is also the case for the millions of teachers working in all the corners of the world. The sense of calling urges them to take actions in seeking ways of improving their teaching practice and service for the students, sustaining their sense of efficacy, promoting their sense of agency, commitment and resilience, and ultimately their effectiveness. Teachers have to play a range of roles to fulfil their commitment and internal calling to serve in education, such as a facilitator, an encourager, a parent, an authority and a friend. All of these roles contribute to the formation of teachers' identities and any change in context leads to further change in these professional and personal identities.

Reading 1.2

Being a learner through years of schooling
Andrew Pollard and Ann Filer

This reading focuses attention on the ways in which, as children and young people grow up, they make their way through a succession of new situations and experiences. Whilst adults may hope to provide security and opportunity within the social settings which are created in homes, schools, playgrounds and online, such contexts also often contain challenges and threats which young children have to negotiate. As children develop, perfect or struggle with their strategies for coping with such situations, so they learn about other people, about themselves and about life.

Thinking about some children you know, how do social factors, such as family life, friendships and relationships with teachers, appear to influence the fulfilment of their learning potential?

Adapted from: Pollard, A. (1996) *The Social World of Children's Learning*. London: Cassell. 8–14, and Pollard, A. (2003) 'Learning through life', in Watson, D. and Slowey, M. *Higher Education and the Lifecourse*. London: Continuum, 167–85.

Six key questions can help us develop an understanding of the social influences on children's learning. The questions are theoretically informed and their apparent simplicity is deceptive for they have many extensions and nuances. Beware then, for they may become a source of endless fascination!

1   *Where and when is learning taking place?* invites consideration of home, school, on-line and informal learning settings in relation to wider political and socio-economic contexts.

2   *Who is learning?* draws attention to children and young people as individuals, to the parents, teachers, peers and siblings who variously influence them, and to the approaches to learning which are characteristically adopted.

3   *What is to be learned?* calls for a consideration of the content of the learning challenges that children and young people face.

4   *How supportive are the learning contexts?* suggests a focus on processes of interaction, on the expectations, constraints and opportunities within specific settings.

5   *What are the outcomes?* then prompts a review of the story and outcomes of each child's story in terms of learning achievements, social status, identity and self-esteem.

6   *Why?* requires reflection on patterns in learning outcomes and trajectories, and on explanations for those patterns. When we stand back, what can we see and understand?

Of course, such questions interlock with and interpolate each other so that an attempt to answer one will immediately make it necessary to pose others. Such spirals of questioning lead, hopefully, to cumulative understanding.

The questions thus constitute a kind of 'tool-kit' for enquiry.

Where and when is learning taking place?

We can identify two ways in which the question, 'where?', is important. First, there is the issue of context at the levels of community, region and country. This has significance because of the social, cultural, political and economic circumstances within which the lives of people are played out.

At a more detailed level, we need to understand the contexts in which children interact with others – the home, the school, on-line and in more informal social settings such as the playground. Each of these settings has specific characteristics with socially constructed rules and expectations guiding behaviour within them. Those of the classroom tend to be more constraining than those, for instance, of the home or playground, but each is important in structuring children's experiences.

The timing and sequencing of events is another aspect of social context. Again there is the historical relationship to developments elsewhere within community, region and country. Teachers, parents and children live *through* particular periods of social and economic development, and experience them sequentially. The era through which childhood occurs thus contributes to biography and identity.

It is also appropriate to consider the development and progress of children and young people year by year, as they pass through the care of successive teachers. There may be patterns which will help in understanding the strengths and weaknesses of the learner.

'Who' is learning?

We must also consider the children and young people directly and, in particular, their 'identity' as learners. How do they see themselves as they strive to fulfil their individual potential within the social contexts in which they live?

To understand influences on identity, we must pay particular attention to the 'significant others' in each child's life – to those who interact with them and influence the ways in which they see themselves. Thus we need to consider the role of parents or carers, siblings, peers and teachers.

Every child also has both physical and intellectual potential which, during the school years, continue to develop. Whether it is through confidence in reading, understanding of early science, or the stirring of sexuality, this gradual realisation of physical and intellectual potential rolls forward to influence self-confidence.

Identity is also influenced by gender, social class and ethnicity, each of which is associated with particular cultural and material resources and with particular patterns of social expectation. Age, status and position, within the family, classroom and playground, are also important for the developing sense of identity of children and young people.

The *perspectives* of children about learning and the *ways in which they respond* to particular challenges will be closely linked to their sense of personal identity. Issues of interest and motivation are particularly important. For instance, children often view self-directed learning through play quite differently from work in response to a task which has been set at school. This brings us to issues of learning stance and strategies.

By *learning stance*, I refer to the characteristic approach which individuals adopt when confronted by a new learning challenge. Obviously a lot will depend on the content of the specific challenge and the context in which it is faced, but there are also likely to be patterns and tendencies in approach. How self-confident do particular children tend to be? Do they feel the need to assert personal control in a learning situation or will they conform to the wishes of others? How are they motivated towards new learning?

Whatever the initial stance of a learner, he or she must then deploy specific *strategies* in new learning situations. The range of strategies available to individual children will vary, with some being confident to make judgements and vary their approach to tasks, whilst others will need guidance and encouragement to move from tried and tested routines.

What is to be learned?

What are the major learning challenges which children and young people face?

At home, for instance, each child also has to develop a place within the family in relation to his or her siblings which, for some, can be stressful and competitive. And as they grow older, the struggle begins for independence and to be taken seriously as a young adult. There are everyday challenges too such as learning to tie laces, be polite to others, swim, ride a bike, go to school, and complete homework.

In the classroom, each child has first to learn a role as a pupil – for instance, to cope with classroom rules and conventions, to answer his or her name at registration, to sit cross-legged on the carpet and to listen to the teacher. Then, as pupils, children must respond to the curricular tasks which they are set. In primary schools, this is likely to include large amounts of work on English and mathematics, with the subjects becoming increasingly specialised through secondary education. Finally, the learning challenges are those of formal examinations.

Among peers and within the playground and other informal settings, considerable learning is involved in maintaining friendships and peer relationships. Reciprocity, a foundation for friendship, requires learning about the social and cultural expectations and needs of others, whether this is manifested in knowledge of the latest 'craze', the rules of games or how to manage falling 'in' and 'out' with friends. In due course, the challenges of adolescence are posed.

How supportive are the learning contexts?

The settings of home, playground or classroom condition the ways in which a child's learning stance and strategies are enacted. Social expectations and taken-for-granted rules influence behaviour.

There are many examples of this. For instance, in the context of many white English middle-class families, social expectations are perhaps at their most structured at set-meals, such as Sunday lunch. The same phenomenon occurs in playgrounds when children assert the overt and tacit rules of games. Of course, there are also many times when actions are far less constrained, when family or peer expectation takes a more relaxed form, allowing more scope for individual action.

The same is true for classroom life. The concept of 'rule frame' describes the nature of the rules-in-play in any particular situation or phase of a teaching session (Pollard, 1985). Such rules derive from the gradual negotiation of understandings about behaviour which routinely takes place between the teacher and pupils. Thus a teacher's introduction and conclusion of a lesson is usually more tightly framed and controlled than the mid-phase of a session in which pupils may engage in various tasks or activities. Similarly, within homes, there are contrasts such as the common tensions of breakfast before getting ready for school and the relative relaxation of chatting whilst going for a walk. Quite different rules and expectations about interaction frame such occasions and these condition the way in which each phase may enable learning.

Of course, the extent of negotiation varies in different settings. In general, adults have the power to initiate, assert, maintain and change rules, whilst children must comply, adapt, mediate or resist. Most teachers and most parents, for most of the time and in most settings, act sensitively towards children and young people. Sometimes this is not the case, there is less legitimacy and the children may well become unhappy or believe that they have been treated 'unfairly'. This will influence future learning. In a context in which the risks and costs of failure are high, only a child with an exceptionally confident learning stance is likely to take any chances. In some classrooms, children may thus 'keep their heads down' and the same may be true in some families or playground situations, perhaps where sibling or peer rivalry creates a risk to status or dignity.

In terms of learning processes, we thus need to consider the *opportunities and risks* which exist for each child to learn within different social settings – the context of power relations and social expectations within which he or she must act and adapt. Some situations may be low key and feel safe, in which the child can feel secure to 'give it a try'. In the case of others, the stakes may be higher and a child's self-esteem may be vulnerable to public critique from siblings, parents, peers or their teacher.

The question, 'how supportive is the specific learning context?', also suggests a focus on *the quality of the teaching and assistance* in which a child receives in different settings. Social constructivist psychology offers a clear analysis of the importance for learning of the guidance and instruction of more skilled or knowledgeable others. Whether support is provided by parents or teachers, siblings or peers, the principle is the same; that children's learning benefits from the 'scaffolding' of their understanding so that it can be extended across the next step in their development.

From this perspective, the *ways* in which adults or other children teach or assist a child's understanding are seen to be of paramount importance. There are affective as well as cognitive aspects of this for it is often necessary to provide a stable emotional framework as well as intellectual challenge. We thus find parents and teachers worrying that a child is 'upset and distracted' when he or she falls out with friends and we can appreciate the emphasis which is placed on children being 'happy and settled'. Although this is a necessary foundation for learning, it is unlikely to be enough without a consistent and well matched input of instruction and support for intellectual growth. This is likely to be found in discussions, questions, advice and other forms of constructive interaction with children which clarify, build on, extend or challenge their ideas. Thus we have the concern with the quality of the teaching and assistance in learning which is available to each child in the home, playground and, in particular, the classroom.

What are the outcomes?

The first and most obvious outcome concerns the *achievement* of intended learning goals. These may vary from school's official curricular aims and performance in tests and examinations, through to the challenges which are presented as part of peer group activities and the learning experiences which confront each child as he or she grows up within the family at home. Learning thus produces relatively overt yardsticks of attainment, whether focus is on letter formation in hand-writing, Mathematics for a GCSE, how to skip, or how to hold their own in family conversation. What has been achieved? What is the new level of attainment? What can the child now do and understand?

Such questions are of particular importance because of their consequences for the ways in which young learners perceive themselves and are perceived by others. The key concepts here are *self-esteem* and *social status*.

Self-esteem is likely to rise as achievements are made. Maturational 'achievements', such as having birthdays or just becoming taller, are often marked with particular pleasure by children as they see themselves 'growing up', but many more attainments are accomplished in the home, playground and classroom as children face new experiences and challenges. The school setting is, of course, particularly important because it is the source of official educational judgements, whilst the home setting offers the support, or otherwise, of parents or carers – the crucial 'significant others'.

Regarding social status, the prominence which is attributed to the child by others, it is arguably relationships within peer groups which are of most significance to children. For many, peer group membership is both a source of great enjoyment in play and a source of solidarity in facing the challenges which are presented by adults. In such circumstances, some children lead whilst others follow and high status may well be associated with popularity, style and achievement in facilitating 'good fun'. On the other hand, peer group cultures can also be exclusive and reject children from membership if they are unable to conform to group norms. Thus, if a child's learning and performance regarding peer expectations is deficient, their social status is likely to be low – with a potentially corrosive effect on their sense of self-esteem and of personal confidence.

Thus then, the process is brought full circle and we return to the first question, *'Who' is learning?*. How personally effective is this person?

Such cycles represent the process of learning in a social context, with the effects of social relationships and learning achievements accumulating over time to contribute to the formation of identity. In fact, the cycle could be represented as a spiral, with learners repeatedly experiencing challenge, support, outcomes and consequence as their personal identities and self-confidence as learners develops in the transition from childhood, through adolescence and towards adulthood.

This brings us to the sixth and final question.

Why do patterns recur about learning in different settings?

As we can see from the readings such as Feinstein et al. (Reading 1.7), there intergenerational patterns do exist in terms of educational outcomes. We know a great deal about learning and how to affect it, but it is not always possible to apply this knowledge. To understand these patterns is a necessary beginning.

These questions can be represented in a simple model, as in Figure 1.2.1.

Figure 1.2.1
Questions on social influences on children's learning

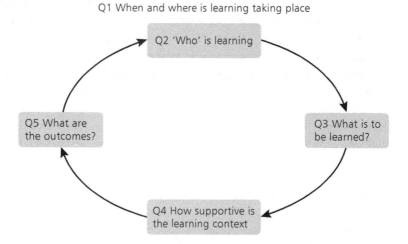

Q1 When and where is learning taking place

Q2 'Who' is learning

Q3 What is to be learned?

Q4 How supportive is the learning context

Q5 What are the outcomes?

The struggle to 'make sense' of our own and other people's lives is an intrinsic part of human behaviour. It is thus something which we all do all the time. For a deeper understanding, appropriately for a professional teacher, it is necessary to combine empathy with analysis. These questions are intended as a starting point.

Reading 1.3

How pupils want to learn
Jean Rudduck and Julia Flutter

> This reading focuses attention on the ways in which, as children and young people grow up, they make their way through a succession of new situations and experiences. Whilst adults may hope to provide security and opportunity within the social settings which are created in homes, schools, playgrounds and online, such contexts also often contain challenges and threats which young children have to negotiate. As children develop, perfect or struggle with their strategies for coping with such situations, so they learn about other people, about themselves and about life.
>
> Thinking about some children you know, how do social factors, such as family life, friendships and relationships with teachers, appear to influence the fulfilment of their learning potential?
>
> *Edited from:* Rudduck, J. and Flutter, J. (2004) How to Improve Your School: Giving Pupils a Voice. London: Continuum, 128–37.

Historically, the character of 'the pupil' has been largely shaped by the resources available in schools – in particular the need to manage quite large numbers of young people with few adults, as in the monitorial system of the nineteenth century. In Victorian times the kind of pupil that the school wanted was thus one who was ready to conform and 'apply' him or herself to the requirements of the school work.

But what kind of learner do we want today?

Rotter (1996) distinguishes between two forms of control, external and internal: people with an *internal locus of control* feel themselves able to determine what happens in their environment. Those with an *external locus of control* feel that the forces outside themselves are always determining what happens to them (see also Dweck, 1976, Reading 2.6).

An observation study based on Rotter's framework found that pupils who felt that they were determining events in their lives tended to be 'active and assertive and exhibit a high degree of exploratory behaviour and excitement about learning' (see Wang, 1983). Such students are more likely to manage either a positive pro-learning stance or sustain a strenuous anti-learning stance. In contrast, in the study that Wang summarizes, students who felt themselves objectified and merely 'acted on' tended to be relatively 'compliant and non-exploratory' and were often inattentive. These students would take their place in a sort of low-energy comfort zone. Pupils here are no trouble: they get on, they do what they are told, and for busy teachers concerned about the increased stress and strain of their professional lives, such qualities in their pupils can, in certain circumstances, seem attractive.

There are other dilemmas in the way we think about pupils today. One is the tension between the aspiration to have pupils in class *now* who are steady and biddable, and the aspiration to help pupils develop the kind of capabilities that will enable them to cope with the complex task of composing a life *beyond school*. As Aronowitz and Giroux said (1986: 9), the way forward is not to programme pupils 'in certain directions so that they will behave in set ways' but to help them towards a reasoned and responsible autonomy. The task for schools is to help young people exercise power over their own lives both in school and as an investment for the future.

Our experience of working with a variety of schools persuades us that opportunities for consultation and for enhanced participation in schools have a direct impact on pupils' engagement. We think it works in this way:

- If pupils feel that they matter in school and that they are respected, then they are more likely to commit themselves to the school's purposes.

- Pupils' accounts of what helps them to learn and what gets in the way of their learning can provide a practical agenda for improving teaching and learning.

- If teaching and the conditions of learning are experienced as congenial then pupils are more likely to commit themselves to learning and develop positive identities as learners.

The figure below is a diagrammatic presentation of our argument.

Figure 1.3.1
Transformation through pupil consultation

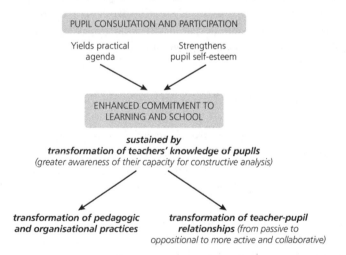

More opportunities for talking about learning can help pupils to understand their own learning and working habits so that they feel more in control of their learning – and this in turn seems to enhance their motivation and engagement. Where pupils are committed to schools and engaged in the learning tasks, then they are more likely to invest energy in managing their own learning well – and they will expect more exciting and productive experiences in lessons.

What conditions of learning do pupils want in schools?

Although we started with a discussion of different perspectives on the kind of pupil adults want in schools and in society, it is also important to ask what kind of pupil *pupils* want to be – and to consider how the conditions of learning in schools influence what pupils can be.

Interviews with pupils in primary and secondary schools confirm that pupils are interested in changing the regimes and relationships that cast them in a marginal role and that limit their agency. Pupils of all ages ask for more autonomy, they want school to be fair and they want pupils, as individuals and as an institutional group, to be regarded as important members of the school community. Policy makers may think about a school primarily in terms of lessons and formal learning but for young people school is a holistic experience: it is about lessons, it is about what happens between lessons, it is about relationships and it is about who and what is valued by the school.

The fragments of testimony that we gathered in interviews appear to be linked by a set of principles that we have constructed from the interview data. The principles operate within and through organizational structures and relationships and together define what we call 'the conditions of learning' (Rudduck et al., 1996). They give weight and colour to the broad institutional frameworks or regimes that define what a pupil is, that determine the regularities of learning, and that, crucially, exert a powerful influence on young people's sense of purpose in learning and their pattern of achievement. According to the degree that they are present for each student they serve to construct different patterns of commitment and confidence. In a context where some students are advantaged and some disadvantaged by social background factors, the conditions of learning are an important factor in equalizing opportunity.

The six principles are not in themselves novel; indeed, they are likely to feature in most schools' statement of aims. What we have done is to come at them from the pupils' perspective and to reassert their central importance. The first three directly affect the student's 'sense of self-as-learner':

- *the principle of respect for students* as individuals and as a body occupying a significant position in the institution of the school;
- *the principle of fairness* to all students irrespective of their class, gender, ethnicity or academic status;
- *the principle of autonomy* (not as an absolute state but as both a right and a responsibility in relation to physical and social maturity).

The next three principles are more about what happens in and out of the classroom and suggest the importance of balancing risk-taking in school work with confidence about one's self and one's image:

- *the principle of intellectual challenge* that helps students to experience learning as a dynamic, engaging and empowering activity;
- *the principle of support* in relation to both academic and emotional concerns;

- *the principle of security* in relation to the physical setting of the school, in social interactions (especially pupils' anxieties about being taunted or mocked) and in relation to intellectual tasks (so that pupils feel confident about learning from mistakes and misunderstandings).

Some aspects of organizational structures are a powerful force in creating different patterns of opportunity and advantage. It is important to understand:

- how material and human resources are allocated to different groups of pupils and tasks and what priorities are reflected;
- how pupils are divided and labelled;
- how well schools explain the rationale for particular rules, regimes or new procedures;
- how rewards and sanctions are handled and how and to whom expectations of high achievement are communicated.

By *relationships* we mean the interactions, within school, of teachers and pupils. Our interviews suggest that what we should be concerned about are the *messages* that such interactions communicate to pupils about themselves as learners. Certain kinds of interactions, or opportunities for interaction, are highlighted in the interviews as carrying strong positive tones – for instance:

- teachers being available to talk with pupils about learning and school work, not just about behaviour;
- teachers recognizing pupils' desire to take more responsibility as they grow older;
- teachers' readiness to engage with pupils in adult ways;
- teachers being sensitive to the tone and manner of their discourse with pupils, as individuals and in groups, so that they do not criticise them in ways that make them feel small (especially in front of their peers);
- teachers being seen to be fair in all their dealings with all pupils;
- teachers' acceptance, demonstrated in action, that an important aspect of fairness is not prejudging pupils on the basis of past incidents;
- teachers ensuring that they make *all* pupils feel confident that they can do well and can achieve something worthwhile.

We are talking here about the *social* conditions or learning but equally important are the *pedagogic* conditions of learning. What pupils say about the kind of teacher and teaching that can capture and sustain their interest in learning can be of great significance if we are prepared to listen!

We have explored factors which influence our conception of the kind of pupil we want in school and indicated how the conditions of learning in school can intervene to define, extend or limit that vision. We are reminded that as well as considering 'What kind of pupil do we want in school' we should also ask 'What kind of school do pupils want to be in?'

Reading 1.4

Learning without limits

Mandy Swann, Alison Peacock, Susan Hart and Mary Jane Drummond

For practising teachers, there is a crucial choice. Deeply embedded in our culture are views about the nature of 'abilities' and ideas about genetic inheritance, social class, ethnicity, gender, etc. Such taken-for-granted ideas emerge and have serious consequences in the form of restricted expectations of what children can achieve.

Swann and her colleagues throw down a gauntlet. Abilities can be developed, and learning has no limits if approached in appropriate ways. Every child has learning capacities. The task of the teacher is to unlock and nurture these capacities. It is also argued that building on learner capacities is the enlightened way to improve standards, but that some national requirements can, ironically, inhibit this.

So where do you stand?

Edited from: Swann, M., Peacock, A., Hart, S. and Drummond, M. J. (2012) *Creating Learning Without Limits*. Maidenhead: Open University Press, 1–7.

We began our research drawn together by some unshakeable convictions:

- that human potential is not predictable;
- that children's futures are unknowable;
- that education has the power to enhance the lives of all.

Few would argue with these simple truths, and yet they are at odds with the prevailing spirit of the age – a time in which teachers are required to use the certainty of prediction as a reliable tool in their planning and organization of opportunities for learning. Targets, levels, objectives, outcomes – all these ways of conceptualizing learning require teachers to behave as if children's potential is predictable and their futures knowable far in advance, as if their powers as educators can have only a limited impact on the lives of many children and young people. Furthermore, closely associated with this view of learning is an equally damaging view of the children who do the learning, who can themselves be known, measured and quantified in terms of so-called ability, a fixed, internal capacity, which can readily be determined.

This determinist thinking is not limited to those of any particular political persuasion. Nor is it an issue of transient significance. It is the legacy of a longstanding and ongoing, deep-rooted and damaging orthodoxy about the nature of 'ability' and how best to set about educating children. This legacy has given rise to limited and limiting thinking on the part of policy makers about children and about how to structure and organize learning and schooling.

Teachers need a much more complex understanding of learning and of the many inter-acting influences that underlie differences of attainment if they are to be able to use their powers as educators to transform children's life chances.

So, what if teachers were to jettison the linear model of learning? What if, instead of being constantly compared, ranked, and fettered by labels, children's learning capacity was enabled to flourish and expand in all its rich variety and complexity? What if planning for preordained and predicted levels was replaced with planning experiences and opportu-nities for learning that promote deep engagement, that fill children with a sense of agency, that endow them with motivation, courage and belief in their power to influence their own futures? And what if school development were to be driven by a commitment on the part of a whole-school community to creating better ways for everybody to live, work and learn together, in an environment free from limiting beliefs about fixed abilities and fixed futures?

In our book, *Creating Learning Without Limits,* we argue that school development inspired by this alternative vision is both necessary and possible. We present the findings of our research study of one primary school which, in just a few years, moved out of 'special measures' to become a successful, vibrant learning community (also rated 'outstanding' by Ofsted). This was not achieved through the use of targets, planning, prediction and exter-nally imposed blueprints for pedagogy, but through a focus on learning (rather than simply attainment) which was nourished by deep belief in the learning capacity of everybody.

The principles which informed developments in this school had their origins in previous work which had explored alternatives to ability-based pedagogy – the *Learning Without Limits* project (Hart et al., 2004). Nine teachers had worked with young people aged from 5 to 16 and drew on expertise across a range of curriculum areas. While their practices were distinctively individual, the research team found that they shared a particular mindset – a way of making sense of what happens in classrooms. This was based on an orientation to the future that came to be called 'transformability'. Rather than accepting apparent differences in ability as the natural order of things, and differentiating their teaching accordingly, these teachers did not see the future of their students as predictable or inevi-table. They worked on the assumption that there is always the potential for change: things can change for the better, sometimes even dramatically, as a result of what both teachers and learners do in the present.

For these teachers the concept of inherent ability, an inaccessible inner force respon-sible for learning, residing in the individual and subject to the fixed, internal limits of each individual learner, had no currency or value. In its place, the research team discerned a powerful alternative concept of *learning capacity*, which resides both in the individual learner and in the social collective of the classroom, and is by no means fixed and stable. This concept of learning capacity, evidenced in the various daily practices of these teachers, released the teachers from the sense of powerlessness induced by the idea of inherent ability. Furthermore, they realized that the work of transforming learning capacity does not depend on what teachers do alone, but on what both teachers *and* learners do together – a joint enterprise, the exercise of co-agency. Convinced of their own (and their students') power to make a difference to future learning, they used their rich fund of knowledge about the forces – internal and external, individual and collective – that shape and limit learning capacity to make transforming choices. Working on the principle that classroom decisions must be made in the interests of all students, not just some – a principle the research team called 'the ethic of everybody' – and rooting their work in the fundamental trust in their students' powers as learners, the project teachers made good their commitment to the essential educability of their learners.

The study amassed convincing evidence that teaching for learning without limits is not a naïve fantasy, but a real possibility, in good working order, accessible to observation and analysis. The research team developed a practical, principled pedagogical model (see Figure 1.4.1), arguing that elements of this model would be recognizable to other teachers who shared similar values and commitments and had themselves developed classroom

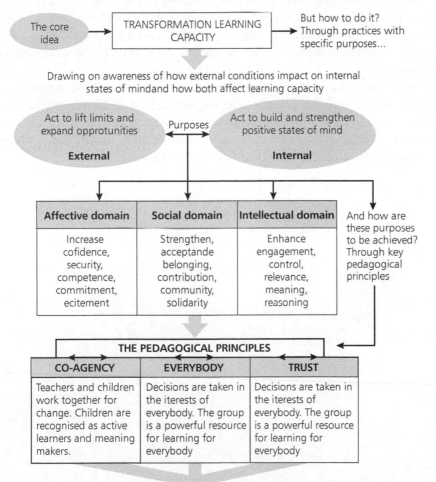

Figure 1.4.1
Creating learning without limits

practices in line with their convictions. They hoped that their work would convince more teachers that the alternative 'transformability' model is a practical and empowering way of realizing their commitment to young people's learning.

The nine teachers in the original study were all working in different schools and their work was inevitably limited to they were able to do individually, within their own class-rooms. The teachers thus recognized that there was so much more that could be done to lift limits on learning if groups of teachers, departments, whole-school staffs or even whole school communities were to work together towards a common vision.

When one of these teachers, Alison Peacock, took up a headship in a primary school, a wonderful opportunity presented itself to explore these wider possibilities. Alison was committed to leading staff in adopting teaching and learning practices devoted to strengthening and transforming children's learning capacity and free from all forms of ability labelling. A new research project was set up, *Creating Learning Without Limits*, to carry out a two-year in-depth study of the work of the staff of The Wroxham School, in Hertfordshire.

Our book thus tells the story of what we learned from this school community about how to create 'learning without limits'. Our enquiry focused on the learning that went on, individually and collectively, as the whole staff worked together, day by day, to create in reality their vision of an education based on inclusive, egalitarian principles, including an unshakeable bedrock belief in everybody's capacity to learn.

Reading 1.5

Assumptions about children and young people
Phil Jones

When we think of childhood and adolescence, do we foreground what children and young people can do, or what they can't? Do we see capability or deficiency? Do we respect their agency or impose controls? How are the issues and dilemmas resolved?

The stance taken by adults makes an enormous difference to the opportunities to learn which children and young people experience. It is reflected in the 'folk pedagogies' described by Bruner (Reading 11.1) and profoundly influences the development of children's attitudes to learning (see Dweck, Reading 2.6).

What are your preconceptions about children and young people?

Edited from: Jones, P. (2009) *Rethinking Childhood: Attitudes in Contemporary Society.* London: Continuum, p. 54–7.

A common way of seeing the period which we name as 'childhood' is that it is a time of maturation and growth, where needs for food and shelter cannot be fully met by the individual without support, and a time where cognitive and emotional development occurs.

The idea of competence in childhood has been defined from a number of different perspectives in relation to this time of maturation, need and development. France, for example, has argued that 'the young are seen as being in a "stage of deficit", where they lack morality, skills and responsibility' (2007, 152). The ideas have become associated with powerful adult definitions often associated with negative images of children. These perspectives are realised through language, attitudes and ways of behaving.

These perspectives regulate the ways in which adults see and treat children, and the ways children see themselves. They define adult-child relationships and the services provided by organizations surrounding the processes or growth, need and maturation of children. They can seem fixed, whereas in fact they are constructions largely made by adults.

One of the central ideas is that adults, often unconsciously, prepare children to be dependent. How do adults encourage children to see themselves in this way?

- Through creating laws that confine children.

- Through creating policies that confirm adults' attitudes that children need adults to make decisions for them.

- Through interacting with each other, and with children, in ways that do not allow children to express themselves or to participate in decision making.

- By using adulthood as a measure that is set as a norm against which other states, such as childhood, are seen as lacking, or in terms of being a deficit.
- By seeing and treating children as incapable and inadequate.

Such practices create a vicious circle for children. Adults have a framework within which children are raised and responded to. This framework sees and treats them as not capable. One of the effects of this is that children's own expectations and ways of seeing themselves are constructed within this incapability. In turn, the way they behave reflects this, which fulfils and confirms adult expectations. This can create situations that are unhelpful and harmful. Bluebond-Langner (1978), in her research with terminally ill children, found that children as young as three years of age were aware of their diagnosis and prognosis without ever having been informed by an adult.

If adult attitudes and the reality of children were congruent, then there would be no need or occasion for tension, challenge and change. However, the rise of different attitudes from children and young people, and from some adults who live and work with children, has created change. In the UK, for example, a series of decisions and counter-decisions regarding the notion of children's competence have occurred. One of the key arenas concerns health-related practices in areas such as medical, dental and surgical treatment. In the UK, from a legal challenge, the notion of the 'Gillick competent' child has arisen.

> Unlike 16- or 17-year-olds, children under 16 are not automatically presumed to be legally competent to make decisions about their healthcare. However, the courts have stated that under 16s will be competent to give valid consent to a particular intervention if they have 'sufficient understanding and intelligence to enable him or her to understand fully what is proposed'. In other words, there is no specific age when a child becomes competent to consent to treatment: it depends both on the child and on the seriousness and complexity of the treatment being proposed. *(Department of Health, 2001)*

These views of children affect different aspects of their lives. They connect to the way children are subordinated, and to the ways in which children relate to the world they live in.

Increasingly, such attitudes have been challenged. The critique points to constraining, traditional ways of perceiving children, and offers a new approach which is appreciative of children's competence. The contrast is illustrated in Figure 1.5.1 overleaf.

Figure 1.5.1
Traditional and
emerging positions

Traditional position	Emerging position
• Incapable • Not able to make valuable decisions • Incomplete adults • As a threat to themselves and others due to deficits in reasoning and experience	• Capable • Active decision-makers with opinions that matter • Seen in terms of own capacities • As able to contribute usefully

This emerging position is not without its challenges and difficulties. The issue of how competence and capability can be defined and seen is complex. The situations within which issues of capability arise also raises questions: Does a child have different competencies in relation to different spheres of their lives? How is competency to be involved in family decision making to be compared to making decisions needing to be made in medical or educational contexts? Questions arise out of the issue of differences regarding capability: How is the issue of age regarded? Are such questions irrelevant if you view the child from a point of view that sees them as capable, and that stresses their right to make decisions about their own, and others, lives?

Reading 1.6

The wider benefits of learning
Leon Feinstein, John Vorhaus and Ricardo Sabates

What is the importance of education?

This reading from a government report looking to the future, argues that the value of education is not simply in terms of qualifications, important though they are.

Additionally, a broad range of skills, competencies and social capabilities have been shown to make a considerable difference to the life-chances of individuals, and to the overall health and cohesion of societies. This reading reviews some of the evidence for these 'wider benefits'. The reading concludes with an interesting discussion of inequality, picked up again in Reading 5.2.

Edited from: Feinstein, L., Vorhaus, J., and Sabates, R. (2008) *Foresight Mental Capital and Wellbeing Project. Learning through life: Future challenges*. London: The Government Office for Science, 34–42.

Positive economic returns of learning to the individual are clearly demonstrated by a range of evidence for different categories of education and training (e.g. Blundell et al., 2000; Card, 1999; Dearden et al., 2002). Wider benefits may be conceptualised as the *prevention* of the many negative outcomes: individual social exclusion and community breakdown encompassing crime, teenage parenthood, anti-social behaviour, intolerance of diversity, mental health problems, social division, and disengagement from educational, social and economic activity, drug abuse and social immobility.

However, the skills, capabilities and social networks that underpin success cannot be acquired in a simple and straightforward way from the mere experience of attending educational institutions over some fixed period of time. Education may also reduce or limit skills, capabilities and networks, diminishing individuals rather than empowering them.

Skills and capabilities develop in part from the complex interactions of individuals in the multiple contexts in which they spend time. The effect of education as one such context for the individual will depend on: the nature of the experience of education for that individual; the interactions with peers, teachers and other individuals; the impact of the experience on the identity, self-concepts, and on his or her beliefs and values.

These impacts depend on the ethos, pedagogy, assessment, curricula and often unintended social interactions experienced in learning environments.

Figure 1.6.1 sets out a simple model of the mediating mechanisms for achievement of the wider benefits of learning. In this model the factors gained through learning are expressed in terms of three particular features of individuals and their relationships with others: skills and capabilities, social networks and qualifications. Each of these is discussed in more detail below.

Figure 1.6.1
Mediating
mechanisms
for achieving
wider benefits of
learning

Educational systems have a crucial role in equipping children and adults to withstand the economic, cultural and technological challenges they face in an increasingly globalised world. The fast pace of new technological developments and the intensification of economic pressures mean that the technical and academic skills of the working population are crucial for the UK economy. However, so are features of personal development such as resilience, self-regulation, a positive sense of self, and personal and social identity. The capability of individuals to function as civic agents with notions of personal responsibility, tolerance and respect depends on these wider features of identity which are strongly influenced by interactions with others in schools, workplaces, communities, neighbourhoods and through the media and other channels.

However, there can be a tension between meeting these wide-ranging objectives for personal development, and focusing on the core question of basic skills and qualifications. To some extent these objectives run in parallel, so that children who are developing well in terms of personal features of development are also more likely to follow positive trajectories with respect to core academic skills, and vice versa. However, there may be occasions when these outcomes conflict in resource terms: for example, space within the curriculum, teacher training, or assessment. Unfortunately, relatively little is known about such trade-offs.

Mediating factors

Three sets of factors mediate between education and the wider benefits of learning:

- Skills and competencies
  - Cognitive skills
  - Technical/vocational skills
  - Resilience
  - Beliefs about self
  - Social and communications skills
- Social networks
  - Bridging
  - Bonding
  - Linking
- Qualifications.

Skills and competencies

Skills and competencies have been conceptualised and measured in a range of different ways.

One approach is that of identity capital. As Côté (2005) expressed it:

> Identity capital represents attributes associated with sets of psychosocial skills, largely cognitive in nature, that appear to be necessary for people to intelligently strategise and make decisions affecting their life courses.

Such skills may ultimately also be of value in the labour market. This distinction between human and identity capital is related to the distinction expressed in the economic literature between hard and soft skills or, alternatively, between what economists call cognitive and non-cognitive development. It has been widely recognised in recent years (Bowles et al. 2001; Dunifon and Duncan (1997); Heckman and Rubinstein (2001); Goldsmith et al. (1997) that soft skills and non-cognitive skills are of value in the labour market. This has led to the inclusion of them in some definitions of human capital (Healy and Côté, 2001). Rather than using the umbrella terms "identity capital" or "human capital", this paper focuses instead on some specific elements that have been stressed in research and policy debate. Below, two particular sets of beliefs and attributes are discussed that are believed to be important for wider outcomes: self-concepts and resilience.

Self-concepts are a key element of identity, including an individual's perception of their own abilities and worth. Such beliefs depend on the information available to the individual and the cognitive ability to process this information. Such self-concepts are multi-dimensional (Shavelson (1976), varying across a range of different domains, for example relating to academic capabilities, social capabilities, or general self-worth.

These self-concepts develop while children are at school but have long-term implications. Among very young children, self-concepts of ability and worth tend to be consistently high, but, with increasing life experience, children learn their relative strengths and weaknesses. School plays an important role in the development of these self-concepts. It provides children with external feedback about their competencies in academic, psychological and social areas. The child also develops perceptions of him or herself from their academic successes and failures, and also from their relationships with peers, and with their teachers.

Self-concepts of ability and worth have an impact upon, and are affected by, other psychosocial factors such as self-efficacy, resilience, and inter-temporal preferences (i.e. decisions over whether to do something immediately or in the future). If an individual has a sufficient regard for themselves generally, and of their abilities in particular, they will consider themselves capable (or efficacious), be more inclined to persevere in the face of adversity (resilience), and take care of themselves not only in the here and now, but also in the future. Through channels involving these psychosocial factors, positive and balanced self-concepts promote positive health-related behaviours, protect mental health and help individuals to manage chronic health conditions (Schuller et al., 2004; Hammond, 2002).

One important self-concept is known as self-efficacy. Bandura (1994) describes self-efficacy as an individual's confidence in their ability to organise and execute a given course of action to solve a problem or accomplish a task. It may apply specifically to a particular competence or more generally. Self-efficacy in relation to learning is an important determinant of motivation which in turn supports active engagement in learning (Eccles et al., 1997). Parents' and teachers' perceptions of children's competencies and likely success are important influences on children's beliefs about their efficacy. These perceptions may be communicated through verbal persuasion and also in more subtle, non-verbal ways. Other factors are also important, such as an environment that provides good emotional and cognitive support (Schoon and Bynner, 2003). Both home and school play important roles in the development of self-efficacy, and they should be understood as parts of an interacting and reinforcing system of influences. Resilience refers to positive adaptation in the face of adversity. It is not a personality attribute, but rather a process of positive adaptation in response to significant adversity or trauma. A major source of adversity in childhood and throughout adulthood is socio-economic disadvantage. This is associated with a number of cofactors, such as poor living conditions, overcrowding, and lack of material resources (Duncan and Brooks-Gunn, 1997). The experience of disadvantage early in life may weaken resilience although this is not necessarily so for specific individuals.

Protective factors fall into three broad categories: attributes of children; characteristics of their families; and aspects of the wider social context (Garmezy, 1985; Rutter, 1987). Thus, resilience can be described as the phenomenon that some individuals show positive adjustment despite being exposed to adversity. It is associated with personality characteristics like self-worth and efficacy, but it is also influenced by factors external to the child, such as having a supportive family and other sources of external support.

Social networks

The effects of education are not limited to effects on the capabilities, competencies and skills of individuals. Another very important aspect of educational experiences is that they are social and involve the engagement of individuals in collective experiences of learning and development. This involvement can have positive and negative effects, bringing benefits but also risks. One of the key influences of education may relate to changes to the social networks in which individuals take part, as well as to the ways in which they develop and maintain such networks. Educational settings may be a source of support or distress depending on the nature of the relationships formed in them.

Education has the capability to promote social integration and civic engagement, and to widen social networks. Schlossberg et al. (1995) suggest that social networks and the ability to draw upon social resources can contribute to resilience, leading to better psychological and physical health-related outcomes.

Crucially, however, education can provide access to particular types of social networks for the individual, or change the type of social networks to which the individual has access. This can usefully be conceptualised in terms of social capital.

The most basic form of social capital is bonding social capital, which coalesces around a single, shared identity, and tends to reinforce the confidence and homogeneity of a particular group. Bridging social capital refers to horizontal social networks that extend beyond homogeneous entities. This form of social capital involves cross-cutting networks among people of various ethnic, cultural, and socio-demographic backgrounds. Linking social capital is characterised by connections with individuals and institutions with power and authority. This is theorised in terms of vertical rather than horizontal networks within the social hierarchy.

It is commonly suggested that those of lower socio-economic status (SES) and education tend to have access to higher levels of bonding social capital, allowing them to use their social networks as a protective factor, but lower levels of access to bridging and linking social capital, limiting their access to resources not available in more local environments. The reverse is commonly thought to be true for higher SES individuals, who may have higher levels of access to bridging and linking social capital, allowing them to tap into a wide range of productive resources.

Putnam (1993) suggests that education and learning can be a valuable source of social capital. In primary education learning can promote societal cohesion and strengthen citizenship when individuals from wide ranging socio-economic backgrounds are enrolled in the public education system. Learning experiences can:

- Provide opportunities to gain and practice skills to improve social capital, such as participation and reciprocity;
- Provide a forum for community-based activity;
- Provide a forum in which students can be taught how to participate responsibly in their society;
- Provide an opportunity to extend and deepen social networks;
- Support the development of shared norms and the values of tolerance, understanding, and respect; and
- Affect individual behaviours and attitudes that influence communities (Schuller et al., 2004)

Thus, education can provide wider benefits for the individual through impacts on access to social networks while also leading to possible tensions in bonding networks, particularly in terms of challenging the ties of individuals to working-class identities.

Peer groups are an example of how education can influence social capital. Education influences the peer group memberships of individuals directly through effects on the nature and range of social interactions and networks experienced in school, HE, or adult learning environments. However, it also acts indirectly, through effects on the occupations individuals can take up. The peer groups formed through educational experience influence norms and values as well as providing direct network-related benefits.

Qualifications

Qualifications are also not features of individuals and also cannot be reduced to the notion of a competency. Although in some circumstances they may provide a measure of a level of achievement, their function is not just as a measure, but also as a signal – the same competency would not have the same benefit in the absence of the qualification. The prospect of a qualification also changes the nature of the learning experience, sometimes adding to the motivation and purpose of learning, at other times distracting from it.

The importance of equity in distribution

Our model recognises that the wider benefits of learning are not only about benefits for an individual flowing from their own participation in learning. The distributional aspect of learning is also important (Green et al., 2006). In other words, what matters for individual health is not only the absolute level of resources available to individuals but also their position in relation to others. At the societal level, recent studies have shown that the degree of relative deprivation within a society is strongly associated with overall mortality and life-expectancy (Daniels et al., 2000). Middle-income groups in relatively unequal societies have worse health than comparable or even poorer groups in more equal societies. This result holds even in countries that have universal health care systems, suggesting an impact of relative differences in income on individual health.

The exact nature of the processes linking social inequality with health inequality is not always readily apparent in research studies, in part due to methodological challenges, but links to education have been demonstrated. Using crime and social dislocation as proxies for social cohesion, a strong statistically negative relationship has been reported between educational inequality and social cohesion (Green et al., 2003). Educational inequality is hypothesised to lead to income inequality, which it is suggested in turn leads to lower levels of social cohesion. Educational inequality was also found to have a direct negative relationship with social cohesion.

Using a psychosocial approach, Wilkinson (1996) argues that the income distribution in a country may directly affect an individual's perception of their social environment, which in turn affects their health. Based on qualitative evidence, Wilkinson finds that more egalitarian societies have better health outcomes. Egalitarian societies are also characterised by high levels of social cohesion, he argues, because market orientation and individualism are restrained by a social morality, thereby allowing the public arena to become a source of supportive social networks rather than of stress and potential conflict. Hence, the structural impact of hierarchical status relations is softened and reduced, with benefits for health. This analysis is extended to a range of social factors in Wilkinson and Pickett (2009).

Learning

How can we understand learner development?

2

The first readings in this chapter illustrate some major approaches to learning. Behaviourism is represented by Skinner (2.1) whilst Piaget's contribution (2.2) reviews key elements of his constructivist psychology. Modern theories of social cognition derive from the work of Vygotsky, as illustrated by his classic account of the 'zone of proximal development' (ZPD) (2.3). An extension of these ideas in relation to learning and culture is provided by Wells (2.4).

Contemporary understanding about human capabilities is being profoundly influenced by new research on neuroscience and genetics. This is represented here by The Royal Society's comprehensive summary of the application of neuroscience to education (2.5).

Teachers have particular influence on learner motivation and disposition, which are of course crucial to achievement. For Dweck (2.6) a 'mastery orientation' is connected to each child's view of his or her own intelligence, as fixed or malleable. Fisher (2.7) marshals arguments on why thinking skills should be taught, whilst James (2.8) elaborates the thinking behind 'learning how to learn'. Claxton (2.9) provides a closely linked analysis of the development of resilience. Finally, Thomas and Pattison (2.10) remind us that much valuable learning takes place informally.

The parallel chapter of *Reflective Teaching in Schools* reviews a similar range of issues and considers them in relation to classroom work. The chapter begins with a discussion of behaviourist, constructivist, social constructivist and socio-cultural models of learning. It then addresses a wide range of factors affecting learning including health and physical development, the brain, 'intelligence', culture, personality and learning style, motivation and meta-cognition. The final section of the chapter takes stock – beginning with a summary of key factors in learning from the Unted States National Research Council. But we also need to 'make sense' of such detail and a famous article on 'two metaphors of learning' is therefore reviewed. Finally, there is a discussion on the challenge of applying school learning in the 'real world'.

There are also suggestions for 'Key Readings' and, of course, many other ideas for more detailed study can be accessed from *reflectiveteaching.co.uk*. To access these, please visit reflectiveteaching.co.uk – then navigate to this book, this chapter and 'Notes for Further Reading'.

Reading 2.1

The science of learning and the art of teaching
Burrhus Skinner

B. F. Skinner made a very important contribution to 'behaviourist' psychology, an approach based on study of the ways in which animal behaviour is shaped and conditioned by stimuli. In this reading, Skinner applies his ideas to the learning of pupils in schools. Taking the case of learning arithmetic, he highlights the production of correct 'responses' from children and considers the forms of 'reinforcement' which are routinely used in classrooms. He regards these as hopelessly inadequate.

What do you see as the implications of behaviourism for the role of the teacher?

Edited from: Skinner, B. F. (1954) 'The science of learning and the art of teaching', *Harvard Educational Review,* 24, 86–97.

Promising advances have been made in the field of learning. Special techniques have been designed to arrange what are called 'contingencies of reinforcement' – the relations which prevail between behaviour on the one hand and the consequences of that behaviour on the other – with the result that a much more effective control of behaviour has been achieved. It has long been argued that an organism learns mainly by producing changes in its environment, but it is only recently that these changes have been carefully manipulated.

Recent improvements in the conditions which control behaviour in the field of learning are of two principal sorts. The Law of Effect has been taken seriously; we have made sure that effects *do* occur and that they occur under conditions which are optimal for producing the changes called learning. Once we have arranged the particular type of consequence called a reinforcement, our techniques permit us to shape up the behaviour of an organism almost at will. It has become a routine exercise to demonstrate this in classes in elementary psychology by conditioning such an organism as a pigeon. Simply by presenting food to a hungry pigeon at the right time, it is possible to shape up three or four well-defined responses in a single demonstration period – such responses as turning around, pacing the floor in the pattern of a figure-8, standing still in a corner of the demonstration apparatus, stretching the neck or stamping the foot. Extremely complex performances may be reached through successive stages in the shaping process, the contingencies of reinforcement being changed progressively in the direction of the required behaviour. The results are often quite dramatic. In such a demonstration one can *see* learning take place. A significant change in behaviour is often obvious as the result of a single reinforcement.

A second important advance in technique permits us to maintain behaviour in given states of strength for long periods of time. Reinforcements continue to be important, of course, long after an organism has learned how to do something, long after it has acquired behaviour. They are necessary to maintain the behaviour in strength of special interest is the effect of various schedules of intermittent reinforcement. We have learned how to maintain any given level of activity for daily periods limited only by the physical exhaustion of the organism and from day to day without substantial change throughout its life. Many of these effects would be traditionally assigned to the field of motivation, although the principal operation is simply the arrangement of contingencies of reinforcement.

These new methods of shaping behaviour and of maintaining it in strength are a great improvement over the traditional practices of professional animal trainers, and it is not surprising that our laboratory results are already being applied to the production of performing animals for commercial purposes.

From this exciting prospect of an advancing science of learning, it is a great shock to turn to that branch of technology which is most directly concerned with the learning process – education. Let us consider, for example, the teaching of arithmetic in the lower grades. The school is concerned with imparting to the child a large number of responses of a special sort. The responses are all verbal. They consist of speaking and writing certain words, figures and signs which, to put it roughly, refer to numbers and to arithmetic operations. The first task is to shape up these responses – to get the child to pronounce and to write responses correctly, but the principal task is to bring this behaviour under many sorts of stimulus control. This is what happens when the child learns to count, to recite tables, to count while ticking off the items in an assemblage of objects, to respond to spoken or written numbers by saying 'odd', 'even', 'prime' and so on. Over and above this elaborate repertoire of numerical behaviour, most of which is often dismissed as the product of rote learning, the teaching of arithmetic looks forward to those complex serial arrangements of responses involved in original mathematical thinking. The child must acquire responses of transposing, clearing fractions and so on, which modify the order or pattern of the original material so that the response called a solution is eventually made possible.

Now, how is the extremely complicated verbal repertoire set up? In the first place, what reinforcements are used? Fifty years ago the answer would have been clear. At that time educational control was still frankly aversive. The child read numbers, copied numbers, memorized tables and performed operations upon numbers to escape the threat of the birch rod or cane. Some positive reinforcements were perhaps eventually derived from the increased efficiency of the child in the field of arithmetic and in rare cases some automatic reinforcement may have resulted from the sheer manipulation of the medium – from the solution of problems or the discovery of the intricacies of the number system. But for the immediate purposes of education the child acted to avoid or escape punishment. It was part of the reform movement known as progressive education to make the positive consequences more immediately effective, but anyone who visits the lower grades of the average school today will observe that a change has been made, not from aversive to positive control, but from one form of aversive stimulation to another. The child at his desk, filling in his workbook, is behaving primarily to escape from the threat of a series of minor aversive events – the teacher's displeasure, the criticism or ridicule of his class-mates, an ignominious showing in a competition, low marks, a trip to the office 'to be talked to' by the principal, or a word to the parent who may still resort to the birch rod. In this welter of aversive consequences, getting the right answer is in itself an insignificant event, any effect of which is lost amid the anxieties, the boredom and the aggressions which are the inevitable by-products of aversive control.

Secondly, we have to ask how the contingencies of reinforcement are arranged. When is a numerical operation reinforced as 'right'? Eventually, of course, the pupil may be able to check his own answers and achieve some sort of automatic reinforcement, but in the early stages the reinforcement of being right is usually accorded by the teacher. The contingencies she provides are far from optimal. It can easily be demonstrated that, unless explicit mediating behaviour has been set up, the lapse of only a few seconds between response and reinforcement destroys most of the effect. In a typical classroom, nevertheless, long periods of time customarily elapse. The teacher may walk up and down the aisle, for example, while the class is working on a sheet of problems, pausing here and there to say right or wrong. Many seconds or minutes intervene between the child's response and the teacher's reinforcement. In many cases – for example, when papers are taken home to be corrected – as much as 24 hours may intervene. It is surprising that this system has any effect whatsoever.

A third notable shortcoming is the lack of a skilful program which moves forward through a series of progressive approximations to the final complex behaviour desired. A long series of contingencies is necessary to bring the organism into the possession of mathematical behaviour most efficiently. But the teacher is seldom able to reinforce at each step in such a series because she cannot deal with the pupil's responses one at a time. It is usually necessary to reinforce the behaviour in blocks of responses – as in correcting a work sheet or page from a workbook. The responses within such a block must not be interrelated. The answer to one problem must not depend upon the answer to another. The number of stages through which one may progressively approach a complex pattern of behaviour is therefore small, and the task so much the more difficult. Even the most modern workbook in beginning arithmetic is far from exemplifying an efficient program for shaping up mathematical behaviour.

Perhaps the most serious criticism of the current classroom is the relative infrequency of reinforcement. Since the pupil is usually dependent upon the teacher for being right, and since many pupils are usually dependent upon the same teacher, the total number of contingencies which may be arranged during, say, the first four years, is of the order of only a few thousand. But a very rough estimate suggests that efficient mathematical behaviour at this level requires something of the order of 25,000 contingencies. We may suppose that even in the brighter student a given contingency must be arranged several times to place the behaviour well in hand. The responses to be set up are not simply the various items in tables of addition, subtraction, multiplication and division; we have also to consider the alternative forms in which each item may be stated. To the learning of such material we should add hundreds of responses concerned with factoring, identifying primes, memorizing series, using shortcut techniques for calculation, constructing and using geometric representations or number forms and so on. Over and above all this, the whole mathematical repertoire must be brought under the control of concrete problems of considerable variety. Perhaps 50,000 contingencies is a more conservative estimate. In this frame of reference the daily assignment in arithmetic seems pitifully meagre.

The result of this is, of course, well known. Even our best schools are under criticism for the inefficiency in the teaching of drill subjects such as arithmetic. The condition in the average school is a matter of widespread national concern. Modern children simply do not learn arithmetic quickly or well. Nor is the result simply incompetence. The very subjects in which modern techniques are weakest are those in which failure is most conspicuous, and in the wake of an every-growing incompetence come the anxieties, uncertainties and aggressions which in their turn present other problems to the school. Most pupils soon claim the asylum of not being 'ready' for arithmetic at a given level or, eventually, of not having a mathematical mind. Such explanations are readily seized upon by defensive teachers and parents. Few pupils ever reach the stage at which automatic reinforcements follow as the natural consequences of mathematical behaviour. On the contrary, the figures and symbols of mathematics have become standard emotional stimuli. The glimpse of a column of figures, not to say an algebraic symbol or an integral sign, is likely to set off – not mathematical behaviour – but a reaction of anxiety, guilt or fear.

The teacher is usually no happier about this than the pupil. Denied the opportunity to control via the birch rod, quite at sea as to the mode of operation of the few techniques at her disposal, she spends as little time as possible on drill subjects and eagerly subscribes to philosophies of education which emphasize material of greater inherent interest.

There would be no point in urging these objections if improvement were impossible. But the advances which have recently been made in our control of the learning process suggest a thorough revision of classroom practices and, fortunately, they tell us how the revision can be brought about. This is not, of course, the first time that the results of an experimental science have been brought to bear upon the practical problems of education. The modern classroom does not, however, offer much evidence that research in the field of learning has been respected or used. This condition is no doubt partly due to the limitations of earlier research, but it has been encouraged by a too hasty conclusion that the laboratory study of learning is inherently limited because it cannot take into account the realities of the classroom. In the light of our increasing knowledge of the learning process we should, instead, insist upon dealing with those realities and forcing a substantial change in them. Education is perhaps the most important branch of scientific technology. It deeply affects the lives of all of us. We can no longer allow the exigencies of a practical situation to suppress the tremendous improvements which are within reach. The practical situation must be changed.

There are certain questions which have to be answered in turning to the study of any new organism. What behaviour is to be set up? What reinforcers are at hand? What responses are available in embarking upon a program of progressive approximation which will lead to the final form of behaviour? How can reinforcements be most efficiently scheduled to maintain the behaviour in strength? These questions are all relevant in considering the problem of the child in the lower grades.

Reading 2.2

The genetic approach to the psychology of thought

Jean Piaget

The present reading provides a concise overview of Piaget's constructivist psychology, but is necessarily packed with ideas. The distinction between formal knowledge and the dynamic of transformations is important, with the latter seen as providing the mechanism for the development of thought. Successive 'stages' of types of thinking are reviewed and are related to maturation, direct experience and social interaction. Finally, attention is drawn to the ways in which children 'assimilate' new experiences and 'accommodate' to their environment, to produce new levels of 'equilibration' at successive stages of learning.

Interpretations of Piaget's work have been of enormous influence on the thinking of primary school teachers. Indeed, it was specifically used as a rationale for the policy recommendations contained in the Plowden Report (Reading 9.4), which emphasised the importance of providing a rich, experiential learning environment which would be appropriate for the 'stage' of each child.

What importance do you attach to concepts such as 'stages of development', 'readiness' and 'learning from experience'?

Edited from: Piaget, J. (1961) 'A genetic approach to the psychology of thought', *Journal of Educational Psychology,* 52, 151–61.

Taking into consideration all that is known about the act of thinking, one can distinguish two principal aspects:

The *formal* viewpoint which deals with the configuration of the state of things to know,
The *dynamic* aspect, which deals with transformations

The study of the development of thought shows that the dynamic aspect is at the same time more difficult to attain and more important, because only transformations make us understand the state of things. For instance: when a child of 4 to 6 years transfers a liquid from a large and low glass into a narrow and higher glass, he believes in general that the quantity of the liquid has increased, because he is limited to comparing the initial state (low level) to the final state (high level) without concerning himself with the transformation. Towards 7 or 8 years of age, on the other hand, a child discovers the preservation of the liquid, because he will think in terms of transformation. He will say that nothing has been taken away and nothing added, and, if the level of the liquid rises, this is due to a loss of width etc.

The formal aspect of thought makes way, therefore, more and more in the course of the development to its dynamic aspect, until such time when only transformation gives an understanding of things. To think means, above all to understand; and to understand means to arrive at the transformations, which furnish the reason for the state of things. All development of thought is resumed in the following manner: a construction of operations which stem from actions and a gradual subordination of formal aspects into dynamic aspects.

The operation, properly speaking, which constitutes the terminal point of this evolution is, therefore, to be conceived as an internalized action bound to other operations, which form with it a structured whole.

So defined, the dynamics intervene in the construction of all thought processes; in the structure of forms and classifications, of relations and serialization of correspondences, of numbers, of space and time, of the causality etc.

Any action of thought consists of combining thought operations and integrating the objects to be understood into systems of dynamic transformation. The psychological criterion of this is the appearance of the notion of conservation or 'invariants of groups'. Before speech, at the purely sensory-motor stage of a child from 0–18 months, it is possible to observe actions which show evidence of such tendencies. For instance: From 4–5 to 18 months, the baby constructs his first invariant, which is the schema of the permanent object (to recover an object which escaped from the field of perception).

When, with the beginning of the symbolic function (language, symbolic play, imagery etc.), the representation through thought becomes possible, it is at first a question of reconstructing in thought what the action is already able to realize. The actions actually do not become transformed immediately into operations, and one has to wait until about 7–8 years for the child to reach a functioning level. During this preoperative period the child, therefore, only arrives at incomplete structures characterized by a lack of logic.

At about 7–8 years the child arrives at his first complete dynamic structures (classes, relations and numbers), which, however, still remain concrete – in other words, only at the time of a handling of objects (material manipulation or, when possible, directly imagined). It is not before the age of 11–12 years or more that operations can be applied to pure hypotheses.

The fundamental genetic problem of the psychology of thought is hence to explain the formation of these dynamic structures. Practically, one would have to rely on three principal factors in order to explain the facts of development: maturation, physical experience and social interaction. But in this particular case none of these three suffice to furnish us with the desired explanations – not even the three together.

Maturation

First of all, these dynamic structures form very gradually. But progressive construction does not seem to depend on maturation, because the achievements hardly correspond to a particular age. Only the order of succession is constant. However, one witnesses innumerable accelerations or retardations for reasons of education (cultural) or acquired experience.

Physical experience

Experiencing of objects plays, naturally, a very important role in the establishment of dynamic structures, because the operations originate from actions and the actions bear upon the object. This role manifests itself right from the beginning of sensory-motor explorations, preceding language, and it affirms itself continually in the course of manipulations and activities which are appropriate to the antecedent stages. Necessary as the role of experience may be, it does not sufficiently describe the construction of the dynamic structures – and this for the following three reasons.

First, there exist ideas which cannot possibly be derived from the child's experience – for instance, when one changes the shape of a small ball of clay. The child will declare, at 7–8 years, that the quantity of the matter is conserved. It does so before discovering the conservation of weight (9–10 years) and that of volume (10–11 years). What is the quantity of a matter independently of its weight and its volume? This abstract notion is neither possible to be perceived nor measurable. It is, therefore, the product of a dynamic deduction and not part of an experience.

Second, the various investigations into the learning of logical structure, which we were able to make at our International Centre of Genetic Epistemology, lead to a unanimous result: one does not 'learn' a logical structure as one learns to discover any physical law.

Third, there exist two types of experiences:

Physical experiences show the objects as they are, and the knowledge of them leads to the abstraction directly from the object. However, logico-mathematical experience does not stem from the same type of learning as that of the physical experience, but rather from an equilibration of the scheme of actions, as we will see.

Social interaction

The educative and social transmission (linguistic etc) plays, naturally, an evident role in the formation of dynamic structures, but this factor does not suffice either to entirely explain its development.

Additionally, there is a general progression of equilibration. This factor intervenes, as is to be expected, in the interaction of the preceding factors. Indeed, if the development depends, on one hand, on internal factors (maturation), and on the other hand on external factors (physical or social), it is self-evident that these internal and external factors equilibrate each other. The question is then to know if we are dealing here only with momentary compromises (unstable equilibrium) or if, on the contrary, this equilibrium becomes more and more stable. This shows that all exchange (mental as well as biological) between the organism and the environment (physical and social) is composed of two poles: (a) of the *assimilation* of the given external to the previous internal structures, and (b) of the *accommodation* of these structures to the given ones. The equilibrium between the assimilation and the accommodation is proportionately more stable than the assimilative structures which are better differentiated and coordinated.

To apply these notions to children's reasoning we see that every new problem provokes a disequilibrium (recognizable through types of dominant errors) the solution of which consists in a re-equilibration, which brings about a new original synthesis of two systems, up to the point of independence.

Reading 2.3

Mind in society and the Zone of Proximal Development

Lev Vygotsky

Vygotsky's social constructivist psychology, though stemming from the 1930s, underpins much modern thinking about teaching and learning. In particular, the importance of instruction is emphasised. However, this is combined with recognition of the influence of social interaction and the cultural context within which understanding is developed. Vygotsky's most influential concept is that of the ZPD, which highlights the potential for future learning which can be realised with appropriate support.

The influence of Vygotsky's work will be particularly apparent in Reading 2.4 but it is also present in many other readings, particularly in Chapters 10, 11, 12 and 13.

Thinking of a particular area of learning and a child you know, can you identify an 'actual developmental level' and a zone of proximal development through which you could provide guidance and support?

Edited from: Vygotsky, L. S. (1978) *Mind in Society: The Development of Higher Psychological Processes.* Cambridge, MA: Harvard University Press, 84–90.

That children's learning begins long before they attend school is the starting point of this discussion. Any learning a child encounters in school always has a previous history. For example, children begin to study arithmetic in school, but long beforehand they have had some experience with quantity – they have had to deal with operations of division, addition, subtraction, and determination of size. Consequently, children have their own pre-school arithmetic which only myopic scientists could ignore.

It goes without saying that learning as it occurs in the preschool years differs markedly from school learning, which is concerned with the assimilation of the fundamentals of scientific knowledge. But even when, in the period of her first questions, a child assimilates the names of objects in her environment, she is learning. Indeed, can it be doubted that children learn speech from adults; or that, through asking questions and giving answers, children acquire a variety of information; or that through imitating adults and through being instructed about how to act, children develop an entire repository of skills? Learning and development are interrelated from the child's very first day of life.

In order to elaborate the dimensions of school learning, we will describe a new and exceptionally important concept without which the issue cannot be resolved: the zone of proximal development.

A well known and empirically established fact is that learning should be matched in some manner with the child's developmental level. For example, it has been established that the teaching of reading, writing and arithmetic should be initiated at a specific age level. Only recently, however, has attention been directed to the fact that we cannot limit ourselves merely to determining developmental levels if we wish to discover the actual relations of the developmental process to learning capabilities. We must determine at least two developmental levels.

The first level can be called the *actual developmental level*, that is, the level of development of a child's mental functions that has been established as a result of certain already *completed* developmental cycles. When we determine a child's mental age by using tests, we are almost always dealing with the actual developmental level. In studies of children's mental development it is generally assumed that only those things that children can do on their own are indicative of mental abilities. We give children a battery of tests or a variety of tasks of varying degrees of difficulty, and we judge the extent of their mental development on the basis of how they solve them and at what level of difficulty. On the other hand, if we offer leading questions or show how the problem is to be solved and the child then solves it, or if the teacher initiates the solution and the child completes it or solves it in collaboration with other children – in short, if the child barely misses an independent solution of the problem – the solution is not regarded as indicative of his mental development. This 'truth' was familiar and reinforced by common sense. Over a decade even the profoundest thinkers never questioned the assumption; they never entertained the notion that what children can do with the assistance of others might be in some sense even more indicative of their mental development than what they can do alone.

The zone of proximal development is the distance between the actual developmental level as determined by independent problem solving and the level of potential development as determined through problem solving under adult guidance or in collaboration with more capable peers.

If we naively ask what the actual developmental level is, or, to put it more simply, what more independent problem solving reveals, the most common answer would be that a child's actual developmental level defines functions that have already matured, that is, the end products of development. If a child can do such-and-such independently, it means that the functions for such-and-such have matured in her. What, then, is defined by the zone of proximal development, as determined through problems that children cannot solve independently but only with assistance? The zone of proximal development defines those functions that have not yet matured but are in the process of maturation, functions that will mature tomorrow but are currently in an embryonic state. These functions could be termed the 'buds' or 'flowers' of development rather than the 'fruits' of development. The actual developmental level characterizes mental development retrospectively, while the zone of proximal development characterizes mental development prospectively.

The zone of proximal development furnishes psychologists and educators with a tool through which the internal course of development can be understood. By using this method we can take account of not only the cycles and maturation processes that have already been completed but also those processes that are currently in a state of formation, that are just beginning to mature and develop. Thus, the zone of proximal development permits us to delineate the child's immediate future and his dynamic developmental state, allowing not only for what already has been achieved developmentally but also for what is in the course of maturing. The state of a child's mental development can be determined only by clarifying its two levels: the actual developmental level and the zone of proximal development.

A full understanding of the concept of the zone of proximal development must result in re-evaluation of the role of imitation in learning. Indeed, human learning presupposes a specific social nature and a process by which children grow into the intellectual life of those around them.

Children can imitate a variety of actions that go well beyond the limits of their own capabilities. Using imitation, children are capable of doing much more in collective activity or under the guidance of adults. This fact, which seems to be of little significance in itself, is of fundamental importance in that it demands a radical alteration of the entire doctrine concerning the relation between learning and development in children.

Learning which is oriented toward developmental levels that have already been reached is ineffective from the viewpoint of a child's overall development. It does not aim for a new stage of the developmental process but rather lags behind this process. Thus, the notion of a zone of proximal development enables us to propound a new formula, namely that the only 'good learning' is that which is in advance of development.

The acquisition of language can provide a paradigm for the entire problem of the relation between learning and development. Language arises initially as a means of communication between the child and the people in his environment. Only subsequently, upon conversion to internal speech, does it come to organize the child's thought, that is, become an internal mental function.

We propose that an essential feature of learning is that it creates the zone of proximal development; that is, learning awakens a variety of internal developmental processes that are able to operate only when the child is interacting with people in his environment and in cooperation with his peers. Once these processes are internalized, they become part of the child's independent developmental achievement.

From this point of view, learning is not development; however, properly organized learning results in mental development and sets in motion a variety of developmental processes that would be impossible apart from learning. Thus, learning is a necessary and universal aspect of the process of developing culturally organized, specifically human, psychological functions.

Reading 2.4

Learning, development and schooling

Gordon Wells

> Gordon Wells criticises three dominant views about the relationship between learning and development: behaviourism (Reading 2.1), constructivist psychology (Reading 2.2) and thinking conceptualised as computer information processes. However, he endorses and extends Vygotsky's social constructivism (Reading 2.3). In so doing, he is one of many contemporary educationalists who have been strongly influenced by versions of this approach because of the ways in which it links history and culture to personal learning through meaningful activity. For example, we inherit and use many cultural as well as material tools – such as language.
>
> Can you identify in your own biography, some examples of how your learning was (or is) influenced by your cultural circumstances, social relationships and activities? And how might this apply to pupils you teach?
>
> *Edited from:* Wells, G. (2008) 'Dialogue, inquiry and the construction of learning communities', in Linguard, B., Nixon, J. and Ranson, S. (eds) *Transforming Learning in Schools and Communities.* London: Continuum, 236–42.

For much of the twentieth century, three views about the relationship between learning and development predominated. The first is behaviourist in origin. It assumes that each individual has a fixed potential, often expressed as IQ, which is said to account for differences in educational achievement. The second view grew out of Piaget's early work on the universal stages of cognitive development, which led to an emphasis on readiness and child-centred discovery learning. The third is modelled on the mind as a computer with innately given cognitive modules. This latter view has tended to be expressed in terms of inputs and outputs, with thinking conceptualized as processing information that is stored in memory like files in a large computer.

However, none of these views does justice to the role of learning in human development. The first ignores what goes on in the mind, treating education as the reinforcement of associations and habits that can be assessed in purely quantitative terms. While the second view emphasizes the constructive nature of learning, it largely ignores the fact that human infants grow up as members of historically ongoing cultures, which strongly influence their development. Finally, the third view comes close to reducing the human mind to a machine and, in so doing, ignores the interdependence of bodily action, thinking and feeling and interaction with others in the activities through which learning occurs. It also has very little to say about development.

In the place of these three inadequate theories, I wish to describe an alternative view, which not only envisages development as ongoing transformation, but also treats it as involving a mutually constitutive relationship between the individual and the society in which she or he is growing up, and between biological endowment and the cultural practices in which, from birth, he or she is continuously involved. Known as cultural historical activity theory (CHAT), this explanation of the relationship between learning and development was first formulated by Vygotsky in Russia and has since been extended and refined by researchers and educators from many different countries. In summary form, the key points of CHAT can be stated as follows:

- The basic 'unit' of human behaviour is purposeful activity jointly undertaken with others in a particular time and place and in relation to a particular culture.

- In all major domains of human activity, goals are achieved by people carrying out actions mediated by tools, both material and symbolic, of which the most powerful and versatile is language.

- Individual development (cognitive, social and affective) results from participation in joint activity with more expert others, in which the individual masters the culturally developed tools and practices and 'appropriates' them as resources for acting and thinking, both alone and in collaboration with others.

- Learning is greatly facilitated by guidance and assistance that is pitched in the learner's 'zone of proximal development'.

While appropriating ways of acting, thinking and feeling from care givers and other community members, the child does not passively copy their knowledge and skills. In contrast, learning is an active and constructive process that involves a triple transformation: of the learner's repertoire for action; of the tools and practices involved, as the learner constructs his or her unique version of them; and of his or her relationship with others and thus of his or her identity. As a result of these transformations, all the individual participants, as well as the cultural situations in and on which they act, are in a constant state of change and development that is the continuously emergent outcome of their actions and transactions. In other words, the developmental relationship between society and its individual members is one of interdependence and co-construction.

Every occasion of joint activity provides a potential occasion for learning. By the same token, assistance given to a learner in his or her attempt to participate is an occasion of teaching. Most often, however, such teaching occurs incidentally and without deliberate intention – as in most parent–child conversations.

There are many occasions when an adult or a more knowledgeable sibling or peer deliberately helps a child with a task, particularly when they judge that the child cannot yet manage on his or her own. Vygotsky (1978) described assistance given in this way as working in the 'zone of proximal development'. In any task we undertake, there is frequently a limit to what we can achieve alone. In such situations, help from another with what is proving difficult both allows us to complete the task and models for us what we need to add to our resources so that, in the future, we shall be able to manage the task unaided. Indeed, in traditional cultures, this is how children learn most of what they know and are able to do.

This kind of situated learning 'on the job' has been described as 'cultural apprenticeship' (Lave and Wenger, 1991; Rogoff, 2003). However, while learning through apprenticeship provides an essential spur to development towards full membership in all cultures, on its own it is insufficient to equip young people today with all the knowledge and skills they need to participate fully in technologically advanced cultures (Lemke, 2002). It is to fulfil this role that educational institutions exist – as they have since it first became necessary to provide a setting for some members of each generation to learn to read and write (Cole, 1996). In the last few centuries, however, as written language and other semiotic systems, such as mathematics, scientific formulae and procedures, graphs, maps and diagrams of all kinds, have come to play an increasingly important role in the development and dissemination of 'formal' knowledge, schools and universities have come to play a more and more significant role in the development of 'higher mental functions'. It is in this relatively novel context that we need to consider the part that deliberate teaching plays in young people's learning.

Schools differ from settings for informal and spontaneous learning-and-teaching in several important ways. First, attendance is compulsory between certain ages (5 or 6 until 16–18 in most cultures); second, there is a prescribed curriculum that sets out – increasingly, in considerable detail – the knowledge and skills that students are required to learn in each year and for which they will be held accountable through tests and other forms of assessment; and third, in each age-based class there is typically a ratio of 25 or more students to each teacher. Furthermore, although the students are all approximately of the same age, they vary considerably in terms of their interests and aspirations, as well as in their physical and intellectual strengths and needs, as a result of their very different backgrounds and life trajectories. Every school class, therefore, is characterized by diversity on a variety of dimensions that need to be taken into account.

Throughout most of the history of schooling, this combination of constraints has led to a transmission approach to education, aimed at ensuring that all students acquire the same set of knowledgeable skills that are considered most useful and important for their future roles in the workforce. With this end in view, the goals of teaching have been those of organizing what is to be learned into appropriately sized and sequenced chunks and of arranging optimal methods of delivery, together with opportunities for practice and memorization. In this approach, little or no attention is given to students' diverse backgrounds, interests and expertise, nor are they encouraged to show initiative and creativity in formulating questions and problems and in attempting to solve them in collaboration with their peers and teachers. Instead, students' success is largely evaluated in terms of their ability to recall what they have been taught and to reproduce it on demand in response to arbitrary questions, often divorced from any meaningful context.

If this pattern were not so historically engrained, its inappropriateness would surely have led to its demise long ago, given the high proportion of students who, each year, fail to master the required curriculum and how little the remainder remember of what they learned a few months after the test. Its one merit is that, from an administrative point of view, both teacher and students can be held accountable for what has to be 'covered', whether or not the actual teaching-and-learning is of long-term value to the learners. With the current preoccupation with efficiency, it is perhaps this administrative convenience that ensures the continuation of practices that, if considered in terms of their effective contribution to student development, would be clearly seen to be unacceptable.

However, these criticisms of the prevailing organization of schooling are not intended to suggest that there should be no guidance given as to what activities students should engage in and as to what they are expected to learn; nor is it intended to suggest that there is no role for deliberate teaching. But teaching certainly cannot be reduced to telling and testing and to maintaining the control necessary to keep students to this externally imposed agenda.

What, then, is the alternative?

I suggest that learning-and-teaching should be seen as complementary aspects of a single collaborative activity we may refer to as 'dialogic inquiry' in a community of learners. In this approach, the teacher has two important roles: as leader, to plan and organize the community's activities; and as facilitator, to provide contingently appropriate assistance to individuals and groups to enable them to achieve goals that they cannot achieve on their own. At the same time, there is a third role that is equally important. As the more expert member of the community, the teacher should also model the dispositions and actions of learning by conducting his or her own inquiries aimed at improving the quality and effectiveness of the community's activity (Wells, 2001).

Reading 2.5

Neuroscience and education
The Royal Society

The text in this reading reflects the work of The Royal Society in promoting greater public understanding of the significance of neuroscience. 'Brain Waves' is a series of reports which apply neuroscientific insights to a range of contemporary issues. Module 2 focuses on education.

The reading begins with eight bullet points from the executive summary of the report, and continues with elaboration and discussion of some of the evidence and issues arising. The full text, with copious citation of evidence, is available at royalsociety.org. Membership of the Working Party which produced Brain Waves Module 2 was Uta Frith (Chair), Dorothy Bishop, Colin Blakemore, Sarah-Jayne Blakemore, Brian Butterworth, Usha Goswami, Paul Howard-Jones, Diana Laurillard, Eleanor Maguire, Barbara Sahakian and Annette Smith.

Edited from: The Royal Society (2011) *Brain Waves Module 2: Neuroscience: Implications for Education and Lifelong Learning.* London: The Royal Society, 3–17.

The brain is the organ that enables us to adapt to our environment – in essence, to learn. Neuroscience is shedding light on the influence of our genetic make-up on learning over our life span, in addition to environmental factors. This enables us to identify key indicators for educational outcomes, and provides a scientific basis for evaluating different teaching approaches.

Education is concerned with enhancing learning, and neuroscience is concerned with understanding the mechanisms of learning. This common ground suggests a future in which educational practice is transformed by science, just as medical practice was transformed by science about a century ago. In this report we consider some of the key insights from neuroscience that could eventually lead to such a transformation.

- The brain changes constantly as a result of learning, and remains 'plastic' throughout life. Neuroscience has shown that learning a skill changes the brain and that these changes revert when practice of the skill ceases. Hence 'use it or lose it' is an important principle for lifelong learning.

- Neuroscience research suggests that learning outcomes are not solely determined by the environment. Biological factors play an important role in accounting for differences in learning ability between individuals.

- By considering biological factors, research has advanced the understanding of specific learning difficulties, such as dyslexia and dyscalculia. Likewise, neuroscience is uncovering why certain types of learning are more rewarding than others.

- Research also shows that resilience, our adaptive response to stress and adversity, can be built up through education with lifelong effects into old age.

- Research also shows that both acquisition of knowledge and mastery of self-control benefit future learning. Thus, neuroscience has a key role in investigating means of boosting brain power.

- Some insights from neuroscience are relevant for the design of adaptive digital technologies. These have the potential to create more learning opportunities inside and outside the classroom, and throughout life. This is exciting given the knock-on effects this could have on wellbeing, health, employment and the economy.

- There is great public interest in neuroscience, yet accessible high quality information is scarce. We urge caution in the rush to apply so-called brain-based methods, many of which do not yet have a sound basis in science. There are inspiring developments in basic science although practical applications are still some way off.

- The emerging field of educational neuroscience presents opportunities as well as challenges for education. It provides means to develop a common language and bridge the gulf between educators, psychologists and neuroscientists.

Both nature and nurture affect the learning brain

Individuals differ greatly in their response to education, and both genes and the environment contribute to these differences. Work with identical twins, who have the same genetic make-up, has shown that they are more similar in, for instance, personality, reading and mathematical ability, than non-identical twins, who differ in their genetic make-up. While it is widely agreed that individual differences can have a genetic basis, genetic influences on brain development and brain function are not yet well understood.

Genetic make-up alone does not shape a person's learning ability; genetic predisposition interacts with environmental influences at every level. Human learning abilities vary, in the same way that human height and blood pressure vary.

The brain is plastic

The brain is constantly changing and everything we do changes our brain. These changes can be short lived or longer lasting. When we sleep, walk, talk, observe, introspect, interact, attend, and learn, neurons fire. The brain has extraordinary adaptability, sometimes referred to as 'neuroplasticity'. This is due to the process by which connections between neurons are strengthened when they are simultaneously activated. This process is often summarised as, 'neurons that fire together wire together'. The effect is known as experience-dependent plasticity and is present throughout life.

Neuroplasticity allows the brain continuously to take account of the environment. It also allows the brain to store the results of learning in the form of memories. In this way, the brain can prepare for future events based on experience. On the other hand, habit learning, which is very fast and durable, can be maladaptive and difficult to overcome, as for example in addiction.

Key findings based on neuroplasticity include the following:

- Changes in the brain's structure and connectivity suggest there are sensitive periods in brain development extending beyond childhood into adolescence. Plasticity tends to decrease with age and this is particularly evident when we consider learning of a second language.

- The overall pattern of neural development appears to be very similar between genders, but the pace of brain maturation appears to differ, with boys on average reaching full maturation at a slightly later age than girls.

- Dynamic changes to brain connectivity continue in later life. The wiring of the brain changes progressively during development for a surprisingly long time.

- Just as athletes need to train their muscles, there are many skills where training needs to be continued to maintain brain changes. The phrase 'use it or lose it!' is very apt. Changes in the adult brain following the acquisition of specific skills has also been shown for music, juggling and dance. This illustrates what we mean by experience-dependent plasticity. The genetic specification of our brains only partly determines what we know and how we behave; much depends on environmental factors that determine what we experience. Education is prominent among these factors.

The brain has mechanisms for self-regulation

Together with findings from cognitive psychology, neuroscience is beginning to shed light on self-regulation and self-control, that is, the inhibition of impulsive behaviour.

Recent research has shown that the ability to inhibit inappropriate behaviour, for example, stopping oneself making a previously rewarded response, develops relatively slowly during childhood, but continues to improve during adolescence and early adulthood. This is probably because the brain regions involved in inhibition, in particular the prefrontal cortex, continue to change both in terms of structure and function, during adolescence and into the twenties. In addition, there are large individual differences in our ability to exert self-control, which persist throughout life. For example, by age three, some children are much better than others at resisting temptation, and the ability to resist temptation (delayed gratification) at this age has been found to be associated with higher education attainment in later childhood and adolescence. Research is under way to investigate to what extent cognitive training programmes can strengthen this ability.

Understanding mechanisms underlying self-control might one day help to improve prospects for boosting this important life skill. In addition, it is important to learners and teachers who are dealing with lack of discipline or antisocial behaviour. Given that the self-reported ability to exert self-control has been found to be an important predictor of academic success, understanding the neural basis of self-control and its shaping through appropriate methods may be valuable.

Education is a powerful form of cognitive enhancement

Cognitive enhancement usually refers to increased mental prowess, for instance, increased problem-solving ability or memory. Such enhancement is usually linked with the use of drugs or sophisticated technology. However, when compared with these means, education seems the most broadly and consistently successful cognitive enhancer of all. Education provides, for instance, access to strategies for abstract thought, such as algebra or logic, which can be applied in solving a vast range of problems and can increase mental flexibility. Literacy and numeracy change the human brain, but also enable human beings to perform feats that would not be possible without these cultural tools, including the achievements of science. The steady rise in IQ scores over the last decades is thought to be at least partially due to education. Findings from neuroscience and cognitive enhancement include the following:

- *Education* can build up an individual's cognitive reserve and resilience, that is, their adaptive response to stressful and traumatic events and illness, including brain injury, mental disorder, and normal ageing. Cognitive reserve and resilience can be built up at any point during life. Research on cognitive reserve has found an inverse relationship between educational attainment and risk of dementia, which means that keeping the mind active slows cognitive decline and improves cognitive abilities in older adults.

- *Physical health, exercise, sleep and nutrition* are crucial to physical and mental wellbeing and their effects on cognitive functions are mediated by the brain. For example, neuroscience research on sleep and sleep deprivation can explain some highly specific effects on memory and other mental functions.

Individual differences in learning ability and the brain

There is wide variation in learning ability; some individuals struggle to learn in all domains, whereas others have specific difficulties for instance, with language, literacy, numeracy or self-control. There is ample evidence that these individuals are at increased risk of poor social adaptation and unemployment. The costs to society are thus substantial and there is an urgent need to find educational approaches that will work.

Current work in neuroscience is directed toward identifying the brain basis of learning difficulties. As this research advances, prospects are raised for identification and diagnosis, and for designing interventions that are suitable for different ages and may overcome or circumvent the learning difficulties. Even for those with severe learning difficulties, improved understanding of specific cognitive and neurological correlates of disorder can be harnessed to make education more effective.

Future challenges

There are major cultural and vocabulary differences between the scientific research and education communities.

Critics of neuroscience fear that it represents:

- a reductionist view that overemphasises the role of the brain at the expense of a holistic understanding of cultural life based on interpretation and empathy
- a determinist view that our neurological inheritance sets us on a path that is unchangeable.

However, a neuroscience perspective recognises that each person constitutes an intricate system operating at neural, cognitive, and social levels, with multiple interactions taking place between processes and levels. Neuroscience is a key component of this system and is therefore a key contributor to enriching explanations of human thought and behaviour. Furthermore, it is a mistake to regard biological predispositions as deterministic; their impact is probabilistic and context-dependent. The important point is that there are educational difficulties that have a biological basis, and cannot be attributed solely to parents', teachers' or society's expectations. If in these cases the biological risk factors are not taken into account, important opportunities to optimize learning will be missed.

A web search using Google with the keywords 'Learning', 'Teaching', and 'Brain' indicates that there is a huge demand for applications of brain science to education. Thus despite philosophical reservations, there is considerable enthusiasm for neuroscience and its applications. This can, however, lead to problems. For example, commercial interests have been quick to respond to the demand of the enthusiasts and promote their credibility with testimonials of reportedly trustworthy individuals. There is already a glut of books, games, training courses, and nutritional supplements, all claiming to improve learning and to be backed by science. This is problematic because the sheer volume of information from a range of sources makes it difficult to identify what is independent, accurate and authoritative. At worst, this industry creates 'neuro-myths' that can damage the credibility and impact of authentic research.

The idea that 'Knowledge needs to go in both directions' typifies the sentiments expressed by neuroscience, policy and teaching communities.

If educational neuroscience is to develop into an effective new discipline, and make a significant impact on the quality of learning for all learners, we need a long-term dialogue between neuroscientists and a wide range of other researchers and professionals from a variety of backgrounds in education.

Reading 2.6

Motivational processes affecting learning

Carol Dweck

> Pupils' motivation and approaches in new learning situations are obviously crucial to outcomes, and this has been the focus of Carol Dweck's research for many years. In this reading, she shows how children's view of intelligence (as fixed or something that can be developed) may lead them to adopt relatively pragmatic performance goals or more developmental learning goals. These are associated with different beliefs in themselves (helpless or mastery-orientated), different forms of classroom behaviour and different learning outcomes.
>
> How can we help children to really believe in themselves and their potential?
>
> *Edited from:* Dweck, C. S., (1986) 'Motivational processes affecting learning', in *American Psychologist,* October, 1040–6.

It has long been known that factors other than ability influence whether children seek or avoid challenges, whether they persist or withdraw in the face of difficulty and whether they use and develop their skills effectively. However, the components and bases of adaptive motivational patterns have been poorly understood. As a result, commonsense analyses have been limited and have not provided a basis for effective practices. Indeed, many 'commonsense' beliefs have been called into question or seriously qualified by recent research – for example, the belief that large amounts of praise and success will establish, maintain, or reinstate adaptive patterns, or that 'brighter' children have more adaptive patterns and thus are more likely to choose personally challenging tasks or to persist in the face of difficulty.

In the past 10 to 15 years a dramatic change has taken place in the study of motivation. This change has resulted in a coherent, replicable, and educationally relevant body of findings – and in a clearer understanding of motivational phenomena. During this time, the emphasis has shifted to a social – cognitive approach – away from external contingencies, on the one hand, and global, internal states on the other. It has shifted to an emphasis on cognitive mediators, that is, to how children construe the situation, interpret events in the situation, and process information about the situation. Although external contingencies and internal affective states are by no means ignored, they are seen as part of a process whose workings are best penetrated by focusing on organizing cognitive variables.

Specifically, the social-cognitive approach has allowed us to (a) characterize adaptive and maladaptive patterns, (b) explain them in terms of specific underlying processes, and thus (c) begin to provide a rigorous conceptual and empirical basis for intervention and practice.

The study of motivation deals with the causes of goal-oriented activity. Achievement motivation involves a particular class of goals – those involving competence – and these goals appear to fall into two classes: (a) *learning goals*, in which individuals seek to increase their competence, to understand or master something new, and (b) *performance goals*, in which individuals seek to gain favourable judgments of their competence.

Adaptive motivational patterns are those that promote the establishment, maintenance, and attainment of personally challenging and personally valued achievement goals. Maladaptive patterns, then, are associated with a failure to establish reasonable, valued goals, to maintain effective striving toward those goals, or, ultimately, to attain valued goals that are potentially within one's reach.

Research has clearly documented adaptive and maladaptive patterns of achievement behaviour. The adaptive ('mastery-oriented') pattern is characterized by challenge seeking and high, effective persistence in the face of obstacles. Children displaying this pattern appear to enjoy exerting effort in the pursuit of task mastery. In contrast, the maladaptive ('helpless') pattern is characterized by challenge avoidance and low persistence in the face of difficulty. Children displaying this pattern tend to evidence negative affect (such as anxiety) and negative self-cognitions when they confront obstacles.

Although children displaying the different patterns do not differ in intellectual ability, these patterns can have profound effects on cognitive performance. In experiments conducted in both laboratory and classroom settings, it has been shown that children with the maladaptive pattern are seriously hampered in the acquisition and display of cognitive skills when they meet obstacles. Children with the adaptive pattern, by contrast, seem undaunted or even seem to have their performance facilitated by the increased challenge.

If not ability, then what are the bases of these patterns? Most recently, research has suggested that children's goals in achievement situations differentially foster the two patterns. That is, achievement situations afford a choice of goals, and the one the child preferentially adopts predicts the achievement pattern that child will display.

The figure below summarizes the conceptualisation that is emerging from the research. Basically, children's theories of intelligence appear to orient them toward different goals: Children who believe intelligence is a fixed trait tend to orient toward gaining favourable judgments of that trait (performance goals), whereas children who believe intelligence is a malleable quality tend to orient toward developing that quality (learning goal). The goals then appear to set up the different behaviour patterns.

Much current educational practice aims at creating high-confidence performers and attempts to do so by programming frequent success and praise. How did this situation arise? I propose that misreadings of two popular phenomena may have merged to produce this approach. First was the belief in 'positive reinforcement' as the way to promote desirable behaviour. Yet a deeper understanding of the principles of reinforcement would not lead one to expect that frequent praise for short, easy tasks would create a desire for long, challenging ones or promote persistence in the face of failure.

Theory of intelligence	Goal orientation	Confidence in present ability	Behaviour pattern
Entity theory – Intelligence is fixed	Performance goal (Goal is to gain positive judgments/avoid negative judgments of competence)	If high ⟶ but If low ⟶	Mastery-orientated Seek challenge High persistence Helpless Avoid challenge Low persistence
Incremental theory (Intelligence is malleable)	Learning goal (Goal is to increase competence)	If high or low ⟶	Mastery-oriented Seek challenge (that fosters learning) High persistence

Figure 2.6.1 Achievement goals and achievement behaviour

Second was a growing awareness of teacher expectancy effects. As is well known, the teacher expectancy effect refers to the phenomenon whereby teachers' impressions about students' ability actually affect students' performance, such that the students' performance falls more in line with the teachers' expectancies (Rosenthal and Jacobson, 1968). The research on this 'self-fulfilling prophecy' raised serious concerns that teachers were hampering the intellectual achievement of children they labelled as having low ability. One remedy was thought to lie in making low-ability children feel like high-ability children by means of a high success rate.

The motivational research is clear in indicating that continued success on personally easy tasks is ineffective in producing stable confidence, challenge seeking and persistence (Dweck, 1975). Indeed, such procedures have sometimes been found to backfire by producing lower confidence in ability. Rather, the procedures that bring about more adaptive motivational patterns are the ones that incorporate challenge, and even failure, within a learning-oriented context and that explicitly address underlying motivational mediators. For example, retraining children's attributions for failure (teaching them to attribute their failures to effort or strategy instead of ability) has been shown to produce sizable changes in persistence in the face of failure, changes that persist over time and generalize across tasks (Andrews and Bebus, 1978).

Motivational processes have been shown to affect (a) how well children can deploy their existing skills and knowledge, (b) how well they acquire new skills and knowledge, and (c) how well they transfer these new skills and knowledge to novel situations. This approach does not deny individual differences in present skills and knowledge or in 'native' ability or aptitude. It does suggest, however, that the use and growth of that ability can be appreciably influenced by motivational factors.

Reading 2.7

Why thinking should be taught

Robert Fisher

> In this reading Fisher defines a range of thinking skills and makes a strong case for the educational value of philosophical enquiry per se. He argues that 'thinking' can certainly be taught in the classroom. School education can, in other words, not only impart knowledge but also teach powerful capabilities for evaluating and applying such knowledge. In later life, independent thinkers are likely to lead innovation in spheres such as the arts, economy and society, but in a democracy this is a capability we should encourage for all our citizens.
>
> How can the development of thinking skills be promoted in your classroom?
>
> *Edited from:* Fisher, R. (2013) *Teaching Thinking: Philosophical Enquiry in the Classroom.* London: Bloomsbury, 2–26.

'Thinking skills' is a generic description of the human capacity to think in conscious ways to achieve certain purposes. Such processes include remembering, translating thoughts into words, questioning, planning, reasoning, analysing, hypothesising, imagining, forming judgements based on reasons and evidence, and so on.

However, a focus on thinking does not mean ignoring the role of knowledge. Knowledge is necessary. But simply knowing a lot of things is not sufficient if children are to be taught to think for themselves. Children need knowledge but they also need to know how to acquire it and use it.

It is true then, that thinking must be about something – but people can do it more or less effectively. The capacity, for example, to assess reasons, formulate hypotheses, make conceptual links and ask critical questions is relevant to many areas of learning. As Gemma, age 10 put it: 'To be a good learner you need to practice training your mind.' Indeed, we want our children to use their skills on a regular basis and get into the habit of thinking critically, creatively and with care. Good thinking requires that cognitive skills become habits of intelligent behaviour learned through practice. We know, for example, that children tend to become better at giving reasons or asking questions the more they practise doing so.

Psychologists and philosophers have helped to extend our understanding of the term 'thinking', by emphasising the importance of *dispositions*. This has prompted a move away from a simple model of 'thinking skills' as isolated cognitive capacities.

If we can systematically cultivate better thinking then we should surely do so.

One reason frequently advanced for the teaching of thinking is that thinking is intrinsic to human development, and that every individual has a right to have their intellect developed. Teaching thinking becomes an end in itself by the very fact that we are thinking animals, and have a right to the education of those faculties that constitute what it is to be human.

Another justification is that we gain pleasure from the right sort of intellectual stimulus and challenge. The Greeks argued that the exercise of the human intellect produced both virtue and satisfaction. In the nineteenth century John Stuart Mill developed this idea further by distinguishing what he called the 'higher' and the 'lower' pleasures of human existence. The higher pleasures of the mind, he said, were more profound and satisfying than the lower pleasures of the body.

Many of the reasons for seeking to develop thinking and learning skills are instrumental or pragmatic, and are to do with the success of individuals and of society. The most important resource any society has is the intellectual capacity of its people. A successful society will be a thinking society in which the capacities for lifelong learning of its citizens are most fully realized. Critical and creative thinking is needed to make sense of knowledge in any subject area.

Another perceived need to teach thinking skills comes from a growing awareness of the rate of change within society. This is accelerating so rapidly that it is difficult to assess what factual knowledge will be needed in the future, and this means that schools should be less focused on imparting information than on teaching students to learn and to think for themselves.

Exercising the mind through intellectual challenge can also promote moral qualities and virtues. Intellectual virtue can be seen as a complex set of attributes including curiosity, thoughtfulness, intellectual courage and perseverance in the search for truth, a willingness to speculate and analyse, to judge and self-correct, and openness to the views of others. Such qualities need to be practised through thinking for oneself and thinking with others. Philosophical enquiry with children can be a means whereby such qualities can become embedded in human character.

Teaching children to be better thinkers is thus both a rational and a moral enterprise. These processes require more than an isolated set of thinking skills. They are also a matter of developing attitudes and dispositions. Teaching thinking cannot be simply a matter of imparting certain skills, for if skills are not used they are redundant. All the finely-honed thinking skills in the world will be for naught if they are not used for positive purposes.

A good thinker displays a number of intellectual virtues. These include:

1 *Seeking truth*
   They care that their beliefs are true, and that their decisions are as far a possible justified. They show this by:

   - seeking alternatives (hypotheses, explanations, conclusions, plans, sources, ideas)
   - supporting views only to the extent that they are justified by available information
   - being well informed, including being informed by the views of others.

   A good thinker is someone who is always trying to find out new things. (Rachel, aged 9)

2 *Being honest*

They care that their position and the position of others are represented honestly: They show this by attending, i.e.:

- being clear about what they mean
- maintaining a focus on the issue in question
- seeking and offering reasons
- considering all factors relevant in the situation
- being aware of their own point of view
- considering seriously other points of view.

To be a good thinker you have to be honest with yourself, and with other people. (Brian, aged 9)

3 *Respecting others*

They care about the dignity and worth of every person. They show this by:

- attentive listening to the views of others
- avoiding scorn or intimidation of others
- showing concern about the welfare of others.

A good thinker listens to what others say, even if you don't agree with them. (Nicholas, aged 9)

Being a person means having a sense of oneself, including oneself as a thinker and learner, and a sense of others through our interaction with them. A broad view of the purposes of education would include developing such intellectual virtues and dispositions as to attend, concentrate, cooperate, organize, reason, imagine and enquire. We need to develop the virtues of seeking truth and being honest, and of respect for others.

Democracy is the political expression of the human urge for freedom, freedom of thought and freedom of expression. Education should be a process whereby the child is gradually helped to recognize the nature of human freedom and of human responsibility. We need to encourage children to think in ways which express their authentic individuality.

Reading 2.8

Learning how to learn

Mary James

In this reading, Mary James describes an influential research project which focused on ways of developing independent learning in schools. It built, in particular, from a new approach to assessment designed to directly support learning processes through the provision of feedback. Among a number of findings are the significance of authentic teacher understanding in developing practices to improve pupil learning. So the big message is that to achieve pupil learning we need to high quality teacher learning. To do that, we need supportive professional networks and school leadership.

In schools you know, can you see how the quality of pupil learning is affected by learning at other levels?

Edited from: James, M. (2007) *Only Connect! Improving Teaching and Learning in Schools*. Professorial Lecture given at the Institute of Education, University of London, 17 October.

The *Learning How to Learn* project (James et al., 2007) was built on the assumption that, in the 21st century, individuals and communities will constantly need to learn new things, apply their knowledge in new contexts, create new knowledge, and exercise wise judgement about what is important and what is not.

This presents a challenge for teachers and for schools who will need to focus on two things simultaneously: teaching the substance of subjects, and helping students to learn the ideas and practices associated with the process of learning itself. For many teachers, this requires them to learn new knowledge about learning, develop new skills, and reassess their roles. Teachers need to learn, as well as their students, and schools need to support them in this. .

The project team worked with 40 secondary, primary and infants schools from seven local authorities.

At the beginning of our work, we assumed that 'learning how to learn' had something to do with self-monitoring and self-regulating aspects of meta-cognition. But our interest in finding out what can be *done* by teachers and students in classrooms led us away from regarding it as a psychological property of learners. Instead we saw it as a set of *practices* that can be developed by students to help them to learn autonomously.

If learning autonomy is the goal, and learning how to learn is the activity oriented towards that goal, then assessment for learning can be viewed as providing tools for the activity.

Figure 2.8.1
The initial design
of *Learning How
to Learn*

Learning Autonomy (outcome)

Learning How to Learn (activity)

Assessment for Learning (tools)

Development work in schools was initiated by the academics in our team (who were the schools' critical friends). A whole-school inset day introduced teachers to the evidence base which was important in convincing them that AfL was worth trying. Then we shared with them some of the practical strategies that other schools had developed. Each school decided how best to implement innovations, often with the help of local authority advisers who acted as local co-ordinators (see James et al., 2007).

The other main intervention from the project team was to feed back the results of the baseline survey we conducted into staff values and practices. This revealed differences among sub-groups of staff and stimulated discussion and action. We provided materials to support more general CPD and school improvement strategies.

Our research used careful and systematic data collection and analysis to enable us to analyse patterns across our sample as a whole, and over time, and to examine school differences on common measures. We developed research instruments at each level (classrooms, schools and networks).

Teachers learning in their classrooms

Many teachers have now adopted what they describe as AfL practices or strategies. One is the practice of 'sharing learning objectives' with students. A second practice is associated with 'traffic lighting' which was first developed as a way of allowing students to communicate their confidence in their learning, during the lesson, so that the teacher could respond appropriately by adjusting the activity as the lesson proceeds. Underpinning both these practices are ideas about the importance of students understanding their learning, becoming active agents in it, and for teaching to be responsive to how learning is progressing through the flow of activity in lessons.

The trouble is that without an understanding of these underlying principles, the first practice can become ritualistic, reduced to writing of the learning objective on the board at the start of every lesson without much reference to it subsequently. Or the learning objective can be reduced to a *task* objective i.e. what students are expected to *do*, not what they are expected to *learn*. The second practice can become equally distorted by becoming just another way of marking students' work. But if this is all that it is, the practice is unlikely to fulfil its formative potential for promoting learning autonomy.

However, some of the teachers that we observed took these same practical suggestions but interpreted and implemented them in ways that did capture what we called the 'spirit' of AfL. What was it that led such teachers towards a deeper understanding and interpretation than others?

Analysis of our questionnaire and interview data suggests that teachers' beliefs about learning affect how they implement AfL in the classroom. Much of the roll out of AfL in England, has focused on giving teachers *procedures* to try out in the classroom without considering what they already *believe* about learning in the first place. Some teachers feel more able to promote student autonomy in their classrooms than others, and those teachers who articulate a clear commitment to student autonomy are more likely to realise it in the classroom.

In understanding these findings, we could not ignore the context in which teachers work. Teachers and students alike work in a system dominated by the demands of the curriculum, tests and examinations. The pressure is to cover the course or teach to the test rather than take the time to explore students' ideas and understanding. This is one way of understanding a gap between what teachers say they believe and what they actually do in the classroom.

Teachers learning in their schools

In order to investigate the *conditions* in schools that might promote changes in classroom practice we investigated: classroom assessment practice and values; teacher learning practice and values; school management and systems practices and values. We examined values-practice gaps, differences between and within schools, changes over time, and associations between factors on the different dimensions.

Gaps between teachers' values and their practices at the beginning of the project were mainly related to *promoting learning autonomy* (practices noticeably behind values – teachers admitted doing *less* than they thought important) and *performance orientation* (practices noticeably ahead of values – teachers did *more* than they thought important). By the end of the project, teachers were reporting to us that they were *rebalancing* their assessment approaches in order to bring their practices into closer alignment with their values. They did this by reducing practices with a *performance orientation* (by an average of 9%) and by increasing practices with a focus on *promoting learning autonomy* (by an average of 7%). Given the size of the sample, these were statistically significant changes.

Some people might ask: Does the reduction of performance orientation affect results? Data from sample schools indicated no negative impact on national test and examination results but there were some interesting success stories. For example one school, towards the end of the project, achieved 84% 5A*–Cs at GCSE in 2004 (and 92% in 2006), and high contextual value-added scores. The majority of its teachers consistently valued *making learning explicit* and *promoting learning autonomy* almost equally highly (and above *performance orientation*), and their values-practice gaps were minimal. The head teacher said:

> AfL has been a joy. It is intellectually profound, yet eminently practical and accessible. The project has enhanced the learning of all of us. I have no doubt that our children are now better taught than ever before.

What appear to be important at the level of the school are:

(i)   a clear sense of direction;

(ii)   systems of support for professional development;

(iii)   systems for locating the strengths of staff as a basis for building on this expertise through networking.

The impact of these factors on classroom practice, particularly those practices associated with learning how to learn and the promotion of learning autonomy are *mediated* by teachers' own learning practice, particularly collaborative classroom-focused inquiry.

Teachers learning through networks

Most of our sample schools were well-equipped with new technology. But these resources were little used for 'school-to-school' electronic networking. There was, however, considerable optimism and anticipation on the part of teachers, managers and LA officials about what network technologies, such as video conferencing, *would* be able to offer in the future.

In our investigations of more general networking we identified weak and strong links. Weak links exist where knowledge is valued but there is not a strong personal relationship. For example, teachers attending a conference might pick up some good ideas and be enthused by a speaker such that they go back to school and try a new approach. Strong links characterise many, so-called, 'learning communities' within and across schools but are sometimes difficult to sustain. We therefore concluded that weak links also need to be valued and exploited.

Another important finding was the difference in the kinds of links that different people within a school had established. Head teachers are usually regarded as the 'networkers' of a school because they have more opportunities to work outside the school and are seen as gatekeepers to knowledge. Project co-ordinators, on the other hand, had to build new networks to go with their role. This brought new knowledge and ideas into the school by *bridging* to other networks and sources of expertise.

Informal networks and links are valuable resources for schools. We concluded that schools could benefit from developing their understanding of different types of networks and links, and by giving teachers opportunities to develop them.

The key challenge for school leaders is to create the space and climate for managers, teachers, support staff and students – especially students – to reflect on and share aspects of their practice, especially their learning practice. This includes encouraging and stimulating reflection, dialogue (even dissent), strategic thinking and risk taking.

In this way, new ways of learning and teaching can be tested, embedded and sustained. Without it, they remain surface changes which decay and disappear when the next initiative comes along.

Reading 2.9

Learning and the development of resilience
Guy Claxton

Guy Claxton has constructed an analysis of how young learners need to develop positive learning dispositions to support lifelong learning. He identifies his 'three Rs' – resilience, resourcefulness and reflection – as being crucial. This reading is focused on the first of these. Resilience is closely associated with having the self-confidence to face problems and the resolve to overcome them. It articulates well with Dweck's concept of 'mastery' (Reading 2.6).

How, through our classroom practices, could we support the development of resilience in our pupils?

Edited from: Claxton, G. (1999) *Wise Up: The Challenge of Lifelong Learning.* Stoke-on-Trent: Network Press, 331–3.

As the world moves into the age of uncertainty, nations, communities and individuals need all the learning power they can get. Our institutions of business and education, even our styles of parenting, have to change so that the development and the expression of learning power become real possibilities. But this will not happen if they remain founded on a narrow conceptualization of learning: one which focuses on content over process, comprehension over competence, 'ability' over engagement, teaching over self-discovery. Many of the current attempts to create a learning society are hamstrung by a tacit acceptance of this outmoded viewpoint, however watered down or jazzed up it may be. The new science of learning tells us that everyone has the capacity to become a better learner, and that there are conditions under which learning power develops. It is offering us a richer way of thinking about learning, one which includes feeling and imagination, intuition and experience, external tools and the cultural milieu, as well as the effort to understand. If this picture can supplant the deeply entrenched habits of mind that underpin our conventional approaches to learning, the development of learning power, and the creation of a true learning society might become realities. In this final chapter, let me summarize the lessons that the new science of the learning mind has taught us.

Learning is impossible without resilience: the ability to tolerate a degree of strangeness. Without the willingness to stay engaged with things that are not currently within our sphere of confident comprehension and control, we tend to revert prematurely into a defensive mode: a way of operating that maintains our security but does not increase our mastery. We have seen that the decision whether, when and how to engage depends on a largely tacit cost-benefit analysis of the situation that is influenced strongly by our subjective evaluations of the risks, rewards and available resources. These evaluations derive from our beliefs and values, our personal theories, which may be accurate or inaccurate. Inaccurate beliefs can lead us to over- or underestimate apparent threats and to misrepresent to ourselves what learning involves.

So when you find people declining an invitation to learn, it is not because they are, in some crude sense, lazy or unmotivated: it is because, for them, at that moment, the odds stack up differently from the way in which their parents or tutors or managers would prefer. Defensiveness, seen from the inside, is always rational. If the stick and the carrot don't do the trick, it may be wiser to try to get a clearer sense of what the learner's interior world looks like. Often you will find that somewhere, somehow, the brakes have got jammed. Sensitivity to the learners' own dynamics is always smart.

Some of these beliefs refer to the nature of knowledge and of learning itself. For example, if we have picked up the ideas that knowledge is (or ought to be) clear and unequivocal, or that learning is (or ought to be) quick and smooth, we withdraw from learning when it gets hard and confusing, or when we meet essential ambiguity. Some beliefs refer to hypothetical psychological qualities such as 'ability'. The idea that achievement reflects a fixed personal reservoir of general-purpose 'intelligence' is pernicious, leading people to interpret difficulty as a sign of stupidity, to feel ashamed, and therefore to switch into self-protection by hiding, creating diversions or not trying. Some beliefs determine how much we generally see the world as potentially comprehensible and controllable ('self-efficacy', we called it). High self-efficacy creates persistence and resilience; low breeds a brittle and impatient attitude. Some beliefs forge a connection between self-worth on the one hand and success, clarity and emotional control on the other, making failure, confusion and anxiety or frustration induce a feeling of shame. All these beliefs can affect anyone, but there are a host of others that specifically undermine or disable the learning of certain groups of people, or which apply particularly to certain types of material. For example, girls and boys have been revealed as developing different views of themselves as learners of mathematics.

These beliefs are rarely spelt out, but are transmitted implicitly and insidiously through the kinds of culture that are embodied in the settings that learners inhabit, such as family, school or workplace. Learning messages are carried by a variety of media. The habits and rituals of the culture enable certain kinds of learning and disable others.

The implications of these conclusions for the kinds of learning cultures we create are self-evident. Parents, teachers and managers have to be vigilant, reflective and honest about the values and beliefs which inform the ways they speak, model and organize the settings over which they have control. Inadvertently create the wrong climate and the development and expression of learning power are blocked. Experience in childhood, at home and at school, is particularly important because these early belief systems, whether functional or dysfunctional, can be carried through into people's learning lives as adults.

Reading 2.10

Informal learning

Alan Thomas and Harriet Pattison

Thomas and Pattison summarise the major conclusion of their study of informal learning at home. Their 'three elements' are relevant to all children's learning, whether being educated in school or otherwise.

Recognition of informal learning is important for teachers, for it makes clear how we merely shape enduring processes of learning and development. Where school efforts are aligned with processes in other learning settings, progress is normally rapid. Sadly for many children and young people, the alignment of home and school cultures is weak (see Readings 5.3 and 5.4).

Edited from: Thomas, A. and Pattison, J. (2007) *How Children Learn at Home.* London: Continuum, 141–6.

We propose three basic elements to the type of learning on which informal home education is based; what is learnt, how it is learnt, and the part played by parents.

First, the culture that surrounds children provides their informal curriculum. Everyday objects, other people and commonplace experiences provide children with a wealth of information on all manner of subjects, including the primary education mainstays of literacy and numeracy. Children are exposed to real-life skills such as shopping, using the telephone, cooking, money calculations, reading, travelling, dealing with people outside the family and so on. These skills are presented holistically, in the situations in which they are actually put to use. The broadening out of the cultural curriculum beyond the immediate and everyday takes place in many ways including conversation, children's own curiosity and investigations, often in the form of play, and the seeing and hearing of snippets of specialized knowledge from a variety of sources including the mass media, visits to museums and other places of interest, books and other people. As children develop they are free to follow up in more deliberate fashion the subjects which hold particular attraction for them by making use of conventional research techniques such as reading, using the internet, joining interest groups, seeking out other specialized sources of information, and of course, thinking out things for themselves.

Second, if the subject matter is there for children in the form of the informal curriculum, they still have to somehow engage with it. There is little doubt that they are very good at doing so. The relevance of the informal curriculum to their own lives is a key factor here. Children are interested in what they see around them and are good at exploring their environment on their own terms; through watching, listening, playing, talking and thinking.

In school, children are assumed to be learning only when they are 'on task' and progressing through prescribed steps within carefully planned lessons. For children learning informally there is no pre-determined approach. Children observe and listen, they ask questions, talk and discuss matters of importance with parents and with each other. As we have seen, they may channel very purposeful energy into finding out for themselves things they find interesting or consider to be important. They sustain research efforts by pursuing longer-term hobbies based on crafts or sports or other interests. They play; working through ideas, setting up scenarios, creating and imitating. The learning taking place through these activities is often barely discernible; even the purposeful pursuance of a hobby is undertaken for pleasure rather than with the intention of becoming an expert. Yet within these activities a number of cognitive strategies are employed, demonstrating that intellectual reasoning and hypothesis testing could be developed without recourse to knowledge of an academic nature. Topics such as the rules of football and the intricacies of step-family relationships provide rich opportunities for the practicing and honing of intellectual skills. Finally practice itself, whether through choice or through the dictates of everyday life, allow children to consolidate new skills and ideas.

Children's individual reaction to the cultural curriculum around them dictate both the pace and structure of their learning. How much they want or are able to take in from a given situation or activity at a given time may be decided by a complex of interest, mood and previous understanding. Some reactions, such as boredom, lack of concentration, inability to apply what they may have previously appeared to understand or simply doing nothing would be considered, in the classroom to be negative and inhibiting to learning. In informal learning however, these reactions may actually be part of a self-regulatory learning system in which learners themselves subconsciously dictate if and when they are ready to take their learning further. Of course with informal learning these reactions are not likely to last for long because children simply move on to something else that has engaged their interest.

The naturalness and efficacy of this type of learning engagement is such that there is very often the feeling that children are simply learning by osmosis: absorbing the information around them in an almost effortless fashion. And indeed, much may be taken in implicitly with barely any learner awareness of the acquisition of new knowledge. The metaphor of the sponge was one which frequently came to mind as parents described the feel of such learning.

Third, parents or carers play an important role in children's informal learning. Good parenting provides a stable home background, intellectual stimulation, parent-child discussion, encouragement and general support of children's activities. Parents share their own knowledge either deliberately or implicitly, act as role models through their own engagement with the informal curriculum and facilitate access to knowledge they do not have, often sharing in the learning themselves. Most of this interaction occurs quite naturally as a consequence of shared lives rather than deliberate pedagogy and is not pre-planned or structured.

The example of literacy, the school learning of which can cause a great deal of stress for children, teachers and parents, exemplifies the ways in which informal learning takes place as a natural part of everyday life. Children who learn to read informally do not do so as a self-contained activity, based on synthetic phonics, graded readers and suchlike. Instead their 'readers' are street and shop names, road and garage signs, cereal packets, brand names, computer prompts, and so on; written language that has real meaning for them, initiated by themselves or pointed out by their parents. They learn to read as they learn the relevance of reading in daily life; they learn what they want to read, when they want to read it. Similarly they build up literacy experience by writing birthday cards, notes, lists, labels and their own literary props when playing. Parents contribute by reading stories, joining in with children's own efforts to read and, through the course of their everyday lives, acting as role models who demonstrate the central part that literacy plays in almost every aspect of modern life.

The overwhelming message from our study has to be the ease, naturalness and immense intellectual potential of informal learning. Children who educated informally learn, not as a separate activity as children do in school, but as an integral part of everything they do as they engage with the world around them.

Reflection

How can we develop the quality of our teaching?

The readings in this chapter illustrate key ideas about the meaning of reflective practice and its relationship with teacher professionalism.

First, we have excerpts from the highly influential work of Dewey (3.1) and Schon (3.2). Dewey contrasts routinised and reflective thinking, and suggests that 'to be genuinely thoughtful, we must be willing to sustain a state of doubt'. Schon identifies the capacity of skilled practitioners to engage in 'reflection-in-action'.

The readings from Stenhouse (3.3) and Pring (3.4) are classic statements of the argument for teachers to engage in research and enquiry in their own classrooms and schools for the improvement of practice.

Calderhead (3.5) demonstrates the complexities and multiple dimensions of teaching, whilst Heilbronn (3.6) shows how this calls for practical judgement and evidence-informed practice.

The selection concludes with discussion from Hodkinson et al. (3.7) of collaboration between teachers in 'communities of practice'. Professional development works best with others.

The parallel chapter of *Reflective Teaching in Schools* emphasises the importance of *processes* of reflection in the development of successive *states* of practical competence. The chapter clarifies the meaning of reflective teaching by identifying seven key characteristics – including the use of evaluative evidence and learning with colleagues. There are also suggestions for further reading both there and on *reflectiveteaching.co.uk*.

The website offers additional 'Reflective Activities', a compendium of terms and many resources for 'Deepening Expertise'. Of particular relevance to reflective practice, it provides supplementary materials on:

- Learning through mentoring in initial training
- Developing an evidence-informed classroom.

Reading 3.1

Thinking and reflective experience

John Dewey

The writings of John Dewey have been an enormous influence on educational thinking. Indeed, his distinction of 'routinised' and 'reflective' teaching is fundamental to the conception of professional development through reflection. In the two selections below Dewey considers the relationship between reflective thinking and the sort of challenges which people face through experience.

Do you feel that you are sufficiently open-minded to be really 'reflective'?

Edited from: Dewey, J. (1933) *How We Think: A Restatement of the Relation of Reflective Thinking to the Educative Process.* Chicago: Henry Regnery, 15–16; and Dewey, J. (1916) *Democracy and Education.* New York: Free Press, 176–7.

The origin of thinking is some perplexity, confusion, or doubt. Thinking is not a case of spontaneous combustion; it does not occur just on 'general principles'. There is something that occasions and evokes it. General appeals to a child (or to a grown-up) to think, irrespective of the existence in his own experience of some difficulty that troubles him and disturbs his equilibrium, are as futile as advice to lift himself by his boot-straps.

Given a difficulty, the next step is suggestion of some way out – the formation of some tentative plan or project, the entertaining of some theory that will account for the peculiarities in question, the consideration of some solution for the problem. The data at hand cannot supply the solution; they can only suggest it. What, then, are the sources of the suggestion? Clearly, past experience and a fund of relevant knowledge at one's command. If the person has had some acquaintance with similar situations, if he has dealt with material of the same sort before, suggestions more or less apt and helpful will arise. But unless there has been some analogous experience, confusion remains mere confusion. Even when a child (or grown-up) has a problem, it is wholly futile to urge him to 'think' when he has no prior experiences that involve some of the same conditions.

There may, however, be a state of perplexity and also previous experience out of which suggestions emerge, and yet thinking need not be reflective. For the person may not be sufficiently *critical* about the ideas that occur to him. He may jump at a conclusion without weighing the grounds on which it rests; he may forego or unduly shorten the act of hinting, inquiring; he may take the first 'answer', or solution, that comes to him because of mental sloth, torpor, impatience to get something settled.

One can think reflectively only when one is willing to endure suspense and to undergo the trouble of searching. To many persons both suspense of judgment and intellectual search are disagreeable; they want to get them ended as soon as possible. They cultivate an over-positive and dogmatic habit of mind, or feel perhaps that a condition of doubt will be regarded as evidence of mental inferiority. It is at the point where examination and test enter into investigation that the difference between reflective thought and bad thinking comes in.

To be genuinely thoughtful, we must be willing to sustain and protract that state of doubt which is the stimulus to thorough inquiry.

The general features of a reflective experience are:

- perplexity, confusion, doubt, due to the fact that one is implicated in an incomplete situation whose full character is not yet determined;
- a conjectural anticipation – a tentative interpretation of the given elements, attributing to them a tendency to effect certain consequences;
- a careful survey (examination, inspection, exploration, analysis) of all attainable consideration which will define and clarify the problem in hand;
- a consequent elaboration of the tentative hypothesis to make it more precise and more consistent, because squaring with a wider range of facts;
- taking one stand upon the projected hypothesis as a plan of action which is applied to the existing state of affairs; doing something overtly to bring about the anticipated result, and thereby testing the hypothesis.

It is the extent and accuracy of steps three and four which mark off a distinctive reflective experience from one on the trial and error plane. They make *thinking* itself into an experience. Nevertheless, we never get wholly beyond the trial and error situation. Our most elaborate and rationally consistent thought has to be tried in the world and thereby tried out. And since it can never take into account all the connections, it can never cover with perfect accuracy all the consequences. Yet a thoughtful survey of conditions is so careful, and the guessing at results so controlled, that we have a right to mark off the reflective experience from the grosser trial and error forms of action.

Reading 3.2

Reflection-in-action

Donald Schon

> Donald Schon's analysis of reflective practice has influenced training, development and conceptions in many professions. His key insight is that there are forms of professional knowledge which, though often tacitly held, are essential for the exercise of judgement as the complexities and dilemmas of professional life are confronted. Such knowledge is *in* professional action, and may be developed by reflection-in-action.
>
> *Edited from:* Schon, D. A. (1983) *The Reflective Practitioner: How Professionals Think in Action.* London: Maurice Temple Smith, 50–68.

When we go about the spontaneous, intuitive performance of the actions of everyday life, we show ourselves to be knowledgeable in a special way. Often we cannot say what it is that we know. When we try to describe it we find ourselves at a loss, or we produce descriptions that are obviously inappropriate. Our knowing is ordinarily tacit, implicit in our patterns of action and in our feel for the stuff with which we are dealing. It seems right to say that our knowing is *in* our action.

Similarly, the workaday life of the professional depends on tacit knowing-in-action. Every competent practitioner makes innumerable judgments of quality for which he cannot state adequate criteria, and he displays skills for which he cannot state the rules and procedures. Even when he makes conscious use of research-based theories and techniques, he is dependent on tacit recognitions, judgments, and skilful performances.

On the other hand, both ordinary people and professional practitioners often think about what they are doing, sometimes even while doing it. Stimulated by surprise, they turn thought back on action and on the knowing which is implicit in action. They may ask themselves, for example, 'What features do I notice when I recognize this thing? What are the criteria by which I make this judgment? What procedures am I enacting when I perform this skill? How am I framing the problem that I am trying to solve?' Usually reflection on knowing-in-action goes together with reflection on the stuff at hand. There is some puzzling, or troubling, or interesting phenomenon with which the individual is trying to deal. As he tries to make sense of it, he also reflects on the understandings which have been implicit in his action, understandings which he surfaces, criticizes, restructures, and embodies in further action.

It is this entire process of reflection-in-action which is central to the 'art' by which practitioners sometimes deal well with situations of uncertainty, instability, uniqueness, and value conflict.

Knowing-in-action

There is nothing strange about the idea that a kind of knowing is inherent in intelligent action. Common sense admits the category of know-how, and it does not stretch common sense very much to say that the know-how is *in* the action.

There are actions, recognitions, and judgments which we know how to carry out spontaneously; we do not have to think about them prior to or during their performance. We are often unaware of having learned to do these things; we simply find ourselves doing them. In some cases, we were once aware of the understandings which were subsequently internalized in our feeling for the stuff of action. In other cases, we may usually be unable to describe the knowing which our action reveals. It is in this sense that I speak of knowing-in-action, the characteristic mode of ordinary practical knowledge.

Reflecting-in-action

If common sense recognizes knowing-in-action, it also recognizes that we sometimes think about what we are doing. Phrases like 'thinking on your feet,' 'keeping your wits about you,' and 'learning by doing' suggest not only that we can think about doing but that we can think about doing something while doing it. Some of the most interesting examples of this process occur in the midst of a performance.

Much reflection-in-action hinges on the experience of surprise. When intuitive, spontaneous performance yields nothing more than the results expected for it, then we tend not to think about it. But when intuitive performance leads to surprises, pleasing and promising or unwanted, we may respond by reflecting-in-action. In such processes, reflection tends to focus interactively on the outcomes of action, the action itself, and the intuitive knowing implicit in the action.

A professional practitioner is a specialist who encounters certain types of situations again and again. As a practitioner experiences many variations of a small number of types of cases, he is able to 'practice' his practice. He develops a repertoire of expectations, images and techniques. He learns what to look for and how to respond to what he finds. As long as his practice is stable, in the sense that it brings him the same types of cases, he becomes less and less subject to surprise. His knowing-in-practice tends to become increasingly tacit, spontaneous, and automatic, thereby conferring upon him and his clients the benefits of specialization.

As a practice becomes more repetitive and routine, and as knowing-in-practice becomes increasingly tacit and spontaneous, the practitioner may miss important opportunities to think about what he is doing. He may find that he is drawn into patterns of error which he cannot correct. And if he learns, as often happens, to be selectively inattentive to phenomena that do not fit the categories of his knowing-in-action, then he may suffer from boredom or 'burn-out' and afflict his clients with the consequences of his narrowness and rigidity. When this happens, the practitioner has 'over-learned' what he knows.

A practitioner's reflection can serve as a corrective to over-learning. Through reflection, he can surface and criticize the tacit understandings that have grown up around the repetitive experiences of a specialized practice, and can make new sense of the situations of uncertainty or uniqueness which he may allow himself to experience.

Practitioners do reflect *on* their knowing-in-practice. Sometimes, in the relative tranquillity of a postmortem, they think back on a project they have undertaken, a situation they have lived through, and they explore the understandings they have brought to their handling of the case. They may do this in a mood of idle speculation, or in a deliberate effort to prepare themselves for future cases. But they may also reflect on practice while they are in the midst of it. Here they reflect-in-action.

When a practitioner reflects in and on his practice, the possible objects of his reflection are as varied as the kinds of phenomena before him and the systems of knowing-in-practice which he brings to them. He may reflect on the tacit norms and appreciations which underlie a judgment, or on the strategies and theories implicit in a pattern of behaviour. He may reflect on the feeling for a situation which has led him to adopt a particular course of action, on the way in which he has framed the problem he is trying to solve, or on the role he has constructed for himself within a larger institutional context.

Reflection-in-action, in these several modes, is central to the art through which practitioners sometimes cope with the troublesome 'divergent' situations of practice. When the phenomenon at hand eludes the ordinary categories of knowledge-in-practice, presenting itself as unique or unstable, the practitioner may surface and criticize his initial understanding of the phenomenon, construct a new description of it, and test the new description by an on-the-spot experiment. Sometimes he arrives at a new theory of the phenomenon by articulating a feeling he has about it.

When he is confronted with demands that seem incompatible or inconsistent, he may respond by reflecting on the appreciations which he and others have brought to the situation. Conscious of a dilemma, he may attribute it to the way in which he has set his problem, or even to the way in which he has framed his role. He may then find a way of integrating, or choosing among, the values at stake in the situation.

When someone reflects-in-action, he becomes a researcher in the practice context. He does not separate thinking from doing. Because his experimenting is a kind of action, implementation is built into his inquiry. Thus reflection-in-action can proceed, even in situations of uncertainty or uniqueness.

Although reflection-in-action is an extraordinary process, it is not a rare event. Indeed, for reflective practitioners it is the core of practice.

Reading 3.3

The teacher as researcher

Lawrence Stenhouse

Lawrence Stenhouse led the Humanities Project during the late 1960s – curriculum development work that revolutionised thinking about professional development. One of his central concerns was to encourage teachers as 'researchers' of their own practice, thereby extending their professionalism. There is a strong link between the argument of this reading and Dewey's conception of 'reflection' (Reading 3.1).

Edited from: Stenhouse, L. (1975) *An Introduction to Curriculum Research and Development.* London: Heinemann, 143–57.

All well-founded curriculum research and development, whether the work of an individual teacher, of a school, of a group working in a teachers' centre or of a group working within the co-ordinating framework of a national project, is based on the study of classrooms. It thus rests on the work of teachers.

It is not enough that teachers' work should be studied: they need to study it themselves. My theme is the role of the teachers as researchers in their own teaching situation. What does this conception of curriculum development imply for them?

The critical characteristics of that extended professionalism which is essential for well-founded curriculum research and development seem to me to be:

The commitment to systematic questioning of one's own teaching as a basis for development;

The commitment and the skills to study one's own teaching;

The concern to question and to test theory in practice.

To these may be added as highly desirable, though perhaps not essential, a readiness to allow other teachers to observe one's work directly or through recordings – and to discuss it with them on an open and honest basis. In short, the outstanding characteristics of the extended professional is a capacity for autonomous professional self-development through systematic self-study, through the study of the work of other teachers and through the testing of ideas by classroom research procedures.

It is important to make the point that teachers in this situation are concerned to understand better their own classroom. Consequently, they are not faced with the problems of generalizing beyond his or her own experience. In this context, theory is simply a systematic structuring of his or her understanding of such work.

Concepts which are carefully related to one another are needed both to capture and to express that understanding. The adequacy of such concepts should be treated as provisional. The utility and appropriateness of the theoretical framework of concepts should be testable; and the theory should be rich enough to throw up new and profitable questions.

Each classroom should not be an island. Teachers working in such a tradition need to communicate with one another. They should report their work. Thus a common vocabulary of concepts and a syntax of theory need to be developed. Where that language proves inadequate, teachers would need to propose new concepts and new theory.

The first level of generalization is thus the development of a general theoretical language. In this, professional research workers should be able to help.

If teachers report their own work in such a tradition, case studies will accumulate, just as they do in medicine. Professional research workers will have to master this material and scrutinize it for general trends. It is out of this synthetic task that general propositional theory can be developed.

Reading 3.4

Action research and the development of practice
Richard Pring

Richard Pring, a leading educational philosopher, builds on the Stenhouse tradition (see Reading 3.3) to take stock of some key characteristics of 'action research'. The reading makes useful comparisons with the characteristics of conventional academic research. Although there are important differences in key objectives, there are also many similarities in the issues that must be faced in any classroom enquiry. Pring emphasizes the need for openness, the importance of dialogue with colleagues and of critical reflection on practice. Action research may thus involve scrutiny of values, including those which might be embedded in centrally prescribed curricula, pedagogies or forms of assessment.

Edited from: Pring, R. (2000) *Philosophy of Educational Research.* Continuum: London, 130–4.

Respect for educational practitioners has given rise to the development of 'action research'. This may be contrasted with conventional research. The goal of research is normally that of producing new knowledge. There will, of course, be many different motives for producing such knowledge. But what makes it research is the systematic search for conclusions about 'what is the case' on the basis of relevant evidence. Such conclusions might, indeed, be tentative, always open to further development and refinement. But the purpose remains that of getting ever 'nearer the truth'. Hence, it makes sense to see the outcomes of research to be a series of propositions which are held to be true.

By contrast, the research called 'action research' aims not to produce new knowledge but to improve practice – namely, in this case, the 'educational practice' in which teachers are engaged. The conclusion is not a set of propositions but a practice or a set of transactions or activities which is not true or false but better or worse. By contrast with the conclusion of research, as that is normally conceived, action research focuses on the particular. Although such a practical conclusion focuses on the particular, thereby not justifying generalization, no one situation is unique in every respect and therefore the action research in one classroom or school can illuminate or be suggestive of practice elsewhere. There can be, amongst networks of teachers, the development of a body of professional knowledge of 'what works' or of how values might be translated into practice – or come to be transformed by practice. But there is a sense in which such professional knowledge has constantly to be tested out, reflected upon, adapted to new situations.

Research, as that is normally understood, requires a 'research forum' – a group of people with whom the conclusions can be tested out and examined critically. Without such openness to criticism, one might have missed the evidence or the counter argument which casts doubt on the conclusions drawn. Hence, the importance of dissemination through publications and seminars. To think otherwise is to assume a certitude which cannot be justified. Progress in knowledge arises through replication of the research activity, through criticism, through the active attempt to find evidence *against* one's conclusions.

Similarly, the growth of professional knowledge requires the sympathetic but critical community through which one can test out ideas, question the values which underpin the shared practice, seek solutions to problems, invite observation of one's practice, suggest alternative perspectives and interpretation of the data.

This is an important matter to emphasize. The temptation very often is to seek to justify and to verify, rather than to criticize or to falsify, one's belief, and to protect oneself by not sharing one's conclusions or the way in which one reached them.

With action research, reflection upon practice with a view to its improvement needs to be a public activity. By 'public' I mean that the research is conducted in such a way that others can scrutinize and, if necessary, question the practice of which it is part. Others become part of the reflective process – the identification and definition of the problem. the values which are implicit within the practice, the way of implementing and gathering evidence about the practice, the interpretation of the evidence. And yet teacher research, in the form of action research, is so often encouraged and carried out as a lonely, isolated activity. Those who are concerned with the promotion of action research – with the development in teachers of well-tested professional knowledge – must equally be concerned to develop the professional networks and communities in which it can be fostered.

There is a danger that such research might be supported and funded with a view to knowing the most effective ways of attaining particular goals – goals or targets set by government or others external to the transaction which takes place between teacher and learner. The teacher researches the most efficient means of reaching a particular educational objective (laid out, for instance. in the National Curriculum or a skills-focused vocational training). But this is not what one would have in mind in talking about research as part of professional judgement or action research as a response to a practical issue or problem. The reflective teacher comes to the problem with a set of values. The problem situation is one which raises issues as much about those values as it does about adopting an appropriate means to a given end. Thus, what makes this an educational practice is the set of values which it embodies – the intrinsic worth of the activities themselves, the personal qualities which are enhanced, the appropriate way of proceeding (given the values that one has and given the nature of the activity).

One comes to science teaching, for example, with views about the appropriate way of doing science – evidence based enquiry, openness to contrary evidence, clarity of procedures and conclusions. The practice of teaching embodies certain values – the importance of that which is to be learnt, the respect for the learner (how he or she thinks), the respect for evidence and the acknowledgement of contrary viewpoints. Therefore, when teacher researchers are putting into practice a particular strategy or are implementing a curriculum proposal, then they are testing out the values as much as the efficaciousness of the strategy or proposal. Are the values the researchers believe in being implemented in the practice? If not, does this lead to shifts in the values espoused or in the practice itself? Action research, in examining the implementation of a curriculum proposal, involves, therefore, a critique of the values which are intrinsic to the practice. Such a critique will reflect the values which the teacher brings to the practice, and those values will in turn be refined through critical reflection upon their implementation in practice. 'Action research' captures this ever shifting conception of practice through the attempt to put into practice certain procedures which one believes are educational.

However, such constant putting into practice, reflecting on that practice, refining of beliefs and values in the light of that reflection, subjecting the embodied ideas to criticism, cannot confine itself to the act of teaching itself. It cannot but embrace the context of teaching – the physical conditions in which learning is expected to take place, the expectations of those who determine the general shape of the curriculum, the resources available for the teachers to draw upon, the constraints upon the teacher's creative response to the issues, the scheme of assessment. It is difficult to see how the clash between the 'official curriculum' and the 'teacher researcher' can be avoided when the latter is constantly testing out the values of the teaching strategies. One can see, therefore, why the encouragement of teacher research is so often defined within official documents in a rather narrow sense.

Action research, therefore, is proposed as a form of research in which teachers review their practice in the light of evidence and of critical judgement of others. In so doing, they inevitably examine what happens to the values they hold, and which they regard as intrinsic to the transaction they are engaged in. Such critical appraisal of practice takes in three different factors which impinge upon practice, and shape the activities within it – the perceptions and values of the different participants, the 'official expectations and values' embodied within the curriculum, and the physical conditions and resources. To do this, various methods for gathering data will be selected – examination results, classroom observation, talking with the pupils. And the interpretation of what is 'working' will constantly be revised in the light of such data. But, of course, others too might, in the light of the data, suggest other possible interpretations. Thus, the dialogue continues. There is no end to this systematic reflection with a view to improving practice.

Reading 3.5

Competence and the complexities of teaching
James Calderhead

In this reading James Calderhead identifies five distinct areas of research on teaching and learning to teach and provides a concise overview of the main issues which have been considered. He summarises by highlighting the complexity of teachers' work and warning against partial and over-simplified conceptions.

How do you feel this analysis relates to the competences listed in Reading 17.3?

Edited from: Calderhead, J. (1994) 'Can the complexities of teaching be accounted for in terms of competences? Contrasting views of professional practice from research and policy'. Mimeo produced for an Economic and Social Research Council symposium on teacher competence, 1–2.

Within recent policy on teaching and teacher education, there has been a popular trend to consider issues of quality in teaching in terms of competences that can be pre-specified and continuously assessed. In particular, the competences that have received most attention have related to subject matter knowledge and classroom management skills, a view which might be simplistically matched to the different responsibilities of higher education institutions and schools as closer working partnerships are formed in initial training. Such a view of teaching, however, is in sharp contrast to the complexity of teachers' work highlighted by empirical research on teaching over the past decade.

Research on teaching and learning to teach falls into several distinct areas, each exploring different aspects of the processes of professional development amongst teachers, and each highlighting some of the influential factors involved.

Socialisation into the professional culture

The material and ideological context in which teachers work has been found to be one of the major influences upon the ways in which teachers carry out their work. New teachers are greatly influenced by traditions, taken-for-granted practices and implicit beliefs within the school, and a powerful 'wash out effect' has been identified (see Zeichner and Gore, 1990). Socialisation studies on professional development have succeeded in highlighting some of the complex interactions that occur between an individual's values, beliefs and practices and those of the school, and also the importance of the individual's capacity to negotiate and manoeuvre within a social system where there may well be several competing professional cultures. This raises issues concerning how student teachers might be appropriately prepared to work as members of teams or as individuals within institutions.

The development of knowledge and skills

This is perhaps the most often cited perspective on learning to teach which emphasises the knowledge and skills that contribute to classroom practice. Studies comparing experienced and novice teachers have demonstrated how the experienced teacher often has a much more sophisticated understanding of their practice. The experienced teacher appears to have access to a wide range of knowledge that can be readily accessed when dealing with classroom situations and which can help in interpreting and responding to them. Recent research on teachers' subject matter knowledge also indicates that teachers, for the purposes of teaching, relearn their subject and also develop a new body of knowledge concerning the teaching of the subject – Shulman's 'pedagogical content knowledge' (see Reading 9.7). Studies of novice and experienced teachers suggest that there is an enormous diversity of knowledge that the experienced teacher possesses, and that acquiring appropriate professional knowledge is often a difficult and extremely time-consuming process for the novice.

The moral dimension of teaching

Teaching as well as being a practical and intellectual activity is also a moral endeavour. Teaching involves caring for young people, considering the interests of children, preparing children to be part of a future society, and influencing the way in which they relate to each other and live. The ethic of caring has been claimed to be a central facet of teaching, often valued by teachers, parents and children, but frequently unacknowledged in discussions of professional development. Teaching in schools inevitably presents several moral dilemmas in the form of decisions about how to allocate time in the classroom, how to cater for individual needs, and how to maintain principles such as 'equality of opportunity'. How are teachers to be prepared for this?

The personal dimension of teaching

Several different aspects of the personal dimension have been emphasised in the research literature. First of all, teachers bring their own past experiences to bear on their interpretation of the teacher's task. Individual past experiences of school, of work, or parenting have been found to provide teachers with metaphoric ways of thinking about teaching that shape their professional reasoning and practice. Secondly, teachers' personalities are themselves an important aspect of teachers' work. In order to establish working relationships with children, to command their attention and respect and to ensure the smooth running of their classes, teachers' personalities are intrinsically involved. Part of the professional development of the novice teacher requires teachers to become aware of their personal qualities and how other people respond to them, so that they can take greater control in their interactions with others. Thirdly, evidence from research on teachers' life cycles suggests that people pass through different phases in their lives in which they adopt different perspectives on life and work, and experience different needs in terms of inservice support.

The reflective dimension of teaching

Notions of reflection have become extremely popular in recent discussions of teacher education. What reflection actually amounts to, however, is considerably less clear. Several notions of reflection are identifiable in the literature – reflection-in-action, reflection-on-action, deliberative reflection, etc. Attempts to generate greater levels of reflection amongst student teachers have taken many forms – reflective journals, action research, the use of theory and research evidence as analytical frameworks, etc. Creating a course that helps students to become more analytical about their practice and to take greater charge of their own professional development is a task with a number of inherent difficulties. For instance, how does the teacher educator reconcile their traditional role as a gatekeeper to the profession with that of mentor and facilitator of reflection? How is reflection fostered when in schools a much higher priority is given to immediate, spontaneous action rather than analysis and reflection? Efforts in this area, however, have stimulated enquiry into identifying the cognitive, affective and behavioural aspects of reflection: what are the skills, attitudes and conditions that promote reflection and enable greater levels of learning from experience to be achieved?

Research on teaching and teachers' professional development points towards the complexity of teachers' work. Each of the dimensions discussed above identifies an important set of variables and provides a partial picture of the whole professional development process. Learning to teach involves the development of technical skills, as well as an appreciation of moral issues involved in education, an ability to negotiate and develop one's practice within the culture of the school, and an ability to reflect and evaluate both in and on one's actions.

Such a view of teaching is in sharp contrast to that promulgated in the current language of 'competences' and 'subject matter knowledge'.

Reading 3.6

Practical judgement and evidence-informed practice

Ruth Heilbronn

This reading explains the deep roots of 'practical judgement' in Aristotle's philosophy and thus confirms the enduring qualities which are required in combining experience and analysis in practical contexts. Interestingly, Bennett writes on managing behaviour (Reading 7.3) from a similar position.

Heilbronn identifies three dimensions of practical judgement: ethics; flexibility; personal rootedness. In this way she affirms that teaching has moral purposes which always require personal judgement from the person who is the teacher. This is what makes it so interesting, and such a responsibility.

What forms of evidence could help you in making practical judgements?

Edited from Heilbronn, R. (2011) 'The nature of practice-based knowledge and understanding', in Heilbronn, R. and Yandell, J. (eds) *Critical Practice in Teacher Education: A Study of Professional Learning*. London: IOE Press, 7–9.

Practical judgement might be characterised as a capacity 'to do the right thing at the right time': to respond flexibly and appropriately in particular situations, whose unique correlation of variables could not be known in advance. Training for professional practice is designed to enable such expert decision making and action.

The concept of 'practical judgement' goes back to Aristotle's concept of *phronesis*. Although this rich notion has been interpreted in a variety of ways, a relevant understanding for teachers is found in Dunne's statement that *phronesis* is: 'an *eye* for what is salient in concrete situations' (Dunne, 1993: 368). Expert practitioners know what to do in specific situations. They have what seems to be 'an intuitive sense of the nature and texture of practical engagement' (Dunne, 1993: 8).

> Phronesis does not ascend to a level of abstraction or generality that leaves experience behind. It arises from experience *and returns into experience*. It is, we might say, the insightfulness – or using Aristotle's own metaphor, 'the eye' – of a particular type of experience, and the insights it achieves are turned back into experience, which is in this way constantly reconstructed or enriched. And the more experience is reconstructed in this way, the more sensitive and insightful phronesis becomes. *(Dunne, 1993: 293)*

In the above quotation the key term is 'experience'. There can be no split between elements encountered in reading, research, university and schools, because these elements make no sense, have no meaning, bear no significance to the practitioner, until and unless they are integrated and able to be applied. Understanding develops through the practical situations in which novices are placed, and with which they grapple. This is true for many kinds of workplaces, where novices may be changed by experience into highly proficient practitioners (Hogan, 2003).

It is possible to outline some characteristics of practical judgement in three main dimensions.

First, there is an ethical dimension to 'the right' response. Professional practices have their codes of ethics and it is expected that practitioners follow these codes and uphold the values of the profession. If we try to think of an example of practitioner action that seems 'value free' we soon give up the attempt. Teaching, nursing, social work, are thoroughly relational practices. They have 'the other', the client, the learner, the patient, whose welfare is inextricably linked to choices and actions. So the right action at any time needs to draw on ethical considerations: a good practitioner will be someone whose actions we can trust as 'wise' or 'judicious'. In acting seemingly spontaneously practitioners draw on their own values, qualities and dispositions, as well as on technical know-how and information based on previous, relevant experiences.

Having professional values and living by them in practice are an essential part of being a practitioner involved with others. The capacity for trustworthiness is fundamental to teaching. The practice of teaching involves the ability to see things from the learners' perspective, to show 'pedagogical thoughtfulness' (van Manen, 1991) and to make adjustments accordingly. Van Manen has described 'tactful' teaching, as that which 'locates practical knowledge not primarily in the intellect or the head but rather in the existential situation in which the person finds himself or herself' (van Manen, 1995: 45–6).

Practical judgement is connected to 'virtue', in the sense that such a practitioner exercises qualities of 'practical wisdom'. A good teacher could be said to be a wise person, someone who exercises an ethical sense of doing what is right, of acting for the good. An example would be a teacher who rejects a strategy for gaining order in the classroom which would involve humiliating pupils, in favour of another, involving more effort based on developing trusting relationships. As Smith (2003) has stated the importance of relationships between pupils, and between them and their teacher cannot be over-emphasised. Teaching is 'thoroughly relational' (Noddings, 2003: 249) and many of the virtues are exercised in relation to others in a pedagogical space of trust (van Manen, 1991).

A second dimension of practical judgement is its flexibility. Expert practitioners can respond flexibly to changing situations. We cannot know in advance what individual situations will throw up in the way of stimuli requiring response. Experts respond flexibly. Since there cannot be a definitive, right way to respond in every circumstance, it follows that any expert response might not be the best one for the circumstance. Therefore, reflecting on practice, interrogating aims, purposes and outcomes of particular choices in particular situations, can be a fruitful source of knowledge and understanding, and can support the development of practical judgement. It follows too that there can be no universally applicable, infallible theory or pedagogical intervention, given the contingency of individual situations of practice. This is significant if there are government promoted pedagogical strategies and educational changes and control over the school curriculum.

A third feature of judgement is its rootedness within an individual person, with a particular character, dispositions and qualities. When a teacher decides what is to be done in any situation, for example with a recalcitrant pupil, even if her decisions seem intuitive they are informed by the teacher's prior experiences and values. There is always more than one available course of action and individual teachers make choices of what they consider the right action in the circumstances. These choices may be based on a number of different factors, involving practical and ethical considerations. A teacher's character, dispositions and capacities underlie the exercise of practical judgement.

Good teachers can be said to exercise sound practical judgement, which involves exercising virtues such as justice, tolerance and courage, and qualities such as patience and optimism. We think of good teachers as acting with integrity and trustworthiness, being open-minded and able to learn from experience. It is an interesting exercise to think of all the qualities required, desired and expected, an exercise fruitfully revisited at various points in a teaching career (Burbules, 1997).

Reading 3.7

Learning in communities of practice
Heather Hodkinson and Phil Hodkinson

Lave and Wenger's (1991) ideas on 'communities of practice' have been hugely influential as a way of representing some kinds of learning and development in workplaces.
Induction into the teaching profession through school-based training is a case in point.
This reading stems from a two-year study of English secondary school teachers, taking as
case studies four subject departments, music, history, art and Information Technology, in
two schools (Hodkinson and Hodkinson, 2005). The authors propose extensions to Lave
and Wenger's work to take greater account of individual teacher identities and contexts
of power relations which in which teachers work.

Are you able to learn from, and contribute to, a community of practice?

Edited from: Hodkinson, H. and Hodkinson, P. (2002) 'Rescuing communities of practice
from accusations of idealism: a case study of workplace learning for secondary school
teachers in England'. Mimeo. London: Teaching and Learning Resource Programme.

Key parts of Lave and Wenger's (1991) argument are captured in the following quotation:

'As an aspect of social practice, learning involves the whole person; it implies not only
a relation to specific activities, but a relation to social communities. … Learning only
partly – and often incidentally – implies becoming able to be involved in new activities,
to perform new tasks and functions, to master new understandings. Activities, tasks,
functions, and understandings do not exist in isolation; they are part of broader systems
of relations in which they have meaning. These systems of relations arise out of and
are reproduced and developed within social communities, which are part of systems of
relations among persons. … [Learning] is itself an evolving form of membership. We
conceive of identities as long-term, living relations between persons and their place and
participation in communities of practice. Thus identity, knowing, and social membership
entail one another.' *(Lave and Wenger, 1991, p 53)*

Within this broad theoretical position, Lave and Wenger (1991, p. 98) state that a
community of practice is 'a set of relations among persons, activity, and world, over
time and in relation with other tangential and overlapping communities of practice'. No
doubt responding to demands for something more precise, Wenger (1998) gives a rather
narrower account, identifying communities of practice as having three dimensions: mutual
engagement, joint enterprise, and a shared repertoire of actions, discourses, tools etc.

The departments where the teachers in our study worked clearly fell within both definitions, in ways that allowed us to label them as communities of practice.

However, we found that the social interactions between members are particularly
important for understanding both the practices and culture of the community and the

learning of everyone within it. Lave and Wenger's theorising needs to be extended to incorporate this.

Teacher dispositions towards their work, their discipline and each other influence their reactions to the community of practice, their contributions to it and, thus, the ways in which that community is (re)constructed. Those dispositions can be related to teachers' previous biographies, to their lives and identities outside school, as well as their on-going participation within the community.

Additionally, we would argue that power relations, both inside and outside any community of practice, have to be given more direct attention. It is not just that such relations influence what individual workers can learn from a community, they also help determine its cultural norms and working practices.

This sort of extension into power relations draws attention to inequalities in learning opportunities in work, with those of higher status getting the greatest opportunities, either through more challenging, varied and innovative work, or through greater access to courses and financial support.

Teacher opportunities to learn stem from the challenges of the job, their interest and ability in taking forward their own subject and teaching interests, through reading etc., the challenges placed before them by new government initiatives, and access to at least some off the job learning. The barriers stem from the isolated nature of much of their work, reinforced by the tyranny of the timetable and bell; the lack of chances to engage with teachers outside their own departments or schools, and a range of government initiatives that stultify activity and increase pressures of performativity.

Principles

What are the foundations of effective teaching and learning?

4

The readings in this chapter illustrate the accumulation of knowledge about learning and effective pedagogic practice which is taking place across the world. Many other examples exist, as TLRP found (see James and Pollard, 2012). Whilst there are variations in different countries and in respect of particular cultures and policy environments, there are also very considerable overlaps in the learning and teaching strategies which are found to be effective, and in the ways which are being developed to understand (or theorise) these practices. Brian Simon's suggestion (11.3) that we should begin from what we share 'in common' is bearing fruit.

This is very good news for the teaching profession, because it means that a scientific foundation for pedagogy and for teacher professionalism is gradually establishing itself.

Each of the six readings draw from an attempt to review what is known about teaching and learning. First we hear from three influential countries – the USA (4.1), then Singapore (4.2) and Finland (4.3). The Organisation for Economic Cooperation and Development (4.4) offers us an international synthesis, and a National Foundation for Educational Research (NFER) team (4.5) provide a UK perspective. Finally, Hattie's meta-analysis (4.6) harvests studies far beyond his native New Zealand to comprehensively summarise the 'effect sizes' of different teaching strategies.

TLRP's ten principles for effective teaching and learning could have provided a further reading, but are the subject of the parallel chapter in *Reflective Teaching in Schools*. There, the rationale for 'evidence-informed principles' to guide policy and practice is rehearsed, together with discussion of each principle in turn. The chapter concludes with a focus on international knowledge accumulation in relation to teaching, learning and schooling.

The relevant parts of *reflectiveteaching.co.uk* maintain this focus and provide links to further work across the world. On the site, navigate to the schools book, and then to this chapter.

Reading 4.1

Brain, mind, experience and school: A US review

John Bransford, Anne Brown and Rodney Cocking

Bransford and his colleagues, drawing on a significant US stocktake of knowledge in the psychology and education, outline recent advances in research which have transformed understanding of how humans learn. They begin with five themes: memory; reasoning; early learning; metacognition; and cultural participation – but they go on to discuss the durability and application of learning, the characteristics of children and young people as learners, and the relationship between mind and brain. These themes are discussed further in Chapter 2 of Reflective Teaching in Schools.

Do you find the nature of these themes sufficiently fascinating to fuel your career in teaching? Hopefully so!

Edited from: Bransford, J. D., Brown, A. L. and Cocking, R. R. (eds) (1999) *How People Learn: Brain, Mind, Experience and School*. Washington, DC: National Academy Press, xi–xvi.

Learning is a basic, adaptive function of humans. More than any other species, people are designed to be flexible learners and active agents in acquiring knowledge and skills. Much of what people learn occurs without formal instruction, but highly systematic and organized information systems – reading, mathematics, the sciences, literature and the history of a society – require formal training, usually in schools. Over time, science, mathematics, and history have posed new problems for learning because of their growing volume and increasing complexity. The value of the knowledge taught in school also begins to be examined for its applicability to situations outside school.

Science now offers new conceptions of the learning process and the development of competent performance. Recent research provides a deep understanding of complex reasoning and performance on problem-solving tasks and how skill and understanding in key subjects are acquired. This summary provides an overview of the new science of learning.

Five themes that changed conceptions of learning

In the last 30 years, research has generated new conceptions of learning in five areas. As a result of the accumulation of new kinds of information about human learning, views of how effective learning proceeds have shifted from the benefits of diligent drill and practice to focus on students' understanding and application of knowledge.

1 *Memory and structure of knowledge*

Memory has come to be understood as more than simple associations; evidence describes the structures that represent knowledge and meaning. Knowing how learners develop coherent structures of information has been particularly useful in understanding the nature of organized knowledge that underlies effective comprehension and thinking.

2 *Analysis of problem solving and reasoning*

One of the most important influences on contemporary learning theory has been the basic research on expert learners. Learning theory can now account for how learners acquire skills to search a problem space and then use these general strategies in many problem-solving situations. There is a clear distinction between learned problem-solving skills in novice learners and the specialized expertise of individuals who have proficiency in particular subjects.

3 *Early foundations*

The development of creative methodologies for assessing infants' responses in controlled research settings has done much to illuminate early learning. Scientific studies of infants and young children have revealed the relationships between children's learning predispositions and their emergent abilities to organize and coordinate information, make inferences, and discover strategies for problem solving. As a result, educators are rethinking the role of the skills and abilities children bring with them to school to take advantage of opportunities for learning in school.

4 *Metacognitive processes and self-regulatory capabilities*

Individuals can be taught to regulate their behaviours. And these regulatory activities enable self-monitoring and executive control of one's performance. The activities include such strategies as predicting outcomes, planning ahead, apportioning one's time, explaining to one's self in order to improve understanding, noting failures to comprehend, and activating background knowledge.

5 *Cultural experience and community participation*

Participation in social practice is a fundamental form of learning. Learning involves becoming attuned to the constraints and resources, the limits and possibilities that are involved in the practices of the community. Learning is promoted by social norms that value the search for understanding. Early learning is assisted by the supportive context of the family and the social environment, through the kinds of activities in which adults engage with children. These activities have the effect of providing to toddlers the structure and interpretation of the culture's norms and rules, and these processes occur long before children enter school.

Transfer of learning

Another aspect of *effective* learning is its durability – does the learning have long-term impact in the ways it influences other kinds of learning or performance? Research studies on the concept of transfer of learning comprise a vast literature that can be synthesized into the new science of learning.

Key conclusions:

- Skills and knowledge must be extended beyond the narrow contexts in which they are initially learned. For example, knowing how to solve a maths problem in school may not transfer to solving maths problems in other contexts.

- It is essential for a learner to develop a sense of *when* what has been learned can be used – the conditions of applicability. Failure to transfer is often due to learners' lack of this type of conditional knowledge.

- Learning must be guided by generalized principles in order to be widely applicable. Knowledge learned at the level of rote memory rarely transfers; transfer most likely occurs when the learner knows and understands underlying principles that can be applied to problems in new contexts.

- Learners are helped in their independent learning attempts if they have conceptual knowledge. Studies of children's concept formation and conceptual development show the role of learners' mental representations of problems, including how one problem is similar *and* different from others and understanding the part-whole relationships of the components in the overall structure of a problem.

- Learners are most successful if they are mindful of themselves as learners and thinkers. A learner's self-awareness as a learner and the role of appraisal strategies keep learning on target or help keep the learner asking if s/he understands. Learners can become independent learners who are capable of sustaining their own learning – in essence, this is how human beings become life-long learners.

Children as learners

While there are remarkable commonalities across learners of all ages, children differ from adult learners in many ways. Studies of young children offer a window into the development of learning, and they show a dynamic picture of learning as it unfolds over time. A fresh understanding of infant cognition and of how young children build on early learning predispositions also offers ideas on ways to ease their transition into formal school settings.

Key findings:

- Humans have a predisposition to learn in certain domains, and young children actively engage in making sense of their worlds. In particular domains, such as biological and physical causality, number, and language, infants and young children have strong predispositions to learn rapidly and readily. These biases towards learning support and may make early learning possible and pave the way for competence in early schooling.

- Children lack knowledge and experience, but not reasoning ability. Although young children are inexperienced, they reason facilely with the knowledge they have.

- Precocious knowledge may jump-start the learning process, but because of limited experience and undeveloped systems for logical thinking, children's knowledge contains misconceptions. Misinformation can impede school learning, so teachers need to be aware of the ways in which children's background knowledge influences what they understand. Such awareness on the part of teachers will help them anticipate children's confusion and recognize why children have difficulties grasping new ideas.

- Strategies for learning are important. Children can learn practically anything by sheer will and effort, but when required to learn about non-privileged domains, they need to develop strategies of intentional learning.

- Children need to understand what it means to learn, who they are as learners, and how to go about planning, monitoring and revising, to reflect upon their learning and that of others, and to learn to determine for themselves if they understand. These skills of metacognition provide strategic competencies for learning.

- Children are both problem solvers and problem generators. They attempt to solve problems presented to them, and they seek novel challenges. They refine and improve their problem-solving strategies in the face of failure and often build on prior successes. They persist because success and understanding are motivating in their own right.

- Adults help children make connections between new situations and familiar ones. Children's curiosity and persistence are supported by adults who direct children's attention, structure experiences, support learning attempts, and regulate the complexity and difficulty levels of information for children.

Children thus exhibit capacities that are shaped by environmental experiences and the individuals who care for them. Developmental processes involve interactions between children's early competencies and the environmental supports – strengthening relevant capacities and pruning the early abilities that are less relevant to the child's community. Learning is promoted and regulated by both the biology and the ecology of the child: learning *produces* development.

Collateral development of mind and brain

Advances in neuroscience are confirming many theoretical hypotheses, including the important role of early experience in development. What is new, and therefore important for the new science of learning, is the convergence of evidence from a number of scientific fields. As developmental psychology, cognitive psychology, and neuroscience, to name but three, have contributed vast numbers of research studies, details about learning and development have converged to form a more complete picture of how intellectual development occurs. Clarification of some of the mechanisms or learning by neuroscience advanced with the advent of non-invasive imaging technologies, such as positron emission tomography (PET) and functional magnetic resonance imaging (fMRI). These technologies enabled researchers to observe directly functions of human learning.

The key finding is the importance of experience in building the structure of the mind by modifying the structures of the brain: development is not solely the unfolding of programmed patterns. Some of the rules that govern learning are now known. One of the simplest rules is that practice increases learning and there is a corresponding relationship between the amount of experience in a complex environment and the amount of structural change in the brain.

Key conclusions:

- Learning changes the physical structure of the brain.
- Structural changes alter the functional organization of the brain; in other words, learning organizes and reorganizes the brain.
- Different parts of the brain may be ready to learn at different times.

Reading 4.2

A tale of two pedagogies: Teaching and learning in Singapore

David Hogan, Phillip Towndrow, Dennis Kwek, Ridzuan Rahim, Melvin Chan and Serena Luo

Singapore's educational system is recognised as world leading, at least as measured by the metrics of international assessments. The authors of this reading draw on findings from a large, national, three-year multi-method research project in secondary English and Mathematics lessons. They describe the contribution that a highly performative pedagogical orientation focused on knowledge transmission and high stakes assessments has made to securing Singapore's international position.

However, they argue that there is now substantial evidence that the value of this particular pedagogical model has run its course. They argue that reform focused on promoting a more balanced twenty-first century pedagogical regime, that supports knowledge building as well as knowledge transmission, will require changes to rules through which schools are held accountable.

Commissioned for this volume: Hogan, D., Towndrow, P., Kwek, D., Rahim, R., Chan, M. and Luo, S. (2012) 'A tale of two pedagogies: teaching and learning in Singapore'. Singapore: National Institute of Education.

Performative pedagogy

Classroom instruction in Singapore's Secondary 3 Mathematics and English is dominated by a coherent, highly institutionalized and authoritative folk pedagogy of the kind that is often termed transmissionist. We have preferred the term *performative* because of its single-minded commitment to optimizing the performance of students in national and international assessments.

The key features of Singapore's performative pedagogy include a determined focus on curriculum coverage, knowledge transmission and exam preparation for national high stakes assessments; a strong and institutionally sanctioned inclination for teachers to 'teach to the test'; fidelity of task implementation to task design; pragmatic, fit-for-purpose instructional choices that draw widely on Eastern and Western pedagogical traditions and models but particularly focus on techniques drawn from direct instruction and traditional instruction (worksheets, textbooks, drill and practice); a pervasive and authoritative ability discourse; and a preponderance of closed questions, limited exchanges and performative talk during lessons. Teachers make limited use of high leverage instructional practices including checking for prior knowledge, communicating learning goals and performance standards, individual monitoring, formative assessment/

feedback, strategic learning support, multi-modal knowledge, collaborative group work and extended elaborated exchanges and understanding talk in classrooms. Teachers routinely compound bureaucratic and epistemic authority, and broadly achieve a high degree of alignment between the curriculum, instruction and assessment. More broadly still, the system delivers a pedagogical regime that is focused, clear-eyed, purposeful, pragmatic, extremely effective (at least on the metrics supplied by international assessments) and taught by teachers who are well-trained, well-paid, well-supported and committed in schools run by carefully selected and highly trained principals (Hogan et al., 2011, 2013a; Hogan, Chan, Rahim, Towndrow and Kwek, 2012a; Hogan, Towndrow, Kwek, Yang and Tan, 2013b).

Still, as effective as it has been, for the past decade or more, the government has been convinced that changes in the broader institutional environment, particularly those associated with globalization and modernization in East Asia, have rendered Singapore's performative pedagogy problematic and in need of reform. The government has by no means sought to replace the system's dominant performative pedagogical orientation but it has supported a range of policy initiatives suitable for a small but very ambitious knowledge economy. Although these initiatives have resulted in significant changes in the cultural order and governance of schooling, pedagogically they have not had substantial or sustainable consequences for classroom teaching and student achievement. This is partly an issue of teacher capacity, but principally it is a consequence of the iron grip that broader meritocratic institutional rules, particularly those associated with national high stakes assessments at the end of primary and secondary school, have on classroom teaching. In Singapore, as teachers do in other systems with similar institutional rules, *teachers teach to the test*. Indeed, although Singapore's performative pedagogical regime has established a relatively high floor under the quality of teaching and learning in Singaporean classrooms, it now constrains rather than encourages responsible risk taking, innovation and instructional improvement. This is not to say that there is no evidence of (or sympathy for) a knowledge building or teaching for understanding pedagogies in Singapore. There is, but they are clearly subordinate to the dominant performative pedagogy and appear to have very little, if any, impact on student performance in conventional assessment tasks. This situation is very unlikely to change until and unless important alternations are made to key institutional aspects of Singapore's pedagogical regime. This has important implications for systems well beyond Singapore's shores seeking to reform classroom pedagogy.

What is to be done?

The tension between a highly institutionalized (and successful) performative pedagogy at the classroom level and ambitious 21st century pedagogical aspirations at the policy level poses a major conundrum for policy makers in Singapore. Caught between their history and their aspirations, policy makers are currently seeking to find ways of enhancing the presence of knowledge building pedagogical practices in the classroom without (explicitly) repudiating the importance of knowledge transmission or the national high stakes assessment regime. Our view is that creating a more balanced (and institutionally relevant) pedagogy will be no easy task, and will take a decade or more to achieve, but that it is possible *provided* the system achieves clarity about the key learning goals of knowledge building pedagogy and secures a number of critical modifications to national curriculum frameworks and the high stakes assessment regime. In addition, these changes will need to be supported by collateral changes to pre-service and in-service teacher education programs.

In broad terms, we take a knowledge building pedagogy to be one that prioritizes, not just factual information and procedural fluency, but conceptual understanding, knowledge building capacity and expertise through learning that is authentic, deep, meaningful, situated, collaborative, transferable and institutionally relevant. Achieving these goals will depend, first and foremost, on task designs that provide extensive access to conceptual, epistemic and metacognitive as well as procedural and factual knowledge and rich opportunities for student participation in domain-specific knowledge practices (particularly those associated with generating, representing, communicating, interrogating, deliberating, justifying and applying knowledge claims), extended understanding talk and cognitively complex ICT mediated activities. Beyond this, implementing a knowledge building pedagogy will depend on the use of high leverage instructional practices that enhance task fidelity and support visible learning, and the use of assessment tasks that focus on elaborated, epistemically rich, cognitively complex, collaborative, ICT mediated knowledge work. But neither the employment of knowledge building tasks, or the adoption of high leverage instructional practices that support them, will happen until and unless knowledge building rather than performativity are explicitly recognized and supported in national curriculum frameworks, national high stakes assessments and professional learning programs. Beyond this, developing and bedding down a successful knowledge building pedagogy will require no little critical attention to broader cultural understandings of teaching, learning and knowledge and the dominant folk pedagogy that it nurtures.

In short, instructional improvement in Singapore will depend on a new alignment of curriculum, assessment, instruction and professional learning and cultural understanding that takes knowledge and learning seriously epistemically and cognitively rather than on a heightened emphasis on the key elements of an outdated and *passé* performative pedagogy. This, it seems to us, is the important lesson of the Singaporean story.

Reading 4.3

What the world can learn from educational change in Finland

Pasi Sahlberg

Finland is system with which the countries of the UK are often compared, and Sahlberg considers what others can learn from their experience. Some particular characteristics of Finnish society are apparent, but so too is the 'main message' that improvement comes enhancing teacher quality, limiting student testing to a necessary minimum, placing responsibility and trust before accountability, and handing over school- and district-level leadership to education professionals. Finland's comprehensive school system is explicitly contrasted with market models for improvement.

Sahlberg offers Finland as a model in which public policy 'builds on teacher strengths' and offers 'fear-free learning for students'.

Edited from: Sahlberg, P. (2011). *Finnish Lessons: What Can the World Learn from Educational Change in Finland.* New York: Teachers College Press, 1–6, 140–5.

The demand for better quality teaching and learning, and more equitable and efficient education is universal. Indeed, educational systems are facing a twin challenge: how to change schools so that students may learn new types of knowledge and skills required in an unpredictable changing knowledge world, and how to make that new learning possible for all young people regardless of their socioeconomic conditions. To be successful with these challenges is both a moral and economic imperative for our societies and their leaders.

At the beginning of the 1990s, education in Finland was nothing special in international terms. All young Finns attended school regularly, the school network was wide and dense, secondary education was accessible for all Finns, and higher education was an option for an increasing number of upper secondary school graduates. However, the performance of Finnish students on international assessments was close to overall averages, except in reading, where Finnish students did better that most of their peers in other countries. The unexpected and jarring recession of that time brought Finland to the edge of a financial breakdown. Bold and immediate measures were necessary to fix national fiscal imbalances and revive the foreign trade that disappeared with the collapse of the Soviet Union in 1990. Nokia, the main global industrial brand of Finland, became a critical engine in boosting Finland from the country's biggest economic dip since World War II. Another Finnish brand, *peruskoulu*, or the 9-year comprehensive basic school, was the other key player in the turnaround of the Finnish economy and society. Interestingly, both Nokia and the Finnish public educational system have their origins in the same time period in Finnish history: the golden years of building the Finnish national identity in the mid-19th century.

Finland as an example

Public educational systems are in crisis in many parts of the world. The United States, England, Sweden, Norway and France, just to mention a few nations, are among those where public education is increasingly challenged because of endemic failure to provide adequate learning opportunities to all children. Tough solutions are not uncommon in these countries. Tightening control over schools, stronger accountability for student performances, firing bad teachers, and closing down troubled schools are part of the recipe to fix failing education systems.

The main message from experience in Finland is that there is another way to improve education systems. This includes improving the teaching force, limiting student testing to a necessary minimum, placing responsibility and trust before accountability, and handing over school- and district-level leadership to education professionals. These are common education policy themes in some of the high performing countries – Finland among them – in the 2009 International Programme for International Student Assessment (PISA) of the OECD (2010a, 2010b). I offer five reasons why Finland is an interesting and relevant source of ideas for other nations that are looking for ways to improve their education systems.

One, Finland has a unique educational system because it has progressed from mediocrity to being a model contemporary educational system and 'strong performer' over the past 3 decades. Finland is special also because it has been able to create an educational system where students learn well and where equitable education has translated into small variations in student performance between schools in different parts of the country at the same time. This internationally rare status has been achieved using reasonable financial resources and less effort that other nations have expended on reform efforts.

Two, because of this proven steady progress, Finland demonstrates that there is another way to build a well-performing educational system using solutions that differ from market-driven education policies. The Finnish way of change is one of trust, professionalism and shared responsibility (Hargreaves and Shirley, 2009). Indeed Finland is an example of a nation that lacks school inspection, standardized curriculum, high-stakes student assessments, test-based accountability, and a race-to-the-top mentality with regard to educational change.

Three, as a consequence of its success, Finland can offer some alternative ways to think about solutions to existing chronic educational problems in the United States, Canada and England (such as high school drop-out rates, early teacher attrition an inadequate special education) and emerging needs to reform educational systems elsewhere (such as engaging students in learning, attracting young talents into teaching, and establishing holistic public sector policies). The Finnish approach to reducing early school leavers, enhancing teacher professionalism, implementing intelligent accountability and student assessment in schools, and improving learning in mathematics, science and literacy can offer inspiration to other school systems looking for a path to success.

Four, Finland is also an international high performer in commerce, technology, sustainable development, good governance, and prosperity and thus raises interesting questions concerning interdependencies between school and other sectors in society. It appears that other public policy sectors, such as health and employment, seem to play a role also in long-term educational development and change. In Finland, this holds true as well regarding income parity, social mobility, and trust within Finnish society.

Finally, we should listen to the story of Finland because it gives hope to those who are losing their faith in public education and whether it can be changed. This case reveals that the transformation of educational systems is possible, but that it takes time, patience and determination. The Finnish story is particularly interesting because some of the key policies and changes were introduced during the worst economic crisis that Finland has experienced since World War I. It suggests that a crisis can spark the survival spirit that leads to better solutions to acute problems than a 'normal situation' would. This speaks against those who believe that the best way to solve chronic problems in many educational systems is to take control away from school boards and give it to those who might run them more effectively, by charters or other means of privatization.

Although there are limits to the ideas that can be transferred from Finland to other nations, certain basic lessons may have general value for other educational systems, such as the practice of building on teacher strengths, securing relaxed and fear-free learning for students, and gradually enchanting trust within educational systems.

There is no single reason why any educational system succeeds or fails. Instead, there is a network of interrelated factors – educational, political and cultural – that function differently in different situations. I would, however, like to cite three important elements of Finnish educational policies since the early 1970s that appear to transcend culture.

The first one is an inspiring vision of what a good public education should be: Finland has been particularly committed to building a good publicly financed and locally governed basic school for every child. This common educational goal became so deeply rooted in politics and public services in Finland that it survived opposing political governments and ministries unharmed and intact. Since the introduction of *peruskoulu* in the early 1970s, there have been 20 governments and nearly 30 different ministers of education in charge of educational reform in Finland.

The second aspect of educational change that deserves attention is the way Finland has treated advice offered externally vis-à-vis its own educational heritage in educational reforms. Much of the inspiration in building independent Finland since 1917 has come from its neighbours, especially from Sweden. The welfare state model, health care system, and basic education are good examples of borrowed ideas from our western neighbour. Later, Finnish education policies were also influenced by guidance from supranational institutions, especially the OECD (which Finland joined in 1969) and European Union (which Finland joined in 1995). And yet, despite international influence and borrowing educational ideas from others, Finland has in the end created its own way to build the educational system that exists today. Many pedagogical ideas and educational innovations are also initially imported from other countries, often from North America or the United Kingdom.

The third aspect of change is a systematic development of respectful and interesting working conditions for teachers and leaders in Finnish schools. This raises an important question that is repeated in almost any situation when whole-system educational reforms are discussed: How do we get the best young people into teaching? Experience from Finland suggests that it is not enough to establish world-class teacher education programs or pay teachers well. The true Finnish difference is that teachers in Finland may exercise their professional knowledge and judgement both widely and freely in their schools.

The future of Finnish education

The Big Dream in the early 1990s was to make the educational system serve the social cohesion, economic transformation and innovation that would help Finland to be a full member of the European Union and remain a fully autonomous nation.

The Big Dream for the future of Finnish education should be something like this: *Create a community of learners that provides the conditions that allow all young people to discover their talent.* The talent may be academic, artistic, creative, or kinesthetic or some other skill set. What is needed for each school to be a safe learning community for all to engage, explore and interact with other people. School should teach knowledge and skills as before but it must prepare young people to be wrong too. If people are not prepared to be wrong, as Sir Ken Robinson says they will not come up with new ideas that have value (Robinson, 2009). That is the only way that we in Finland will be able to make the best use of our scarce human resources.

Many changes are required to the existing format of schooling. First and foremost, Finnish schools must continue to become more pupil-friendly so that it allows more personalized learning paths. Personalization doesn't mean replacing teachers with technology and individualized study. Indeed, the new Finnish school must be a socially inspiring and safe environment for all pupils to learn the social skills that they need in their lives. Personalized learning and social education lead to more specialization but build on the common ground of knowledge and skills. The following themes of change would emerge:

1 *Development of a personal road map for learning*

   It is important for each young person to acquire certain basic knowledge, such as reading, writing, and using mathematics. In the future, it will be important that students have alternative ways to learn these basic things. Children will learn more and more of what we used to learn in school out of school, through media, the Internet, and from different social networks to which they belong. This will lead to a situation in which an increasing number of students will find teaching in schools irrelevant because they have already learned what is meaningful for them elsewhere.

   A good solution to address this is to rethink schools so that learning in them relies more on individual customized learning plans and less on teaching drawn from a standardized curriculum for all. The art of future education will be to find a balance between these two.

2 *Less classroom-based teaching*

   Developing customized and activity-based learning eventually leads to a situation in which people can learn most of what is now taught in schools through digital devices wherever and whenever. Hand-held portable devices will provide online access to knowledge and other learners. Shared knowing and competences that are becoming an integral part of modern expertise and professional work will also become part of schools and traditional classrooms. Finland and some other countries have shown that it is not the length of the school year or school day that matters most. Less teaching can lead to more students learning if the circumstances are right and solutions smart. Such circumstances include trust in schools, adequate support and guidance for all students, and curriculum that can be locally adjusted to meet the interests and requirements of local communities.

3 *Development of interpersonal skills and problem solving*

In the future people will spend more time on and give more personal attention to media and communication technologies than they do today. It means two things from the educational point of view. First, people in general will spend less time together in a concrete social setting. Social interaction will be based on using social networking and other future tools that rely on digital technological solutions. Second, people will learn more about the world and other people through media and communication technologies. Especially expanding engagement in social media and networks will create a whole new source of learning from other people who have similar interests.

Schools need to rethink what their core task in educating people will be. It cannot remain as it is today: to provide the minimum basic knowledge and skills that young people need in the future. The future is now and many young people are already using those skills in their lives today. Schools need to make sure that all students learn to be fluent in reading, mathematics, and science concepts, and possess the core of cultural capital that is seen as essential. Equally important, however, is that all students develop attitudes and skills for using available information and opportunities. They will also need to develop better skills for social interaction, both virtual and real, learn to cooperate with people who are very different from themselves, and cope in complex social networks.

4 *Engagement and creativity as pointers of success*

Current education systems judge individual talent primarily by using standardized knowledge tests. At worst these tests include only multiple choice tasks. At best they expand beyond routine knowledge and require analytical, critical thinking, and problem solving skills. However, they rarely are able to cover the non-academic domains that include creativity, complex handling of information, or communicating new ideas to others.

Conventional knowledge tests will gradually give space to new forms of assessment in schools. As schools move to emphasize teaching skills that everybody needs in a complex and unpredictable world, the criteria of being a successful school will also change. People will learn more of what they need through digital tools and media, and therefore it will become increasingly difficult to know what role schools have played in students' learning (or not learning if you wish) of intended things. Two themes will be important as we move toward the end of this decade.

First, engaging all students in learning in school will be more important than ever. Lack of engagement is the main reason for the challenge that teachers face in schools and classrooms today. It is well known from research and practice that as children get older their interest in what schools offer declines. By the end of *peruskoulu* a growing number of young people find school learning irrelevant, and they are seeking alternative pathways to fulfil their intentions. Therefore, engagement in productive learning in school should become an important criterion of judging the success or failure of schools.

Second, students' ability to create something valuable and new in school will be more important than ever – not just for some students, but for most of them. If creativity is defined as coming up with original ideas that have value, then creativity should be important as literacy and treated with the same status. Finnish school have traditionally encouraged risk taking, creativity, and innovation. These traditions need to be strengthened. When performance of students or success of schools is measured, the creative aspect of both individual learning and collective behaviour should be given. In other words, a successful school is able to take each individual – both students and teachers – further in their development that they could have gone by themselves.

The Finnish way of educational change should be encouraging to those who have found the path of competition, choice, test-based accountability, and performance-based pay to be a dead end. It reveals that creative curricula, autonomous teachers, courageous leadership and high performance to together.

Reading 4.4

The nature of learning: An OECD stocktake

Hanna Dumont, David Istance and Francisco Benavides

> The OECD's Centre for Educational Research and Innovation set out to answer key questions: What do we know about how people learn? How do young people's motivations and emotions influence their learning? What are the benefits of group work, formative assessment, technology or project-based learning, and when are they most effective? How is learning affected by family background? Answers were expressed through seven principles for practical application – as indicated below.
>
> Can you identify overlaps in the OECD summary and the themes proposed by Bransford et al. from the US (Reading 4.1) or TLRP's principles (Chapter 4 of Reflective Teaching in Schools)? Knowledge and understanding accumulates in such ways.
>
> *Edited from:* Dumont, H., Istance, D. and Benavides, F. (2010) 'Executive summary', in *The Nature of Learning: Using Research to Inspire Practice.* Paris: OECD, 13–8.

Why such interest in learning?

Over recent years, learning has moved increasingly centre stage for a range of powerful reasons that resonate politically as well as educationally across many countries.

OECD societies and economies have experienced a profound transformation from reliance on an industrial to a knowledge base. Global drivers increasingly bring to the fore what some call '21st century competences'. The quantity and quality of learning thus become central, with the accompanying concern that traditional educational approaches are insufficient.

Similar factors help to explain the strong focus on measuring learning outcomes (including the Programme for International Student Assessment [PISA]) over the past couple of decades, which in turn generates still greater attention on learning. *To move beyond the diagnosis of achievement levels and shortcomings to desirable change requires the development of deeper understanding of how people learn most effectively.*

The sense of reaching the limits of educational reform invites a fresh focus on learning itself. Indeed, education has been reformed and reformed again in most OECD countries, leading many to wonder whether we need new ways to influence the very interface of learning and teaching.

The research base on learning has grown enormously but many researchers observe how inadequately schools tend to exemplify the conclusions of the learning sciences. At the same time, far too much research on learning is disconnected from the realities of educational practice and policy making. Can the bridges be made to inform practice by this growing evidence base?

The nature of learning

This summary aims to help in building bridges and 'using research to inspire practice'. Leading researchers from Europe and North America were invited to take different perspectives on learning, summarising large bodies of research and identifying their significance for the design of learning environments.

Their work provides a powerful knowledge base for the design of learning environments for the 21st century.

The conclusions are summarised below with a small selection of the key arguments made by the different authors.

1 *The learning environment recognises the learners as its core participants, encourages their active engagement and develops in them an understanding of their own activity as learners.*

A learning environment oriented around the centrality of learning encourages students to become 'self-regulated learners'. This means developing the 'meta-cognitive skills' for learners to monitor, evaluate and optimise their acquisition and use of knowledge (De Corte, 2010; Schneider and Stern, 2010). It also means to be able to regulate one's emotions and motivations during the learning process (Boekaerts, 2010; Hinton and Fischer, 2010).

Wiliam (2010) notes that many have called for a shift in the role of the teacher from the 'sage on the stage' to the 'guide on the side.' He warns against this characterisation if it is interpreted as relieving the teacher, individually and collectively, of responsibility for the learning that takes place.

Resnick, Spillane, Goldman and Rangel (2010) identify as critical the gap between the 'technical core' (i.e. classroom teaching) and the formal organisation in which it is located and the wider policy environment, a gap which reduces learning effectiveness and innovative capacity.

2 *The learning environment is founded on the social nature of learning and actively encourages well-organised co-operative learning.*

'Effective learning is not purely a 'solo' activity but essentially a 'distributed' one: individual knowledge construction occurs throughout processes of interaction, negotiation and co-operation' (De Corte, 2010). Neuroscience shows that the human brain is primed for interaction (Hinton and Fischer, 2010). However valuable that self-study and personal discovery may be, learning depends on interacting with others.

There are robust measured effects of co-operative forms of classroom learning when it is done properly as described by Slavin (2010). Despite this, such approaches still remain on the margins of much school activity. The ability to co-operate and learn together should be fostered as a '21st century competence', quite apart from its demonstrated impact on measured learning outcomes.

3 *The learning professionals within the learning environment are highly attuned to the learners' motivations and the key role of emotions in achievement.*

The emotional and cognitive dimensions of learning are inextricably entwined. It is therefore important to understand not just learners' cognitive development but their motivations and emotional characteristics as well. Yet, attention to learner beliefs and motivations is much further away from standard educational thinking than goals framed in terms of cognitive development (Boekaerts, 2010).

Being highly attuned to learners' motivations and the key role of emotions is not an exhortation to be 'nice' – misplaced encouragement will anyway do more harm than good – but is first and foremost about making learning more effective, not more enjoyable.

Powerful reasons for the success of many approaches using technology (Mayer, 2010), co-operative learning (Slavin, 2010), inquiry-based learning (Barron and Darling-Hammond, 2010) and service learning (Furco, 2010) lie in their capacity to motivate and engage learners.

4 *The learning environment is acutely sensitive to the individual differences among the learners in it, including their prior knowledge.*

Students differ in many ways fundamental to learning: prior knowledge, ability, conceptions of learning, learning styles and strategies, interest, motivation, self-efficacy beliefs and emotion, as well in socio-environmental terms such as linguistic, cultural and social background. A fundamental challenge is to manage such differences, while at the same time ensuring that young people learn together within a shared education and culture.

Prior knowledge is one of the most important resources on which to build current learning as well as one of the most marked individual difference among learners: '… perhaps the single most important individual differences dimension concerns the prior knowledge of the learner' (Mayer, 2010). Understanding these differences is an integral element of understanding the strengths and limitations of individuals and groups of learners, as well as the motivations that so shape the learning process.

'Families serve as the major conduit by which young children acquire fundamental cognitive and social skills' (Schneider, Keesler and Morlock, 2010), meaning that prior knowledge is critically dependent on the family and background sources of learning and not only what the school or learning environment has sought to impart.

5 *The learning environment devises programmes that demand hard work and challenge from all without excessive overload.*

That learning environments are more effective when they are sensitive to individual differences stems also from the findings stressed by several authors that each learner needs to be sufficiently challenged to reach just above their existing level and capacity. The corollary is that no-one should be allowed to coast for any significant amounts of time on work that does not stretch them.

Learning environments should demand hard work and effort from all involved. But the findings reported in this volume also show that overload and de-motivating regimes based on excessive pressure do not work because they do not make for effective learning. For Schneider and Stern (2010), a fundamental cornerstone is that 'learning is constrained by capacity limitations of the human information-processing architecture' (also stressed by Mayer, 2010).

6   *The learning environment operates with clarity of expectations and deploys assessment strategies consistent with these expectations; there is strong emphasis on formative feedback to support learning.*

Assessment is critical for learning. 'The nature of assessments defines the cognitive demands of the work students are asked to undertake' (Barron and Darling-Hammond, 2010). It provides 'the bridge between teaching and learning' (Wiliam, 2010). When assessment is authentic and in line with educational goals it is a powerful tool in support of learning; otherwise it can be a serious distraction.

Formative assessment is a central feature of the learning environment of the 21st century. Learners need substantial, regular and meaningful feedback; teachers need it in order to understand who is learning and how to orchestrate the learning process.

The research shows strong links between formative assessment practices and successful student learning. Such approaches need to be integrated into classroom practice to have such benefits (Wiliam, 2010).

7   *The learning environment strongly promotes 'horizontal connectedness' across areas of knowledge and subjects as well as to the community and the wider world.*

Complex knowledge structures are built up by organising more basic pieces of knowledge in a hierarchical way; discrete objects of learning need to be integrated into larger frameworks, understandings and concepts. (Schneider and Stern, 2010).

The connectedness that comes through developing the larger frameworks so that knowledge can be transferred and used across different contexts and to address unfamiliar problems is one of the defining features of the 21st century competences. Learners are often poor at transferring understanding of the same idea or relationship in one domain to another.

Meaningful real-life problems have a key role to play in bolstering the relevance of the learning being undertaken, supporting both engagement and motivation. Inquiry- and community-based approaches to learning offer extensive examples of how this can be done (Barron and Darling-Hammond, 2010; Furco, 2010). An effective learning environment will at the least not be at odds with the influences and expectations from home; better still, it will work in tandem with them (Schneider, Keesler and Morlock, 2010).

A demanding educational agenda

The force and relevance of these overall conclusions or 'principles' do not reside in each one taken in isolation from the others. Instead, they provide a demanding framework and all should be present in a learning environment for it to be judged truly effective. The educational agenda they define may be characterised as: *learner-centred, structured, personalised, inclusive and social.*

Reading 4.5

'Good teaching': A UK review

Naomi Rowe, Anne Wilkin and Rebekah Wilson

This reading is drawn from the findings of a literature review conducted by the UK's National Foundation for Educational Research. Their report summarises what research since 2006 tells us about the characteristics of 'good teaching'. It is organised under the themes of teaching environment, teaching approaches and teacher characteristics.

Again, can you find overlaps with other reviews on learning and on teaching?

Edited from: Rowe, N., Wilkin, A. and Wilson, R. (2012) *Mapping of Seminal Reports on Good Teaching* (NFER Research Programme: Developing the Education Workforce). Slough: NFER, 2–5, 8, 10, 15–17.

What do we understand by the term 'effective teaching' – or 'pedagogy' as it is often described? Alexander (2008) argued that the two terms are not synonymous and that pedagogy is often too narrowly defined as merely what teachers do in the classroom: the action, but without the values, theories and evidence that underpin it. The term 'pedagogy' involves 'acquiring and exercising rather more expertise – intellectual and ethical – than is often understood by the term 'teaching'' (GTCE, 2011, p. 88).

The notion of 'expert professional knowledge' is said to be central to the concept of effective pedagogy. It is not just about individual teachers' practices and values but 'encompasses the domains of curriculum and assessment, together with the social, cultural and policy context of young people's learning' (GTCE, 2011, p. 88), thus building on Alexander's (2008) notion of teachers as educators rather than mere technicians. Such expert knowledge needs to include teachers' subject knowledge, but also how teachers then apply that knowledge to their teaching in order to facilitate their pupils' knowledge and understanding.

The NFER review is based on 25 reports, mainly but not exclusively from the UK, and seeks to develop a map of significant evidence since 2006 of what good teaching looks like. This is summarised in Figure 4.5.1.

Teaching environment

A number of reports emphasised the benefits for learners of a calm, well-disciplined and orderly classroom environment in which pupils feel safe and secure (Dunne et al., 2007; Sammons et al., 2008; OECD, 2009; Siraj-Blatchford et al., 2011). The establishment of clear boundaries and behavioural expectations within a culture of mutual respect was reported to encourage pupils' confidence and facilitate their learning (Day et al., 2008; Siraj-Blatchford et al., 2011).

Figure 4.5.1 Some key features of effective teaching

Teaching environment	Teaching approaches	Teacher characteristics
Calm, well-disciplined, orderly	Interactive teaching	Good subject knowledge
Safe/secure	Use of teacher-pupil dialogue, questioning	Self-efficacy/belief
An ethos of aspiration and achievement for all	Monitoring pupil progress (including the use of feedback)	High expectations
Positive emotional climate	Pupil assessment (including AfL)	Motivational
Purposeful, stimulating	Pupil agency and voice (active engagement in their learning)	Provides challenge
Bright, attractive and informative displays	Enquiry-based	Innovative/proactive
Clean, tidy and well organised	Effective planning and organisation	Calm
New or redesigned buildings and spaces	Scaffolding learning	Caring
	Building on the prior experience and learning of pupils	Sensitive
	Personalisation, responding to individual needs	Gives praise
	Home-school learning, knowledge exchange	Uses humour as a tool
	Use of new technology/ICT	Engenders trust and mutual respect
	Collaborative practice	Flexible (where appropriate)
	Good use of teaching assistants (TAs)	Builds positive relationships with pupils
	Creative use of visits/visiting experts	Self-reflecting

Dunne et al. (2007), in a report on effective teaching and learning for low-attaining groups, noted that an 'explicit disciplinary context' was particularly appreciated by low attainers as it enabled them to avoid 'distraction and disruption' and allowed a greater focus on learning (p. 5).

Teaching approaches

The use of interactive approaches to teaching, such as those afforded through group work, was reported to have a number of benefits (Muijs and Reynolds, 2010; James and Pollard, 2006; Day et al., 2008; Leadbeater, 2008; Siraj-Blatchford et al., 2011). Chief amongst these was the sense of cooperation and collaboration which led to developments in social skills, empathy and problem solving skills.

A dialogic approach, which enables teachers and their pupils to participate in interactive dialogue about the learning, characterised by skilful open-ended questioning from the teacher, was reported to foster independent thinking and enhance understanding (Ofsted, 2010; Siraj-Blatchford et al., 2011). Alexander (2008) argued that 'talk' is a powerful pedagogical tool which: [...] 'mediates the cognitive and cultural spaces between adult and child, among children themselves, between what the child knows and understands and what he or she has yet to know and understand' (p. 92).

A number of reports emphasised the importance for effective practice of continuous monitoring of pupil progress in order to target support effectively, guide future planning and enhance learning outcomes (Sammons et al., 2008; Ofsted, 2009b; Ofsted, 2009c; Day et al., 2009; Sharples et al., 2011). Inherent in this was the need to provide pupils with regular feedback on their progress which was said to move pupils' thinking forward and encourage motivation and engagement (Dunne et al., 2007; Sammons et al., 2008; Ofsted, 2009b; Ofsted, 2009c; Pollard, 2010).

The contribution that pupil assessment can make to effective teaching and learning was highlighted in several reports (Muijs and Reynolds, 2010; James and Pollard, 2006; Ofsted, 2009a; Mourshed et al., 2010; Pollard, 2010; DfE, 2010; GTCE, 2011). James and Pollard (2006) and the GTCE (2011) both made the case for the primacy of the teacher in the assessment process rather than using external tests. The data then produced can be used by teachers, pupils and their parents to inform future teaching and learning (GTCE, 2011). Assessment for Learning (AfL), an extension of dialogic teaching and learning (Siraj-Blatchford et al., 2011), uses assessment in the classroom in order to raise levels of achievement and makes pupils partners in their learning (Alexander, 2008; Siraj-Blatchford et al., 2011). Pollard (2010) found that when pupils were involved in discussing and setting their own targets, this enhanced aspirations and motivated them to be more confident about reaching for higher goals (p. 18). The GTCE (2011) noted that AfL is 'underpinned by: [...] the proposition that pupils will improve most if they understand the aim of their learning, where they are in relation to this aim and how they can achieve the aim or reduce the gap' (p. 131).

Another strategy gaining prominence in the literature is the use of pupil agency and voice; actively engaging pupils as partners in their learning (James and Pollard, 2006; Dunne et al., 2007; Alexander, 2008; Sammons et al., 2008; OPM, 2008; Ofsted, 2009a; OECD, 2009; Pollard, 2010). The OECD (2009), in its report on the first results from the Teaching and Learning International Survey (TALIS), referred to this approach as being underpinned by 'constructivist beliefs' (p. 220), i.e. that knowledge is not something that can just be delivered to pupils via direct instruction from the teacher, but requires active involvement and participation from pupils.

An effective way of promoting the active involvement of pupils and fostering independent learning was a focus on developing an enquiry-based approach (Leadbeater, 2008; Ofsted, 2009a, 2010). This approach encouraged pupils to develop their questioning and investigative skills (and thus links to dialogic and constructivist approaches), to make connections, challenge their assumptions and then 'reflect critically' on their ideas and results (Ofsted, 2010, p. 5).

Effective planning and organisation, with clear objectives and appropriate pace so as to provide a broad, balanced, relevant and stimulating curriculum, was identified as an effective teaching strategy (Ofsted, 2009a, 2009b, 2010; Siraj-Blatchford et al., 2011).

A number of reports examined for this review emphasised personalisation – the importance for teachers of gearing approaches and resources to the needs of each individual child – thus placing the child at the heart of what they do (Muijs and Reynolds, 2010; Dunne et al., 2007; Leadbeater, 2008; Siraj-Blatchford et al., 2011; Day et al., 2008, 2009; Ofsted, 2009b; Pollard, 2010). Siraj-Blatchford et al. (2011) noted that prior knowledge of pupils' experience and learning facilitated personalisation, in that teachers were then in a better position to 'adapt their teaching to the specific interests and needs of their students' (p. 75).

Several reports focused on the importance of home-school learning and knowledge exchange (Muijs and Reynolds, 2010; James and Pollard, 2006; Dunne et al., 2007; Leadbeater, 2008; Sammons et al., 2008; Alexander, 2008; Day et al., 2009; Ofsted, 2009b; Pollard, 2010; Sharples et al., 2011; Siraj-Blatchford et al., 2011).

In the 2010 Schools White Paper (DfE, 2010), the DfE referred to the value of teachers learning from others by observing and being observed, as well as being provided with opportunities to 'plan, reflect and teach with other teachers' (p. 19). The OECD (2009) found that in all 23 participating Teaching and Learning International Survey (TALIS) countries, collaborative practice usually involved sharing ideas and information. This type of activitywas described by the GTCE (2011) as facilitating the development of the 'self-sustaining professional learning community' (p. 79).

Teacher characteristics

Within the literature, a number of intrinsic characteristics of individual teachers were identified as being influential factors in pupils' learning experiences and outcomes.

Of prime importance was the requirement for both primary and secondary teachers to have good subject knowledge (James and Pollard, 2006; Day et al., 2008; Ofsted, 2009a; DfE, 2010), as well as a good understanding of how to teach the subject, termed 'pedagogical content knowledge' (James and Pollard, 2006, p. 8), combined with a strong sense of professional values (Day et al., 2009). However, Ofsted (2009a), in a report on improving primary teachers' subject knowledge, found that 'the range and quality of teachers' subject knowledge' could differ substantially in any one school and where teaching in a lesson was judged to be good, this was often because teachers' general teaching skills 'more than made up for any weaknesses in their knowledge of the subject they were teaching' (p. 7).

The OECD (2009) identified teachers' self-efficacy, a belief in their own capabilities, as a key feature of effective teaching. It is reported to be an indicator of aspects of productivity, but also of the manner in which teachers act in the classroom. The report suggested that teachers with higher levels of self-efficacy might be 'more likely to adapt to and moderate dynamics' in schools with pupils from different backgrounds or those that 'present particular challenges' (OECD, 2009, p. 223).

Teachers identified as more effective were said to have high expectations that were clear, consistent and understood (Dunne et al., 2007; Day et al., 2008; Alexander, 2008; Ofsted, 2009b, 2009c), and to be able to motivate their pupils through a variety of teaching approaches such as pupil-led or interactive lessons (Day et al., 2008; Ofsted, 2009a, 2009b).

A number of affective characteristics were highlighted in the literature. Day et al. (2008) referred to the need for teachers to be calm and caring during lessons and display sensitivity to pupils. personal and learning needs. Pollard (2010) argued that with sensitive teachers, even those pupils who may have had a negative experience of formal schooling could 'enjoy learning, gain new skills and contribute to society' (p. 28). Ofsted (2009b) found that outstanding primary schools were characterised by such teachers, who provided affection and stability. Effective teachers gave praise frequently, and for a variety of purposes (Day et al., 2008; Ofsted, 2009b) and often used humour as a tool to make the topic or subject seem more relevant to pupils' own experiences (Day et al., 2008). They were also able to engender trust and mutual respect and made every effort to be flexible in order to provide a learning environment that encouraged pupil participation (Dunne et al., 2007; Day et al., 2008).

The ability to create and develop positive relationships with pupils was reported to be very important in terms of building rapport, facilitating interaction and communication, and nurturing mutual wellbeing, thus leading to more positive behaviour and higher standards (Dunne et al., 2007; Day et al., 2008; Leadbeater, 2008; OECD, 2009; Pollard, 2010; DfE, 2010; Siraj-Blatchford et al., 2011). Leadbeater (2008) introduced the term 'relationships for learning' to describe effective teacher-pupil relationships predicated on the following four key aspects:

- children need relationships that build participation
- children need relationships that provide them with recognition
- children need relationships that make them feel cared for, safe and secure
- children need relationships that motivate them to learn. (p. 19)

Conclusion

The NFER review highlighted particular key features that have been identified. However, listing a repertoire of effective teaching strategies is not in itself enough to ensure effective teaching. Although there are generic features of effectiveness, 'these features alone cannot illuminate the attitudes, characteristics and skills of effective and more effective teachers in action' (Day et al., 2008, p. 8). James and Pollard (2006) argued that, as well as being provided with useful strategies, teachers also need to understand the principles that underpin their practice so that teaching does not run the risk of becoming 'ritualised' (p. 8).

Equally, different schools have different expectations and operate in very different contexts (Mourshed et al., 2010) so each journey towards effectiveness is necessarily different. It is therefore of fundamental importance that any repertoire of strategies be adapted and refined to suit the particular needs, context and experience of the school, its teachers and its pupils (Emery, 2011).

Reading 4.6

Visible learning: A global synthesis

John Hattie

As this reading points out, many teaching strategies do work – but some work better than others. Hattie used statistical techniques to compare measurements of the effects of teaching strategies and harvested findings from across the world. The result is a synthesis of over 800 meta-analyses relating to achievement – and it is possible to 'read off' the most effective strategies. But by offering an explanation, Hattie tries to do more than this. The key themes, 'visible teaching, visible learning', have many resonances with the other readings presented in this chapter, and are developed further throughout *Reflective Teaching in Schools*.

How do you feel about your own practice and experience in relation to the 'six signposts towards excellence' which Hattie identifies?

Edited from: Hattie, J. (2009) *Visible Learning: A Synthesis of Meta-Analyses Relating to Achievement.* Abingdon: Routledge, 1–3, 236–40 and 244.

In the field of education one of the most enduring messages is that 'everything seems to work' to some extent. However, a lot is also known about what makes a major difference in the classroom. A glance at the journals on the shelves of most libraries, and on web pages, would indicate that the state of knowledge in the discipline of education is healthy.

Why does this bounty of research have such little impact? One possible reason is the past difficulties associated with summarizing and comparing all the diverse types of evidence about what works in classrooms. In the 1970s there was a major change in the manner we reviewed the research literature. This approach offered a way to tame the massive amount of research evidence so that it could offer useful information for teachers. The predominant method has always been to write a synthesis of many published studies in the form of an integrated literature review. However, in the mid-1970s, Gene Glass (1976) introduced the notion of meta-analysis – whereby the effect in each study, where appropriate, are converted to a common measure (an effect size), such that the overall effects could be quantified, interpreted, and compared, and the various moderators of this overall effect could be uncovered and followed up in more detail. The method soon became popular and by the mid-1980s more than 100 meta-analyses in education were available. My book is based on a synthesis of more than 800 meta-analyses about information on learning that have now been completed, including many recent ones. It demonstrates how the various innovations in these meta-analyses can be ranked from very positive to very negative effects on student achievement.

An explanatory story, not a 'what works' recipe

Figure 4.6.1 provides examples of effects associated with teaching methods and working conditions.

Teaching	d	Working Conditions	d
Quality of teaching	0.77	Within-class grouping	0.28
Reciprocal teaching	0.74	Adding more finances	0.23
Teacher-student relationships	0.72	Reducing class size	0.21
Providing feedback	0.72	Ability grouping	0.11
Teaching students self-verbalization	0.67	Multi-grade/age classes	0.04
Meta-cognition strategies	0.67	Open vs. traditional classes	0.01
Direct Instruction	0.59	Summer vacation classes	-0.09
Mastery learning	0.57	Retention	-0.16
Average	0.68		0.08

There are many teaching strategies that have an important effect on student learning. Such teaching strategies include explanation, elaboration, plans to direct task performance, sequencing, drill repetition, providing strategy cues, domain-specific processing, and clear instructional goals. These can be achieved using methods such as reciprocal teaching, direct instruction, and problem solving methods. Effective teaching occurs when the teacher decides the learning intentions and success criteria, makes them transparent to the students, demonstrates them by modelling, evaluates if they understand what they have been told by checking for understanding, and re-telling them what they have been told by tying it all together with closure. These effective teaching strategies involve much cooperative pre-planning and discussion between teachers, optimizing peer learning, and require explicit learning intentions and success criteria.

Peers play a powerful role, as is demonstrated in the strategies involving reciprocal teaching, learning in pairs on computers, and both cooperative and competitive learning (as opposed to individualistic learning). Many of the strategies also help reduce cognitive load and this allows students to focus on the critical aspects of learning, which is particularly useful when they are given multiple opportunities for deliberative practice.

The use of resources, such as computers, can add value to learning. They add a diversity of teaching strategies, provide alternative opportunities to practice and learn, and increase the nature and amount of feedback to the learner and teachers. They do, however, require learning how to optimize their uses.

It is also clear that, repeatedly, it is the difference in the teachers that make the difference in student learning. Homework in which there is no active involvement by the teacher does not contribute to student learning, and likewise the use, or not, of technologies does not show major effects on learning if there is no teacher involvement. Related to these teacher influences are the lower effects of many of the interventions when they are part of comprehensive teaching reforms. Many of these reforms are 'top down' innovations, which can mean teacher do not evaluate whether the reforms are working for them or not. Commitment to the teaching strategy and re-learning how to use many of these methods (through professional development) seems important.

Any synthesis of meta-analyses is fundamentally a literature review, and thus it builds on the scholarship and research of those who have come before. My major purpose has been to generate a model of successful teaching and learning based on the many thousands of studies in 800 and more meta-analyses. The aim is not to merely average the studies and present screeds of data. This is not uncommon; so often meta-analyses have been criticized as mere number crunching exercises, and a book based on more than 800 meta-analyses could certainly have been just that. That was not my intent. Instead, I aimed to build a model based on the theme of 'visible teaching, visible learning' that not only synthesized existing literature but also permitted a new perspective on that literature.

The conclusions are recast here as six signposts towards excellence in education:

1 Teachers are among the most powerful influences in learning.

2 Teachers need to be directive, influential, caring, and actively engaged in the passion of teaching and learning.

3 Teachers need to be aware of what each and every student is thinking and knowing, to construct meaning and meaningful experiences in light of this knowledge, and have proficient knowledge and understanding of their content to provide meaningful and appropriate feedback such that each student moves progressively through the curriculum levels.

4 Teachers need to know *the learning intentions* and success criteria of their lessons, know *how well they are attaining* these criteria for all students, and know *where to go next* in light of the gap between students' current knowledge and understanding and the success criteria of:'Where are you going?', 'How are you going', and 'Where to next?'.

5 Teachers need to move from the single idea to multiple ideas, and to relate and then extend these ideas such that learners construct and reconstruct knowledge and ideas. It is not the knowledge or ideas, but the learner's construction of this knowledge and these ideas that is critical.

6 School leaders and teachers need to create schools, staffroom, and classroom environments where error is welcomed as a learning opportunity, where discarding incorrect knowledge and understanding is welcomed, and where participant can feel safe to learn, re-learn and explore knowledge and understanding.

In these six signposts, the word 'teachers' is deliberate. Indeed, a major theme is the importance of teachers meeting to discuss, evaluate and plan their teaching in light of the feedback evidence about the success or otherwise of their teaching strategies and conceptions about progress and appropriate challenge. This is *critical reflection in light of evidence* about their teaching.

Note what is *not* said. There are no claims about additional structural resources, although to achieve the above it helps not to have the hindrance of a lack of resources. There is nothing about class size, about which particular students are present in the school or class, or about what subject is being taught – effective teaching can occur similarly for all students, all ethnicities, and all subjects. There is nothing about between-school differences, which are not a major effect in developed countries. There is little about working conditions of teachers or students – although their effects, though small, are positive and positive means we should not make these working conditions worse.

Teachers and principals need to collect the effect sizes within their schools and ask 'What is working best?', 'Why is it working best', and 'Who is it not working for?'. This will create a discussion among teachers about teaching. This would require a caring, supportive staffroom, a tolerance for errors, and for learning from other teachers, a peer culture among teachers of engagement, trust and shared passion for improvement.

part two

Creating conditions
for learning

Contexts
What is, and what might be?

5

These readings address the broad contexts in which teachers work.

The first draws from a classic text, in which Mills (4.1) analyses the relationship between individuals and society. He accounts for social change through the continuous interaction of biography and history. This analysis underpins a reflective and questioning attitude towards taken-for-granted structures, policies and assumptions: for 'personal troubles' can often be seen in relation to more enduring 'public issues'. In a related, later reading, Power (17.5) discusses the idea of 'the imaginative professional'.

Green and Janmaat (5.2) demonstrate how public policies vary in particular countries, and highlight the underlying assumptions upon which taken-for-granted thinking is based. International comparisons show how things can be thought about, and developed, in a variety of ways.

The readings from Ball (5.3) and a Government education department (5.4) highlight the influence of social class on education. Across the UK, this remains powerful and pervasive. These particular readings focus on how some families are able to benefit from their circumstances, and on policies and school practices which may enhance opportunities for more children and young people.

In a final reading, from the last days of the General Teaching Council for England (GTCE) before its abolition, the case is made for a constructive and educationally sound model of accountability for schools and the profession.

The parallel chapter of *Reflective Teaching in Schools* engages with many additional issues. The 'social context' of education is analysed in terms of the concepts of ideology, culture, opportunity and accountability, as these influence schools in each country within the UK. Teachers, pupils and families are then considered, both as individuals and as groups, with particular attention to how they act within their circumstances.

Extensive 'Notes for Further Reading' on such factors are available on *reflectiveteaching.co.uk*. The social context within which teachers and pupils work is, after all, a topic with a great many avenues for exploration in sociology, economics, history, politics, cultural studies, anthropology, comparative education, etc. The available literature is very extensive indeed.

Whilst the selections in this chapter are heavily constrained by space, see also the readings in Chapter 17 of this book. For example, there are echoes of Mills' analysis in the reading by Power (17.5) and in the discussion of policy formation by Bowe and Ball (17.7).

Reading 5.1

The sociological imagination
C. Wright Mills

This reading comes from a classic sociological text. Wright Mills focused on the interaction between individuals and society, and thus on the intersection of biography and history. Teachers have particular responsibilities because, though acting in particular historical contexts, we shape the biographies of many children and thus help to create the future. Mills poses several questions which can be used to think about our society and the role of education in it.

How do you think what you do today, may influence what others may do in the future?

Edited from: Mills, C. W. (1959) *The Sociological Imagination.* New York: Oxford University Press, 111–13.

The sociological imagination enables its possessor to understand the larger historical scene in terms of its meaning for the inner life and the external career of a variety of individuals. It enables him (sic) to take into account how individuals, in the welter of their daily experience, often become falsely conscious of their social positions. Within that welter the framework of modern society is sought, and within that framework the psychologies of a variety of men and women are formulated. By such means the personal uneasiness of individuals is focused upon explicit troubles and the indifference of publics is transformed into involvement with public studies.

The first fruit of this imagination – and the first lessons of the social science that embodies it – is the idea that the individual can understand his own experience and gauge his own fate only by locating himself within his period, that he can know his own changes in life only by becoming aware of those of all individuals in his circumstances. In many ways it is a terrible lesson; in many ways a magnificent one. We do not know the limits of man's capacities for supreme effort or willing degradation, for agony or glee, for pleasurable brutality or the sweetness of reason. But in our time we have come to know that the limits of 'human nature' are frighteningly broad. We have come to know that every individual lives, from one generation to the next, in some society; that he lives out a biography, and that he lives it out within some historical sequence. By the fact of his living he contributes, however minutely, to the shaping of this society and to the course of its history, even as he is made by society and by its historical push and shove.

The sociological imagination enables us to grasp history and biography and the relations between the two within society. That is its task and its promise. To recognize this task and this promise is the mark of the classic social analyst. And it is the signal of what is best in contemporary studies of man and society.

No social study that does not come back to the problems of biography, of history, and of their intersections within a society, has completed its intellectual journey. Whatever the specific problems of the classic social analysts, however limited or however broad the features of social reality they have examined, those who have been imaginatively aware of the promise of their work have consistently asked three sorts of questions:

- *What is the structure of this particular society as a whole?*

  What are its essential components, and how are they related to one another? Within it, what is the meaning of any particular feature for its continuance and for its change?

- *Where does this society stand in human history?*

  What are the mechanics by which it is changing? What is its place within and its meaning for the development of humanity as a whole? How does any particular feature we are examining affect, and how is it affected by, the historical period in which it moves? And this period – what are its essential features? How does it differ from other periods? What are its characteristic ways of history-making?

- *What varieties of men and women now prevail in this society and in this period?*

  And what varieties are coming to prevail? In what ways are they selected and formed, liberated and repressed, made sensitive and blunted? What kinds of 'human nature' are revealed in the conduct and character we observe in this society in this period? And what is the meaning for 'human nature' of each and every feature of the society we are examining?

Reading 5.2

Regimes of social cohesion

Andy Green and Jan Janmaat

This reading is based on analysis of data on inequality and social attitudes in over 25 developed countries. The study shows how educational inequality undermines key aspects of social cohesion, including trust in institutions, civic cooperation and the rule of law. The authors argue that more egalitarian education systems tend to promote both economic competitiveness *and* social cohesion. The work highlights the significance for social cohesion of the distribution of opportunities and the nature of the values that people acquire.

Through its work with young people, education influences the future and is infused with moral purpose. We must recognise 'What is', but may also ask 'What should be?'.

How do you feel that the policy context in which you work affects educational provision?

Edited from: Green, A. and Janmaat, J. G. (2011) *Education, Opportunity and Social Cohesion.* Centre for Learning and Life Chances in Knowledge Economies and Societies. London: Institute of Education, 2–5.

Regimes of social cohesion

Different traditions of thought and policy on social cohesion have evolved within the western world. Comparative analysis identifies three distinctive types of social cohesion in contemporary states. These can be characterised as 'liberal', 'social market' or 'social democratic'. We refer to these as 'regimes of social cohesion' to emphasise their systemic properties, which are relatively durable over time.

Liberal (English-speaking countries, e.g. particularly the UK and the USA)
In liberal societies, such as the United Kingdom and the United States, social cohesion has traditionally relied on the triple foundations of market freedoms, an active civil society, and core beliefs in individual opportunities and rewards based on merit. A wider set of shared values has not been regarded as essential for a cohesive society – and nor, in the British case at least, has a tightly defined sense of national identity. The state was not, historically, considered the main guarantor of social cohesion, beyond its role in the maintenance of law and order.

Social Market (NW continental Europe, e.g. Belgium, France, Germany and the Netherlands)
The social market regime, by contrast, has relied on a strong institutional embedding of social cohesion. Solidarity has depended relatively more on the state and less on civil

society, and rates of civic participation have generally been lower. Trade union coverage and public spending on welfare and social protection are high. These factors, along with concerted and centralized trade union bargaining, have helped to reduce household income inequality. Maintaining a broad set of shared values – and a strong national identity – has also, historically, been considered important for holding societies together.

Social Democratic (The Nordic countries, e.g. Denmark, Finland, Norway and Sweden) The social democratic regime, like the social market regime, institutionalises social solidarity. However, here, egalitarian and solidaristic values make a greater contribution to social cohesion. Levels of social and political trust are also much higher. This cannot be attributed solely to greater ethnic homogeneity in these societies, although this may have once played a part in Denmark and Norway. Sweden is both ethnically diverse and highly trusting.

Social cohesion during economic crisis

Every country is affected by the challenges of globalisation and particularly so during periods of economic crisis. However, societies differ in what holds them together.

The core beliefs of liberal societies, such as the UK (e.g. active civil society and individual opportunities), are seen to be embodied in the 'free market' which has become more dominant under globalisation. However, social cohesion in such societies is likely to be undermined by the rapid erosion of people's faith in individual opportunity and fairness.

The UK has high levels of income inequality and relatively low rates of social mobility. Inequality and lack of mobility are likely to grow due to the disproportionate effects of the economic crisis (in unemployment and public expenditure cuts, for example) on young people, women, the low paid and those in areas of socio-economic disadvantage. As the prospects of secure jobs and home ownership diminish for many people, belief in the core unifying values of opportunity, freedom and just rewards are likely to decrease, causing social and political trust to diminish further.

Education, inequality and social cohesion

Education systems play a key role in determining future life chances and in mitigating or exacerbating social inequalities. These have been linked with various negative health and social outcomes, including high rates of depression, low levels of trust and cooperation, and high levels of violent crime.

We found that education systems which select students to secondary schools by ability and make extensive use of ability grouping within schools tend to exhibit more unequal educational outcomes than non-selective comprehensive systems with mixed ability classes.

The four education systems in the UK perform somewhat differently. Those in Scotland

and Wales produce slightly more equal educational outcomes at 15 than those in England and Northern Ireland, according to the OECD Programme for International student Assessment (PISA).

The 2009 PISA study of literacy skills amongst 15 years olds shows that educational outcomes in the UK are more unequal than in most of the OECD countries where tests were conducted (Green and Janmaat, 2011).

The gap between the mean scores of UK students in the 90th and 10th percentiles was 246 points – the equivalent of six years of schooling on the average across OECD countries. PISA 2009 showed that the variance in scores in the UK have only reduced marginally since the 2000 survey. Amongst the 34 countries tested, the UK had the 11th highest total variance in scores.

The UK is also notable for degree to which the average performance within a school is influenced by the social characteristics of its intake. Across all OECD countries, on average, 57% of the performance difference between schools can be attributed to the social character of the intake. In the UK (and in Luxembourg, New Zealand and the USA) the social intake accounts for over 70% of performance difference between schools.

Skills distribution and social cohesion

Variation in performance among school students is one of the factors which, over time, determines the overall distribution of skills within the adult population. We found strong links between social cohesion and the distribution of adult skills.

The more unequal the skills distribution among adults, the higher the rates of violent crime and civic unrest, and the lower the levels of social trust and civil liberties. For several of the indicators, these correlations also hold over time, suggesting that the relationships may be causal. It seems likely that wide educational disparities generate cultural gaps and competition anxieties which undermine social bonds and trust.

Our research suggests that it is not so much the average level of education in a country which matters most for social cohesion, but rather how the skills acquired are spread around.

Education systems and civic competences

Civic competences are an important component of social cohesion. These refer to the knowledge, skills and values that people need to participate effectively in a liberal democratic society. We examined the links between education system characteristics and the levels and distributions of civic competences across countries.

When compared with comprehensive systems, selective education systems have:

- higher levels of social segregation across classrooms
- greater disparities in civic knowledge and skills and
- larger peer effects on civic knowledge and skills (meaning that the latter are

strongly affected by the social backgrounds and achievement levels of other students in the class).

Implications for policy

We urge policymakers in the UK to take account of the potentially negative impact that educational inequality can have on social cohesion.

Social cohesion in the UK has always depended on high levels of civic participation and a widespread belief in the availability of individual opportunities and rewards based on merit. In the current period of austerity, where opportunities for young people are substantially reduced, there is a serious danger that these shared beliefs will be eroded, thus weakening social bonds. In such circumstances it is particularly important that the education system is seen to offer opportunities for all students.

Reading 5.3

Schooling, social class and privilege
Stephen Ball

This reading illustrates and analyses how social class inequalities are reproduced, in part, by the strategies adopted by some families to secure educational advantage. It suggests that, behind arguments about the efficacy of quasi-markets and choice of school, there are significant social consequences which deepening inequalities within our societies. Ball suggests that parental investment in children by middle-class families, through broadening their experiences and understanding, creates 'abilities' which schools then develop further.

How does this analysis illuminate patterns of attendance and performance at schools you know?

Edited from: Ball, S. (2003) *The More Things Change: Educational Research, Social Class and 'Interlocking' Inequalities.* Professorial Inaugural Lecture, Institute of Education, University of London. 12 March.

I see sociological theories as a toolbox which provides levers and mechanisms for analysis and interpretation. This is particularly important, I think, in the understanding of social class.

I am interested in the pro-active tactics of certain families as a way of understanding 'success' rather than failure in education. This enables the construction of a theory of privilege rather than a theory of deficits – a distinction which is crucial to my endeavours here.

Class is never more potent and damaging than when inequality is no longer explained in its terms, when classed policy is naturalised, becomes common sense – when class policy is simply good policy. The naturalisation of policy makes possible the tracing back of social problems, and the allocating of blame, to social subjects. This kind of transference is centrally embedded in policies which allocate resources through systems of choice, within which families are expected to act as 'risk managers'. Such choice systems call for particular resources and skills which are unevenly distributed across the population.

If we want to understand the production of social inequalities in and through education we thus need to take families seriously. Greater attention has to be given to the ways in which inequalities are produced in the complex interactions between the cultural, social and material sites of home, school and policy – to the interlocking of inequalities.

Education policy, school choice and social practices

Choice policies and a market system of education, in the current socio-economic context, are a response to the current interest anxieties of the middle class.

In effect education policy is a focus of class struggles: very immediate and down-to-earth struggles for opportunity, advantage and closure, and over the distribution of scarce resources. The policies in play at any point in time bear the hallmarks of those struggles. They may be overt, through campaigns and interventions – particularly those articulated around curriculum, modes of instruction, student grouping and the distribution of rewards and success roles; or through the privileging of opportunity over and against equity; or through the mechanism of the market itself which values some qualities and some kinds of students and devalues others.

The anxieties, concerns and efforts which underlie these struggles are of an enduring nature, but the middle classes are particularly anxious and active. Current social and economic conditions have raised the stakes of competition for educational success; and moves to empower parents have given a specific legitimacy to diverse forms of inter-vention and participation. For these, middle-class parents possess the relevant skills and resources.

Additionally, there is an overlap of interests from the two sides of the market: parental consumers and school providers.

In a performative system of education, this process is also driven by the differential valuing of students by schools needing to compete within league tables of achievement and to reach exam and test targets. Middle-class students, on the whole, are cheaper and easier to teach in relation to achieving targets and performance improvements, and many schools will do whatever they can to woo them (Woods et al., 1998).

On the consumer side, it is interesting to note examples of the efforts of middle-class parents in socially diverse metropolitan settings to colonise and capture particular schools of choice. Butler and Robson (2001) note examples in their research into gentrification in six London settings. One is a 'success' story in Telegraph Hill, where they report a primary school which has been '"made" by the middle class and transformed' ; the second, in Brixton, is, at least for the time being, a failure. Here, despite concerted efforts, 'the middle classes have not been successful in establishing hegemony over any particular primary school'. Ball, Vincent and Kemp (2003) found similar, and successful 'captures' of primary schools, as class 'enclaves', in Stoke Newington and Battersea.

Clearly, in all of this the most distinct and decisive strategy of choice is for private schooling. Private schools offer a cultural milieu which is coherent and undiluted, and constitutes a 'protected enclave for class formation' (Sedden, 2001: 134).

As I have noted already, middle-class families work hard and deploy their resources to establish a monopoly over routes of and locations of privilege, ensuring for their children high-status trajectories through the education system, and insulating them from the untoward influence of social 'others'. This is a process of drawing and maintaining lines of distinction, between and within schools: it is a process of social closure.

Loads of children there had special needs and they have lots of children who are refugees who really didn't speak English, and I just thought, it's not appropriate for a bright little girl who, you know, is going to need quite a lot of stimulation. *(Mrs Henry)*

I liked the fact that they catered specifically for children's abilities in subjects that I think are difficult to teach in a mixed-ability group…. It was one of the points we thought were positive…. They set in maths and languages straight off. *(Mrs McBain)*

The state school down the road would have been lovely, except that *nobody* sends their children there. *(Mrs Henry, my emphasis)*

The 'nobody' referred to in the final extract is striking and telling – the school in question, the 'state school down the road' has children in it, but it is full of 'nobodies', the point is here that 'nobody' is 'not us'. People like us do not send our children to a school like that. It is a school 'of' and 'for' 'others'. These sorts of cultural and calculative evaluations, and their concomitant recognitions and rejections, the 'us's' and 'others', are part of the parents' 'reading' of schools in the process of making choices between them.

Access to routes of privilege and success roles and their associated identities ensures the storing up of valuable cultural capital 'within' the student.

Parenting and investment in the child

Within the educational life of the middle-class family enormous effort is devoted to the assembly and maintenance of a well-adapted educational subject, a 'reasoning and reasonable' child, as Vincent puts it (2001). In a risk society the prudent family can no longer leave their child's fate to the state. This may be thought of as a process of investment in the child and involves the deployment of a range of capitals – economic, social, cultural and emotional – and 'the gratuitous expenditure of time, attention, care and concern' (Bourdieu, 1986b: 253). Let me offer some glimpses of these capitals at work.

A couple of months ago I got a studies skills teacher and I started working, it's through my mum's friends, so I've been seeing this woman weekly, and she's helping me, you know, how to work, when to work and actually getting down and doing it [Anick wants to be a lawyer]. Neither of my parents are lawyers, we have lawyer friends but I mean at school, my parents just saw me, because I argue, they said that would just fit a lawyer…. I think I am going to America this summer. I've got the opportunity of working at McDonald's law firm in Chicago. Because one of my Dad's best friends is head lawyer at McDonalds. So I could go there for a couple of months. *(Anick: Hemsley Girls)*

…. yeah, but A level's beyond my field. A level maths. So sort of like, six months ago we got him a tutor anyway. And he was happy talking to him. So I think he sort of … LAUGHS … overcame a lot of the problems. He didn't have many, I must say, actually. But anything he did have, the tutor sorted out with him, and he felt happier doing that than actually speaking to them. And I said – do you want me to talk to them? And he said no. So I thought I wouldn't interfere, especially as he seemed all right about it. *(Carl's mother: Maitland Union)*

Part of this process of social formation, the support and encouragement, the bought-in expertise and supplementary activities, the long-term sculpting of decision-making, is focused on the child's needs – but it also establishes for the child a sense of their best interests. They are made clear about what is important and possible, and what is not. 'Cultural scripts' are acted out with little scope for improvisation – and where improvisations do occur they can lead to family crises and thence to organised remediation. Again, at these points of crisis and potential failure the deployment of relevant capitals is crucial to the maintenance of trajectories. Emotional resources are particularly important at times of uncertainty (Devine, 1998: 33), but so too is the ability to 'buy in' specialist support or to lobby for special services.

These experiences develop in the child a particular orientation to schooling and develop certain skills and capabilities – a role readiness. They also work to constitute the child as able.

In this sense we can see 'ability' and 'achievement' partly at least as a social assembly achieved within the family, as a collective endeavour, which often extends beyond the family itself (through, for example, the employment of tutors) and requires various forms of capital investment in order to be maintained. This is a point made by Bourdieu: 'ability or talent is itself the product of an investment of time and cultural capital' (Bourdieu, 1986b: 244). Viewed in this way ability and achievement can be understood as the composite productions of families, which at times involve enormous emotional exertions and capital expenditures – rather than either a natural or individual phenomenon.

Only a part of this activity is visible in the classroom: the middle-class child in the classroom is in part a cipher of attentive, surveillant, participant parenting – or, to borrow a phrase, 'intensive parenting' – or more often and more accurately 'intensive mothering'. The vast majority of the work of assembly and support is done in the vast majority of middle-class families by mothers. Responsibility weighs heavily on the mother in a whole variety of senses.

In such ways, the values and incentives of market policies being pursued and celebrated by the states of almost all western societies give legitimation and impetus to certain actions and commitments – enterprise, competition, excellence – and inhibit and de-legitimise others – social justice, equity, tolerance.

I am a sociologist and as such, for me, the task is 'to show that things are not as self-evident as one believed; to see that what is accepted as self-evident will no longer be accepted as such' (Foucault, 1988: 154). 'Thinking otherwise' is thus possible.

Reading 5.4

Disadvantage and low attainment
Department for Children, Schools and Families (DCSF)

> The government report on which this reading is based explores the links between disadvantage and low attainment.
>
> Some of patterns are identified, of which the most salient is that home experiences in the early years lead to significant developmental differences. To avoid a 'continuing cycle of underperformance' it is necessary for teachers to try to offset and compensate for disadvantage – hence recommendations for deployment of the best teachers, maintaining high expectations, working to improve social and emotional skills and maintaining aspirations. Whilst teachers cannot ultimately compensate for society, they can make a difference to the life chances of some pupils, and this reading tries to show how.
>
> Thinking of the children you teach, how might you contribute to closing attainment gaps?
>
> *Edited from: Breaking the Link between Disadvantage and Low Attainment,* Department for Children, Schools and Families (2009). Nottingham: DCSF, 17–23.

For most pupils school is a rich and rewarding experience, but it is an uncomfortable fact that at every ability level in the system, pupils from poor backgrounds achieve less well than their counterparts. The reasons are complex, and not purely linked to money. Of course, absolute levels of poverty may mean children suffer from poor housing or an inadequate diet. But, even in families above the poverty line, parents may be sceptical about the value of education and not see that success at school is important for their children.

There is much that can be done to support schools to address these issues. But real progress in breaking the link between deprivation and low educational attainment relies most of all on the leadership of every teacher in every school, and on their ability to transmit their own passion for transforming opportunity.

Early years and the home

Even when children are very young, the link between cognitive development and family deprivation is already apparent. For example, research (e.g. Feinstein, 2003) has identified significant gaps in developmental tasks have opened up at 22 months, and the Millennium Cohort Study shows lower vocabulary at age three for children from poorer households. Investment in early years services for children and families such as Sure Start and free nursery education will address these early gaps, and specific new interventions including "Every Child a Talker" are designed to tackle some of the key issues.

Nevertheless, children may not experience the benefits at home which more advantaged children take for granted, for example access to a wide range of books or educational software. Parents want to help their children succeed, but do not necessarily know the best way to do this. We are providing targeted support, for example through promoting family reading and seeking to help parents who may themselves have had a poor experience of schools not to pass on those negative perceptions to their children.

In the classroom

When children start school already behind their peers, this can set up a continuing cycle of underperformance. They find it hard to keep up and so may learn more slowly, hence falling even further behind. Disadvantaged pupils make slower progress than others. No

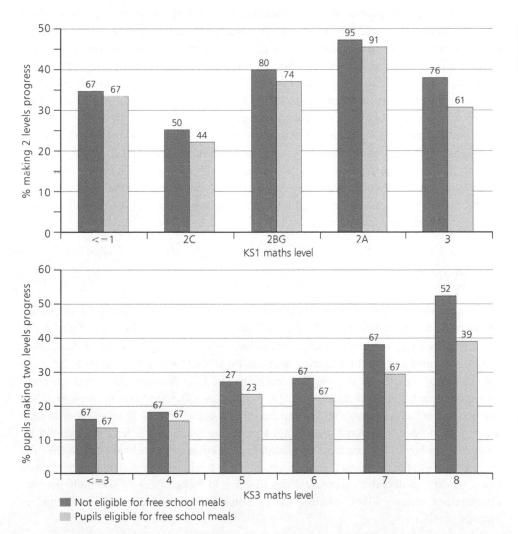

Figure 5.4.1
Differences in progress in maths by disadvantaged and affluent pupils

■ Not eligible for free school meals
■ Pupils eligible for free school meals

matter what their starting point, disadvantaged pupils are less likely to make two levels of progress between key stages than their more advantaged peers with the same prior attainment. The size of the progress gap differs by prior attainment band. Low attaining disadvantaged pupils typically find it slightly harder to catch up if they fall behind; and high attaining ones typically find it *much* harder to excel. This is why the personalisation approach focuses so strongly on rates of progress, and on all pupils making good progress regardless of the level from which they start. Figure 5.4.1 illustrates this for progress in mathematics.

The best way to ensure that pupils progress regularly is to ensure they never fall behind.

Teachers

The most disadvantaged children need and deserve the best teachers. But this is not just about attracting new people into the profession, it is also about deployment of teachers within a school. Hobbs (2007) found that the quality of teaching and learning in bottom groups contributed to low achievement and low expectations. Where senior leaders are making a difference for all children, they ensure their strongest teachers spend most of their teaching time where they can have greatest impact – often in the lower sets. And they will make sure that practice in the classroom means that skilled teachers focus their efforts on accelerating the progress of those who are struggling.

Ofsted's report (2008), *Twelve Outstanding Secondary Schools: Excelling Against the Odds,* examines the elements that have contributed to their success. It is no surprise that they all have in common well-distributed leadership and outstanding teaching. They also tend to have stable staffing, being successful at attracting, recruiting and retaining staff. Ofsted note that the leaders are driven by a moral purpose, wanting to see other schools' pupils succeed as well as their own.

Behaviour

Pupils eligible for free school meals (FSM) are seven times more likely to be permanently excluded from primary school than those who are not eligible, and three and a half times as likely to be permanently excluded from secondary school. Sir Alan Steer (2009) presented a report highlighting the need for school behaviour policies to be set in the context of policies on learning and teaching. The links between poor behaviour and low attainment are not straightforward, but if pupils are failing to keep up in lessons they can become bored and disruptive, preferring to gain notoriety amongst their friends than admit they do not understand something. Expressing emotion can be a cultural taboo, especially for boys. Children from disadvantaged backgrounds sometimes do not have the skills or self-confidence to deal with criticism or set-backs, which may make them more likely to express denial or to respond negatively and inappropriately when challenged. Programmes such as SEAL address this by helping pupils develop self-belief and to manage conflict.

Outside influences

Aspiration is a key issue: what do young people want to do with their lives, and do they understand how to achieve that? At puberty, the influence of peer groups becomes much stronger which can create a culture of it being "not cool to learn". Recent research has shown a significant disparity in aspirations, with young people from traditional working-class communities showing less ambition than more recently arrived groups. An intergenerational pattern of worklessness can lead to insularity and low horizons. Schools can begin to change this by providing access to positive role-models from similar backgrounds with whom young people can identify. Schools can also provide a range of experiences, in arts, sport or community volunteering, which gives children a glimpse into other worlds and helps them to find something they can succeed at. And schools are making sure that they all have productive links to business and to Universities, so that young people learn early what is possible for them and are motivated to take advantage of the opportunities.

Schools can make a much wider contribution to a community. For example, schools themselves can have a significant effect on local culture: those which succeed in the most disadvantaged areas respect the local community, employing local people wherever possible, but insisting upon high standards and expectations for everyone.

Schools cannot do this in isolation. We know that teachers, particularly in disadvantaged areas, often spend a lot of time dealing with pupils' and parents' wider problems. Extended services can make a big difference: having integrated health and social care on school sites means that problems getting in the way of children's learning can be more easily dealt with.

Wider opportunities

Ensuring the curriculum is relevant and engaging is, of course, important for all pupils but especially those who have not been well served by the traditional curriculum. A mix of theoretical and practical learning gives an opportunity to motivate pupils and demonstrate the relevance of education to what they want to do in their lives. Many schools are exploring how to improve the match between the basic curriculum and the needs and aspirations of their pupils, extending the range of curricular pathways where possible. They also take every chance to celebrate success, so that pupils can see that they are making progress and have tangible, realistic goals to work towards.

Links to SEN and other additional needs

An FSM child is also more likely to have been identified with special educational needs (SEN). There is a very large overlap between FSM status and either having a statement of SEN. A child who is eligible for free school meals may also come from one of the minority ethnic groups that underperform compared to the rest of the cohort. There is often an interaction effect between these factors. The interventions which will help a child to succeed are likely to be very similar in each case – a clear assessment of where they are starting from, personalised learning to make sure they have the basic educational and personal skills in place, a rigorous approach to tracking their progress, high aspirations and stretching, relevant targets.

All of this demonstrates why pupils from deprived backgrounds are likely to underperform, and explains why schools should identify and closely monitor the progress of their FSM pupils. The evidence is clear: given two pupils on the same level of attainment who are both performing below expectations, the child from the deprived background is more likely to fall behind.

Symptoms, issues and responses

The chart below summarises the main symptoms and causes of the atttainment gap for disadvantaged pupils, and the strategies which schools and local authorities can adopt to address them:

Figure 5.4.2
The attainment
gap: some causes
and remedies

Why do disadvantaged children progress less well?	
Some symptoms and issues	School and local authority responses
Cognitive gaps already evident before age 5	Children's Centres, support for families and early reading
Weaker home learning environment	
Lower prior attainment at each Key Stage	Schools working closely with parents
Harder to recover from stalled learning	Personalisation, progress, 'keep up not catch-up'
Quality of teaching for children in lower sets	
Behaviour, exclusion and absence issues	Tracking, early intervention, one-to-one tuition
Aspirations, peer influences, "not cool to learn"	In-school teacher deployment, training
Weak family/community networks	Policies on behaviour, exclusion and absence, SEAL, an engaging curriculum
Narrow experiences and opportunities	Positive role-models, active information, advice and guidance policies
SEN/disadvantage overlap	School/cluster/LA action to compensate
Gaps are too often an "invisible issue"	Broader curriculum; extended school services
	Ensure SEN policies focus on progress
	Use new accountability framework

The effects of disadvantage are cumulative and pervasive because poor pupils typically make slower progress than pupils with similar attainment from more affluent backgrounds.

To weaken the link between disadvantage and achievement we must continue to raise attainment overall, *and* accelerate the rate of progress made by the lowest performers. And at the same time we must focus resources on children from disadvantaged backgrounds because without extra help and support they will fall even further behind.

This is not an impossible task. Schools can achieve impressive rates of improvement for children from deprived backgrounds. Nor does it require a whole new pedagogy or approach. Repeated examples show that what really makes a difference is the consistency with which schools engage all their pupils, always being determined to go the extra mile to help them to achieve.

Reading 5.5

Accountability in teaching
General Teaching Council for England (GTC E)

> The General Teaching Councils (GTC) of Northern Ireland, Scotland, Wales and the Republic of Ireland collaborate together and promote the profession in many ways. This reading derives from the swan-song of the English GTC, published just prior to abolition. The importance of school and teacher accountability is affirmed but, it is argued, must be fulfilled in ways which enhance the development of teaching quality rather than undermining it. As a contribution towards this, the General Teaching Council for England (GTCE) proposes a 'new contact' between the government and the teaching profession. There are contemporary initiatives to create a Royal College of Teaching in England, and the issues raised in this reading would need to be faced.
>
> What forms of professional representation do you feel are most appropriate in your country?
>
> *Edited from: Teaching Quality: Policy Papers,* GTCE (2011). London: GTCE, 44–60.

Why does accountability matter?

Education and wider children's services provided by the state are taxpayer-funded; they are complex and require the exercise of both expertise and ethics; what they do is sensitive and can touch on issues of confidentiality and safeguarding. They are political in that they raise questions of entitlement, equity, justice and ideology, about the distribution of resources and the respective roles of the family and the state in influencing children's outcomes. For all these reasons accountability is appropriate, necessary, and highly political.

The case for change

We contend that there are three principal shortcomings of the *status quo* in accountability:

- there is too much of it;
- it does not focus enough on improving teaching quality; and
- it is inadequate to ensure the quality of teaching.

In this section, we will examine each of these in turn.

There is too much accountability

- Excessive accountability can obscure what matters most.
- Too much 'top-down' accountability can inhibit personal responsibility and professional initiative.
- An element of proportionality has been introduced, but not enough.
- The cost of accountability appears to outweigh the benefits, and this is not sustainable in the current economic climate.

'High stakes' institutional inspection may have been a justifiable model at a time when the state lacked comprehensive data on each school and thereby a picture of the performance and range of 'the system'. Although elements of proportionality have been introduced to inspections, there are few substantial changes, in the shape of additional freedoms or opportunities for those schools routinely deemed good or outstanding, or a varied menu of support and challenge for those schools struggling to improve. The economic climate suggests a more nuanced approach is needed, targeting accountability resources carefully in the public interest. The Coalition government has already taken steps in this direction.

The Government is encouraging greater diversity among schools, and the Secretary of State acknowledges that the *quid pro quo* is improved accountability. He also asserts that there will be greater autonomy and more opportunity for the exercise of professional judgement by teachers. If the profession is to respond creatively to these circumstances it needs to feel entrusted and empowered.

But teaching has been caught in what Onora O'Neill termed 'the accountability paradox': the more we want professionalism, the more requirements and systems we pile on a service to 'ensure' standards of practice, the less likely are practitioners to feel and take professional responsibility, as they do not believe they are trusted to deliver appropriately without surveillance and micromanagement. This is but one of the perverse consequences of overlaying new accountability requirements upon old. The account-ability to which schools are subject takes many forms and focuses on a very wide range of activities. Typically, new themes are added (community cohesion, healthy lifestyles, partnership working etc) without consolidating them with existing themes. The practice of layering new expectations upon old makes it harder for account-holders (inspectors, School Improvement Partners, line managers) to focus their attention squarely on teaching quality.

Accountability does not focus enough on improving teaching quality

- It does not encourage improvement-focused behaviour – e.g. collaboration.
- It does not contribute as much as it might to the generation of improvement-focused knowledge.

Collaborative work between schools is increasingly important (e.g. delivering a comprehensive 14–19 offer within a locality), as is schools' work with other children's services (e.g. safeguarding, team around the child work). Other developments, including academies and the new teaching schools, depend on partnership in different ways. Collaboration is predicated on transparency: on a willingness to open the doors on one's own practice and be receptive to learning from the practice of others. Institutional accountability is at odds with these developments.

Research into school improvement and effective teacher development emphasises the importance of knowledge transfer between schools, and of learning across schools, as well as within them. Without external links and benchmarks, a school's perspectives on matters such as standards and methods can become parochial and limited. And teachers need to engage with evidence about effective practice that is generated beyond as well as within their schools. For these reasons accountability mechanisms need to support knowledge transfer and system improvement, as well as assuring acceptable standards of teaching, learning and leadership.

Accountability is inadequate to ensure the quality of teaching

- Teachers are not sufficiently required or supported to account for the quality of teaching.
- Accountability is too heavily focused on institutional accountability as distinct from teaching accountability, despite what is known about the extent of in-school variation in teaching standards.
- Successive administrations have tinkered with the scope, frequency and manner of inspection and performance management, suggesting dissatisfaction with the resulting insights into teaching quality.
- Parents and pupils have an insufficient stake in teaching quality.

This set of concerns is at the heart of the GTCE's public interest remit and concern for teaching quality. We therefore now explore more fully stakeholder perceptions of accountability.

Teacher accountability

'Accountability without adequate support and development opportunities serves to undermine teacher confidence and professionalism'.

Teachers as professionals accept the legitimacy of and necessity for being accountable for the results of their teaching. In 2009 the GTCE sought to explore teachers' attitudes to and experiences of accountability through its annual survey of teachers. We found that there was a high degree of support for accountability from teachers.

These responses demonstrate that teachers understand and accept accountability for their work and its outcomes. But school accountability discussions in the media over the last couple of decades, involving teachers, their representatives, successive governments, and at times HMCI, suggest otherwise. Moreover, our research suggests that teachers' first associations with the term 'accountability' tend to be mainly negative: they associate it with sanctions, burdens, centralisation, and mistrust.

It is important to distinguish between the principle of accountability and the practice of specific accountability mechanisms. Doing so provides a more constructive starting point for the negotiation of a new 'contract' between the teaching profession and its stake-holders about accountability. Teachers accept the need for accountability. The question is, what forms of accountability are most likely to realise stakeholders' legitimate aspirations – assurance of standards and conduct, support for improvement, information on pupil outcomes, or guaranteeing proper use of public funds?

Below, we review various mechanisms through which accountability can be realised.

Performance management

As performance management is the principal means by which individual teachers are held to account for their teaching and their pupils' learning in the employment setting, the 2010 GTCE survey asked how teachers experienced performance management. 49 per cent agreed that performance management was an effective way of holding teachers to account for the quality of their teaching, and 32 per cent disagreed. 18 per cent said they neither agreed nor disagreed. School leaders are much more likely than other teachers to believe that performance management is effective for teaching accountability (71 per cent of head teachers, and 60 per cent of deputy/assistant head teachers and Advanced Skills Teachers).

We contend that improving performance management is a priority for ensuring teaching quality and upholding the public interest in teaching.

School self-evaluation

The survey revealed more support for school self-evaluation. 77 per cent of teachers agreed that school self-evaluation was useful, and only nine per cent disagreed that it was a useful tool for improvement as well as accountability.

Agreement was particularly high among heads (91 per cent) and deputy/assistant heads (89 per cent), who have most involvement with school self-evaluation. The Coalition government has announced an end to the use of a standardised self-evaluation format as part of the inspection process.

External observation of teaching

Research in 2008 suggested that only 25 per cent of teachers were regularly observed – the current picture is not known. The GTCE survey found only 24 per cent of teachers agreed that external observation of teaching should be part of public accountability via inspection. 51 per cent disagreed and 22 per cent neither agreed nor disagreed. Younger and newer teachers were less likely to disagree with this proposition.

Providing an account to parents

26 per cent of teachers agree that teachers do not have sufficient opportunity to give parents a full and rounded account of their children's learning. Agreement rises to 31 per cent among secondary school teachers, and to 32 per cent among teachers at schools working with socioeconomic or linguistic challenges. Younger teachers (40 per cent) and those newest to teaching (33 per cent) are also more likely to agree.

Exercising professional judgement

86 per cent of teachers agreed that they needed more opportunities to exercise their professional judgement.

Accountability for professional development

The GTCE's 2010 Survey was conducted at a time when the previous government was considering the introduction of a licence to practise for teachers. The licence was intended to ensure that teachers upheld and enhanced their teaching standards throughout their careers in order to remain registered professionals.

The survey gauged teachers' responses to the proposition that teachers should be accountable for their continuing professional development (CPD) in order to be permitted to practise. 57 per cent agreed and 25 per cent disagreed. Agreement among heads and assistant/deputy heads was stronger (80 per cent and 69 per cent respectively). These responses to the *principle* of revalidation or licensing were more positive than the reception that teachers' organisations gave the specific proposals advanced by the then Government.

The survey found a strong correlation between support for this proposition and environmental factors such as strong opportunities for or engagement with CPD, and good evaluation of CPD impact. This suggests that teachers' views about a licence to practise are likely to be more positive if their access to high quality, good impact CPD is improved. Schools' engagement with CPD – effective or otherwise – is known to be variable.

Here we offer some propositions for the reform of accountability for schools in general and for teaching in particular. Movement is needed – not only on the part of the government but also on the part of the profession and its stakeholders – in order to arrive at a system *and a culture* of intelligent accountability. School accountability should be a process that provides an authoritative and credible account of teaching quality, and it should result in improvements in children's educational and wider outcomes. What is needed to get there? We make three core propositions, and examine each below.

1 *A new 'contract'*

A new contract needs to be negotiated between the state (or government) representing the community of interest in teaching and the teaching profession. This would not be a contract in the employment sense, but a published memorandum of understanding, governing what stakeholders can expect of teachers and what teachers can expect from their stakeholders.

The contract needs to underpin a more productive, respectful and creative relationship, and an understanding about accountability needs to be at its heart. As we have argued, if the relationship between the state and the profession is not right – for example, if it is overly concerned with compliance, even with regard to demonstrably healthy institutions – accountability is contaminated and ineffective. Reform of accountability means also addressing wider issues of understanding and respect. Teachers have a responsibility to accept accountability, and the state has a responsibility to devise an accountability system that meets the needs of all stakeholders, including teachers.

2 *Teachers should have better opportunities to give an account of their teaching practice*

Teachers should have better opportunities to give an account of their teaching practice, and account-giving should be seen as a right and a responsibility of a professional teacher.

Although many teachers say they experience accountability as a significant burden, many are seldom asked to give an account of their practice – to explain why they opted for one intervention over another, or to describe the thinking behind a particular goal or the steps taken to reach it. We have argued elsewhere for improving the status and quality of pedagogy, or the discipline of teaching. Pedagogic language and dialogue should be a stronger part of teaching accountability. Fine judgements about teaching quality need to be made and should inform improvements in teaching practice.

Performance management and any future system of professional revalidation need to be recast as opportunities for account-giving using pedagogic dialogue. Schools might also want to think about how the routine conversations that occur around progress-checking and target-setting could be recast as opportunities for pedagogic account-giving. In some schools performance management is described as an annual encounter, and something borne by teachers. It needs to be more like supervision at its best in other disciplines. If accountability exposes poor teaching quality, the steps to remedial support and, where necessary, capability procedures need to be fair but swift. Teacher training needs to develop new entrants with these skills. Conversations between school leaders and SIPs, or between inspectors and teachers, should also have this character.

In terms of the relational nature of accountability, teachers are currently held accountable by proxy through mechanisms that purport to uphold their interests. It is arguable that teachers should be engaged in account giving directly with their primary stakeholders. This notion can raise concerns, conjuring fears of teachers having to justify their practice to those who are insufficiently skilled to make much of the experience, or too partisan to evaluate the account fairly. On balance we believe there is more to be gained than risked by improving face-to-face account giving in appropriate circumstances between teachers and parents or pupils, though the processes and conditions for this would require sensitive design. This implies that the language of pedagogy needs to be accessible to service users (and other children's practitioners), otherwise it risks reinforcing traditional hierarchies and impeding public accountability.

3   *Recasting the stake held by parents and pupils*

The stake held in education by parents and pupils needs to be recast, to improve their opportunities for hearing an account, and their capacity to be productive stakeholders. There are rights and responsibilities associated with being a stakeholder, and sometimes the responsibilities are overlooked. While it is not possible to guarantee that parents and pupils will always use their stake responsibly, it should be possible to devise accountability processes that encourage and support responsible account-holding. The bottom line is that parents' and pupils' stake in teaching is a right, whether or not they hold that stake responsibly. This is the fundamental difference between accountability and responsiveness, the latter being the mode in which many schools conduct their everyday relationships with parents. Responsiveness might be described as meeting the needs of those parents who press for more or different information or engagement. Accountability is what all parents are due regardless of their receptiveness, skill or inclination.

Relationships
How are we getting on together?

6

Good classroom relationships minimise behavioural difficulties and provide positive conditions for learning. The readings in this group confirm this significance, analyse underlying processes and suggest practical strategies to develop excellent teacher–pupil relationships.

The first reading is a classic, from the pupil perspective, in which the experience of schooling is described by Jackson (6.1) in terms of 'crowds, praise and power' – so it is potentially stressful. Immordino-Yang and Damasio then deploy a neuroscientific analysis to support 'what every teacher knows' – that the emotional climate in a classroom is crucial for learning.

Two articles directly on teacher–pupil relationships, then offer further support. Pollard (6.3) analyses processes in negotiating classroom rules, whilst Chaplain (6.4) rehearses ways in which rules, routines and rituals can be used to establish authority and maintain a smooth-running classroom.

Finally, the chapter focuses on teacher expectations and their consequences. Evidence of their impact, both positive and negative, are reviewed by Gipps and MacGilchrist (6.5). Lawrence, in Reading 6.6, offers a very clear account of self-esteem. For pupils, this may be enhanced or diminished by a great many influences, but teacher actions are among the most significant.

The parallel chapter of *Reflective Teaching in Schools* addresses similar issues and provides more practical classroom guidance. There are specific sections on developing good classroom relationships and on their role in advancing learning. The professional skills of teachers are discussed and, finally, the chapter focuses on enhancing classroom climate, supporting self-esteem and developing an inclusive classroom. 'Key Readings' are suggested.

On *reflectiveteaching.co.uk* there are additional ideas on the issues raised in this chapter in its supplementary 'Reflective Activities' and 'Notes for Further Reading'. Within the section on 'Deepening Expertise', you will find that 'relationships' are at the heart of its organising conceptual framework.

Reading 6.1

Life in classrooms

Philip Jackson

> This a short extract from Jackson's classic book which revolutionised ways of thinking about classrooms by highlighting the *experience* of pupils. He sets out the nature of school attendance and of the school context: schooling is compulsory; a pupil is one in the classroom crowd, is subject to praise or sanction, and is constrained by the power of the teacher. Crowds, praise and power are inevitable elements of children's school experiences, and they gradually learn to adapt and cope with them. The most rapid adaption is needed at school entry but the issues never entirely go away.
>
> Can you identify children in your class who adapt particularly well, and others who have difficulties? How does this issue of social adaption affect their learning?
>
> *Edited from:* Jackson, P. W. (1968) *Life in Classrooms.* New York: Teachers College Press, 4–11.

School is a place where tests are failed and passed, where amusing things happen, where new insights are stumbled upon, and skills acquired. But it is also a place in which people sit, and listen, and wait, and raise their hands, and pass out paper, and stand in line, and sharpen pencils. School is where we encounter both friends and foes, where imagination is unleashed and misunderstanding brought to ground. But it is also a place in which yawns are stifled and initials scratched on desktops, where milk money is collected and lines are formed. Both aspects of school life, the celebrated and the unnoticed, are familiar to all of us, but the latter, if only because of its characteristic neglect, seems to deserve more attention than it has received to date from those who are interested in education.

In order to appreciate the significance of trivial classroom events it is necessary to consider the frequency of their occurrence, the standardization of the school environment, and the compulsory quality of daily attendance. We must recognize, in other words, that children are in school for a long time, that the settings in which they perform are highly uniform, and that they are there whether they want to be or not. Each of these three facts, although seemingly obvious, deserves some elaboration, for each contributes to our understanding of how students feel about and cope with their school experience.

The magnitude of 7,000 hours spread over six or seven years of a child's life is difficult to comprehend. Aside from sleeping, and perhaps playing, there is no other activity that occupies as much of the child's time as that involved in attending school. Apart from the bedroom there is no single enclosure in which he spends a longer time than he does in the classroom. From the age of six onward he is a more familiar sight to his teacher than to his father, and possible even to his mother.

Thus, when our young student enters school in the morning he is entering an environment with which he has become exceptionally familiar through prolonged exposure. Moreover, it is a fairly stable environment – one in which the physical objects, social relations, and major activities remain much the same from day to day, week to week, and even, in certain respects, from year to year. Life there resembles life in other contexts in some ways, but not all. There is, in other words, a uniqueness to the student's world. School, like church and home, is some place special. Look where you may, you will not find another place quite like it.

There is an important fact about a student's life that teachers and parents often prefer not to talk about, at least not in front of students. This is the fact that young people have to be in school, whether they want to be or not. The school child, like the incarcerated adult, is, in a sense, a prisoner. He too must come to grips with the inevitability of his experience. He too must develop strategies for dealing with the conflict that frequently arises between his natural desires and interests on the one hand and institutional expectations on the other.

In sum, classrooms are special places. The things that make schools different from other places are not only the paraphernalia of learning and teaching and the educational content of the dialogues that take place there. There are other features, much less obvious though equally omnipresent, that help to make up 'the facts of life', as it were, to which students must adapt.

They may be introduced by the key words: *crowds, praise, and power*.

Learning to live in a classroom involves, among other things, learning to live in a crowd. Most of the things that are done in school are done with others, or at least in the presence of others, and this fact has profound implications for determining the quality of a student's life.

Of equal importance is the fact that schools are basically evaluative settings. The very young student may be temporarily fooled by tests that are presented as games, but it doesn't take long before he begins to see through the subterfuge and comes to realize that school, after all, is a serious business. It is not only what you do there but what others think of what you do that is important. Adaptation to school life requires the student to become used to living under the constant condition of having his words and deeds evaluated by others.

School is also a place in which the division between the weak and the powerful is clearly drawn. This may sound like a harsh way to describe the separation between teachers and students, but it serves to emphasize a fact that is often overlooked, or touched upon gingerly at best. Teachers are indeed more powerful than students, in the sense of having greater responsibility for giving shape to classroom events, and this sharp difference in authority is another feature of school life with which students must learn how to deal.

In three major ways then – as members of crowds, as potential recipients of praise or reproof, and as pawns of institutional authorities – students are confronted with aspects of reality that at least during their childhood years are relatively confined to the hours spent in classrooms. It is likely during this time that adaptive strategies having relevance for other contexts and other life periods are developed.

Reading 6.2

We feel, therefore we learn

Mary Helen Immordino-Yang and Antonio Damasio

This reading illustrates the fascinating contributions which biologists and neuroscientists are able to make to educational understanding. Drawing on evolutionary theory, the authors argue that thinking and emotions cannot be separated. To achieve the cognitive performance which is typically valued in education systems, it is thus essential to provide emotionally affirming learning environments in classroom and schools. Sahlberg's analysis of Finland's education system may come to mind here (Reading 4.3) but experienced teachers of course know the quality of relationships underpins what it is possible to achieve in a classroom.

How do you seek to balance emotional and cognitive factors within your teaching?

Edited from: Immordino-Yang, M. H. and Damasio, A (2007) 'We feel, therefore we learn: the relevance of affective and social neuroscience to education'. *Mind, Brain and Education*, 1 (1) 3–10.

Recent advances in the neuroscience of emotions are highlighting connections between cognitive and emotional functions that have the potential to revolutionize our understanding of learning in the context of schools. In particular, connections between decision making, social functioning, and moral reasoning hold new promise for breakthroughs in understanding the role of emotion in decision making, the relationship between learning and emotion, how culture shapes learning, and ultimately the development of morality and human ethics. These are all topics of eminent importance to educators as they work to prepare skilled, informed, and ethical students who can navigate the world's social, moral, and cognitive challenges as citizens. In this article, we sketch a biological and evolutionary account of the relationship between emotion and rational thought, with the purpose of highlighting new connections between emotional, cognitive, and social functioning, and presenting a framework that we hope will inspire further work on the critical role of emotion in education.

Modern biology reveals humans to be fundamentally emotional and social creatures. And yet those of us in the field of education often fail to consider that the high-level cognitive skills taught in schools, including reasoning, decision making, and processes related to language, reading, and mathematics, do not function as rational, disembodied systems, somehow influenced by but detached from emotion and the body. Instead, these crowning evolutionary achievements are grounded in a long history of emotional functions, themselves deeply grounded in humble homeostatic beginnings. Any competent teacher recognizes that emotions and feelings affect students ' performance and learning, as does the state of the body, such as how well students have slept and eaten or whether they are feeling sick or well. We contend, however, that the relationship between learning, emotion and body state runs much deeper than many educators realize and is interwoven with the notion of learning itself. It is not that emotions rule our cognition, nor that rational thought does not exist. It is, rather, that the original purpose for which our brains evolved was to manage our physiology, to optimize our survival, and to allow us to flourish. When one considers that this purpose inherently involves monitoring and altering the state of the body and mind in increasingly complex ways, one can appreciate that emotions, which play out in the body and mind, are profoundly intertwined with thought. And after all, this should not be surprising. Complex brains could not have evolved separately from the organisms they were meant to regulate.

But there is another layer to the problem of surviving and flourishing, which probably evolved as a specialized aspect of the relationship between emotion and learning. As brains and the minds they support became more complex, the problem became not only dealing with one's own self but managing social interactions and relationships. The evolution of human societies has produced an amazingly complex social and cultural context, and flourishing within this context means that only our most trivial, routine decisions and actions, and perhaps not even these, occur outside of our socially and culturally constructed reality. Why does a high school student solve a math problem, for example? The reasons range from the intrinsic reward of having found the solution, to getting a good grade, to avoiding punishment, to helping tutor a friend, to getting into a good college, to pleasing his/her parents or the teacher. All of these reasons have a powerful emotional component and relate both to pleasurable sensations and to survival within our culture. Although the notion of surviving and flourishing is interpreted in a cultural and social framework at this late stage in evolution, our brains still bear evidence of their original purpose: to manage our bodies and minds in the service of living, and living happily, in the world with other people.

This realization has several important implications for research at the nexus of education and neuroscience. It points to new directions for understanding the interface of biology, learning, and culture, a critical topic in education that has proven difficult to investigate systematically. It promises to shed light on the elusive link between body and mind, for it describes how the health and sickness of the brain and body can influence each other. And importantly, it underscores our fundamentally social nature, making clear that the very neurobiological systems that support our social interactions and relationships are recruited for the often covert and private decision making that underlies much of our thought. In brief, learning, in the complex sense in which it happens in schools or the real world, is not a rational or disembodied process; neither is it a lonely one.

Taking an evolutionary perspective, emotions and the mechanisms that constitute them as behaviours, which humans experience as resulting in punishment or reward, pain or pleasure, are, in essence, nature's answer to one central problem, that of surviving and flourishing in an ambivalent world. Put simply, the brain has evolved under numerous pressures and oppressions precisely to cope with the problem of reading the body's condition and responding accordingly and begins doing so via the machinery of emotion. This coping shows up in simple ways in simple organisms and in remarkably rich ways as brains get more complex. In the brains of higher animals and people, the richness is such that they can perceive the world through sensory processing and control their behaviour in a way that includes what is traditionally called the mind. Out of the basic need to survive and flourish derives a way of dealing with thoughts, with ideas, and eventually with making plans, using imagination, and creating. At their core, all of these complex and artful human behaviours, the sorts of behaviours fostered in education, are carried out in the service of managing life within a culture and, as such, use emotional strategies (Damasio, 1999). Emotion, then, is a basic form of decision making, a repertoire of know-how and actions that allows people to respond appropriately in different situations. The more advanced cognition becomes, the more high-level reasoning supports the customization of these responses, both in thought and in action. With evolution and development, the specifications of conditions to which people respond, and the modes of response at their disposal, become increasingly nuanced. The more people develop and educate themselves, the more they refine their behavioural and cognitive options. In fact, one could argue that the chief purpose of education is to cultivate children's building of repertoires of cognitive and behavioural strategies and options, helping them to recognize the complexity of situations and to respond in increasingly flexible, sophisticated, and creative ways. In our view, out of these processes of recognizing and responding, the very processes that form the interface between cognition and emotion, emerge the origins of creativity — the artistic, scientific, and technological innovations that are unique to our species. Further, out of these same kinds of processing emerges a special kind of human innovation: the social creativity that we call morality and ethical thought.

In teaching children, the focus is often on the logical reasoning skills and factual knowledge that are the most direct indicators of educational success. But there are two problems with this approach. First, neither learning nor recall happen in a purely rational domain, divorced from emotion, even though some of our knowledge will eventually distil into a moderately rational, unemotional form. Second, in teaching students to minimize the emotional aspects of their academic curriculum and function as much as possible in the rational domain, educators may be encouraging students to develop the sorts of knowledge that inherently do not transfer well to real-world situations. As both the early- and late-acquired prefrontal damage patients show, knowledge and reasoning divorced from emotional implications and learning lack meaning and motivation and are of little use in the real world. Simply having the knowledge does not imply that a student will be able to use it advantageously outside of school.

As recent advances in the neurobiology of emotions reveal, in the real world, cognition functions in the service of life-regulating goals, implemented by emotional machinery. Moreover, people's thoughts and feelings are evaluated within a sociocultural context and serve to help them survive and flourish in a social, rather than simply opportunistic, world. While the idea that learning happens in a cultural context is far from new (Tomasello, Carpenter, Call, Behne and Moll, 2005), we hope that these new insights from neurobiology, which shed light on the nested relationships between emotion, cognition, decision making, and social functioning, will provide a jumping-off point for new thinking on the role of emotion in education.

Reading 6.3

Teachers, pupils and the working consensus
Andrew Pollard

> This reading provides a sociological analysis of how teacher–pupil relationships are formed. At the start of each new year it is suggested that a 'process of establishment' takes place, through which understandings and tacit rules about classroom life are negotiated. This 'working consensus' reflects the needs and coping strategies of both pupils and teacher as they strive to fulfil their classroom roles. Given the power of each to threaten the interests of the other, the working consensus represents a type of moral agreement about 'how we will get on together'. It thus frames future action and relationships.
>
> Do you feel that you have successfully negotiated a working consensus with the children or young people you teach?
>
> *Edited from:* Pollard, A. (1985) *The Social World of the Primary School.* London: Cassell, 158–71.

The interests of teachers and children are different in many ways and yet, in a sense, teachers and children face an identical and fundamental problem: they both have to 'cope' if they are to accomplish their daily classroom lives satisfactorily. I contend that this is possible only with some degree of accommodation of each other's interests. This is the essence of the interaction concept of working consensus, which encapsulates the idea of teacher and children mutually negotiating interdependent ways of coping in classrooms. This working consensus is created through a process of establishment (Ball, 1981b) at the start of the school year. For instance one experienced teacher at Moorside commented:

> I always start off the year carefully, trying to be well organised and fairly strict so that the children get into a routine, and then we get to know each other gradually. Usually by the summer term I can relax the routine, do more interesting topics, have a few more jokes and discussions. By then everyone knows what sort of things are allowed, and I know the children well enough to do that kind of thing without them trying things on.

In this 'getting to know each other' period the teacher usually attempts to set up routines, procedures and standards which are offered as 'the way to do things'. This attempt to impose routines is not surprising, since the most salient threat to a teacher's interests is that of the large numbers of children, and routines will to some extent absorb some of the pressure. Meanwhile the teacher watches the children, interpreting their actions from the point of view of her perspective and evaluating the effect of them on her interests.

The teacher often holds the initial advantage and may think that everything is going well. However, from the point of view of the children, the salient threat to their interests is that of teacher power, the particular use of which is initially unknown. Thus the children have good reason to watch and evaluate, gradually accumulating a stock of knowledge and experience of the teacher and of situations, most of which is defensively organised around the threat of teacher power. For instance, one boy said:

> Last year was great; Mrs Biggs, she was very strict to start with, but then she used to sit at her desk and mark books a lot, so we could talk and send notes. I used top play noughts and crosses with Nigel and draw pictures. If she got up we'd just slide the papers under our books. When she was explaining things to people – that was good, but we had to hand our work in or if we didn't we'd get lines, and it had to be reasonable or we'd get into bother. It wasn't too bad really.

Gradually, as incidents occur and as sparring goes on, classes are seen to settle down and children feel they have got to know their teacher better.

This more settled accord is often described by teachers and other educationists as a 'good relationship'. It is rightly regarded as being extremely important and a teacher may well be judged by colleagues partly by his or her ability to foster such a relationship with pupils. However, the concept of a good relationship has always been a rather vague one, only accessible in some accounts to those with particular levels of sensitivity and intuition.

In fact it is possible to be more analytical. In my view the process of establishment normally and naturally leads to a stabilisation of relationships because of mutuality of the coping needs of the teacher and pupils. What emerges is essentially a negotiated system of behavioural understandings for the various types of situations which routinely occur in the classroom. Through interaction, incidents and events, a type of case law of inter-subjectively understood rule systems, expectations and understandings emerges and begins to become an assumed, taken-for-granted reality which socially frames each situation. These socially understood, but tacit, conventions and rules constrain the behaviour of the children to varying degrees, depending on the quality and definition of the working consensus, but it is not unusual to find classes in some primary schools which a teacher can confidently leave for a time in the secure expectation that productive activities will continue just as they would have done had the teacher been present.

It is significant that these rules and understandings constrain not only the children, but also the teacher. This point follows from the fact that the rules are interactively constructed through negotiating processes to which teachers are party. Thus, from the child perspective, teachers can be seen as morally bound, and indeed the working consensus can be seen as providing a type of moral order in the classroom.

If the teacher breaks the understood rules then the action is considered unfair. Children commented:

> Well, I just dropped this marble in class and usually she just tells us off, but she took it and wouldn't give it back. It wasn't hers to take just because I dropped it.

> I answered the register in a funny voice and he went right mad. Yesterday he was cracking jokes himself. He's probably had a row with his wife.

These examples are instances of the most common teacher infringement of the working consensus – that of reaction to a routine deviant act which is seen as being too harsh. Such a reaction tends to produce bad feeling and often provokes more deviance.

It is thus the case that if the working consensus and the good relationship are to be maintained, both teacher and pupil strategies are partially circumscribed by them.

Of course it has to be recognised that a teacher's absolute power resources are greater than those of pupils. However, it can be argued that to an extent the working consensus incorporates and accepts differentiated status and behaviours, that it takes into account material realities and differences in socially sanctioned authority, differences in knowledge and differences in experience, and that these become accommodated into the relationships and understandings which are established between teachers and children.

The working consensus is thus an interactive product; indeed it can be seen as a collective, interdependent adaptation by the teacher and children to survival problems which are, in different ways, imposed on them both.

As we have seen, a crucial feature of classroom life which derives directly from the working consensus is the system of intersubjectively understood rules. These are tacit and take-for-granted conventions which are created through the dynamics of interaction and through negotiation. They develop through incident and case law as the teacher and children come to understand each other and to define the parameters of acceptable behaviour in particular situation. The result is that such tacit understandings influence and 'frame' the actions of both teacher and pupils.

Two further points have to be made. In the first place such rules are not static; they change depending on the situation, which can be analyzed in terms of the time, place, activity and people involved. In the second place they vary in strength. On some occasions the rule frame may be high and the expected behaviour is very clearly defined, while on other occasions, when the rule frame is weak, action is less circumscribed.

The concepts of working consensus and rule frame provide a means of analyzing the social context *within* classrooms. They relate to self, and are the product of processes of classroom interaction in which the coping necessities and interests of each party play a major part.

The working consensus – the 'good relationship' – represents a mutual agreement to respect the dignity and fundamental interests of the other party. As such it is produced by creative and interactive responses to the structural position which teachers and pupils face in their classrooms. The additional point, though, is that these responses themselves create a micro social structure and context – analyzable in terms of rule frame – to which individuals also have to relate as they act.

Reading 6.4

Classroom rules, routines and rituals
Roland Chaplain

> This reading combines the knowledge of a social psychologist with the expertise of a classroom practitioner. Whilst facing the need for the teacher to 'be in charge', Chaplain shows how careful use of rules, routines and rituals can contribute enormously to creating a positive environment for learning. He draws attention to the nesting of classroom behaviour policies within those of the school.
>
> Is there any scope for the further development of rules, routines or rituals to help in achieving your classroom goals?
>
> *Edited from:* Chaplain, R., (2003) *Teaching Without Disruption in the Primary School.* New York: Routledge, 140–55; also in *Teaching Without Disruption in the Secondary School.* New York: Routledge.

In the classroom, the teacher should be in charge.

Rules

Intelligently constructed rules can help establish teacher control and facilitate learning, provided that their meaning is clear, they are supported by the relevant rewards and sanctions, and the teacher behaves assertively. The main function of classroom rules is to set limits to pupils' behaviour and to make them aware of the conditions required for success. They operate in a preventative or feed forward way to establish and maintain order and momentum. This does not mean pupils are not treated warmly or that humour, developing relationships and mutual respect are also not important. Indeed, a principal objective of having rules is to create a safe and warm environment through making clear what the teacher values as important to ensure pupils' success and to develop positive working relationships.

Rules operate at both the classroom and whole-school levels, the latter representing the core behavioural expectations for the school to provide consistency and predictability for both staff and pupils.

Classroom rules should focus on making a classroom safe, keeping pupils on legitimate tasks and promoting appropriate social behaviour.

Rules to avoid the dangers of running in class, messing about in science lessons, or not checking gym equipment before it's used, are clearly necessary and need little, if any, qualification. In addition to physical safety, rules provide psychological safety at both cognitive and emotional levels. Disruption in class interferes with the learning process in various ways; cognitively by disturbing concentration and attention and emotionally by making people feel anxious or worried.

A teacher's behaviour towards a class will support pupils' needs, changing its emphasis from early encounters to later in the school year. Early stages focus on defining expectations and boundaries and involve relatively high levels of direction, whereas in later stages, pupils are given differentiated levels of responsibility and diversity in learning experiences, informed by performance feedback. In such ways, in addition to signalling the rights and responsibilities of pupils, rules help to create the conditions for learning (Rudduck, et al., 1996).

To have a set of rules to cover all possible situations would result in a rather long unmemorable and unmanageable list, so the number of rules should be kept to a minimum. I recommend a maximum of five simply worded and easy to remember rules. Hargeaves et al. (1975) recommended five types of rules which relate to: movement; talking; time; teacher-pupil relationships; and pupil-pupil relationships. There are clear overlaps between the different types.

Five basic principles to consider when deciding how to develop rules are:

1 *keep 'em positive*. The wording of a rule can make or break it. Rules should reflect what you value and want to encourage in your classroom.

2 *keep 'em brief*. Rules should include only key concerns. Make sure they are kept brief and snappy as this makes them easier to remember.

3 *keep 'em realistic*. Set rules which reflect expectations that are appropriate and achievable by you or the class.

4 *keep 'em focused*. The overall objective for having rules is self-regulation. Rules should concentrate on key issues, including being aware of personal safety and the safety of others; consideration of others; cooperation; honesty; friendliness; as well as attending to legitimate classroom activity and maintaining appropriate nose levels for specific contexts.

5 *keep 'em*. If the rule is worth having in the first place, then it needs to be regularly reinforced. If you find it is not working or has lost its relevance, then either modify it or drop it. Do not make rules ineffective by applying them one minute and letting them slide the next.

Rules supported by rewards and sanctions, which demonstrate clear cause and effect relationships, remove ambiguity for staff and pupils. Sanctions should be predictable and hierarchical. 'Fuzzy' sanctions or threats which are not carried through are a waste of time. Being clear about what sanctions are available in school and which are appropriate for particular types of misdemeanour, how they are organised and who has the authority to issue and carry them through, helps to remove ambiguity and allows both teacher and class to focus on the task in hand – that is, teaching and learning.

Routines

Routines are used to manage everyday social behaviour around school and in class, as well as supporting teaching and learning. They are often organised around a particular time (such as the start of a lesson, for example), a place (classroom) or context (group work). Their object is to add meaning to rules and to translate their spirit into action. If being polite is an important rule, then the routines established for greeting pupils and staff when they arrive in school or class, how equipment is shared and empowering people to have their thoughts and feelings heard should reflect this. If not disturbing other pupils while working is a rule, then a routine for checking or marking pupils' work, distributing materials and moving around the classroom should ensure that disruption to pupils is minimalised. Well thought-out and communicated routines facilitate the smooth running of lessons, keeping pupils on-task and maintaining the efficient and well-ordered operation of your classroom.

Some routines operate at the school level (lunchtime, assemblies), others at the classroom level (getting work out, changing activities). There are a great many routines roughly similar to all schools, whilst others vary significantly between schools to reflect different cultures and contexts, as well as the values and beliefs of those responsible for running the schools. Common routines include those used to control movement around the school, entering classrooms, getting work out, issuing materials, asking questions, putting things away and so on.

Particular teachers and subjects require different routines. Non-teaching activities such as getting pupils ready to learn, distributing materials and marking work, whilst necessary, can take up substantial amounts of teaching time, but well thought-out routines can streamline these activities, increasing the time available for learning.

Efficient routines thus provide teachers with more time to teach, and pupils with more time to learn. Spending time planning and reviewing routines beforehand pays dividends, since it provides pupils with a sense of organisation and order. Experienced teachers spend considerable time in their early encounters with pupils teaching them routines. This is not to suggest that routines are only important in early encounters; spending time establishing and practising routines results in them becoming automatic and triggered by simple ritualised behaviours – clapping hands, a stare, or folding arms, for example.

Rituals

Rituals also offer a very powerful form of demonstrating authority to all members of the school community. They give shape to, and facilitate, the smooth running of the school day. A ritual, such as assembly, requires participants to behave in a formalised way and includes particular actions, words and movements. It involves a series of routines occurring in a particular sequence. How pupils enter assembly often reflects how they are expected to enter other formal areas, such as classrooms. There may be modifications to give the assembly more status, such as playing music when people enter. The rules about who is expected, or permitted, to speak, and in what order, is usually fairly easily understood. These routines and procedures are usually learnt at first by instruction and prompting, and later by internalising the various routines involved.

Rituals also provide a sense of community and social identity, incorporating feelings of belonging and security which can be emotionally uplifting and within which personal development can take place. Assemblies are events which promote the social identity of the school and are used as a vehicle for reminding pupils of what is valued – for example, giving prizes for positive behaviour or publicly admonishing unacceptable behaviour. Similar processes operate in the classroom, but with less formality.

In the classroom, a rule (respecting others, for example) will be supported with routines (in this example, pupils raising their hands before asking questions) and is often triggered by a teacher's ritual of moving to a particular place or through the use of a gesture (such as a raised finger to forewarn an individual eager to shout out an answer). Other rituals include standing or sitting in particular places in the classroom and clapping hands or folding arms in order to elicit particular behaviour such as gaining attention.

Reading 6.5

Teacher expectations and pupil achievement
Caroline Gipps and Barbara MacGilchrist

> In this review, Gipps and MacGilchrist summarise key evidence on the significance of teachers' maintaining high expectations and pupil performance. There seems to be little doubt that this is a crucial factor in effective teaching, as children's self-confidence flourishes from the affirmation and encouragement of their teachers. Again, as in the previous readings, teacher and pupil behaviour are seen to be inextricably linked. Interestingly, however, research studies of classroom practice often document relatively low levels of explicit encouragement, praise and communication of expectations.
>
> Can you support the performance of your children by explicitly conveying your confidence in them? How will they respond?
>
> *Edited from:* Gipps, C. and MacGilchrist, B. (1999) 'Primary school learners', in Mortimore, P. (ed) *Understanding Pedagogy and its Impact on Learning.* London: Paul Chapman, 52–5.

One of the hallmarks of effective teachers is their belief that all children can achieve. This belief manifests itself in a variety of ways in the classroom, the most common being through the high expectations teachers set for the children they are teaching. When drawing attention to some of the knowledge and skills teachers need to have in order to bring about effective learning, Mortimore (1993) identified the essential need for teachers to have psychological and sociological knowledge: 'Psychological knowledge so that they can understand how young minds operate and how young people cope with different cultural patterns and family traditions. Sociological knowledge of the way factors such as race, gender, class or religion operate to help or hinder successful teaching' (p. 296).

The research literature that has focused on the relationship between disadvantage and achievement and the extent to which schools can enhance the achievement of pupils whatever their background provides important sociological knowledge for teachers. Two common themes emerge from the literature. The first is that socioeconomic inequality is a powerful determinant of differences in cognitive and educational attainment (Mortimore and Mortimore, 1986). Longitudinal studies support this finding (Douglas, 1964; Davie et al., 1972). Social class, along with ethnic background, gender and disability, has been found to have a substantial influence on the life chances of young people. The other common theme is that schools can and do make a difference, but that some schools are much more effective than others at counteracting the potentially damaging effects of disadvantage (Edmunds, 1979; Rutter et al., 1979; Reynolds, 1982; Mortimore et al., 1988; Smith and Tomlinson, 1989; Sammons et al., 1995).

There have been numerous studies to identify the characteristics of highly successful schools (Sammons et al., 1995). Whilst researchers are rightly cautious about identifying causal relationships, the review of the effectiveness literature by Sammons et al. (1995) has revealed a set of common features that can be found in effective schools. The majority of these concern the quality and nature of teaching and learning in classrooms along with the overall learning ethos of the school. Some draw attention in particular to the relationship between teachers' beliefs and attitudes and pupils' progress and achievement.

The idea of a selffulfilling prophecy was first introduced by Merton (1968), and the wellknown study by Rosenthal and Jacobson (1968) demonstrated how this concept can operate in the classroom. They showed that it was possible to influence teachers' expectations of certain pupils even though the information they had been given about those pupils was untrue. In their review of the literature Brophy and Good (1974) and Pilling and Pringle (1978) identify the power of teacher expectation in relation to pupils' learning.

In two studies of primary age pupils (Mortimore et al., 1988; Tizard et al., 1988), the importance of teacher expectations emerged. Tizard and colleagues focused on children aged four to seven in 33 inner London infant schools. The purpose of the research was to examine factors in the home and in the school that appeared to affect attainment and progress during the infant school years. Particular attention was paid to the different levels of attainment of boys and girls, and of white British children and black British children of AfroCaribbean origin. The team found that there was a link between disadvantage and pupil progress and attainment. The literacy and numeracy knowledge and skills that children had acquired before they started school were found to be a strong predictor of attainment at age seven.

The study was able to identify those school factors that appear to exert a greater influence on progress than home background. The two most significant factors were the range of literacy and numeracy taught to the children and teachers' expectations. Whilst each of these factors was independently associated with progress, the team found that the school and class within it that the child attended proved to be an overriding factor in terms of the amount of progress made. A relationship was found between teacher expectations and the range of curriculum activities provided for children, especially in the areas of literacy and numeracy. The team reported that, of the schoolbased measures we looked at, we found that teachers' expectations of children's curriculum coverage showed the strongest and most consistent association with school progress' (*op cit.,* p. 139). Where teachers had low expectations of children they provided a narrower curriculum offering.

The Junior School Project (Mortimore et al., 1988) was a longitudinal study of a cohort of seven year old pupils in fifty London schools. The project drew together different aspects of disadvantage. Using sophisticated research techniques the team was able to account for what were called pupil and school 'givens'; for example, they were able to take account of pupil factors such as home language, family circumstances, age and sex, and school factors such as size and the stability of staffing. This enabled the team to focus on those factors over which the school had control, such as teaching methods, record keeping and curriculum leadership. They were able to examine which of these factors appear to have a positive impact on pupils' progress and achievement.

The research revealed significant differences in children's educational outcomes during the Junior years. Age, social class, sex and race were each found to have an impact on cognitive achievement levels at age seven and eleven. For example, at age seven those children whose parents worked in nonmanual jobs were nearly ten months further ahead in reading than pupils from unskilled manual homes. By the end of the third year the gap had widened. It was also found that with noncognitive outcomes, such as behaviour and selfconcept, there were differences according to age, social class, sex and race. Overall, however, it was found that it was the social class dimension that accounted for the main differences between groups of pupils.

It was the focus on progress that the pupils made over the four years of the study that demonstrated that some schools (and the teachers within them) were far more effective than others. With reading, for example, the average child in the most effective school increased his or her score on a ten point reading test by 25 points more than the average child attending the least effective school. The team found that schools which did better on one measure of academic progress tended to do better on others, and that effective schools tended to be effective for all pupils regardless of social class, ethnic group, sex or age.

High teacher expectations were a common characteristic of these schools. The team looked at ways in which expectations were transmitted in the classroom. They found, for example, that teachers had lower expectations of pupils from socioeconomically disadvantaged backgrounds. Denbo's (1988) analysis of the research literature over a twenty year period supports the importance of teacher expectation. Denbo found that many studies demonstrated that both low and high teacher expectation greatly affected student performance. It has been demonstrated that if appropriate teaching styles and teaching expectations are used (OFSTED, 1993a) then pupils can become positive about learning and improve their levels of achievement.

If learner is seen as an active partner in the learning process, then his/her motivational and emotional state becomes more relevant. One of the school outcomes studied by Mortimore et al. was the attitude of students towards themselves as learners. The team designed a measure of selfconcept which revealed clear school differences. Some schools produced pupils who felt positive about themselves as learners regardless of their actual ability. Others produced pupils who were negative about themselves even though, according to their progress, they were performing well. Kuykendall (1989) argues that low teacher expectations have been shown to reduce the motivation of students to learn, and that 'perhaps the most damaging consequence of low teacher expectations is the erosion of academic selfimage in students' (p. 18). Mortimore (1993) supports this view: 'for a pupil who is regularly taught by a teacher with low expectations, the experience can be demoralizing and too often leads to serious underachievement' (p. 295). Not unrelated to this, he draws attention to the need for teachers to provide good role models for pupils.

It is interesting that these findings mirror, in many respects, some of the studies about the brain and learning referred to earlier. Drawing on the work of LeDoux (1996), Goleman (1996) argues that emotions play a key role in cognitive development. He takes the view that emotional intelligence, as he calls it, is a vital capacity for learning. It involves, for example, motivation, the ability to persist and stay on task, control of impulse, regulation of mood and the capacity for keeping distress from swamping the ability to think. Not unrelatedly, Smith (1998) comments that many learners in the classroom avoid taking risks and prefer to stay in 'the comfort zone'. He reminds us that young learners will happily 'copy out in rough, copy it out in neat, draw a coloured border around it, highlight the key words in primary colour, draw you a picture' but that this 'rote, repetitive comfort zone activity is not where real learning takes place' (p. 43). He describes how studies of the brain indicate that 'the optimal conditions for learning include a positive, personal leaning attitude where challenge is high and anxiety and selfdoubt is low' (p. 41). In her review of the literature on effective primary teaching, Gipps (1992) identified some important factors that mark out effective primary teaching. Amongst these is 'the importance of a good positive atmosphere in the classroom with plenty of encouragement and praise, high levels of expectations of all children and high levels of workrelated talk and discussion' (p. 19). She came to the conclusion that, over and above what theories inform us about good teaching, theorists tell us that children are capable of more than we expect.

So, it seems clear that teachers do have beliefs about how children learn and that they need a teaching strategy able to negotiate a path among the rocks and hard places of context, content, child and learning. This resonates with the complexity of real class-rooms. Furthermore, those teachers who see children as thinkers, and therefore capable of achieving more and more, are the ones who can enable children to view themselves as able to learn. This is a virtuous circle which needs to be encouraged.

Reading 6.6

What is self-esteem?

Denis Lawrence

> Denis Lawrence provides a wonderfully clear account of the collection of ideas associated with self-esteem. Distinguishing between self-concept, self-image and the sense of ideal self, he describes self-esteem in terms of an individual's evaluation of their personal worth. Such self-conceptions initially derive from family relationships but during the school years these are augmented by the impressions offered by teachers and peers.
>
> Self-esteem is a vital issue in respect of the formation of identity and self-confidence. However, it also has a direct effect on the ways in which pupils approach learning challenges. Clearly, teacher expectations are a particularly significant influence on the ways in which pupils see themselves, and these are the subject of Reading 6.5 .
>
> How could you build up the self-esteem of your pupils?
>
> *Edited from:* Lawrence, D. (2006) *Enhancing Self-Esteem in the Classroom.* London: Paul Chapman, 1–9.

What is self-esteem? We all have our own idea of what we mean by the term, but in any discussion of self-esteem amongst a group of teachers there are likely to be several different definitions. The chances are that amongst these definitions the words *self-concept, ideal self* and *self-image* will appear.

Self-concept

Firstly, the term *self-concept* is best defined as the sum total of an individual's mental and physical characteristics and his/her evaluation of them. As such it has three aspects: the cognitive (thinking); the affective (feeling) and the behaviourial (action). In practice, and from the teacher's point of view, it is useful to consider this self-concept as developing in three areas – self-image, ideal self and self-esteem.

The self-concept is the individual's awareness of his/her own self. It is an awareness of one's own identity. The complexity of the nature of the 'self' has occupied the thinking of philosophers for centuries and was not considered to be a proper topic for psychology until James (1890) resurrected the concept from the realms of philosophy. As with the philosophers of his day, James wrestled with the objective and subjective nature of the 'self' – the 'me' and the 'I' – and eventually concluded that it was perfectly reasonable for the psychologist to study the 'self' as an objective phenomenon. He envisaged the infant developing from 'one big blooming buzzing confusion' to the eventual adult state of self-consciousness. The process of development throughout life can be considered, therefore, as a process of becoming more and more aware of one's own characteristics and consequent feelings about them. We see the *self-concept* as an umbrella term because subsumed beneath the 'self' there are three aspects: self-image (what the person is); ideal self (what the person would like to be); and self-esteem (what the person feels about the discrepancy between what he/she is and what he/she would like to be).

Each of the three aspects of self-concept will be considered in turn. Underpinning this theoretical account of the development of self-concept will be the notion that it is the child's *interpretation* of the life experience which determines self-esteem levels. This is known as the phenomenological approach and owes its origin mainly to the work of Rogers (1951). It attempts to understand a person through empathy with that person and is based on the premise that it is not the events which determine emotions but rather the person's interpretation of the events. To be able to understand the other person requires therefore an ability to empathize.

Self-image

Self-image is the individual's awareness of his/her mental and physical characteristics. It begins in the family with parents giving the child an image of him/herself of being loved or not loved, of being clever or stupid, and so forth, by their non-verbal as well as verbal communication. This process becomes less passive as the child him/herself begins to initiate further personal characteristics. The advent of school brings other experiences for the first time and soon the child is learning that he/she is popular or not popular with other children. He/she learns that school work is easily accomplished or otherwise. A host of mental and physical characteristics are learned according to how rich and varied school life becomes. In fact one could say that the more experiences one has, the richer is the self-image.

The earliest impressions of self-image are mainly concepts of *body-image*. The child soon learns that he/she is separate from the surrounding environment. This is sometimes seen amusingly in the young baby who bites its foot only to discover with pain that the foot belongs to itself. Development throughout infancy is largely a process of this further awareness of body as the senses develop. The image becomes more precise and accurate with increasing maturity so that by adolescence the individual is normally fully aware not only of body shape and size but also of his/her attractiveness in relation to peers. Sex-role identity also begins at an early age, probably at birth, as parents and others begin their stereotyping and classifying of the child into one sex or the other.

With cognitive development more refined physical and mental skills become possible, including reading and sporting pursuits. These are usually predominant in most schools so that the child soon forms an awareness of his/her capabilities in these areas.

This process of development of the self-image has been referred to as the 'looking-glass theory of self' (Cooley, 1902) as most certainly the individual is forming his/her self-image as he/she receives feedback from others. However, the process is not wholly a matter of 'bouncing *off* the environment' but also one of 'reflecting *on* the environment' as cognitive abilities make it possible for individuals to reflect on their experiences and interpret them.

Ideal self

Side by side with the development of self-image, the child is learning that there are ideal characteristics he/she should possess – that there are ideal standards of behaviour and also particular skills which are valued. For example, adults place value on being clean and tidy, and 'being clever' is important. As with self-image the process begins in the family and continues on entry to school. The child is becoming aware of the mores of the society. Peer comparisons are particularly powerful at adolescence. The influence of the media also becomes a significant factor at this time with various advertising and show-business personalities providing models of aspiration.

So, what is self-esteem?

Self-esteem is the individual's *evaluation* of the discrepancy between self-image and ideal self. It is an affective process and is a measure of the extent to which the individual cares about this discrepancy. From the discussion on the development of self-image and ideal self it can be appreciated that the discrepancy between the two is inevitable and so can be regarded as a normal phenomenon.

Indeed, there is evidence from clinical work that without this discrepancy – without levels of aspiration – individuals can become apathetic and poorly adjusted. For the person to be striving is therefore a normal state.

What is not so normal is that the individual should worry and become distressed over the discrepancy. Clearly, this is going to depend in early childhood on how the significant people in the child's life react to him/her. For instance, if the parent is overanxious about the child's development this will soon be communicated and the child, too, will also become overanxious about it. He/she begins first by trying to fulfil the parental expectations but, if he/she is not able to meet them, he/she begins to feel guilty.

The subject of reading is probably the most important skill a child will learn in the primary school and normally will come into contact with reading every day of school life. It is not surprising therefore, that the child who fails in reading over a lengthy period should be seen to have developed low self-esteem, the end product of feeling guilt about his/her failure. The child then lacks confidence in him/herself.

It can be appreciated from the foregoing description of the development of self-concept that teachers are in a very strong position to be able to influence self-esteem.

In summary, it is not failure to achieve which produces low self-esteem, it is the way the significant people in the child's life react to the failure. Indeed, it could be argued that failure is an inevitable part of life. There is always someone cleverer or more skilful than ourselves. This must be accepted if we are to help children develop happily without straining always to be on top. Eventually, of course, children become aware of their own level of achievement and realize that they are not performing as well as others around them. Then they can develop low self-esteem irrespective of the opinion of others; they have set their own standards. It is probably true to say, however, that the primary schoolchild is still likely to be 'internalizing' his/her ideal self from the significant people around him/her.

Self-esteem as defined so far refers to a 'global self-esteem' – an individual's overall feeling of self worth. This is relatively stable and consistent over time. In addition to this overall, or global, self-esteem we can have feelings of worth or unworthiness in specific situations. Accordingly we may feel inadequate (low self-esteem) with regard to mathematics or tennis playing. However, they do not affect our overall feeling of self-worth as we can escape their influences by avoiding those situations. If, of course, we cannot avoid them and regularly participate in these activities which make us feel inadequate they may eventually affect our overall self-esteem. Also if we continue to fail in areas which are valued by the significant people in our lives then our overall self-esteem is affected. It is worth reflecting on how children cannot escape school subjects which is why failure in school so easily generalizes to the global self-esteem.

In summary, self-esteem develops as a result of interpersonal relationships within the family which gradually give precedence to school influences and to the influences of the larger society in which the individual chooses to live and to work. These extraneous influences lose their potency to the extent to which the individual becomes self-determinate. For the student of school age, however, self-esteem continues to be affected mainly by the significant people in the life of the student, usually parents, teachers and peers.

Engagement
How are we managing behaviour?

7

The readings in this chapter are concerned with the particular issue of managing behaviour. The theme is that, it is helpful to develop a range of strategies (including those which are assertive), but in principle good behaviour is best achieved by engaging pupils constructively.

Doyle (7.1) analyses the complexity of classrooms and the challenges of teacher decision-making.

The remaining readings focus directly on class management and discipline. Watkins (7.2) is reassuring in arguing that behaviour in most schools is generally good, and that we need to keep media reports in perspective. School policies, however, do make a difference. Of specific reference to each of us, Bennett (7.3) focuses on the personal qualities of teachers – and there is much in what he says about the five virtues which are needed.

Moving into action, Cowley (7.4) suggests ten practical strategies which should make a difference in achieving good behaviour. Meanwhile, Kounin (7.5) draws on his classic analysis of class management and its consequences for behaviour and learning. His work is well worth detailed study – and practice! Merrett and Wheldall (7.6) conclude with further strategies for behaviour management, this time based on careful reinforcement of desired behaviours.

There is a wealth of practical ideas for managing behaviour in this set of readings.

The parallel chapter of *Reflective Teaching in Schools* has sections on understanding classroom behaviour; establishing authority; and the skills needed for engaging pupils, managing classroom episodes and cycles of behaviour (including the management of challenging behaviour). It concludes with Key Reading suggestions for additional sources of support.

Supplementary materials are also available on *reflectiveteaching.co.uk*. These include 'Reflective Activities', Notes for Further Reading, a Compendium and links to further resources.

Reading 7.1

Learning the classroom environment
Walter Doyle

This reading from Doyle highlights some of the reasons why classroom teaching is so difficult to do well, and gives some useful pointers to making it easier. In his view, classroom environments are highly complex and events often unfold simultaneously in ways which cannot be forseen. Doyle believes that teachers develop strategies and skills for reducing some of this complexity, and identifies five ways in which this is done.

Does your classroom sometimes feel complex in the ways which Doyle describes? How helpful are the skills which he suggests?

Edited from: Doyle, W. (1977) 'Learning the classroom environment: an ecological analysis', *Journal of Teacher Education*, XXVIII (6) 51–4.

Deliberation about the nature of teaching skills has generally centered on the teacher's ability to manage subject matter – to explain content, formulate questions, and react to student answers. Naturalistic studies of classrooms suggest, however, that knowing how to manage subject matter sequences represents only a small part of the skill necessary to be a teacher.

Salient features of classrooms

The most salient features of the classroom for the student teachers in my study were *multidimensionality, simultaneity and unpredictability*. The following brief discussion of these categories will clarify the nature of environmental demands in classrooms.

Classrooms were *multidimensional* in the sense that they served a variety of purposes and contained a variety of events and processes, not all of which were necessarily related or even compatible. In classrooms, student teachers confronted groups with a wide range of interests and abilities as well as a diversity of goals and patterns of behaviour. In addition, they faced a multiplicity of tasks that included such matters as processing subject matter information, judging student abilities, managing classroom groups, coping with emotional responses to events and behaviours, and establishing procedures for routine and special assignment, distribution of resources and supplies, record keeping, etc. These tasks also interacted in the sense that ways of dealing with one dimension (e.g. distributing resources and supplies) had consequences for other dimensions (e.g. managing classroom groups) and in the sense that procedures at one point established a precedent that restricted options at a later time It was not uncommon to find student teachers initially over-whelmed to some degree by the sheer quantity of activities, many of which were seen to interfere with their primary interest in managing subject matter.

In addition to the quantity of dimensions in classrooms, many events occurred *simultaneously*. In a discussion, for instance, teachers needed to attend to the pace of the interaction, the sequence of student responses, fairness in selecting students to answer, the quality of individual answers and their relevance to the purposes of the discussion, and the logic and accuracy of content while at the same time monitoring a wide range of work involvement levels and anticipating interruptions. While giving assistance to individual students, teachers also had to remember to scan the rest of the class for signs of possible misbehaviour or to acknowledge other students who were requesting assistance. Examples such as these can be easily multiplied for nearly any set of classroom activities.

The simultaneous occurrence of multiple events, together with the continuous possibility of internal and external interruptions, contributed to an *unpredictability* in the sequence of classroom events, especially for student teachers who had not yet learned to anticipate consequences. Student teachers often found it difficult to predict student reactions to a set of materials or to judge how much time it would take to complete an activity. They were also frequently frustrated by changes in the normal schedule, breakdowns in equipment, and interruptions. The fact that classrooms can go in many different directions at any given point in time often complicated the task of enacting lesson plans in intended ways.

Strategies and skills for reducing complexity

Analysis of induction sequences indicated that all teachers developed strategies that could be interpreted as attempts to reduce the complexity of the classroom environment. There appeared to be considerable variations, however, in the success of different strategies.

In cases labelled 'unsuccessful', student teachers appeared to attempt to reduce classroom complexity by ignoring the multiplicity and simultaneity of the environment. In many instances, this method of reducing complexity involved (a) localizing attention to one region of the classroom; and (b) being engrossed in one activity at a time.

Successful strategies tended to be more congruent with the multiplicity and simultaneity of the environment. A preliminary attempt to codify these skills produced the following categories:

Chunking, or the ability to group discrete events into large units;

Differentiation, or the ability to discriminate among units in terms of their immediate and long-term significance;

Overlap, or the ability to handle two or more events at once (Kounin, 1970, Reading 7.5);

Timing, or the ability to monitor and control the duration of events; and

Rapid judgement, or the ability to interpret events with a minimum of delay.

Discussions with cooperating teachers during the three-year course of the present research

suggested that these categories represent a part of the tacit knowledge experienced teachers have about the way classrooms work.

The first two skills, *chunking* and *differentiation*, suggest that student teachers undergo a concept formation process during which they learn to classify and interpret classroom events and processes in ways that are relevant to the demands created by multi-dimensionality, simultaneity, and unpredictability. In describing pupils, for instance, successful student teachers tended to classify individuals in terms of their potential for disruption, skills in classroom tasks, inclinations to participate in lesson activities, etc. They seemed to know that the movement of some students around the room to secure supplied or sharpen pencils could be ignored whereas the movement of other students required careful monitoring. Similarly, successful teachers learned to judge content in terms of how students would react to it and how difficult it would be to implement in the classroom, in contrast to those who retained purely academic criteria for content adequacy. In sum, successful student teachers transformed the complexity of the environment into a conceptual system that enabled them to interpret discrete events and anticipate the direction and flow of classroom activity. In addition they learned to make rapid judgments about the meaning and consequences of events and to act decisively.

The skills of *overlap* and *timing* supplement the interpretive strategies of chunking, differentiation, and rapid judgment in ways that enable successful student teachers to regulate classroom demands to some degree. The need for overlap was a continuing condition in classrooms. Successful teachers were able to divide attention between several simultaneous dimensions of classroom activity structures. They were also easily distracted by changes in sound or movement in the classroom. Hence they were in a position to react to developing circumstances as necessary. During the course of the observations, timing also emerged as an especially salient skill for managing classroom demands, one that operated on several levels. It was apparent, for example, that timing was related to the effectiveness of directives to individual students (e.g. 'Stop talking and get back to work!'). Successful managers tended to pause and continue to gaze at the target student for a brief period after issuing such a directive. The target student typically returned to work immediately after receiving the directive, but looked up again in one or two seconds. If the teacher was still monitoring the student, there was a greater likelihood that the directive would be followed. Unsuccessful managers, on the other hand, tended to issue directives and continue on as if compliance had been achieved. Over time, this latter pattern seemed to result in directives being ignored and, therefore, reappeared more frequently with less effect.

Reading 7.2

The big picture on behaviour
Chris Watkins

This reading challenges regular but misleading press reports, and affirms the achievement of UK teachers in ensuring that 'behaviour in most schools is good'. Watkins then goes on to demonstrate just how the policies and practices of schools can make a difference. Among the factors identified, he suggests that behaviour is enhanced by schools that 'promote self-discipline and active involvement in the learning process'.

How would you characterise the behaviour policies and practices in schools you know?

Edited from: Watkins, C. (2011) *Managing Classroom Behaviour.* London: ATL, 5–6, 24–5.

Behaviour in most schools is good. The national picture from inspection reports regularly shows this. But it is a different picture to that which is portrayed in some sections of the press. Such reports have a role in amplifying deviance. As a result, many people in the UK believe there is much more crime than there actually is in the country as a whole, and difficulties in pupil behaviour are especially distorted. The problem is that people do seem to believe such accounts. The media paint a portrait of schools where teachers are regularly subject to intimidation and assault. Yet this is not the case from available records. Research and teacher surveys find that the behaviours that teachers most often deal with are repetitious low-level forms such as 'talking out of turn', 'calculated idleness or work avoidance', 'hindering other pupils' or 'making unnecessary (nonverbal) noise'; all of which are frustrating and stressful, but they are not the level of difficulties more frequently reported.

It is useful to consider what purpose is served by amplifying a problem. Such amplification promotes a distorted picture, and action based on such a picture can bring about a deterioration rather than improvement to a situation. In many staffrooms there are voices which seem to amplify difficulties, and it is sometimes difficult to know how to respond. One approach is to seek clear evidence to place alongside their view, so that whatever action follows is based on fact, not just feeling. So what are the facts on school behaviour?

Schools make a difference

The behaviour which pupils display in school is not always a simple reflection of their behaviour elsewhere, including at home. When teachers and parents report on the same children at home and at school, there is comparatively little overlap in the difficulties identified. Further, most teachers know model pupils who they have later found to live under very adverse home circumstances.

Different schools make different differences

Different schools have different overall effects, independent of the make-up of their student intake. Some schools are high excluding schools, some have high levels of truancy, and so on. Key staff in different schools vary in the extent to which they believe that the problem of disruptive behaviour is within the power of schools to resolve. These beliefs are crucial for they inform action and can become self-perpetuating. It is suggested that higher rates of difficulty and exclusion are to be found amongst those schools with lower confidence in their own powers to tackle the problem. So when explaining difficult behaviour, we cannot leave the school out of the picture. Aspects of it as an organisation need to be engaged. The four statements below use key research studies.

1   *Pro-active schools have better behaviour.*

   Schools which aim to pre-empt and prevent difficulties do well. They recognise they contribute to the patterns of behaviour in the school, take steps to understand and analyse such patterns, and intervene through preventive approaches at organisational, classroom and individual level. Reactive schools can experience further deterioration in response to reactive practices.

2   *Schools with a strong sense of community have better behaviour.*

   Schools that form tight communities do well. They give attention to how students feel affiliated to the school, they provide a rich spectrum of adult roles, and adults engage with students personally and challenge them to engage in the life of the school. Teachers display a 'diffuse' teacher role, having frequent contact with staff and students in settings other than the classroom.

3   *Schools with teacher collaboration have better behaviour.*

   In collaborative settings, teachers share information about particular students to find ways to help the student learn more effectively. When they have a particularly difficult problem with a student, they seek help widely, and look for causes and then solutions. In contrast, teachers in isolated settings share information about students by swapping stories about a child's errant behaviour or sympathising with one another. For them, problems invariably means behaviour problems, and punishment is seen as the solution.

4   *Schools that promote pupil autonomy have better behaviour.*

   Schools that promote self-discipline and active involvement in the learning process, and show an interest and concern for pupil development, do well. In contrast, schools that generate a climate of conflict, with severe punishment and a sense of constant tension, or schools that generate a libertarian climate with low severity of punishment and a lack of self-direction are both linked with high levels of misbehaviour.

This implies working towards policies which help the school monitor and learn codes which promote an effective community, resources for teachers to work together and respect for a wide range of learners. If some of the above are being worked for, we may get nearer to a situation in which both teachers and pupils are learning the same things about behaviour in their school:

- it pays not to react
- it pays to care about the organisation
- it pays to work together
- it pays to be responsible.

Reading 7.3

Virtues of great teachers: Justice, courage, patience, wisdom and compassion

Tom Bennett

In this reading an experienced secondary practitioner speaks plainly about the characteristics of 'great teachers'. Tough-minded talk is underpinned by more tender-minded commitments, and this combination gives food for thought about the personal characteristics which contribute to the establishment of classroom authority and enactment of the teacher role.

How do you stand in relation to the five 'virtues' which Bennett identifies?

Edited from: Bennett, T. (2012) *Teacher: Mastering the Art and Craft of Teaching.* London: Continuum, 71–121.

To Aristotle, there were many virtues – of the mind (like intelligence, knowledge and memory), of the body (such as dexterity and strength), and of character (such as courage, forbearance and temperance). It's virtues of character that concern us here – and I identify five below.

Justice

Justice is a vital ingredient in the repertoire of a teacher. Children are HYPERsensitive to justice – particularly when they inhabit the lighter side of the scales. Funnily enough, kids rarely cry foul when the wheel of fortune lands them on the jackpot.

If you were trying to alienate and annoy children – if you were, for some kamikaze reason, in the mood to see exactly how quickly you could piss the kids off to the point where they refuse to even breathe if you ask them, then simply do this; be arbitrary, be unfair. Treat some as favourites for no discernible reason, and others as enemies with equally random justification. Watch how quickly they start to hate you with a vigour that can actually be weighed by a set of kitchen scales. It won't take long, I promise.

Your ability to provide justice is intrinsically tied in with your role as an adult. Remember that for most children, adults are still seen as the masters of the universe, the law-givers and the magistrates of all that is good and reasonable. Adults are supposed to be fair.

It is an act of appalling betrayal for an adult to be unfair to a child, precisely because it is an attribute so valued by society that we need to encourage it as much as possible. Sure, we can never remedy the intrinsic unfairness of the world, but that's the point – we create communities for mutual benefit, not merely egoism. And if you want children to grow up with a sense of fairness, they have to be treated fairly themselves.

Courage

Now we turn to courage, the virtue of appropriate bravery. Bravery concerned Aristotle very much; he regarded it as being pivotal in a person's character. With this virtue, possessed in correct proportions, all other moral actions were possible. In teaching, as in life, courage is the quality that precedes all others. You can be a tyrant and teach (although I wouldn't advise it), but you cannot be a mouse. The question for any classroom practitioner is; do you have the willpower to say to another human being, I know what is best for you?

Courage is the root and the soil of authority. I have never seen a job where it is so tested, so frequently, as those which involve dealing with the public. And dealing with the children of the public is just as demanding, if not more so.

Classroom life is primarily a battle of wills, make no mistake. You may have very agreeable classes, but you are unlikely to have a class so blissfully helpful that you won't have to bend them to your will at some point. And it is more than likely that you will have to do it a lot.

Patience

Patience, far from being the mousy virtue of the librarian, is closely linked to courage. It describes fortitude under pressure, and the ability to bear intolerable loads with tolerance and calm.

The role of the teacher demands patience because students, being human, don't always show linear progress in their learning. This is because understanding doesn't follow the straight line of graph paper: small mental breakthroughs happen in fits and starts; eureka moments occur in the unlikeliest of environments; effort varies from child to child and from day to day, so that children who have been working at straight Ds all year can suddenly put in a fit of effort towards their exams and leap up to a B.

It also takes a new teacher a long, long time to build up relationships with their class – maybe a year, maybe more or less, depending on the demographic, the rigour of the school, the teacher, and a million other factors. How often have I heard a teacher wail at me, 'I tried the things you advised; detentions, praise, clear boundaries, and they're still acting up.' The teacher is usually talking to me after a few weeks of these methods, oblivious to the fact that such strategies can take months and months and months of time. But they have been trained to expect results that happen as swiftly as sodium dropped into water, buzzes and bubbles. The human character is far less prescribed than that.

Wisdom

Wisdom is far more apparent in demonstration than by definition. Aristotle makes a distinction between theoretical and practical wisdom. Theoretical is the one we could identify with knowledge: to know a lot. Practical wisdom is when we see it put into practice. It is thus far closer to comprehension and understanding than it is to mere memorization. But skills are non-existent without content: to be wise about something is both to know a great deal about it, and to be able to put that knowledge to sound effect. Wisdom is a rational process of evaluating and identifying processes that reach from aims towards successful outcomes. It requires speculation, imagination and creative thinking, and application through practice.

Wisdom in the classroom allows us to understand the bigger picture of what is going on. For example, in my experience, broadly speaking, noisy classes learn less than ones that can be quiet on a regular basis; I base this axiom on the simple truth that being quiet allows one to listen and to think, and to write and to work without distraction. But this is not always the case: some activities require noise; some thrive because of it, like debates or hot-seating. Wisdom is the ability to remember that a noisy class might not be the worst thing in the world; to take a step back and ask oneself, what is the aim of the task I have set these students? And if the answer isn't impeded by the noise they produce, then wisdom asks, is the noise so bad after all? In this context, wisdom is a way of seeing the forest and not focusing on the bark of the trees.

This ability to discern the bigger picture also applies to teacher/student relationships. There is a tension that exists between general rules for everyone to follow and exceptions to those rules depending on circumstances. For example, every decent classroom will have general rules about conduct and behaviour, at least for reference when they are broken. But equally every teacher will be aware of times when exceptions could – or in fact should – be made. The teacher needs to have the wisdom to realize when the greater ends of education are served by enforcing rules and when they are not.

Compassion

The idea that compassion is an important virtue in teaching is simultaneously both obvious and controversial. In the first instance, it is a profession where the wellbeing of others is part of the intrinsic aim of the role. You are there to better the education of the children in your charge, and that is automatically directed towards others. What could be more compassionate than that? Well, for a start teachers haven't always been associated with the engines of delight and charm that we now know them to be; in fact it would be fair to say that until the second half of the twentieth-century, many people's experiences of formal education would have been characterized equally with punishment and discomfort as with cuddles. Indeed, some would say that in order to be a teacher, an adult, an authority and a professional, it is best if one doesn't suffer too much compassion, and that one should treat students with a dispassionate regard for nothing other than their academic wellbeing. But this is a false dichotomy, for the emotional and intellectual aspects of compassion will always exist together. The key question for teachers is this: how do you balance them?

Compassion is important because, whilst learning can be enormous fun, it can also be enormously dry. Those who say that all learning and all lessons must engage or entertain are, to be honest, a bit simple. I regard them as well-meaning but essentially quite stupid.

The teacher's job is to direct the children through education; to teach them the best that we have learned so far, to enable them to exceed us, to exceed even themselves. But it isn't always enjoyable. And it is perfectly normal for a child at times to resist the delights of the classroom. In other words, sometimes some children won't enjoy doing as they're told. I do hope this isn't a shock. But as teachers, our job, our duty is to consider the long-term interests of the child even if they themselves do not perceive the benefit.

Reading 7.4

Ten strategies for managing behaviour

Sue Cowley

Sue Cowley's books, despite their provocative titles, contain a great deal of grounded and educationally effective advice on classroom practice. In this illustrative reading, as she explains: 'Controlling a large group of people is difficult in any situation, but when some of your students have no wish to be in school, let alone in your lesson, life can become very difficult indeed. The ten strategies described below are relatively easy to apply, and should cost you little in the way of stress.'

Might some of these strategies work for you?

Edited from: Cowley, S. (2010) *Getting the Buggers to Behave*. London: Continuum, 39–53.

1. Learn to 'read and respond'

You can hype up a class, and equally you can calm it down. Sometimes you'll catch yourself getting the students overexcited, and you'll automatically take measures to bring down the excitement levels. This effect is particularly vivid with young children: even the way your voice sounds is enough to get some classes hyped up. You can also have exactly the same effect on individual students, particularly when you are dealing with their behaviour.

The ability to 'read and respond' to a class or an individual, by adapting what you do instantly, is a subtle skill to learn. It comes more easily with experience, and also as you get to know your class and the people within it. To 'read and respond', you need to: make on-the-spot judgements during the lesson; base these judgements both on how students are responding to the activities that you're doing, and also on how your approaches to behaviour are working; adapt or even throw away a lesson activity if it's not working; change your behaviour management techniques if necessary; be particularly flexible on days when there are already high levels of tension in the class or with particular individuals.

2. Wait for silence

Waiting for silence is one of the most important techniques a teacher can use to encourage and enhance learning. When I say 'wait for silence', I don't mean get your students silent and then talk at them endlessly. What I mean is when you need to talk to the whole class you should not address the students until they are completely silent and fully focused on you (or on whoever is speaking). This applies at the start of the day or lesson, for instance when taking the register, and also at any time when you wish to talk to the class (whatever age the students are). When you get silent attention you send a clear message: the learning is important and you will not allow it to be jeopardized.

In your quest to get silence, it is better to use non-verbal, rather than verbal, techniques. These create less stress for you and add less noise to your classroom. They also give a sense of control and confidence.

Talk about your expectation of silent attention in your first lesson with a class. Get them thinking about why this boundary is so important. Model the behaviour you're after – listen really carefully to your students when they are talking, and try never to talk over a class.

3. Make use of cues

A lot of teacher stress is caused by fairly low-level misbehaviour. The idea behind the use of cues is to get the students doing the behaviour you do want, rather than letting them behave incorrectly first, and then having to tell them off. You can use cues for any behaviour that is repeated regularly, and they can be verbal or non-verbal. Cues often change over time, becoming a form of shorthand understood by all.

Take, for example, 'answering questions'. Start any whole-class question with the phrase: 'Put your hand up if you can tell me …'. By specifying the behaviour you want (hands up), you anticipate and overcome the incorrect response (calling out). This can gradually be abbreviated to 'Hands up' or just a slight raise of your hand.

4. Give them 'the choice'

We cannot actually force our students to behave – we can only make it seem like the best of all possible options. Ideally, we want them to take responsibility for their own actions, and for the consequences of those actions. This is important in creating a positive and effective environment for learning. It is also vital in setting people up for their lives beyond education, when the choices they make about behaviour become potentially that much more crucial.

This is where the technique of 'the choice' comes in. There are essentially two choices: either the students do as you ask, or they accept the consequences of a refusal to comply. You want to get on with teaching and learning – if their behaviour makes that impossible, you utilize the rules of the organization to impose a consequence. This is only fair on the majority who do want to learn. If we make the choices and consequences simple and clear enough, this can prevent misbehaviour occurring or escalating. It also encourages students to consider and change their negative behaviours, to avoid unwelcome consequences in the future.

'The choice' helps you depersonalize a range of tricky situations, because it puts responsibility in the hands of the student. It is up to her to decide how she wishes to behave, and which consequences she is willing to receive. Your role is that of 'police officer' – applying the code of conduct of the place where you work. When using 'the choice': state the behaviour you require; make clear the positive benefits of doing as you ask; make clear the consequences of refusing to comply; give the student a short time to consider her decision. If she decides not to comply, apply the consequences. Aim to sound disappointed, rather than vengeful when doing this.

5. Be reasonable, but don't reason with them

So long as you are reasonable with your students, and you don't have unrealistic expectations about how they will work or behave, then there is no need to actually reason with them over what you do ask them to do. Here are some examples of how this might work with different age groups:

Early years: It's perfectly reasonable to insist they don't paint on the walls. So long as you don't get cross about the odd splash on the floor.
Primary: It's perfectly reasonable to have silence to explain an activity. So long as you don't take 15 minutes to explain it.
Secondary: It's perfectly reasonable to ask students to write in silence. So long as you don't expect them to write for hours at a time.

The 'being reasonable' part of the equation is tricky to manage – you need to make difficult decisions about the right balance to strike. Set high standards, and expect the very best, but be realistic as well. If you are too authoritarian with your demands, then confrontations and difficulties will arise. Similarly, if you're too relaxed, students will take advantage.

6. Use statements, not questions, and assume compliance

Learn to use statements about what you want in relation to behaviour. This is much more helpful than questioning student actions – you state what they should be doing, rather than complaining about what they are not. It also gives the impression of someone who knows what she wants, and who has confidence that the children will comply.

Here are a few examples of questions, and how they might be rephrased as statements:

'Why aren't you doing the work?' becomes 'I want you to get on with the activity now, so you can leave on time.'
'Why are you being so silly?' becomes 'I want you to sit properly on your chair and focus on the learning, thanks.'
'Why aren't you listening?' becomes 'Everyone looking this way and listening in silence, thanks.'

When you're making these positive statements about what you want, you can also use a technique called 'assumed compliance'. All that is meant by this term is that you say 'thanks' (you assume they'll do it) rather than 'please' (you're hoping they will). If you use these two techniques simultaneously, it gives the added benefit of making you sound like a teacher who is very positive, certain and confident about getting what she wants.

7. Use repetition

Much of the time, when we say something, we expect it to be heard and understood the first time around. This is not necessarily a sensible expectation to have, and it can lead to unnecessary misunderstandings and confrontations. Classrooms and other teaching spaces can be noisy and confusing places for our students: there might be many different reasons why they do not respond immediately to your directions. Here are some of the times when you might usefully use repetition with your students: to get their attention before you give an instruction; to ensure they are listening if you need to warn them about a potential sanction; because they might not hear your instructions the first time you give them; to clarify any possible misunderstandings and make your wishes perfectly clear; to reinforce your instructions and make it clear that they must be followed.

8. Set targets and time limits

Learning always works best when you've got clear objectives – a specific target at which to aim. Targets can help you harness our natural sense of competition: perhaps against others, but more importantly against our own previous best. Having a clear amount to achieve, within a set time frame, helps create a sense of urgency and pace to the work. It gives a clear structure – something definite towards which the students can work. Targets also help your less able children feel a sense of achievement. When the teacher asks the class to work in groups to find five ideas in 3 minutes, even the least able should be able to contribute to this task. You might use a whole range of different targets: a target for how many words or answers the students must complete; a time for completing the activity; a target for improving behaviour, such as staying in seats. When setting targets, use the following tips to help you get it right: make sure your targets suit the students; keep targets short and specific for maximum impact; add visual prompts to aid understanding; use your voice, or even some music, to create a sense of pace and urgency; use language to enhance your students' motivation levels: words such as 'competition', 'prize' and 'challenge'; make sure any rewards offered for completion of targets are ones that really appeal to the group or the individual.

9. Use humour

Humour is incredibly powerful in the classroom. Teachers who make their students laugh, and who can laugh with them when appropriate, inevitably form good relationships with their classes. Of course there are times when you can't see the funny side. On a Monday morning/Friday afternoon, when you're tired, hungover, getting a cold or are just plain cranky, you might not feel in the mood for a stand-up comedy routine. But if you can take a fun approach to the job, and make the work and the lessons seem like light relief, this will definitely help you to manage behaviour.

Alongside its beneficial effects on your students, humour: offers a respite from the tension that can build up in a poorly behaved class; makes your work fun for yourself and your students; helps you stay relaxed and rational; helps you avoid defensiveness.

Use humour to dissipate the threat of low-level personal insults: be clear that you refuse to take this kind of stuff seriously and your students will soon give up on doing this. With older students, you can turn an insult on its head by agreeing with what the student has said. So, if a student says, 'Your hair looks really stupid like that, Miss', you might answer (deadpan), 'Yes, I know, I'm planning to sue my hairdresser'. Learn to laugh at yourself when you make a mistake, for instance tripping over or saying something daft. Students love a teacher who is willing to be self-deprecating. It's a good way of undermining the image of teacher as authoritarian figure, and it shows that you don't take yourself too seriously.

10. Put yourself in their shoes

When you're dealing with persistent misbehaviour, it is easy to lose your sense of perspective. You may begin to feel that students are deliberately being awkward, and even that they have a personal vendetta against you. In turn, this leads to overreactions to what is actually relatively minor misbehaviour.

Develop the ability to step outside yourself, and to view what happens from your students' perspective. Become a reflective teacher, constantly engaged in a process of self-analysis. This in turn will feed into every aspect of your practice.

When an activity doesn't seem to be working, or the students start misbehaving, put yourself in their shoes to try to work out why: is there too much listening and not enough doing? Is the concept too hard for the class to grasp? Do the students find this particular topic area boring? Is this work too easy for the group?

Sometimes you can't do much about the situation – they have to get through a particularly tough bit of learning. But at least if you put yourself in their shoes, you can understand why they might fidget. Similarly, you can analyse your own teaching by using this approach. If your students often become confrontational with you when you try to discipline them, step back and view the way that you deal with behaviour from the outside. Are you saying or doing something to exacerbate the situation? Are there external factors at work?

Reading 7.5

Discipline and group management in classrooms
Jacob Kounin

Kounin's book on group management is a classic text which has been of enormous influence in the analysis of classroom management. Based on careful study of videotapes of US classrooms, Kounin's insights are well grounded in observation of teacher actions and pupil response. Do not be deceived or put off by the language of this reading, for it has immensely practical implications. The term 'recitation' describes a whole-class, teacher-directed teaching session.

Amongst the attractions of Kounin's work are the amusing names which he gave to some of the patterns which he identified: when did you last do a 'dangle', or subject your class to a 'slowdown'?

Edited from: Kounin, J. (1970) *Discipline and Group Management in Classrooms.* New York: Holt, Rinehart and Winston, iv and 74–101.

The planned and unplanned realities of a classroom necessitate a teacher having skills that go beyond curricular planning and managing individual children. These skills pertain to *group* management.

Study of videotapes showed that there *were* specific categories of teachers' behaviour that correlated with their managerial success as measured by pupil work involvement, deviancy rate, contagion of misbehaviour, and effectiveness of desists. Some of the dimensions of teachers' behaviours that made a difference in the behaviour of pupils were, as we termed them: *withitness* (demonstrating that she knew what was going on); *overlapping* (attending to two issues simultaneously), *transition smoothness* (absence of dangles, flip-flops, and thrusts); *slowdowns* (where momentum is lost) and maintaining *group-focus*.

Withitness

Withitness was defined as a teacher's communicating to the children by her actual behaviour that she knows what the children are doing, or has the proverbial 'eyes in the back of her head'. What kinds of teacher behaviours, and in what circumstances, provide cues to pupils as to whether the teacher does or does not know what is going on? It is not adequate to measure what a teacher knows in order to obtain a score for the degree of her withitness. It is necessary to measure what she *communicates* she knows. The children, after all, must get the information that she knows or doesn't know what they are doing.

Desist events are examples of incidents where a teacher does something that communicates to the children whether she does or doesn't know what is happening. In desist events a child is doing something and the teacher does something about it. Does she pick the correct target and does she do it on time? Or, does she make some kind of mistake that communicates the information that she doesn't know what is happening?

Overlapping

Overlapping refers to what the teacher does when she has two matters to deal with at the same time. Does she somehow attend to both issues simultaneously or does she remain or become immersed in one issue only to the neglect of the other? These kinds of 'overlapping' issues occur in both desist events and in child intrusion events

An overlapping issue is present at the time of a desist event when the teacher is occupied with an ongoing task with children at the time that she desists a deviancy. Thus, if she is in a recitation setting with a reading group and she notes and acts upon a deviancy occurring in the seatwork setting, she is in an overlapping situation.

The Videotape Studies show that overlapping and withitness are significantly related to each other. Teachers who show signs of attending to more than one issue when there is more than one issue to handle at a particular time are likely to pick correct deviancy targets and do something about the deviancy on time – before the deviancy becomes more serious or begins to spread to other children. Overlapping correlates to withitness but does not, in and of itself, relate to managerial success, whereas withitness does. The reality of classrooms dictates that both are essential skills.

Transition smoothness

A teacher in a self-contained classroom must manage considerable activity *movement*: she must initiate, sustain, and terminate many activities. Sometimes this involves having children move physically from one part of the room to another, as when a group must move from their own desks to the reading circle. At other times it involves some psychological movement, or some change in props, as when children change from doing arithmetic problems at their desks to studying spelling words at the same desks.

There are two major categories of movement mistakes. First are behaviours producing jerkiness. These are actions of teachers that interfere with the smoothness of the flow of activities. The second category of movement mistakes is of teacher behaviours producing slowdowns that impede the momentum of activities.

Jerkiness: The categories associated with jerkiness in transitions are stimulus-boundedness, thrusts, dangles and flip-flops. *Stimulus-boundedness* may be contrasted with goal-directedness. Does the teacher maintain a focus upon an activity goal or is she easily deflected from it? In a stimulus-bound event, a teacher behaves as though she has no will of her own and reacts to some unplanned and irrelevant stimulus as an iron filing reacts to a magnet: she gets magnetized and lured into reacting to some minutia that pulls her out of the main activity stream. A *thrust* consists of a teacher's sudden 'bursting in' on the children's activities with an order, statement, or question in such a manner as to indicate that her own intent or desire was the only determinant of her timing and point of entry. That is, she evidenced no sign (pausing, looking around) of looking for, or of being sensitive to, the group's readiness to receive her message. A *dangle* was coded when a teacher started, or was in, some activity and then left it 'hanging in mid-air' by going off to some other activity. Following such a 'fade away' she would then resume the activity. *Flip-flops* were coded at transition points. In a flip-flop a teacher terminates one activity, starts another, and then initiates a return to the activity that she had terminated.

Slowdowns: Slowdowns consisted of behaviours initiated by teachers that clearly slowed down the rate of movement in a recitation activity and impede the forward momentum of an activity. Two major categories of slowdowns are overdwelling and fragmentation. *Overdwelling* was coded when the teacher dwelled on an issue and engaged in a stream of actions or talk that was clearly beyond what was necessary for most children's understanding or getting with an activity. Overdwelling would produce a reaction on the part of most children of: 'All right, all right, that's enough already!'. Overdwelling could apply to either the behaviour of children or to the task. A *fragmentation* is a slowdown produced by a teacher's breaking down an activity into sub-parts when the activity could be performed as a single unit.

Movement management, including both smoothness and momentum is a significant dimension of classroom management. Indeed, techniques of movement management are more significant in controlling deviancy than are techniques of deviancy management as such. In addition, techniques of movement management possess the additional value of promoting work involvement, especially in recitation settings.

Maintaining group focus

A classroom teacher is not a tutor working with one child at a time. Even though she may work with a single child at times, her main job is to work with a group of children in one room at one time. Sometimes the group is the entire class and sometimes it is a subgroup or subgroups. Given this partial job analysis, it may be fruitful to see what techniques teachers use in recitation sessions to maintain group focus.

Group alerting: This refers to the degree to which a teacher attempts to involve children in the task, maintain their attention, and keep them 'on their toes' or alerted. Positive group alerting cues were:

any method used to create 'suspense' before calling on a child to recite: pausing and looking around to 'bring children in' before selecting a reciter, saying 'Let's see now, who can …' before calling on a reciter;

keeping children in suspense in regard to who will be called on next; picking reciters 'randomly' so that no child knows whether he will be called on next or not;

teacher calls on different children frequently or maintains group focus: intersperses 'mass unison' responses; says, 'Let's put our thinking caps on; this might fool you'; asks group for show of hands before selecting a reciter;

teacher alerts non-performers that they might be called on in connection with what a reciter is doing; They may be called on if reciter makes a mistake; presignals children that they will be asked about recitation content in the immediate future.

Accountability: Accountability refers to the degree to which the teacher holds the children accountable and responsible for their task performances during recitation sessions. This entails her doing something to get to know what the children are actually doing and to communicate to the children in some observable manner that she knows what they are doing. The degree to which she goes out to obtain this knowledge and to communicate it, is the degree to which she holds the children in the group accountable for their performances. The most usual means of securing information is for the teacher to require children to produce or demonstrate work that is being done in the current setting and to check these demonstrations. Thus, the following are the kinds of behaviours associated with accountability:

The teacher asks children to hold up their props exposing performances or answers such a manner as to be readily visible to the teacher.

Teacher requires children to recite in unison while the teacher shows signs of actively attending to the recitation.

Teacher brings other children into the performance of a child reciting. (Teacher says: 'Jimmy, you watch Johnny do that problem and then tell me what he did right or wrong.')

Teacher asks for the raised hands of children who are prepared to demonstrate a performance and requires some of them to demonstrate.

Our findings show that teachers who maintain group focus by engaging in behaviours that keep children alerted and on their toes are more successful in inducing work involvement and preventing deviancy than are teachers who do not. This aspect of teacher style is more significant in recitation settings than in seatwork settings.

Satiation: This important further issue is concerned with the nature of the activities programmed in the classrooms. What are the groups of children required to do – what is the teacher moving them into and out of? Does the nature of the classroom activity program relate to work involvement and deviancy? Answers entail an analysis of the curriculum. Indeed, even within the same grades of the same school, teachers do vary in what they emphasize, in how they sequence the activities, and in what they do beyond the school's basic curricular commonalities.

Does a teacher do anything beyond the usual routine in a recitation session that would be likely to produce either a clear feeling of repetitiousness or a clear feeling of progress in an academic activity? In our research, the code for progress cues consisted of three categories. 'Routine' was coded when the teacher engaged in ordinary and usual kinds and amounts of behaviour relating to progress or repetition: She did nothing special to induce feelings of progress nor did she impose special repetitiousness during recitations. 'Positive cues' were noted whenever a teacher did something beyond the immediate call of duty to get a child or group to feel that they were making progress and accomplishing something in the activity. 'Negative cues' were coded whenever a teacher repeated an explanation or demonstration beyond what was necessary for clarity, or when she had a child or children repeat a performance when it was already correct.

Conclusion

It is possible to delineate concrete aspects of teacher behaviour that lead to managerial success in the classroom.

Running a classroom is a complicated technology having to do with: developing a non-satiating learning programme; programming for progress, challenge, and variety in learning activities; initiating and maintaining movement in classroom tasks with smoothness and momentum; coping with more than one event simultaneously; observing and emitting feedback for many different events; directing actions at appropriate targets; maintaining a focus upon a group; and doubtless other techniques not measured in these researches.

The master of classroom management skills should not be regarded as an end in itself. These techniques are, however, necessary enabling tools which allow the teacher to accomplish her teaching goals.

Reading 7.6

Positive teaching in the classroom
Frank Merrett and Kevin Wheldall

This reading provides advice on achieving and maintaining class discipline and task engagement from a behaviourist perspective, and it might thus be read in conjunction with Skinner's work (Reading 2.1). The emphasis is on changing pupil behaviour using *positive* reinforcement in a controlled, skilful and managed way, rather than becoming negative, as can all too easily happen when discipline problems arise in classrooms. The use of such techniques may seem to jar with some aspirations for classroom relationships, but in one form or another they contribute to the repertoire of many experienced teachers.

Are you able to manage positive reinforcements consistently?

Edited from: Merrett, F. and Wheldall, K. (1990) *Identifying Troublesome Classroom Behaviour.* London: Paul Chapman, 11–22.

There are five principles of 'positive teaching'.

1 Teaching is concerned with the observable.

2 Almost all classroom behaviour is learned.

3 Learning involves change in behaviour.

4 Behaviour changes as a result of its consequences.

5 Behaviours are also influenced by classroom contexts.

These five principles sum up what we mean by positive teaching. The main assumption is that pupils' behaviour is primarily learned and maintained as a result of their interactions with their environment, which includes other pupils and teachers. Consequently, behaviour can be changed by altering certain features of that environment. As we have said, the key environmental features are events which immediately precede or follow behaviour. This means that classroom behaviours followed by consequences which the pupils find rewarding will tend to increase in frequency. Similarly, certain changes in behaviour may be brought about merely by changing the classroom setting.

One way of thinking about positive thinking is in terms of the ABC in which:

A – refers to the *antecedent conditions*, i.e. the context in which a behaviour occurs or what is happening in that environment prior to a behaviour occurring.

B – refers to the *behaviour itself*, i.e. what a pupil is actually doing in real physical terms (not what you think he or she is doing as a result of inferences from his or her behaviour).

C – refers to the *consequences of the behaviour*, i.e. what happens to the pupil after the behaviour.

Let us look at consequences in a little more detail.

A major concern within Positive Teaching is with the identification of items and events which pupils find rewarding and to structure the teaching environment so as to make access to these rewards dependent upon behaviour which the teacher wants to encourage in class.

Consequences may be described as rewarding punishing. Rewarding consequences, which we call *positive reinforcers*, are events which we seek out or 'go for', whilst we try to avoid *punishing* consequences. Neutral consequences are events which affect us neither way. Behaviours followed by positive reinforcers are likely to increase in frequency. Behaviours followed by punishers tend to decrease in frequency whilst neutral consequences have no effect. In Positive Teaching, infrequent but appropriate behaviours (for example, getting on with the set work quietly) are made more frequent by arranging for positive reinforcers, such as teacher attention and approval, to follow their occurrence. This is called *social reinforcement*.

Undesired behaviours may be decreased in frequency by ensuring that positive reinforcers do not follow their occurrence, i.e. a neutral consequence is arranged. Occasionally it may be necessary follow undesired behaviours with punishers (for example, a quiet reprimand) in an attempt to reduce the frequency of behaviour rapidly but there are problems associated with this procedure. Punishment plays only a minor and infrequent role in Positive Teaching not least because sometimes what we believe to be punishing is, in fact, reinforcing to the pupil. Pupils who receive little attention from adults may behave in ways which result in adult disapproval. Such pupils may prefer disapproval to being ignored and will continue to behave like this because adult attention, in itself, whether praise or reprimand, is positively reinforcing. This is what some people call attention-seeking behaviour.

We should note that terminating a punishing consequence is also reinforcing and can be, and often is, used to increase desired behaviours. This is known as *negative reinforcement*. Again this has problems associated with its use since pupils may rapidly learn other, more effective, ways of avoiding the negative consequence than you had in mind. For example, some teachers continually use sarcasm and ridicule with their pupils. They cease only when their pupils behave as they wish. However, another way for pupils to avoid this unpleasant consequence is to skip lessons or stay away from school.

Finally, one can punish by removing or terminating positive consequences (for example, by taking away privileges). This is known as *response cost* but again there are similar problems associated with this. Pupils may find alternative ways of avoiding this unpleasant consequence. Lying, cheating and shifting the blame are common strategies employed. These are all behaviours we would wish to discourage but by creating consequences which we believe to be aversive we may be making them more likely to occur.

When we want to teach pupils to do something new, or to encourage them to behave in a certain way more frequently than they normally do, it is important that we ensure that they are positively reinforced every time they behave as we want them to. This normally leads to rapid learning and is known as *continuous reinforcement*. When they have learned the new behaviour and/or are behaving as we want them to do regularly, then we may maintain this behaviour more economically by reducing the frequency of reinforcement.

Another important reason for wanting to reduce the frequency of reinforcement is that pupils may become less responsive if the positive reinforcer becomes too easily available. Consequently, once pupils are regularly behaving in an appropriate way we can best maintain that behaviour by ensuring that they are now reinforced only intermittently. Intermittent reinforcement can be arranged so that pupils are reinforced every so often (i.e. in terms of time) or, alternatively, after so many occurrences of the behaviour. These different ways of organising the frequency of reinforcement are known as reinforcement schedules.

It should be emphasised that positive teaching is not about creating robots who just do as they are told, mindlessly following the teacher's instructions. Rather, positive teaching is about helping children to become effective, independent learners. Positive teachers should, in effect, like all good teachers, have the ultimate aim of making themselves redundant.

Spaces
How are we creating environments for learning?

8

The readings in this chapter are intended to help with understanding class-rooms as 'learning environments'.

Bronfenbrenner (8.1) begins with his classic analysis of layered contexts for development and learning – and, as teachers, we of course have responsibility for part of this ecology. Indeed, what is the nature of the learning environments that we create through our classroom provision? Bransford et al. (8.2) summarise much accumulated knowledge when they answer that effective learning environments should centre on learners, knowledge, assessment and community.

Three readings focus on space, time and technology in classrooms – and on how they can support teaching and learning. Clegg and Billington (8.3) begin with a practical discussion of the organization space, resources and display. Berliner's classic paper (8.4), offers ideas for describing and analysing the use of time – thus enabling or constraining 'opportunities to learn'. Edwards (8.5) introduces the concept of 'affordance' to highlight the potential uses to which resources can be put, and illustrates this in relation to the affordances of ICT.

Kress (8.6) illustrates the importance of an ecological analysis in reviewing the impact of the 'digital revolution' on schools. In the contemporary world, we now experience multimodal forms of communication and design which afford radically new learning experiences and challenge traditional curricula and teaching methods.

And yet, as Muijs and Reynolds (8.7) demonstrate, the role of a good teacher in providing whole-class instruction remains 'tried and tested'. If done well, direct, interactive teaching remains effective and efficient – and should certainly be part of a teacher's repertoire.

The parallel chapter of *Reflective Teaching in Schools* addresses similar issues and suggests activities to increase the effectiveness of classroom organisation. The first section discusses learning environments – formal and informal, school and home. We then focus on the classroom environment, including the use of space, resources and time. Section 3 is concerned with the use of technology for learning and again considers this both within and beyond schools. Finally, in section 4, the emphasis is on the management of pupils and of adults. It includes extensive discussion on individual, group and whole-class organisation, and of working with parents, carers and teaching assistants.

The emphasis throughout is on achieving coherence between learning aims and the selected form of classroom organisation, and then working towards consistency between the various organisational elements. The chapter concludes with suggestions of 'Key Readings'. Of course, reflectiveteaching. co.uk offers many further ideas and activities.

Reading 8.1

Environments as contexts of development
Urie Bronfenbrenner

Bronfenbrenner's work on the 'ecology' of social environments and their effects on child development and learning has been extremely influential since publication of his *The Ecology of Human Development* (1979). His model highlights life-wide and life-long dimensions in the contexts which learners experience. In the summary below, four terms are used to describe layers of life-wide context. These range from the direct interaction of significant others in a child's life (microsystem) to the characteristics of broader culture, social and economic circumstances (macrosystem). The final term adds the life-long dimension of time (chronosystem).

Can you see, with or without these terms, the key dimensions which Bronfenbrenner represents?

Edited from: Bronfenbrenner, U. (1993), 'Ecological models of human development'. *International Encyclopedia of Education*, Vol. 3, 2nd edn. Oxford: Elsevier, 37–43.

Environments as contexts of development

The ecological environment is conceived as a set of nested structures, each inside the other like a set of Russian dolls. Moving from the innermost level to the outside, these structures are described below.

Microsystems

A microsystem is a pattern of activities, social roles, and interpersonal relations experienced by the developing person in a given face-to-face setting with particular physical, social, and symbolic features that invite, permit, or inhibit engagement in sustained, progressively more complex interaction with, and activity in, the immediate environment. Examples include such settings as family, school, peer group, and workplace.

It is within the immediate environment of the microsystem that proximal processes operate to produce and sustain development, but as the above definition indicates, their power to do so depends on the content and structure of the microsystem.

Mesosystems

The mesosystem comprises the linkages and processes taking place between two or more settings containing the developing person (e.g. the relations between home and school, school and workplace, etc.). In other words, a mesosytem is a system of microsystems.

An example in this domain is the work on the developmental impact of two-way communication and participation in decision-making by parents and teachers. Pupils from classrooms in which such joint involvement was high not only exhibited greater initiative and independence after entering high school, but also received higher grades. The effects of family and school processes were greater than those attributable to socioeconomic status or race.

Exosystems

The exosystem comprises the linkages and processes taking place between two or more settings, at least one of which does not contain the developing person, but in which events occur that indirectly influence processes within the immediate setting in which the developing person lives (e.g. for a child, the relation between the home and the parent's workplace; for a parent, the relation between the school and the neighbourhood peer group).

Research has focused on exosystems that are especially likely to affect the development of children and youth indirectly through their influence on the family, the school, and the peer group.

Macrosystems

The macrosystem consists of the overarching pattern of micro-, meso-, and exosystems characteristic of a given culture or subculture, with particular reference to the belief systems, bodies of knowledge, material resources, customs, life-styles, opportunity structures, hazards, and life course options that are embedded in each of those broader systems. The macrosystem may be thought of as a societal blueprint for a particular culture or subculture.

This formulation points to the necessity of going beyond the simple labels of class and culture to identify more specific social and psychological features at the macrosystem level that ultimately affect the particular conditions and processes occurring in the microsystem.

Chronosystems

A final systems parameter extends the environment into a third dimension. Traditionally in the study of human development, the passage of time was treated as synonymous with chronological age. Since the early 1970s, however, an increasing number of investigators have employed research designs in which time appears not merely as an attribute of the growing human being, but also as a property of the surrounding environment not only over the life course, but across historical time.

A chronosystem encompasses change or consistency over time not only in the characteristics of the person but also of the environment in which that person lives (e.g. changes over the life course in family structure, socioeconomic status, employment, place of residence, or the degree of hecticness and ability in everyday life).

An excellent example of a chronosystem design is found in Elder's classic study *Children of the Great Depression* (1974). The investigation involved a comparison of two otherwise comparable groups of families differentiated on the basis of whether the loss of income as a result of the Great Depression of the 1930s exceeded or fell short of 35 percent. The availability of longitudinal data made it possible to assess developmental outcomes through childhood, adolescence, and adulthood. Also, the fact that children in one sample were born eight years earlier than those in the other permitted a comparison of the effects of the Depression on youngsters who were adolescents when their families became economically deprived with the effects of those who were still young children at the time.

The results for the two groups presented a dramatic contrast.

Paradoxically, for youngsters who were teenagers during the Depression years, the families' economic deprivation appeared to have a salutary effect on their subsequent development, especially in the middle class. As compared with the non-deprived, deprived boys displayed a greater desire to achieve and a firmer sense of career goals. Boys and girls from deprived homes attained greater satisfaction in life, both by their own and by societal standards. These favourable outcomes were evident among their lower-class counterparts as well, though less pronounced.

Analysis of interview and observation protocols enabled Elder to identify what he regarded as a critical factor in investigating this favourable developmental trajectory: the loss of economic security forced the family to mobilize its own human resources, including its teenagers, who had to take on new roles and responsibilities both within and outside the home and to work together toward the common goal of getting and keeping the family on its feet. The experience provided effective training in initiative, responsibility, and cooperation.

Reading 8.2

Designs for learning environments
John Bransford, Ann Brown and Rodney Cocking

This is a second reading from a classic US review of contemporary knowledge on learning (see also Reading 4.1). In this case, the focus is on the design of learning environments. The four characteristics identified, with central foci on learners, knowledge, assessment and community, have been much cited.

What implications, in your view, does this analysis of effective learning environments have for practice?

Edited from: Bransford, J. D., Brown, A. L. and Cocking, R. R. (1999) *How People Learn: Brain, Mind, Experience and School.* Washington, DC: National Academy Press, xvi–xix.

Theoretical physics does not prescribe the design of a bridge, but surely it constrains the design of successful ones. Similarly learning theory provides no simple recipe for designing effective learning environments, but it constrains the design of effective ones. New research raises important questions about the design of learning environments – questions that suggest the value of rethinking what is taught, how it is taught, and how it is assessed.

A fundamental tenet of modern learning theory is that different kinds of learning goals require different approaches to instruction; new goals for education require changes in opportunities to learn. The design of learning environments is linked to issues that are especially important in the processes of learning, transfer and competent performance. These processes, in turn, are affected by the degree to which learning environments are student centred, assessment centred, and community centred.

We propose four key characteristics of effective learning environments:

Learner-centred environments
Effective instruction begins with what learners bring to the setting: this includes cultural practices and beliefs, as well as knowledge of academic content. A focus on the degree to which environments are learner centred is consistent with the evidence showing that learners use their current knowledge to construct new knowledge and that what they know and believe at the moment affects how they interpret new information. Sometimes learners' current knowledge supports new learning; sometimes it hampers learning.

People may have acquired knowledge yet fail to activate it in a particular setting. Learner-centred environments attempt to help students make connections between their previous knowledge and their current academic tasks. Parents are especially good at helping their children make connections. Teachers have a harder time because they do not share the life experiences of all their students, so they have to become familiar with each student's special interests and strengths.

Knowledge-centred environments

The ability to think and solve problems requires knowledge that is accessible and applied appropriately. An emphasis on knowledge-cantered instruction raises a number of questions, such as the degree to which instruction focuses on ways to help students use their current knowledge and skills. New knowledge about early learning suggests that young students are capable of grasping more complex concepts than was believed previously. However, these concepts must be presented in ways that are developmentally appropriate by linking learning to their current understanding. A knowledge cantered perspective on learning environments highlights the importance of thinking about designs for curricula. To what extent do they help students learn with understanding versus promote the acquisition of disconnected sets of facts and skills? Curricula that are a "mile wide and an inch deep" run the risk of developing disconnected rather than connected knowledge.

Assessment to support learning

Issues of assessment also represent an important perspective for viewing the design of learning environments. Feedback is fundamental to learning, but feedback opportunities are often scarce in classrooms. Students may receive grades on tests and essays, but these are summative assessments that occur at the end of projects. What are needed are formative assessments, which provide students with opportunities to revise and improve the quality of their thinking and understanding. Assessments must reflect the learning goals that define various environments. If the goal is to enhance understanding and applicability of knowledge, it is not sufficient to provide assessments that focus primarily on memory for facts and formulas.

Community-cantered environments

The fourth, important perspective on learning environments is the degree to which they promote a sense of community. Students, teachers, and other interested participants share norms that value learning and high standards. Norms such as these increase people's opportunities and motivation to interact, receive feedback, and learn. The importance of connected communities becomes clear when one examines the relatively small amount of time spent in school compared to other settings. Activities in homes, community centers, and after-school clubs can have important effects on students' academic achievement.

New technologies

A number of the features of new technologies are also consistent with the principles of a new science of learning.

Key conclusions:

- Because many new technologies are interactive, it is now easier to create environments in which students can learn by doing, receive feedback, and continually refine their understanding and build new knowledge.

- Technologies can help people visualise difficult-to-understand concepts, such as differentiating heat from temperature. Students are able to work with visualisation and modelling software similar to the tools used in nonschool environments to increase their conceptual understanding and the likelihood of transfer from school to nonschool settings.

- New technologies provide access to a vast array of information, including digital libraries, real-world data for analysis, and connections to other people who provide information, feedback, and inspiration, all of which can enhance the learning of teachers and administrators as well as students

There are many ways that technology can be used to help create such environments, both for teachers and for the students whom they teach. However, many issues arise in considering how to educate teachers to use new technologies effectively. What do they need to know about learning processes? About the technology? What kinds of training are most effective for helping teachers use high-quality instructional programs? What is the software and teacher-support tools, developed with full understanding of principles of learning, have not yet become the norm.

Reading 8.3

Classroom layout, resources and display
David Clegg and Shirley Billington

In this reading Clegg and Billington offer further practical advice on the organisation and use of classroom space, on the management of resources and on display. They maintain a clear focus on the contribution which these factors can make to the processes of teaching and learning for which the teacher aims.

Do you feel you have the best possible layout and system for resource management? And what is the balance of celebrating, stimulating and informing in the display or other affirmation of learners work?

Edited from: Clegg, D. and Billington, S. (1994) *The Effective Primary Classroom: Management and Organisation of Teaching and Learning*. London: David Fulton, 123–5.

Classrooms are not passive environments in which teaching and learning happens to take place – they should be designed to promote and enhance learning. They should motivate and stimulate, and they should be planned to make the most efficient use of the most important resource – namely the teacher.

There is no one way to organise and run classrooms. All we are saying is that the way they are set up and managed should be just as much a part of a teacher's pedagogy as curriculum planning, teaching strategies or assessing learning.

Classroom layout

When thinking about how classrooms are organised and managed most teachers will begin by considering how the furniture is laid out. However, this is a much more complex process than simply fitting all the furniture in, and making sure that everyone has a seat.

Depending on their approach to teaching and learning, teachers have broadly three options in terms of layout. The first of these options is to create a series of working areas within the classroom. These could include a reading area, a writing area, science area and maths area and possibly others depending on the age of the children. Within these working areas children would have easy access to an appropriate range of resources and materials. There are some clear advantages to this type of layout. It is easy for children to understand, and by providing a specific area designated for a particular activity pupils can be motivated and develop a sense of purpose. Resources and materials can be carefully matched to learning experiences, and will introduce children to the idea of specific resources relating to specific activities.

The second and third options concerning classroom layout have a different focus. Rather than limiting resources to specific areas they look to organising the classroom in a more holistic way. Essentially the choice is between putting the resources and materials around the outside of the room, with children working in the middle, or putting the resources in the middle and children round the edges. The former is the more predominant pattern, but has the disadvantage of creating potentially more movement around the room. In the latter option, the theory is that all children have equal access to resourcing.

If we consider all three of these options, the reality is that many teachers opt for a mixture. Most classrooms have some designated areas, most commonly for wet or practical work, and a reading area. Other resources are usually stored around the edges of the room.

The ways in which teachers wish to operate will also have a bearing on how pupils are arranged. The teacher who, when talking at length to the whole class, prefers children sat together in a carpeted area, and then disperses the children to a variety of areas, with a variety of working partners, may not see the necessity for every child to have his or her own place. If one group will always be working on an activity that does not require desks or table space, then there is no need to have a place for every pupil. When space is limited this could be an important factor. When children are older, and sitting on the floor is less comfortable, or when there are an increasing number of occasions when everybody needs some desk or table space, then clearly this must be provided. The important message is to maintain a degree of flexibility. Modern furniture enables most teachers to provide a range of options. Putting tables together can save space, and enable a group of six or eight children to work together. Similarly the same tables arranged differently can provide space for individual or paired work.

Managing classroom resources

The following are key issues for consideration by every teacher when thinking about the organisation of resources in the classroom.

Quality: This is a far more important element than quantity. Teachers are natural hoarders, and loathe to discard items which may have outlived their usefulness, but there is little point in shelf space being taking up by outdated or tatty books (which children will avoid using) or cupboards being full of games or jigsaws with pieces missing. The quality of the resources will affect the quality of the learning.

Appropriateness: Is there a variety of equipment suitable for the planned curriculum, and for the range of abilities within the class? If the school has a policy on centralised resources it may be important to think in terms of a basic equipment list for each classroom and planning activities which will make use of centralised resources at specific times.

Storage: Resources and materials should be appropriately stored so that a system is evident to the children. Resource areas (not necessarily work areas) can be established, so that all the equipment for a particular subject is collected in a clearly defined location. Colour coding for drawers, and storage boxes with pictorial labels for younger children can help with efficient use of equipment by pupils.

Accessibility: The more that children can organise resources for themselves the less time should be spent by a teacher on low-level tasks such as giving out paper. Children need to be clear about what they have immediate access to, and what can only be used with permission or under supervision. However, the vast majority of materials in a classroom should be available for children to select for appropriate use.

Consideration should be given to providing basic equipment for continual use such as pots of pencils, a variety of types of paper, and to organising other materials for ease of access. In order to do this in some classrooms, it may be necessary to remove cupboard doors to provide open shelving, or to purchase some inexpensive and colourful storage such as stackerjacks or plastic baskets.

If children are to make good use of the facilities available in a classroom they need to be clear about the system which operates. They may need to be trained in making appropriate use of resources, and in selecting materials for a particular task. They can play a role in managing classroom resources, and it may be useful to involve them in preliminary planning when organising the equipment for a particular curriculum area.

Giving children responsibility for ensuring that the resource system works well is an important aspect of developing independence from the teacher. They should be able, or if young be trained, in the collection, use, return and replacement of materials with minimal reference to the teacher. Where equipment is limited, they can be encouraged to negotiate with other children over the use of a particular resource. Negotiation and sharing equipment are important elements in planning tasks.

Display in the classroom

The business of display is much more than brightening up dull corners, covering cracks, and double mounting: it is another important factor in ensuring classrooms are places in which effective learning can take place.

Display has three distinct uses: it can celebrate, stimulate and inform. How display is used to promote these three functions will also transmit values and messages to children, parents and colleagues. For example, what you choose to celebrate will begin to give messages about what is valued or who is held in high esteem. How you begin to stimulate and inform through display will illustrate some clear ideas about how you regard children and their learning. The transmission of values and attitudes is a dimension that touches all aspects of display, but it is worthwhile thinking about each of the three ways display can be used.

Celebration: Enjoying and acknowledging children's achievement is an important aspect of any classroom. Displaying those achievements is just one way of demonstrating the regard in which their work is held, but there are many others. One of the restrictions of displaying pupils' work has been that it has led to an over emphasis on the product or outcome, at the expense of the process. It is not too difficult to redress this imbalance. If we consider for a moment the way modern libraries and museums have been eager not only to display authors' and artists' finished items, but to acquire the notebooks, jottings, sketch pads and rough drawings to demonstrate the development of the works, we can perhaps begin to see how schools can also start to acknowledge the process. As teachers who are concerned with process and outcome, it is important that we place equal value on each. Efforts at drafting can be displayed alongside the finished stories, sketches and jottings shown next to the completed art work. This gives clear messages, not least that behind good outcomes, there is usually a great deal of hard work, and that hard work is worth acknowledging and displaying.

There are other, perhaps more fundamental, considerations about displaying work. Display is one way of promoting children's self-image, and giving them a sense of worth. The converse is also true. Failing to display some pupils' work may go some way to alienating those children from the classroom. This is an area where teachers must use their judgment. It is important that all children have work displayed (not all at the same time!) but it is equally important that such work is worthy of display, and is of some significance. Display can also demonstrate the achievements of groups of pupils working towards a common end, as well as the achievements of individuals.

The most effective displays of children's work pay some regard to basic aesthetic considerations. The most attractive displays are the result of some thought concerning shape, colour, form and texture. This not only boosts children's confidence in seeing their work promoted in this way, but, perhaps more importantly, it provides an opportunity to discuss these features, for when children begin to set up their own displays.

Stimulation: What is displayed in classrooms can form part of the learning process. A good dramatic, thought-provoking display can provide great stimulation for learning. There are countless ways in which children can be motivated by something they can see, observe, smell, touch or hear. Science investigations can start with a display which challenges through effective questioning, and promotes the development of skills, for example, 'use the magnifying glass to observe, record what you see …', 'what do you think will happen if …?', all of which can begin to make children think, discuss, predict and hypothesise. Similarly, display can stimulate an aesthetic or artistic response through careful use of colours, textures, and forms. In the humanities, a collection of artefacts can be the starting point for enquiry and investigation. The most effective displays are often those which not only stimulate and motivate, but also show the results. These uses of display to celebrate, stimulate and inform are not mutually exclusive and they will often be interlinked.

Informing: The notion that display within the classroom can support young children's learning is the aspect that is least recognised. Stimulation and motivation are starting points for learning, but display can provide support once children have embarked upon their work. What is actually stuck up on the walls, or stood in a corner, or displayed on a table can act as a resource for the learner. This will vary from classroom to classroom, but it could include such items as current word lists, key phrases to reinforce an ongoing activity, the display of resource material alongside guidance on how to use it, or simple instructions about what to do in particular circumstances.

The possibility of displaying the process alongside the outcomes can provide a source of support for other pupils and a focus for discussion.

Display makes a very significant contribution to the classroom climate. It is by its very nature a public statement which is there for children, colleagues and parents to see. As it is a significant factor in creating classroom atmosphere it is vital that we do not fall into the trap of 'surface rather than substance' (Alexander, 1992), and that requires thought and consideration about how good display contributes to effective learning rather than simply making the room look nice.

Reading 8.4

Instructional time – and where it goes
David Berliner

The use of time in the classroom is a fundamental consideration when providing opportunity for students to learn. This reading introduces some ways to think about the use of time in the classroom, and offers some different ways to classify such time. Opportunity to learn is quite closely correlated with outcomes, and yet contemporary empirical studies still record very large amounts of time in schools in which curricular learning is not taking place. Somehow, time 'evaporates'.

What could you do, to increase the proportion of time in which your pupils actually spend on curricular learning?

Edited from: Berliner, D. (1990). 'What's all the fuss about instructional time?', in Ben-Peretz, M. and Bromme, R. (eds) *The Nature of Time in Schools*. New York: Teacher College Press, 3–35.

- *Allocated time*, usually defined as the time that the state, district, school, or teacher provides the student for instruction. For example a school may require that reading and language arts be taught 90 minutes every day in the second grade. Allocated time is the time block set aside for that instruction–90 minutes a day, or 7 .5 hours a week or 300 hours a school year. Sometimes this is called *scheduled time*, to distinguish it from the time actually allocated by teachers. This can prove in important distinction when the *concept* of allocated time is used to create a *variable* for a research study. When that is the case it has been found that measures of allocated time derived from any source other than direct observation of teachers invariably overestimate the actual time provided in schools for instruction in a curriculum area. In the original 'model of school learning,' the article that began contemporary research on instructional time, allocated time was called 'opportunity to learn.

- *Engaged time,* usually defined as the time that students appear to be paying attention to materials or presentations that have instructional goals. When the concept of engagement is used to create the variable of student engaged time the variable is usually measured by classroom observers or coded from videotapes of students in learning situations. Students' self-reports of engagement have also been used as a variable. Engaged time is always a subset of allocated time. A synonym for engaged time is 'attention.'

- *Time-on-task,* usually defined as engaged time on particular learning tasks. The concept is not synonymous with engaged time, but is often used as if it were. The term *time-on-task* has a more restricted and more complex meaning than does the term *engaged time*. It makes clear that engagement is not all that is desired of students in educational environments. Engagement in particular kinds of tasks is what is wanted. Thus, engagement may be recorded when a student is deeply involved in mathematics or a comic book during a time period allocated to science. Time-on-task, however, would not be recorded because the task in which students were to be attentive was science. Time-on-task should be thought of as a conjunctive concept, not nearly as simple a concept as engagement. This distinction, though often lost, makes clearer that time is, in a sense, a psychologically empty vessel. Time must be filled with activities that are desirable. Time-on-task as a variable in empirical research is usually measured in the same ways as engagement, though when the distinction noted above is kept in mind, the curriculum, instructional activities, or tasks in which the student engages are also recorded.

- *Academic learning time*, usually defined as that part of allocated time in a subject-matter area (physical education, science, or mathematics, for example) in which a student is engaged successfully in the activities or with the materials to which he or she is exposed, and in which those activities and materials are related to educational outcomes that are valued. This is a complex concept related to or made up of a number of other concepts, such as allocated time (the upper limit of ALT); time-on-task (engagement in tasks that are related to outcome measures, or, stated differently, time spent in curriculum that is aligned with the evaluation instruments that are in use); and success rate (the percent of engaged time that a student is experiencing a high, rather than low, success experience in class). Academic learning time is often and inappropriately used as a synonym for engagement, time-on-task, or some other time-based concept. Its meaning, however, is considerably more complex than that, as will be elaborated on below.

- *Transition time*, usually defined as the non-instructional time before and after some instructional activity. The occurrence of transition time would be recorded within a block of allocated time when a teacher takes roll or gives back homework at the beginning of an instructional activity; and it would be recorded when books are put away or jackets and lunches are brought out at the end of an instructional activity. The concept describes the inevitable decrease in time allocated for instruction that ordinarily accompanies mass education.

- *Waiting time*, usually defined as the time that a student must wait to receive some instructional help. The time spent waiting to receive new assignments from the teacher, on a line to have the teacher check work, or waiting for the teacher's attention after raising one's hand in class are examples of waiting time. This member of the family of instructional time concepts is concerned with instructional management and is not to be confused with wait-time the time between the end of a question asked by the teacher and beginning of a response by a student. The latter member of the family of instructional time concepts is concerned with instruction and cognition, rather than classroom management.

- *Aptitude*, usually defined as the amount of time that a student needs, under optimal instructional conditions to reach some criterion of learning. High aptitude for learning something is determined by fast learning; low aptitude is reflected in slow learning. This time-based definition of aptitude is unusual and will be elaborated on below. A definition of this type serves to point out how some members of the instructional time family do not, at first glance, seem to be family members.

- *Perseverance*, usually defined as the amount of time a student is willing to spend on learning a task or unit of instruction. This is measured as engagement, or the time-on-task that the student willingly puts into learning. Perseverance is another of the instructional time concepts that do not at first appear to belong to the family. Although this concept is traditionally thought to be a motivational concept, when operationalized in a certain way, it becomes a variable that is measured in time, and thus becomes an instructional time concept as well.

- *Pace*, usually defined as the amount of content covered during some time period. For example, the number of vocabulary words covered by Christmas, or the number of mastery units covered in a semester will differ from classroom to classroom. In educational systems where standardized tests are used as outcomes, and where those tests sample items from a broad curriculum, students whose teacher exposes them to the most content ordinarily have a better chance of answering the test questions. As the pace of instruction increases, however, depth of coverage usually decreases.

Reading 8.5

Environment, affordance and new technology

Anthony Edwards

The concept of 'affordance' is a powerful idea in relation to classroom provision and practice. It refers to the *potential uses* of something (perhaps maths equipment, art materials or a new software programme), and to the activities which such potential uses make possible. The term invites teachers to consider the environment of their classrooms and the available resources, and to reflect creatively on possibilities and constraints for teaching and learning activities. Affordance is often used in discussion of software, and the reading describes a taxonomy of ICT affordances.

What are the main affordances of your working environment, and what others might be developed?

Edited from: Edwards, A. (2012) *New Technology and Education*. London: Continuum, 86–8.

The theory of affordances was first developed by the American psychologist James Gibson (1904–79) as a result of work he did with pilots during the Second World War on the depth of perception. He argued that there are features of the environment 'that afford (i.e. enable) perception and action in that environment'.

> They are not constructed by the person. They exist independently in the environment, and are discovered rather that constructed by the actor. Thus, a rigid surface stretching to the horizon under our feet affords locomotion; an object of a certain size affords grasping and so on. (*Boyle et al., 2004: 296*)

Affordances, therefore, are the perceived 'and actual properties of a thing, primarily those functional properties that determine just how a thing could possibly be used' (Salmon, 1993: 51).

Wertsch (1998) applied Gibson's theory to digital technologies. He regarded the computer as a tool that amplified opportunities to combine physical with symbolic forms of action. This interchange often reflects complex thought processes that are dependent on both the learning environment and the capability for action of the learner.

Teachers appear to go through a number of developmental stages when employing technology in the classroom. They begin by regarding the computer in particular as either a substitute for pencil and paper, or as a machine tutor. Some move towards viewing it as a support for cognitive activity, which learners could not undertake without it (Somekh, 1994).

The rate at which teachers move through these stages is not only dependant on pedagogy, the local context and the subject discipline in which they are working, but also on their own ICT competence. Research indicates that once they have acquired an appropriate level of proficiency, they adopt an integrated, enhanced or complimentary approach to utilizing technology (Laurillard, 2007). An integrated approach involves carefully reviewing the curriculum and only employing ICTs when they can contribute to specific aims and objectives. An enhanced approach is one in which the technology is used to enrich the learning experience in the classroom. A complimentary approach is one in which the technology is used to support aspects of pupils' work, such as helping to bridge the gap between school and home. Competence by itself is not sufficient to guarantee that teachers, regardless of pedagogy, use ICTs effectively in the classroom. They must also understand the potential the technology has to affect teaching and learning. This is its 'affordance' – that which the tool makes possible.

A taxonomy of affordances

Conole et al. (2004) have developed a taxonomy of ICT affordances. The taxonomy seeks to establish the possibilities for action that ICTs offer not only to the teacher but to the learner, as well. They are categorized as accessibility, change, collaboration, diversity, multimodality, nonlinearity and reflection, and are explained below.

Accessibility A vast amount of information is now readily available to teachers and learners from many sources, including shared networks and websites. For the teacher, the challenge is helping learners to know how to use what is available. For the learner, the challenge is not searching but selecting.

Change Rapid change to the information available can be made as a result of new technologies. News about political unrest or freak weather can be transmitted around the world in an instant, regardless of the proximity of the recipient to the event. While this provides unprecedented opportunities to remain *au courant*, the information can be subject to inaccuracies, lacking in authority and posted with little reflection. For the educator, the challenge is to help learners to make informed decisions despite this immediacy.

Collaboration Digital technologies have the potential to link people together through new forms of online communication, including chat rooms, forums and mailing lists. This can foster discourse but also lead users to engage with each other on a superficial level, and for them to lack a clear identity. For the educator, the challenge is to ensure that learners have the appropriate communication and literacy skills (Deed et al., 2010).

Diversity ICTs can expose learners to things beyond their immediate environment and can draw on the experiences of others, including subject experts who are necessarily close by or teachers. Computer simulations also offer the user the opportunity to model complex behaviours and systems that would not be available otherwise. For the teacher, it raises questions about how well those in their care are taught to distinguish what 'is real and what is rendered real via the technology' (Conole et al., 2004: 117).

Multimodality A combination of touch, vision and voice can be used to access some technologies. By employing voice-activated software, users can issue commands at the same time as writing, reading or sending a message. This not only enables multitasking, but it makes it more possible for learning to take different forms. Learners can easily hear, figuratively feel (through simulation), read and see material in whatever combination is appropriate to their needs.

Nonlinearity Some technologies such as the World Wide Web allow those using search engines to approach their task in any number of different ways. Web pages, unlike the rooms in a house, can be entered or exited from any point, not just by the equivalent of the front or back door. This equates to a system in which output is not directly related to input and from an educational perspective is an important facility. It allows learning to be based on experimentation and trial and error rather than as a series of graded steps with none of the shortcuts that the behaviourists are so fond of. ICT affordances may not only reside in a computer but also in software packages, websites and multimedia, or connected peripheral devices.

Reflection Technologies which allow for discourse to occur over an extended period time (asynchronous) and can make use of archived material (such as forums) without the need for immediate responses have the potential to nurture reflection and present 'new opportunities for knowledge claims to be considered and subject to the critical gaze of much wider and more diverse communities of practice' (Conole et al., 2004: 118). For the educator, the challenge is how to make sure the learners take the time to reflect properly.

Reading 8.6

The profound shift of digital literacies
Gunther Kress

The range of technological experience, and digital sophistication, of many children and young people is now very considerable – and often leaves schools and teachers behind. Kress discusses how new textual learning spaces and modes of communication are being created by screen-based technologies, and considers how children are developing skills and capabilities to exploit these. The challenges for schools, both today and in the future, are profound.

How is your school adapting to contemporary developments in communication technology and popular culture?

Edited from: Kress, G. (2010) 'The Profound Shift of Digital Literacies', in Gillen, J. and Barton, D. (eds) *Digital Literacies. TLRP – Technology Enhanced Learning.* London: Institute of Education, 2–3.

My interest is meaning-making in communication. Communication is a social activity, and as such it is embedded in the wider social environment. That environment is marked by great instability, so that communication is becoming ever more problematic. Digital literacies are in a deep and profound sense *new* literacies, not merely the traditional concept of literacy – reading and writing – carried on in new media.

I wish to draw attention to the radically changing forms and functions of texts, which go beyond traditional conceptions of what literacy is and has been. I consider productive aspects to be at least as significant as receptive – text-making as important as text-receiving – though I also suggest that distinction is increasingly challenged in the environment of digital technologies.

In the current period writing is being affected by four factors:

1 Texts are becoming intensely multimodal, that is, image is ever-increasingly appearing with writing, and, in many domains of communication, displacing writing where it had previously been dominant.

2 Screens (of the digital media) are replacing the page and the book as the dominant media.

3 Social structures and social relations are undergoing fundamental changes, as far as writing is concerned, predominantly in changes of structures of authority, and in the effects of changing gender formations.

4 Constellations of mode and medium are being transformed. The medium of the book and the mode of writing had formed a centuries-long symbiotic constellation; this is being displaced by a new constellation of medium of the screen and mode of image. The consequences of this shift are profound.

The effect of these four together amount to a revolution in the world of communication.

Multimodality

Contemporary texts are becoming ever more multimodal, that is, they combine writing and image (on screen or page); writing, image, moving image, music and speech (on a DVD, on a website); or gesture, speech, image, spatial position (in f2f interaction). This requires that we think newly about reading and writing, but also that we think about the meaning-contribution of all other modes that appear in texts. We can no longer treat image as merely decorative, or even just as 'illustration': images are now being used to make meaning just as much – though in different ways – as is writing.

The increased use of images is not making texts simpler, as is often claimed. Multimodal texts demand new ways of reading: the meaning of each mode present in the text has to be understood separately, and its meaning conjoined with all others that are present, and brought into a single coherent reading. The demands on writing have both changed and multiplied. Socially, there is now recognition of much greater cultural and social diversity and an expectation that this diversity is acknowledged. Writing now has to be considered in relation to audience, and in relation to the other modes which may be present in the textual ensemble, and their communicational functions. Writing is becoming part of a larger and encompassing design effort in the making of texts.

Design

The new environments are encouraging a new disposition towards making texts and towards reading texts. Readers, as indeed writers and designers, will now need to treat all features of the graphically presented text as meaningful. Where before their training had disposed them to attend to language in a much more abstract way – to grammar, words, syntax – now they need to attend to all features of a text. In other words their disposition has changed from a linguistic to a semiotic one.

Both the making of text and the reading of text demands much more attention to all possible means of making meaning. Design requires the apt use of all resources (modes, genres, syntax, font, layout, etc.) to content and to audience. So, the facility offered by digital media shifts notions of making texts from 'using the available resource of writing in relation to my purposes and according to convention' to 'using apt resources for that which I wish to represent in order to implement the design that I have, given my understanding of the relevant characteristics of the social environment in which I am producing this text.'

It is relatively straightforward to see design in text-making; however design is also at work in text 'reception'. Where more traditional texts such as books have strict order at various levels, and given entry-points, multimodal texts, with their organisation on visual principles, and their multiple entry-points offer and even expect the reader to construct the order of reading for her/himself. In effect, reading the multimodal text makes readers into the designers of the texts they read.

Reading with digital media makes reading into an activity in which in many or most instances it is possible to change the text that I am reading as I read it. This changes the status of author and of text radically. In reading I can become author in a way which before had been possible only 'inwardly' (and in theory).

Implications

The use of screens and the implications of that use for pedagogies as well as for forms of writing, need to be fully understood. Screens encourage profoundly different approaches to reading than did the traditional page. The phenomenon of hyper-textuality chimes with larger social moves away from hierarchical and towards more lateral structures. A user of the screen who has several windows open at the same time – attending to chat, surfing the internet, listening to sound-as-music, is engaged in forms of 'attention' management entirely unlike the withdrawing, reflective modes of reading traditional written text, a mode still encouraged and rewarded in schools. The task will be to attend to both dispositions, bringing out, in ways plausible and relevant to young text-makers, the continuing value of each.

Those who have grown up in a world where the screen and its potentials have already become naturalised, are taking as natural all the potentials of the screen, including its social potentials and consequences – in terms of action, agency, modes to be used, modes which are focal, forms of production and reading.

If the school remains obliged to adhere to the characteristics of the former semiotic and social world, there will be an increasingly vast gap of practice, understanding, and disposition to knowledge.

Reading 8.7

Direct and interactive whole-class instruction
Daniel Muijs and David Reynolds

Direct instruction refers to a teaching strategy in which the teacher works actively with the whole class in structured and purposive ways. This has long been an important aspect of effective teaching, and a number of studies that have shown that what the teacher does has a strong influence on pupil outcomes (see, for a recent synthesis, see Hattie, 2009, Reading 4.6). Recent examples of direct instruction models were provided by the National Literacy and Numeracy Strategies in England.

In what ways do you use direct instruction and how might you be able to further develop your practice?

Edited from: Muijs and Reynolds (2011) *Effective Teaching.* London: Sage, 35–63.

Direct instruction

Whole class teaching has been employed in schools for a long time, but the effectiveness of direct instruction has not been scientifically studied until quite recently. Interest in this style of teaching took off with the 'teacher effectiveness' school of research, in which researchers study the actual practices of teachers in classrooms, observing lessons and linking their behaviours to pupil outcomes such as scores on standardised tests.

For many purposes, including the teaching of basic skills, whole-class teaching has been found to be more effective than individualised learning approaches. One reason is that whole class teaching actually allows the teacher to make more contacts with each pupil than is possible with individualised work. Pupils have also been found to be more likely to be on task during whole class sessions than during individualised instruction. This is mainly because it is easier for the teacher to monitor the whole class while teaching than to monitor individual pupils. Whole class teaching also allows the teacher to easily change and vary activities and to react quickly to signs that pupils are switching off, either through lack of understanding of the content or through boredom. It also allows mistakes and misconceptions made by pupils to be illustrated to the whole class.

Furthermore, some other arrangements, in particular those in which different pupils or groups of pupils are doing different activities within the classroom, are more complex, and therefore more difficult to manage effectively than a whole-class setting in which pupils are mainly doing the same thing.

This, however, does not mean that teachers should spend the whole lesson teaching the whole class. Individual or group practice remains an essential part of the lesson if pupil learning is to be maximised, as pupils have to have the opportunity to reinforce their learning. It would also be wrong to equate whole class teaching with passive reception of learning by students. Learners need to be active to learn, and active engagement in the lesson is necessary.

It is thus not enough merely to teach the whole class in order to have an effective direct instruction lesson. A number of conditions need to be met:

- Direct instruction is based on an active role for the teacher, who must be expert in appropriately presenting the content of the lesson to pupils.
- The lesson as a whole needs to be well structured, with the objectives of the lesson clearly laid out, key points emphasised, and main points summarised at the end.
- Teachers need to present the material they are teaching in small steps. Pupils need to fully master these before going on to the next part. Each step itself needs to be well-structured and clear.
- The pace of the lesson needs to be fast for lower-level skills, while leaving more time for reflection when the goal of the lesson calls for higher levels skills.
- Use of advance organisers and modelling can help aid lesson clarity.

Direct instruction does have its limitations. It is not effective with all pupils and is more suited to teaching basic skills than to teaching higher order thinking skills.

Individual practice, also known as seatwork, is an important part of direct instruction, but again certain conditions need to be in place to make it effective. Seatwork needs to be well prepared and needs to tie in clearly with the objectives and goals of the lesson. While it is normal that seatwork will often take the form of doing exercises in a workbook or on worksheets, it is important to not slavishly follow a publishers' scheme, but to tailor seatwork to the objectives of the lesson and the pupils taught.

Teachers need to monitor the whole class during seatwork to ensure all pupils stay on task and to provide help to pupils experiencing problems.

Interactive teaching

As we have seen, in order to be effective, direct instruction has to be far more than lecture-style delivery of content to pupils. Teaching must be interactive. For example, Mortimore et al. (1988) found positive effects for the use of frequent questioning, communicating with the class and the use of 'higher order' questions and statements. Muijs and Reynolds (1999) also demonstrated the importance of factors such as using a high frequency of questions, use of open-ended questions, asking pupils to explain their answers and using academic questions – which were significantly related to pupil achievement. American researchers had already demonstrated the importance of interaction in their research. Rosenshine and Furst (1973) found the use of a wide variety of questions to be a crucial factor in their research from the 1960's and early 1970's.

The interaction between teacher and pupil is thus one of the most important aspects of direct instruction. Questioning can be used to check pupils' understanding, to 'scaffold' pupils' learning, to help them clarify and verbalise their thinking and to help them develop a sense of mastery.

Effective questioning is one of the most widely studied aspects of teaching, and a solid body of knowledge exists on which strategies are most effective.

In direct instruction lessons, questions need to be asked at the beginning of the lesson when the topic of the last lesson in that subject is being reviewed, after every short presentation and during the summary at the end of the lesson. Teachers need to mix both higher and lower level questions, product and process questions, and open and closed questions.

- The cognitive level of questions refers to the difficulty of the questions, in particular whether they require relatively sophisticated thinking skills from pupils ('higher' level) or more basic application of rules or retention of facts ('lower' level).

- A related distinction is that between open and closed questions. Closed questions have one clear answer (e.g. 'how much is 4 times 8'), while open questions have open ended answers (e.g. 'what do you think makes a country democratic').

- Product questions are designed to find the answer to a particular problem, while process questions are meant to elicit procedures, processes and rules used to get to the answer. There is a move towards emphasising process more strongly, as obtaining generic skills such as 'problem solving' is seen as more important in a rapidly changing world than accumulating factual knowledge.

The exact mix depends upon the lesson topic, but teachers need to ensure that enough open, higher level, process questions are used.

Correct answers need to be acknowledged in a positive but businesslike fashion. When a pupil answers a question partially correctly the teacher needs to prompt that pupil to find the remaining part of the answer before moving on to the next pupil. When a pupil answers a question incorrectly, the teacher needs to point out swiftly that the answer was wrong. If the pupil has answered incorrectly due to inattention or carelessness, the teacher must swiftly move on to the next pupil. If the answer is incorrect due to lack of knowledge, the teacher needs to try and prompt the pupil to answer correctly, call on other pupils, or offer further appropriate instruction.

Another form of interaction that may be effective in certain lessons is classroom discussion. In order for discussion to be effective it needs to be carefully prepared. The teacher needs to give pupils clear guidelines on what the discussion is about. During the discussion pupils need to be kept on task, and the teacher needs to write down the main points emerging from the discussion. After the discussion, these main points (the product of the discussion) can be summarised, and pupils can be debriefed by asking them to comment on how well the discussion went (the process of the discussion).

Teachers need to make sure that all pupils get the chance to answer questions.

part three

Teaching for learning

Curriculum

What is to be taught and learned?

9

A curriculum reflects the values and understanding of those who construct it, and the readings in this chapter, together with the parallel text in *Reflective Teaching in Schools*, are intended to support a new era in curriculum planning. In a nutshell, whilst controversy about specific requirements continues and performance priorities remain, teachers and governors are increasingly invited to construct their own 'school curriculum' and to organise specific provision in ways they judge appropriate.

We begin therefore with advice from Male and Waters (9.1) on curriculum design and its relationship to school aims.

Key issues about knowledge are then introduced. Young (9.2) argues that a concern with knowledge should not be seen as old-fashioned, but as a means of gaining access to powerful ways of thinking. Extending this, Wilson (9.3) rehearses the relationship between 'interests', 'forms of thought' and school subjects.

The emphasis on knowledge is then challenged by those who start from a concern with learning. A classic is that of the Plowden Report (9.4) which, whilst acknowledging subject knowledge, strongly promoted the view that learning should be routed in direct experience and realised through the 'agency' of the learner. Bruner (9.5) may offer a way through this with his concept of the 'spiral curriculum'. This suggests that knowledge and development can be reconciled through *appropriate* curricular design. In Reading 9.6, by Unwin, the argument is extended to vocational education with an assertion of the importance of the intrinsic value of practical learning and of relevance.

The chapter concludes with another classic, this time from Shulman (9.7). He analyses three forms of subject knowledge needed by teachers, and argues that each makes an important contribution to effective teaching. Whilst content knowledge is important, so too is 'pedagogical content knowledge', and we again see the crucial teacher role in managing the interaction between subject knowledge and learner development.

The parallel chapter of *Reflective Teaching in Schools* begins with a discussion of principles for curriculum provision, drawing attention to the importance of aims, values, knowledge and development. Section 2 then reviews other key elements of curriculum design – in particular, how knowledge, concepts, skills and attitudes make up a balanced curriculum. The third major part of the chapter describes the structure and content of national curricula within the UK. It contrasts subject-based and integrated curricula, and academic versus vocational education. Finally, there is a section on subject knowledge and teacher expertise. This includes discussion on developing confidence in subject knowledge and on its application through the curriculum.

There are also suggestions for 'Key Readings' in relation to each of the topics covered. 'Reflective Activities', 'Notes for Further Reading' and suggestions for 'Deepening Expertise' are offered in the relevant section of *reflectiveteaching.co.uk*.

Reading 9.1

Designing the school curriculum
Brian Male and Mick Waters

Following decades or relatively tight control by UK governments over the curriculum, the trend of policy is to balance national expectations with greater school autonomy. The 'national curriculum' is thus complemented by the 'local curriculum' – with scope for enhancing relevance and adaption to the specific circumstances of the communities which each school serves. Together, national and local curricula comprise the 'school curriculum' as a whole. Teachers, governors and school communities can thus plan to achieve their particular educational priorities through the school curriculum. This reading discusses the principal elements of such provision.

Edited from: Male, B. and Waters, M. (2012) *The Primary Curriculum Design Handbook.* London: Continuum; and Male, B. and Waters, M. (2012) *The Secondary Curriculum Design Handbook.* London: Continuum, 8–14.

How we can create an exciting, engaging and spontaneous curriculum, and at the same time ensure that students achieve high standards in assessments and examinations? Is it possible to design such a curriculum?

There are three levels of understanding the curriculum:

1 The curriculum as set out by the nation: all those things the nation thinks our young people should learn.

2 The curriculum as set out by the school or the teacher: the mediation of those national expectations into a form that is relevant to the particular students in the school or class.

3 The curriculum as experienced by the children: which might vary from student to student even within a class.

The curriculum of each school is thus much more than the national curriculum.

School aims

What students learn in any school goes way beyond the subjects on the timetable. They are learning all the time, whether we want them to or not, and by the age of 16 they are very different people from the children who started in Year 1. This breadth of learning is often reflected in school aims, which almost always refer to aspects of personal, social and emotional development and to a range of knowledge and skills. Aims may reflect this breadth – for instance, that young people should become:

- Successful learners
- Confident individuals
- Responsible citizens.

Personal and social development

Most teachers and parents see personal and social development as a very important part of the work of the school. Indeed, most countries make reference to personal and social development in their national curricula and some set specific targets. In England for example, the Early Years Foundation Stage (EYFS) guidance for children up to the age of 5 details aspects of personal development.

Key skills

Most countries also refer to a range of skills that apply across and beyond subjects (see Reading 10.5 for an example). These might be general, such as critical thinking, problem solving, communicating or investigating, or they might be more specific such as analysing, synthesizing and evaluating. Since they apply across the curriculum, these are often referred to as generic or key skills. If we take these sorts of skills seriously, then they will have significant implications for the curriculum and for the nature of learning within it.

Knowledge

Within subjects themselves, there can be a tension between subject knowledge, skills and understanding. These three terms have been used to denote different forms of learning:

1 Knowledge is the possession of information.

2 A skill is the ability to do something (either mental or physical).

3 Understanding goes beyond knowledge into a comprehension of general principles and concepts.

Much of the debate about the importance of knowledge arises because the term 'knowledge' is used in a variety of ways in education: from 'knowing that' (simple information to be recalled) to 'knowing how to' (which implies skills) and 'knowing about' (which implies understanding). There is general agreement that conceptual development (understanding) is at the deepest level of learning.

It is important to note two things here: first, the distinction between knowledge, skills and understanding is key to curriculum design because they each involve a different type of learning that the curriculum needs to take account of. Second, the curriculum must equip young people with more than knowledge. A curriculum without skills or under-standing would be shallow – the curriculum of the pub quiz.

Competencies

When education is successful, learners are able to make use of the knowledge, skills and understanding they have acquired because they have developed the right attitudes and approaches to use them effectively. This coming together of knowledge, understanding, skills and personal development is usually referred to as a 'competency'.

Schools in many countries make use of this idea in developing their curricula. For example, Singapore's national curriculum has at its heart: 'Social and Emotional Competencies' and 'Twenty-first Century Competencies'. The latter are listed as:

- Civic literacy
- Global awareness
- Cross-curricular skills
- Critical and media skills
- Information and communication skills.

The key to a school's curriculum design is how aims, knowledge, skills and personal development can be brought together for their mutual benefit and to achieve competency. Curriculum design is the methodology for putting these together.

Beyond lessons

Most curriculum planning focuses on what goes on in lessons, but students also learn from the routines of the school, the things that happen every day or week such as going to assembly, lunchtimes and breaks, performing duties, playing for teams, organizing activities. Some of these routines can be rich sources of learning.

Schools also frequently organize events: things that do not happen every day or week. These can provide a series of experiences over a long period of time like putting on a school concert or play, or of short duration, such as a visit to a museum. Unlike the routines, events are usually planned as part of the overt curriculum.

There are also all those things that happen outside normal hours. They may not involve all the students all the time, but a huge amount of learning takes place in clubs, societies, sports, music groups, school councils and home-school activities and the like. These are seldom part of the planned curriculum, but are another rich source of learning.

There is also the ethos of the school and the set of relationships that prevail. These are not part of the planned curriculum, but will impact on it, especially when our list of educational objectives includes things like: 'show respect' or 'be sensitive to others'. This can impact on the school as a 'learning community' in which both adults and other students contribute to learning (Lave and Wenger, 1991).

There will be very few schools indeed where all these things do not go on in some form. Altogether, they comprise the school curriculum, as experienced by pupils.

Reading 9.2

Powerful knowledge

Michael Young

> The role of subject knowledge in curriculum is surprisingly controversial – and debate sometimes becomes politicised. Michael Young helpfully distinguishes between 'knowledge of the powerful' (which might be deemed elitist), and 'powerful knowledge' (which is expected to provide opportunities for all). He argues that powerful knowledge is increasingly specialised and distinct from everyday experience – so schools must accept responsibility, in pupils' best interests, for teaching subject matter which is *not* familiar to students. This argument makes an interesting contrast with the position of the Plowden Report (see **Reading 9.4**).
>
> Do you see subject knowledge in the curriculum as a constraint on learning or a source of opportunities?
>
> *Commissioned for this volume:* Young, M. (2013) *Powerful Knowledge in Education.* London: University of London, Institute of Education.

What knowledge?

In using the very general word 'knowledge' I find it useful to distinguish between two ideas '*knowledge of the powerful*' and '*powerful knowledge*'. 'Knowledge of the powerful' refers to who defines 'what counts as knowledge' and has access to it. Historically and even today when we look at the distribution of access to university, it is those with more power in society who have access to certain kinds of knowledge. It is this that I refer to as 'knowledge of the powerful'. It is understandable that many sociological critiques of school knowledge have equated school knowledge and the curriculum with 'knowledge of the powerful'. It was, after all the upper classes in the early nineteenth century who gave up their private tutors and sent their children to the Public Schools to acquire powerful knowledge (as well, of course, to acquire powerful friends). However, the fact that some knowledge is 'knowledge of the powerful', or high-status knowledge as I once expressed it (Young 1971, 1998), tells us nothing about the knowledge itself. We therefore need another concept in conceptualising the curriculum that I want to refer to as 'powerful knowledge'. This refers not to whose has most access to the knowledge or who gives it legitimacy, although both are important issues; it refers to what the knowledge can do – for example, whether it provides reliable explanations or new ways of thinking about the world. This was what the Chartists were calling for with their slogan 'really useful knowledge'. It is also, if not always consciously, what parents hope for in making sacrifices to keep their children at school; that they will acquire powerful knowledge that is not available to them at home.

Powerful knowledge in modern societies in the sense that I have used the term is, increasingly, specialist knowledge. It follows therefore that schools need teachers with that specialist knowledge. Furthermore, if the goal for schools is to 'transmit powerful knowledge', it follows that teacher–pupil relations will have certain distinctive features that arise from that goal. For example:

- they will be different from relations between peers and will inevitably be hierarchical;
- they will not be based, as some recent government policies imply, on learner choice, because in most cases, learners will lack the prior knowledge to make such choices.

This does not mean that schools should not take the knowledge that pupils bring to school seriously or that pedagogic authority does not need to be challenged. It does mean that some form of authority relations are intrinsic to pedagogy and to schools. The questions of pedagogic authority and responsibility raise important issues, especially for teacher educators, which are beyond the scope of this chapter. The next section turns to the issue of knowledge differentiation.

Knowledge differentiation and school knowledge

The key issues about knowledge, for both teachers and educational researchers, are not primarily the philosophical questions such as 'what is knowledge?' or 'how do we know at all?' The educational issues about knowledge concern how school knowledge is and should be different from non-school knowledge and the basis on which this differentiation is made. Although the philosophical issues are involved, school/non-school knowledge differences raise primarily sociological and pedagogic questions.

Schooling is about providing access to the specialised knowledge that is embodied in different domains. The key curriculum questions will be concerned with:

- the differences between different forms of specialist knowledge and the relations between them;
- how this specialist knowledge differs from the knowledge people acquire in everyday life;
- how specialist and everyday knowledge relate to each other; and
- how specialist knowledge is pedagogised.

In other words, how it is paced, selected and sequenced for different groups of learners. Differentiation, therefore, in the sense I am using it here, refers to:

- the differences between school and everyday knowledge;
- the differences between and relations between knowledge domains;
- the differences between specialist knowledge (e.g. physics or history) and pedagogised knowledge (school physics or school history for different groups of learners).

Underlying these differences is a more basic difference between two types of knowledge. One is the *context-dependent* knowledge that is developed in the course of solving specific problems in everyday life. It can be *practical* – like knowing how to repair a mechanical or electrical fault or how to find a route on a map. It can also be *procedural*, like a handbook or set of regulations for health and safety. Context-dependent knowledge tells the individual how to do specific things. It does not explain or generalise; it deals with particulars. The second type of knowledge is *context-independent* or *theoretical knowledge*. This is knowledge that is developed to provide generalisations and makes claims to universality; it provides a basis for making judgments and is usually, but not solely, associated with the sciences. It is context-independent knowledge that is at least potentially acquired in school, and is what I referred to earlier as *powerful knowledge*.

Inevitably schools are not always successful in enabling pupils to acquire powerful knowledge. It is also true that schools are more successful with some pupils than others. The success of pupils is highly dependent on the culture that they bring to school. Elite cultures that are less constrained by the material exigencies of life, are, not surprisingly, far more congruent with acquiring context-independent knowledge than disadvantaged and subordinate cultures. This means that if schools are to play a major role in promoting social equality, they have to take the knowledge base of the curriculum very seriously – even when this appears to go against the immediate demands of pupils (and sometimes their parents). They have to ask the question 'is this curriculum a means by which pupils can acquire powerful knowledge?' For children from disadvantaged homes, active participation in school may be the only opportunity that they have to acquire powerful knowledge and be able to move, intellectually at least, beyond their local and the particular circumstances. It does them no service to construct a curriculum around their experience on the grounds that it needs to be validated, and as a result leave them there.

Conceptualising school knowledge

The most sustained and original attempt to conceptualise school knowledge is that developed by the English sociologist Basil Bernstein (Bernstein, 1971, 2000). His distinctive insight was to emphasise the key role of knowledge boundaries, both as a condition for the acquisition of knowledge and as embodying the power relations that are necessarily involved in pedagogy. Bernstein begins by conceptualising boundaries in terms of two dimensions.

First he distinguished between the *classification* of knowledge – or the degree of insulation between knowledge domains – and the *framing* of knowledge – the degree of insulation between school knowledge or the curriculum and the everyday knowledge that pupils bring to school.

Second, he proposed that classification of knowledge can be *strong* – when domains are highly insulated from each other (as in the case of physics and history) – or *weak* – when there are low levels of insulation between domains (as in humanities or science curricula). Likewise, framing can be *strong* – when school and non-school knowledge are insulated from each other, or *weak*, when the boundaries between school and non-school knowledge are blurred (as in the case of many programmes in adult education and some curricula designed for less able pupils).

In his later work Bernstein (2000) moves from a focus on *relations between* domains to the *structure of the domains* themselves by introducing a distinction between vertical and horizontal knowledge structures. This distinction refers to the way that different domains of knowledge embody different ideas of how knowledge progresses. Whereas in vertical knowledge structures (typically the natural sciences) knowledge progresses towards higher levels of abstraction (for example, from Newton's laws of gravity to Einstein's theory of relativity), in horizontal (or as Bernstein expresses it, segmental) knowledge structures like the social sciences and humanities, knowledge progresses by developing new languages which pose new problems. Examples are innovations in literary theory or approaches to the relationship between mind and brain.

Bernstein's primary interest was in developing a language for thinking about different curriculum possibilities and their implications. His second crucial argument was to make the link that between knowledge structures, boundaries and learner identities. His hypothesis was that strong boundaries between knowledge domains and between school and non-school knowledge play a critical role in supporting learner identities and therefore are a condition for learners to progress.

Conclusions

I have argued that, whatever their specific theoretical priorities, their policy concerns or their practical educational problems, educational researchers, policy makers and teachers must address the question 'what are schools for?' This means asking how and why school have emerged historically, at different times and in very different societies, as distinctive institutions with the specific purpose of enabling pupils to acquire knowledge not available to them at home or in their everyday life. It follows, I have argued, that the key concept for the sociology of education (and for educators more generally) is *knowledge differentiation*.

The concept of knowledge differentiation implies that much knowledge that it is important for pupils to acquire will be non-local and counter to their experience. Hence pedagogy will always involve an element of what the French sociologist Pierre Bourdieu refers to, over-evocatively and I think misleadingly, as *symbolic violence*. The curriculum has to take account of the everyday local knowledge that pupils bring to school, but such knowledge can never be a basis for the curriculum. The structure of local knowledge is designed to relate to the particular; it cannot provide the basis for any generalisable principles. To provide access to such principles is a major reason why all countries have schools.

The concept of *knowledge differentiation* sets a threefold agenda for schools and teachers, for educational policy makers and for educational researchers.

First, each group (separately and together) must explore the relationship between the purpose of schools to create the conditions for learners to acquire powerful knowledge and both their *internal structures* – such as subject divisions – and their *external structures* – such as the boundaries between schools and professional and academic 'knowledge producing communities' and between schools and the everyday knowledge of local communities.

Second, if schools are to help learners to acquire powerful knowledge, local, national and international groups of specialist teachers will need to be involved with university-based and other specialists in the ongoing selection, sequencing and inter-relating of knowledge in different domains. Schools therefore will need the autonomy to develop this professional knowledge; it is the basis of their authority as teachers and the trust that society places in them as professionals. This trust may at times be abused; however, any form of account- ability must support that trust rather than try to be a substitute for it.

Third, educational researchers need to address the tension in the essentially *conservative* role of schools as institutions with responsibility for knowledge transmission in society – especially as this aspect of their role is highlighted in a world increasingly driven by the instabilities of the market. However, 'conservative' has two very different meanings in relation to schools. It can mean preserving the stable conditions for acquiring 'powerful knowledge' and resisting the political or economic pressures for flexibility. A good example is how curricular continuity and coherence can be undermined by modularisation and the breaking up of the curriculum into so-called 'bite-sized chunks'. The 'conservatism' of educational institutions can also mean giving priority to the preservation of particular privileges and interests, such as those of students of a particular social class or of teachers as a professional group. Radicals and some sociologists of education have in the past tended to focus on this form of conservatism in schools and assume that if schools are to improve they have to become more like the non-school world – or more specifically the market. This takes us back to the tension between differentiation and de-differentiation of institutions that I referred to earlier.

In summary, I have made three related arguments.

The first is that although answers to the question 'what are schools for?' will inevitably express tensions and conflicts of interests within the wider society, nevertheless educational policy makers, practising teachers and educational researchers need to address the distinctive purposes of schools.

My second argument has been that there is a link between the emancipatory hopes associated with the expansion of schooling and the opportunity that schools provide for learners to acquire 'powerful knowledge' that they rarely have access to at home.

Third, I introduce the concept of *knowledge differentiation* as a principled way of distinguishing between school and non-school knowledge. Contemporary forms of accountability are tending to weaken the boundaries between school and non-school knowledge on the grounds that they inhibit a more accessible and more economically relevant curriculum. I have drawn on Basil Bernstein's analysis to suggest that to follow this path may be to deny the conditions for acquiring powerful knowledge to the very pupils who are already disadvantaged by their social circumstances. Resolving this tension between political demands and educational realities is, I would argue, one of the major educational questions of our time.

Reading 9.3

Teaching a subject

John Wilson

This reading focusses further on the nature of subjects. John Wilson's philosophical approach asserts the inevitability of engaging in subject matter when engaged in teaching. Further, he offers an analysis of four different 'forms of thought', based on philosophical analysis. Interestingly, these articulate quite closely with the curriculum areas to be found in Scotland and Northern Ireland, although some of the subjects of the curriculum in England and Wales are harder to place.

Can need to recognise both learner development (Reading 9.4) and subject study be reconciled?

Edited from: Wilson, J. (2000) *Key Issues in Education and Teaching.* Cassell: London, New York, 48–52.

If we are going to do anything we could seriously call educating children (rather than just being nice to them), we will be concerned that they should have some kind of knowledge, or abilities, or skills, or types of competence. But we cannot give them knowledge or competence in general: it is bound to be knowledge *of* something or competence *at* something; it is bound to be some kind, or different kinds, of knowledge and competence. For instance, a child can learn to play football and/or chess and/or badminton, but cannot learn to play them all at the same time, just because they are different games. Similarly, you can teach children about animals and plants or about geology and rock formations, or introduce them to the beauties of the countryside, but you cannot do all these at exactly the same time because they are different kinds of knowledge and experience. You might or might not want to bring them all under one subject title, like perhaps 'nature study' or 'the natural environment', but they would still be different.

This difference is a matter of logic and has nothing to do with wanting to 'break down subject barriers' or any other educational idea. It just is the case that some kinds of interests and questions are different from others. Being interested in why birds migrate is different from being interested in how rocks are formed, and still more different from being interested in what makes a beautiful landscape or what sort of houses would spoil it. Of course, there may be connections between these interests, but they are still different.

These differences are what make 'subjects' inevitable. Suppose you take some children to see a church. Sooner or later, whatever your views about 'subjects', they are going to be interested in it in different ways. Some children will be interested in how it is built or how the spire manages to stay up when it is so tall—that is the start of 'mechanics' or part of 'architecture'. Other children will be interested in who built it and why, how it got to be there, and who wanted it—the start of 'history'. Others may want to know what it is for and what goes on in it—'religion' or perhaps 'sociology'. And so on. It is inevitable that you should cater for these different interests in different ways simply because they *are* different. If a child asks, 'How does the spire manage to stand up?' and you reply, 'Yes, isn't it beautiful? It cost £5,000 and was built in 1876,' you will not be able to educate that child at all; what the child wants to know, now anyway, is something about stresses and structures and building.

So we have to make 'subjects' fit different interests. This is a long and difficult business because many subjects have grown up in a rather haphazard way, not necessarily because of the differences in the particular angles from which people might be interested in things but for quite other reasons. Some of the reasons have to do with our history: for instance, when science becomes important we began to do less Latin, Greek and theology and more tradition or inertia. This gives us a very mixed bag of subject-titles. But what we have to do is not to try to scrap the lot but to look much more closely and carefully at all of them, so that we can find out what we are trying to do. Before we start some major operation that we might call 'changing the curriculum', we have to be clear about what we are doing now, and this brings us inevitably back to questions like 'What is it to teach such and such?'

It would obviously be useful to compile a list of the disciplines: that is, a list of the various angles from which pupils can be interested in things, of the kinds of questions and answers and knowledge that apply to different aspects of them. This is not easy because it is not easy to know just how to chop up different kinds of human knowledge and experience. But certainly one of the more promising lists has been made by Hirst (Hirst and Peters, 1970), and it is worth looking at it to see how the disciplines or 'forms of thought' (as he calls them) might relate to subject titles as they appear in school curricula.

Logic/mathematics: This kind of knowledge is not about the world of our sense experience at all but about logical derivations from certain rules or axioms. In some ways, it is like playing a game. You start with the axioms of Euclid or rules about the meaning of certain signs and symbols, and then you derive further knowledge from these. We all have a fairly clear idea what sort of operation this is, and the school subjects that come under the general title 'mathematics' are clear examples of it.

Science: This kind of knowledge is about the physical world, about causes and effects in nature, why things fall downwards, why planets move in ellipses and so on. Again, this is pretty clear, and we can identify this discipline in subjects entitled 'chemistry', or 'physics', or 'biology'.

Personal knowledge: This is more difficult. But you can see that when we ask questions about why *people* do things (not why planets or light waves do things), it is a different sort of study. People have intentions, purposes and plans, which planets do not have. So 'Why did he …?' means something very different from 'Why did it …?' And, as we would expect, the sort of evidence with which we need to work is different: for people we need evidence about what goes on in their heads—about their intentions and designs. The clearest case of a subject-title that uses this discipline is 'history', which is surely about why people did things in the past. (If we were interested in why eclipses or earthquakes happened in the past, that would be more like science.) Some aspects of what goes on under title like 'psychology', or 'sociology' may be also concerned with personal knowledge, though other aspects may be more like science: it all depends what sort of answers and knowledge we are after.

Morality, aesthetics and religion: These are more difficult still. We lump them together partly because it is not clear what ground each of the three word covers, and there may be some overlap. (Thus for some people 'morality' is part of 'religion', or at least importantly connected with it.) But it seems plausible to say that there are questions about what is morally right and wrong, which are different from questions about what is beautiful, or ugly, or dainty, or elegant ('aesthetics'), and perhaps different again from questions about what one should worship or pray to ('religion'). Philosophers have been working on these areas, trying to help us get clearer about them, but even now we can see that some subject-titles include some of the disciplines. Thus if under the title of 'English' I try to get children to appreciate the elegance or effectiveness of a poem or a play, that looks like 'aesthetics' — and it is similar to (the same sort of discipline as) what the French teacher might do with a French poem or what the music teacher might do in musical appreciation classes.

It is worth noting here, incidentally, that not being as clear as we ought to be about these disciplines holds up all possible progress in some cases. The most obvious example is RE. We have the subject title 'RE' (or 'RI' or 'scripture' or 'divinity' or anything we like to choose), but it does not help unless we know what *sort* of knowledge—what discipline—is involved in teaching RE. We can sidestep the problem by, say, teaching church history in RE periods, but that is the discipline of history or personal knowledge and might well be left to the history teachers; or we can encourage children to appreciate the beauty of biblical language, but that is the discipline of aesthetics or literary appreciation and might well be left to the English teacher. Religious people at least will feel that there is something missing if that is all we do. The problem for such people is to point out a special kind of discipline, with a special kind of knowledge, that should go on under 'RE'.

This kind of list is very useful to bear in mind when we are considering rather vaguely entitled new subjects, as perhaps 'social studies' or 'the environment' or 'sex education'. For we at once want to know what disciplines are going to be involved, and the list allows us to raise the question against a useful background.

Reading 9.4

Aspects of children's learning
Central Advisory Council for England

> This reading from the Plowden Report conveys the tone and emphasis of what has been taken as the most influential statement of 'progressivism' in primary education, with its concern that provision should be appropriate in terms of child development. The role of play in early learning is clearly set out, together with the conception of 'the child as the agent of his or her own learning', and the necessity of building a curriculum based on children's interests and experiences. But note too, in that context, the affirmation of 'knowledge and facts'.
>
> There has been much debate since Plowden – but how enduring, in your opinion, are the issues about learning and development which it addressed?
>
> *Edited from:* Central Advisory Council for Education (England) (1967) *Children and their Primary Schools*, Plowden Report. London: HMSO, 193–7.

Play is the central activity in all nursery schools and in many infant schools. This sometimes leads to accusations that children are wasting their time in school: they should be 'working'. But this distinction between work and play is false, possible throughout life, certainly in the primary school. Its essence lies in past notions of what is done in school hours (work) and what is done out of school (play). We know now that play – in the sense of 'messing about' either with material objects or with other children, and of creating fantasies – is vital to children's learning and therefore vital in school. Adults who criticise teachers for allowing children to play are unaware that play is the principal means of learning in early childhood. it is the way through which children reconcile their inner lives with external reality. In play, children gradually develop concepts of causal relationships, the power to discriminate, to make judgements, to analyze and synthesise, to imagine and to formulate. Children become absorbed in their play and the satisfaction of bringing it to a satisfactory conclusion fixes habits of concentration which can be transferred to other learning.

From infancy, children investigate the material world. Their interest is not wholly scientific but arises from a desire to control or use the things about them. Pleasure in 'being a cause' seems to permeate children's earliest contact with materials. To destroy and construct involves learning the properties of things and in this way children can build up concepts of weight, height, size, volume and texture.

Primitive materials such as sand, water, clay and wood attract young children and evoke concentration and inventiveness. Children are also stimulated by natural or manufactured materials of many shapes, colours and textures. Their imagination seizes on particular facets of objects and leads them to invent as well as to create. All kinds of causal connections are discovered, illustrated and used. Children also use objects as symbols for things, feelings and experiences, for which they may lack words. A small girl may use a piece of material in slightly different ways to make herself into a bride, a queen, or a nurse. When teachers enter into the play activity of children, they can help by watching the connections and relationships which children are making and by introducing, almost incidentally, the words for the concepts and feelings that are being expressed. Some symbolism is unconscious and may be the means by which children come to terms with actions or thoughts which are not acceptable to adults or are too frightening for the children themselves. In play are the roots of drama, expressive movement and art. In this way too children learn to understand other people. The earliest play of this kind probably emerges from play with materials. A child playing with a toy aeroplane can be seen to take the role of both the aeroplane and the pilot apparently simultaneously. All the important people of his world figure in this play: he imitates, he becomes, he symbolises. He works off aggression or compensates himself for lack of love by 'being' one or other of the people who impinge on his life. By acting as he conceives they do, he tries to understand them. Since children tend to have inflexible roles thrust on them by adults, they need opportunities to explore different roles and to make a freer choice of their own. Early exploration of the actions, motives and feelings of themselves and of others is likely to be an important factor in the ability to form right relationships, which in its turn seems to be a crucial element in mental health. Adults can help children in this form of play, and in their social development, by references to the thoughts, feelings and needs of other people. Through stories told to them, children enter into different ways of behaving and of looking at the world, and play new parts.

Much of children's play is 'cultural' play as opposed to the 'natural' play of animals which mainly practises physical and survival skills. It often needs adult participation so that cultural facts and their significance can be communicated to children. The introduction into the classroom of objects for hospital play provides opportunities for coming to terms with one of the most common fears. Similarly the arrival of a new baby in the family, the death of someone important to the child, the invention of space rockets or new weapons may all call for the provision of materials for dramatic play which will help children to give expression to their feelings as a preliminary to understanding and controlling them. Sensitivity and observation are called for rather than intervention from the teacher. The knowledge of children gained from 'active' observation is invaluable to teachers. It gives common ground for conversation and exchange of ideas which it is among the most important duties of teachers to initiate and foster.

The child is the agent in his own learning. This was the message of the often quoted comment from the 1931 Report: 'The curriculum is to be thought of in terms of activity and experience rather than of knowledge to be acquired and facts to be stored'. Read in isolation, the passage has sometimes been taken to imply that children could not learn from imaginative experience and that activity and experience did not lead to the acquisition of knowledge. The context makes it plain that the actual implication is almost the opposite of this. It is that activity and experience, both physical and mental, are often the best means of gaining knowledge and acquiring facts. This is more generally recognised today but still needs to be said. We certainly would not wish to undervalue knowledge and facts, but facts are best retained when they are used and understood, when right attitudes to learning are created, when children learn to learn. Instruction in many primary schools continues to bewilder children because it outruns their experience. Even in infant schools, where innovation has gone furthest, time is sometimes wasted in teaching written 'sums' before children are able to understand what they are doing.

The intense interest shown by young children in the world about them, their powers of concentration on whatever is occupying their attention, or serving their immediate purposes, are apparent to both teachers and parents. Skills or reading and writing or the techniques used in art and craft can best be taught when the need for them is evident to children. A child who has no immediate incentive for learning to read is unlikely to succeed because of warnings about the disadvantages of illiteracy in adult life. There is, therefore, good reason for allowing young children to choose within a carefully prepared environment in which choices and interest are supported by their teachers, who will have in mind the potentialities for further learning. Piaget's observations support the belief that children have a natural urge to explore and discover, that they find pleasure in satisfying it and that it is therefore self-perpetuating. When children are learning new patterns of behaviour or new concepts, they tend both to practise them spontane-ously and to seek out relevant experience, as can be seen from the way they acquire skills in movement. It takes much longer than teachers have previously realised for children to master through experience new concepts or new levels of complex concepts. When understanding has been achieved, consolidation should follow. At this stage children profit from various types of practice devised by their teachers, and from direct instruction.

Children will, of course vary in the degree of interest that they show and their urge to learn will be strengthened or weakened by the attitudes of parents, teachers and others with whom they identify themselves. Apathy may result when parents show no interest, clamp down on children's curiosity and enterprise, tell them constantly not to touch and do not answer their questions. Children can also learn to be passive from a teacher who allows them little scope in managing their own affairs and in learning. A teacher who relies only on instruction, who forestalls children's questions or who answers them too quickly, instead of asking the further questions which will set children on the way to their own solution, will disincline children to learn. A new teacher with time and patience can usually help children who have learnt from their teachers to be too dependent. Those who have been deprived at home need more than that. Their self-confidence can only be restored by affection, stability and order. They must have special attention from adults who can discover, by observing their responses, what experiences awaken interest, and can seize on them to reinforce the desire to learn.

External incentives such as marks and stars, and other rewards and punishments, influence children's learning mainly by evoking or representing parents' or teachers' approval. Although children vary temperamentally in their response to rewards and punishments, positive incentives are generally more effective than punishment, and neither is an damaging as neglect. But the children who most need the incentive of good marks are least likely to gain them, even when, as in many primary schools, they are given for effort rather than for achievement. In any case, one of the main educational tasks of the primary school is to build on and strengthen children's intrinsic interest in learning and lead them to learn for themselves rather than from fear of disapproval or desire for praise.

Learning is a continuous process from birth. The teacher's task is to provide an environment and opportunities which are sufficiently challenging for children and yet not so difficult as to be outside their reach. There has to be the right mixture of the familiar and the novel, the right match to the stage of learning the child has reached. If the material is too familiar or the learning skills too easy, children will become inattentive and bored. If too great maturity is demanded of them, they fall back on half remembered formulae and become concerned only to give the reply the teacher wants. Children can think and form concepts, so long as they work at their own level, and are not made to feel that they are failures.

Teachers must rely both on their general knowledge of child development and on detailed observation of individual children for matching their demands to children's stages of development. This concept of 'readiness' was first applied to reading. It has sometimes been thought of in too negative a way. Children can be led to want to read, provided that they are sufficiently mature. Learning can be undertaken too late as well as too early. Piaget's work (see Reading 2.2) can help teachers in diagnosing children's readiness in mathematics, and gives some pointers as to how it can be encouraged.

At every stage of learning children need rich and varied materials and situations, though the pace at which they should be introduced may vary according to the children. If children are limited in materials, they tend to solve problems in isolation and fail to see their relevance to other similar situations. This stands out particularly clearly in young children's learning of mathematics. Similarly, children need to accumulate much experience of human behaviour before they can develop moral concepts. If teachers or parents are inconsistent in their attitudes or contradict by their behaviour what they preach, it becomes difficult for children to develop stable and mature concepts. Verbal explanation, in advance of understanding based on experience, may be an obstacle to learning, and children's knowledge of the right words may conceal from teachers their lack of understanding. Yet it is inevitable that children will pick up words which outstrip their understanding. Discussion with other children and with adults is one of the principal ways in which children check their concepts against those of others and build up an objective view of reality. There is every justification for the conversation which is characteristic feature of the contemporary primary school. One of the most important responsibilities of teachers is to help children to see order and pattern in experience, and to extend their ideas by analogies and by the provision of suitable vocabulary. Rigid division of the curriculum into subjects tends to interrupt children's trains of thought and of interest and to hinder theme from realising the common elements in problem solving. These are among the many reasons why some work, at least, should cut across subject divisions at all stages in the primary school.

Reading 9.5

The spiral curriculum

Jerome Bruner

Bruner's classic text, *The Process of Education* (1960), is premised on the idea that students are active learners who construct their own knowledge and understanding. Challenging the constraining effects of those advocating subject-based and developmental progression, he argued that all knowledge can 'be taught in some intellectually honest form to any child at any stage of development' (p. 33). It is then revisited, successively, at further levels of difficulty. He drew particular attention to the place of narrative in learning and in 'making sense' through life.

If there is value in these ideas, they have significant implications for progression in curriculum planning.

Edited from: Bruner, J. S., (2006) *In Search of Pedagogy Volume II: The Selected works of Jerome S. Bruner.* New York: Routledge, 145–6.

A very long time ago I proposed something which was called a spiral curriculum (1960). The idea was that when teaching or learning a subject, you start with an intuitive account that is well within the reach of the student, then circle back later in a more powerful, more generative, more structured way to understand it more deeply with however many recyclings the learner needs in order to master the topic and turn it into an instrument of the mind, a way of thinking. It was a notion that grew out of a more fundamental view of epistemology, about how minds get to know. I stated this view almost in the form of a philosophical proverb: Any subject could be taught to any child at any age in some form that was honest. Another way of saying the same thing is that readiness is not only born but made. You make readiness.

The general proposition rests on the still deeper truth that a domain of knowledge can be constructed simply or complexly, abstractly or concretely. The kid who understands the intuitive role of the lever and can apply it to the playground see-saw is getting within reach of knowing the meaning of quadratic functions. He now has a grasp of one instantiation of an idea that makes teaching him about quadratics a cinch. I'm saying this because we have done it. Give me a balance beam with hooks placed at equal distances along it, some weights that you can hang on the hooks of the balance beam to make it balance, and I will show you. A ten-year-old I was working with once said to me: 'This gadget knows all about arithmetic'. That gave me pause, and I tried to convince him that it was he who knew arithmetic, not the balance beam. He listened politely, but I don't think I succeeded; maybe that will come later along the curriculum spiral. Anyway, he had learned a meaning of expressions like $x^2 + 5x + 6$ and why they balance – mean the same – as ones like $(x +2)(x + 3)$.

The research of the last three decades on the growth of reasoning in children has in the main confirmed the rightness of the notion of the spiral curriculum in spite of the fact that we now know about something called domain specificity. It is not true now, nor was it ever true, that learning Latin improves your reasoning. Subject matters have to be demonstrably within reach of each other to improve each other. There isn't infinite transfer. On the other hand, there is probably more than we know, and we can build up a kind of general confidence that problems are solvable. That has a huge transfer effect. The kid says, 'Now how would we do that?' using a kind of royal 'we'. A good intuitive, practical grasp of the domain at one stage of developmental leads to better, earlier, and deeper thinking in the next stage when the child meets new problems. We do not wait for readiness to happen. We foster it by making sure they are good at some intuitive domain before we start off on the next one.

However, it's interesting that we don't always do it. It is appalling how poorly history, for example, is taught at most schools and at most universities. Teachers needs to give students an idea that there are models for how events happened historically, even if we give them a sort of Toynbeyan model, to the effect that there is challenge and response, or the kind of Paul Kennedy model of what happens to wealthy nations. The particular model doesn't matter, just so it is clear and coherent so that kids can say, 'Pretty smart, but it doesn't work'. We need models that can be given some basic sense even though they are rejected later. One way to do it is by placing emphasis upon what is story-like about the model. For what we grasp better than anything else are stories, and it is easy for children (or adults) to take them apart, retell them, and analyse what's wrong with them.

The most natural and earliest way in which we organize our experience and our knowledge is by use of narrative. It may be that the beginnings, the transitions, the full grasps of ideas in a spiral curriculum depend upon embodying those ideas initially into a story of narrative form in order to carry the kid across any area where he is not quite grasping the abstraction. The story form is the first one grasped by kids, and is the one with which they all seem most comfortable.

Reading 9.6

Vocational education matters

Lorna Unwin

> Despite the high quality provision in many parts of Europe, vocational education has rarely been taken seriously in the UK. In this reading, Unwin highlights the intrinsic value of practical learning in all forms, and the contribution which it can make to personal wellbeing and social cohesion as well as to economic productivity. In schools, early work and later learning, practical learning and vocational education deserves to be taken very seriously.
>
> In what ways does practical activity enhance your own learning?
>
> *Edited from:* Unwin, L (2009) *Sensuality, Sustainability and Social Justice: Vocational Education in Changing Times.* Professorial Inaugural Lecture, Institute of Education, University of London, 4 February.

Over the past 150 years or so, many commentators have been concerned to expose the serious deficiencies in provision for vocational education and training (for contemporary critiques and reviews of the historical commentary, see, Unwin, 2004; Warhurst et al., 2004; Wolf, 2002; Keep and Mayhew, 1999; Green, 1990; Bailey, 1990). These critiques have drawn attention to. the separation of vocational education from general education; the failure to establish dedicated vocational institutions; the lack of investment in the development of vocational teachers; the acceptance by successive governments that only employers should determine the content and form of vocational qualifications; and the lack of labour market regulation.

But let's step back from the critiques of government policy and consider the meaning and purpose of vocational education in contemporary society.

One of the few academics to devote time and energy to the study of vocational education was the American philosopher, John Dewey. He placed the concept of the 'vocational' in the wider context of viewing one's life as a whole. Dewey (1915) argued that vocational education helps people consider what kind of lives they want to lead and to identify the type of skills and knowledge they might require to achieve their goals. He added that vocational education was more than preparation for an occupation, rather it was a means to develop an understanding of the historical and social meanings of that occupation, paid or unpaid. As such, participation in vocational education is an important means for all individuals to connect their interests and abilities with the world around them.

Three stages of vocational education can be identified. First, there is vocational preparation prior to entering the labour market. Provision at this stage faces particular challenges in relation to the creation of satisfactory simulated work environments, access to up-to-date equipment, and the vocational expertise of teachers. Second, apprenticeship, where it exists, is an age-old model of learning (still used in occupations as diverse as medicine and hairdressing) that conceives vocational preparation as a combination of work experience, job-specific training and vocational education. Done well, apprenticeship creates a space within which the development of occupational expertise and induction into an occupational community will also involve wider conversations about the aesthetic and moral dimensions of working life. Finally, further vocational development relates to the stage beyond apprenticeship when the work itself becomes the source of learning. All workers need to improve their expertise and extend their knowledge to some degree, and they and their employers need to regularly reappraise the relationship between the worker's capability and the changing requirements of the workplace (Fuller and Unwin, 2004).

All three phases demand a sophisticated understanding of the importance of what Richard Sennett (2008: 9) terms 'craftsmanship'. He writes:

> Craftsmanship may suggest a way of life that waned with the advent of industrial society – but this is misleading. Craftsmanship names an enduring, basic human impulse, the desire to do a job well for its own sake.

In his book, Sennett calls for a 'vigorous cultural materialism' in order to bring together concern for culture and the objects and activities of everyday life. Crucially, this relates to the process of making and mending. It is, he suggests, through making things that people can learn about themselves.

Further, Sennett argues that three basic abilities form the foundation of craftsmanship:

- the ability to localise (making a matter concrete);
- to question (reflecting on its qualities);
- and to open up (expanding its sense).

Sennett states that, to deploy these capabilities, 'the brain needs to process in parallel visual, aural, tactile, and language-symbol information' (p. 277).

Certainly, practical activity motivates a great many people to learn. It also tends to be a much more social and collective process and, hence, is an excellent vehicle for building the inter-personal skills that are important in the workplace.

Such arguments go way beyond the view that 'practical learning' is simply a panacea for the need to engage young people who are not amenable to traditional subject-centred general education.

Indeed, these points challenge the reductionist conception of competence that still underpins the design of the vocational qualifications.

Vocational education done well will inspire young people, and will motivate older workers to up-skill and re-skill. It is different to academic education and demands a more sophisticated pedagogy as it requires learning to switch across environments – from classroom to workplace to workshop – it demands that teachers really are expert and up-to-date and that equipment is appropriate and of the highest quality – above all, it is expensive.

Vocational education is central to social justice and social cohesion and to the renewal of the economy. We need a new approach that situates the development of vocational expertise within a social partnership that allows employers, vocational educators and institutions, local government, and trade unions to create programmes for all grades of workers.

Reading 9.7

A perspective on teacher knowledge
Lee Shulman

The final reading in this chapter on curriculum is not about its organisation and content, but about the forms of teacher knowledge which are required to teach a curriculum effectively. It is derived from Shulman's classic paper in which he identifies three forms of teacher knowledge, subject content, pedagogic and curricular. This thinking has been extremely influential in teacher training, provision for continuous professional development and in endorsing the need for domain-based expertise.

Thinking of your own curricular strengths, can you identify these three forms of knowledge in yourself? And regarding subjects about which you feel less secure, what forms of knowledge particularly concern you?

Edited from: Shulman, L. S. (1986) 'Those who understand: knowledge growth in teaching', *Educational Researcher,* February, 9–10.

How might we think about the knowledge that grows in the minds of teachers, with special emphasis on content? I suggest we distinguish among: subject matter content knowledge, pedagogical content knowledge, and curricular knowledge.

Content knowledge

This refers to the amount and organization of knowledge per se in the mind of the teacher.

To think properly about content knowledge requires going beyond knowledge of the facts or concepts of a domain. It requires understanding the structures of the subject matter in the manner defined by such scholars as Joseph Schwab (1978).

For Schwab, the structures of a subject include both the substantive and the syntactive structures. The substantive structures are the variety of ways in which the basic concepts and principles of the discipline are organized to incorporate its facts. The syntactic structure of a discipline is the set of ways in which truth or falsehood, validity or invalidity, are established. When there exist competing claims regarding a given phenomenon, the syntax of a discipline provides the rules for determining which claim has greater warrant. A syntax is like a grammar. It is the set of rules for determining what is legitimate to say in a disciplinary domain and what 'breaks' the rules.

Teachers must not only be capable of defining for students the accepted truths in a domain. They must also be able to explain why a particular proposition is deemed warranted, why it is worth knowing, and how it relates to other propositions, both within the discipline and without, both in theory and in practice.

Thus, the biology teacher must understand that there are a variety of ways of organizing the discipline. Depending on the preferred text, biology may be formulated as: a science of molecules from which one aggregates up to the rest of the field, explaining living phenomena in terms of the principles of their constituent parts; a science of ecological systems from which one disaggregates down to the smaller units, explaining the activities of individual units by virtue of the larger systems of which they are a part; or a science of biological organisms, those most familiar of analytic units, from whose familiar structures, functions, and interactions one weaves a theory of adaptation. The well-prepared biology teacher will recognise these and alternative forms of organization and the pedagogical grounds for selecting one under some circumstances and others under different circumstances.

The same teacher will also understand the syntax of biology. When competing claims are offered regarding the same biological phenomenon, how has the controversy been adjudicated? How might similar controversies be adjudicated in our own day?

We expect that the subject matter content understanding of the teacher be at least equal to that of his or her lay colleague, the mere subject matter major. The teacher need not only understand that something is so; the teacher must further understand *why* it is so, on what grounds its warrant can be asserted, and under what circumstances our belief in its justification can be weakened and even denied. Moreover, we expect the teacher to understand why a given topic is particularly central to a discipline whereas another may be somewhat peripheral. This will be important in subsequent pedagogical judgments regarding relative curricular emphasis.

Pedagogical content knowledge

A second kind of content knowledge is pedagogical knowledge, which goes beyond knowledge of subject matter per se to the dimension of subject matter knowledge *for teaching*. I still speak of content knowledge here, but of the particular form of content knowledge that embodies the aspects of content most germane to its teachability.

Within the category of pedagogical content knowledge I include, for the most regularly taught topics in one's subject area, the most useful forms of representation of ideas, the most powerful analogies, illustrations, examples, explanations, and demonstrations – in a word, the ways of representing and formulating the subject that make it comprehensible to others. Since there are no single most powerful forms of representation, the teacher must have at hand a veritable armament of alternative forms of representation, some of which derive from research whereas others originate in the wisdom of practice.

Pedagogical content knowledge also includes an understanding of what makes the learning of specific topics easy or difficult: the conceptions and preconceptions that students of different ages and backgrounds bring with them to the learning of those most frequently taught topics and lessons. If those preconceptions are misconceptions, which they so often are, teachers need knowledge of the strategies most likely to be fruitful in reorganizing the understanding of learners, because those learners are unlikely to appear before them as blank slates.

Here, research on teaching and on learning coincide most closely. The study of student misconceptions and their influence on subsequent learning has been among the most fertile topics for cognitive research. We are gathering an ever growing body of knowledge about the misconceptions of students and about the instructional conditions necessary to overcome and transform those initial conceptions. Such research-based knowledge, an important component of the pedagogical understanding of subject matter, should be included at the heart of our definition of needed pedagogical knowledge.

Curricular knowledge

The curriculum is represented by the full range of programs designed for the teaching of particular subjects and topics at a given level, the variety of instructional materials available in relation to those programs, and the set of characteristics that serve as both the indications and contraindications for the use of particular curriculum or programme materials in particular circumstances.

The curriculum and its associated materials are the *materia medica* of pedagogy, the pharmacopoeia from which the teacher draws those tools of teaching that present or exemplify particular content and remediate or evaluate the adequacy of student accomplishments. We expect the mature physician to understand the full range of treatments available to ameliorate a given disorder, as well as the range of alternatives for particular circumstances of sensitivity, cost, interaction with other interventions, convenience, safety, or comfort. Similarly, we ought to expect that the mature teacher possesses such understandings about the curricular alternatives available for instruction.

How many individuals whom we prepare for teaching biology, for example, understand well the materials for that instruction, the alternative texts, software, programmes, visual materials, single-concept films, laboratory demonstrations, or 'invitations to enquiry?' Would we trust a physician who did not really understand the alternative ways of dealing with categories of infectious disease, but who knew only one way?

Planning

How are we implementing the curriculum?

10

The seven readings in this chapter address key issues curriculum planning and implementation.

First, we have a classic Her Majesty's Inspectorate of Schools (HMI) analysis of key 'characteristics of any curriculum' (10.1) – breadth, balance, relevance, differentiation, progression and continuity. This is extremely important, since it offers a conceptual framework for thinking about, and evaluating, curriculum provision. Reading 10.2, from Northern Ireland, then provides practical advice for the development of the 'school curriculum' based on aspiration, audit, adaption and action.

Readings 10.3, 10.4 and 10.5 explore three particular features of curriculum implementation. Turner-Bissett leads on forms of 'integrated curricula' – provision which is supported now in primary by Cornerstones or IPC systems. Thomas reports on the Royal Society of Arts (RSA)'s work on area-based curricula, which foregrounds local relevance and community engagement in the curriculum. The Welsh Government documents how skill development should be promoted through all years of education. These three cross-curricular dimensions should complement explicit provision for core and foundation subjects.

Three particularly challenging issues are then tackled. Haynes (10.6) provides a fresh account of progression and differentiation, drawing on his own experience. Personalised pedagogy is the subject of Reading 10.7, written by a '2020 Review Group' under the leadership of the Chief Inspector of Schools of the time.

The parallel chapter of *Reflective Teaching in Schools* moves through successive levels of curriculum planning. It begins with whole-school planning and policies, before moving to focus on the structuring of programmes of study and then schemes of work. Characteristics of the curriculum, such as breadth, balance, progression and relevance are interwoven. Short-term planning, for lessons, activities and tasks are then considered, including sections on differentiation and personalisation. As usual, the chapter conclude with suggestions for 'Key Readings'.

reflectiveteaching.co.uk provides additional, and regularly updated, materials. For example, 'expert questions' on curriculum, embedded within *Reflective Teaching in Schools*, are drawn together in the section on 'Deepening Expertise'.

Reading 10.1

Characteristics of the curriculum
Her Majesty's Inspectors (HMI)

> HMI's Curriculum Matters series, and the pamphlet entitled 'The Curriculum from 5 –
> 16', from which this reading is edited, can be seen as an attempt to pre-empt legis-
> lation by offering a non-statutory framework for a national curriculum. The pamphlet
> identified nine 'areas of learning and experience' (related to subject areas), four 'elements
> of learning' (knowledge, skills, concepts and attitudes), and the five 'characteristics of
> curriculum' which are discussed below.
>
> It is interesting to see the importance of 'relevance' here (see **Reading 10.4**) for,
> whilst the other 'characteristics' were emphasised, it was to disappear from the official
> documents of the 1990s.
>
> What do you see as the relevance of 'relevance'?
>
> *Edited from:* Department of Education and Science (1985) *The Curriculum from 5–16,*
> *Curriculum Matters 2,* An HMI Series. London: HMSO, 10–48.

The curriculum provides a context for learning which, as well as providing for the
progressive development of knowledge, understanding and skills, recognises and builds
on the particular developmental characteristics of childhood and adolescence. Active
learning, and a sense of purpose and success, enhance pupils' enjoyment, interest, confidence and sense of personal worth; passive learning and inappropriate teaching styles can
lead to frustration and failure. In particular, it is necessary to ensure that the pupils are
given sufficient first-hand experience, accompanied by discussion, upon which to base
abstract ideas and generalisations.

If the opportunities for all pupils to engage in a largely comparable range of learning
are to be secured, certain characteristics are desirable.

Breadth

The curriculum should be broad. The various curricular areas should reinforce one another:
for example the scientific area provides opportunities for pupils to learn and practise mathematical skills. Breadth is also necessary within an area and within its components: thus in
the linguistic and literary area pupils should read a variety of fiction and non-fiction myths,
legends, fairy tales, animal stories, stories based on family life, adventure stories, historical
fiction, science fiction, reference books, factual accounts, documents, directories and articles.

Class teachers in primary schools are in a strong position to arrange the interplay of the
various aspects of learning since, as *Primary Education in England* (DES, 1978) pointed out:

The teacher can get to know the children and know their strengths and weaknesses; the one teacher concerned can readily adjust the daily programme to suit special circumstances; it is simpler for one teacher than for a group of teachers to ensure that the various parts of the curriculum are coordinated and also to reinforce work done in one part of the curriculum with work done in another.

This does not mean that the class teacher can or should be expected to cover the whole curriculum unaided, especially with the older pupils. He or she should be able to call on the support of teachers who, as well as having responsibilities for their own classes, act as consultants in particular subjects or areas of the curriculum.

Primary schools generally offer a broad curriculum in the sense that all the areas of learning and experience are present to some extent. However, care is needed to ensure that breadth is not pursued at the expense of depth since this may lead to superficial work.

Balance

A balanced curriculum should ensure that each area of learning and experience and each element of learning is given appropriate attention in relation to the others and to the curriculum as a whole. In practice this requires the allocation of sufficient time and resources for each area and element to be fully developed. Balance also needs to be preserved within each area and element by the avoidance, for example, of an undue emphasis on the mechanical aspects of language or mathematics, or on writing predominantly given over to note taking and summarising. There should also be a balance in the variety of teaching approaches used: didactic and pupil-initiated; practical and theoretical; individual, group and full-class teaching.

Balance need not be sought over a single week or even a single month since in some cases it may be profitable to concentrate in depth on certain activities; but it should be sought over a period of, say, a term or a year.

Relevance

The curriculum should be relevant in the sense that it is seen by pupils to meet their recent and prospective needs. Overall, what is taught and learned should be worth learning in that it improves pupils' grasp of the subject matter and enhances their enjoyment of it and their mastery of the skills required; increases their understanding of themselves and the world in which they are growing up; raises their confidence and competence in controlling events and coping with widening expectations and demands; and progressively equips them with the knowledge and skills needed in adult working life. Work in schools can be practical in a number of ways. First it can be directly concerned with 'making and doing'.

Second, pupils at all stages need to work and enjoy working with abstract ideas and to come to an understanding of them by drawing on their own concrete experience, observation and powers of reasoning and, whenever possible, by testing out and reinforcing their learning by reference to real examples.

Third, all that pupils learn should be practical, and therefore relevant, in ways which enable them to build on it or use it for their own purposes in everyday life. For example being read to, reading, hearing music, or taking part in a discussion, all have both a specific and a cumulative effect on the individual, especially if teachers use opportunities to relate what is being learnt to pupils' interests, to contemporary realities and general human experience.

Fourth, the more that knowledge and skills learned in school can be developed within and applied to activities that have real purpose and place in the wider world, the more clearly their relevance will be perceived by the pupils.

Differentiation

As stated in HMI's discussion document *A View of the Curriculum* (HMI,1980):

> The curriculum has to satisfy two seemingly contrary requirements. On the one hand it has to reflect the broad aims of education which hold good for all children, whatever their capabilities and whatever the schools they attend. On the other hand it has to allow for differences in the abilities and other characteristics of children, even of the same age…. If it is to be effective, the school curriculum must allow for differences.

A necessary first step in making appropriate provision is the identification of the learning needs of individual pupils by sensitive observation on the part of the teacher. This may indicate a need for smaller, more homogeneous groups, regrouping for different purposes, or the formation of sub groups for particular activities. Individual work and assignments can be set to allow for different interests, capabilities and work rates so long as this does not isolate pupils or deprive them of necessary contact with other pupils or the teacher. Finally there should be differentiation in the teaching approaches; some pupils need to proceed slowly, and some need a predominantly practical approach and many concrete examples if they are to understand abstractions; some move more quickly and require more demanding work which provides greater intellectual challenge; many have a variety of needs which cannot be neatly categorised.

Progression and continuity

Children's development is a continuous process and schools have to provide conditions and experiences which sustain and encourage that process while recognising that it does not proceed uniformly or at an even pace. If this progression is to be maintained there is a need to build systematically on the children's existing knowledge, concepts, skills and attitudes, so as to ensure an orderly advance in their capabilities over a period of time. Teaching and learning experiences should be ordered so as to facilitate pupils' progress, with each successive element making appropriate demands and leading to better performance.

The main points at which progression is endangered by discontinuity are those at which pupils change schools; they also include those at which children enter school, change classes or teachers, or change their own attitudes to school or some aspect of it. Not all change is for the worse, however, and many pupils find a new enthusiasm or aptitude in new situations. Nevertheless, curricular planning within and between schools should aim to ensure continuity by making the maximum use of earlier learning.

Primary schools have to build on and allow for the influences to which children entering school have already been exposed and to take account of what will be expected of them in the schools to which they will transfer in due course. Continuity within schools may best be achieved when there are clear curricular policies which all the staff have been involved in developing and which present a clear picture of the range of expectations it is reasonable to have of individual pupils. If the foals are as clear as possible, progress towards them is more likely to be maintained.

Reading 10.2

Implementing a revised curriculum
Partnership Management Board of Northern Ireland

This reading suggests a process for curriculum implementation whilst maintaining a strong grip on overall educational aspirations and building on previous provision. It was prepared as advice to schools during the introduction of a 'Revised Curriculum' in Northern Ireland, but its implementation model is applicable anywhere. In addition to subjects and 'areas of learning', various cross-curricular themes are identified. Because of the extent of curriculum change in contemporary education systems internationally, there are many similar examples of advice to schools from government agencies. Such guidance often affirms the importance of school autonomy in decision-making, whilst also trying to ensure national entitlements.

What opportunities for curriculum development exist in your school?

Edited from: Partnership Management Board (2007) *Planning for the Revised Curriculum.* *Belfast: Council for Curriculum,* Examinations and Assessment (CCEA).

The Revised Curriculum seeks to prepare young people for a rapidly changing world.

We recognise that implementation needs to be planned, incremental and facilitated in ways that take account of your school's individual circumstances and readiness. What's more, teachers need time to access training and support to develop confidence with and expertise in all of the areas of curriculum change.

This 'Big Wheel' model (See Figure 10.2.1) shows the range and scale of issues that you must focus on and how these issues are inter-connected. The model also reveals the centrality of the learner. Pupils are the reason for change and the Revised Curriculum is designed to best meet their needs.

Figure 10.2.1
The 'Big Wheel'
model: Starting
points for
implementing a
Revised Curriculum

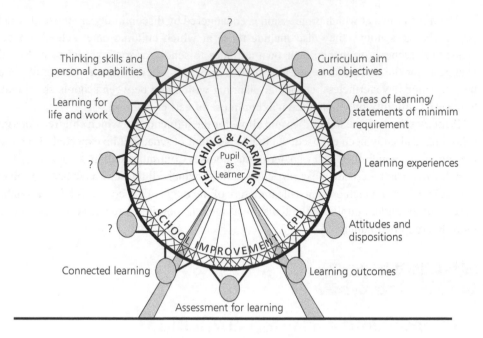

Although all the areas of curriculum change (the 'pods') are inter-related and moving at once, you can decide which pod to jump on as a starting point. You may have your own starting points not named here – hence the unspecified pods.

Because the areas of curriculum change are so inter-related, whichever pod you begin with should inevitably lead you to planning for the other pods. To ensure manageability and thoroughness, however, we recommend that you devise a plan for each area of curriculum change.

Once you choose your starting point, you can begin to plan change. We recommend using the 4A's planning model, shown below. This model has been developed as a result of schools' experiences in trial and pilot work.

The 4 A's model comprises four steps – Aspire, Audit, Adapt, and Action.

The approach offers an incremental process that you can repeat as you plan the various elements of the Revised Curriculum. Schools involved in pilot studies have reported that the 4 A's approach provides:

- a deeper understanding of the changes in the Revised Curriculum;
- opportunities for staff to identify creative opportunities to meet the requirements of the Revised Curriculum;
- increased engagement and commitment from staff; and
- vital information to inform decision-making.

We encourage you to adapt and amend the model in ways that harmonise with your existing school development plan and best suit the needs and interests of your pupils.

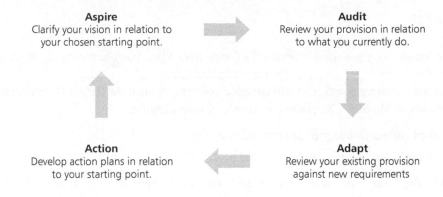

Figure 10.2.2
The 4 A's model
of curriculum
implementation

Aspire

During the Aspire stage, you must clarify your vision for the Revised Curriculum in relation to your chosen starting point (pod).

You can use the following questions to encourage staff involvement:

- 'What do we want our pupils to know about?'
- 'What do we want our pupils to be (attitudes, dispositions and values)?'
- 'What do we want our pupils to be able to do (skills and capabilities)?'

Audit

During the Audit stage, you must review your current provision in relation to the pod you have chosen to start with. We recommend that you audit your current provision on a departmental subject level.

Each department's audit should show:

- the department's and/or subjects' focuses for learning;
- what learning is being delivered and when (the knowledge, understanding and skills that your *Area of Learning* currently delivers);
- the learning experiences that are currently being delivered to pupils;
- the learning outcomes (*Thinking Skills and Personal Capabilities*); and
- how pupils are being assessed.

You then use these audit findings to create a key stage or year-by-year Curriculum Map. Record everything that is happening in every subject on the Curriculum Map.

Adapt

At the Adapt stage, you need to review the Curriculum Maps you created during the Audit stage against the requirements of the Revised Curriculum.

For some starting points, you will compare your map against the Revised Curriculum's Statements of Minimum Requirement. Your goal is to identify:

- duplications and/or gaps in learning; and
- strengths and weaknesses.

In the Adapt stage, you also begin to look forward at how you can revise what you currently offer in order to meet the requirements of the Revised Curriculum in relation to the pod you have chosen as your starting point. You need to consider:

- what you want your pupils to know, understand and be able to do;
- what learning experiences you want to deliver to pupils; and
- what can be done better.

In addition, you may see natural opportunities in your Curriculum Map to also implement some of the other areas of change. If so, take advantage of this by identifying:

- what *Thinking Skills and Personal Capabilities* you want to deliver to pupils;
- opportunities for *Assessment for Learning*;
- opportunities for *Connected Learning* (for example through topics such as health, the environment or identity); and
- opportunities for *Learning for Life and Work*.

Action

During the Action stage, you must develop action plans in relation to your chosen starting point and your agreed areas of change and aims/scope of change.

Separate action plans should be prepared for each of the following:

- the whole school
- departments;
- *Areas of Learning;*
- individual subjects; and
- individual teachers.

Reading 10.3

Constructing an integrated curriculum

Rosie Turner-Bisset

Learners must 'make sense' of their experiences, and that includes making sense of things they are taught in school. An established way of doing that, in both primary and secondary contexts, is through the application of subject knowledge within more integrated curricular topics. In this reading, Turner-Bisset explores this strategy and other forms of integration to make provision, for example, for the development of concepts and skills. This anticipates innovation in the 'school curriculum'. There are also commercial providers offering online systems to support integrated curricular work.

Of the important educational aims to which you subscribe, which would benefit from cross-curricular or integrated provision?

Edited from: Turner-Bisset, R. (2000) 'Reconstructing the primary curriculum: integration revisited', *Education*, 3–13, 28 (1), 3–8.

There are several different ways in which the curriculum can be integrated, and five possible forms are discussed below. The first two look back, as it were, on classroom practice which was common from the 1960s to the mid-nineties. The last three are suggestions for the future.

Integration by topic or theme

This is probably the most widespread form of integration. Exponents of topic work exhibit a particular attitude towards epistemology. They suggest that knowledge, at least at the primary level, cannot be compartmentalised into separate subjects. Such a view may not be clearly articulated by teachers, but it tacitly underpins their curriculum planning and organisation. It is further underpinned by Piagetian notions of children in the primary years needing immediate, first-hand experiences as concrete starting points for discovery and enquiry. These forms of learning, with their roots in the ideas of Rousseau, Dewey and Kilpatrick are intrinsic to topic or project work as originally conceived. However, in practice, much topic work in the 1970s and 1980s was seen as a vehicle for the practice of basic skills.

Topic work has been criticised by HMI (e.g. DES, 1978) for comprising too much low-level copying from texts, rather than the development of enquiry and cognitive skills. The original notions of enquiry were too often replaced by 'finding out' from books. Note-taking skills, which would have enabled some selection of relevant material from texts, were not always taught. If assessment of topic work was problematic, its low status compared to 'the basics' of reading, writing and maths meant that teachers could safely give assessment of topic work a low priority.

Teaching through topics, particularly the tried and tested topics popularised and sanctioned by Plowden (Central Advisory Council for Education, 1967), seemed to provide a flexible solution to difficult problems of curriculum organisation and planning. For teachers faced with mixed-ability classes and wide variations in motivation, topic work has often been a method of curriculum organisation: '...wherein subject boundaries and differences in levels can be blurred, where it is still legitimate to assign different tasks to children of different abilities and where all can be deemed to finish work at the same time ready to move on to the next project' (Eggleston, 1980).

Integration by organisation

The next form or method is integration by organisation. This was particularly common during the 1970s, 1980s and early 1990s. The idea is that the curriculum is integrated because a range of different activities are happening simultaneously in one lesson, sometimes called multi-curriculum focus, or in some forms, the integrated day. In the ORACLE studies (Galton et al., 1980), the authors labelled one teaching style 'rotating changers' because the children rotated around different activities in a one or one or two-teacher base, sometimes changing on a signal from the teacher such as a bell. The advantages of such organisation were supposedly greater freedom for the children, but often, since the activities were teacher chosen, what happened was that children moved on to another activity before they were ready. The subjects were not integrated except in that they were happening at the same time; so whether or not this is true integration is debatable.

Integration by concept

The next form is integration by concept. Concepts are so fundamental to learning that some consideration of this idea is important. All subjects have their concepts: some are major over-arching ones such as, for example, energy and power in science, tone and line in art, pitch and melody in music, and cause and effect in history. Each subject discipline also has its second or third order concepts (Dean, 1995), for example, oxygen in science or the Church in history. Such concepts need teaching, for children may have a concept of a church as that building on the corner of the road on the way to school, or a place of worship on Sundays, whereas the teacher working through the Tudors with a Key Stage 2 class would need to teach the concept of the Church as an abstract idea; a large, powerful organisation, not located in any specific building. Such an understanding would be essential for children to read with full understanding one of the many topic books available on the Tudors. To take a practical example: time is a difficult concept in both history and mathematics. Lessons that aim to increase children's understanding of time can be taught in both subjects. This can be done at a simple level by work on sequencing and chronology. At a more sophisticated level, a numberline with BC and AD on it would both reinforce work on positive and negative numbers and use this analogy to help teach the idea of counting backwards for years BC. To teach the concepts of urbanisation and change in both history and geography, mapwork can be used, with children identifying similarities and differences between the same places, particularly of the numbers of buildings. Maps, more usually associated with geography, can act as the representation of a difficult, abstract concept in each subject.

Integration by skill or process

Some skills and processes are common to a number of subjects. For example, sequencing is found in various guises in maths, English or language work, history, PE, dance and music. Observation is common to art, science, history, geography and design technology. In particular, developing visual literacy is of fundamental importance in art and history. Comparing and contrasting are used in a number of subject areas. Reasoning is a skill necessary to maths, science, geography and history. Hypothesising is integral to science, geography and history. Enquiry of different forms of evidence is an essential part of science, history and geography; interpretation of the evidence is also fundamental to all three of these subjects. It is also part of our understanding of stories and books encountered in English, but used in various ways across the curriculum, including religious education. Synthesis of a number of different elements is found in all the arts, as well as English, in the creation of narratives, and history, where one of the key elements requires children to put together reasoned accounts or arguments using a number of different sources of evidence. Thus it would seem reasonable to decide which skills or processes are to be used and developed in children, and devise activities within a particular subject area, which is maybe the focus of a block of work designed for those skills.

Integration by content

By this I mean putting together two or more subjects where the content fits together, or, to express it differently, one subject acts as the vehicle to teach another. One example I have used successfully in schools is that of music and dance to teach about the particular cultures of the Tudors and the Victorians. Songs and dances from each era and culture were taught, and the children learned or practised, depending on their previous level of attainment, skills of fitting written words to a tune, clapping to a beat, moving to a beat, sequencing of steps and patterns, social skills, and listening skills. However, the songs and dances were also treated as historical evidence: the children were asked what they knew or could find out about these people from their music and dance. The children thought such people had some beautiful tunes that they liked to sing and use to write songs, that they were very fit, that they liked enjoying themselves, and that they were not stupid because quite ordinary people could do difficult dances.

Foundation subjects, in particular, can often be integrated into a literacy strategy. For example, in Music and English the singing of a song ensures practice of musical skills, while the repeated experience of reading the words aids word recognition and familiarity with letter strings.

The role of the teachers

Teachers must creatively interpret the demands of the National Curriculum. They must turn the printed prescription into action, and they will need all their professional skills and knowledge to do so.

What needs to be done is a kind of curriculum mapping of the factual knowledge, concepts, skills, processes and values embedded in the subjects of the National Curriculum. It will then be possible to prioritise what is taught and consider possible forms of integration.

Some concepts, skills and processes cut across the curriculum and are intrinsic to more than one subject. To map these gives a different perspective on the curriculum than that engendered by a subject-focused view. This is not to argue that the distinctive nature of each subject should be lost; this is not intended. Indeed, the distinctiveness of each subject must be understood, before aspects of subjects can be integrated.

A question remains as to who is to do this mapping. I have said it is for the teachers, but some guidance could and should be provided by curriculum experts both within and outside government departments, and by local authority advisory services, such as remain. A combination of external advice and whole-school thinking could be the ideal.

Reading 10.4

An area-based curriculm

Louise Thomas

This reading promotes the development of unique 'school curricula', drawing on resources within local communities. Its origins lie in a concern to ensure that the curriculum is as meaningful and relevant to learners as possible – and in a critique of constraining national requirements from the Royal Society of Arts.

To what extent does the curriculum you teach relate to the communities and local areas in which your pupils live?

Edited from: Thomas, L. (2010) *Engaging the Local: The RSA Area Based Curriculum.* London: Royal Society of Arts, 1–4, 29–30.

The aim of an Area Based Curriculum is to engage a wide range of people and organisations in a local area in providing young people with a curriculum that is meaningful and challenging; that recognises and values their neighbourhoods, communities, families, cultures and wider locality; and equips them to shape their own futures and that of their local area for the better. The aim is not to reduce learning to the local, but rather to diversify the kinds of knowledge that are valued by schools, ensuring that the resources provided by local areas of all kinds are recognised, valued, and engaged in young people's learning.

Many schools feel compelled by national requirements to provide a generic curriculum which fails to engage or enthuse young people, and that misses opportunities to draw on local resources to support young people's learning. Failure to take proper account of the lived worlds and identities of young people can impede the engagement required for achievement.

National policy tends to treat schools and children as without context (unless their context is seen to be problematic in some way), rather than ensuring the system takes proper account of the areas it serves. This construction of certain areas as problematic can be damaging, and risks undermining efforts to reduce the impact of social class, ethnicity and neighbourhood on educational success.

What's the solution?

The RSA sees local areas and the communities within them as crucially important to the education of children. We propose an alternative way of looking at the relationship between areas and the education provided therein: one that values and takes seriously the knowledge, expertise, culture, and ambition of local areas and the people who live and work within them *wherever and whoever they may be*. We argue that every locality is as meaningful as the next and that every child should be given the opportunity to see their lived worlds recognised and valued by their curriculum – across or between the subjects or areas of learning outlined in the National Curriculum.

An Area Based Curriculum would draw on diverse stakeholders (including young people) in a local area to develop a curriculum through which all children might be critically engaged in the realities and richness of their local area. This model could empower pupils and parents as well as other local representatives from outside the school, and secure their investment in local children's education; drawing on local resources to support the curriculum and school.

In order to do this we posit the concept of an Area Based Curriculum: a curriculum that challenges our usual way of seeing local areas in terms of:

- The people: who is or can be involved in education
- The places: where learning happens, and what places have educational value
- The cultures and knowledge: what is worth knowing, and who constructs and holds this knowledge.

Development and implementation of an Area Based Curriculum is by no means easy, but there is a large amount of evidence that supports a range of positive outcomes that could be attained through this work.

We propose a way forward underpinned by the below key principles.

1 There is not a single, uniform model that can be applied across areas. Any local area should develop and own its own curriculum designed to address the specific history, socio-economic context, needs and resources of the locality.

2 An approach to local areas that starts by mapping the resources, opportunities and expertise already held within an area, and the 'lived worlds' of the young people in the area

3 Curriculum co-developed in collaborative and equal partnerships between schools, and community partners (organisations, groups, or individuals), supported by a charter of principles

4 The engagement of young people as partners in curriculum development, and an insistence on ensuring the involvement of those young people least engaged in school

5 Provision of support for curriculum design and partnership skills, and opportunities for the development of activist professionalism in teachers and community practitioners

6 Monitoring of experiences and indicators of engagement and achievement among pupils learning from the Area Based Curriculum.

Although we propose principles, such as the above, as a basis for moving forward, we approach this work in a spirit of enquiry. We thus also pose a range of questions that may be answered through practical attempts to implement Area Based Curricula.

- What structures, policies, protocols and systems (e.g. around CRB checks, risk assessments) need to be or can be changed at a local level to facilitate and enable the involvement of a wider range of people in the enactment of an Area Based Curriculum?

- Can mutual and collaborative partnerships be established between school and curriculum partners through a focus on mutual enquiry?

- What can local authorities and decision makers do to make it easier for students to learn outside the classroom?

- What structures might be best to ensure that learning opportunities and resources in localities are recognized, used and shared by schools?

- How do we develop a framework for deciding between local resources and those farther afield?

- How might assumptions about what local, regional, national and global mean, and how they are valued, be challenged and critiqued by practitioners, partners and students?

- What can Local Authorities and networks of stakeholders and schools do to support curriculum innovation in a context of national accountability?

- How can local contexts be engaged to make learning exciting and meaningful even for the traditionally marginalized, without losing equal access to a national entitlement for all children?

- Can we ensure that all children are able to construct their own pathways to success through enabling them to position themselves critically with respect to their local context and their national and global position?

Education is one of the most situated of all public services, and yet schools still struggle to make use of the vast resources afforded by local areas. Many of those local areas are treated by policy makers and schools alike as problems that it would be better to remove children from, rather than as real places of value, with real resources to offer. We assert local communities have the means to be more fully engaged with the education of the children that live there, and that this engagement will benefit pupils and schools.

Reading 10.5

Skills for 3 to 19-year-olds
Welsh Assembly Government

This publication is part of the 'revised, more learner-centred and skills-focused curriculum' which was implemented in Wales from September 2008. It illustrates government guidance about continuity and progression in thinking, communication, ICT and number for learners from 3 to 19 and beyond. Government policies in particular countries do change from time to time – but the characteristics of learners and of learning stay much the same.

How do policies and practices in your school compare with the advice offered below?

Edited from: Welsh Assembly Government (2008) *Skills Framework for 3 to 19-year-olds in Wales.* Cardiff: Welsh Assembly Government, 2–22.

The Education Reform Act of 1988 set out the requirements for a balanced and broadly based curriculum which: *'prepares… pupils for the opportunities, responsibilities and experiences of adult life.'*

There is, however, strong consensus in schools that subject Orders cannot alone adequately fulfil this requirement since many emphasise detailed subject knowledge rather than skills development. Whilst it is important to retain a common entitlement, there is also a need to offer different pathways through learning in order to suit the aptitudes and interests of learners and to meet the requirements of employers and others.

These requirements are outlined in the summary report of the *Future Skills Wales 2003 Generic Skills Survey* that states:

'Of the employers reporting skills gaps, lack of IT skills is the most common problem, followed by communication skills… showing initiative, problem solving and ability to learn.' *(Future Skills Wales, 2003)*

In the publication, *Excellent Schools*, Estyn had already recognised this situation and stated that:

'Schools will need to devote attention to developing attitudes to learning – affecting the disposition of learners and developing their learning skills – as well as to delivering formal instruction.' *(Estyn, 2002)*

These comments were reflected by ACCAC in its advice, *Review of the school curriculum and assessment arrangements 5–16* (2004), where there is a recommendation that:

'The National Curriculum Orders are revised to develop a learner-centred, skills-focused curriculum that is relevant to the 21st century and inclusive of all learners. The aim should be for the revised curriculum to be first taught in September 2008.'

The advice also suggests that:

> 'The Welsh Assembly Government should consider, as a long-term goal, the vision of a radically revised curriculum that is more overtly learner-centred and skills-focused, and not necessarily subject-based.'

ACCAC concluded that a revised curriculum should have a clear focus on the needs of learners and the process of learning, accompanied by fuller attention to the development and application of skills. The goal should be to develop a curriculum with appropriate learning activities that:

- focuses on and meets learners' needs
- is inclusive and provides equality of opportunity
- equips learners with transferable skills
- supports bilingualism
- is relevant, challenging, interesting and enjoyable for all learners
- transforms learning to produce resourceful, resilient and reflective lifelong learners
- is achievable and adequately resourced.

If learning can be personalised to meet the needs of individuals, their education will be correspondingly more successful and enduring. Hence the current commitment to focus on the learner in the revised curriculum.

Developing thinking across the curriculum

Developing thinking can be defined as developing patterns of ideas that help learners acquire deeper understanding and enable them to explore and make sense of their world. It refers to processes of thinking that we have defined as plan, develop and reflect. These processes enable learners to think creatively and critically to plan their work, carry out tasks, analyse and evaluate their findings, and to reflect on their learning, making links within and outside their formal learning environment. Although we are born with a capability to think, there is ample evidence that we can learn to think more effectively.

It could be said that, in the past, the process of learning has been taken for granted and has at times seemed mysterious. As evidence from research and practice has been increasingly aligned and interwoven, a number of barriers have been overcome. The most notable have been in the fields of developing thinking and assessment for learning. Both developing thinking and assessment for learning rely on basic principles of pedagogy such as questioning technique and articulating strategies.

Developing communication across the curriculum

The communication section of the framework leads on from much of the work done over the past few years on developing literacy across the curriculum. It links elements from the proposals for Language, Literacy and Communication Skills and Welsh Language Development in the Foundation Phase, levels for early literacy, the national curriculum Orders for Welsh, Welsh second language, English and modern foreign languages, and the Key Skills qualification, also called Communication. Communication requirements aim to support bilingual and multilingual development. Indeed, language skills learned in one language should support the development of knowledge and skills in another.

Developing communication should take place across the whole curriculum and should cover four elements relating to oracy, reading, writing and wider communication skills. Communication is taken to mean all forms of communication, not only that which depends on developed, unimpaired speech and hearing. The use of the word 'talk' in relation to oracy, therefore refers to any kind of communication made by a speaker at an early stage of development. Wider communication skills include non-verbal communication of all kinds – including gesture, mime, signing – and the expression of ideas and emotions through other mediums such as music and art.

Developing ICT across the curriculum

As with the sections for communication and number, the ICT section of the framework leads on from much of the work done on developing ICT across the curriculum in recent years. It sets out six stages of progression in ICT capability and brings together skills from the *Information and Communication Technology in the National Curriculum for Wales* Order and the ICT Key Skills requirements.

The framework has two strands:

- finding and developing information and ideas
- creating and presenting information and ideas.

The first strand is about searching for information for specific purposes, and bringing together or processing that information in different forms to develop new information, which could be used to inform judgements and help make decisions. The second strand maps capability in using ICT to communicate ideas, thoughts and intentions, selecting appropriate ways of giving information with the intended recipient or audience in mind.

The main indicators of progression in ICT capability are:

- a developing sense of purpose and audience for the work
- increasing competence and sophistication in the creative use of software functions
- the gradual change from using given ICT resources to choosing and selecting resources to suit the task and purpose.

Developing number across the curriculum

The section for developing number across the curriculum leads on from much of the work done over the last few years on developing numeracy across the curriculum, most of which was focused on Key Stage 2 and Key Stage 3. There has been much discussion over the past twenty years or so about what numeracy is, but there is general agreement that it involves more than just calculating correctly; it also involves 'the ability to use number correctly and appropriately across a wide range of situations and contexts. This includes using number and graphical techniques to represent, interpret and analyse data as well as, for example, measuring, saving and spending, describing and comparing properties of shapes' (ACCAC, 2003).

Guidance in the Framework is intended to be as inclusive as possible. For this reason, the title was chosen to be 'number' rather than 'numeracy' in order to be equally valid for the youngest and oldest learners, as well as those with additional learning needs. Number skills can be applied at all ages in different situations across the curriculum, as appropriate to learners' abilities, achievements and stages of development, contributing to a deeper understanding of subject knowledge.

Reading 10.6

Progression and differentiation

Anthony Haynes

This reading offers insights on the significance of progression and differentiation for curriculum planning and classroom practice. It concludes with a refreshing acknowledgement of the challenge of achieving differentiation in classrooms and a realistic appreciation of the potential for improvement as skills and expertise develop with experience.

Acknowledging its difficulty, do you envisage providing progression and differentiation as a positive professional challenge?

Edited from: Haynes, A. (2010) *The Complete Guide to Lesson Planning and Preparation.* London: Continuum, 135–47.

The planning and preparation stage of teaching could be thought of in terms of a building. First we put in place the four cornerstones – our understanding of:

- Educational aims
- The needs of stakeholders, especially pupils
- The context in which we are teaching
- The cognitive structure of what we teach.

These cornerstones both delimit and support what we do. Next we construct the first storey – the curriculum. This provides the basis on which we can add the second storey, medium term planning and the third – short-term planning, including three rooms of particular importance: time, space and language.

Now we need to put a roof on the building. This entails putting two concepts into place: (a) progression and (b) differentiation. I figure these in terms of the building's roof because they are over-arching concepts. They apply throughout and across the curriculum, in every class at every stage.

To understand these two concepts, it may help now to switch metaphors. Think, for a moment, of teaching as an activity that has two dimensions.

- There is what we might call the vertical axis, namely time. Progression in education is a vertical concept: that is, it is concerned with the order in which we do things and the question of when we do them.
- Differentiation, on the other hand, is a horizontal concept. It is concerned with differences, at any particular stage in the curriculum – differences between pupils, differences in the provision we make for them and, crucially, the relationship between these two set of differences.

Progression

In order to decide how to sequence the curriculum, we need to examine it from the point of view of the learner. The question that matters is not, 'What do we want teach when?' but rather, 'What would make sense to the learners and help them to learn?' How can we help them to move on from one thing to another, both onwards and upwards, building as they do so on previous learning?

To do this, we need to look both forwards and backwards in the curriculum. For a moment, let's take the example of English teaching in secondary schools. Suppose we want pupils in one year group to be able to compare characters from two different stories. This poses two challenges: they have not only to understand each of the characters, but also to organize their ideas within a comparative structure (e.g. they may need to learn how to employ phrases such as 'The main similarity' or 'In contrast'). In this case it may well help if at a previous stage in the curriculum the pupils have had some experience of comparative study based on simpler material – a couple of short articles, for example. Thus we might plan backwards, as it were, by deciding to include such an exercise in the scheme of work for the preceding term. And we can plan forwards too. If, to continue our example, pupils complete a comparative study of two characters from different stories now, what could they move on to later? Perhaps a comparative study of the stories as a whole, including more characters or other aspects such as plot? Perhaps a comparative study of two longer texts?

As always, it helps to integrate our thinking here with our model of the curriculum. That is, it helps to think through the potential continuities not only in terms of subject matter (perhaps the most obvious type), but also in terms of cognitive structure and modes of learning.

Differentiation

Differentiation is the process of adapting educational activity to suit the diverse needs and characteristics of the learners. The aim of course, is to optimize the learning of each pupil. That aim is very easy to state, but difficult to achieve in practice.

Essentially, there are three ways of proceeding.

First, one may differentiate by outcome. The teacher may set the same task for all pupils, who might then produce very different outcomes. That isn't necessarily a bad thing. For example, in art each pupil may be asked to produce a collage from a certain selection of materials. The results may differ wildly. Well, differences in personal style are one of the things that make art fun. The results may differ in level of achievement too (some may be more inventive, composed, etc. than others). That too is not necessarily a problem. It is useful for assessment purposes (this is, after all, how examinations commonly work). And it may be useful developmentally too: the question would be how much the task had done to help each pupil's collage-making abilities develop.

But although differentiation by outcome isn't necessarily a problem, it can be. If some pupils are set a task that is beyond them and they simply flail and fail, that is no good to anyone. The pupils don't develop and they become dispirited. It isn't even very useful for the purposes of assessment. (After all, if you were to set a degree-level Mathematics paper to the population at large, most people would score zero – which would reveal nothing.) To rely willy-nilly on differentiation by outcome is less than professional.

The second way to differentiate is by task. That is, one sets different tasks to different pupils based on one's baseline assessment of them. This method clearly has one advantage: it can help the teacher to ensure that each pupil is working in what psychologists call the Zone of Proximal Development (ZPD). 'ZPD' refers to that area of learning that takes pupils beyond what they already know, but within achievable limits.

There are, however, disadvantages to differentiating by task. The main problem is that the success of the method depends on the matching of task to pupil, which in turn depends on the accuracy of the teacher's judgement and the baseline assessment on which it is based. If the selection is poor, the classroom will be full of bored or dispirited pupils.

A third way to differentiate is by support. That is, one can vary the level and means of support that pupils receive. For example, a teacher might set a task such as practising their tennis serves. Some pupils might be able to do that unaided (or by aiding each other). They might know what a good serve is supposed to be like and which parts of their own serves they need to work on. Others might have little or no idea what to do. They would need to receive some additional support, at least to get them underway.

Here educators sometimes use the analogy of scaffolding. Asking pupils to complete a task can be like asking them to climb an object a tree, say. Some might be able to climb without any scaffolding. Some might need scaffolding to support them throughout. Others might need some at first but then find they can do without.

These, then – differentiation by outcome, by task and by support – are three main ways to differentiate. In most contexts the teacher will probably need to use each of the three at some point.

Let me finish with some reflections on my own experience. Differentiation is an issue that has concerned me a great deal: the more I've thought about teaching, the more it has figured – and the more aware I've become of how my own practice has fallen short. But I have also realized that, in this area at least, perfectionism probably isn't a helpful frame of mind. I suggest that even if you could decide what a perfectly differentiated lesson for your class might be, you probably couldn't provide it. If, like me, you find that perfection is beyond you, my suggestion is rather that you aim for proficiency. I've found in any case that often the first few steps in differentiation can carry you quite a long way – not least because when pupils sense you making those steps they are more likely to try to meet you half way.

When I began teaching I certainly approached lesson planning in terms of 'one size fits all.' I then gradually moved into a second phase, where typically I would start by designing a 'one size fits all' lesson and then work out ways of differentiating for particular pupils or groups. Now, I tend to use a more flexible approach. I first ask myself, 'What are we trying to do here?' and then try to think of a range of ways of getting there. I like this kind of creative approach, but I don't think I could have worked like that when starting out. In teaching, it seems to me, one can't do everything at once.

Reading 10.7

Personalised pedagogies for the future
Teaching and Learning in 2020 Review Group

> Her Majesty's Chief Inspector of Schools, Christine Gilbert, led a group to review innovative UK practice and international evidence and to make recommendations for effective teaching and learning in the classrooms and schools of the future. As can be seen in this reading, their report included a vision of new forms of school experience which combine use of data, respect for learner agency, excellent pedagogies, engaging curricula and assessment to support learning processes. The ideas and practices suggested below echo TLRP's principles and the international evidence rehearsed in the readings of Chapter 4.
>
> What forms of pedagogy do you believe will be essential as the twenty-first century develops?
>
> *Edited from:* Teaching and Learning in 2020 Review Group (2006) *2020 Vision.* Nottingham: Department for Education and Skills (DfES) Publications, 13–5.

Any strategy for personalising learning must focus on improving the consistency of teaching to meet learners' needs as effectively as possible. This means strengthening the relationship between learning and teaching through:

- using data and assessment information rigorously, together with knowledge of factors that might influence pupils' progress, to shape teaching and assess its impact

- matching teaching to the different and developing abilities of pupils, focused on breaking down barriers to learning and progress and underpinned by high expectations

- regular monitoring of progress and rapid responses at the point at which pupils begin to fall behind, so that there is a relentless focus on pupils 'keeping up'

- dialogue between teachers and pupils, encouraging pupils to explore their ideas through talk, to ask and answer questions, to listen to their teachers and peers, to build on the ideas of others and to reflect on what they have learnt

- collaborative relationships which encourage and enable all pupils to participate and which develop pupils' skills of working independently and in groups, enabling teachers and pupils to move learning forward together

- judicious use of whole-class teaching, as well as one-to-one, paired and group work

- using more open-ended tasks with pupils, either individually or in groups, based on specific projects or areas of inquiry

- developing pupils' appetite for and attitude to lifelong learning.

Securing these will benefit all children and young people and help them to become better learners. They are at the heart of effective learning and teaching. However, in a MORI survey of 11–16 year olds (Greany and Rodd, 2004), many pupils reported that their experience of school is still marked by long periods of time listening to teachers or copying from the board or a book. Personalising learning involves changing – and challenging – such routines.

The following are likely to be particularly beneficial for lower attaining pupils and so contribute to closing attainment gaps:

- a broad and rich curriculum that takes account of prior learning and experiences and helps pupils to develop the full range of knowledge, skills, understanding and attitudes

- attention to appropriate curriculum materials – for example, engaging boys in reading through providing non-fiction as well as fiction

- securing expected levels and good progress for all pupils in speaking, listening, reading and writing, particularly in the early stages of learning

- strategies that enable pupils to see clearly how they are progressing, such as setting and reviewing individual targets in lessons, drawing attention to small steps in learning, and frequent, task-based feedback (HMI, 2003).

- an explicit focus on higher order thinking skills and learning how to learn, using group work, including academic peer tutoring, paired and cooperative learning (Ellis et al., 1994; McKinstery et al., 2003)

- study support and out-of-classroom learning that give pupils from disadvantaged backgrounds additional access to and support for learning (Macbeath et al., 2003).

In personalising learning, teachers use their understanding of achievement data and other information about their pupils to benefit particular groups, for example, the gifted and talented, by matching teaching and opportunities for learning more accurately to their needs. When this is done in a structured and consistent way across the school, within a culture of mutual respect, the experience of those schools that are already engaged in personalising learning suggests that it leads to establishing good learning behaviours (Steer, 2005).

Personalising learning is equally relevant to primary schools and secondary schools, although it will look quite different as children develop and move through their own 'learning journey'. Primary and secondary schools face specific challenges in personal-ising learning, related to their different organizational structures and the age and maturity of their learners. In the early years and in primary schools, while children can be – and in many schools are – engaged as partners in learning, teachers and parents have a far greater role in determining what and how they learn, with an emphasis on developing literacy and numeracy alongside positive attitudes to learning, and social skills. The structures of primary schools tend to make it easier for teachers and support staff to gain a rounded picture of children's learning needs, although continuity as children move through the school remains important.

The breadth and depth of learning and the number of teachers with whom pupils have contact increase as they enter secondary school and parents may find it more difficult to engage with their children's learning. It is at this stage that, for some pupils, the problem of disengagement becomes most acute. The extent to which all pupils are able to make choices about their learning increases during the 14–19 phase and also has an impact.

Primary schools to date have not been drawn into discussions about putting personalising learning into practice to the same extent as secondary schools. This is at least in part a result of the view that the challenge of personalising learning is greater in secondary schools. However, many of its principles are seen in the most effective practice in good primary schools. The introduction of the Early Years Foundation Stage will also provide a solid basis for later learning (Rose, 2006).

We recommend that:

all schools should reflect a commitment to personalising learning and teaching in their policies and plans, indicating the particular strategies the school is exploring to fulfil that commitment for all children. As part of the self-evaluation process, schools should consider and report how effectively this commitment is being fulfilled.

Pedagogy

How can we develop effective strategies?

This chapter begins with a reading from Bruner (11.1) which encourages us to reflect on how our culture influences our intuitions about learning, learners and teaching. In a sense, this reading is a warning. To be effective, we need to deepen our thinking about learning and pedagogy – to move beyond the taken-for-granted.

A Teaching Council takes this forward, in Reading 11.2, to stake out the rationale for teacher professionalism and the role of pedagogic expertise. It is seen as an essential foundation.

And yet there is still a struggle. Why is it that the role of pedagogy is not fully understood in our societies, as it is in many other parts of the world? Simon's answer (11.3) provides an historical explanation in terms of core beliefs. Put crudely, if abilities are relatively fixed, then teaching is not of great consequence. But if we believe that everyone has potential, then pedagogic skill is essential to provide opportunities. And here perhaps lie deep-seated beliefs with ramifications for policies on teacher education and professional development. Simon's recommendation to build a science of pedagogy on learning processes that we share in common was the source of TLRP's commitment to establish generic 'principles' for effective teaching and learning (see Chapter 4).

Tharp and Gallimore (11.4) summarise the Vygtskian underpinning of much modern teaching with their concept of learning as 'assisted performance'. Their four-stage model is worthy of careful study and reflection. For instance, can you apply it to aspects of your own learning, and what was the role of the teaching of 'more capable others' in that?

Max van Manen (11.5) reverses the gaze to consider student perspectives on pedagogy. How do pupils experience different teachers and classroom practices?

Finally, Mercer and Littleton (11.6) offer an analysis of ways in which pupils talk and think together. Their typology of such talk as disputational, cumulative or exploratory is a useful device for evaluating the nature of joint talk in a classroom. As with earlier discussion of direct, interactive instruction (8.7), capability to promote such dialogue is an important element of a teacher's repertoire.

The associated chapter of *Reflective Teaching in Schools* makes a particular feature of case studies in which teachers put pedagogic principles into practice. For example, the art, craft and science of classroom pedagogy illustrated through a case, before providing information on key educationalists who have contributed to thinking on pedagogy. There is a section on building from learners' prior knowledge and a more elaborate one on the development of pedagogic repertoire for whole-class, group and individual teaching. Progression through a series of lessons is also discussed and illustrated.

At the end of the chapter, 'Key Readings' are suggested – and these can be amplified as usual by those on *reflectiveteaching.co.uk*. On the website, there are also many additional 'Reflective Activities' and other resources. The section on 'Deepening Expertise' is particularly relevant to the development of pedagogy.

Reading 11.1

Folk pedagogy

Jerome Bruner

> Bruner, from the perspective of an educational psychologist and strongly influenced by Vygotsky (see **Reading 2.3**), is interested in how theories of the mind affect teachers' practice. He argues that teachers who theorise about learning need to take into account intuitive beliefs (which he terms 'folk pedagogy') because such beliefs may be deeply ingrained. However, teachers will also seek to change them in the light of their developing understanding of theories of mind. In this extract, he sets out why it matters that teachers understand how their perceptions of learners' minds affect how they teach.
>
> How would you characterise your 'folk pedagogies', and how do these relate to your professional understanding of teaching and learning?
>
> *Edited from:* Bruner, J. S. (1996) *The Culture of Education.* Cambridge, MA: Harvard University Press, 45–50.

Our interactions with others are deeply affected by everyday, intuitive theories about how other minds work. These theories are omnipresent but are rarely made explicit. Such lay theories are referred to by the rather condescending name of *folk psychology*. Folk psychologies reflect certain 'wired-in' human tendencies (like seeing people normally as operating under their own control), but they also reflect some deeply ingrained cultural beliefs about 'the mind'. Not only is folk psychology preoccupied with how the mind works here and now, it is also equipped with notions about how the child's mind learns and even what makes it grow. Just as we are steered in ordinary interaction by our folk psychology, so we are steered in the activity of helping children learn about the world by notions of *folk pedagogy*. Watch any mother, any teacher, even any babysitter with a child and you'll be struck by how much of what they do is steered by notions of 'what children's minds are like and how to help them learn', even though they may not be able to verbalize their pedagogical principles.

From this work on folk psychology and folk pedagogy has grown a new, perhaps even a revolutionary insight. It is this: in theorizing about the practice of education in the classroom (or any other setting, for that matter), you had better take into account the folk theories that those engaged in teaching and learning already have. For any innovations that you, as a 'proper' pedagogical theorist, may wish to introduce will have to compete with, replace, or otherwise modify the folk theories that already guide both teachers and pupils. For example, if you are convinced that the best learning occurs when the teacher helps lead the pupil to discover generalizations on her own, you are likely to run into an established cultural belief that a teacher is an authority who is supposed to *tell* the child what the general case it, while the child should be occupying herself with memorizing the particulars. And if you study how most classrooms are conducted, you will often find that most of the teacher's questions to pupils are about particulars that can be answered in a few words or even by 'yes' or 'no.' So your introduction of an innovation in teaching will necessarily involve changing the folk psychological and folk pedagogical theories of teachers – and, to a surprising extent, of pupils as well.

Teaching, in a word, is inevitably based on notions about the nature of the learner's mind. Beliefs and assumptions about teaching, whether in a school or in any other context, are a direct reflection of the belief and assumption the teacher holds about the learner. Of course, like most deep truths, this one is already well known. Teachers have always tried to adjust their teaching to the backgrounds, abilities, styles, and interests of the children they teach. This is important, but it is not quite what we are after. Our purpose, rather, is to explore more general ways in which learners' minds are conventionally thought about, and pedagogic practices that follow from these ways of thinking about mind. Nor will we stop there, for we also want to offer some reflections of 'consciousness raising' in this setting: what can be accomplished by getting teachers (and students) to think *explicitly* about their folk psychological assumptions, in order to bring them out of the shadows of tacit knowledge.

To say only that human beings understand other minds and try to teach the incompetent, is to overlook the varied ways in which teaching occurs in different cultures. The variety is stunning. We need to know much more about this diversity if we are to appreciate the relation between folk psychology and folk pedagogy in different cultural settings.

Understanding this relationship becomes particularly urgent in addressing issues of educational reform. For once we recognize that a teacher's conception of a learner shapes the instruction he or she employs, then equipping teachers (or parents) with the best available theory of the child's mind becomes crucial. And in the process of doing that, we also need to provide teachers with some insight about their own folk theories that guide their teaching.

Folk pedagogies, for example, reflect a variety of assumptions about children: they may be seen as wilful and needing correction; as innocent and to be protected from a vulgar society; as needing skills to be developed only through practice; as empty vessels to be filled with knowledge that only adults can provide; as egocentric and in need of socialization. Folk beliefs of this kind, whether expressed by laypeople or by 'experts', badly want some 'deconstructing' if their implications are to be appreciated. For whether these views are 'right' or not, their impact on teaching activities can be enormous.

A culturally oriented cognitive psychology does not dismiss folk psychology as mere superstition, something only for the anthropological connoisseur of quaint folkways. I have long argued that explaining what children *do* is not enough; the new agenda is to determine what they *think* they are doing and what their reasons are for doing it. Like new work on children's theories of mind, a cultural approach emphasizes that the child only gradually comes to appreciate that she is acting not directly *on* 'the world' but on beliefs she holds *about* that world. This crucial shift from naive realism to an understanding of the role of beliefs, occurring in the early school years, is probably never complete. But once it starts, there is often a corresponding shift in what teachers can do to help children. With the shift, for example, children can take on more responsibilities for their own learning and thinking. They can begin to 'think about their thinking' as well as about 'the world'.

Advances in how we go about understanding children's minds are, then, a prerequisite to any improvement in pedagogy.

Reading 11.2

What is pedagogy and why is it important?
The General Teaching Council for England

> Pedagogy, according to Alexander (2000), combines both the act of teaching and its rationale. In Europe, this conceptualisation goes back to at least the 1630s when Comenius published his *Didactica Magna*, and it remains well established today. Understanding has been more limited in some parts of the UK, but is changing rapidly – and this reading explains why. To move forward, it is essential to establish beneficial synergies between theory and practice, research and application. The establishment of Teaching Schools in England is one example of this, and TLRP's principles are another.
>
> Do you agree that, to be a really effective teacher, it is necessary to think pedagogically?
>
> *Edited from:* GTCE (2010) 'Introduction' in Pollard, A. (ed.) *Professionalism and Pedagogy: A Contemporary Opportunity*. London: TLRP, 4–6.

International evidence is clear that the single most significant means of improving the performance of national educational systems is through excellent teaching (e.g. Barber and Mourshed, 2007; OECD, 2005). The quality of pedagogy, of what teachers actually do, is thus firmly on the contemporary agenda. Since the UK already has a qualified and trained teaching workforce, relatively modest investment in supporting teachers' professionalism could be very cost-effective. There is both a need and an excellent opportunity for the profession to demonstrate and strengthen its expertise and to improve its status in the public mind.

The relative lack of reference to pedagogy in educational discussion in the UK, compared with practice in many other successful countries, has been the focus of academic debate for the best part of thirty years. The concern was first raised by Brian Simon's 1981 paper, Why no pedagogy in England? (see Reading 11.3).

In a world-class educational workforce – Finland might be used as an example – teachers are the ones who initiate discussions about pedagogy, and then evaluate and critique the ideas they develop. This 'pedagogic discourse' aspires to be explicitly grounded in the scrutiny of ideas, theories, ethical values and empirical evidence. It goes well beyond simplified prescription, for instance of 'what works', and supersedes reliance on centrally-imposed performance targets. In their place is greater trust in teachers' capacity for self-improvement as an inherent element of their professional identity. However, this trust has to be earned – hence the focus on the nature of pedagogic expertise.

Teaching is a professional activity underpinned by qualifications, standards and accountabilities. It is characterised by complex specialist knowledge and expertise-in-action. In liberal democratic societies, it also embodies particular kinds of values, to do with furthering individual and social development, fulfilment and emancipation.

'Pedagogy' is the practice of teaching framed and informed by a shared and structured body of knowledge. This knowledge comprises experience, evidence, understanding moral purpose and shared transparent values. It is by virtue of progressively acquiring such knowledge and mastering the expertise – through initial training, continuing development, reflection and classroom inquiry and regulated practice – that teachers are entitled to be treated as professionals. Teachers should be able and willing to scrutinise and evaluate their own and others' practice in the light of relevant theories, values and evidence. They should be able to make professional judgements which go beyond pragmatic constraints and ideological concerns, and which can be explained and defended.

Furthermore, pedagogy is impoverished if it is disconnected from the capacity and responsibility to engage in curriculum development and to deploy a range of appropriate assessment methodologies. Indeed, in most European countries, these elements are treated as a whole, enabling a broad conception of pedagogy. Teachers should be knowledgeable about curriculum and assessment principles as a part of their pedagogical expertise. To promote the further development of professional expertise in the UK, we have included these dimensions, and the interrelationships between them, in the conceptual framework later in the Commentary.

Pedagogic expertise can be thought of as a combination of science, craft and art.

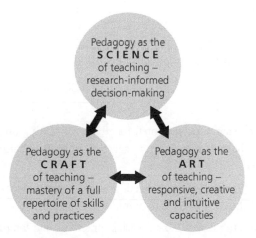

Figure 11.2.1
The science, craft and art of pedagogic expertise

This representation helps us to understand the complementary needs for collectively created knowledge, professional skills and personal capacities. It is also important to remember that all these are grounded in ethical principles and moral commitment – teaching is never simply an instrumental activity, a question just of technique.

One of the challenges for pedagogical discourse is to distinguish between what is known in a scientific sense of being explicit, cumulative and generalisable, and what are the irreducibly intuitive and creative elements of teaching.

It is generally accepted now that good teaching requires strategic decisions informed by evidence. But it also requires a large number of implicit and often instantaneous judgements and decisions. These are responses to the dynamic situation in the classroom, often shaped by the 'community of practice' to which the teacher belongs. They are also expressions of each teacher's individual relationship with his or her pupils: how s/he generates a positive classroom climate or takes advantage of unexpected teaching and learning opportunities. This is the 'craft' and the 'art' of teaching.

And we all need to acknowledge this paradox of teaching – that the more expert a teacher becomes, the more his or her expertise is manifested in sensitivity to contexts and situations, in imaginative judgements in-the-moment sourced from tacit knowledge. The importance of these forms of expertise is often underestimated. Indeed, they often become so embedded, instinctive and taken-for-granted that they are barely recognised.

Such behaviours need to be analysed and discussed, so that the profession can become more confident about its expert practice, its professionalism. The development of a conceptual framework for the discussion of pedagogy is a contribution to that goal (see Chapter 16 of *Reflective Teaching in Schools*).

The GTCE believes that teaching should be based on the development of a pedagogic discourse that arises from teachers sharing and scrutinising the practices and kinds of knowledge which they build, and the values in which these are rooted. The issue is not about theorising about practice since many teachers naturally do this. It is more about whether:

> 'The theories they espouse ... have been justified and developed by being exposed to the critical scrutiny of other practitioners, whether they are based on a consideration of evidence from research...whether they have been interrogated in terms of the values and assumptions on which they are based' *(Furlong, 2000:13)*.

This integration of theory, practice and values into a discourse of pedagogy would mean amongst other things:

- strengthening the shared professional language for talking about teaching, learning and children so that it can stand up to scrutiny in terms of argument, evidence and espoused values;
- developing communities of 'warranted' practice which contribute to the development of this language in dynamic ways; and
- enabling teachers to present their theories, practices and language in more confident and accessible ways.

Reading 11.3

Why no pedagogy in England?

Brian Simon

In his classic paper, Simon explains the history of pedagogic thinking in England and the reasons why, despite early promise, it has not been as influential as elsewhere in Europe. He draws attention to assumptions about learning which became embedded within British culture and which are still in some tension today. Are abilities simply inherited? What is the 'human capacity for learning?'. If one affirms the latter, argues Simon, then a science of pedagogy is essential, and should be focused on learning processes we share in common. This argument is the basis on which TLRP's principles of effective teaching and learning are based (see Chapter 4 of *Reflective Teaching in Schools*).

Do you agree that we share fundamental processes of learning 'in common'?

Edited from: Simon, B. (1981) 'Why no pedagogy in England?' in B. Simon and W. Taylor (eds) *Education in the Eighties: The Central Issues*. London: Batsford, 128–40.

Education, as a subject of enquiry and study, still less as a 'science', has historically had little prestige in this country, having been to all intents and purposes ignored in the most prestigious education institutions. As Matthew Arnold tirelessly pointed out over one hundred years ago, in France, Prussia and elsewhere, the problems of education for the middle class were taken really seriously. In Britain, on the other hand, everything was neglected; a laissez-faire pragmatism predominated (Arnold, 1874). This situation has, to some extent, been perpetuated. The dominant educational institutions of this country have had no concern with theory, its relation to practice, with pedagogy.

But this is only part of the picture. For whilst the public schools expressed a total disregard for pedagogy, in fact a systematic, rational approach was being developed elsewhere.

Alexander Bain's *Education as a Science* was published in 1879, reprinted six times in the 1880s, and a further ten times before 1990. Examination of student-teacher manuals indicates their indebtedness to Bain. The crucial basis for this approach lay in the theory, announced by Bain as fact, that the formation of associations of ideas in the mind was accompanied by new connections, linkages, or 'paths', in the substance of the brain. The process of education, since it consisted in the planned ordering of the child's experiences, must therefore have a necessary effect. This, of course, had been the basis of the theory of human perfectibility characteristic of the Enlightenment. The approach not only posited the educability of the normal child, it stressed the 'plasticity', as Bain put it, of brain functioning and processes. Education then, was concerned with *acquired* capacities and functions. It was about human change and development.

Empirical support for the theory of the formation of new connections in the brain as underlying the acquisition of new associations was available to Bain, particularly from the work of his contemporary, the neuro-psychologist Henry Maudesley. Every sense impression resulting in a 'current of molecular activity' from one part of the brain to another, Maudsely wrote, 'leaves behind it ... some after-effect' or 'modification of the nerve elements concerned in its function'. This physiological process, he claimed, 'is the physical basis of memory', the 'foundation of our mental functions'.

It followed from this approach that, to order education aright in terms of the acquisition of knowledge, two things were necessary. First, to obtain a psychological (and physiological) understanding of the growth of human powers through infancy, childhood and youth; and second, to analyse the content of subject matter in terms of its own inner logic. Together these underlay the determination of the curriculum. But Bain was also closely concerned with motivation, discipline, teacher-pupil relationships, moral education, as well as with the mode of teaching the main curriculum areas. Seeing 'education 'specifically as schooling, he covered in his book almost every relevant aspect of teaching, learning, and classroom organisation.

Of course the theories, and the practices advocated by Bain and the authors of derivative teaching manuals, had their limitations as well as theoretical weaknesses. This goes without saying. But in the 1890s, the approach was serious, systematic and all-embracing. The pedagogy of this specific decade pointed the way to universal education, and was seen as such by its progenitors. What happened? Why was this embryo pedagogy not systematically developed? What went wrong?

One reason was that the social and political context underwent an abrupt change. The development based on Bain's work took place within the *elementary* system with, at the time, a realistic prospect of organic growth. This was the backcloth, the crucial feature, of this movement as a whole. The administrative and legislative events of 1899 to 1904, almost traumatic in their effects, put a stopper on this. It abolished the School Boards, confined elementary education within precise limits, and established a new system of *secondary* schooling parallel to, but quite separate from, the elementary system.

This created a new situation. The social-disciplinary function of elementary education was now especially emphasised and a positive pedagogy based on scientific procedures and understanding and relevant for *all* was no longer seen as appropriate, or required.

However, there now emerged new local authority-controlled systems of secondary education. The more advanced local authorities, determined to extend educational provision, approached this new field with energy and developed considerable pride in the schools systems so created.

It was the establishment and rapid development of this new system of secondary schools which underlay new developments in the theory and practice of education. Thus we find, in the period 1900–1914, a renewed concern to develop a relevant pedagogy and it is this that lies behind the great interest in the work of Herbart and of the Prussian educators who had developed Herbartianism into a system. Once again basing himself on associationism, Herbart set out to explain the process of human acquirements, seeing them as the result of education, of teaching and learning. His ideas were developed and their practical application modified and refined in the work of Rein at the University of Jena and other educators, and found expression in the German schools and thinking from the 1860s.

It was not until the turn of the century however, that Herbart's ideas began to make a serious impact in Britain. By the first decade of the twentieth century, most existing universities were developing and expanding their departments of education and a number of chairs in the subject now existed. These wrote books for teachers either explaining or interpreting Herbart. There was then, a brief new flowering of pedagogy – a serious concern with the theory and practice of education.

The rational foundation for pedagogical theories – for the concept of education as a science – had lain in associationist psychological theories concerning learning. These were espoused by Bain, as we have seen, and also by Herbart and his elaborators. So it was theory and practice based on these ideas which gave rise both to the positive, or optimistic, pedagogics of the 1890s relating to elementary education, and to those of the period 1900–1920 relating to the new system of secondary education.

But it was just at this period that new approaches came to predominate in the field of psychology which either relegated associationism to the background, or denied its significance altogether.

The two major influences were, on the one hand, the rise of philosophic idealism, which denied the material basis of mind and decisively rejected the model of human formation; and, on the other hand, the triumph of Darwinism with its emphasis on heredity.

The demands of the system and the movement of ideas now coincided. In the field of educational theory, psychometry (or mental testing) now established its hegemony which lasted over forty years from the 1920s. The triumph of psychometry tied in with a new stress on individualism after World War I and a kind of reductionist biologism. This spelt the end of pedagogy – its actual death. If education cannot promote cognitive growth, as the psychometrists seemed to aver, its whole purpose or direction was lost.

This, I suggest, is the background to our present discontents. For a combination of social, political and ideological reasons, pedagogy – a scientific basis to the theory and practice of education – has never taken root and flourished in Britain.

For a single decade in the late nineteenth century in the field of elementary education; for a similar short period early this century in secondary education, pedagogic approaches and analyses flowered – though never in the most socially prestigious systems of the public schools and ancient Universities. Each 'system', largely self-contained, developed its own specific educational approach, each written within its narrowly defined field, and each 'appropriate' to its specific social function. In these circumstances the conditions did not exist for the development of an all-embracing, universalised, scientific theory of education relating to the practice of teaching. Nor is it an accident that, in these circumstances, fatalistic ideas preaching the limitation of human powers were in the ascendant.

Education and the technological revolution

We can no longer afford to go on in the old way, muddling through on a largely pragmatic, or historically institutionalised basis, tinkering with this and that. In spite of what must surely be temporary setbacks in the provision of educational facilities, the conditions now exist for a major breakthrough in terms of pedagogy. This statement is made on the basis of two contemporary developments, the one structural and the other theoretical. Of major importance here is the insistent tendency towards unification of the historically determined separate systems of schooling through the transition to comprehensive secondary education. This has been accomplished, in the realm of ideas or theory, by a shift in the concern of educators and psychologists from the static concepts of the child (derived from intelligence testing) towards dynamic and complex theories of child development. Both open new perspectives relating to the grounding of educational theory and practice on science (or on scientific procedures).

A revitalised pedagogy?

What then, are the requirements for a renewal of scientific approaches to the practice of teaching – for a revitalised pedagogy?

First, we can identify two essential conditions without which there can be no pedagogy having a generalised significance or application. The first is recognition of the human capacity for learning. It may seem unnecessary, even ridiculous, to single this out in this connection, but in practice this is not the case. Fundamentally, psychometric theory, as elaborated in the 1930s to 1950s, denied the lability of learning capacity, seeing each individual endowed, as it were, with an engine of a given horse-power which is fixed, unchangeable and measurable in each particular case, irrevocably setting precise and definable limits to achievement (or learning). It was not until this view had been discredited in the eyes of psychologists that serious attention could be given to the analysis and interpretation of the *process* of human learning.

The second condition is the recognition that, in general terms, the process of learning among human beings, is similar across the human species as a whole. As Stones (1979) puts it: 'except in pathological cases, learning capability among individuals is similar', so that, 'it is possible to envisage body of general principles of teaching' that are relevant to 'most individual pupils'. The determination, or identification, of such general principles must comprise the objectives of pedagogical study and research.

One further point must be made at the start. The term 'pedagogy' itself implies structure. It implies the elaboration or definition of specific means adapted to produce the desired effect – such-and-such learning on the part of the child. From the start of the use of the term, pedagogy has been concerned to relate the process of teaching to that of learning on the part of the child. It was this approach that characterised the work of Comenius, Pestalozzi and Herbart, and that, for instance, of Joseph Priestly and the associationist tradition generally.

Both the conditions defined above are today very widely accepted among leading psychologists directly concerned with education and with research into human cognitive development. When Bruner (1972) claimed, in a striking and well-known statement, that 'any subject can be taught to anybody at any age in some form that is both interesting and honest', he was basing himself on a positive assessment of human capacity for learning, and deliberately pointing to the need to link psychology with pedagogy. In an essay aimed at persuading American psychologists of the need to concern themselves with education – to provide assistance in elucidating the learning process for practicing educators – he stressed his central point, 'that development psychology without a theory of pedagogy was as empty an enterprise as a theory of pedagogy that ignored the nature of growth'. 'Man is not a naked ape,' writes Bruner, 'but a culture clothed human being, hopelessly ineffective without the prosthesis provided by culture.' Education itself can be a powerful cultural influence, and educational experiences are ordered and structured to enable people more fully to realise their humanity and powers, to bring about social change – and to create a world according to their felt and recognised objectives. The major problem humanity faces it not the general development of skill and intelligence but devising a society that can use it wisely' (Bruner, 1972: 18, 131, 158).

When writing this, Bruner was clearly concerned with social change, and with the contribution that pedagogical means might make to this, as we must be in Britain in face of the dramatic social challenge that technological change now presents. And in considering the power of education, rightly ordered, to play a central part in this, it may be as well to recall that, while the simplified and certainly over-mechanistic interpretations of the associationist psychologies of the nineteenth century are no longer acceptable in the form, for instance, expressed by Alexander Bain and his predecessors, the concept of learning as a process involving the formation of new connections in the brain and higher nervous systems has in fact not only retained its force, but has been highly developed by neuro-physiologists and psychologists specifically concerned to investigate learning. Amongst these, perhaps the greatest contribution has been made by A. R. Luria in a series of works relevant to teaching, education and human development generally; but perhaps particularly in his work on the role of language in mental development, and in his theory of what he calls 'complex functional systems' underlying learning (Luria, 1962).

It is now generally accepted that in the process of mental development there takes place a profound qualitative reorganisation of human mental activity, and that the basic characteristic of the reorganisation is that elementary, direct activity is replaced by complex functional systems, formed on the basis of the child's communication with adults in the process of learning. These functional systems are of complex construction, and are developed with the close participation of language, which as the basic means of communication with people is simultaneously one of the basic tools in the formation of human mental activity and in the regulation of behaviour. It is through these complex forms of mental activity ... that new features are acquired and begin to develop according to new laws which displace many of the laws which govern the formation of elementary conditioned reflexes in animals. *(1962: 4)*

The work and thinking of both Luria and Bruner (as representative of their respective traditions) point in a similar direction – towards a renewed understanding both of the power of education to effect human change and especially cognitive development, and of the need for the systematisation and structuring of the child's experiences in the process of learning.

The main thrust of my argument is this: that to start from the standpoint of individual differences is to start from the wrong position. To develop effective pedagogic means involves starting from the opposite standpoint, from what children have in common as members of the human species: to establish the general principles of teaching and in the light of these, to determine what modifications of practice are necessary to meet specific individual needs. If all children are to be assisted to learn, to master increasingly complex cognitive tasks, to develop increasingly complex skills and abilities or mental operations, then this is an objective that schools must have in common; their task becomes the deliberate development of such skills and abilities in all their children. And this involves importing a definite structure into the teaching, and so into the learning experiences provided for the pupils. Individual differences only become important, in this context, if the pedagogical means elaborated are found not to be appropriate to particular children (or groups of children) because one or other aspect of their individual development or character. In this situation the requirement becomes that of modifying the pedagogical means so that they become appropriate for all: that is, of applying general principles in specific instances.

Reading 11.4

Teaching as the assistance of performance
Roland Tharp and Ronald Gallimore

This reading is an elaboration of Vygotsky's ideas (see **Reading 2.3**), and sets out with particular clarity a four-stage model of learning in which different types of assistance in performance are characteristic: support from others; from self-regulation; from internalisation; and where performance declines and new learning is necessary.

How does Tharp and Gallimore's four-stage model relate to your own learning? Think, for instance, about how you learned to swim, ride a bicycle or speak a language. And how does it relate to your classroom teaching?

Edited from: Tharp, R. and Gallimore, R. (1988) *Rousing Minds to Life: Teaching, Learning and Schooling in Social Context.* New York: Cambridge University Press, 28–39.

To explain the psychological, we must look not only at the individual but also at the external world in which that individual life has developed. We must examine human existence in its social and historical aspects, not only at its current surface. These social and historical aspects are represented to the child by people who assist and explain, those who participate with the child in shared functioning:

> Any function in the child's cultural development appears twice, or in two planes. First it appears on the social plane, and then on the psychological plane. First it appears between people as an interpsychological category, and then within the child as an intrapsychological category. This is equally true with regard to voluntary attention, logical memory, the formation of concepts, and the development of volition *(Vygotsky, 1978: 163)*.

The process by which the social becomes the psychological is called *internalization*: The individual's 'plane of consciousness' (i.e. higher cognitive processes) is formed in structures that are transmitted to the individual by others in speech, social interaction, and the processes of cooperative activity. Thus, individual consciousness arises from the actions and speech of others.

However, children reorganize and reconstruct these experiences.

Indeed, the child is not merely a passive recipient of adult guidance and assistance; in instructional programs, the active involvement of the child is crucial (Bruner, 1966).

In summary, the cognitive and social development of the child proceeds as an unfolding of potential through the reciprocal influences of child and social environment. Through guided reinvention, higher mental functions that are part of the social and cultural heritage of the child will move from the social plane to the psychological plane, from the socially regulated to the self-regulated. The child, through the regulating actions and speech of others, is brought to engage in independent action and speech. In the resulting interaction, the child performs, through assistance and cooperative activity, at developmental levels quite beyond the individual level of achievement. For skills and functions to develop into internalized, self-regulated capacity, all that is needed is performance, through assisting interaction. Through this process, the child acquires the 'plane of consciousness' of the society and is socialized, acculturated, made human.

Assisted performance defines what a child can do with help, with the support of the environment, of others, and of the self. For Vygotsky, the contrast between assisted performance and unassisted performance identified the fundamental nexus of development and learning that he called the zone of proximal development (ZPD).

The development of any performance capacity in the individual thus represents a changing relationship between self-regulation and social regulation. We present progress through the ZPD in a model of four stages. The model focuses particularly on the relationship between self-control and social control.

Figure 11.4.1
Genesis of performance capacity: progression through the ZPD and beyond

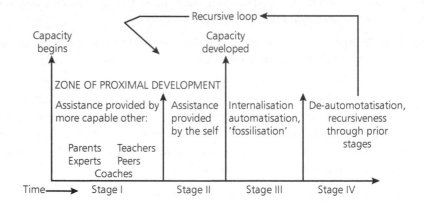

Stage I: Where performance is assisted by more capable others

Before children can function as independent agents, they must rely on adults or more capable peers for outside regulation of task performance. The amount and kind of outside regulation a child requires depend on the child's age and the nature of the task: that is the breadth and progression through the ZPD for the activity at hand.

Such assistance of performance has been described as *scaffolding*, a metaphor first used by Wood, Bruner and Ross (1976) to describe the ideal role of the teacher.

During Stage I, we see a steadily declining plane of adult responsibility for task performance and a reciprocal increase in the learner's proportion of responsibility. This is Bruner's fundamental 'handover principle' – the child who was a spectator is now a participant (Bruner, 1983: 60). The developmental task of Stage I is to transit from other-regulation to self-regulation.

Stage II: Where performance is assisted by the self

If we look carefully at the child's statements during this transition, we see that the child

> has taken over the rules and responsibilities of both participants in the language-game. These responsibilities were formerly divided between the adult and child, but they have now been taken over completely by the child, *(Wertsch 1979: 18)*

Thus, in Stage II, the child carries out a task without assistance from others. However, this does not mean that the performance is fully developed or automatized.

During Stage II, the relationships among language, thought, and action in general undergo profound rearrangements. Control is passed from the adult to the child speaker, but the control function remains with the overt verbalization.

The phenomenon of self-directed speech reflects a development of the most profound significance. According to Vygotsky, and his follower Luria, once children begin to direct or guide behaviour with their own speech, an important stage has been reached in the transition of a skill through the ZPD. It constitutes the next stage in the passing of control or assistance from the adult to the child, from the expert to the apprentice. What was guided by the other is now beginning to be guided and directed by the self.

Stage III: Where performance is developed, automized, and 'fossilized'

Once all evidence of self-regulation has vanished, the child has emerged from the ZPD into the *developmental stage* for that task. The task execution is smooth and integrated. It has been internalized and 'automatized'. Assistance, from the adult or the self, is no longer needed. Indeed 'assistance' would now be disruptive. It is in this condition that instructions from others are disruptive and irritating; it is at this stage that self-consciousness itself is detrimental to the smooth integration of all task components. This is a stage beyond self-control and beyond social control. Performance here is no longer developing; it is already developed. Vygotsky described it as 'fossilized', emphasizing its fixity and distance from the social and mental forces of change.

Stage IV: Where de-automatization of performance leads to recursion back through the ZPD

The lifelong learning by any individual is made up of these same regulated, ZPD sequences – from other-assistance to self-assistance – recurring over and over again for the development of new capacities. For every individual, at any point in time, there will be a mix of other-regulation, self-regulation, and automatized processes. The child who can now do many of the steps in finding a lost object might still be in the ZPD for the activities of reading, or any of the many skills and processes remaining to be developed in the immature organism.

Furthermore, once children master cognitive strategies, they are not obligated to rely only on internal mediation. They can also ask for help when stuck or during periods of difficulty. Again, we see the intimate and shifting relationship between control by self and control by others. Even for adults, the effort to recall a forgotten bit of information can be aided by the helpful assistance of another so that the total of self-regulated and other-regulated components of the performance once again resembles the mother and child example of shared functioning. Even the competent adult can profit from regulation for enhancement and maintenance of performance.

Indeed, a most important consideration is that *de-automatization and recursion* occur so regularly that they constitute a Stage IV of the normal developmental process. What one formerly could do, one can no longer do. The first line of retreat is to the immediately prior self-regulating phase. A further retreat, to remembering the voice of a teacher, may be required, and consciously reconjuring the voice of a tutor – is an effective self-control technique.

But in some cases no form of self-regulation may be adequate to restore capacity, and a further recursion – the restitution of other regulation – is required. Indeed, the profession of assisting adults (psychotherapy) is now a major Western institution. In all these instances, the goal is to reproceed through assisted performance to self-regulation and to exit the ZPD again into a new automatization.

Reading 11.5

Student experiences of pedagogy
Max van Manen

In this extract from a book about researching teaching, especially aspects of pedagogy, van Manen gives an account of students describing their classroom experiences. He considers what their 'anecdotes' tell us about their experiences of pedagogy. Crucially, we see the interweaving of classroom relationships, instruction and learning.

Do you feel able to view your pedagogy through learners' eyes?

Edited from: van Manen, M. (1999) 'The language of pedagogy and the primacy of student experience' in J. Loughran (ed.) *Researching teaching: Methodologies and Practices for Understanding Pedagogy*. London: Falmer Press, 19–22.

When we ask students to describe their classroom experiences with teachers, it becomes immediately evident how students often see teaching in terms of style, personality, and qualities such as fairness, patience, commitment, and kindness. In a project aimed at discovering how students experience the interactive dimension of teaching, the narratives collected from these students are strongly suggestive of pedagogical qualities that students admire or criticize in their teachers.

Students were asked to write a simple 'anecdote,' a short story, about a single classroom event. Before this assignment was given, students learned how to write vivid accounts of personal experiences. Next they were provided with the following suggestion:

Think back to one teacher and describe, in an anecdote, a particular experience with this teacher. In your anecdote refer to how the teacher talked, acted, behaved, or used certain gestures. Describe the kinds of things that were said, showed, taught, or learned in this lesson or school situation. What manner of speaking, choice of words, personal demeanour, or way of behaving may have been part of this situation? What was this experience like for you? Describe, for example, how this particular teacher in this particular moment seemed to help you understand something, to make you feel interested in a topic. Describe how in this situation you felt secure or insecure, capable or incapable, challenged or bored, smart or dumb, good about yourself or self-critical, and so forth.

Students were also taught to edit the anecdotes. For the purpose of anonymity and plausibility some further editing was sometimes done. The following suggestions were given to enhance the narrative power of the anecdote:

1 an anecdote is a very short and simple story

2 an anecdote usually relates one incident

3 an anecdote begins close to the central idea

4 an anecdote includes important concrete detail

5 an anecdote often contains several quotes

6 an anecdote closes quickly after the climax.

Some stories that students tell are straightforward, other anecdotes are more intriguing. But in almost all cases there is a strong sense of relationality involved in the descriptions. The way that the teacher relates to the students is a dominant theme. For example, in the following anecdote a student describes a teacher holding a class discussion; the student implicitly seems to criticize the teacher for a poor instructional style, as well as for a less than encouraging manner of interacting. The students' account creates a strong sense of classroom atmosphere.

'Okay, close your note books,' Mr Lam said.

The class did so without delay, except for a few students who quickly glanced over their work in an attempt to memorize fast their answers for the 'discussion'.

'Okay now…' he continued slowly while taking his elevated position on the desk. In a relaxed manner he supported his body with one arm stretched behind him while his other arm formed into one huge finger, 'When was Hong Kong returned to Chinese rule?' He looked around with his finger poised to strike like a stinger of death.

Momentarily each one of us froze, expecting the finger to terminate its searching movement right at his or her person.

Before the finger came to a stop the teacher already mocked with a grimace of disgust on his face: 'You are going to have lots of trouble on the test.' Then he pointed his finger first at some of the regulars who usually knew the answers. William guessed almost in a whisper, 'Earlier this year?'

Mr Lam performed a silly laugh. His finger pointed to Darlene.

'Five years ago?'

Mr Lam groaned as if in pain. Then his finger came straight at me, 'In 1988?' I offered hesitatingly.

He did not even acknowledge that my answer was wrong too. But his face was disapproving. His finger danced three or four more times from one student to the other. Finally he stopped and said slowly, 'Hong Kong was returned to Chinese rule in 1997.' Then, as if tortured, Mr Lam pulled himself from his comfortable position off the top of the desk and wrote our assignment on the board.

That ended our 'discussion.' *(Grade 8 boy)*

The following anecdote also reports on an incident of classroom interaction. The student seems to experience the action of the teacher as causing her embarrassment.

'Mr Jones!'

Mr Jones turned his head slowly. He looked down at me.

'What is it, Jennifer?' he asked. He was now leaning on the counter and assumed a grimace of exasperated waiting. I hated that. Whenever I had to say something he did not seem to want to hear it. As if I were unintelligent and slow. But whenever he wanted me to say something I did not have anything to say. And so again I would feel stupid.

Mr Jones was so good at making me feel worthless and like an idiot. I don't think I am dumb, but whenever I tried to prove it he always thought of something to throw me off-guard.

'Well, Jennifer? Did you have some ingenious comment or question to ask me? I have an answer for everything you know.' He smiled smugly while he was demonstratively awaiting my response.

'I... no, it was nothing,' I replied. My neck and face grew hot with embarrassment. Again I had made myself look like an idiot in his eyes.

As Mr Jones continued with the lesson I stared at my book, mulling over what I had wanted to ask. Why did I suddenly lose courage to speak up? I felt flustered and defeated as I could not help but focus on my inner confusion.

'Jennifer! ... are you awake? No time to go to sleep yet!' Mr Jones' mock sarcasm made me sit up with a shock. A flush of desperation make my whole body tremble. Then my feeling of embarrassment turned into frustrated anger. I don't know why but I slammed my book shut. My reaction caused a stir of laughter in the whole class. I felt like exploding.

The next day I stayed home... 'sick!' *(Grade 9 girl)*

Is it fair to take seriously these stinging accounts of classroom lessons? Are the student accounts exaggerated, perhaps? How would these teachers have described the situations? Of course, they may have been dismayed, arguing that they do not intend to cause embarrassment. In fact the teachers may claim adamantly that they care deeply about their students and that they want them to feel successful in their studies. Indeed, we may be convinced that the teachers are very sincere. But no matter what teachers say their feelings and intentions really are, what seems ultimately more important is how the students *experience* them.

Teacher encouragement is often cited as important by young people. In the next anecdote, written by a Grade 9 student, we gain a strong sense of how important it is for a teacher to relate supportively to the student.

'Kathleen, your turn!' I heard the shrill voice of Mrs Shean, and could feel my face turn red. This teacher had a way of making you feel just awful by simple giving you 'the look,' or what some kids referred to as 'the evil eye'.

Slowly I stood up, hoping my legs wouldn't give up on me, and partially wishing we would have a fire drill right then. No such luck! 'Kathleen, we're waiting,' I could hear Mrs Shean say.

Very cautiously I began to read the words off the paper I was holding, and hoping I wasn't boring Mrs Shhean and the rest of the class to death.

As my hands began to tremble, with fear no doubt, I just barely saw a nice smile spreading across my teacher's face. I continued to read, but now with more flair and confidence. As I was reading my assignment aloud I started to recall the thoughts and feelings I had last night when I was doing this writing. Out of the corner of my eyes I could see how the teacher was slightly leaning forward, paying close attention to what I was saying. Somehow I could now speak with more conviction.

Just as I finished the last few words of my report, I looked up, and was utterly surprised to see a sparkle in Mrs Shean's eyes as she said, 'Very good Kathleen. That's the best presentation I've heard all day.'

I sat down in my desk, hardly able to believe what I had just heard. Mrs Shean hardly ever gave out compliments, and now she had just given one to me, me of all people!

Ring! 'Time to go class,' said Mrs Shean. As I left the classroom, I took one last glance at my teacher, who suddenly didn't seem as mean or cold as I used to think she was. As I looked over at her, she gave me a really warm smile, which stayed with me for the rest of the day. *(Grade 9 girl)*

In the above anecdote we can see how important it can be for students to be positively acknowledged by a teacher. The teacher needs to demonstrate that he or she believes in the student. The belief that a teacher shows in a student can indeed transform the student. Negative beliefs can weaken and positive beliefs can strengthen the student's actual performance. It is important for teachers to realize that 'belief' has the creative power to actually bring forth what is believed about the other person. Being encouraging, believing in the students, and giving students recognition seem critical qualities. A teacher who truly believes in a student can have incredible pedagogical power. These beliefs may strengthen the positive faculties that the teacher presumes present in the student. It is almost as if the teacher lures these abilities out of the young person with his or her belief. If the teacher thinks highly about a student's ability, attitude, and efforts, then his or her belief may actually awaken and corroborate these qualities in the student.

Reading 11.6

Talking and thinking together
Neil Mercer and Karen Littleton

Talking and discussion is one of the most powerful forms of learning, and promoting it is thus crucial in teachers' pedagogic repertoire. In this extract, Mercer and Littleton outline a three-part typology of talk – disputational, cumulative and exploratory. They exemplify this typology through transcripts of classroom talk. Their aim is to focus attention on how children can use talk to think together.

Do these forms of talk occur in your classroom?

Edited from: Mercer, N. and Littleton, K. (2007) *Dialogue and the Development of Children's Thinking: A Socio-cultural Approach.* London: Routledge, 57–63.

By encouraging children's use of talk as a thinking tool, teachers support the development of intellectual habits that will not only enhance children's study of the curriculum but should also serve them well in their future lives.

In the *Thinking Together* approach (Mercer, 2000), children are encouraged to give reasons, seek clarification, ask questions, listen to each others' ideas and so on. But they learn much more than a model set of talk strategies. The main goal is children's active appropriation of a particular 'educated' way of talking and thinking, one that they understand and appreciate, so that in time they are able to apply, adapt and develop their use of language flexibly and creatively in their discussions.

At the heart of the approach is the negotiation by each teacher and class a set of 'ground rules' for talking and working together. These ground rules then become established as a set of principles for how the children will collaborate in groups. The ground rules effectively open up and maintain an *intersubjective space* in which alternative solutions to problems are generated and allowed to develop and compete as ideas, without threatening either group solidarity or individual identity.

Many studies have suggested that interaction between peers can be of potential benefit for children's learning, reasoning and problem-solving. However, research has also highlighted the seeming paradox of children working *in* groups but rarely *as* groups. Whilst they may be seated in close proximity, children frequently work alongside each other rather than with each other – their joint work, such as it is, being characterised by disagreements, disputes and turn-taking. That is, they may interact, but rarely 'interthink'. Moreover, it is not uncommon to see children seated in groups but working individually.

A typology of children's classroom talk

Building on work by Barnes and Todd (1995), researchers on a project on Spoken Language and New Technology (Fisher, 1993; Mercer, 1995) devised a three part typology of talk. This was designed to reflect the different ways in which children talked together in classrooms:

- *Disputational Talk*, is characterised by disagreement and individualised decision making. There are few attempts to pool resources, to offer constructive criticism or make suggestions. Disputational talk also has some characteristic discourse features – short exchanges consisting of assertions and challenges or counter assertions ('Yes, it is.' 'No it's not!').

- *Cumulative Talk,* in which speakers build positively but uncritically on what the others have said. Partners use talk to construct 'common knowledge' by accumulation. Cumulative discourse is characterised by repetitions, confirmations and elaborations.

- *Exploratory Talk*, in which partners engage critically but constructively with each other's ideas. Statements and suggestions are offered for joint consideration. These may be challenged and counter-challenged, but challenges are justified and alternative hypotheses are offered. Partners all actively participate, and opinions are sought and considered before decisions are jointly made. Compared with the other two types, in Exploratory Talk knowledge is made more publicly accountable and reasoning is more visible in the talk.

The reader might like to test the application of the typology by considering each of the following short examples of discussions, Sequences 1–3 below. In all three of the transcripts, the participants are primary school children who are working at the computer. They are all engaged in the joint task of making up a conversation between two cartoon characters portrayed on a computer screen, and also have to decide what the characters are thinking as they speak. They then type the words into the relevant 'speech' and 'thought' bubbles. (Whenever it seemed to the researchers that the children were speaking the voices of the characters, the words have been placed in inverted commas. Interjections are indented.)

Sequence 1: Jo and Carol

Carol: Just write in the next letter. 'Did you have a nice English lesson.'

Jo: You've got to get it on there. Yes that's you. Let's just have a look at that. 'Hi, Alan did you have a nice English lesson. Yes thank you, Yeah. Yes thank you it was fine.'

Carol: You've got to let me get some in sometimes.

Jo: You're typing.

Carol: Well you can do some, go on.

Jo: 'Yes thank you.'

Carol: [*unintelligible.*]

Jo: You're typing. 'Yes thank you' 'I did, yeah, yes, thank you I did.'

Carol: You can spell that.

Jo: Why don't *you* do it?

Carol: No, because *you* should.

Sequence 2: Sally and Emma

Sally: Yeah. What if she says erm erm 'All right, yeah.' No, just put 'Yeah all right.' No, no.

Emma: No. 'Well I suppose I could.'

Sally: 'spare 15p.' Yeah?

Emma: Yeah.

Sally: 'I suppose.'

Emma: 'I suppose I could spare 50p.'

Sally: '50?'

Emma: Yeah. 'Spare 50 pence.'

Sally: '50 pence.'

Emma: '50 pence.' And Angela says 'That isn't enough I want to buy something else.'

Sally: Yeah, no no. 'I want a drink as well you know I want some coke as well'.

Emma: 'That isn't enough for bubble gum and some coke.'

Sally: Yeah, yeah.

Sequence 3: Tina, George and Sophie

George: We've got to decide.

Tina: We've got to decide together.

George: Shall we right, right, just go round like – take …

Tina: No, go round. You say what you think, and she says ….
          I think she should be saying: 'Did you steal my money from me?'

Tina: Your go.

Sophie: I think we should put: 'I thought that my money's gone missing and I thought it was you'.

George: 'I think it was you'.

Sophie: Which one?

Tina: Now what was it I was going to say, Um, um.

George: No because she's thinking, so we need to do a thought. So we could write her saying ….

Sophie: 'My money's gone missing so ….'.

Tina: I was going to say, if we're doing the one where she's saying, this is saying not thinking.

Sophie: 'My money's gone do you know where it is?'

Tina: No. On the saying one, she could say …

George   You should be saying.

Tina: Like she could be thinking to say to Robert, she could be saying: 'Do you know where's my money?' 'Do you know anything about my money going missing?'

George: Yeah, what, yeah that's good. When she's thinking, I think she should be thinking: 'Oh my money's gone missing and it's definitely Robert.'

Tina: Yeah.

Sophie: No, 'cos she's saying it to him isn't she?
Tina: No, she's thinking at the moment.
George: No, she's thinking.
Tina: That's the speech bubble.

The talk in Sequence 1 has characteristics of Disputational Talk. Both participants take an active part, but there is little evidence of joint, collaborative engagement with the task. Much of the interaction consists of commands and assertions. The episode ends with a direct question and answer, but even this exchange has an unproductive, disputational quality.

Sequence 2 has obvious features of Cumulative Talk. There is no dispute, and both participants contribute ideas which are accepted. We can see repetitions, confirmation and elaborations. The interaction is cooperative, but there is no critical consideration of ideas.

Sequence 3 has some characteristics of Exploratory Talk. It begins with Tina and George making explicit reference to their task as requiring joint decision making, and they attempt to organise the interaction so that everyone's ideas are heard. They then pursue a discussion of what is appropriate content for the character's 'thought' and 'speech' bubbles in which differing opinions are offered and visibly supported by some reasoning (For example 'No, because she's *thinking,* so we need to do a thought.' '…if we're doing the one where she's *saying,* this is *saying* not thinking.'). However, their reasoning is focused only on this procedural issue: they do not discuss explicitly or critically the proposed content of the character's thoughts and words. Were the space available to include longer examples, we could show that their later discussion also has some 'cumulative' features.

Evaluating talk

The three-part typology described and exemplified above is not only meant to be descriptive: it has an evaluative dimension, reflecting our concern with educational effectiveness. Our analysis of children's talk supports the view that not all kinds of talk are of similar educational value. Talk of a mainly 'disputational' type, for example, is very rarely associated with processes of joint reasoning and knowledge construction. Whilst there may be a lot of interaction between children, the reasoning involved is mainly individualised and tacit. Furthermore, the kind of communicative relationship developed through disputation is defensive and overtly competitive, with information and ideas being flaunted or withheld rather than shared. It is common for this type of talk to comprise tit-for-tat 'yes it is', 'no it isn't' patterns of assertion and counter-assertion. Judgemental comments such as 'you're stupid' and 'don't do that thicko' are typically heard. Disputational argument of this kind has little in common with the kind of reasoned argument that is represented by Exploratory Talk. Children engaged in a disputational type of talk are not, however, orientated to the pursuit of reasoned argument, they are being 'argumentative' in the negative sense of squabbling and bickering.

In contrast to Disputational Talk, Cumulative Talk characterises dialogue in which ideas and information are shared and joint decisions are made: but there is little in the way of challenge or the constructive conflict of ideas in the process of constructing knowledge. Cumulative Talk represents talk which seems to operate more on implicit concerns with solidarity and trust, hence the recourse to a constant repetition and confirmation of partners' ideas and proposals.

Exploratory Talk represents a joint, co-ordinated form of co-reasoning in language, with speakers sharing knowledge, challenging ideas, evaluating evidence and considering options in a reasoned and equitable way. The children present their ideas as clearly and as explicitly as necessary for them to become shared and jointly analysed and evaluated. Possible explanations are compared and joint decisions reached. By incorporating both constructive conflict and the open sharing of ideas, Exploratory Talk constitutes the more visible pursuit of rational consensus through conversation. Exploratory Talk foregrounds reasoning. Its ground rules require that the views of all participants are sought and considered, that proposals are explicitly stated and evaluated, and that explicit agreement pre-cedes decisions and actions. It is aimed at the achievement of consensus. Exploratory Talk, by incorporating both conflicting perspectives and the open sharing of ideas represents the more visible pursuit of rational consensus through conversations. It is a speech situation in which everyone is free to express their views and in which the most reasonable views gain acceptance.

The purpose of this three part analytic typology is quite circumscribed: to focus attention on the extent that talk partners use language to think together when pursuing joint problem-solving and other learning activities. It offers a frame of reference for making sense of the variety of talk in classrooms.

Communication
How does language support learning?

There are seven readings in this chapter and they address a wide range of issues concerning the use of language in school contexts.

The first group are directly concerned with the communication skills of inter-active teaching (see **Reading 8.7**). Nystrand (12.1) begins with an illustration of classroom discussion and teachers' use of authentic questions to engage students in learning. This is contrasted with more routine interaction and 'listless classrooms'. Extending this further, Perrot (12.2) provides a detailed analysis of questioning skills, including the 'development of an overall questioning strategy'.

Alexander's discussion of pedagogic repertoire (**Reading 12.3**) is structured in terms of the organization of interaction and then in relation to 'teaching talk' and 'learning talk'. We see how various forms of communication form the essence of pedagogic repertoire. Alexander applies this to contrast 'dialogic' and 'transmissive' teaching.

Reading 12.4, from Harrison, asserts the significance of reading across the curriculum. It supports children in making sense of experience and building on existing knowledge. This theme is extended by Barrs and Cork (12.5) who discuss the interconnections of reading, listening, discussing and writing within the curriculum, and ways in which these skills and capabilities reinforce each other. Bereiter and Scardamalia (12.6) focus on the particular development of writing – the least favourite activity of generations of pupils. They show how knowledge can be 'transformed' through the process of writing, and how texts can be used as an expression of agency. Finally, Blackledge (12.7) shows how the cultural and linguistic backgrounds of bilingual learners can be used as a rich resource for classroom learning.

As a whole, these readings convey the richness and educational potential of classroom communication and the shared responsibility of teachers for the development of communication skills. However, they also highlight the pedagogic expertise which is needed.

The parallel chapter of *Reflective Teaching in Schools* considers the major characteristics of classroom communication. There are sections on talking and listening, on reading and on writing. The chapter concludes with discussion on grammar, differences between spoken and written language, and on English as an additional language.

'Key Readings' provides suggestions for taking the issues further, and *reflectiveteaching.co.uk* offers additional activities and ideas for more detailed reading and other resources.

Reading 12.1

Engaging students, through taking them seriously

Martin Nystrand

Nystrand presents an extract from his study of classroom discussion. He analyses how far the teacher successfully uses questions to engage students in thinking about texts. He makes a particular point about the value of 'authentic' questions designed to seek information rather than to test students' knowledge.

In the example below, can you detect the authenticity of interaction – and see the consequences?

Edited from: Nystrand, M. with Gamoran, A., Kachur, R., Prendergast, C. (1997) *Opening Dialogue: Understanding the Dynamics of Language and Learning in the English Classroom.* New York: Teachers College Press, 1–7.

An engaging classroom

Ms. Lindsay is writing on the board, trying hard to keep up with John, one of her students in this ninth-grade class, who has just read aloud his plot summary for a chapter from Mildred Taylor's *Roll of Thunder, Hear My Cry.*

'I had a lot of trouble,' says Ms. Lindsay, 'getting everything down [on the board], and I think I missed the part about trying to boycott.' She reads from the board: 'and tried to organize a boycott.' Did I get everything down, John, that you said?'

'What about the guy who didn't really think these kids were a pest?' replies John.

'Yeah, okay,' says Ms. Lindsay. 'What's his name? Do you remember?' John shakes his head, indicating he can't remember.

Without waiting to be called on, Alicia, another student, volunteers, 'Wasn't it Turner?'

Looking around the class, Ms. Lindsay says, 'Was it Turner?'

Several students say, 'Yes.'

'Okay,' continues Ms. Lindsay, 'so Mr. Turner resisted white help. Why? Why would he want to keep shopping at that terrible store?'

John quickly answers, 'There was only one store to buy from because all the other ones were white.'

'Well,' Ms. Lindsay objects, 'the Wall Store was white too.'

Another student, Tom, now addressing John, wonders, 'Is it Mr. Hollings's store? Is that it?'

'No,' John answers. 'Here's the reason. They don't get paid till the cotton comes in.

But throughout the year they still have to buy stuff – food, clothes, seed, and stuff like that. So the owner of the plantation will sign for what they buy at the store so that throughout the year they can still buy stuff on credit.'

'So,' Ms. Lindsay says, reading aloud what she puts up on the board, 'he has to have credit in order to buy things, and this store is the only one that will give it to him.'

Another student, Felice, speaks up. 'I was just going to say, it was the closest store.'

Barely looking away from the board now, Ms. Lindsay replies while continuing to flesh out the paragraph building on the board, 'Okay – it's the closest store; it seems to be in the middle of the area; a lot of sharecroppers who don't get paid cash – they get credit at that store – and it's very hard to get credit at other stores. So it's going to be very hard for her to organize that boycott; she needs to exist on credit.'

'Yeah?' she says as she then nods to yet another student. Discussion continues.

In the 2 years that my colleagues and I visited hundreds of eighth- and ninth-grade literature classrooms, this brief excerpt of class classroom discourse came to represent the most important qualities we found of instruction that works: that is, instruction that helps students understand literature in depth, remember it and relate to it in terms of their own experience, and – most important for literature instruction – respond to it aesthetically, going beyond the who, what, when, and why of nonfiction and literal comprehension. In this classroom, students were *engaged*, not merely 'on task.' Unlike most, this class was not about the transmission and recitation of information, and the teacher's role was not that of asking questions to see how much students knew and going over the points they did not yet understand. This session was about figuring things out – in class, face-to-face, teacher and students together.

Traditional teacher and learner roles were here reversed. Rather than lecturing or quizzing students about the main points, this teacher instead took notes from them about their ideas. There was no penalty for error in this class; feigning a lapse, the teacher allowed a student to help her with a character's name. In this class, students as well as the teacher asked key questions, and in the end it was the students, not the teacher, who explained the main point.

Most instruction is about what is already known and figured out. Indeed, learning and being prepared for class typically mean reliably remembering what is already known. This class went further, and instruction here was ultimately about working collaboratively to understand what was not yet understood. Clearly this teacher took her students seriously, and clearly they knew it. Instruction of this sort is described inadequately by the main points in a lesson plan. Capturing instruction and learning of this sort requires constructing a narrative of unfolding understanding involving thoughtful interaction between and among teacher and students.

This kind of instruction, we also learned, is rare in American schools. Most schooling is organized, we found, for the plodding transmission of information through classroom recitation. Teachers talk and students listen. And the lower the track, we found, the more likely this is to be true.

Listless classrooms

American high schools are all too often 'orderly but lifeless.' Teachers tend to avoid controversial topics, simplifying complex issues into bite-sized pieces of information distilled into countless worksheets and continual recitation. These teachers maintain control through dull, plodding coverage of content. In response, students tend to do their work but show little enthusiasm for learning, and their work is often superficial, mindless, and quickly forgotten. In the classes we observed, only about a quarter of the students participated in question-and-answer recitation, and the actual discussion of the sort examined above occurred, on average, less than one minute a day. Indeed, in the vast majority there was none at all. Almost all teachers' questions, moreover, required students to recall what someone else thought, not to articulate, examine, elaborate, or revise what they themselves thought.

Listless classrooms are sometimes attributed to problems of motivation, methods, and curriculum, and no doubt many are. Yet for too long now, debates about curriculum and instruction and mental life in classrooms have been polarized by debates about which is better: teacher control or student control, direct instruction or collaborative learning. Indeed, a long tradition of research and polemic pitting of teacher versus student as the appropriate theoretical centre for understanding curriculum and instruction has precluded our understanding that more basic than either teacher or student *is the relationship between them*. Lifeless instruction and reluctant student engagement and thinking may be viewed as fundamental problems of instructional discourse – of the kind of language that defines students' interactions with their teachers, peers, and texts. Instruction is 'orderly but lifeless' when the teacher predetermines most of its content, scope, and direction.

In other, far fewer, classrooms – like Ms. Lindsay's – teachers engage their students in more probing and substantive interactions, and the talk is more like conversation or discussion than recitation (Nystrand and Gamoran, 1991). In these classrooms, the teacher validates particular students' ideas by incorporating their responses into subsequent questions, a process Collins (1982) calls 'uptake.' In the give-and-take of such talk, students' responses and not just teacher questions shape the course of talk. The discourse in these classrooms is therefore less predictable and repeatable because it is 'negotiated' and jointly determined – in character, scope, and direction – by both teachers and students as teachers pick up on, elaborate, and question what student say. Such interactions often are characterized by 'authentic' questions, which are asked to get information, not to see what the students know and do not know; that is, authentic questions are questions without 'pre-specified' answers (Nystrand and Gamoran, 1991). These questions convey the teacher's interest in students' opinions or thoughts. Hence, in contrast to the 'test questions' of recitation, or what Mehan (1979) calls 'known information questions.' They indicate the priority the teacher places on thinking and not just remembering. These 'instructional conversations,' as Tharp and Gallimore (1988) call them, engage students because they validate the importance of students' contributions to learning and instruction. The purpose of such instruction is not so much the transmission of information as the interpretation and collaborative co-construction of understandings. In this kind of classroom talk, teachers take their students seriously.

Ultimately, the effectiveness of instructional discourse is a matter of the quality of teacher-student interactions and the extent to which students are assigned challenging and serious epistemic roles requiring them to think, interpret, and generate new understandings.

Reading 12.2

Using questions in classroom discussion
Elizabeth Perrot

This is a detailed reading on the various skills and strategies involved in the use of questions in classroom discussion. This is an essential part of any teaching repertoire. Perrot considers how to use questioning to improve both the quality of children's thinking, particularly with reference to 'higher order thinking' and the extent of their participation. Finally, she reviews some of the most important issues in the development of an effective overall questioning strategy.

Questioning is one of the most important techniques of teaching and taping a session when using questioning is always revealing. What does Perrot's analysis of skills offer to you?

Edited from: Perrot, E. (1982) *Effective Teaching: A Practical Guide to Improving Your Teaching*. London: Longman, 56–91.

Research studies carried out in many parts of the world have shown that the majority of teacher's questions call for specific factual answers, or lower cognitive thought. But higher cognitive questions, which cause pupils to go beyond memory and use other thought processes in forming an answer, have an important role. While both types of questions have their part to play in teaching, a heavy reliance on lower-order questioning encourages rote learning and does little to develop higher-order thinking processes.

Teaching skills associated with helping pupils to give more complete and thoughtful responses are: pausing, prompting, seeking further clarification and refocusing a pupil's response.

Teaching skills associated with increasing the amount and quality of pupils' participation are: redirecting the same question to several pupils, framing questions that call for sets of related facts, and framing questions that require the pupil to use higher cognitive thought.

Such teaching skills are a means to an end (pupils' behaviour) . Therefore, you must have clearly in mind the particular end you wish to achieve. Additionally you must become a careful observer of pupils' behaviour, since their reactions can give you valuable clues about the effectiveness of your own performance.

Helping pupils to give more complete and thoughtful responses

Pausing: If the teacher's object is to sample what the class knows within a relatively short time and to elicit brief answers, 'rapid-fire' questioning is an appropriate skill. On the other hand, if the teacher's objective is to provide an atmosphere more conducive to discussion, in which pupils will have time to organize longer and more thoughtful responses, he must adopt a more appropriate questioning procedure. One skill that may be used to encourage longer and more thoughtful responses is to pause for three to five seconds after asking a question, but before calling on a pupil. The use of this skill should eventually result in longer responses because your pupils will be able to discriminate between pausing behaviour and your 'rapid-fire questioning'.

However, they will not automatically give longer answers when you first begin using pausing in your discussions. Depending upon their previous classroom experiences, relatively few pupils may respond appropriately. Some may begin to day-dream, hoping they will not be called on; others may raise their hands without first thinking. Therefore, when you first start using pausing behaviour, you should help the pupils learn what you want them to do. Immediately after the question verbal prompts can be presented, such as, 'Please think over your answer carefully', 'When I call on you, I want a complete answer', then pause for three to five seconds before you call on someone. Success lies in using questions which require longer and more thoughtful responses, pausing to allow ample time to organize those responses and reinforcing pupils for such responses.

If the pupil's response does not come up to the level you are seeking, you must be prepared to help him to develop a better answer. Good ideas however, should not be rejected simply because you did not previously consider them. You should always be prepared to evaluate and accept good answers, and to reinforce the pupil for them.

Prompting: This strategy is based on a series of questions containing hints that help the pupil develop his answer. Sometimes a single prompt will be sufficient to guide the pupil to a better answer. More commonly, it is necessary for the teacher to use a series of prompts which lead the pupil step by step to answer the original question. Teacher prompts may be in the form of intermediate questions, clues or hints that give the pupil the information he needs to arrive at a better answer. If the initial response is partly correct, first reinforce the correct part by telling the pupil what was right. Then begin by modifying the incorrect part. The exact questions used in a prompting sequence cannot be specified in advance, since each depends on the pupils' previous response. However, you should always have in mid the criterion response. Equally important, you should praise the final answer as much as if the pupil gave it at the beginning.

Seeking clarification: In some instances, a pupil may give a response which is poorly organized, lacking in detail or incomplete. Here you face a situation in which the pupil is not wrong, but in which his answer still does not match the response you seek. Under these circumstances you can use the probing skill of seeking clarification. Unlike prompting, seeking clarification starts at a different point on the response continuum. The teacher is not adding information; he is requesting the pupil to do so.

Refocusing: There are numerous occasions when the teacher receives a response that matches the one he wants. Refocusing may then be used to relate the pupil's response to another topic he has studied. The skill is used to help the pupil consider the implications of his response within a broader conceptual framework. He is asked to relate his answer to another issue. Refocusing is the most difficult form of probing since the teacher must have a thorough knowledge of how various topics in the curriculum may be related. You will be able to refocus more effectively if you study the content of your planned discussion beforehand, and note relationships with other topics the class has studied.

Improving the amount and quality of pupils' participation

Redirection: In using the technique of redirection, the same question is directed to several pupils. The question is neither repeated nor rephrased even though more than one pupil responds. To use redirection effectively, you must choose a question which calls for an answer of related facts or allows a variety of alternative responses. A poor question for redirection is one requiring only a single answer, such as 'What is the capital of France?' In this case, the first correct response effectively shuts off further questioning.

The first result of redirection is that you will talk less and the pupils will participate more. A second gain, which can be used to advantage later, is that by requiring several pupils to respond to the same question you can begin encouraging pupils to respond to each other.

Questions calling for sets of related facts: You undoubtedly encounter pupils in your classes who respond to almost any type of question as briefly as possible; that is, they answer 'yes' or 'no', or use only short phrases. Before you blame the pupils for not achieving more, be sure you are not at fault. You may be using types of questions associated with short answers that are not recognizable by their stem. When you ask, 'Isn't the purpose of your local police force the protection of life and property?' you are actually seeking a simple 'yes' or 'no' response. The question is so phrased that confirmation by the pupil is an acceptable answer. If on the other hand, you want discussion, you should phrase the same questions as follows: 'What are the duties of our local police force?' A 'yes' or 'no' response will not suffice here. But what if you have good questions and the pupils are still not responding adequately? Where do you start? As we have suggested, the question itself is only part of the story. Pupils previously allowed to respond briefly or to give memory-type responses are not likely to respond to your expectations at first. Praise the pupil for what he has stated and ask him to contribute more. Success lies in using questions which require longer and better responses and in reinforcing the pupils for their successively longer and better responses.

Higher-order questions: Besides encouraging pupils to give longer responses you should also try to improve the quality of their responses. Indeed, the kinds of questions the teacher asks will reveal to the pupil the kind of thinking which is expected of him. Since different kinds of questions stimulate different kinds of thinking, the teacher must be conscious of the purpose of his questions and the level of thinking they evoke.

An effective questioning sequence is one that achieves its purpose. When your purpose is to determine whether pupils remember certain specific facts, ask recall questions, such as: What is the capital of Canada? When did Henry VIII become King of England?

When your purpose is to require pupils to use information in order to either summarize, compare, contract, explain, analyse, synthesize or evaluate ask higher-order questions. For instance: Explain the kinds of problems caused by unemployment. How did life in the eighteenth century differ from life today?

Developing an overall questioning strategy

In order to be effective, skills must be appropriately incorporated into a questioning strategy planned to achieve particular learning objectives. The following summary indicates the relationships between functions and skills.

Function	Skill	Participant
To increase readiness to respond	Pausing	Class
	Handling incorrect responses	Individual
	Calling on non-volunteers	Individual
To increase quantity of participation	Redirecting questions	Class
	Calling for sets of related facts	
To improve quality of response	Asking higher-order questions	Individual
	Prompting	Individual
	Seeking clarification	Individual
	Refocusing	Individual
To increase quantity of participation while improving quality of response	Redirecting higher-order questions	Class

Figure 12.2.1 Relationships between functions and skills in questioning

A common problem in questioning sequences is a lack of emphasis on higher-order questions. This may be due to failure in planning a strategy where the primary objective is the improvement of the quality of thought. It may also be related to the fact that questioning is taking place in a group situation where the teacher is concerned with the quantity of pupil participation. In his effort to increase the quantity of pupil participation a teacher might rely on redirecting a disproportionate number of multiple-fact questions. Such tactics tend to emphasize recall and decrease the time available for asking higher-order questions and probing.

A second problem relates to the teacher's failure to refocus. A primary task of the teacher is to help pupils relate what they are presently learning to what they have previously learned. Perhaps an even more significant task is to help pupils to understand that the idea which they are studying are often relevant to other situations. Refocusing is probably the most difficult probing skill. Although the use of this skill depends on the preceding answer of the pupil teachers who have clearly in mind the conceptual content of their lesson can plan for questioning sequences which enable them to use refocusing.

A third problem arises from the teacher's failure to have clearly in mind criteria for evaluating pupil responses. As previously mentioned, skills provide a means to an end.

Only by specifying a particular end can a teacher determine which means are appropriate. To increase the quality of pupils' answers teachers should:

Carefully plan questions which require higher-order responses.

Have in mind the criteria for an acceptable answer.

Identify previously learned facts which are essential to the initiation of the higher-order questions.

Review for essential information to determine what the pupils know.

Frame questions that can be used systematically to develop the original pupil response and meet the higher order criteria.

Reading 12.3

The need for pedagogical repertoire
Robin Alexander

In this extract from Alexander's essays, he writes about the idea of teachers' pedagogical *repertoires* being paramount.

Alexander argues that classroom teaching requires the judicious selection from three repertoires concerning the organisation of interaction, teaching talk and learning talk. He further suggests that dialogic talk provides the best conditions for high quality learning. Underpinning such teaching strategies, of course, are knowledge about learners, the subject to be taught and the context in which the teaching and learning take place.

Is this three dimensional analysis of pedagogic repertoire useful to you in reviewing your present practice, and ways in which you might decide to develop it?

Edited from: Alexander, R. J. (2008) *Essays on Pedagogy.* Abingdon: Routledge, 109–13.

Here is the essence of the approach on which I have been working.

First, the idea of *repertoire* is paramount. The varied objectives of teaching cannot be achieved through a single approach or technique. Instead, teachers need a repertoire of approaches from which they select on the basis of fitness for purpose in relation to the learner, the subject-matter and the opportunities and constraints of context.

The idea of repertoire can be extended infinitely, down to the finest nuance of discourse. But to make it manageable, we concentrate in the first instance on three broad aspects of pedagogical interaction: *organisation*, *teaching talk* and *learning talk*.

Repertoire 1: Organising interaction

The *organisational* repertoire comprises five broad interactive possibilities reflecting our earlier distinction between individualism, community and collectivism, or child, group and class:

- *whole class teaching* in which the teacher relates to the class as a whole, and individual students relate to the teacher and to each other collectively;
- *collective group work*, that is group work which is led by the teacher and is therefore a scaled-down version of whole class teaching;
- *collaborative group work* in which the teacher sets a task on which children must work together, and then withdraws;
- *one-to-one activity* in which the teacher works with individual children;
- *one-to-one activity* in which children work in pairs.

Thus the organisational possibilities are whole class, group and individual, but group and individual interaction subdivide according to whether it is steered by the teacher or the children themselves. A competent teacher, arguably, needs to able to manage all five kinds of interaction, and select from them as appropriate.

Repertoire 2: Teaching talk

The *teaching talk* repertoire comprises the five kinds of talk we observed in use across the five countries in the international study. First, the three most frequently observed:

- *rote*: the drilling of facts, ideas and routines through constant repetition;
- *recitation*: the accumulation of knowledge and understanding through questions designed to test or stimulate recall of what has been previously encountered, or to cue students to work out the answer from clues provided in the question;
- *instruction / exposition*: telling the student what to do, and/or imparting information, and/or explaining facts, principles or procedures.

These provide the familiar and traditional bedrock of teaching by direct instruction. Less frequently, but no less universally, we find some teachers also using:

- *discussion*: the exchange of ideas with a view to sharing information and solving problems;
- *dialogue*: achieving common understanding through structured, cumulative questioning and discussion which guide and prompt, reduce choices, minimise risk and error, and expedite the 'handover' of concepts and principles.

Each of these, even rote, has its place in the teaching of a modern and variegated curriculum, but the last two – discussion and dialogue – are less frequently found than the first three. Yet discussion and dialogue are the forms of talk which are most in line with prevailing thinking on children's learning.

It's important to note that there's no necessary connection between the first and second repertoires. That is to say, whole class teaching doesn't have to be dominated by rote and recitation, and discussion isn't confined to group work. Discussion and dialogue, indeed, are available in all five organisational contexts (see Figure 12.3.1).

The possibility in Figure 12.3.1 that students can, without teacher intervention, achieve dialogue (which as defined here guides learners cumulatively towards understanding) as well as discussion (which is more exploratory in intent) may elevate some eyebrows. But this is perfectly feasible, given heterogeneous grouping and the different ways and rates in and at which children learn. Vygotsky envisaged the zone of potential development being traversed 'under adult guidance or in collaboration with more capable peers.' (Vygotsky, 1978: 6).

Indeed, Bell and Lancaster exploited peer tuition 200 years ago in their monitorial systems, though admittedly with rote and memorisation rather than dialogue in mind.

	Rote	Recitation	Exposition	Discussion	Dialogue
Whole class teaching	✓	✓	✓	✓	✓
Collective group work (teacher led)		✓	✓	✓	✓
Collaborative group work (pupil led)				✓	✓
One-to-one (teacher led)		✓	✓	✓	✓
One-to-one (pupil pairs)				✓	✓

Figure 12.3.1 Combined repertoires for classroom teaching

The idea has been revived in more ambitious form through peer mentoring/tutoring (Hargreaves, 2005), and 'learning partners' (Williamson, 2006).

Repertoire 3: Learning talk

The third repertoire is the child's rather than the teacher's. It constitutes not how the teacher talks or organises interaction, but how the children themselves talk, and the forms of oral expression and interaction which they need to experience and eventually master. This *learning talk* repertoire includes the ability to:

- *narrate*
- *explain*
- *instruct*
- *ask different kinds of question*
- *receive, act and build upon answers*
- *analyse and solve problems*
- *speculate and imagine*
- *explore and evaluate ideas*
- *discuss*
- *argue, reason and justify*
- *negotiate.*

Such abilities are associated with four contingent abilities which are vital if children are to gain the full potential of talking with others:

- *listen*
- *be receptive to alternative viewpoints*
- *think about what they hear*
- *give others time to think.*

Learning talk repertoires such as this depending on how one conceives of human development on the one hand and the curriculum on the other – are often missing from discussion of classroom interaction. Because the teacher controls the talk, researchers tend to start and finish there, focusing on teacher questions, statements, instructions and evaluations and how children respond to them, rather than on the kinds of talk which children themselves need to encounter and engage in.

Principles of dialogic teaching

So far we have a view of classroom talk which requires the judicious selection from three repertoires – organisation, teaching talk and learning talk. Now we come to the heart of the matter. I submit that teaching which is dialogic rather than transmissive, and which provides the best chance for children to develop the diverse learning talk repertoire on which different kinds of thinking and understanding are predicated, meets five criteria. Such teaching is: *collective*: teachers and children address learning tasks together, whether as a group or as a class;

- *reciprocal*: teachers and children listen to each other, share ideas and consider alternative viewpoints;
- *supportive*: children articulate their ideas freely, without fear of embarrassment over 'wrong' answers; and they help each other to reach common understandings;
- *cumulative*: teachers and children build on their own and each other's' ideas and chain them into coherent lines of thinking and enquiry;
- *purposeful*: teachers plan and steer classroom talk with specific educational goals in view.

The genealogy of these criteria is complex. Suffice it to say that it combines (i) a positive response to what I and others have observed by way of effective classroom interaction in the UK and elsewhere; (ii) an attempt to counter the less satisfactory features of mainstream classroom interaction (which, for example, tends not to exploit the full collective potential of children working in groups and classes, is one-sided rather than reciprocal, is fragmented or circular rather than cumulative, and is often unsupportive or even intimidating to all but the most confident child); (iii) distillation of ideas from others working in this and related fields – thus, for example, the criterion of *reciprocity* draws on the pioneering work of Palincsar and Brown (1984) among others, while *cumulation* reflects not only Bakhtin (e.g. 1986) but also the entire weight of post-Enlightenment understanding of how human knowledge, collectively as well as individually, develops.

Reading 12.4

Why is reading so important?
Colin Harrison

In this extract from *Understanding Reading Development*, Harrison reminds us to think about why reading is so important and hence why it forms a central part of any teacher's practice. Drawing on Bruner, he argues that narrative is crucial to human development but that information books are equally important, because from both, young readers learn how texts, like people, can communicate.

Why, in your view, is reading so important across the curriculum?

Edited from: Harrison, C. (2004) *Understanding Reading Development*. London: Sage, 3–8.

Why should teachers devote so much time to supporting children in becoming confident and fluent readers? My starting point in answering this question is not taken from government statements identifying national goals in reading; rather, it is a quotation from a letter written by Gustave Flaubert in 1857:

> Do not read, as children do, to amuse yourself, or like the ambitious, for the purpose of instruction. No, read in order to live. *(Flaubert, 1857, in Steegmuller, 1982)*

Teachers can be forgiven for forgetting sometimes the joy and delight that most young children experience as they discover what words can do. But I want to make no distinction between reading stories and reading for information in relation to the question of what we gain from reading. I want to affirm that reading not only increases our life skills and extends our knowledge, but goes much deeper. Indeed, I want to argue that in many respects reading determines how we are able to think, that it has a fundamental effect on the development of the imagination, and thus exerts a powerful influence on the development of emotional and moral as well as verbal intelligence and therefore on the kind of person we are capable of becoming.

Many teachers of my generation were influenced by Barbara Hardy's essay on *Narrative as a primary act of mind*, taken from the book *The Cool Web* in which she argued that 'inner and outer storytelling' plays a major role in our sleeping and waking lives. She wrote:

> … For we dream in narrative, daydream in narrative, remember, anticipate, hope, despair, believe, doubt, plan, revise, criticise, construct, gossip, learn, hate, and love by narrative. In order really to live, we make up stories about ourselves and others, about the personal as well as the social past and future. *(Hardy, 1977, p. 13)*

The importance of narrative, she argues, is not simply about enjoyment of stories, or even about understanding ourselves; narrative is a fundamental tool in the construction of inter-subjectivity – the ability to recognise mental states in ourselves, and through imagination and projection, to recognise the potential reciprocity of mental states in others – their beliefs, intentions, desires, and the like. It is this (and not simply the existence of language) that makes us distinctive as human beings. Jerome Bruner put this point very powerfully:

> I want to propose that this deep, primitive form of human cognition [ie: inter-subjectivity] is captured linguistically in the form of narrative. *(Bruner 2000, 33)*

Bruner was arguing here that inter-subjectivity, our very ability to relate to other people in characteristically human ways, is fundamentally related to our use of the linguistic form of narrative.

If narrative is fundamental to human development, then reading is about much more than gaining a skill: it is about learning to be. And it is precisely because this is such a difficult and sensitive subject to talk about that we avoid talking about it, and this leaves an enormous vacuum. Because reading is so important, that vacuum becomes filled by other discourses, and often these have an emphasis on skills, on employment, on the economy and on reading for practical purposes. Of course, these practical purposes are extremely important, but I would nevertheless wish to emphasise that, when we are looking at reading development, we are talking about giving people tools to be human. Indeed, if learning to read opens significant additional possibilities in terms of understanding how we might live, then we can argue that we have a moral duty to read, and, therefore as teachers, a moral duty to teach reading.

It is enormously valuable for all teachers to have some understanding of how children learn to read, and of the remarkable potential of early literacy experiences to influence children's development.

In a nursery that I visit regularly, I heard the following story from the mother of Henry, then a cheerful little boy of 22 months. His language was developing well, which is to say that he was beginning to talk confidently, even though he was sometimes frustrated because he did not yet have the words to explain everything he wanted to say. But the remarkable incident which followed his being bitten by another child showed that Henry could use a book to communicate his feelings, even before he had learned the words to utter them.

One afternoon, when Henry's mum arrived to pick him up from nursery, Henry's key worker took her aside and asked her to sign her section of an accident form. 'Everything's alright,' said the key worker, 'but I have to tell you that I'm afraid Henry was bitten this afternoon by another child. I have had a conversation with the other child and explained how serious it is to bite someone, and have asked him not to do it again.' Naturally, this being a modern nursery, there was no mention of the name of the biter. When Henry's mum went to pick up Henry, there was no sign of anguish, anger or upset, but Henry proudly rolled up his sleeve and revealed a fine set of teeth marks on his forearm. He then became increasingly agitated and clenched his little fists with frustration, as he realised he could not tell his mum what had happened. Suddenly, he rushed over to the book corner, and fetched a book, ran back to his mum and opened it. The book had a number of pictures of reptiles, and Henry turned the pages determinedly until he found the picture he wanted. It was a photograph of a very large crocodile with its jaws wide open revealing a full set of sharp teeth. Henry pointed to the photograph, then he pointed to the bite on his arm. Then he pointed to his best friend, another little boy, who was sitting across the room, working with great concentration on a drawing. 'Snap! Snap!' said Henry as he pointed to his pal. His mum understood.

What is intriguing about this anecdote are the connections between the infant's intentionality, his communication strategies, and his emergent literacy. Henry understood, even before his speech was anything like fully developed, that books, as well as people, can communicate, and he used this understanding to make an announcement that was richer and far more dramatic than would have been possible without access to the book. What exactly was happening here? First, Henry was initiating a literacy event: a child who was not yet two was demonstrating an awareness that a book could be used as a bridge – a third possible world that might be used to link his own mental world to the mental world of his mum. Second, he already understood the potential of metaphor – that one event or object which had a partial set of correspondences with another event or object could be used to stand proxy for that event or object, and could evoke a set of associations in the mind of another. Third, he implicitly understood how powerful a metaphor could be: his little pal, the biter, had not sprung from a jungle river and torn off his arm – but Henry used the evocative image of the crocodile to striking effect, and to call up in his mother's mind associations with the atavistic fear of being attacked by a giant reptile. And these things did not just happen: they occurred because Henry inhabited a world surrounded by books – in the kitchen of his home, in his bedroom, at his grandparents' house, and in the nursery that he had attended daily since he had been six months old. They happened because since before he had been just a few months old, adults had been sharing books with him, and initiating him into the awareness of possible worlds that are accessed through books, and into the visual and linguistic representations that made up those worlds.

It is interesting that this example of developing inter-subjectivity used an information book. Indeed, whilst narrative and story are important in distinctive ways in human development, information books are important, too. Historians tell us that the first written texts were not stories or poetry, but information texts – facts about ownership, law, the permanent recording of important details and events. Stories offer us models of how to live, but information books give us the power to store, to name, to retrieve, to share, to explore, to wonder at, and to bring order to our representations of the world.

Reading 12.5

Reading, listening, discussing and writing
Myra Barrs and Valerie Cork

Research by Barrs and Cork explored how teachers can bring reading and writing together effectively. In this extract they outline some of the ways readers learn how written language works, for example through hearing literature read aloud, and are able to use it in their own writing to shape a reader's response. All teachers, whatever their role, have responsibilities to support the development of basic skills such as literacy. This reading highlights the interconnected elements which contribute.

In what ways does your teaching contribute to generic literacy skills?

Edited from: Barrs, M. and Cork, V. (2001) *The Reader in the Writer: The Links Between the Study of Literature and Writing Development at Key Stage 2*. London: The Centre for Literacy in Primary Education, 38–42.

Reading aloud

The recognition that we learn the large-scale structures of written language above all by learning to listen to its tunes and rhythms, and that these become part of our auditory memory, helps to explain why hearing texts read aloud is such an important experience for young language learners.

Where reading aloud is effective, it is often strongly performative and dramatic in character, with teachers taking on the voices of the characters and bringing the world of the text to life. Such reading provides an important way into unfamiliar texts for inexperienced readers.

In our research we became particularly interested in the way in which teachers reading aloud to children helped them to attend to the tunes of literary texts. Their reading enlarged the text for children, helping them to hear the author's voice and characteristic stylistic rhythms – the chatty contemporary speech-like rhythms of Betsy Byars, the spare poeticised speech of Kevin Crossley-Holland's prose.

But such readings also helped children by enabling them to attend more closely to the language of the text. Reading aloud does this partly, of course, by slowing the experience of reading down from the more rapid pace of silent reading. In reading aloud, text cannot be scanned or skipped over; the full effect of the text as it is written must be experienced and given voice. The reading-aloud pace enables readers not only to read to get at the meaning, but also to take in many more of the subtleties of the writing: to register the effect of the 'particular words in their particular order' (Rosenblatt, 1978).

Through artful and expressive reading aloud these teachers framed the 'reading event' which is the encounter between the reader and the text.

Learning listening

The point has often been made that reading aloud is a form of interpretation: we speak, in fact, of a 'reading' of a text. Reading aloud always involves a reader in many decisions about the appropriate ways to render the multiple aspects of a text, decisions which are often taken at a relatively unconscious level.

Similarly, listening to a text read aloud can be seen as a way of internalising these interpretations of multiple aspects of the text, and doing so at a level beyond conscious analysis. Aspects of the text such as its genre, tone, register, style, voice, rhythm, and tune are taken in holistically, as children learn to 'read through their ears' (Manguel, 1996). As children hear stories read aloud in this way they are learning a kind of attuned and responsive listening to written language which mirrors the listening that was part of their learning of spoken language (Pradl, 1988).

The development of an ear for language is one of a writer's (and a reader's) most valuable attributes, and this 'inner ear' is likely to be developed above all by such aural experiences of language. James Britton (1982) considered that the store of language that children internalise is acquired 'through reading and being read to'. He argued that in this way we build up a store of written language forms on which we draw as writers.

By the end of our research we had identified skilful reading aloud as a key feature of the teaching of the especially effective teachers in our sample. The children in these teachers' classes were regularly involved in listening to their teachers' performances of literary texts. These readings were a source of intense interest and enjoyment, engaging children with new texts and providing them with dramatic interpretations of familiar texts. Their responsiveness to the language of these texts became apparent in their writing. When Yossif wrote:

> I ran away because I was scared of the people. Guy found me and put a flower in my hand. He made me warm, comfortable and confident. We went back home and we danced together.

He is clearly echoing the tune and patterns of the Kevin Crossley-Holland text. But he is also creating entirely new structures in this mould, without using the words of the original. Reading aloud and re-reading was an especially notable feature of Yossif's teacher's approach to teaching reading and writing; he had had many experiences of hearing *The Green Children* read and of reading it for himself, and was steeped in its rhythms. Listening to texts read aloud in this way is likely to be a particularly important language experience for children like Yossif, who are learning English as a second language.

Listening to one's own text

It is clear that the interplay between reading and writing in learning to write is likely to be constant, and that the teaching of writing needs continually to foster and emphasise this interplay. Reading aloud is a way of encouraging children to listen to their own texts, as well as those of others. We were interested in the way in which some experienced teachers help children to hear their own text by reading it aloud to them, and by encouraging them to read their own texts aloud.

Manguel observes that 'when you read your own text aloud you can feel the weakest part'. The creation of opportunities for children to hear their texts read and to read them aloud themselves, sometimes to a writing partner, is often an effective way of enabling them to see how they can revise and improve their texts. In 'learning to listen to their own texts' (Barrs, 1992) children are also learning to become their own 'first reader' and to develop the kind of 'ear' for written language which will be an important resource in their reading and their writing.

Discussing reading

Closely linked to the reading aloud and re-reading of texts, in the classrooms we visited, was the discussion of texts and of children's responses to those texts. Discussions of this kind are a central part of a literature programme, and help to illuminate 'problems of perception and interpretation' (Harding, 1963) for inexperienced readers. But such discussions also enlarge and demonstrate to children what it is that readers take from a literary experience, how they respond to a text, and what it is that goes on as they read. They can also make them more conscious of, and observant of, their own reactions.

Discussion may raise many different kinds of issues. One fundamental area of response for discussion will be the readers' responses to the content of the text. Children in our sample responded to *Fire, Bed and Bone* in a markedly empathetic manner, clearly identifying with the dog-narrator and the plight of the family in the book. In discussion children made links between the text and their own experiences, often moving from 'text to life'.

But discussions of texts also lead to a more developed sense of how readers interpret texts, and of the 'multiple perspectives' present in a rich text, its 'polyphonic' (Iser, 1978) character. By sharing and discussing responses, children begin to appreciate that other readers might read the same text somewhat differently, and to search for evidence of how their own interpretation is supported by the text. Discussions of this kind extend children's awareness of their own responses to the text.

Learning to write reading

Our research supposed that reading and writing are, as Vygotsky suggests, two halves of the same process: that of 'mastering written language' (Vygotsky, 1978).

Young writers are not simple learning to use written language structures, they are also learning to 'write reading' and to shape a reader's response. This is always a difficult thing to do for, as David Olson (1996) points out, written text 'preserves the words, not the voice'. The problematic task for a writer is to decide how to render what Olson terms the 'illocutionary force' of an utterance – such features of spoken language as stress, pause, tone, pitch and intonation, which do so much to affect the meaning. Alberto Manguel describes *public reading* as a form of publishing and suggests that it offers the writer an important opportunity to 'give the text a tone', something which, he implies, it is difficult to do through the written words alone.

Olson suggests that 'writing modern prose is nothing more than the attempt to control how the reader takes the text'. While we must acknowledge that this is never completely possible, we also know that good writers develop a wide repertoire of means of representing those 'illocutionary' aspects of text, ranging from the precise choice of words and the word order to the use of all the resources of punctuation and layout. Attentive reading will help to alert young writers to the way these features are used.

In developing their own resources, an apprentice writer's main assets will therefore be their reading and their growing sense of how experienced writers work, which skilful teaching will help them to develop. As children become more aware of themselves as both writers and readers, they begin to learn to 'read like writers' and to 'write like readers'.

Reading 12.6

From 'knowledge telling' to 'knowledge transforming'

Carl Bereiter and Marlene Scardamalia

In this extract, Bereiter and Scardamalia outline the distinction between knowledge telling and knowledge transforming. Seeing the two as different, but closely related, is helpful to teachers when developing writing in the classroom. They argue for the importance of writers paying discrete attention to what they are writing about and the style in which they are composing, moving back and forth between the two rather than necessarily trying to concentrate on both at once.

How could this categorisation help in structuring tasks for your pupils?

Edited from: Bereiter, C. and Scardamalia, M. (1987) *The Psychology of Written Composition.* Hillsdale, NJ: Lawrence Erlbaum Associates, 6–12.

Everyday thinking, which is easy and natural, seems to follow a different model from formal reasoning, which is more problematic (Bartlett, 1958). Similar contrasts may be drawn between casual reading and critical reading, between talking and oratory, between the singing people do when they light-heartedly burst into song and the intensely concentrated effort of the vocal artist.

In each case the contrast is between a naturally acquired ability, common to almost everyone, and a more studied ability involving skills that not everyone acquires. The more studied ability is not a matter of doing the same thing but doing it better. There are good talkers and bad orators, and most of us would prefer listening to the former. And there are surely people whose formal reasoning is a less reliable guide to wise action than some other people's everyday thought. What distinguishes the more studied abilities is that they involve deliberate, strategic control over parts of the process that are unattended to in the more naturally developed ability. That is why different models are required to describe these processes.

Such deliberate control of normally unmonitored activity exacts a price in mental effort and opens up possibilities of error, but it also opens up possibilities of expertise that go far beyond what people are able to do with their naturally acquired abilities. In the case of writing, this means going beyond the ordinary ability to put one's thoughts and knowledge into writing. It means, among other things, being able to shape a piece of writing to achieve intended effects and to reorganize one's knowledge in the process.

From conversation to knowledge telling to knowledge transforming

Although children are often already proficient users of oral language at the time they begin schooling, it is usually some years before they can produce language in writing with anything like the proficiency they have in speech. Longitudinal studies by Loban (1976) suggest that the catch-up point typically comes around the age of twelve. The most immediate obstacle, of course, is the written code itself. But that is far from being the only obstacle. Other less obvious problems have to do with generating the content of discourse rather than with generating written language. Generating content is seldom a problem in oral discourse because of the numerous kinds of support provided by conversational partners. Without this conversational support, children encounter problems in thinking of what to say, in staying on topic, in producing an intelligible whole, and in making choices appropriate to an audience not immediately present.

In order to solve the problem of generating content without inputs from conversational partners, beginning writers must discover alternative sources of cues for retrieving content from memory. Once discourse has started, text already produced can provide cues for retrieval of related content. But they are not enough to ensure coherent discourse, except perhaps of the stream-of-consciousness variety. Two other sources of cues are the topic, often conveyed by an assignment, and the discourse schema. The latter consists of knowledge of a selected literary form (such as narrative or argument), which specifies the kinds of elements to be included in the discourse and something about their arrangement. Cues from these two additional sources should tend to elicit content that sticks to a topic and that meets the requirements of a discourse type. In essence, the knowledge-telling model is a model of how discourse production can go on, using only these sources of cues for content retrieval – topic, discourse schema, and text already produced.

A typical child's way of generating text was described for us by a 12-year old student as follows:

> I have a whole bunch of ideas and write down until my supply of ideas is exhausted.
> Then I might try to think of more ideas up to point when you can't get any more ideas
> that are worth putting down on paper and then I would end it.

Knowledge telling provides a natural and efficient solution to the problems immature writers face in generating text content without external support. The solution is efficient enough that, given any reasonable specification of topic and genre, the writer can get started in a matter of seconds and speedily produce an essay that will be on topic and that will conform to the type of text called for. The solution is natural because it makes use of readily available knowledge – thus it is favourable to report of personal experience – and it relies on already existing discourse-production skills in making use of external cues and cues generated from language production itself. It preserves the straight-ahead form of oral language production and requires no significantly greater amount of planning or goal-setting than does ordinary conversation. Hence it should be little wonder if such an approach to writing were to be common among elementary school students and to be retained on into university and career.

Knowledge telling versus knowledge transforming

In the preceding discussion of the knowledge-telling model, it was allowed that there could be large differences in outcome depending on the writer's knowledge of the topic of discourse and on the writer's sophistication in the literary genre. In addition, of course, quality of the written product will vary depending on language abilities, such as diction and syntactic fluency, that are not dealt with in the knowledge-telling model. With all this allowance for individual differences and for improvement through learning, it is not obvious that a second model is required to account for the different ways writers go about generating text content.

Consider, however, the following description by Aldous Huxley of his composing process:

> Generally, I write everything many times over. All my thoughts are second thoughts. And I correct each page a great deal, or rewrite it several times as I go along … Things come to me in driblets, and when the driblets come I have to work hard to make them into something coherent. *(Cited in Writers at Work, 2nd series, 1963, 197.)*

The process described here does not sound like merely a more sophisticated or elaborate version of the process 12-year olds describe of writing down thoughts that they already have in their minds. The process Huxley describes is one in which the thoughts come into existence through the composing process itself, beginning as inchoate entities ("driblets") and gradually, by dint of much rethinking and restating, taking the form of fully developed thoughts. This is the process that we shall call "knowledge transforming". It is a process that cannot be accounted for by the knowledge telling model and that seems to require a differently structured model.

This reworking or transforming of knowledge has been described in a variety of ways by professional writers. But it is, then, a process found only in exceptionally talented people who have writing their life's work? No. Evidence of a knowledge-transforming approach to writing can be found even, among people who have no particular talent for or commitment to writing, some of whom would even be judged to be bad writers by literary standards.

Where are writers who use knowledge-transforming strategies to be found? We find them among talented young students, undergraduates and graduate students in psychology, education and English, but they could probably be found among people at advanced levels in any intellectual discipline. These are people who, like Huxley, actively rework their thoughts. While they may not have Huxley's skill in expressing these thoughts, they are used to considering whether the text they have written says what they want it to say and whether they themselves believe what the text says. In the process, they are likely to consider not only changes in the text but also changes in what they want to say. Thus it is that writing can play a role in the development of their knowledge.

To account for this interaction between text processing and knowledge processing, it is necessary to have a model of considerably greater complexity than the model of knowledge telling. Such a model is sketched in Figure 12.6.1.

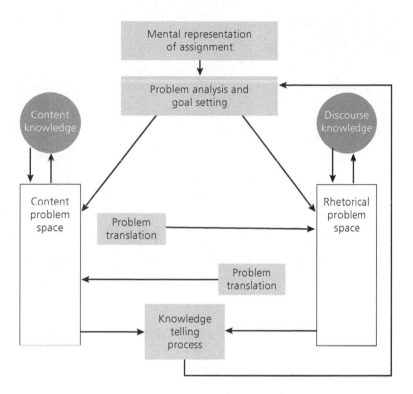

Figure 12.6.1
Structure of
the knowledge-
transforming
model

It will be noted that the knowledge-telling process is still there, but it is now embedded in a problem-solving process involving two different kinds of problem spaces. In the content space, problems of belief and knowledge are worked out. In the rhetorical space, problems of achieving goals of the composition are dealt with. Connections between the two problem spaces indicate output from one space serving as input to the other. For instance, a writer might be working in the rhetorical space on a problem of clarity and might arrive at the decision that she needs to define the concept of *responsibility* that she is building her argument around. This is a content problem, however, and so one might imagine a message going from the rhetorical problem space to the content problem space, saying "*What do I really mean by responsibility?*" Work on this problem within the content space might lead to determining that responsibility is not really the central issue after all but that the issue is, let us say, *competence to judge*. This decision, transferred to the rhetorical space, might initiate work on problems of modifying the text already written so as to accommodate the change in central issue. This work might give rise to further content problems, which might lead to further changes in the writer's beliefs, and so on until a text is finally created that successfully embodies the writer's latest thinking on the subject.

It is this kind of interaction between problem spaces that we argue is the basis for reflective thought in writing.

The distinctive capabilities of the knowledge-transforming model lie in formulating and solving problems and doing so in ways that allows a two-way interaction between continuously developing knowledge and continuously developing text.

Reading 12.7

Language, culture and story in the bilingual school

Adrian Blackledge

This reading draws attention to the diversity of languages is the UK and to the rich resource they provide for language learning. In particular, Adrian Blackledge draws on his classroom experience to show how bilingual children can develop their confidence and enhance their learning when drawing on their home languages and cultures. Story is shown to be an important means for connection and affirmation.

There is a more general point here about the valuing of home languages. Is there more that could be done in relation to the language of the children or young people with whom you work?

Edited from: Blackledge, A. (1994) 'Language, culture and story in the bilingual primary school', in Blackledge, A. (ed.) *Teaching Bilingual Children.* Stoke-on-Trent: Trentham, 43–7, 55–7.

Children in British schools speak more than two hundred languages. As many as five hundred thousand children learn to speak a language other than English at home before they encounter English at school. It has long been recognised that children's primary learning medium is their first language. Yet at policy-making level there has been scant recognition of these other languages of Britain, of their immense value as a resource, or of the crucial part they have to play in the education of bilingual children. Still less have governments encouraged teachers to promote the development of children's languages in the classroom, preferring to turn a deaf ear to the voices of more than half a million children.

As a teacher in a multilingual primary classroom I became aware that bilingual children's work would sometimes improve dramatically when they used their home language. This was particularly evident when children were telling stories to each other in their own languages.

In a large, multilingual school in Birmingham children from Year 6 told stories to children from Year 3 in homogeneous linguistic groups. During a series of weekly story-telling sessions, stories were told in Sylheti, Mirpuri and Malay. Some groups of bilingual children were asked to tell their stories in English. All children were then asked to write one of their stories in English. It soon became clear that most of the children telling stories in their first language were relating tales which originated in the narrative wealth of their home culture. In the course of this work children discussed their experiences of telling and listening to stories. The following is a transcript of part of a conversation with four Mirpuri-speaking girls in Year 6.

Teacher:	Where do your stories come from?
Shakila:	No, it doesn't matter. It depends who I am telling it to I suppose. If I was telling it to a teacher, or to Saima, I would use English. If I was telling it to my little brother, he's four and doesn't know English really yet, I would use Mirpuri.
Teacher:	But you don't think you tell the story better in Mirpuri, even though it is told to you in Mirpuri?
Shakila:	No, it's just who I'm talking to.
Teacher:	What about you two — do you prefer to tell stories in English or Mirpuri?
Noreen:	I think English, because I can explain them better in English.
Sabrina:	Yes, I think so, too. You can explain the stories better in English.
Teacher:	Even if the stories are told to you in Mirpuri?
Sabrina:	Yes, even when my aunt or grandma tells me a story in Mirpuri, I can tell it better in English, because I usually hear more stories in English.
Teacher:	What about you, Saika, which language do you prefer to use to tell stories?
Saika:	I don't know, it doesn't matter. I can tell it the same in both.
Teacher:	You don't think, like Noreen and Sabrina, that you tell stories better in English?
Saika:	No I don't think so.
Teacher:	The story you told today, where did you first hear it, and in which language?
Saika:	My grandma told it to me in Mirpuri. She doesn't speak English.
Teacher:	Is it just as easy to tell that story in English as in Mirpuri?
Saika:	Yes, it's the same.

Savva (1990) reminds us that 'bilingual children's language experience is not the same: each of them has a different linguistic background'. The four girls in this conversation apparently have very similar linguistic histories—each born in Britain to Mirpuri-speaking parents and educated at the same school from the age of four—yet they have different perceptions of their abilities to tell sophisticated stories in their first language. While Saika and Shakila feel that they have equal narrative facility in Mirpuri and English, Norren and Sabrina have a different view of their storytelling skills in the two languages. Noreen and Sabrina both feel that they are better able to 'explain' their story in English than in Mirpuri. This perception of their language preferences raises an important question: are Noreen and Sabrina's narrative skills (and therefore, by implication other language skills) being *replaced* by the skills they are learning in English? Levine (1990) emphasises the importance of a dialectical relationship between the languages children already know and their becoming adept in the new one:

> It is our hope, and what we work for, that English will become an *additional*, not a displacing language in our pupils' lives.

If English is to replace rather than add to the languages of the children we teach, we must ask what is the effect of such a programme on their cultural identity, their self-esteem and sense of their place in the community.

The monolingual teacher can do much to encourage an additive rather than a subtractive bilingual environment; that is, a classroom environment in which children are *adding* a new language to their existing skills rather than *replacing* their first language with that of the school. A bilingual education programme will be successful if the school actively promotes the value and use of children's languages. The curriculum need not be taught through those languages. If children are encouraged to use their languages at their convenience, and these languages are accorded genuine value in the classroom, it is likely that existing and new languages will develop side-by-side.

Cummins and Swain (1986) provide evidence from a range of bilingual education programmes to show that experience with either first or second language can promote development of the linguistic proficiency underlying both languages. Skills learned in one language will transfer readily to another. Thus if children speak in their home language for part of the curriculum they are not wasting time that could be spent 'learning English'. In fact their development of skills in the home language enables them to learn English more proficiently and with greater sophistication. Children are able to add a new language to their existing skills when their first language is strongly reinforced by a committed bilingual education programme in the school.

Most of the fifty children in our study were aware of using languages at the mosque which they rarely used elsewhere, e.g. Urdu for instruction, Arabic for reading the Quran. All of the children said they used English and the home language at school; many added that they used English in the classroom, and the home language mainly in the playground. Although most of the children said they hear stories in English and the home language, a majority said they prefer to tell stories in English. However, almost all of the children qualified this by saying, as Shakera (Sylheti) does, that their language of narrative depends on their audience.

> If I tell it to someone who speaks my language I would tell it in my language because they won't understand the words that are hard for that person. So it would be easy in my language for them.

When encouraged to use their home language for storytelling, bilingual children will bring to the classroom the narrative riches of their culture. Of the bilingual children telling stories in their home language as part of our project, the vast majority told a story which originated in their home culture. Of those bilingual children telling stories in English, fewer than half told a story which originated in their home culture. The majority of children working in English wrote stories drawn from experiences in their own domestic lives in Birmingham. In general, the stories originating in the home culture were more sophisticated then those of local origin. Shakila's story of "The King and his Seven Wives", told in Mirpuri, was based in the rich narrative tradition of the Indian sub-continent; Saima's story, "Three Wishes, No More!" was set in Pakistan, an adaptation of a tale she first heard in Mirpuri. She told the story in Mirpuri and wrote it in English. The children's stories originating in the home culture tended to have folk/fairy-tale characteristics, while stories set in local contexts tended to be more mundane accounts of daily life. Umar's Malaysian folk-tale of "The Elephant and The Ants" provided a further example of a story told in home language, then written in English.

Children and their families hold a wealth of learning opportunities. The stories they tell, which have perhaps never been written down before they write them; the chance to share part of their culture, and for that to be valued by other children; their knowledge of language use in different contexts; the opportunity to accord status to a variety of languages by making authentic use of them in the curriculum—all of these valuable resources are easily overlooked. If bilingual children are to use their whole linguistic repertoire in schools, they must be confident that their languages have a genuine role to play in all areas of the curriculum and in all areas of school life.

By these means schools will begin to provide an additive orientation to bilingual education, developing in children the ability, confidence and motivation to succeed.

Assessment

How can assessment enhance learning?

The readings in this chapter provide clarification of types of assessment and suggest the positive contribution assessment can make to teaching and learning.

In the first reading (13.1) Harlen and her colleagues review the relationship between the purposes and form of different types of assessment. This is absolutely crucial. If powerful forms of assessment are misaligned with educational purposes, there will be distortion. Major assessment purposes include formative and summative feedback, evaluation of system-wide performance, and school accountability.

The next four readings concern the development of 'assessment for learning'. The first of these (13.2) is a classic from the Assessment Reform Group and sets out its key features. Spendlove (13.3) focuses on creating conditions for giving feedback to learners and also on ways of eliciting feedback on our own teaching. Pupil self-assessment of learning is the particular focus of Muschamp (13.4) and she offers practical suggestions drawn from extensive classroom action research. Sue Swaffield (13.5) takes us back to core principles. She emphasises the responsiveness of assessment for learning to pupil progress and perspectives, and its unique role in the classroom learning of teachers.

Finally, Stobart (13.6) reminds us of how assessment shapes the ways in which we understand ourselves, our institutions and our societies. Both the conduct of assessment and interpretation of its outcomes are social process – and there are decisions to be made. As Stobart puts it: 'there is no neutral assessment'.

The parallel chapter of *Reflective Teaching in Schools* is also focused on assessment to enhance learning. It begins with a discussion of 'guiding principles' of assessment for learning and then provides detailed guidance on the five main classroom strategies – with strong links to the readings below. A final section affirms the principles of assessment for learning. There is also a useful list of 'Key Readings'.

On *reflectiveteaching.co.uk*, updated sources for further study are provided in 'Notes for Further Reading'. The website also offers a number of other resources on assessment, including further 'Reflective Activities'. Within the section on 'Deepening Expertise', a range of Expert Questions on assessment are discussed and research highlights are showcased.

Reading 13.1

Assessment purposes and principles

Wynne Harlen, Caroline Gipps, Patricia Broadfoot and Desmond Nuttall

There are many types of assessment, but each is suited to particular purposes and cannot safely be used in other ways. This reading provides an excellent overview of assessment purposes, key principles and four of the most important types of assessment.

Assessment purposes have often been conflated by policymakers, but what type would be most helpful to you in your work?

Edited from: Harlen, W., Gipps, C., Broadfoot, P. and Nuttall, D. (1992) 'Assessment and the improvement of education', *Curriculum Journal*, Vol. 3., No. 3, 217–25.

Assessment in education is the process of gathering, interpreting, recording and using information about pupils' responses to an educational task. At one end of a dimension of formality, the task may be normal classroom work and the process of gathering information would be the teacher reading a pupil's work or listening to what he or she has to say. At the other end of the dimension of formality, the task may be a written, timed examination which is read and marked according to certain rules and regulations. Thus assessment encompasses responses to regular work as well as to specially devised tasks.

All types of assessment of any degree of formality involve interpretation of a pupil's response against some standard of expectation. This standard may be set by the average performance of a particular section of the population or age group, as in norm-referenced tests. Alternatively, as in the National Curriculum context, the assessment may be criterion-referenced. Here the interpretation is in terms of progression in skills, concept or aspects of personal development which are the objectives of learning, and the assessment gives direct information which can be related to progress in learning. However, the usefulness of criterion-referenced assessment depends on the way in which the criteria are defined. Too tightly defined criteria, while facilitating easy judgement of mastery, require an extensive list which fragments the curriculum. On the other hand, more general criteria, which better reflect the overall aims of education, are much less easily and reliably used in assessing achievement.

The roles of assessment in education are as a means for:

providing feedback to teachers and pupils about on-going progress in learning, has a direct influence on the quality of pupils' learning experiences and thus on the level of attainment which can be achieved (formative role);

communicating the nature and level of pupils' achievements at various points in their schooling and when they leave (summative role), summarizing, for the purposes of selection and qualification, what has been achieved (certification role);

recording information for judging the effectiveness of educational institutions and of the system as a whole (evaluative or quality control role).

There is an unavoidable backwash on the curriculum from the content and procedures of assessment. The higher the stakes of the assessment, the greater this will be. Multiple-choice and other paper-and-pencil tests provide results which are easily aggregated and compared but their used encourages teachers to ignore much of what pupils should learn as they 'teach to the test'.

Not all assessment purposes are compatible. Strong evidence from experience in the US, combined with that now accumulating in England and Wales, indicates that information collected for the purposes of supporting learning is unsuitable and unreliable if summarized and used for the purposes of quality control, that is, for making judgements about schools, and its use for this purpose severely impairs its formative role.

There is likely to be a trade-off between, on the one hand, cost and quality and, on the other, effectiveness. The cheapest assessment techniques, such as multiple-choice, machine-markable tests, may be convenient instruments to use but provide poor quality information for the purposes of communication and little or no support for the learning process itself.

Key principles

These issues are the purposes of assessment are borne in mind in proposing the following set of principles to inform policy-making on assessment:

assessment must be used as a continuous part of the teaching-learning process, involving pupils, wherever possible, as well as teachers in identifying next steps;

assessment for any purpose should serve the purpose of improving learning by exerting positive force on the curriculum at all levels. It must, therefore, reflect the full range of curriculum goals, including the more sophisticated skills and abilities now being taught;

assessment must provide an effective means of communication with parents and other partners in the learning enterprise in a way which helps them support pupils' learning;

the choice of different assessment procedures must be decided on the basis of the purpose for which the assessment is being undertaken. This may well mean employing different techniques for different assessment purposes;

assessment must be used fairly as part of information for judging the effectiveness of schools. This means taking account of contextual factors which, as well as the quality of teaching, affect the achievement of pupils;

citizens have a right to detailed and reliable information about the standards being achieved across the nation through the educational system.

Formative assessment

A major role identified for assessment is that of monitoring learning and informing teaching decisions on a day-to-day basis. In this role, assessment is an integral part of the interactions between teacher, pupil and learning materials. Because of this relationship, some teachers, who practise formative assessment well, may not recognize that what they are doing includes assessing.

What is required from a formative assessment scheme is information that is: gathered in a number of relevant contexts; criterion-referenced and related to a description of progression; disaggregated, which means that distinct aspects of performance are reported separately; shared by both teacher and pupil; on a basis for deciding what further learning is required; the basis of an on-going running records of progress.

A scheme of formative assessment must be embedded in the structures of educational practice; it cannot be grafted on to it. Thus there are implications in the foregoing for the curriculum, for teachers, in terms of required supporting materials and pre-service or in-service training, and for record-keeping practice.

Summative assessment

Summative assessment is similar to formative assessment in that it concerns the performance of individual pupils, as opposed to groups. In contrast with formative assessment, however, its prime purpose is not much to influence teaching but to summarize information about the achievements of a pupil at a particular time. The information may be for the pupils themselves, for receiving teachers, for parents, for employers or for a combination of these.

There are two main ways of obtaining summative information about achievements: summing up and checking up (Harlen, 1991).

Summing up provides a picture of current achievements derived from information gathered over a period of time and probably used in that time for formative purposes. It is, therefore, detailed and broadly based, encompassing all the aspects of learning which have been addressed in teaching. To retain the richness of the information it is best communicated in the form of a profile (i.e. not aggregated), to which information is added on later occasions. Records of achievement (RoA) provide a structure for recording and reporting this information, combining some of the features of formative assessment with the purposes of summative assessment in that they involve pupils in reviewing their own work and recognizing where their strengths and weaknesses lie.

Checking up offers no such additional benefits as an approach to summative assessment. It is generally carried out through providing tests or tasks specially devised for the purpose of recording performance at a particular time. End of year tests or examinations are examples, as are the end of module tests for checking performance in modular programmes and external public examinations.

Checking up and summing up approaches have contrasting advantages and disadvantages. Tests used for checking up are limited in scope unless they are inordinately long and so are unlikely to cover practical skills and some of the higher level cognitive skills. On the other hand, they do provide opportunities for all pupils to demonstrate what they have learned. Summative assessment which is based only on formative assessment depends on the opportunities provided in class for various skills and understandings to be displayed and, further, may be out of date in relation to parts of work covered at earlier points and perhaps not revisited.

This suggests that a combination of these two approaches may be the most appropriate solution. There are several advantages to having test materials available for teachers to use to supplement, at the end of a particular period, the information they have from on-going assessment during that time. The emphasis is on 'test materials' and not tests. These would ideally be in the form of a bank from which teachers select according to their needs. The items in the bank would cover the whole range of curriculum objectives and the whole range of procedures required for valid assessment. This provision would also serve the purposes of the non-statutory Standard Assessment Tasks.

The main advantages are that the availability of a bank of test material would provide teachers with the opportunity to check or supplement their own assessment in a particular area where they felt uncertain about what pupils can do. This would ensure that all aspects of pupils' work were adequately assessed without requiring extensive testing. Checking their own assessments against those arising from well-trialled and validated tasks would also build up teachers' expertise and lead to greater rigour in teachers' assessments.

Assessment for evaluative and quality assurance purposes

Information about pupils' achievement is necessary in order to keep under review the performance of the system as a whole – the quality assurance role of assessment. In the absence of such information it is possible for rumour and counter-rumour to run riot.

To serve this purpose, assessment has to be carried out in a way which leads to an overall picture of achievement on a national scale. It requires measures of achievement of a large number of pupils to be obtained and summarized. For this purpose testing in controlled conditions is necessary. However, if every pupils is tested, this leads to adverse effects on both teaching practice and on the curriculum and an over-emphasis on formal testing generally. Further, surveys which test every pupil cannot provide the depth of data required to provide a wide-range and in-depth picture of the system. Thus testing every pupil at a particular age is not appropriate for assessing performance at the national level.

To serve the evaluative role, assessment at the national level does not need to cover all pupils nor to assess in all attainment targets those who are included. The necessary rigour and comparability in assessment for this purpose can be provided by the use of a sample of pupils undertaking different assessment tasks.

Assessing school effectiveness

It is well established that the attainment of an individual is as much a function of his or her social circumstances and the educational experiences of his or her parents as it is of the effectiveness of the school or schools attended. To judge the effectiveness of a school by the attainment of its pupils is therefore misleading and unfair. What is wanted is a model that disentangles the effect on attainment of the school from that of the pupils' background. The value-added approach, that looks at the gain in achievement while the pupils is at a particular school (that is, the progress he or she makes there) offers a way forward and is, indeed, the basis of school effectiveness research such as that reported in *School Matters* (Mortimore et al., 1988; see also McPherson, 1992).

The assessments of attainment used (both on entry to the school and on leaving) should be as broad as possible to ensure that school effectiveness is not reduced to efficiency in teaching test-taking skills but reflects the full range of the aims of the school.

To counter the narrowness of outcomes implied by test results, even when shown in value-added form, it is suggested that schools should publish detailed reports covering such areas as: the aims of the schools; details of recent inspection reports (if any); particular areas of expertise offered; cultural and sporting achievements; community involvement; destinations of leavers. In short, the school should show its test results as part of its record of achievement.

Reading 13.2

Assessment for learning
Assessment Reform Group

This extract comes from an influential pamphlet which helped to popularise the concept of 'assessment for learning'. Produced by a working group of educational researchers, it identified how feedback processes and active pupil engagement could have significant effects on learning, and how these could be embedded in routine classroom practice.

How could you investigate your own practice in respect of the 'five, deceptively simple key factors' (see below)?

Edited from: Assessment Reform Group (1999) *Assessment for Learning: Beyond the Black Box.* Cambridge: University of Cambridge School of Education, 5–8.

In a review of research on assessment and classroom learning, Paul Black and Dylan Wiliam synthesised evidence from over 250 studies (Black and Wiliam, 1998). The outcome was a clear and incontrovertible message: that initiatives designed to enhance effectiveness of the way assessment is used in the classroom to promote learning can raise pupil achievement. The scale of the effect would be the equivalent of between one and two grades at GCSE for an individual. The gain was likely to be even more substantial for lower-achieving pupils.

The research indicates that improving learning through assessment depends on five, deceptively simple, key factors:

- the provision of effective feedback to pupils;
- the active involvement of pupils in their own learning;
- adjusting teaching to take account of the results of assessment;
- a recognition of the profound influence assessment has on the motivation and self-esteem of pupils, both of which are crucial influences on learning;
- the need for pupils to be able to assess themselves and understand how to improve.

At the same time, several inhibiting factors were identified. Among these are:

- a tendency for teachers to assess quantity of work and presentation rather than the quality of learning;
- greater attention given to marking and grading, much of it tending to lower the self-esteem of pupils, rather than to providing advice for improvement;
- a strong emphasis on comparing pupils with each other which demoralises the less successful learners;

- teachers' feedback to pupils often serves social and managerial purposes rather than helping them to learn more effectively;
- teachers not knowing enough about their pupils' learning needs.

There is also much relevant evidence from research into the impact of National Curriculum Assessment in England and Wales during the 1990s, one of the most far-reaching reforms ever introduced into an educational system. That evidence suggests that the reforms encouraged teachers to develop their understanding of, and skills in, assessment. However, the very high stakes attached to test results, especially at Key Stage 2, are now encouraging teachers to focus on practising test-taking rather than on using assessment to support learning. Pupils are increasingly seeing assessment as something which labels them and is a source of anxiety, with low-achievers in particular often being demoralised.

Assessment for learning in practice

It is important to distinguish assessment for learning from other current interpretations of classroom assessment. What has become known in England and Wales as 'teacher assessment' is assessment carried out by teachers. The term does not imply the purpose of the assessment, although many assume that it is formative. This often leads to claims that what is already being done is adequate. In order to make the difference quite clear it is useful to summarise the characteristics of assessment that promotes learning.

These are that it:

- is embedded in a view of teaching and learning of which it is an essential part;
- involves sharing learning goals with pupils;
- aims to help pupils to know and to recognise the standards they are aiming for;
- involves pupils in self-assessment;
- provides feedback which leads to pupils recognising their next steps and how to take them;
- is underpinned by confidence that every student can improve;
- involves both teacher and pupils reviewing and reflecting on assessment data.

This contrasts with assessment that simply adds procedures or tests to existing work and is separated from teaching, or on-going assessment that involves only marking and feeding back grades or marks to pupils. Even though carried out wholly by teachers such assessment has increasingly been used to sum up learning, that is, it has a summative rather than a formative purpose.

The term 'formative' itself is open to a variety of interpretations and often means no more than that assessment is carried out frequently and is planned at the same time as teaching. Such assessment does not necessarily have all the characteristics just identified as helping learning. It may be formative in helping the teacher to identify areas where more explanation or practice is needed. But for the pupils, the marks or remarks on their work may tell them about their success or failure but not about how to make progress towards further learning.

The use of the term 'diagnostic' can also be misleading since it is frequently associated with finding difficulties and errors. Assessment for learning is appropriate in all situations and helps to identify the next steps to build on success and strengths as well as to correct weaknesses.

A particular point of difference with much present practice is the view of learning that the approach to assessment implies. Current thinking about learning acknowledges that learners must ultimately be responsible for their learning since no-one else can do it for them. Thus assessment for learning must involve pupils, so as to provide them with information about how well they are doing and guide their subsequent efforts. Much of this information will come as feedback from the teacher, but some will be through their direct involvement in assessing their own work. The awareness of learning and ability of learners to direct it for themselves is of increasing importance in the context of encouraging lifelong learning.

So what is going on in the classroom when assessment is really being used to help learning? To begin with the more obvious aspects of their role, teachers must be involved in gathering information about pupils' learning and encouraging pupils to review their work critically and constructively. The methods for gaining such information are well rehearsed and are, essentially:

- observing pupils – this includes listening to how they describe their work and their reasoning;
- questioning, using open questions, phrased to invite pupils to explore their ideas and reasoning;
- setting tasks in a way which requires pupils to use certain skills or apply ideas;
- asking pupils to communicate their thinking through drawings, artefacts, actions, role play, concept mapping, as well as writing;
- discussing words and how they are being used.

Teachers may, of course, collect information in these ways but yet not use the information in a way that increases learning. Use by the teacher involves decisions and action – decisions about the next steps in learning and action in helping pupils take these steps. But it is important to remember that it is the pupils who will take the next steps and the more they are involved in the process, the greater will be their understanding of how to extend their learning. Thus action that is most likely to raise standards will follow when pupils are involved in decisions about their work rather than being passive recipients of teachers' judgements of it.

Involving pupils in this way gives a fresh meaning to 'feedback' in the assessment process. What teachers will be feeding back to pupils is a view of what they should be aiming for: the standard against which pupils can compare their own work. At the same time, the teacher's role – and what is at the heart of teaching – is to provide pupils with the skills and strategies for taking the next steps in their learning.

Reading 13.3

Feedback and learning
David Spendlove

We know that 'feedback' is crucial for learning – but why is so little of it routinely provided? There are workload considerations of course, but the more fundamental challenge is interpersonal and relational – as this reading explores. David Spendlove argues that an appropriate emotional climate in a classroom must be established. When such trusting relationships exist, then the feedback loop can take another turn so that learners communicate back to the teacher. Various ideas for supporting this are offered. Complementary feedback loops then exist – from teacher to pupils, and from pupils to teacher.

How could you develop your skills for giving, and receiving, feedback?

Edited from: Spendlove, D. (2009) *Putting Assessment for Learning into Practice*. London: Continuum, 10–13.

Creating an emotional environment which enables feedback

Part of emotional literacy in schools lies in recognizing the vulnerability of children in the learning process.

Assessment processes, and in particular negative feedback, have often been used inappropriately as a short, sharp disciplinary tool – i.e. a means of paying back a pupil.

The difficulty with feedback is that we tend to take it personally and therefore will often respond personally. For instance, during research on Assessment for Learning (AfL) it was found that children who got a low summative mark would often not engage with the feedback as they felt it was merely further criticism adding more anguish to the process.

In order for all children to attempt to view feedback, even though it is personal, as a positive way to improvement means removing personalities from the situation. So although some children will feel it is teachers picking on them all of the time, the reality is often different. A process of reframing is necessary to focus on what needs to change and why, rather than blanket statements of despondency. Negative or critical feedback must be viewed as providing the key to unlocking the path to improvement while no feedback or limited feedback keeps the path locked.

One final point to remember – most of the time difficult feedback is given by someone because they care and because they are not willing to take the easy option of merely saying something palatable. Why? Because it takes much longer and is far more difficult to give what is perceived by the receiver as negative feedback.

Suggestions for improving the emotional environment for feedback

Comment-only feedback (rather than marks or grades) provides a means of preventing pupils being able to easily compare themselves with each other and also provides information on how to improve.

- Link feedback to learner's own self-assessment, thus focusing on the quality of the self-evaluation.

- Create a trusting environment – explain why we have feedback and how it leads to improvement.

- Share stories about when you have had feedback that was difficult to accept at the time but which was correct and which made you focus on improvement.

- Peer-assessment often makes the feedback process more effective.

- The timing of feedback is important – make sure that time is spent allowing children to engage and reflect on feedback that you have provided, so early on rather than at the end of the lesson if possible.

- Make sure the assessment and feedback remain focused on the learning objectives and criteria.

- Use appropriate emotive, motivating and engaging language and avoid words such as 'failed' or 'underachieved'.

- Be sensitive to the needs of the learner and look for opportunities to praise.

- As part of developing emotional literacy it is valuable to ask and discuss with learners how they feel when they get feedback that is difficult to accept.

- Look to see how your emotional literacy policy ties in with your policy on assessment for learning – they should complement each other.

Gaining feedback from learners

As well as the teacher feeding back to the learner at regular intervals about their performance, an essential part of AfL (in fact all learning) is the feedback of the learner to the teacher. This takes place throughout the lesson and is the means of the teacher adapting the learning journey according to need.

There are two key pieces of information that we are trying to obtain from learners which will ultimately shape how we teach. These are: first, the extent that the learners have understood the learning related to the objectives of the lesson; and second, the extent that learners understand and are able to make connections with the learning related to the bigger picture (such as where the new learning fits with a continuum of experiences). Making these connections is an essential part of learning as application contextualizes the learning more effectively.

Feedback should be gained at regular intervals throughout the lesson, for example, through using class plenaries to stocktake.

The two key aims of this feedback are: first, so that diagnostic teaching can take place – therefore the teaching can be adjusted in real time to ensure the most effective learning is occurring; second, to have as many learners as possible engaged and challenged for the greatest amount of time during the lesson. Central to this is making the feedback process regular, familiar and accessible for all learners.

Opportunities to gain feedback from learners

The opportunities below are the means of getting regular feedback from learners so that teaching can be adjusted to aid the next learning phase.

- *Regular starters/plenaries:* Interactive starters and plenaries don't just take place at the start and end of the lesson but throughout the learning – often marking each phase of learning.
- *Targeted questions:* Pre-planned deep questions targeted at individuals or groups to ensure that all learners are challenged in to providing feedback.
- *Think-pair-share:* Whole class engaged in thinking in pairs then sharing their thinking/ learning with group.
- *Learners assessing their own/peers' work:* Learners feedback what they have had difficulty with.
- *Learners plan questions* (with model answers) for teacher or partner: The quality of questions and answers will provide feedback on the extent of the understanding.
- *Self-assessment of understanding:* Learners feedback on their own assessments.
- *Traffic lights:* At the end of the lesson, learners are asked to indicate their understanding of each objective using red, yellow or green circle, according to whether they feel they have achieved the objective fully (green), partially (yellow) or not at all (red). Thumb-o-meter: Similar to traffic lights – thumbs up if you are confident understanding objective X, thumbs down if not.
- *Mini-whiteboards:* For a whole range of feedback from learners relating to questions or objectives, from smiley faces to drawing, spellings, equations, etc.
- *Mind maps:* Used by learners to tag and map their learning to make connections to other areas of learning.

Reading 13.4

Pupil self-assessment

Yolande Muschamp

Yolande Muschamp and a team of seconded teachers spent two years working with colleagues in 24 classrooms to develop practical ways of encouraging pupil self-assessment in primary school classrooms. One product of this action research study was this reading. It contains practical advice, based around the negotiation and use of 'targets'. The idea of pupil self-assessment is closely related Vygotsky's conception of self-regulation (see **Reading 2.3**).

Do you see a role for pupil self-assessment in your classroom?

Edited from: Muschamp. Y. (1991) 'Pupil Self Assessment', *Practical Issues in Primary Education,* No 9. Bristol: National Primary Centre (South West), 1–8.

Our discussions with teachers revealed a strong commitment to, 'on-going assessment that could be built upon every day'. Teachers wanted to support children's learning through careful use of formative assessment. What is more, many felt that children should themselves be involved in their own assessment. As one teacher put it:

> 'We are now more conscious about making children independent and responsible for their own learning. It is fascinating to see how they view their role and work, and want to look back'.

Working alongside children we were initially able to record the evaluations that they made of their work. We also asked them to comment on the work of other children presented to them in a folder. This showed that children were making assessments, but in a relatively limited way. For instance, we asked children what, specifically, made a piece of work 'good'. Although we received a wide range of answers the comments which predominated related to presentation.

> 'The writing must be neat.'
> 'The letters are very big, I think the 'g' is the wrong way round.'

Without exception the children commented on how neat or tidy they felt each piece of work to be; how large the letters were; or how accurately drawings had been coloured. Often this was given as the only reason for the work to have any worth. When questioned further, some children were able to explain some of the specific features which made a piece of work satisfactory.

> 'The answers are all right.'
> 'You mustn't repeat things like 'and then' and you must put in a lot of details and describing words.'
> 'The lines don't go over the edges.'

However, when asked why they thought they were doing a particular activity, very few children understood the specific aims of their teacher. Their comments were often very general.

> 'So when we grow up we will know how to write.'
> 'To help you get a good job.'

As a group we shared our findings and decided to see if extending children's understanding of the purpose of activities, would widen the range of comments that they made. We hoped that children would develop a fuller picture of the progress they made if more aspects of the learning aims were shared with them. It was agreed that, in each of the classes, children would be encouraged to move through three stages.

Stage 1 Sharing aims and using targets

Teachers felt that by introducing plans at the beginning of the year, and then monthly or half termly, children were provided with *an overview or context* for their work. Three parts to this strategy emerged.

The first was establishing learning objectives in which children were given, or helped to plan, clear learning objectives. The skills, knowledge and understanding that activities were designed to develop were discussed. These were presented to even very young children in such ways as, 'learning how to …' and 'learning all about…'.

Second, was selecting a focus. Here we found it was important to be very precise and explicit about what it was the children were going to do. Within activities we selected one or two specific areas to focus on, for example, 'good beginnings for stories', 'measuring accurately to the nearest centimetre' and 'concentrating on the sequence of an account'.

Finally, we made decisions on forms of learning support. For instance, children did not always have the technical language to talk about their work and rarely had considered which method to use. Introducing a few helpful terms and discussing the range of methods available became part of the sharing of aims. These might have included words such as, 'description', 'design', 'fair test', 'account'. The methods might include, 'looking closely and drawing', 'taking notes', 'using an index' and 'drafting'.

Once a child had a clear idea of what it was they were trying to do, then *planning targets* became much easier.

The targets were particularly important because, when matched closely the activities that had been planned, they allowed children to decide when the activity had been successfully completed and to monitor what they had learnt. We found that it was helpful to plan the targets as questions that the children could ask themselves. Thus, when learning a skill, the child could ask: 'What will I be able to do?'. When the learning objective was finding out or acquiring knowledge, the child could ask: 'What do I know now?'. When the objective was to develop understanding, the child could ask: 'Can I explain?'

Having planned the targets, assessing them became relatively straight forward. Children were encouraged to refer to their targets alongside their work. One pleasing effect was that children often kept on course and did not become bored with the assessments. There were also noticeable improvements in the pacing of work. The following approaches were used:

teacher assessment: with the targets planned and documented, teachers found it effective to assess them in a short discussion with a child. A child could be asked to perform, explain or give an account of a topic. This was supplemented by an open question about unexpected outcomes and general questions about activities that the child had enjoyed or taken a particular interest in.

peer assessement: working in groups, children soon found it easy to discuss and assess their targets with their friends. Many teachers were surprised at how sophisticated the questioning of each other became. In a few schools this led to the development of pupil designed questionnaires for self-assessment.

self-assessment: the children's initial comments were rather basic, such as, 'this is good, for me'. Some targets were simply ticked with no comment. However, with encouragement children soon illustrated how targets had been met and moved quickly on to planning new ones, 'I have counted threes with Daniel. I went up to 39. My next pattern is sixes'.

Stage 2 Reviewing, 'feeding forward' and recording

The main purpose of the review stage was for the child to stand back and assess the progress that they had been making over a few weeks, a month or a term. This stage also included: selecting documentation to record this progress, looking back and editing old records. A valuable outcome was the creation of a basis for reporting to parents, transferring to a new class and planning for the future.

Many different ways of reviewing were tried. The most successful often reflected the way the classrooms already operated and did not therefore appear unusual or artificial to the children. For example:

conferencing: in which time was put aside for the teacher and pupil to talk together about how targets had been met, what should be followed up and 'fed forward' into future planning. The children were already used to reading with the teacher in a one to one situation. A card index was used to keep track of who's turn it was to talk with the teacher. Notes for future planning were written on the cards.

quiet time: was provided to allow children to look through their work alone or with a partner. They were encouraged to take notes for planning and development activities.

questionnaires: were designed by the teacher and by the children as a basis for review. Some were adapted so that they could be used to annotate any work chosen to be stored as a record.

Although we found teachers continuously responding to, and advising children, it was felt that a lot of good ideas for future action were still being lost or forgotten at the review stage. Several ways of developing a system for managing this 'feed forward' were tried and proved successful. For instance:

ideas box: at a class level many ideas for future investigations were collected and stored on cards for all to use. This system operated rather like the floor book.

'how to' books: children wrote up things that they had learnt to do in a class book for others to use. However more was often learnt by children during the writing up than by other children reading the books. They were very popular and of great interest to other children.

notebooks: a small notebook or a page set aside in a larger book, folder or profile were used in some classes for children to record their own plans, areas for development and interests. These were often used to complete planning sheets.

Two particular challenges faced us at the recording stage. First, how could the recording that the children did themselves become part of everyday classroom life? Many solutions were determined by what was already happening in the classrooms. For instance, loose leaf records were selected and moved to a profile or record of achievement folder; photocopying or photography were used where schools felt able to afford them, and were already using them for other purposes; children's comments were written down for them by an older child or adult in schools where this sort of shared activity was encouraged.

Second, on what basis should a selection for a record be made? The reasons for selection varied from school to school, reflecting the policies that had been developed for similar areas such as the selection of work for displays or the participation in assemblies. In many schools children were encouraged to select their 'best work' as a record of their achievement, whereas another school decided to select 'before and after' pieces, such as, a first draft and a final desk top published version of a story; a list from a brainstorming and a drawing of the final result of an investigation in science. Additionally, sampling by subject or over time was tried.

Stage 3 Helping to report on progress

An exciting highlight of the self-assessment strategies that we were developing occurred when the children were given the opportunity to share their assessments with their parents or carers. This worked most successfully where this was part of an overall policy for home-school liaison. Schools where parents were already fully involved in classroom activities found it easier to encourage children's involvement in the reporting process. The children's role in this process varied enormously. For instance:

helping in the preparation of reports occured when children were encouraged to write a short report of their progress and thoughts about school based on the reviews that they had carried out. Teachers and the parents then added their comments.

playing host was a role undertaken when parents and carers visited the school during an ordinary day. The children took them on a tour of specially prepared displays; showed them the work they were doing; and shared their profiles or records of achievement with them.

preparing for parent interviews was an important role for children in lots of different ways, such as putting out a display of their work or taking their profiles home to share before a parent/teacher interview. Some accompanied their parents, or actually organised a parents' afternoon themselves.

It is always hard to evaluate development projects, for what may be proved to be possible in the short term may not be sustained over a longer period. However, we can record teacher opinion that the encouragement of pupil self-assessment through the use of targets had a very worthwhile effect on teaching and learning processes in the classrooms in which we worked. Furthermore, everyone – teachers, parents and pupils themselves – seemed to enjoy working in this way.

Reading 13.5

Authentic assessment for learning
Sue Swaffield

In distinguishing *assessment for learning* from its commonly used synonym *formative assessment,* Sue Swaffield draws attention to some key features of AfL. These include its focus and prime beneficiaries, its timing, the role of learners, and the fact that AfL is in itself a learning process.

Are you clear about the principles underlying authentic AfL?

Edited from: Swaffield, S. (2011) 'Getting to the heart of authentic Assessment for Learning', *Assessment in Education: Principles, Policy and Practice,* 18 (4), 441–3.

The focus of Assessment for Learning (AfL) is on the enhancement of student learning.

The prime concern is with the here and now of learning, as it occurs in the flow of activity and transactions occurring in the classroom. This is what Perrenaud (1998) refers to as the regulation of learning, and what Wiliam (2008) describes as 'keeping learning on track'. The focus is on the learning of these students now, although there is also consideration given to their learning in the near future. The immediacy and clear focus on learners and their teachers are captured in the depiction of formative assessment by Thompson and Wiliam (2007, p. 6) as:

'Students and teachers,
    … using evidence of learning,
        … to adapt teaching and learning,
            … to their immediate learning needs,
                … minute-by-minute and day-by-day.'

The emphasis is thus on everyday practice. Indeed, teachers are concerned with the learning of the pupils they are responsible for at the present, as well as for those they will teach in the future. When they review the results of periodic tests and assessments, they use that information to evaluate and revise provision, perhaps in terms of schemes of work and lesson plans, teaching approaches or classroom organisation. The information can also be used for longer-term curriculum improvement. Black et al. (2003, p. 122) point out that in this scenario, assessment is 'formative for the teacher'.

Assessment 'as' learning

AfL is, in itself, a learning process. Definitions often talk of seeking or eliciting evidence that is then used to enhance teaching and learning, but they don't always capture the constructivist, metacognitive and social learning elements of more sophisticated elaborations.

The strategies which are established as beingcentral to assessment for learning have been presented in slightly different formulations by various authors but, in essence, the practices identified by Black and Wiliam in their 1998 review (see Reading 13.2) have been repeatedly affirmed.

Sharing criteria with learners, developing classroom talk and questioning, giving appropriate feedback, and peer and self-assessment are accepted as being at the heart of assessment for learning, and yet they are not always made explicit. Indeed, introductions to AfL often give less prominence to the learning aspects of these practices than their to their formative potential.

- Sharing criteria enables learners to develop a clear sense of what they are aiming at and the meaning of quality in any particular endeavour which, coupled with self and peer assessment, helps students learn not only the matter in hand but also to develop metacognition.

- Classroom talk and questioning are very good methods for teachers to elicit evidence of pupils' understanding and misunderstandings in order to inform the next steps in learning and teaching.

- Engaging in dialogue and listening to the flow of arguments enable students to construct their knowledge and understanding – irrespective of whether the teacher uses the information gleaned formatively.

- Dialogue and peer assessment help students learn socially, through and with others.

- When students are given appropriate feed-back and the opportunity to apply it, they can learn through improving their work. More importantly, they learn that they can in effect 'become smarter' through judiciously focused effort.

Distinguishing assessment for learning from formative assessment

The terms 'assessment for learning' and 'formative assessment' are often used synonymously, but the discussion above suggests this is erroneous.

Assessment for learning differs from formative assessment in a number of ways:

- Assessment for learning is a learning and teaching process, while formative assessment is a purpose and some argue a function of certain assessments;

- Assessment for learning is concerned with the immediate and near future, while formative assessment can have a very long time span;

- The protagonists and beneficiaries of assessment for learning are the particular pupils and teacher in the specific classroom (or learning environment), while formative assessment can involve and be of use to other teachers, pupils and other people in different settings;

- In assessment for learning pupils exercise agency and autonomy, while in formative assessment they can be passive recipients of teachers' decisions and actions;
- Assessment for learning is a learning process in itself, while formative assessment provides information to guide future learning; and
- Assessment for learning is concerned with learning how to learn as well as specific learning goals, while formative assessment concentrates on curriculum objectives.

Making the distinction between formative assessment and assessment for learning clear is important particularly because the practice of using the terms synonymously has enabled assessment for learning to be misappropriated. An influential example of this was the English National Assessment for Learning Strategy introduced in 2008. For example, a list of adjectives used to describe 'good assessment for learning' was revealing, including as it did emphases on 'accuracy' and 'reliability' (DCSF, 2008, p. 5). But these are properties of summative rather than formative assessment. Although the strategy states that AfL 'focuses on how pupils learn' (DCSF, 2008, p. 5), its approach belies this by emphasising more formal and regular testing. Research has shown that frequent testing and assessment against national standards is detrimental to students' learning and motivation, especially for the lower attaining students.

Any misrepresentation of assessment for learning matters because of its power to affect people's view of the practice. Students, parents, teachers, school leaders, local authority personnel, and policy makers may be socialised into a flawed interpretation of AfL. It seems likely that this normalisation will be pervasive, self-reinforcing, and seen by the vast majority (if it is noticed at all) as unproblematic, even though enlightened teachers, school leaders and advisers undoubtedly mediate the strategy to remain as close as possible to authentic AfL.

We know from research and practice that authentic interpretations and enactments of assessment for learning improve pupils' learning – their engagement with learning, their attainment as measured by tests, and most importantly their growth in becoming more self-regulating, autonomous learners. Teachers' motivation and professional practice are enhanced. The relationships among pupils and teachers, and the culture of the classroom, are transformed.

Unless we get to the heart of authentic assessment for learning these precious prizes will not be widely realised. Teachers' professional lives will be impoverished, and the biggest and ultimate losers will be students.

Everyone committed to enhancing learning needs to strengthen and develop further our understanding of authentic assessment of learning. We need to take every opportunity to assert and explain the fundamental principles and features of AfL, including clarifying the similarities and differences between authentic assessment for learning and formative assessment. Academics, teachers, school leaders, policy makers, pupils, and parents should all be involved.

Learners, who as essential actors as well as beneficiaries are the beating heart of authentic assessment, deserve nothing less.

Reading 13.6

Creating learner identities through assessment
Gordon Stobart

> Gordon Stobart's book is concerned with the way assessment shapes the way we see ourselves, and it opens with pen portraits of two pupils whom Stobart tellingly labels 'Hannah the nothing' and 'Ruth the pragmatist'. For a related analysis, see Reading 14.7.
>
> Considering your own school career, how did assessment outcomes influence the way you thought about yourself?
>
> *Edited from:* Stobart, G. (2008) *Testing Times: The Uses and Abuses of Assessment.* London: Routledge, 1–4.

Assessment, in the form of tests and examinations, is a powerful activity which shapes how societies, groups and individuals understand themselves. Three specific arguments are developed here:

- Assessment is a value-laden social activity and there is no such thing as 'culture-free' assessment;

- Assessment does not objectively measure what is already there, but rather creates and shapes what is measured – it is capable of 'making up people';

- Assessment impacts directly on what and how we learn, and can undermine or encourage effective learning.

These characteristics invest assessment with considerable authority, and lead to constructive or destructive consequences.

Some illustrations

To flesh out these claims, we consider the ways in which school assessment began to create the learning identities of three children, Hannah, Sharon and Stuart.

Hannah is the name given to an 11 year old pupil in England in a class studied by Diane Reay and Dylan Wiliam (1999). This class was being prepared for the national tests (SATs) which children take in the last year of junior schools in England. These tests carried no major selection consequences for the pupils, since their secondary schools have already been chosen, but the results were critically important for their schools and teachers as they were publicly judged by them. Great emphasis was therefore placed on preparation for the tests, because for teachers, the task was to get as many children at level 4 and above as possible, as school and national targets were based on this. As a result of the testing and drilling, children become well aware of their expected level. It is in this context that the following exchange took place:

Hannah:	I'm really scared about the SATs. Mrs O'Brien [a teacher at the school] came in and talked to us about our spelling and I'm no good at spelling and David [the class teacher] is giving us times tables tests every morning and I'm hopeless at times tables so I'm frightened I'll do the SATS and I'll be a nothing.
Researcher:	I don't understand Hannah. You can't be a nothing.
Hannah:	Yes, you can 'cos you have to get a level like a level 4 or level 5 and if you're no good at spellings and times tables you don't get those levels and so you're a nothing.
Researcher:	I'm sure that's not right.
Hannah:	Yes it is 'cos that's what Miss O'Brian was saying. *(Reay and Wiliam, 1999, p. 345)*

To make this claim of nothingness even more poignant, the authors point out that Hannah was 'an accomplished writer, a gifted dancer and artist and good at problem solving, yet none of those skills make her somebody in her own eyes. Instead she constructs herself as a failure, an academic non-person' (p. 346).

This was not an isolated example. By the time of the SATs the children described each other in terms of levels and these had begun to affect social relationships, with the 'level 6' Stuart becoming a target for bullying in the playground. When asked about the consequences of their SAT results, this conversation followed:

Sharon:	I think I'll get a two, only Stuart will get a six.
Researcher:	So if Stuart gets a six what will that say about him?
Sharon:	He's heading for a good job and a good life and it shows he's not gonna be living on the streets and stuff like that.
Researcher:	And if you get a level two what will that say about your?
Sharon:	Um, I might not have a good life in front of me and I might grow up and do something naughty or something like that. *(p. 347)*

Tamara Bibby found very similar attitudes in her research: 'Children start to think of themselves as levels. And it's wrapped up with morality and goodness. Good people work hard and listen in class. If it suddenly becomes clear your mate gets lower levels than you, are they a good person? It can put real pressure on a friendship' (Bibby, 2010).

The power of assessment

Assessment, in the broad sense of gathering evidence in order to make a judgement, is part of the fabric of life. Our ancestors had to decide where to cross rivers and mountains and when to plant crops. Choosing the site for Stonehenge and the astronomical lining up of the rocks remains to this day an impressive assessment exercise.

However, the deliberate gathering of evidence in order to make specific judgements about individuals or groups is particularly important. Allan Hanson (1994) defines a test as 'a representational technique applied by an agency to an individual with the intention of gathering information' (p. 19). This definition can be applied more generally to constructed forms of assessment. Its value as a definition is that it signals the *representational* nature of tests; a test often stands in for, and acts as a metaphor for, what a person can do. How appropriate the metaphor is (for example, how well does a personality test represent a person's character) is at the heart of validity arguments in assessment. This definition also emphasises the social dimension of assessment, including the power that test givers have over the test taker. This gathering of information has often rested on assumptions that testing reveals objective truths that are concealed from direct observation. Hanson disputes this:

> These assumptions are mistaken. Because of their representational quality, tests measure truth as culturally construed rather than as independently existing.... By their very existence, tests modify or even create that which they purport to measure. (p. 47)

This reflects one of our initial propositions, *that assessment shapes who and what we are and cannot be treated as a neutral measure of abilities or skills that are independent of society*. Assessment of the individual is, paradoxically, an intrinsically social activity.

The philosopher of science Ian Hacking (2007) has developed a broader argument about this. As he puts it, 'sometimes our sciences create kinds of people that in a sense did not exist before. This is making up people' (p. 2). His argument provides a useful framework for understanding how assessment can classify people in ways which are then treated as representing some objective reality.

People, of course, exist independently of measurement and they differ in many ways; it is the *social choice* of how they are assessed, labelled and sorted that shapes identities. For example, labels such as Dyslexic, ADHD, and Asberger's Syndrome have recently come into common usage and assumptions are now made about people who are so labelled. One of Hacking's other examples is the 'discovery' of the Multiple Personality in the 1970s. This led to a rapid increase in the number of people exhibiting the syndrome and the number of personalities exhibited (the first person had two or three, by the end of the decade the average number was seventeen). A series of social processes was part of this development, the end result of which was that a recognisable new person, *the multiple*, came into being with a recognisable identity. There were even 'split bars' where multiples would socialise (you could meet a lot of personalities there).

Hacking proposed a framework of five interactive elements through which this assessment category was created:

1 *Classification.* This behaviour was quickly associated with a 'disorder', for example the Multiple Personality Disorder.

2 *The people.* These are the unhappy/inadequate individuals who will express this identity (or fortunate individuals in the case of 'genius').

3 *The institutions.* Clinics, training programmes and international conferences address the disorder.

4 *Knowledge.* This is both from the institutions and popular knowledge, for example the public perception that Multiple Personality Disorder was caused by early sexual abuse and that five per cent of the population suffer from it.

5 *Experts.* These generate the knowledge, judge its validity and use it in practice. They work within institutions which guarantee their status and then give advice on how to treat the people who they classify as having it.

Hacking also introduced the *looping effect*, which refers to the way those classified respond to their new identities. This may at some point take the form of resistance, for example Gay Rights seeking to restore control of the legal classifications into which homosexuals fall.

The mechanisms by which these socially created classifications are brought into being are particularly relevant to arguments about intelligence testing, multiple intelligences and learning styles, as these have followed much the same pattern. Hacking describes these as ten *engines of discovery* that drive this process: 1. Count, 2. Quantify, 3. Create Norms, 4. Correlate, 5. Medicalise, 6. Biologise, 7. Geneticise, 8. Normalise, 9. Bureaucratise, 10. Reclaim our identity (p. 10).

To provide a flavour of how these engines work I use his example of obesity, the incidence of which has risen dramatically in the last two decades. This first becomes quantified as a Body Mass Index of over 30 (*count, quantify*) and then we are given norms for underweight, normal, overweight and obese for any given age (*create norms*). It is then correlated with ill-health, for example diabetes. This is accompanied by the medical treatments, chemical and surgical, to reduce weight (*medicalise*). We then look for biological causes, not least because it relieves the person of responsibility, obesity becomes a chemical imbalance rather than personal choice. This inevitably leads to the search for the genetic basis of obesity. At the same time the effort is made to help the obese become as normal as possible through anti-craving drugs and weight loss programmes (*normalise*). The bureaucratic engine often has positive intentions, for example the recent introduction of obesity screening programmes into school to pick up young children who are already obese. The resistance sets in when the obese begin to feel persecuted and assert that bigness is good – like the ironic French 'Groupe de Re/flexion sur l'Obe/site/ et le Surpoids (GROS).

This sequence makes sense of some key educational classifications which have been generated by similar assessment and social processes. For example, the development of IQ testing followed precisely this trajectory, even to the extent of the early IQ testers creating new statistical techniques (for example scaling, normal distribution and correlational techniques) to develop engines 1–4. IQ was then *biologised* and *geneticised* by giving it a physiological basis and treating it as largely inherited. This was then built into schooling provision (engines 8 and 9), for example,11+ selection in the UK. The resistance came with the social recognition of the unfairness of this form of selection.

In short, there is no neutral assessment. Assessment shapes how societies, groups and individuals understand themselves.

part four

Reflecting on consequences

Outcomes

How do we monitor student learning achievements?

14

The focus of this chapter is on the summative use of assessment for monitoring achievements, and we start with a reading by Broadfoot (14.1) reminding us of the complexity of the issues. It is apparent that clarity of purpose is the best guide to effective use of assessment.

Reading 14.2, from the Scottish Government, provides an example of a national assessment system which appears to have been carefully configured to reinforce learning intentions. In England, a wide range of assessment arrangements are expected to develop, in place of a state system of 'levels'. In any event, multi-layered forms of target setting seem likely to remain. The use of targets to reinforce learning objectives is the subject of Butt's reading (14.3) and Ofsted's contribution (14.4) indicates how data on comparative performance can be used in school improvement processes.

The final readings are cautionary. Mansell et al. (14.5) discuss the fragility of national assessment systems and highlight the educational side-effects of systems with an overdependence on performance indicators. Sturman (14.6) records the strengths and weaknesses of international comparisons and warns against inappropriate 'policy tourism'. Finally, Filer and Pollard (14.7) argue that the social construction of assessment outcomes needs to be understood. Drawing on a sociological analysis of teacher–pupil interaction processes, they offer reasons why the notion of objective assessment is a myth.

Within *Reflective Teaching in Schools* there are four main sections. The first tackles key issues such as accountability and improvement, validity and reliability. The second concerns summative assessment using statutory and non-statutory tests, tasks, surveys, examinations and teacher assessment. A third section deals with the application of assessment data to support pupil learning, school transfer or school accountability. Finally, there is a section on record keeping and on reporting to parents – and, of course, suggestions of 'Key Readings'.

reflectiveteaching.co.uk offers extensive 'Notes for Further Reading' and additional 'Reflective Activities'. Within 'Deepening Expertise', there is discussion of a wide range of assessment issues.

Reading 14.1

Assessment: Why, who, when, what and how?
Patricia Broadfoot

This reading provides a wide-ranging overview of most of the key issues in the use of assessment in education. It demonstrates that, beyond the apparent simplicity of the examination results with which we are all familiar, lie crucial issues about purposes, processes and effects. Assessment is also powerful – in measuring or accrediting performance, enhancing or distorting learning, and in many other ways. Expert teachers need to understand it, and use it beneficially.

Which aspect of assessment, as reviewed by Broadfoot, are most relevant to your practice?

Edited from: Broadfoot, P. (2007) *Assessment Policy and Practice: The 21st Century Challenge For Educational Assessment.* London: Continuum, 3–14.

Assessment should be "the faithful servant and not the dominating master" of teaching and learning (Mortimore and Mortimore, 1984). An essential first step to achieving this is the development of 'assessment literacy' amongst all those with responsibility for teaching and learning in institutions. Teachers, lecturers and education professionals of all kinds now readily accept that an understanding of the central issues around assessment and an ability to use assessment constructively is a key element of their professional repertoire of skills.

The scope of assessment

In seeking to understand the role that assessment plays in educational activity, it is convenient to divide the discussion in terms of five central questions. The first of these is the most profound, namely: *why do we assess?* For it is in the light of the decision about purpose that we may consider other options – who is to be assessed and who is to do the assessing, what is to be assessed, when is it to be assessed, and how is the assessment to be undertaken?

Why assess?

Four generic purposes of assessment were identified by the Task Group on Assessment and Testing for England and Wales – the body which provided the blueprint for the original national assessment system. These were:

- diagnostic assessment to identify students' learning needs

- formative assessment to support and encourage learning
- summative assessment to identify learning outcomes
- evaluative assessment which is directed at assessing the quality of provision in institutions and in the system as a whole (DES, 1988).

A more sociological way of looking at the question of assessment purposes identifies the four functions of educational assessment as:

- certification of achievement (*competence)*
- selection (*competition)*
- the evaluation of provision (*content)*
- the control of both individual aspirations and systemic functioning *(control)* (Broadfoot, 1996).

Clearly, assessment serves a number of different purposes. Many of the purposes for which assessment is used are based on assumptions about its utility and effect which are rarely questioned. Our schools and universities, colleges and training centres are increasingly driven by assessment requirements. Yet, despite the enormous impact of this culture on all our lives, its desirability is rarely questioned, its effects rarely debated. The undoubted convenience of tried and tested assessment procedures underpins a web of assumptions and practices that seems almost inevitable.

In the past, it would have been possible to make a broad distinction concerning the overall purpose of assessment between its retrospective role in measuring and reporting *past* learning and achievement as in, for example, exam certificates, and its prospective role in identifying *future* potential and aptitudes when it is used as the basis for selection. However, recently there has developed a great deal of interest about the ways in which assessment can be used to support the learning process itself. This is often expressed as a distinction between assessment *for*, rather than assessment *of*, learning. It is a development that has considerable significance in terms of how we think about assessment in that it has opened up the spectrum of assessment purposes much more widely.

Central to such considerations is the distinction between 'formative' and 'summative' assessment.

- *Formative assessment* is intended to contribute directly to the learning process through providing feedback which models success and guides future efforts, as well as giving encouragement.
- *Summative assessment* is a point in time measure. It is for 'checking up' or 'summing up' what an individual learner has achieved. It is often associated with reporting, certification and selection.

In discussing the purposes of assessment, it is also useful to make a distinction between assessment for *curriculum*, that is assessment which is an integral part of the ongoing teaching and learning process and assessment for *communication* which concerns all those aspects of assessment which have to do with providing information for potential users, whether this is about students, teachers, institutions or systems. Although there are many parallels here to the distinction between formative and summative assessment, the distinction between assessment for curriculum and assessment for communication makes more emphatic the fundamental tension between the different roles of educational assessment.

At one extreme of the continuum of assessment purposes is the 'diagnostic discourse' – the private evaluative conversation that both teachers and students engage in their heads as they monitor the learning process on an on-going basis. 'How am I doing? This is so boring! Will I be finished first?' are some of the thoughts that may typically be going through learners' minds. 'Is she paying attention? He looks unhappy – he may need me to explain this again' – are some of the many monitoring observations teachers will make as part of their internal 'diagnostic discourse'.

By contrast, the collection of marks and grades that typically sits in books and on record forms and reports is much more likely to be 'dead data'. It often makes very little contribution to the business of teaching and learning itself where its primary function is reporting progress, accountability and selection (Broadfoot, 1996).

It should already be apparent that there is a fundamental tension between the two broad roles of assessment – for curriculum and for communication.

Who assesses?

This question is closely related, clearly, to the previous one of 'why assess'? The purpose of assessment will dictate who carries it out. The decision will also be influenced by who is paying for the assessment. A moment's thought will serve to highlight the inherent tensions between the purposes that teachers and other professionals might have for assessment as opposed to the candidates themselves, parents, the government and society as a whole. There will be aspects of common ground between these various groups in their shared concern with quality and with the need for fairness, but there will be important differences of emphasis too. For Government, for example, the acceptability of the assessment, its perceived legitimacy by the public, is usually paramount. For parents, by contrast, the priority may be that of motivation or minimizing the degree of stress the assessment causes for their children. However, traditionally and still today, most assessment has been conducted by those responsible for teaching.

More recently, however, two other partners have joined the ranks of the assessors. The first of these is the students themselves who, increasingly, are being called upon to engage in self-assessment and also assessment of each other, as a means of helping them understand their own learning. The other new member of the assessment team is the government. Although school inspectors are a familiar feature of most education systems, in recent years the activities of these individuals have been greatly strengthened by the advent of various new kinds of monitoring device aimed at enhancing both the accountability and the overall performance of the education system. It is the advent of the government as a major source of assessment which is fundamental to the advent of assessment as a key policy tool.

What is assessed?

Traditionally, most forms of formal student assessment have involved reading and writing – the so-called 'paper and pencil tests'. However, traditional tests and exams cover a very small portion of the potential range of skills, competencies and aptitudes that might usefully be included. As long ago as 1992, an influential report suggested that all the following aspects are potential areas for assessment:

- written expression, knowledge retention, organization of material, appropriate selection
- practical, knowledge application, oral, investigative skills
- personal and social skills, communication and relationships, working in groups, initiative, responsibility, self-reliance, leadership
- motivation and commitment, perseverance, self-confidence, constructive acceptance of failure (Hargreaves, 1992).

Hargreaves subsequently stressed the particular importance of 'learning how to learn' (Hargreaves, 2004) (see Reading 2.8).

Perhaps the most central point to bear in mind in any consideration of what is to be assessed is that the assessment tail tends to wag the curriculum dog. Teachers and students both know very well that what is assessed will be likely to form the priorities for learning, just as governments have recently realised that what is assessed in terms of institutional quality and subsequently translated into the indicators which form the basis of public judgement and league tables, is also likely to be a key driver of institutional priorities. This phenomenon, often called 'the washback effect', is one of the most important, yet least often studied aspects of assessment.

When to assess?

At first sight this may seem a less important question. However, the issue of when to assess closely reflects the underlying purpose of the assessment. Clearly, teachers' monitoring of students' understanding and engagement is likely to be continuous. If the major purpose of assessment is to encourage better learning, the need for good quality feedback is likely to be frequent.

However, assessment which is more about communication and accountability, is likely to be more spasmodic and come at the end of a particular unit of learning. This might be, for example, for coursework assessment or school reports. Assessment for certification and/or national monitoring might take place at the end of a key stage of schooling. Assessment for selection is likely to take place when there is the need for a choice to be made, either because there is a requirement to ration among those potentially qualified, and to choose the best of this group, or because such assessment is needed to help students themselves make choices about where to go next.

Where the focus is not student learning but institutional performance, the decision about when to assess is likely to be driven as much by practicalities such as cost and the availability of suitable personnel, as by more educational concerns. School inspections, for example, demanding as they are in terms of preparation and time, are likely not to take place more often than every few years. However, internal self-evaluation for the same purpose, given its more formative character, is likely to be a much more ongoing process.

It should, therefore, be clear that there is a subtle inter-action between decisions about what the assessment is for, what is to be assessed and when the assessment should take place.

How to assess?

Reference has already been made to the various forms that evidence for assessment purposes might take. This includes insights gained from informal questioning, from diagnostic tests, from various kinds of observation, self-assessment documents, portfolios and appraisal reports, as well as more conventional teacher assessments and tests and external examinations. Formal public examination is the most visible expression of assessment activity, but it is certainly the tip of a much larger iceberg.

Fundamental to any decision regarding 'how to assess' is the issue of purpose, as this will drive the kind of comparison for which the data generated will be used. Perhaps the most familiar type of assessment is *norm-referenced,* in which candidates are compared with one another. This is an approach that is closely associated with competition. Apart from the widespread belief that such competition is motivating for learners, as in, for example, sport, it has also arisen because of the need for assessment that discriminates between individuals where a selection has to be made.

However, a great deal of assessment has always been, and remains, what is called '*criterion referenced* assessment', that is, assessment in relation to a standard. Some of the earliest forms of assessment were of this kind. In practice, of course, many tests have elements of both. The process of deciding, for example, the appropriate level children ought to achieve in a national curriculum assessment, has been initially identified by some exercise in norm referencing, although the assessment itself will be criterion-referenced. Driving tests are often cited as the classic example of a criterion-referenced test since they lay down the competencies an individual needs to demonstrate if they are to be allowed a driving license. However, here again, the decision about what constitutes competence has, at some point, been made on a more norm-referenced basis.

The key distinction here is that, where the emphasis is on criterion referenced assessment, the goal is that the assessed, whether this is an individual student, a group of students, a teacher or an institution, should be capable of being successful and that all those who do meet this defined standard should pass the test. In contrast, a norm-referenced test is almost inevitably associated with a number of candidates failing, in that it distributes those being assessed in terms of the best to the worst.

More recently, a third basis for comparing performance has become widely recognised. This is so-called *ipsat*ive assessment in which the standard for comparison is that of the individual learner with himself or herself. Here the concern is to identify an individual learner's progress in relation to their own previous performance. Ipsative assessment is an approach that is, of course, just as relevant for institutions and systems as it is for individuals. It is closely associated with the more recent development of interest in assessment for learning as part of the overall concern with formative assessment.

Two other crucial concepts are needed in the toolbox of the assessor when thinking about 'how to assess'. These are the concepts of *reliability* and *validity*. These terms are now very widely used and have become a familiar part of professional vocabulary. Reliability simply relates to the *dependability* of an assessment. It reflects the degree of confidence that if a different test was to be used or a student was to be re-tested on some future occasion, the result would be broadly similar.

Validity, on the other hand, concerns the degree to which an assessment is a faithful representation of what it purports to be assessing. There are several ways of looking at validity. *'Face validity'* refers to whether the assessment being used is convincing in terms of its content as a test of the skill or knowledge in question. *Construct validity* is by contrast, a more technical term that refers to the extent to which the assessment represents the underlying knowledge or skill that it is intended to.

Validity has been a particular problem in relation to standardised multiple choice testing. This is because such tests cannot easily represent a real-life performance situation. As a result there is now a powerful trend towards more teacher assessment in the pursuit of more "authentic evidence" of student achievement and through more 'performance-based' assessment. It is increasingly being recognised that a great deal of important information about student competencies has not, in the past, been captured because of the limitations of so-called 'objective' tests. Unfortunately, efforts to introduce more complex and authentic tasks which are capable of capturing some of the more ephemeral learning objectives, such as 'creativity', have often been bedevilled by the almost inevitably low levels of reliability.

The tension between reliability and validity is one of the most enduring features of contemporary educational assessment as it weaves its way through many of the debates that take place around the questions of why, who, when, what and how.

Reading 14.2

Principles of assessment in Curriculum for Excellence

The Scottish Government

This reading illustrates national advice on reporting on progress and achievement. In particular, it shows an explicit attempt to align assessment and curriculum systems. The guidance it offers to schools legitimates and encourages use of a wide range of assessment processes and forms of evidence, so that a rounded appreciation of learning achievements can be obtained. It is also notable for its direct focus on assessing learning, rather than on making judgements about 'levels'.

To what extent in your practice can you also maintain authenticity and capacity for meaningful feedback and reporting?

Edited from: The Scottish Government (2011) *Principles of Assessment in Curriculum for Excellence, Building the Curriculum 5. A Framework for Assessment.* Edinburgh: The Scottish Government, 10, 29–31.

Curriculum for Excellence sets out the values, purposes and principles of the curriculum for 3 to 18 in Scotland. The revised assessment system is driven by the curriculum and so necessarily reflects these values and principles. A Framework for Assessment is designed to support the purposes of Curriculum for Excellence.

The purposes of assessment are to:

- support learning that develops the knowledge and understanding, skills, attributes and capabilities which contribute to the four capacities

- give assurance to parents and carers, children themselves, and others, that children and young people are progressing in their learning and developing in line with expectations

- provide a summary of what learners have achieved, including through qualifications and awards

- contribute to planning the next stages of learning and help learners progress to further education, higher education and employment

- inform future improvements in learning and teaching

Designing, discussions, tasks and activities

Assessment is part of the process of directing learning and teaching towards outcomes through enriched experiences and needs to be planned as such. Staff need to design effective discussions, tasks and activities that elicit evidence of learning. They need to ensure that assessment is fit for purpose by carefully considering the factors outlined in the previous section.

Staff should consider the following questions:

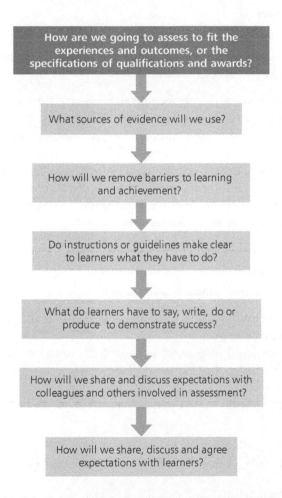

Figure 14.2.1
Questions for developing a curriculum for excellence

Staff should plan discussions, tasks and activities so that learners can provide evidence of their knowledge and skills from a range of sources and with choice of approach. These should include both in-school and out-of-school activities and should provide opportunities for learners to progress over time and across a range of activities. Staff should decide, with learners, on the most appropriate approach to assessment for a particular outcome or set of outcomes.

Sources of evidence can include:

- observations of learners carrying out tasks and activities, including practical investigations, performances, oral presentations and discussions
- records (oral, written, audio-visual) created by children and young people which may include self-assessment and/or peer assessment or may be assessed by the teacher
- information obtained through questioning in high quality interactions and dialogue
- written responses
- a product, for example, piece of artwork, report, project
- accounts provided by others (parents, other children or young people, or other staff) about what learners have done

Staff should consider ways to remove any unnecessary barriers including ensuring that language used to describe what is expected of learners is accessible. They should consider the amount of support required to ensure fairness and provide sufficient challenge.

In designing assessments staff should decide what would be appropriate evidence of achievement. This should involve reviewing exemplar materials, including those available through the National Assessment Resource, deciding on what learners would need to say, write, do or produce to demonstrate success and indicate, for example:

- expected responses to questions
- expected skills and attributes to be demonstrated
- success criteria for performances and products

Consideration should be given to how to reflect, share, discuss and agree these expectations with learners and with colleagues.

For specifically designed assessment tasks or tests, teachers should make sure that learners are clear about what they have to do. How assessment is carried out can provide opportunities for learners to demonstrate a number of skills, for example higher order thinking skills, working with others, enterprise and employability.

Assessment of interdisciplinary learning

Carefully-planned interdisciplinary learning provides good opportunities to promote deeper understanding by applying knowledge and understanding and skills in new situations and taking on new challenges. Interdisciplinary learning can take place not only across classes and departments, but also in different contexts and settings involving different partners, including colleges and youth work organisations.

This requires careful planning to ensure validity and reliability. Interdisciplinary learning needs to be firmly focused on identified experiences and outcomes within and across curriculum areas, with particular attention to ensuring progression in knowledge and understanding, skills, attributes and capabilities.

Recording progress and achievements

It is important that staff keep regularly updated records of children's and young people's progress and achievements. These should be based on evidence of learning. Learners and staff will need to select whatever best demonstrates the 'latest and best' exemplars of learning and achievement.

Much recording will take place during day-to-day learning and teaching activities. In addition, staff will periodically complete profiles of individual and groups of learners when they have been looking in-depth at a particular aspect of learning.

Approaches to recording should be:

- manageable and practicable within day-to-day learning and teaching
- selective and focused on significant features of performance

Effective recording can be used as a focus for discussions during personal learning planning to identify next steps in learning. It also helps staff to ensure that appropriate support and challenge in learning is in place for each child and young person. It can be used to share success with staff, learners and parents.

Reading 14.3

Target setting in schools
Graham Butt

Setting and monitoring targets for pupil learning can be very helpful as part of reflective practice. In particular, if targets are valid, they focus efforts and provide tangible feedback on achievement. The process thus, in principle, enables improvement – as Butt's reading describes. Targets are also used by school leaders and inspectors to hold teachers, departments and schools to account, and sophisticated systems for data entry, analysis and comparison have been developed. It is crucial, of course, that targets are appropriately aligned with educational objectives.

In the school you know best, how well aligned are stated educational objectives and measured targets?

Edited from: Butt, G. (2010) *Making Assessment Matter.* London: Continuum, 89–94.

Considerable emphasis is given to targeting the performance of underachieving students, as well as students for whom a small improvement in their performance will have beneficial effects for both them and their school (such as raising the performance of students on grade borderlines at GCSE). Despite the government's commitment to meeting the needs of every child, there are often tangible differences in how target-setting and support is delivered according to different students' abilities. This is perhaps understandable–with limited time and resources available it is necessary to take a strategic approach to setting and achieving targets.

A whole-school approach has been recommended for tackling under performance through the use of targets:

1   *Review*: Identify strengths, weaknesses and lessons learned from students' previously assessed performance. Review progress of current students – identify those on target to meet or exceed national expectations at the end of their key stage; identify groups or individual students who are not making sufficient progress, or who are at risk of 'failing'.

2   *Plan*: Adapt schemes of work and teaching plans to address weaknesses shared by many students. Create an intervention plan, set targets and organize support for students at risk.

3   *Implement*: Apply revised schemes of work and teaching plans. Ensure subject teams, year teams and support staff work collaboratively to implement the plan.

4   *Monitor and evaluate*: Monitor the implementation. Track students' progress towards their targets, particularly those receiving additional support. Evaluate the impact of the revised schemes of work, teaching plans and intervention plan and adjust as necessary. *(Adapted from DfES, 2004)*

At the classroom level, national and local data of student performance can be used to help set targets. However, there is also a mass of assessment data that is already 'in front of you' that can be used for setting targets – assessed work from your students, ephemeral teacher assessments, test and exam results, observations, moderation of work across the department or school, and subject reports. All of these sources of evidence can combine to build up a picture of what are appropriate, achievable, realistic and timely targets to set.

Target-setting is a professional activity, usually performed at departmental and individual class level. It must value the professional judgement of teachers and should be based on accurate summative and formative assessment practices. In many schools the setting of targets is par to a system of monitoring and evaluating student performance, sometimes referred to as an 'improvement cycle' (see Figure 14.3.1).

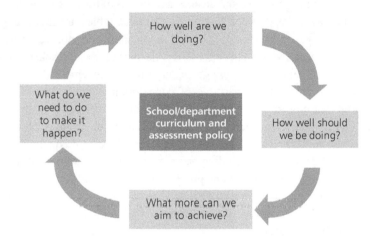

Figure 14.3.1
An improvement cycle (after Finders and Flinders, 2000: 78)

Flinders and Flinders (2000) draw an important distinction between forecasts and targets. Forecasts are what school, department, teacher or student might reasonably be expected to achieve based on measures of current practice and performance. Targets build on forecasts, but with the important addition of a degree of challenge designed to drive up standards. This may be modest or ambitious according to circumstances.

Target-setting uses a range of diagnostic, predictive and comparative data in relation to the school's performance. These are combined with assessment information gathered at classroom levels which takes into account the strengths, weaknesses and potential of individual students. All of this data should be considered within the context of the school's general performance levels and any information available on its overall achievements and expectations, such as inspection reports. It is important that whatever targets are set are realistic and achievable. There is no point in setting targets that are clearly unattainable given the context of the levels of resource input and the nature of the school.

Target-setting should be related to plans which aim to improve student learning. Such a process often refers to the setting of 'curricular targets' – targets in which numerical and descriptive data are translated into an achievable outcome, often involving specific teaching and learning objectives. The DfES (2004) represented this process as follows:

Information gathering (evidence base from which areas for improvement are identified)

information analysis (identification of areas of weakness which provide the basis for establishing curricular targets)

action planning (intervention, support and monitoring – activities that work towards achieving curricular targets)

success criteria (the possible outcomes for specific cohorts of students that will show that targets have been achieved).

Targets, particularly short-term targets, should be shared with students in an appropriate form.

One approach could be to setup a spreadsheet as a means of tracking performance against the targets. Data may be represented though into graphs, tables, averages, aggregates or statistical diagrams, as appropriate. Spreadsheets might show current level of performance, test scores, external data as well as target grades/levels and records of teacher-assessed work.

Carr (2001) has developed a technique of targeting achievement through the use of narrative. Drawing on the work of early years' educators in New Zealand she shows how teachers built up 'learning stories' for each of their students on a day-to-day basis, based on a narrative of their achievements. The principle which underpins such stories is that they recognize the individuality of the learner and seek to give credit for what they can do. The story is comprehensive, including accounts of learning at home, engaging whole families in the learning and assessment process. Here the view of learning is holistic, recognizing that it cannot be easily broken down into lists of areas, content, skills and abilities to be learnt. As Drummond (2008: 14) notes with reference to the teachers in New Zealand who use this approach:

> Their construction of learning is very different; they see it as a moving event, dynamic and changeful, practically synonymous with living. They see no need to restrict their assessment to the building blocks of literacy or numeracy: the learning stories are comprehensive in their scope.

Clarke (1998) makes the important point that targets are most meaningful and relevant to students if they are set from their starting points, rather than being filtered down from the objectives and goals of teachers and senior managers in schools. Here students have to be able to see short-term, achievable steps within the targets, which must be carefully constructed to match their particular needs as reflected by their current performance levels. As Harlen (2008: 145) states:

> Openness about goals and criteria for assessment not only helps students to direct their effort appropriately but removes the secrecy from the process of summative assessment, enabling them to recognize their own role in their achievement instead of it being the result of someone else's decisions.

The setting of targets has always gone on in schools. Traditionally, teachers have carried with them a professional appreciation of where individuals and groups of students 'should be' within their learning – particularly as they have progressed towards high stakes assessment points. Schools have also made judgements about their aggregate performance, and made comparisons with other schools.

Today, the recording and achievement of school targets, as well as the assessed performance of individual students, is a more open, publicly accountable exercise than in the past. Meeting targets is an annual, national expectation for the education sector – with ever more elaborate means of ensuring that neither students nor teachers fall by the wayside.

However, grades and levels do not, of themselves, motivate students to improve their performance – feedback from teachers needs to be personal, inclusive and practical to ensure such changes.

Reading 14.4

Using data to improve school performance
Office for Standards in Education

> This reading is an official view from England's Ofsted on how schools can use performance data – and it illustrates some key principles. The most important is that, because schools are complex and multi-dimensional, a range of information and forms of analysis are essential. Viewing the achievements of a school too narrowly risks giving a distorted impression – though Ofsted then emphasise the particular importance of performance data. This contemporary dilemma has to be managed.
>
> What forms of data does your school use, and how are they interpreted?
>
> *Edited from:* Office for Standards in Education (2008) *Using Data, Improving Schools*. London: Ofsted, 10–12.

Why each kind of data is important

No single kind of data or analysis can tell the whole story about a school. To make an accurate three-dimensional image of a human being, photographs from as many angles as possible would be needed. Similarly, to achieve a rounded and comprehensive picture of a school's recent performance, a range of different kinds of data and analyses is required.

In schools of all kinds, it is always important to know what the pupils have attained in comparison with pupils of their age nationally. When evaluating a school's performance, it is fair to make suitable allowances for the context in which it is working, but for the pupils' prospects in their future lives, no allowances will be made. The raw results are all that matter to them and to their future chances.

It is also important to know how different groups of pupils have performed in absolute terms. It is no help to pupils from a particular ethnic group who have not performed well to know that other pupils from the same group nationally have not performed well. The priority is to improve the performance of all individuals and, if a particular group is underachieving, to focus particular efforts on improving the performance of individuals in that group.

The 'floor targets' set by the Government are framed in terms of absolute attainment at particular thresholds. The rationale for these targets is to improve the life chances of all pupils by identifying expectations of minimum standards which all pupils should reach at key stages. A further function of the 'floor targets' could be seen as ensuring that no pupil attends a mainstream school at which the overall attainment outcomes fall below a certain level – it having been shown that the overall attainment of a cohort influences the attainment of individuals within that cohort.

When evaluating school performance, however, value added data are important. [Simple value added data record gains in attainment by a schools' pupils over a period. Contextualised value added augment these data by comparing the schools' performance with those of other schools in matched circumstances.] Both simple and contextual value added data have roles to play in building up an overall picture of a school's effectiveness, and each can be a corrective for the other. Contextual data illustrate the extent to which non-school factors can legitimately be regarded as having influenced the pupil progress in relation to prior attainment. Simple value added measures can bring a sense of perspective if a school's contextual value added measure is particularly high or low. But 'absolute' success remains crucial.

How schools can use performance data

School performance data matter because they provide the basis for schools' accountability to their users and the local community, for their own monitoring and self-evaluation and for their planning for improvement. Such data also inform judgements about whether a school is providing value for money.

Although schools in England operate within a statutory framework and respond to priorities and initiatives produced nationally, they retain considerable scope to make local decisions about how to manage their affairs. Therefore, although what they do is at least partly prescribed, how they do it and how well they do are matters over which the school has considerable control.

Schools are responsible and therefore accountable in a number of ways and in a number of directions. In the first instance they are accountable to their users, those for whom they provide a service, principally, pupils and their parents, but also (and increasingly) to others in the local community who may use the extended services for which schools are now taking responsibility. In a sense, too, schools are also accountable to those who will be responsible for the next stages of the education or training that their pupils will receive, and to the employers for whom they will eventually work. Schools are also accountable to the national and local bodies that fund education and ultimately to the taxpayers and others who provide the resources.

Some key accountability questions are:

- How good are the results attained by the pupils?

- How good is the education and care provided by the school?
- How much value is provided for the money and other resources made available to the school?

Responding satisfactorily to these questions requires evidence. The most powerful evidence, and that which best facilitates comparison, is that provided by data relating to the performance of pupils.

Schools can, and do, make extensive use of performance data for self-evaluation and planning for improvement, and also when reporting on their performance to a range of external audiences, notably parents and the local community. For the latter purpose, they generally use the same widely understood threshold measures as are used for national reporting.

For self-evaluation and planning for improvement, however, a more detailed analysis is required, enabling the school to identify the strengths and weaknesses of its performance not only across phases, subjects and groups of pupils, but also class by class, pupil by pupil and question by question, using the full range of data: raw results, value added and contextual information. The purpose is to enable the school to diagnose the reasons for any variations in performance, to identify priorities for improvement, and to plan the actions and put in place the support to bring about that improvement.

Neither contextual value added nor any other system of evaluation should be used to set lower expectations for any pupil or group of pupils. The focus must be on helping schools and their pupils achieve the best outcomes possible.

Reading 14.5

The reliability, validity and impact of assessment

Warwick Mansell, Mary James and the Assessment Reform Group

This reading raises concerns about the reliability, validity and impact of the national assessment system in England during the 2000s, but illustrates issues which are of relevance anywhere. There are crucial issues about 'dependabilty' – can you really rely on national assessment scores for the sorts of decisions you need to take? And there is another set of issues around congruence, or the lack of it – does national assessment reinforce or distort educational objectives.

Could you discuss these issues with a group of colleagues?

Edited from: Mansell, W., James, M. and Assessment Reform Group (2009) *Assessment in schools. Fit for purpose?* A Commentary by the Teaching and Learning Research Programme. London: TLRP, 12–13.

Assessment data, for the most part based on pupil performance in tests and examinations, are now used in an extraordinary variety of ways, underpinning not just judgments of pupils' progress, but helping measure the performance of their teachers, schools and of the nation's education system as a whole. These uses can have far-reaching consequences for those being judged by the data.

Reliability

A first important question for research, policy and practice, therefore, should be the *reliability* of this information. In simple terms, how accurate is the assessment data generated, particularly, through national tests and examinations, as an indicator of what we might want to measure?

Research suggests that we should treat national test results in England, as measures of pupil performance, with caution. Dylan Wiliam estimated in 2000 that at least 30 per cent of pupils could be misclassified in such tests. In December 2008, Paul Newton suggested a figure closer to 16 per cent. In March 2009, the Qualifications and Curriculum Authority published research based on tests taken in 2006 and 2007. This analysed the number of times markers agreed on the level to award to pupils' answers in the now-discontinued key stage 3 tests in English, maths and science. The extent of agreement varied from 95 per cent in maths to 56 per cent in English writing, the latter suggesting that markers disagreed on the 'correct' level to award in nearly half of these cases.

There is thus a need for published health warnings around the reliability of the tests and examinations. The question of the impact on public confidence, of being open about the degree of error in the testing system, needs of course to be taken seriously. However, the argument that there is a need to be transparent about the limits and tentativeness of the judgments being made about individuals under the testing regime carries greater weight. There is also a clear need for more research on reliability.

Validity

The second key question surrounds the *validity* of national tests and examinations: do they measure the aspects of education which society feels it is important to measure?

There has been a continuing debate around the validity of national curriculum tests, particularly in England. For example, the absence of any assessment of oracy within the external Key Stage 1, 2 and 3 English tests has been a source of contenti on for many, especially as speaking and listening is often seen as the foundation for children's mastery of the subject. If English national test data are central to the construction of performance information on schools but leave out this central part of the subject, how valid are the judgments that follow? Similar arguments by science organisations in relation to Key Stage 2 science tests – that they failed to measure all that was important about that subject, including experimental and investigative work – helped persuade the government in England to scrap these assessments.

Impact

The third key question surrounds the impact of publishing information on pupils' test and examination scores on classroom practice. This is, arguably, the defining question of the English government's education policies, and an extraordinary amount has been written about it. There is little doubt that policies such as performance tables, targets and Ofsted inspections that place great weight on test and examination data have driven behaviour in schools. Advocates of this system argue that it has helped teachers focus on what those designing the performance measures regard as essential to the educational experience, such as facility with English and mathematics.

Yet there is now a great volume of material cataloguing the educational side-effects of a structure which is too focused on performance indicators. These include the often excessive and inequitable focus of many schools on pupils whose results may be key to a school hitting particular achievement targets; the repetition involved in months of focusing on what is tested and on test practice, which also serves to narrow the curriculum; and the consequent undermining of professional autonomy and morale among teachers.

The impact on pupil motivation to learn is an area of particular interest. If one of the central aims of assessment for learning is to encourage independent motivation to understand among pupils, findings from research that learners in high-stakes testing systems can become dependent on their teacher to guide them towards answers should be taken seriously.

More generally on pupil motivation, the most extensive review of research in recent years on the effect of the tests found that those that were seen as 'high stakes' de-motivated many children. Only the highest attainers thrived on them, with many showing high levels of anxiety. After the introduction of national testing in England, the research found, self-esteem of young children became tied to achievement, whereas before there was little correlation between the two. This effect was found to increase the gap between low- and high-achieving pupils, with repeated test practice tending to reinforce the poor self-image of the less academic. The review also found that pupils tended to react by viewing learning as a means to an end – the pursuit of high marks – rather than as an end in itself.

On the other hand, it has been argued that some children and young people thrive in the face of stressful challenges and that external tests and examinations do motivate pupils to take what they are learning seriously. Indeed, the government in England has suggested this recently, when arguing that the possible introduction of new tests, which Key Stage 2 pupils could take up to twice a year, could increase motivation. There is as yet little evidence for this claim.

Making best use of international comparison data

Linda Sturman

For more than 50 years, the International Association for the Evaluation of Educational Achievement (IEA) has been conducting comparative studies of educational achievement in a number of curriculum areas, including mathematics and science. For exemplary information on such tests, see http://timssandpirls.bc.edu and for IEA's cautionary approach to application, see Mirazchiyski (2013). Similarly, the OECD has been providing comparative evidence on student achievement, through their Programme for International Student Assessment (PISA), see www.oecd.org/pisa. In this reading, Sturman (Director of International Comparison at the NFER) summarises the strengths of these studies but also emphasises the need for care when interpreting their findings.

   With others, could you list the value, and dangers, of international comparison?

Edited from: Sturman, L. (2012) 'Making best use of international comparison data', *Research Intelligence,* 119, Autumn/Winter, 16–17.

International comparison studies are increasingly high profile, providing large-scale datasets that focus on a range of areas. Recent studies include PIRLS (reading literacy at ages 9–10), TIMSS (mathematics and science at ages 9–10 and 13–14), CivEd and ICCS (civics and citizenship at secondary school), PISA (reading, mathematical literacy, scientific literacy and problem solving at age 15), ESLC (European languages at secondary school), and PIAAC (adult competences). The studies collect achievement data and a wealth of data relating to background variables (at school-, class- and pupil-level, and in the home context) that might impact on achievement.

   As well as direct involvement in the international coordination of some of these studies, NFER has long-standing experience as the National Centre coordinating such studies on behalf of the UK education departments. This provides us with a unique insight into the value of the surveys and the context in which their data is collected and can be interpreted.

The value of international comparison surveys

These large-scale surveys are conducted by two key organisations, the IEA and the OECD. Their aims in relation to these studies are to describe the current situation with a view to monitoring, evaluating and supporting future policy and development:

'Fundamental to IEA's vision is the notion that the diversity of educational philosophies, models, and approaches that characterize the world's education systems constitute a natural laboratory in which each country can learn from the experiences of other.' *(Martin and Mullis, 2012)*

'Parents, students, teachers, governments and the general public – all stakeholders – need to know how well their education systems prepare students for real-life situations. Many countries monitor students' learning to evaluate this. Comparative international assessments can extend and enrich the national picture by providing a larger context within which to interpret national performance.' *(OECD, 2009, p. 9)*

Outcomes from the studies have certainly been used for policy development in the UK. For example, outcomes from PIRLS, TIMSS, PISA and ICCS have informed policy and curriculum review in England, and PISA outcomes have prompted a review of standards in Wales. Other uses of the data can also support evaluation and development. For example, specific findings from some studies have been shared with teachers and subject associations, with a view to supporting reflections on how to improve teaching and learning. So the value of international comparisons seems clear.

But is it really that simple?

Unfortunately not. Probably the greatest risk in the use of large-scale international datasets is the ease with which it is possible to draw overly simplistic – or erroneous – conclusions. The datasets tend to be descriptive. They rank each country's attainment relative to other participants. They identify strengths and weaknesses in performance and trends over time. They describe the national context of achievement, and highlight apparent associations between achievement and context. Even so, despite this wealth of data, there are some things that large scale international datasets cannot do.

A major potential pitfall in using outcomes from international datasets is the risk of inappropriate 'policy tourism'. A policy or practice that suits its home country perfectly may not transfer so comfortably to a country where the culture, context and educational system are very different. In using outcomes from these studies, therefore, it is important to consider which countries' outcomes are useful for policy development. Some examples of different types of useful comparator group are:

- High performing countries (can offer insights into how to improve others' education systems).

- Countries with a similar context (may offer insights based on a similar education system, similar socio-economic or linguistic profile, or similar economic goals).

- Countries which have previously performed less well than expected and have reformed their education systems (can provide a model for consideration).

A key factor in any decision about comparator groups is the extent to which their respective contexts are likely to support transferability.

A second potential pitfall is that international comparison outcomes generally do not indicate causality: they cannot say (for example, where there is an apparent association between factor A and achievement at level B), whether A causes B, or B causes A, or whether the association is caused by a third, related variable.

Another limitation is that, for countries where more than one survey of a subject area is carried out, it is tempting to draw conclusions across the surveys. However, this can be complex if they appear to show different results. The surveys tend to report outcomes on a standardised scale, often set to a mean of 500. This gives the illusion of being able to compare scores on different surveys directly. However, because of the different content and focus of each survey, comparison is only possible within a scale not across scales.

Another illusion is that, even if scores cannot be compared directly across surveys, the respective country rankings can be compared. This is, of course, an illusion because rankings are affected not only by performance, but also by the combination of countries in a survey. Once the combination of countries in a survey changes, any attempt at direct comparison becomes invalid. Rankings can also be affected by measurement error. Tests of statistical significance can mediate the risk and this means that intra-survey ranking of countries into *bands* of similar achievement may be more reliable than absolute rankings. The issue of rankings being affected by the combinations of countries within each survey remains, however.

So can these limitations be overcome?

Valid use of the data and outcomes can be achieved by treating the international findings not as end-points, but as useful indicators and starting points for further investigation. The datasets for these studies are usually made available for further research and, because they are complex, are accompanied by detailed technical guidance and, sometimes, training. Because the international study reports are designed to identify international trends, they do not give complete analysis in the national context.

However, further analysis can be useful, based on the national dataset of a single country or subset of countries. This can provide more targeted outcomes to inform national policy and development. Such analysis allows data to be used in the context of the survey from which it was sourced, but integrated with and contributing to other research outcomes.

Reading 14.7

The myth of objective assessment
Ann Filer and Andrew Pollard

This reading highlights the social factors that inevitably affect school assessment processes, pupil performance and the interpretation of assessment outcomes. The consequence, it is argued, is that national assessment procedures cannot produce 'objective' evidence of pupil, teacher or school performance. Whilst much assessment evidence may have valuable uses in supporting learning and has a massive impact in the development of pupil identity, it is an insecure source of comparative data for accountability purposes.

How do circumstances affect assessment in your school?

Edited from: Pollard, A. and Filer, A. (2000) *The Social World of Pupil Assessment: Processes and Contexts of Primary Schooling.* Continuum: London, 8–11.

The assessment of educational performance is of enormous significance in modern societies. In particular, official assessment procedures are believed to provide 'hard evidence' on which governments, parents and the media evaluate educational policies and hold educational institutions to account; pupil and student learners are classified and counselled on life-course decisions; and employers make judgements about recruitment.

Underpinning such confident practices is a belief that educational assessments are sufficiently objective, reliable and impartial to be used in these ways. But is this belief supported by evidence? Can the results of nationally required classroom assessments be treated as being factual and categoric?

Our longitudinal, ethnographic research (Filer and Pollard, 2000) focused on social processes and taken-for-granted practices in schools and homes during the primary years. In particular, it documented their influence on three key processes: the production of pupil performance, the assessment of pupil performance and the interpretation of such judgements. On the basis of this analysis we argue that, despite both politicians' rhetoric and the sincere efforts of teachers, the pure 'objectivity' of assessment outcomes is an illusion. More specifically, we suggest that:

- individual pupil performances cannot be separated from the contexts and social relations from within which they develop;
- classroom assessment techniques are social processes that are vulnerable to bias and distortion;
- the 'results' of assessment take their meaning for individuals via cultural processes of interpretation and following mediation by others.

Our argument thus highlights various ways in which social processes *inevitably* intervene in assessment.

In this reading we confine ourselves to describing and selectively illustrating the core analytic framework which we have constructed. In particular, we identify five key questions concerned with assessment. These are set out in Figure 14.7.1.

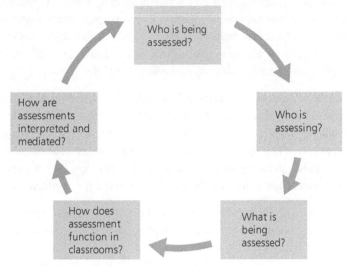

Figure 14.7.1
Questions
concerning social
influences on
assessment

Who is being assessed?

The key issue here concerns the pupil's personal sense of identity. Put directly, each pupil's performance fulfils and represents his or her sense of self-confidence and identity as a learner.

We see self-perceptions held *by* individuals and judgements made *about* individuals as being inextricably linked to the social relationships through which they live their lives. Of course, there certainly are factors that are internal to the individual in terms of capacities and potentials, but realisation of such attributes is a product of external social circumstances and social relationships to a very significant extent (see Pollard with Filer, 1996). Amongst these are school assessments, of various forms, which constitute formalised, partial, but very powerful social representations of individuals. In our full account (Filer and Pollard, 2000), we provide extensive case-study examples of such influences on the development of children's identities – for instance, through the story of Elizabeth and her primary school career.

In the autumn of 1988, five year old Elizabeth entered Mrs Joy's reception class with about twenty-seven other children and began her schooling at Albert Park. She was a physically healthy, attractive and lively child and assessments made during that first year relate to such characteristics, as well as to her intellectual and linguistic competence. Teacher records recorded a range of Elizabeth's communication, physical and intellectual skills.

> Vocabulary good – a clear ability to express herself – confident – can communicate with adults. Can concentrate and talk about her observations.
> Good language and fine motor skills – reading now enthusiastic – writing good.
> Can organise herself, is able to take turns.
> *(Profile for Nursery and Reception Age Children, Summer 1989, Reception)*

However, Mrs Joy perceived Elizabeth's classroom relationships in a more negative light, as her records from the time also show:

> Elizabeth is loud during class activity time – she never looks particularly happy unless doing something she shouldn't be. Elizabeth is a loud boisterous child who needs constant correction of negative behaviour. When corrected she often cries and becomes morose for a short period. Elizabeth doesn't mix well with the girls and disrupts them at any given opportunity. *(Teacher records, Reception, 1988–89)*

Elizabeth's mother related to her daughter's identity as a girl and a wish that she was 'more dainty' and, in the opinion of her Year 2 teacher, a wish that she could have 'a neat, quiet child'. Certainly Eleanor Barnes held gendered expectations regarding the learning styles of girls and boys. Though, of course, she certainly wished for Elizabeth to do well at school, she revealed in many of her conversations in interview an expectation for a physical and intellectual passivity in girls that Elizabeth did not conform to. For instance:

> ...I mean, in some ways I think she should have been a boy because she's got so much *energy*, and she just wants to know about *everything* – How does this work? Why does it work like that? What do you do with this? – I mean, probably that is *her*. That is her personality. She wants to know everything and she wants to know what everybody else is doing. *(Eleanor Barnes, parent interview with Ann Filer, July 1995, Year 6)*

Even these brief illustrative snippets of data convey the interaction between the evolving identity of children and the views and actions of significant others in their lives. The data demonstrates just how diverse, complex and enduring such influences can be. However, variability in such social support for children is likely to be echoed by variability of their performance – with the result that this may not reflect their true potential. Performance is thus, in part, a social product which reflects self-belief and circumstances.

Who is assessing?

Having argued that pupil identity can only be understood in context, we clearly need to focus on teachers – since they are undoubtedly the most powerful classroom participants with whom pupils must interact.

In particular, we need a sociological conception of pedagogy and its link to each teacher's own sense of personal identity. For this, we have used the concept of 'coping strategy' and traced how satisfying role expectations and the constant pressures of teaching must be balanced with maintaining sense of personal integrity and fulfilment. In the immediacy of classroom dynamics, this can be seen as teachers juggle to resolve endemic dilemmas. At the level of the school, it is played out through negotiation between different interest groups and the formation of taken-for-granted institutional assumptions. In *The Social World of Pupil Assessment* (Filer and Pollard, 2000), we relate such issues to the context of the early 1990s in which the National Curriculum and new assessment requirements were introduced. A case study of Marie Tucker and her classroom practice demonstrates the detailed application of this analysis, showing how her coping strategies, classroom organisation and associated pedagogies produced particular contexts which satisfied her, but within which pupils such as Elizabeth then had to learn and perform. It also documents how Mrs Tucker began to perceive and assess pupils in terms of their actions in relation to her personal criteria.

Teachers thus mediate national policy, and this is likely to be a constructive process as requirements are adapted to particular classroom and pupil circumstances. However, whatever the settlement achieved by the teacher, the pupil has to respond to that situation and accept assessment in terms of his or her teacher's interpretation. This, we argue, will reflect both standard national requirements and local, or personal, adaptions.

What is being assessed?

An official answer to such a question might point to the subject content of a test, or to listed criteria of judgement, and would draw conclusions in terms of the 'attainment' of pupils. More colloquially, inferences about the particular 'abilities' of children may be legitimated by faith in the objectivity and categoric techniques of 'standardised assessment'. However, we argue that such confident conclusions are misplaced, because pupil knowledge, skills and understandings are embedded in particular socio-cultural understandings and further conditioned by factors such as gender, ethnicity and social class.

To put the problem simply, to what extent does National Curriculum Assessment measure the inherent capability of a pupil, and to what extent the influence of socio-economic and cultural factors on a child? Would we be assessing Elizabeth's performance as a distinct entity, or must we also recognise the circumstances that enable or restrict her capabilities? This could lead into an analysis of the material, cultural and social capital available to families, and the extent to which children embody such advantages or disadvantages and are thus more, or less, able to cope with the school curriculum. Similarly, at the level of the peer group, we could focus on the ways in which cultural factors can enable or constrain performance. Whilst the school performance of some children may be enhanced by being with a 'good group of friends', a well understood influence is also that of an anti-learning culture. In many comprehensive schools this is a very serious problem, through which 'swots', 'ear-oles', and 'keeners' are denigrated. Sadly, we also found signs of it in the primary schools we studied, with some children wanting to avoid achievement because 'it's so embarrassing when you get praised by everybody'.

Thus, whilst pupils' subject knowledge, skill or understanding may seem to be 'objectively' revealed by the neutral, standardisation technique of a test or assessment procedure, test results also reveal the facilitation or constraint of socio-cultural influences and forms of understanding. In *The Social World of Pupil Assessment* we illustrated the latter through a detailed analysis of a Year 3 'news' session at Albert Park Primary School. In particular, we showed how classroom meanings were created through interaction of circumstances, strategies and identities, and how language was used to satisfy pupil agendas as well as in response to teacher-led instruction.

Assessment, this analysis suggests, can never tap pure knowledge or capability – any result will also always reflect the wider socio-cultural circumstances of its production. Beyond the formal subject-matter, what *else* is being assessed?

How does assessment function in classrooms?

To really try to understand classroom assessment, we felt that we needed to trace the links between assessment and other sociologically important influences on classroom life – ideology, language and culture.

As a whole, these factors are played out through particular power relations between teachers and pupils, and have significant consequences for social differentiation. We have explored these ideas drawing on some of Basil Bernstein's work (1975) to analyse how assessment and other classroom processes are bound together in patterns of authority and control. We contrasted ways in which particular forms of assessment give rise to patterns of teacher-pupil relationships and interactions in the teaching process, and patterned goals for learning. In particular, we analysed ways in which testing and other assessment practices associated with 'performance goals' can act to polarise pupil attainment and thus, unwittingly, can promote 'learned helplessness' in some children. Additionally, we considered ways in which contrastive forms of teachers' assessment language can act to promote or inhibit pupils' responses. This highlights the ways in which classroom language is conditioned by patterns and forms of control, which are embedded in teachers' routine, everyday practices.

The consequence of this analysis, we would argue, is that it is not possible for teachers to be 'neutral' in their impact on pupil performance or in their assessment of pupil performance. Irrespective of intentions, each teacher's assessment practices generates a *particular* set of evaluative circumstances within which interaction with each child takes place. Elizabeth's experience was particular – it was not entirely shared by her classmates, nor was it consistent from year to year. The scope for variability in the overall effect of assessment practices is enormous.

How are assessment interpreted and mediated?

In following-through the assessment process, we needed to consider the various 'audiences' for assessments, with particular reference to families and, to a lesser extent, peers. How do they react to the assessment judgements that are made, and what effect does their reaction have?

For pupils such as Elizabeth, parents, siblings, families and peers are important 'significant others'. We traced their influence throughout our case-study children's lives from age 4 to age 11, and found that their response to seemingly official assessment results was particularly important. Most specifically, in *The Social World of Pupil Assessment* we analysed how families interpret, mediate and give meaning to assessment outcomes so that their impact on their child is shaped and filtered. Whilst a few parents appeared to take assessment results at face value, far more engaged in supportive conversations with their children. Knowing their children very well, they were able to explore the test outcomes in relation to their previous experiences, aptitudes and future interests. In this way, the personal meaning and significance of the tests was negotiated, endorsed and concluded as the latest episode in the family narrative of each pupil's childhood. Such meanings and conclusions were crucial for future self-confidence and engagement with new learning.

Once again then, we would argue that the outcomes of assessment cannot be seen as categoric and direct in their consequence. Rather, their meaning is malleable and is drawn into existing frames of reference, relationships and patterns of social interaction. For each learner, this is an extremely important process in the development of further phases of their personal narrative and in the construction of identity.

Conclusion

Overall then, in relation to each of the five major questions set out in our cyclical model, we emphasise the influence of social factors on assessment. In particular, learner, assessor, focus, process and interpretation are all embedded in particular socio-cultural contexts and caught up in webs of social relationships.

In such circumstances, we believe that the technical 'objectivity' of assessment is a myth too far. Certainly, it is an insecure foundation on which to base categoric and high-stakes measures of performance for teacher, school and LEA comparison. Indeed, we would go further and argue that because of these, and other, sociological factors, presently established assessment practices are likely to yield patterns and systematic effects which are fundamentally divisive. As a consequence, policy-makers' attempts to configure the education system to meet the demands of international competition, may also unwittingly reinforce social divisions and widen the life-chance gaps which many children already face. The relationship between performance and circumstances cannot be removed or wished away.

Inclusion

How are we enabling opportunities?

15

The readings in this chapter reflect the prolific research that exists concerning inequalities within our societies and on the provision of inclusion within schools.

Richardson's Reading (15.1) reviews ten principles underpinning legislation on equality and diversity. In so doing, he provides an overview of dimensions of inequality and the challenges facing schools. In Reading 15.2, Pollard draws on a range of social research to offer a model for analysing processes of differentiation and polarisation within schools.

Focusing on the case of children with special educational needs, Thomas and Loxley (15.3) challenge us to be clear about the nature of 'difference'. Is it, and the diversity with which it is associated, to be welcomed, or feared?

An even more prevalent criterion of difference is that of 'ability'. Hallam (15.4) reviews research on how many grouping practices in schools are based on this concept. She suggests that, whilst grouping by attainment can have positive academic effects in the short term, it can also have significant unintended consequences. For the future, Hallam recommends flexible grouping based on systematic monitoring of all pupil's progress. It may be that contemporary technologies are now making this possible. Thorne (15.5) provides more immediate ideas on how, with particular reference to gender, to avoid divisive effects and promote cooperative classroom relationships.

The chapter concludes with a reading from Kershner (15.6) on 'learning in inclusive classrooms'. She brings together powerful ideas on learning environments (see Chapter 8) and psychological analyses on learner expectations and self-perception (see Chapter 2).

The parallel chapter of *Reflective Teaching in Schools* considers the social consequences of children's classroom experiences. It begins with a review of the major dimensions of difference: disability, gender, ethnicity, social class, age, appearance, sexuality and learning capabilities. The chapter then moves to address how differentiation occurs in routine school practices and may be reinforced through pupil culture.

Difference though, is discussed as part of the human condition – thus generating commitments to diversity and inclusion. Needs are discussed as a dimension of difference. Finally, the chapter focuses on practical ways of developing inclusive classroom policies and practices.

There are suggestions for 'Key Readings' at the end of the chapter. The resources on *reflectiveteaching.co.uk* extend this.

Reading 15.1

Principles underlying UK legislation for equality and diversity

Robin Richardson

National legal frameworks work vary in some details, but in this reading Richardson picks out generic principles on which equality and diversity legislation in the UK is based. A key challenge for teachers, or any other provider of services, is to provide equality of treatment whilst also affirming difference. Guidance may come from consultation, participation and the use of evidence.

Considering particular individuals or groups who you teach, are there ways in which you could improve provision for equality and diversity?

Edited from: Richardson, R. (2009) *Holding Together.* Stoke-on-Trent, Trentham Books, 24, 26–8.

Legislation about equality and diversity in Great Britain is concerned with six separate strands or areas: age; disability; ethnicity; faith, religion or belief; gender, including gender reassignment; and sexuality. The ten principles summarised here apply to all six strands and each one is explicit in at least one piece of UK legislation.

Principle 1: Equality

All people are of equal value and should be treated with equal respect, dignity and consideration:

- whatever their age
- whether or not they are disabled
- whatever their ethnicity, culture, national origin or national status
- whatever their faith tradition, religion or belief
- whichever their gender
- whatever their sexual identity

Principle 2: Difference and reasonable accommodation

People have a range of different interests, needs and experiences. Treating people equally (Principle 1) does not necessarily mean treating them all the same. Policies, procedures and activities must not discriminate, but also must take account of differences of experience, outlook and background – one size does not 'fit all'. In particular policies must take account of the kinds of specific barrier, inequality and disadvantage which people may face, and must make reasonable adjustments and accommodation.

Principle 3: Cohesion

Positive attitudes, relationships and interaction should be fostered, and a shared sense of cohesion and belonging. Therefore, hate-crime and prejudice related incidents and harassment should be addressed and prevented. Policies, procedures and activities should promote:

- mutually positive attitudes between older people and younger, and mutually beneficial relationships
- positive attitudes towards disabled people, good relations between disabled and non-disabled people, and an absence of harassment of disabled people
- positive interaction, good relations and dialogue between groups and communities different from each other in terms of ethnicity, culture, national origin or national status, and an absence of racism-related bullying and incidents
- mutual respect and good relations between girls and boys, and women and men, and an absence of sexual harassment and bullying
- positive interaction, good relations and dialogue between groups and communities different from each other in terms of faith tradition, religion or belief, and an absence of racism-related bullying and incidents
- good relations between people regardless of their sexual identity, and an absence of homophobic incidents and bullying

Principle 4: Being proactive to create greater equality of outcome

Opportunities should be taken to reduce and remove inequalities of outcome and the barriers that already exist, with a view to producing not only equality of opportunity but also equality of outcome.

It is not enough just to avoid discrimination and negative impacts. In addition to avoiding or minimising possible negative impacts of our policies, we must take opportunities to maximise positive impacts by reducing and removing inequalities and barriers that may already exist.

Principle 5: Consultation and involvement

People affected by a policy or activity should be consulted and involved in the design of new policies, and in the review of existing ones – 'nothing about us without us'. Views and voices should be collected, directly and through representative bodies.

Principle 6: Participation

All people should be enabled to take a full part in economic, political, social and cultural life at local and national levels. Policies and activities should benefit society as a whole, both locally and nationally, by fostering greater participation in public life, and in the affairs of voluntary and community sector organisations and institutions.

Principle 7: Evidence

Policies should be based on reliable evidence. When new policies are proposed, and existing policies are monitored and reviewed, a range of quantitative and qualitative evidence should be collected and used about the likely impact.

Principle 8: Complexity

All people have multiple identities. No one is just one thing. All have a range of different affiliations and loyalties. Many of the terms and categories used in the equalities field are necessarily imprecise and have the potential to be misleading.

Principle 9: Social class

The inequalities cited above in respect to age, ethnicity, disability, faith, gender and sexuality should not be considered independently of inequalities of social class. Differences of wealth, income, occupation, status, educational qualifications, influence, leisure activities, consumption patterns, health levels, aspirations and outlooks are relevant when we are designing, implementing and improving services.

Principle 10: Action

Principles are not enough. There must also be action. Every public body must draw up an action plan or delivery plan showing the specific measures it will adopt to create greater equality in its sphere of influence.

Reading 15.2

Social differentiation in schools
Andrew Pollard

This reading provides one way of taking stock of issues associated with the provision of equal opportunities in schools. Initially, the reasons why teachers differentiate amongst pupils and also the possible unintended consequences of doing so are considered. Criteria of judgement for facing this major dilemma are then offered, together with a model for thinking about school processes and social consequences.

Can you see the connection between this reading and others in this chapter?

Edited from: Pollard, A. (1987) 'Social differentiation in primary schools', *Cambridge Journal of Education*, 17 (3) 158–61.

'The act or process of distinguishing something by its distinctive properties' – that is how my dictionary defines differentiation and, of course, it is a process in which we all engage as we go about our daily lives. Indeed, we could make few effective decisions without recourse to judgements about the particular qualities of people and things. However, serious responsibilities and potential problems are introduced when 'processes of distinguishing' are applied by those with a degree of power and authority to the qualities and lives of other people; for instance, as applied by us regarding the children in our classes at school. Further importance accrues if it can be shown that some of the judgements of differentiation, on which practices are based, are often inaccurate and may thus lead to injustices occurring. In such circumstances the issues raised inevitably extend beyond the practical ones of the moment, which may have provided an initial impetus for distinctions to be drawn, to encompass personal, ethical and moral concerns.

Of course, it can reasonably be argued that differentiation is both necessary and inevitable in classrooms. Classroom life is characterised by complexity, and rapid decisions certainly have to be made by teachers. As an exercise in information processing the challenges are considerable. Perhaps it is thus inevitable that teachers develop ways of thinking about children which make it possible both to anticipate potential difficulties before they arise and to interpret circumstances and events so that effective action can be taken. To this extent, differentiation may be seen as the product of a range of strategies which enable teachers to 'cope' with the demands of classroom life.

There seem to be three particular areas around which teacher knowledge of pupil differences tends to accumulate. The first relates to the issue or control and discipline, for teachers know very well that the maintenance of classroom order provides an infrastructure without which many essential activities cannot take place. The second concerns the interpersonal relationships which are developed with children – who is 'good to have in the class' and who is 'difficult to get on with' – and, of course, 'good relationships' have been a much prized quality of classroom life for many years and seen as one vital source of fulfilment and security for both teachers and children. Finally and by no means unimportantly, there is teacher knowledge about children's learning achievements, needs and capacities.

Differentiation of children can thus be seen partly as a response to the practicalities of classroom life and partly as a necessary attribute of forms of 'good teaching' in which responsiveness to individuals is made a priority.

On the other hand there is a great deal of sociological and historical evidence, collected in many countries and with different age groups, which demonstrates socially divisive effects when patterns in differentiation practices evolve in settings such as schools and classrooms. The most obvious criteria around which such patterns occur are those of 'race'. social class, sex, academic ability, age and physical disability.

Of course, to varying degrees which one which one might want to discuss, these criteria represent 'objective' attributes which may call for different treatment. Yet, at the same time they are applied to people who share certain fundamental freedoms and human rights. Thus, if it can be shown that such rights are denied or adversely affected by patterns in social practices then a cause for concern certainly exists.

Differentiation thus poses some severe dilemmas. Is it to be seen as an evil or a good? On the one hand one can argue that to fail to differentiate is to deny individuality and the unique qualities and needs of people. On the other hand it can be argued that differentiation is iniquitous, for in making distinctions of any sort, some children may be advantaged over others.

How then should we, as teachers, face such dilemmas? Perhaps dilemmas can only be resolved by making reflective judgements of appropriateness and of worthwhileness for specific situations. However, such judgements need to be supported both by principled criteria and by social awareness of what actually happens – for instance, as highlighted by available research on the topic. I will discuss each of these elements in turn.

Criteria of judgement

On this point one cannot avoid facing the issue of value commitments and beliefs about the basic purposes of education. As an example, and in full recognition of my own commitments and of the rights of others to make different choices, I offer the following educational priorities which might be adopted with regard to children: to foster children's intellectual growth; to facilitate children's personal and social development; to maximise children's opportunities in life; and to prepare children to exercise rights and accept responsibilities as individuals and as future citizens.

If these four educational priorities are accepted for the moment, then we can consider the effects of differentiation in terms of them. For instance:

intellectual growth: Does differentiation depend children's thinking or lead to superficiality? Does differentiation open horizons or lead to closure?

personal and social development: Does differentiation facilitate children's growth or stunt it?

opportunities: Is differentiation enabling or disabling?

rights and responsibilities: Does differentiation enfranchise or disenfranchise, increase social awareness or decrease it?

To answer such questions we need to consider the second ingredient – awareness and knowledge of the types and processes of differentiation which may occur in schools.

Awareness of differentiation processes

I am not going to attempt a review of all the research which is relevant to this issue – that would take volumes. In any event, on this matter the detail is arguably less important than principles which might be applicable to a range of situations and practices. I will therefore simply attempt to set up and discuss the relatively concise analytical model below:

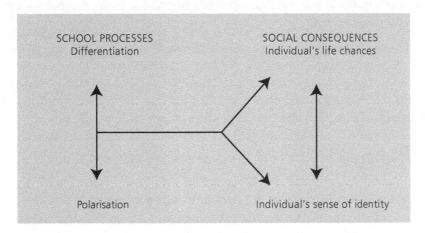

Figure 15.2.1
The differentiation-polarisation process and its consequences

Differentiation

Differentiation refers here to any way in which individual children are distinguished, one from another, by teachers. I thus use the term explicitly to describe processes of distinction which children have relatively little control over. There are various aspects of this at a classroom level and I offer below some examples:

There are those to do with the content and form of the curriculum – e.g. how are girls, the disabled and ethnic minorities represented in reading books? Are the positions of children on a maths scheme taken as an indicator of a status which children acquire?

There are aspects of differentiation which are related to classroom management – e.g. do children line up by sex, are the 'second years' and the 'third years' regularly dismissed at different times?

Some aspects of differentiation are particularly explicit such as when it is reflected in classroom organisation – e.g. to what extent are children ability-grouped in your school, how often is gender used as an organisational device in activities?

Powerful forms of differentiation can also occur through the language which is used in school which may, or may not, be equally meaningful and appropriate to all social groups. For instance, how are the needs of those for whom English is a second language catered for? Do some children understand the register and vocabulary of the teachers better than others?

Another rather subtle but powerful form of differentiation concerns interpersonal relationships. Are there differences in the quality of the rapport which is established with different children? Are there differences in the number of times boys and girls, younger and older children, 'good' and 'naughty' children have contact with and get the attention of the teacher?

Another issue concerns reinforcement and the differential valuing of children's efforts. Are merit points or other extrinsic rewards given and, if so, is there a pattern in who gets them? Whose work is displayed and praised? Is any particular social group over-represented?

For each aspect of differentiation there are hundreds of such questions and, of course, it is not my purpose to suggest that all such forms of differentiation are, in some inevitable way, 'wrong'. The question which has to be asked though is whether there are *patterns* of differentiation which might represent a less than just and fair treatment of the individual attributes and rights of each child and each social group.

Polarisation

In simple terms, polarisation can be seen as a response by children to the differentiation which they experience. The effect of polarisation is thus to multiply, amplify and compound the social consequences of the initial differentiation.

This can be seen to work in the studies of children's social relationships and perceptions. For instance, friendship groups are often related to academic status as well as to criteria such as race and sex and they may even reveal the influence of seat places where these are dictated by the organisation of the classroom. Status and popularity within child culture can also be seen to depend partly on the relationship of each child with the teacher. Children who find it hard to succeed in school, or who get into trouble a lot, may develop relatively antagonistic attitudes to school and may act in conjunction with others in similar positions. On the other hand, children who are successful in school, who are well trusted by their teachers and stimulated by the form and content of the curriculum may well feel very positive about it. Status in child culture is often obtained by demonstrating that one can cope with school life, that one is strong, able enough and independent enough. Polarisation thus occurs every time a child is teased because he is she is 'only on red level books' or when, say 'John's gang' develops its reputation for 'mucking about' and is contrasted with the quieter groups who 'just walk around' and 'do what the teacher says'.

Another way of approaching this is to see children in school as having to cope in two social spheres at the same time. They have to cope with the formal requirements of teachers and normally have to accept the judgements which may be made of them. They also have to cope with the social world of the playground and of their peers. In both contexts they have to retain their dignity as individuals. The result of this is that, if they are treated in particular ways in class then, in the playground, they are likely to either play on the prestige they have gained or try to recoup some of the dignity they may have lost. In any event, the effects of the initial differentiation is likely to be increased by the polarisation which then follows.

The model above postulates that these two processes exist in interaction together. For instance, the effect of polarisation of attitudes and of peer group association could well lead to increased differentiation as teachers respond to them. The danger is thus that the two processes mesh together to produce a vicious circle in which, in the midst of everyday school life, the overall differentiation effect is steadily increased.

What are the social consequences of these processes?

Social consequences of two main sorts result. The first concerns the self-image and sense of identity which each child develops – how do they see themselves, how much self-confidence do they have? The second concerns life-chances more directly – how are future possibilities for each child affected by school processes and experiences?

The self-image and identity of individuals is constructed through social interaction with others. We thus come to 'know' ourselves gradually and continuously throughout life. At any point though, we 'present' our self to others in particular ways – usually in ways which we feel are appropriate for the situation as we perceive it and in ways which support our existing image of 'who we are'. Schools have a very significant role to play in this process of identity formation for they are, for most children, the first formal organisation which they will have experienced. In a sense therefore, school life provides the primary medium through which the public identities of each child are created, explored, tested, evolved and adopted. Children take forward a particular sense of self and act upon it as they experience new situations. In turn, others then react to the presentation of this identity.

It does not take much imagination to see that the prospects for children who have developed a sense of failure and dissatisfaction in school are likely to be very different from those of children who have had their efforts praised, valued and reinforced. Because of the links between education, assessment, credentialism and employment, schools play a very important gate-keeping role through their influence on the long-term prospects of children. Indeed, the processes of differentiation and polarisation, which may be identified in the classrooms of even very young children, may well manifest themselves in terms of income, housing, occupation and status thirty years on.

This seems to me to be the major challenge of socially aware teaching, with any age of child.

Difference or deviance?

Gary Thomas and Andrew Loxley

> This extract draws particular attention to the ways in which we respond to the charac-
> teristics of others, and how this works within institutions such as schools. It warns of
> how routine practices can 'make difference' and may even interpret it as deviance from
> an imagined norm.
>
> The quest for inclusion requires constant awareness of language, concepts, categories,
> statistics and other forms of representation.
>
> Can you identify processes in your daily life which, in the terms of this reading, 'create
> difference'?
>
> *Edited from:* Thomas, G. and Loxley, A. (2007) *Deconstructing Special Education and
> Constructing Inclusion.* Maidenhead: Open University Press. 76–8, 87.

To be called 'special' is to be given a new identity within the schooling system. How far
this social identity becomes transferable to (or resisted by) other institutions or forms
part of an individual's personal identity is highly debatable. However, it is clear that this
accreditation of difference represents in practice two phenomena: first, a transition from
one state to another – that is from the 'non-special' to the 'special'; second, a set of interventions which reinforces this state of difference. There is at work a process of re-ordering
which positions a pupil into different and possibly new sets of social relations – with
teachers, peers and support staff.

This is what Munro (1997) calls a continual 'labour of division', and it is characteristic
of much activity of institutions, not just schools. This notion of labour of division is, of
course, an inversion of Marx's (1995) concept of the division of labour, and it is used to
signify the way institutions actively go about splintering and fragmenting previously given
categories. It is about the drawing and continual redrawing of boundaries; of constructing
points of demarcation which in turn are used as indices to 'map' individuals or groups into
appropriate classifications. This making of difference seems almost to be an endemic part
of the process of being an institution. If this is the case, it presents problems for those who
wish to see more inclusion in social and institutional life.

What can be discovered about the process?

It is clear, first of all, that the recognition of difference is not necessarily anti-inclusional.
Williams (1992), draws useful distinctions between diversity, difference and division:

> By *diversity* I mean difference claimed upon a shared collective experience which is
> specific and not necessarily associated with a subordinated or unequal subject position
> ... *difference* denotes a situation where a shared collective experience/identity ... forms
> the basis of resistance against the positioning of that identity as subordinate. By *division* I

mean the translation of the expression of a shared experience into a form of domination. *(Williams, 1992: 70)*

Williams is arguing that we cannot assume that difference will automatically be translated into some anti-inclusive domination. Not all forms of difference automatically imply marginalisation and exclusion. Likewise, Munro (1997) points out that:

> ... considered as a feature of society, difference might be said to enjoy mixed fortunes. Sometimes difference is in vogue; it is a thing to be welcomed and may be referred to wholesomely in such terms as 'diversity'. On other occasions ... it is viewed as something more shadowy, even malevolent, with any difference being treated as deviant. *(Munro, 1997: 14)*

This then is the key issue: is difference something to be welcomed, or is it, in Munro's terms, to be made into something 'shadowy', 'malevolent', 'deviant'? There are clearly variations in the way that educators handle kinds of difference. In the case of certain systems of symbols – sexuality, clothing, patterns of speech and behaviour – there is strong evidence that exclusionary pressure associates itself with this kind of difference.

But it is not just with difficult behaviour at school that the process of making difference works. While it is not as conspicuous in other areas it nevertheless occurs, despite the outward impression that inclusion is happening. As Barnes et al. (1999) and Geertz (1973) remark, different cultural groups mark out and categorise social difference by reference to localised criteria. And this has been especially the case as far as education is concerned and the concept of 'need' has played its part in this. The mark of difference has been used as a rationale for segregation rather than celebration, even though the markers of that difference are subtle and elude definition. For instance, notions of 'need' in physical impairment or, even more relevantly, 'learning difficulties' may have referents which are difficult to be specific about outside a local context. There is certainly evidence of this as far as reading difficulty is concerned: Thomas and Davis (1997) showed that 'reading difficulty' is not a clear-cut, unambiguous label; teachers in different schools will have different ideas about what constitutes 'a child with reading difficulty', depending on their local experience.

With Warnock (DES, 1978), the number of children 'with special needs' rose from around two per cent of the school population – that is, those who were educated in special schools – to 20 per cent. People who were clever with numbers worked out that this meant that 18 per cent of children in ordinary schools had special needs, and this became a commonplace: 18 per cent of children in ordinary schools had special educational needs. It is extraordinary that this figure – 18 per cent – came to be accepted as uncritically as it was. The figure '18 per cent' even made its way into the title of a respectable book about special needs (Gipps, 1987). For 18 per cent to be accepted (not 17 per cent or 19 per cent, note) as the proportion of children with special needs in ordinary schools shows a faith in the power of statistics which has probably never been rivalled in the history of serious discourse on public policy.

As Giddens (1990) puts it:

> Concepts ... and the theories and empirical information linked to them, are not merely handy devices whereby agents are somehow more clearly able to understand behaviour

… they actively constitute what that behaviour is and inform the reasons for which it is undertaken. *(Giddens, 1990: 42)*

Giddens implies that as we 'discover' new ways of making sense of phenomena, these explanations in turn become inseparable from what those phenomena are. The empirical and epidemiological information drawn on by the Warnock Committee in 1978 (DES, 1978) did not merely hold a mirror up to some reality which could be used by educators. Rather, it actively generated a 'reality' which had to be lived up to.

Difference and identity are constructed in and through social relations. Whether difference is seen positively, as diversity, or negatively as deviance or deficit depends on the mindset of the person or group of people who observe that difference.

Various thinkers – Lyotard (1984), Foucault (1991), Bourdieu (1984), the labelling theorists – have helped to show how the words we use and the systems of thought and enquiry we employ, shape the interpretation of difference. One of their most important insights is that instruments of enquiry, including our very discourse, not only reveal the nature and extent of difference, but also go to construct that difference. They reveal also the imperative to seek homogeneity in institutional life and the corresponding imperative to delineate and differentiate those who differ from the norm. Their analyses, while in some ways depressing, are important for thinking about how to counteract the processes they reveal.

Reading 15.4

Ability grouping in schools: A literature review
Sue Hallam

This is a more complex subject than many people would like it to be and, as Hallam demonstrates, there are dilemmas to be faced. However, a range of practical strategies provide alternatives to organisational inflexible forms of grouping by 'ability'. This term, incidentally, should be avoided where possible because, whilst we may understand attainment levels and processes of achievement, we cannot accurately know intrinsic potential.

In schools you know, what organisational strategies are used to group pupils – and what are their strengths and weaknesses?

Edited from: Hallam, S. (2002) *Ability Grouping in Schools: A Review of the Literature*. London: Institute of Education, 1–5, 32–5, 71–95.

Ability grouping has been the subject of research for most of the twentieth century since Whipple (1919) carried out a study of the effects of special class placement on a group of high-aptitude 5th and 6th graders in the USA. Since then hundreds of studies have been undertaken and there have been many literature reviews and syntheses of research findings.

Despite this ever increasing body of evidence, the field has been characterised by controversy and polemic. There are several reasons for this, but perhaps most importantly, particular types of grouping seem to benefit different groups of pupils. Streaming and setting tend to benefit the more able, whereas mixed ability structures tend to benefit the less able. The type of pupil grouping which is adopted is therefore underpinned by different philosophical values. Because of this, policy decisions about pupil grouping have often been based on ideological principles rather than educational ones.

Cross cultural studies comparing the educational systems in Japan and Taiwan with those in the USA suggest that the Western stress on ability grouping minimises the importance of student, teacher and parental effort. The concept of differential ability sets a ceiling on what can be expected from a child. In Japan and Taiwan, pupils, with support from parents and teachers, are expected to put in additional effort if they are not successful. No one expects pupils to be removed from the classroom for special interventions or to make it easier to move ahead. There is no ability grouping in state schools prior to 10th grade in Japanese schools. The school day is longer and people are encouraged to work hard. The Western emphasis on ability may serve to lower our expectations of what pupils can achieve.

Current thinking about the nature of intelligence, the many factors which affect learning outcomes and the evidence indicating the importance of effort, indicate a need for grouping structures within school which increase pupil motivation and are sufficiently flexible to meet pupils' ever changing needs. As early as 1931, Turney outlined advantages and disadvantages of systems of streaming, banding or setting – as indicated below.

Figure 15.4.1
Perceived advantages and disadvantages of structured ability grouping

Advantages	Disadvantages
1. helps to maintain interest and incentive, because bright students are not bored by the participation of the dull permits pupils to make progress commensurate with their abilities	1. slow pupils need the presence of the able students to stimulate them and encourage them
2. encourages slower pupils to participate more because they are not eclipsed by those who are much brighter	2. a stigma is attached to low groups, classes or streams, which discourages pupils in these sections
3. makes possible adaption of techniques of instruction to the needs of the group	3. teachers are unable, or lack time, to differentiate the work for different levels of ability
4. makes teaching easier	4. teachers object to the slower groups

Taken together, the evidence from the reviews of Slavin (1987, 1990) and Kulik and Kulik (1992) indicate that where there are differential effects on achievement related to pupil grouping procedures, they depend mainly on the extent of access to the curriculum, or as Carroll (1963) first described it 'opportunity to learn'. Where pupils are given greater access or opportunity to proceed through the curriculum more quickly, they achieve more. Where pupils are taught in mixed ability classes the overall differentiation of the curriculum is less and lower ability pupils tend to perform better (Ireson and Hallam, 2001)

However, structured ability grouping, of itself, does not appear to lead to consistently better or worse performance in any group of pupils. This may be because pupil performance is primarily related to access to the curriculum and the quality of teaching on offer. In some circumstances, where the curriculum is differentiated, allowing faster progress and more in depth work, structured ability grouping can be beneficial in raising the attainment of those who are more able. Where the grouping structures lead to low expectations, a reduced curriculum and teaching which is focused on control rather than learning, lower ability groups are likely to do worse. Neither of these scenarios is inevitable. Teaching in the top sets may be too time pressured and competitive to enable in depth understanding for some pupils, thus leading to poor performance. In the bottom sets, teachers with high expectations who have positive relationships with the pupils, engender high levels of motivation and set interesting challenging work are likely to improve performance.

Nonetheless, grouping structures have a powerful influence on teacher's attitudes, expectations and pedagogy, and on the way that pupils view themselves and interact with teachers. There is therefore a tendency for structured ability grouping to increase differences in performance between the more and less able. In contrast, in mixed ability classes, there is less extreme differentiation of the curriculum and pupils experiences of pedagogy are more similar. This is likely to lead to reduction in differences in performance between the more and less able, although the quality of the teaching is likely to determine whether there is a levelling up or down. If the work is challenging, stimulating and appropriately differentiated where necessary, the performance of the high ability pupils is likely to be maintained and that of the lower ability pupils raised.

These conclusions leave policy makers with difficult choices. A more palatable approach may be to explore different types of innovative grouping structures which may promote greater attainment for all pupils more consistently.

Practical solutions

The major factor for educationally effective grouping of pupils is that it offers sufficient flexibility to meet changing demands at school, class, group and individual levels. Highly structured school based systems tend to lack this flexibility. The most appropriate ways for individual schools to develop flexibility in grouping depends on their size, resources and pupil intake. There is no simple 'off the shelf' recipe for success.

A major consideration is the age of the pupils and how the grouping system can not only ensure their attainment academically but promote positive social and personal development.

Setting: One option for schools is to adopt structured grouping systems, such as banding or setting but to attempt to minimise their negative effects. The particular benefit of setting is that it allows work to be set at an appropriate level for the pupil and makes the management of learning easier for the teacher. The danger for schools is the development of an ethos which stresses academic achievement to the exclusion of all else; an environment where high ability is reified – thus leaving the majority of pupils feeling unvalued with a subsequent loss to their self-esteem, confidence and academic attainment.

Vertical grouping: A large proportion of small primary schools, of necessity, have to adopt vertical grouping structures, that is putting children in classes which include more than one year group. There are advantages, for instance:

- The student stays with the same teacher for several years allowing closer and more secure relationships to develop;
- Vertical grouping promotes cooperation and other forms of positive social behaviour;
- The use of different learning materials provides opportunities for younger students to benefit from exposure to more advanced curricula while providing older students with the opportunity to benefit from reviewing earlier work.

Special activity groups: Withdrawing children from classes has traditionally been used in the UK to provide additional support for children experiencing difficulties in specific areas, often literacy. However, the principle of providing 'special activities' can be applied to groups formed across or within year groups or within classes for a very wide range of purposes.

Co-operative learning: Co-operative learning techniques can be applied in several ways. All the methods have in common that pupils work together to learn and are responsible for one another's learning as well as their own. There are three fundamental principles; rewards are given to teams; each individual is accountable for their own contribution; each team member must have an equal opportunity of being successful.

Mastery learning: Mastery learning (Bloom, 1976) involves the teacher introducing a topic which has clearly identifiable criteria for attainment. Pupils spend time learning and working on relevant materials and are then tested. Those students who do not achieve mastery are given feedback and corrective activities by the teacher or pupils who were successful on the test and the topic is explained again using alternative methods and materials. Those pupils who initially failed the test retake it. When a specified number of pupils have mastered the topic (usually 80%) the class move on to another topic. In some cases this cycle may be repeated more than once to ensure a higher level of mastery.

Mixed ability teaching: Despite the difficulties which were outlined earlier, this approach has some advantages. The evidence suggests that mixed ability teaching:

- can provide a means of offering equal opportunities;
- can address negative consequences of structured ability grouping by encouraging co-operative behaviour and social integration;
- can promote good relations between pupils;
- encourages teachers to identify pupil needs and match learning tasks to them.

For mixed ability teaching to be successful teachers need to be highly skilled and supported by a wide range of resources differentiated to satisfy pupil needs across the ability range.

Within class ability grouping: There may be circumstances where teachers wish to group pupils within the class by ability for instructional purposes and the setting of work. The main advantage of adopting grouping structures within, as opposed to between, classes is their flexibility. Pupils can be moved between groups easily and teachers can restructure groupings regularly based on their knowledge of pupil progress, levels of achievement, behaviour and rates of work. Different groupings can be adopted for different purposes.

A tiered curriculum: An alternative to grouping pupils by ability within the class to enable differentiated instruction to take place is to develop a tiered curriculum which enables whole class exposition but differentiates the work which follows (Ireson, 1998). For instance, one UK school adopted such a system applying a four-tier system in all subjects in Years 7–13 (Ireson, 1998). The levels were:

Basic- the minimum acceptable for a student of a particular age to achieve;

Standard – the average performance expected for a student of a particular age;

Extended – above average performance for a student of a particular age;

Advanced – at least one year in advance of an average student of a particular age.

This differentiated structure was used by all departments. All pupils learnt the same topic or skill and differentiation was through the level of difficulty. Students selected for themselves the level of work that they wished to attempt with the teacher negotiating change with the student should the aim prove unrealistic. In the higher age groups, pupils were able to select their own set placement. Their choices invariably were realistic. In some lessons teaching strategies were identical for all tiers whilst in others they were partly differentiated.

The advantage of the system was that pupils were at the centre of learning within a tightly structured system. There was a common language of achievement which was used by pupils, parents and teachers, which was clear and simple to understand and provided a framework for planning, reporting and recording. This facilitated cross subject comparisons and ensured that teachers had accurate perceptions of what pupils could do. Students took responsibility for their own work, acquired considerable metacognitive skills, became well motivated, developed a clear understanding of their own capabilities and were encouraged to work independently. Because students selected the levels that they worked at there was no stigmatisation of the lower ability levels and self esteem was improved as was behaviour and overall achievement. The weakness of the system related to the heavy workload for the staff in preparing differentiated materials.

*Individualised instruction: S*uccessful individualised programmes are based on instruction tailored to the assessed abilities of each student; students working at their own pace, receiving periodic reports on their mastery, and planning and evaluating their own learning; and the provision of alternative materials and activities. Where these criteria are satisfied, individualised programmes have been shown to be more effective than whole-class instruction in relation to cognitive and affective outcomes.

The future

Schools were designed for the industrial age (Bayliss, 1998), yet are attempting to provide education for the changing needs of the twenty-first century. More flexibility is required.

However, if schools are to adopt flexible grouping to maximise the academic, personal and social development of their pupils, they need to have ways of monitoring the effectiveness of grouping structures so that change can be instigated internally when necessary. This requires that schools develop ways of systematically monitoring progress across all curriculum subjects, pupils' attitudes towards learning and school, pupils' self-esteem, and levels of disaffection (through attendance, unauthorised absence and fixed term and permanent exclusions). Such data can then be used to inform decisions about grouping structures between and within classes. Learning-focused groupings could then play a key role in raising educational attainment.

Reading 15.5

How to promote cooperative relationships among children

Barrie Thorne

> Barrie Thorne's book 'Gender Play' is well worth reading as a study of how boys' and girls' identities are formed. In this extract, she considers the practical implications of her work and offers advice to teachers on promoting cooperation among children. She particularly considers the classroom management of groups, reinforcing cooperative behaviour, providing opportunities and challenging stereotyping. This advice is applicable to all forms of differentiation.
>
> How do your pupils interact together, and how you could influence this?
>
> *Edited from:* Thorne, B. (1993) *Gender Play: Girls and Boys in School.* Buckingham: Open University Press, 157–67.

In my ethnographic study of children's daily lives in school, I have sought to ground and develop, with detailed substance and a sense of process and activity, the claim that gender is socially constructed. I have argued that kids, as well as adults take an active hand in constructing gender, and that collective practices – forming lines, choosing seats, teasing, gossiping, seeking access to or avoiding particular activities animate the process.

Thus, I showed how kids construct 'the girls' and 'the boys' as boundaried and rival groups through practices that uphold a sense of gender as an oppositional dichotomy. But I also examined practices that have the effect of neutralizing, or, as in situations of 'crossing', even challenging the significance of gender.

Some of these practices have been developed by teachers and researchers trying to challenge racial separation and inequality and in this brief review I will try to encompass some of the interactive dynamics of race and gender. The ideas may also apply to the handling of other differences, such as religion or disability.

In grouping students, use criteria other than gender or race.
When teachers and aides divide girls and boys into competing teams or tell them to sit at different tables, they ratify the dynamics of separation, differential treatment, stereotyping and antagonism. Organizing students on other grounds, such as random sorting, and using terms of address like 'class' or 'students' rather than the ubiquitous 'boys and girls' will help undermine gender marking.

This suggestion raises a basic dilemma. When granted autonomy and left on their own, kids tend to separate by gender and sometimes also by race. Should school staff determine all seating, even in lunchrooms? Should playground aides bustle into situations kids have set up and urge girls and boys to play together? Obviously this is neither practical nor desirable. Kids do not flourish when they are perpetually watched and controlled; they need, and will struggle to claim, at least some independence from adults.

On the other hand, when adults form mixed-gender groups, I have observed that some kids look a little relieved; the adult action takes away the risk of teasing and makes girl-boy interactions possible. One boy told me: 'You get to talk to kids you usually wouldn't get to know'. When they do choose to form groups, for whatever purpose, I believe that school staff should try, self-consciously, to maximize heterogeneity.

Affirm and reinforce the values of cooperation among all kids regardless of social categories.
A teacher recently told me about her efforts to undermine 'girl-boy staff' and foster more cooperative cross-gender relations among her students. 'We're one class, not boys and girls; we're going to get together as a class,' she repeatedly told them. By emphasizing 'the class', she affirmed a more inclusive basis of solidarity.

To be effective, affirmation of the value of mixed-gender and mixed-race, interaction may need to be explicit and continual. Lisa Serbin and her colleagues (who found extensive gender separation among children in a pre-school), trained the teachers to positively reinforce co-operative cross-gender play, for example with comments like 'John and Cathy are working hard together on their project'. This behaviour-modification effort lasted for two weeks, during which the amount of cross-gender play increased significantly. But when the programme was discontinued, the children returned to the earlier pattern.

Whenever possible, organize students into small, heterogeneous, and cooperative work groups.
Unfortunately, we can't lessen the crowding of most schools, but small group instruction may create pockets of less public and thus, perhaps, more cooperative interaction. Indeed, social psychologists who study the dynamics of intergroup relations have found that when people from different racial or gender groups interact in smaller groups focused on a shared goal requiring interdependence, they are more likely to see one another as individuals rather than through the lens of 'us-versus-them'.

Elliot Aronson and his colleagues entered the de-segregated classrooms and organized small multiracial groups to work together on reports, studying for quizzes, and other collaborative tasks. They called this a 'jigsaw classroom', referring to the principle of a jigsaw puzzle in which each person has pieces of information the entire group needs to complete the task. The result was a de-emphasis on racial divisions and in increase in friendships among African-American, Chicano, and white students.

Facilitate kids' access to all activities.
In many activities, especially on playgrounds and even in classrooms, girls and boys may not have equal access to particular activities, for example in some classrooms boys have been found to have more access than girls to computers.

To broaden access to gender-typed activities school staff can make a point of teaching the skills to everyone and, if possible, setting an example by challenging stereotypes.

School staff might consider introducing playground games, like handball, that have the potential to increase the amount of cross-gender play. A playground rule that would-be players cannot be 'locked out' of a game unless there are already too many players can also lessen opportunities for exclusion and may embolden more kids to join activities stereotypically associated with the other gender. By introducing new activities and teaching relevant skills in a gender-neutral way, teachers and aides can create conditions in which kids themselves may more often form mixed-gender groups. The transformative elements of play – a sense of the voluntary and of control over the terms of interaction – can be drawn on to facilitate social change.

Actively intervene to challenge the dynamics of stereotyping and power.
Proximity does not necessarily lead to equality, as critics of the philosophies of assimilation and integration have long pointed out. Boys and girls and kids of different racial and ethnic backgrounds may be encouraged to interact more frequently, but on whose terms? Groups may be formally integrated, but tensions and inequalities may persist. In the de-segregated middle school where Schofield observed, the teachers by and large affirmed a neutral or colour-blind ideology, trying to ignore the presence of race divisions, though teachers more readily marked gender in their interaction with students. But the students often divided and sometimes hassled one another along lines of both race and gender, and there was persistent mistrust and fear between black and white students. The teaching staff were so intent on pretending that race made no difference that they did little to help white and black students learn how to interact with one another or explore the nature and meaning of cultural difference and the dynamics of racism. In some situations, it may be important for teachers to open deal with rather than ignore social divisions.

My observations of antagonistic mixed-gender interactions suggest that the dynamics of stereotyping and power may have to be explicitly confronted. Barbara Porro and Kevin Karkau engaged their classes in discussions about gender stereotyping, persistent separation between girls and boys, and the teasing ('sissies', 'tomboys', 'you're in love') that kept them apart. Porro explained sexism to her students by finding terms that six-year-olds could understand; the class began to label sexist ideas (e.g. that women could not be doctors, or men could not be nurses as old-fashioned.

Such accounts suggest ways in which teachers can engage in critical thinking about and collaborative ways of transcending social divisions and inequalities.

Learning in inclusive classrooms

Ruth Kershner

This is a valuable reading because it draws together a number of threads in relation to learning, organisation and inclusion in classrooms. It reaches between psychological theory and the practicalities of classroom provision, and maintains an awareness of learners throughout. Significantly too, the issue of inclusion is related to understanding of learning processes and direct interactions with pupils.

How does your understanding of learning relate to your provision for inclusion?

Edited from: Kershner, R. (2009) 'Learning in inclusive classrooms', in Hick, P., Kershner, R. and Farrell, P. (eds) *Psychology for Inclusive Education: New Directions in Theory and Practice*. London: Routledge, 157–67.

Inclusive education involves schools in welcoming children to participate as pupils, without setting arbitrary boundaries based on previous attainment, social characteristics, behaviour, linguistic proficiency, sensory and physical skills, or assumptions about intellectual potential. However, inclusive education also implies that the children are not just present in classrooms, but they learn and succeed in this context.

Day-to-day experience with children and psychological research studies of children's mathematical, problem-solving, reasoning, memory, language and conceptual understanding (e.g. Siegler, 1996) show that there is wide variability in how children of the same age think and behave. This can apply to the same child at different points of an activity, or in different contexts, as well as to differences between peers. So grouping school pupils by age or by 'ability' oversimplifies the educational task (Ireson and Hallam, 2001). Organisational decisions like pupil grouping do not work as strategies for inclusion in themselves unless they are informed by an understanding of how children learn.

A more explicit interest in learning processes focuses attention on how children engage with learning activities, respond to teaching and develop knowledge, skills and understanding across the curriculum. The central importance of the classroom environment, the sharing of knowledge, and the different forms of communication between teacher and pupils emerges particularly strongly.

Towards inclusive learning environments

Teaching approaches which seem intrinsic to inclusive learning are already represented in many classrooms where emphasis is placed on pupils' dialogue, collaboration, choice, exploration and learning to learn, and where it is assumed that all pupils are capable of learning. The concept of the inclusive classroom implies that the teacher's decision-making about classroom activities and the whole learning environment is embedded in a thoughtful, active and positive attention to the children as individuals and groups of pupils, who themselves support and extend each others' learning.

However Jackson (1968: 10) famously remarks that classrooms are intrinsically about 'crowds, praise and power', reminding us that attempts to create inclusive learning environments all have to face up to the fact that most formal school activities take place with or in the presence of others who are not there by choice or preference, that what children say and do is constantly evaluated, and that there are hierarchies of power and responsibility which do not tend to favour the children in any significant and consistent sense. These and other characteristics of schools seem to work against the responsiveness, respect and flexibility intrinsic to inclusion.

More optimistically, there are many accounts of learning and teaching which succeed in demonstrating how the values and beliefs associated with inclusion may appear in classroom practice. For instance, the teachers involved in Hart, Dixon, Drummond and McIntyre's (2004) *Learning Without Limits* project are seen to have a common belief in the 'transformability of learning capacity' (p. 192) which contrasts with the fatalism of defining fixed ability levels or assuming that classroom conditions cannot change (see Reading 1.4). Certain teaching principles emerge which underpin their classroom practice, including notions of 'co-agency' and power-sharing, acting in the interests of everybody, and trusting the pupils to learn when the conditions are right for them. This is a perspective on inclusive learning that acknowledges the classroom context as a potentially supportive reality for the pupils involved if the principles and values are explicitly in place.

As Doll, Zucker and Brehm (2004: 15) discuss, it is the classroom rather than the child which can be seen to become more resilient when strategies are embedded for promoting pupils' autonomy, self-regulation and self-efficacy alongside an emphasis on caring and connected relationships between teachers and pupils, peers and the home and school. In considering the inclusion of children identified with learning disabilities, Keogh and Speece (1996) draw attention to certain classroom features, including the relevance of the teaching method, the curricular content, the management of learning activities in time and space, the use of resources, and the interactions between peers and teachers – all being experienced differently by individuals and groups of pupils. Some recent approaches to educational research have aimed to tackle the complexity of classroom life, including Könings, Brand-Gruwal and Van Merriënboer (2005) who consider the whole learning environment in terms of the reciprocal relationships between the perceptions, preferences and activities of students, teachers and educational designers. Similarly, Wortham (2006) investigates the connections between pupils' academic learning and their changing social identification, using the techniques of linguistics and anthropology.

Understanding 'learning' to support inclusion?

Psychological conceptions of learning have traditionally focused separately on changes at behavioural, cognitive and neural levels – these representing broadly behaviourist, constructivist and neuroscientific schools of thought. The associated mechanisms or processes of learning range from simple behaviourist stimulus-response associations and rote learning to more complex accounts of information handling, language use and meaning making or the workings of the brain and neural connectionism. Each of these psychological perspectives on learning also potentially says something useful about specific educational tactics – for instance, how to reinforce desired behaviour, how to make certain material more memorable, how to support the transfer of learning between different situations and build on previous learning.

Yet one of the problems in gaining a coherent view of children's full experience of learning in school is that the psychological perspectives outlined above are not simply operating at different levels of analysis in which, for example, changes at behavioural level are 'explained' by cognitive changes which in turn are 'explained' by brain functions. Within these alternative models the human learner's knowledge is seen primarily in terms of *either* behavioural responses, *or* mental schemata *or* biological effects, and researchers in each tradition do not necessarily seek connections between them.

This splitting of research into different strands may be due in part to the use of metaphors which underlie different accounts of learning. For instance, Sfard (1998) distinguishes the 'acquisition metaphor' and the 'participation metaphor'. The former identifies learning in terms of the accumulation of knowledge and concepts by reception or active construction, '....gaining ownership over some kind of self-sustained entity' (p. 5). The latter, in contrast, focuses on the ongoing learning activity which involves becoming a member of a particular community with its own language and norms, ie. understanding participation in terms of becoming 'part of a greater whole' (p. 6). Sfard remarks on the meaning and promise of the participation metaphor: 'The vocabulary of participation brings the message of togetherness, solidarity and collaboration ....'. The new metaphor promotes an interest in people in action rather than in people 'as such' (p. 8). This apparent affinity between the participation metaphor and inclusion seems to open up the possibilities for reframing pedagogy as a more inclusive process.

The need to acknowledge and respond to people's different ways of understanding learning applies as much to the learner as to the teachers. Marton and Booth (1997) use evidence from their interviews with young people and adults to identify the particular ways in which learning may be experienced. For instance they contrast 'learning as memorizing and reproducing' with 'learning as understanding' or 'learning as changing as a person'. They remark on the motivational implications of associated 'surface' or 'deep' approaches which may be adopted: 'the former focusing on the tasks themselves and the latter going beyond the tasks to what the tasks signify' (p. 38). Marton and Booth go on to argue that 'the approach to learning adopted by an individual .... in a particular situation is a combination of the way in which that person experiences learning and the way that he or she experiences the situation' (p. 47). Carr and Claxton (2004) make a similar point about individuals' tendencies to respond or learn in certain ways. Their view is that personal learning dispositions such as resilience and playfulness are closely linked to the perceived opportunities and constraints in each new setting.

Inclusive learning and teaching are intimately connected to the ways in which educational activity is conceived, the perceptions of opportunities and constraints in the school setting, and the employment of particular tools and operations which allow participants to achieve the desired educational goals.

part five

Deepening understanding

Expertise
Conceptual tools for career-long fascination?

16

The readings in this chapter offer different perspectives on change and professional development.

We start with Collarbone (16.1) whose experience in a national agency leads her to call on teachers to embrace professional development as part of workforce development to meet future needs. However, Hargreaves (16.2) explains an inherent conservatism which is rooted in the practice of teaching.

More optimistically, for Eaude (16.3), the development of teacher expertise is the essence of professionalism and its nature can be codified. He draws particular attention to the structuring of knowledge (with links to Expert Questions) and to the responsiveness of experts. Wiliam (16.4) takes this further with a discussion of how expertise develops in the form of 'practical wisdom' – a position not unlike that of Heilbronn (3.6). Hattie's text (16.5) extends his work on the effectiveness of particular teaching strategies. Interestingly though, he offers the notion of 'mind frames' to conceptualise 'visible learning' as a way of structuring expert knowledge.

Timperley and her colleagues (16.6) provide lessons from a comprehensive review of effective approaches to teacher learning and development.

The associated chapter of *Reflective Teaching in Schools* is entirely devoted to the structuring of expert knowledge. It draws together Expert Questions, seeded throughout the book, into a single conceptual framework based on the enduring issues of curriculum, pedagogy, assessment and aims, contexts, processes and outcomes. Case study illustrations relating to key concepts are offered. 'Key Readings' for this chapter suggest a number of classic studies on teacher expertise.

This approach to structuring expert knowledge is significantly extended in the 'Deepening Expertise' section of *reflectiveteaching.co.uk*. Advice on Useful Links to internet resources for evidence-informed expert practice will also be found there, together with links to a selection of TLRP publications.

Reading 16.1

Contemporary change and professional development

Pat Collarbone

This reading explains the need to look forwards, and to continually develop the individual and collective expertise of teachers. Collarbone argues that this is essential to respond to the pace of contemporary change and this rationale certainly underpins the 'remodelling' policies of governments to enhance and focus the professionalism of the 'education workforce'.

Do you like being 'remodelled'? How can you take control of your own professional development in the contexts in which you work?

Edited from: Collarbone, P. (2009) *Creating Tomorrow Planning, Developing and Sustaining Change in Education and Other Public Services.* London: Continuum, 2, 4.

This is a time of profound and seismic global shifts. Our world is changing fundamentally; at an exhilarating, or terrifying, speed – depending on your perspective.

The changes and challenges we face today are even greater than those of the nineteenth century, when the industrial revolution exploded into being and fundamentally and permanently changed the way we work and live.

Today, the miracles and curses of the technological revolution are having a similar level of impact on our work and lives, only this time the change is even faster and the impact is even more ubiquitous. Today, things are becoming possible, even commonplace, on a daily basis that only a few short years ago seemed like outlandish science fiction.

The technological revolution isn't happening in isolation of course. At the same time, new economies are growing at an unprecedented pace, destabilizing the old economic status quo and creating uncertainty and conflict as well as opportunity: reserves of oil and other key resources are depleting at an alarming rate; our security is threatened by a real and sometimes over-imagined terrorist threat; and the earth itself is under dire environmental threat from our profligacy.

These momentous changes – and numerous others – are happening, here and now, whether we acknowledge them or do anything about them or not. They are affecting all our lives in a myriad of ways: political, economic, social, technical, legal, environmental … you name it. And the stakes are higher than at any other time in our history.

Such changes are fast making the old top-down organizational model that grew out of the industrial revolution a thing of the past. For effective organisations today, inclusively and collaboratively involving all staff in all aspects of planning, production and delivery, and putting the customer at the heart of delivery (and often development), is becoming the norm.

At the core of all this change is workforce development.

The movement to greater personalization is not only customer facing, it is also an internal process. A strong focus on individuals, both customers and staff, is becoming more and more important to success. To do this effectively, organizations need to become more demand led, reforming their staffing models and making them more inclusive and flexible. The following points illustrate the need for workforce development:

- Intellectual capital (and those that hold it) has become one of organizations' most valuable resources, if not the most valuable. This gives employees a great deal more power, importance and influence than they have ever previously had.

- The increasing mobility of all levels of workers, added to the importance of intellectual capital, is dramatically changing the way employees are viewed and treated.

- The nature of leadership is changing, from the 'hero' leader of old to a more democratic, inclusive and collaborative model.

- Organizations are looking more and more to develop new collaborative partnerships (locally, nationally and internationally), often supported by the efficiencies and capabilities of new technology, to enhance their work.

- The speed of change is increasing and this demands correspondingly flexible organizations – with flexible and talented staff – that are able to adapt and change equally quickly.

- Ongoing training and continual professional development for staff, i.e. a high level of staff expertise, is becoming increasingly key to organizations' long-term success.

These changes are not news. In fact, many of our more forward thinking organizations have already addressed them head on – and continue to address them. For example, in England, our schools, local authorities and range of support agencies and other organizations, have used and continue to use the remodelling change process to direct, manage and adapt to these changes in a successful and sustainable way.

Reading 16.2

Contemporary change and professional inertia
Andy Hargreaves

This reading discusses a tendency towards professionally conservative thinking by teachers – focused on present, practical realities. The nature of teachers' work is identified, and the ways in which this underpins a cautious approach to change, are discussed. Hargreaves suggests that contemporary educational reforms increase pressure for short term performance and thus reinforce 'addictive presentism'. He calls for inspiring vision and principled collaboration to build expertise for long-term improvement (see also Hargreaves and Fullan, 2012).

How do you feel about your work, and your future in the profession?

Edited from: Hargreaves, A. (2007) *The Persistence of Presentism and the Struggle for Lasting Improvement,* Professorial Lecture. Institute of Education, University of London, 24 January.

Dan Lortie's *Schoolteacher* (1975) is a great classic of the field. At the core of the book lay a simple but compelling argument: that teaching is characterised by three orientations which impede educational improvement – conservatism, individualism and presentism.

Conservatism is the most evident obstacle to change. The only changes that teachers deemed desirable, Lortie argued, were ones that amounted to 'more of the same'; confirming current 'institutional tactics' by 'removing obstacles and providing for more teaching with better support'. Teachers had 'a preference for doing things as they have been done in the past' (1975: 209).

Individualism, Lortie claimed, was reinforced and rewarded by a job that had uncertain criteria for successful performance and which led them to align their goals with their 'own capacities and interests' (Lortie, 1975: 210). Teachers therefore had a stake in their own autonomy and were likely to resist changes in conditions that would threaten it.

Presentism springs from what Lortie termed the 'psychic rewards' of teaching:

Teachers perceive their psychic rewards as scarce, erratic and unpredictable. They are vulnerable to the ebb and flow of pupil response; even highly experienced teachers talk about 'bad years'. Uncertainties in teaching inhibit the feeling that future rewards are ensured, and such doubts support the position that it is unwise to sacrifice present opportunities for future possibilities. *(1975: 211)*

Presentism reinforces individualism and conservatism. Teachers at the time of Lortie's study showed little enthusiasm 'in working together to build a stronger technical culture' (Lortie, 1975: 211). They 'punctuate their work' into small study units, 'concentrating on short-range outcomes as a source of gratification', and they 'do not invest in searching for general principles to inform their work' (Lortie, 1975: 212).

In the decades following Lortie's classic study, there has been an accumulating assault on individualism in teaching. There have been significant efforts to *re-culture* schools so as to develop greater collaboration among teachers, in cultures of interactive professionalism. More recently, this has acquired greater precision through the idea of schools becoming strong professional communities where teachers use achievement data and other evidence to guide collective improvement efforts. These communities promote cultures of continuous and shared learning, distributed teacher leadership, and professional learning and assistance across schools through networked learning communities that expand school-to-school lateral capacity for improvement.

Lortie's legacy has therefore been to highlight the existence of and connection between *individualism* and *conservatism* in teaching as interrelated obstacles to improvement and change, and to inspire antidotes in the form of teacher collaboration and collegiality.

However, Lortie's legacy in relation to *presentism* has been much less urgent or evident, and antidotes to its effects on teaching, learning and educational change are weak or absent.

Three forms of presentism

Endemic presentism: Lortie's classic explanation of presentism is that it is an ingrained feature of teaching that results from the way teaching is organized. Jackson referred to this quality as one of immediacy: the pressing and insistent nature of classroom life for teachers who are responsible for organising, orchestrating and reacting to the needs and demands, the vagaries and vicissitudes, of large groups of energetic children gathered together in one place (Jackson, 1968).

Events at school-level may also breed cynicism towards long-term thinking. For example, missions collapse when headteachers leave and others replace them in rapid succession; whole-school self-evaluation exercises are often experienced as so exhausting that teachers do not want to endure them more than once; and after repeated failures at long-term, whole-school change, teachers in mid-to-late career become cynical and concentrate on immediate issues in their own classrooms even more than they did before (Hargreaves, 2005; Huberman, 1993).

Adaptive presentism: In recent years, presentism has changed from being an endemically 'natural' condition of teaching to an acute and unwanted one. Years of encroaching standardisation of teaching, characterised by increasingly detailed and prescribed curriculum and assessment systems, have separated teachers from their purposes and pasts (Helsby 1999; Woods et al., 1997).

This process was described by Apple (1989) and others as one of increasing intensification in teachers' work, where teachers were expected to respond to increasing pressures and comply with multiple innovations. Intensification and initiative overload led to reduced time for relaxation and renewal, lack of time to retool skills and keep up with the field, increased dependency on externally prescribed materials, and cutting of corners and of quality.

The age of standardisation and marketisation also placed many schools in increasingly competitive relationships with each other, in relation to criteria determined by high-stakes tests, along with serious sanctions for those who do not make satisfactory progress on the short-term targets measured by the tests.

A pervasive and predictable consequence has been the proliferation of a calculative approach to meeting short-term, high-stakes targets. Such success in delivering short-term targets may be achieved at the price of long-term sustainability in lifelong learning and higher-order proficiencies within a broader curriculum.

Addictive presentism: The major reason for the persistence of presentism lies in an emergent and professionally appealing variant that shows signs of becoming even more potent than its predecessors. Indeed, short-term improvement measures are at risk of acting like lids on efforts to attend to longer-term, more sustainable transformation. Instead of building people's confidence to break out of the existing culture, the affirming success of short-term strategies seems to entrench schools in the culture of presentism even more deeply. Schools become almost addicted to them.

The logic of short-term funding, of a policy culture characterised by immediacy and a teaching culture steeped in endemic presentism, along with a performance-driven discourse that addresses itself more to short-term targets of achievement and improved management of pupil learning than to long-term transformations of teaching and learning, all exert a combined pressure to preserve and perpetuate the short-term orientation as a substitute for, rather than a stimulant of, long-term transformation.

The persistence of presentism in teaching in an era of more collaborative teacher involvement in data-informed improvement and educational reform, is therefore not merely professionally *endemic*, nor even organisationally and politically *adaptive*. It is now also personally, professionally and institutionally *addictive.*

To understand the persistence of presentism as an educational phenomenon poses the challenge of how to deal with it. Perhaps, most important of all, is a need at all levels for an inclusive, inspiring vision and discourse of educational improvement that connects the learning of individuals to the lives of their communities and the future of their societies – a vision that does not merely personalise the curriculum through increased management, monitoring and mentoring, but that connects pupils' learning with who they are, where they are from, where they are headed, and how they will live among and contribute to the welfare of others in a prosperous, just and secure world.

Reading 16.3

The development of teacher expertise

Tony Eaude

> This excerpt is from a short summary of the literature on teacher expertise and addresses the background research, the structure of expert knowledge, practical flexibility and responsiveness, and processes of expert development. The importance of practice is worth noting, as is the significance of conceptual understanding. Of course, Chapter 16 of *Reflective Teaching in Schools* is centrally concerned with the latter.
>
> Can you relate these ideas about expertise to teachers you know?
>
> *Edited from:* Eaude, T. (2012) *How Do Expert Primary Class-teachers Really Work?* Knutsford: Critical Publishing, 8–10, 13, 61–2.

Berliner (2001) summarises research-informed propositions about expertise as follows:

- expertise is specific to a domain, developed over hundreds and thousands of hours, and continues to develop;

- development of expertise is not linear, with plateaus occurring, indicating shifts of understanding;

- expert knowledge is structured better for use in performance than is novice knowledge;

- experts represent problems in qualitatively different – deeper and richer – ways than novices;

- experts recognise meaningful patterns faster than novices;

- experts are more flexible and more opportunistic planners and can change representations faster, when appropriate, than novices;

- experts impose meaning on, and are less easily misled by, ambiguous stimuli;

- experts may start to solve a problem slower than a novice but overall they are faster problem solvers;

- experts are usually more constrained by task requirements and the social constraints of the situation than novices;

- experts develop automaticity to allow conscious processing of more complex information;

- experts have developed self-regulatory processes as they engage in their activities.

The list above was initially provided by Glaser (1999). It shows clearly that expertise is very difficult to develop, requiring a lot of practice over a long period of time. In many fields, such as music and sport, the figure of 10,000 hours is used and Berliner (2004) cites research that expert radiologists were estimated to have looked at 100,000 X-rays. In relation to teaching, Berliner (2001) suggests at least four and a half years, though this depends on how expertise is defined and at what level.

Second, expertise develops at an uneven pace, as the individual's understanding changes; and separate aspects of expertise develop at different times and speeds. So a chess player's opening play and his tactical awareness may develop at different rates, probably according to which aspects he practises and concentrates on. And an engineer is likely to acquire expertise more in design, construction, maintenance or repair, according to which she focusses on. While all teachers can, and should be expected to, become increasingly expert, they are unlikely to have a high level of expertise in every respect.

Third, experts do not just do the same things as novices but better, or quicker, or more economically. They think and operate in different ways. Consider the hockey goalkeeper's expertise. Aspects such as body position, balance and timing are crucial, but this does not just entail doing what a club goalkeeper does, but much better. It involves using and combining varying aspects of knowledge to act in qualitatively different ways.

How experts structure knowledge

One key aspect of expertise is how the individual thinks about problems to be solved. Shulman (2004) provides valuable insights from his work on the thought processes of doctors when diagnosing a patient's medical condition. These processes are usually assumed to be rational, based on collecting all the evidence and then coming to a conclusion on the basis of this. However, Shulman's research suggests that, in practice, doctors intuitively formulate a series of tentative hypotheses, altering these, or formulating new ones, as fresh information becomes available.

A GP to whom I spoke recently stated that she relied heavily on intuition, but added that knowledge of the family often helps to make links which would otherwise be missed, though this could also be a hindrance if 'one loses the capacity to be surprised', in her words, or 'makes too many presuppositions', in mine.

Such processes are necessary to manage complex situations without oversimplifying. In Glaser's words, (1999: 91) expertise involves the selective search of memory or use of general problem-solving tactics, with an 'efficiency that derives primarily from this knowledge being structured for retrieval, pattern recognition and inferencing.' In other words, experts' knowledge is arranged so that what matters most can be recalled easily, possible patterns identified and reasonable hypotheses be formulated. Selecting which information or cues to take note of, and which to ignore, is one mark of the real expert.

Shulman (2004) emphasises that, in most fields, experts increasingly work in teams with other people who have specific skills or expertise that they do not have. So, for instance, a surgeon will rely on a whole team, including anaesthetists and specialist nurses; and an architect will work with engineers, quantity surveyors and others. One implication is that different sorts of expertise are – or should be – complementary. A second is that responsibility is collective rather than residing with one individual, helping to reduce the sense of isolation and of being on one's own which tends to make one more cautious, when faced with uncertainty. However, teachers rarely work in teams – at least when actually teaching – and so are often left isolated in the very situation where they most need the support of others.

How experts respond to events and feedback

Bereiter and Scardalmalia (cited in Berliner, 2001: 473) distinguish between crystallized and fluid (or adaptive) expertise. The former 'consists of intact procedures that have been thoroughly learned through experience, brought forth and used in relatively familiar tasks. Fluid expertise consists of abilities that come into play when an expert confronts novel or challenging tasks.' Those working in complex situations and dynamic environments, such as teachers, require fluid expertise. This involves reliance on intuition and hunch, but supported by a deep knowledge both of the task and the context – and assessment of what might go well or otherwise and noticing signs that it is.

Glaser (1999: 89) writes that 'the central underlying properties or meaningful deep structure of the situation is key to experts' perceptions, whereas the surface features and structural properties organise the less-than-expert individuals' perceptions.' This indicates that experts recognise significant patterns and use these to inform practice; and that expertise involves models and routines based on an initial analysis of the situation, but adapted in the light of circumstances.

Glaser's list above included 'automaticity to allow conscious processing of more complex information.' Experts use routines to help cope with complexity and to decide quickly which information is relevant and which not. For example, the expert doctor or therapist will go through various routine checks and look out for symptoms or responses, especially unexpected ones. Experts know, and try to work at, the limits of their own expertise, but they do so economically, simplifying the situation to make it manageable but without oversimplifying. This allows them to concentrate on, and respond to, what is going on around them. Someone less expert tends to take too much account of what does not matter and either to oversimplify or to adopt an overcomplicated strategy. Oversimplifying limits the opportunities for novelty and improvisation, while overcomplicating leads to confusion and to wasted time.

Experts use self-regulatory processes with great skill, enabling them to step back at appropriate points and observe the process and outcomes of their actions. Their self-awareness is shown in the allocation of attention and sensitivity to what is happening, adapting their initial hypotheses in response to feedback of different types. This is because they need to, and do, see what is not going according to plan, so that they can adapt, with an expert being better than a novice at judging when, and to what extent, an activity or an approach should be modified.

As Sternberg and Horvath (1995: 16) suggest, an expert 'neither jumps into solution attempts prematurely nor follows a solution path blindly ... and is able selectively to encode, combine and compare information to arrive at insightful solutions.' So, those with a high level of expertise are likely to move more rapidly to find the best way forward than non-experts when the situation or the problem is relatively simple. However, in complex or unfamiliar territory, they may move more slowly, more deliberatively, testing hypotheses against new evidence, though they are usually likely to be quicker overall and certainly more successful than non-experts. Experts sense when to act and when to hold off, neither panicking nor being indecisive, when faced with uncertainty. And when to stick by the rules and when to bend them.

Ways of developing expertise

When developing expertise, teachers gradually build better-informed and greater confidence in their own professional judgement.

Ideally, developing expertise is a collective as well as an individual process, where individuals can draw on the wisdom of others, from research and the practice of those with greater experience.

Teachers benefit from watching other teachers at work, or working alongside them, looking to identify and discuss dilemmas and successful patterns of resolution rather than concentrating on shortcomings.

Experts recognise the limits of their expertise and are prepared to call on others, where need be. In teaching, this involves drawing on the expertise of other people both within and beyond the school and sharing their own. This is much easier in a school context where others provide support. Just as the learning environment influences profoundly how children learn, the school and policy environment affects how teachers are encouraged, or otherwise, to exercise and develop their expertise. This requires headteachers and colleagues who encourage each other to explore, to risk, to innovate – and support each other through the successes and the difficulties.

Shulman highlights the value of case studies in developing professional expertise, suggesting (2004: 564) that these are valuable because 'participants are urged to elaborate on … what actually happened, what was said and done, how all that occurred made them feel … to dig deep into the particularity of the context because it is in the devilish details that practice differs dramatically from theory.'

Watching and discussing with others with a high level of expertise is a necessary part of teachers developing expertise. But it is not enough. Underlying how teachers act is how they think. So teachers have to challenge – and often try to change – how they think about ideas such as intelligence and inclusion, behaviour and breadth, curriculum and challenge. For instance, Twiselton's (2006) research into primary student teachers characterises some as 'task managers', with little emphasis on children's learning, some as 'curriculum deliverers' where the focus is more on learning but largely based on external demands, and some as 'concept/skill builders' where they understand and encouraged patterns of learning beyond the task. If teachers are to see themselves as curriculum creators rather than deliverers, initial teacher education must at least open up this possibility; and continuing professional development must encourage it.

Reading 16.4

Improving teacher expertise

Dylan Wiliam

This reading focuses on the development of teacher expertise and on professional development activity. Wiliam suggests how professional understanding develops through
practice, and argues that the content of professional development should focus on
teaching strategies of proven effectiveness and on practical processes of classroom application. The lecture from which this reading is drawn describes Wiliam's collaboration
with Paul Black on *Assessment for Learning* (Black et al., 2003).

   Thinking of your own development plans, do you first analyse what is likely to be most
effectiveness, as Wiliam suggests?

Edited from: Wiliam, D. (2007) *Assessment for Learning: Why, what and how?* Inaugural
lecture. Institute of Education, University of London, 24 April.

In England, there is a four-fold difference in the speed of learning between the most
effective and least effective classrooms. The obvious factors — class size or grouping
strategies — make relatively little difference. What matters is the quality of the teacher.

Aristotle's perspective on the nature of expertise (or intellectual virtue as he called it)
is informative here. Aristotle identified three main intellectual virtues: *episteme*, *techne*,
and *phronesis*. The first of these, *episteme* (science), is the knowledge of timeless universal
truths. For example, the base angles of an isosceles triangle are always equal. Once you
have proved this to be true, there is no need to check it tomorrow, it will still be true. The
second intellectual virtue, *techne* (craft), deals with the realm of things that are variable.
For example, there is no one perfect form for a table, but the ability to make a table for
a specific purpose is an important virtue. Yet it is the third intellectual value, *phronesis*
(practical wisdom), that Aristotle regarded as the highest. As an example of *phronesis,*
Aristotle gave the leadership of the state. For this task a person needs to be aware of
important principles, but these must always be tempered by the knowledge of specific
contexts.

This perspective is fruitful when thinking about the nature of expertise in teaching
because governments, and agencies employed by governments, are often engaged in a
search for 'what works'. However, in education 'what works' is a particularly useful
question to ask because almost everything works somewhere, and nothing works everywhere. The important question is, '*Under what conditions does a particular initiative
work.*' Expertise in teaching would therefore appear to be mainly a matter of *phronesis*
rather than *episteme* or indeed, *techne*. This is why so much educational research appears
to teachers either to tell them what they already know or something they know to be
inappropriate to their particular circumstances.

Promoting 'practical wisdom'

If expertise in teaching is 'practical wisdom', how can we promote its development? The organizational theorists Nonaka and Takeuchi (1995) looked at processes of knowledge creation and knowledge transfer in commercial organizations. In particular, they explored the interplay of explicit and implicit or tacit knowledge (often described as the kind of knowledge that an organization does not know it has until the people who have it leave).

Nonaka and Takeuchi outline four basic modes of knowledge conversion (see Figure 16.4.1). Perhaps the most familiar is the process they call 'combination' where one person communicates their explicit knowledge to another, for example, when one person tells another that lessons in a particular school are all of 40 minutes' duration. A second form of knowledge conversion occurs when one person's implicit knowledge is picked up by others, implicitly, through a process of socialization. An individual learns, 'That's the way things are done round here.'

Figure 16.4.1
Processes for transferring professional knowledge

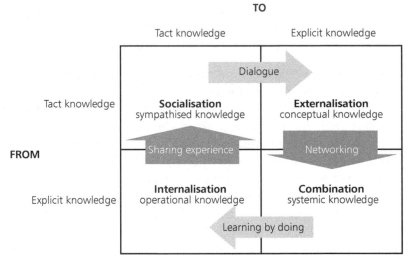

(After Nanaka and Takucuchi, 1995)

'Externalization' is a process in which one person's implicit knowledge is made explicit for the purpose of communication to another. When I started training teachers in the 1980s, I wasn't particularly helpful to the student teachers I was supporting because I had no way of describing what it was that I was doing. I had been reasonably successful as a practitioner, but had not developed a language for describing what I was doing. However, being forced to reflect on practice, and being forced to develop a language of description, I was developing a deeper understanding of my own practice.

Complementary to this is internalization—the process of moving from explicit to implicit knowing. One example of this process is what happens when one is told how to do something, which creates a basic knowledge of the process, only for a much deeper understanding to emerge later—often months later. A friend of mine is a very keen golfer, and his coach was telling him that in order to improve his swing, he needed 'to quieten his lower body'. For weeks, he worked on trying to put this into practice, and eventually, he understood what his coach had meant, but only when he could actually do what his coach was suggesting. The phrase 'to quieten his lower body' looked like an instruction, but it was really a description of what it would feel like to have internalized this new knowledge, and make it into operational knowledge.

As well as these four modes of knowledge conversion, Nonaka and Takeuchi propose a 'knowledge spiral' that is generated by moving around the four modes of knowledge conversion through four processes: *sharing experience, dialogue, networking* and *learning by doing*. It is this model of knowledge creation and knowledge conversion that drives our approach to teacher professional development.

The fundamental insight contained in the Nonaka and Takeuchi model is that knowing something is not the same as being able to do it. In our conversations with teachers, Paul Black and I realized that many of the teachers knew the research we were talking about quite well. What they did not do was to enact this knowledge in their practice. The problem was not lack of knowledge but a lack of understanding of what it meant to do this in the classroom.

That is why I do not believe we should tell teachers what to do. This is not out of some misguided sense of wanting to be kind to teachers of to value their experience. If there were something that we could tell teachers to do with a guarantee that it would improve student outcomes, then there would be a strong case for telling them what to do (and perhaps even sacking those who refused!). After all, schools are there for students, not teachers. But telling teachers what to do doesn't work because it is impossible to prepare teachers for every situation they are going to face in the classroom. Teaching is just too complex.

On the other hand, we also know that experience alone is not enough. Just leaving teachers to their own devices does not work either—if it were then the most experienced teachers would generate the greatest progress in their students, and we know that is not true. Instead, what is needed are ways to support teachers to reflect on their practice in systematic ways, to build on their accessible knowledge base and, perhaps most importantly, to learn from mistakes.

Twenty years ago this would have resulted in a very gloomy prognosis, because there was relatively little evidence that it was possible to improve teacher practice. However, in recent years, it has become clear that the relative ineffectiveness of teacher professional development efforts in the past means nothing for what we might to in the future, because we have not engaged consistently in the kinds of activities that the research indicates are necessary in order to help teachers change their practice.

Content, *then* process

If we are to help teachers improve student outcomes, the starting point must be on those things that make most difference to student outcomes. In other words, we start from the changes in teacher practice that make the most difference to students, and only then work out how to help teachers make the change—content, *then* process.

The content and efficacy of teaching

The first element of our content model is evidence of efficacy. This is essential because without such evidence, teachers say, 'I would love to teach this way, but I can't because I've got to raise my test scores.' For example, if Assessment for Learning (AfL) is being promoted, it is essential that teachers know that their students are likely to have higher achievement on tests and examinations. Fortunately, as discussed above, the evidence in favour of AfL is strong.

The second content element of the model is a number of practical techniques for implementation in classrooms. Here are some examples associated with AfL.

> To highlight learning intentions, a very simple technique is to discuss examples, before students are asked to complete a task themselves. So, if the task is to write a story, examples of stories from last year's class might be considered—some good, some middling, and some weaker ones. There can then be discussion, either in pairs, groups or as a whole class, about what is good about the good ones.
>
> Techniques for effective feedback typically involve ensuring that the feedback creates more work for the student. For example, a mathematics teacher once said to me, 'If you're marking a student's work and tick 15 of the answers as correct and mark five of them as incorrect, then the child can work out for themselves that they've got 15 out of 20.' So I suggested that instead, the teacher could explain an error and then tell the student, 'Five others are also wrong for the same reason. Find them and fix them.'
>
> Teachers can increase the extent to which students act as learning resources for one another. For example, secondary science teachers typically have a number of requirements for laboratory reports, including a margin for each page, headings being underlined, diagrams drawn in pencil and labelled and so on. One way to engage students in supporting each others' learning is to insist that before students are allowed to submit their report to the teacher they have to get a 'buddy' to certify that all the basic requirements have been satisfied by signing the 'pre-flight checklist'. The teacher then marks the assignment, and reports back to the student who wrote the report on the quality of the report, and to the 'buddy' on the extent to which they accurately assessed their partner's work in terms of how well the basic requirements had been met.

The process of teaching to improve outcomes

The second part of our professional development model focuses on the process. For example, how we can support teachers in making greater use of AfL in their classrooms? From work with teachers over a ten-year period, five aspects of the process seem to be particularly important: choice, flexibility, small steps, accountability and support.

First, teachers need to be given a choice about what aspects of practice to develop. It is often assumed that to improve, teachers should work on the weakest aspects of their practice, and for some teachers, these aspects may indeed be so weak that they should be the priority for professional development. But for most teachers, students will benefit more from teachers becoming even more expert in their strengths. In our work with teachers in Oxfordshire and Medway, one of the teachers, Derek was already quite skilled at conducting whole-class discussion sessions, but he was interested in improving this practice further. He is now one of the most skilled practitioners we have ever observed in this regard. A colleague of his at the same school, Philip, was much more interested in helping students develop skills of self-assessment and peer-assessment and he too is now highly skilled at these aspects of practice. To make Philip work on questioning, or to make Derek work on peer-assessment and self-assessment is unlikely to benefit their students as much as supporting each teacher to become excellent in their own way. When teachers themselves make the decision about what it is that they wish to prioritize for their own professional development, they are more likely to 'make it work'.

Second, teachers need the flexibility to be able to modify the A*f*L techniques they use to fit their own classroom context. The danger in this is that a teacher may so modify an idea that it is no longer effective.

The third element of the process model is that of taking small steps. In implementing this professional development model, we have to accept that teacher learning is slow. This is, to borrow a rather well-known phrase, an 'inconvenient truth'. Social inequalities are everywhere, and the knowledge that high-quality education can largely alleviate many of these inequalities means that policymakers are understandably in a hurry to make a difference. However, for changes in practice to be lasting, they must be integrated into a teacher's existing routines, and this takes time. Many of those involved professional development are familiar with the experience of encouraging teachers to try out new ideas, and seeing them being enacted when they visit teachers' classrooms only to hear that as soon as they have left, the teachers revert to their former practices.

Any kind of change in one's teaching practice is hard. But the kinds of changes I am calling for here are particularly hard, because they go 'against the grain' of current educational orthodoxy. In our pre-service courses with teachers, we talk about the importance of 'opening up' the classroom, providing space for students to talk, both because it is beneficial to their development, but also because by careful listening to what the students say, teachers can gain insights into their development. However, opening up the classroom in this way is seen by many teachers as 'giving up control'—faddish ideas being advocated by ivory tower academics who don't know what real teaching is. A*f*L practices would be hard to develop even in the most supportive climate, but are even harder when there is active hostility to their introduction. That is why, even if we are in a hurry to help teachers improve their practice, we should 'hasten slowly'.

The last two elements of the process model are support and accountability, which can be thought of as two sides of the same coin: supportive accountability. The idea here is that we create structures that while making teachers accountable for developing their practice, also provide the support for them to do this. Developing one's practice of formative assessment is different from learning new facts. It requires developing new habits, and traditional models of teaching are much better at imparting knowledge than changing habits. If we want to change teachers' habits, we would do well to look at organizations such as *Weight Watchers*. After all, everyone who wants to lose weight knows they have to do two things: eat less and exercise more. The knowledge base for weight loss is actually very simple. What is hard is changing the habits that result in weight gain. In the same way, if we are going to change what teachers do in classrooms then helping teachers change habits is as important as giving teachers new knowledge.

Clearly, creating this 'supportive accountability' could be done in a number of ways, but one particular mechanism—teacher learning communities within school and beyond—is particularly suited to supporting teachers in their development. Through in participation in learning communities, teachers can experiment, share, discuss, network—and thus develop their expertise.

Reading 16.5

Mind frames for visible learning
John Hattie

Hattie picks up on his meta-analysis of the effect-sizes of teaching strategies (see **Reading 4.6**), and proposes that adopting 'mind frames' for visible teaching and learning will make a significant difference to student learning. Rather like TLRP's principles, this is a way of structuring knowledge for expert interpretation of rapidly changing classroom circumstances. Fragmentary research findings make more practical sense when placed within theoretically robust frameworks of professional understanding.

As your expertise develops, can you see the shape of an emerging framework of understanding? It will need to be your own.

Edited from: Hattie, J. (2012) *Visible Learning for Teachers: Maximizing Impact on Learning.* Abingdon: Routledge, 1–20.

What are the attributes of schooling that truly make the difference to student learning? The 'visible' aspect refers first to making student learning visible to teachers, ensuring clear identification of the attributes that make a visible difference to student learning, and *all* in the school visibly knowing the impact that they have on the learning in the school (of the student, teacher, and school leaders). The 'visible' aspect also refers to making teaching visible to the student, such that they learn to become their own teachers, which is the core attribute of lifelong learning or self-regulation, and of the love of learning that we so want students to value. The 'learning' aspect refers to how we go about knowing and understanding, and then doing something about student learning. A common theme is the need to retain learning at the forefront and to consider teaching primarily in terms of its impact on student learning.

Figure 16.5.1 sums up the high-level principles which I propose:

Visible teaching and learning occurs when learning is the explicit and transparent goal, when it is appropriately challenging, and when the teacher and the student both (in their various ways) seek to ascertain whether and to what degree the challenging goal

I see learning through the eyes of my students

Figure 16.5.1
Know thy impact:
mind frames for
visible learning

Mind frames

- I am an evaluator/ activator
- I am a change agent
- I am a seeker of feedback
- I use dialogue more than monologue
- I enjoy challenge
- I have high expectations for all
- I welcome error
- I am passionate about and promote the language of learning

A cooperative and critical partner

- I use learning intensions and success criteria
- I am for surface and deep outcomes
- I consider prior achievement and attitudes
- I set high expectation targets
- I feed the gap in student learning

An adaptive learning expert

- I create trusting environments
- I know the power of peers
- I use multiple strategies
- I know when and how to differentiate
- I foster deliberate practice and concentration
- I know I can develop confidence to succeed

A reciever of feedback

- I know how to use the three feedback questions
- I know how to use the three feedback levels
- I give and receive feedback
- I monitor and interpret my learning/teaching

I help students to become their own teachers

is attained. Visible teaching and learning occurs when there is deliberate practice aimed at attaining mastery of the goal, when there is feedback given and sought, and when there are active, passionate, and engaging people (teacher, students, peers) participating in the act of learning. It is teachers seeing learning through the eyes of students, and students seeing teaching as the key to their ongoing learning. The remarkable feature of the evidence is that the greatest effect on student learning occurs when teachers become learners of their own teaching, and when students become their own teachers. When students become their own teachers, they exhibit the self-regulatory attributes that seem most desirable for learners (self-monitoring, self-evaluation, self-assessment, self-teaching).

A key premise is that the teacher's view of this or her role is critical. It is the specific mind frames that teachers have about their role – and most critically a mind frame within which they ask themselves about the effect they are having on student learning. Fundamentally, the most powerful way of thinking about a teacher's role is for teachers to see themselves as *evaluators* of their effects on students. Teachers need to use evidence-based methods to inform, change, and sustain these evaluation beliefs about their effect. These beliefs relate to claims about what each student can do as a consequence of the teacher's actions, and how every resource (especially peers) can be used to play a part in moving students from what they can do now to where the teacher considers they should be

– and to do so in the most efficient, as well as effective, manner. It matters what teachers do – but what matters *most* is having an appropriate mind frame relating to the impact of what they do. An appropriate mind frame combined with appropriate actions work together to achieve a positive learning effect.

As I argued in *Visible Learning* (Hattie 2009, Reading 4.6), when teachers see learning occurring or not occurring, they intervene in calculated and meaningful ways to alter the direction of learning to attain various shared, specific, and challenging goals. In particular, they provide students with multiple opportunities and alternatives for developing learning strategies based on the surface and deep levels of learning some context or domain matter, leading to students building conceptual understanding of this learning, which the students and teachers then use in future learning. Learners can be so different, making it difficult for a teacher to achieve such teaching acts: student can be in different learning places at various times, using a multiplicity of unique learning strategies, meeting different and appropriately challenging goals. Learning is a very personal journey for the teacher and the student, although there are remarkable commonalities in this journey for many teachers and students. It requires much skill for teachers to demonstrate to all of their students that they can see the students' 'perspective, communicating it back to them so that they have valuable feedback to self-assess, feel safe, and learn to understand others and the content with the same interest and concern' (Cornelius-White, 2007: 23).

The act of teaching requires deliberate interventions to ensure that there is cognitive change in the student; thus the key ingredients are being aware of the learning intentions, knowing when a student is successful in attaining those intentions, having sufficient understanding of the student's prior understanding as he or she comes to the task, and knowing enough about the content to provide meaningful and challenging experiences so that there is some sort of progressive development. It involves a teacher who knows a range of learning strategies with which to supply the student when they seem not to understand, who can provide direction and redirection in terms of the content being understood and thus maximize the power of feedback, and show the skill to 'get out the way' when learning is progressing towards the success criteria.

Of course, it helps it these learning intentions and success criteria are shared with, committed to, and understood by the learner – because in the right caring and idea-rich environment, the learner can then experiment (be right and wrong) with the content and the thinking about the content, and make connections across ideas. A safe environment for the learner (and for the teacher) is an environment in which error is welcomes and fostered – because we learn so much from errors and from the feedback that then accrues from going in the wrong direction or not going sufficiently fluently in the right direction. In the same way teachers themselves need to be in a safe environment to learn about the success or otherwise of their teaching from others.

To create such an environment, to command a range of learning strategies, and to be cognitively aware of the pedagogical means that enable the student to learn requires dedicated, passionate people. Such teachers need to be aware of which of their teaching strategies are working or not, need to be prepared to understand and adapt to the learner(s) and their situation, contexts, and prior learning, and need to share the experience of learning in this manner in an open, forthright, and enjoyable way with their students and their colleagues.

It is teachers with certain mind frames that make the difference. Powerful, passionate, accomplished teacher are those who:

- focus on students' cognitive engagement with the content of what it is that is being taught;

- focus on developing a way of thinking and reasoning that emphasizes problem-solving and teaching strategies relating to the content that they wish students to learn;

- focus on imparting new knowledge and understanding, and then monitor how students gain fluency and appreciation in the new knowledge;

- focus on providing feedback in an appropriate and timely manner to help students to attain the worthwhile goals of the lesson;

- seek feedback about their effects on the progress and proficiency of *all* of their students

- have deep understanding about how we learn; and

- focus on seeing learning through the eyes of their students, appreciating their fits and starts in learning, and their often non-linear progressions to the goals, supporting their deliberate practice, providing feedback about their errors and misdirections, and caring that the students get to the goals and that the students share the teacher's passion for the material being learnt.

This focus is sustained, unrelenting, and needs to be shared by all in a school.

Teacher professional learning and development
Helen Timperley, Aaron Wilson, Heather Barrar and Irene Fung

> This is an excerpt from a comprehensive, international review of what is known about
> teachers' professional development. The authors establish that the right sort of profes-
> sional development provision can make a big difference to student outcomes. The trick
> though, is to bring together suitable learning contexts, appropriate content and focus,
> and relevant, engaging activities.
>
>   What professional development activities are available to you?
>
> *Edited from:* H. Timperley, A. Wilson, H. Barrar and I. Fung (2007) *Teacher Professional
> Learning and Development: Best Evidence Synthesis Iteration.* Wellington. New Zealand:
> Ministry of Education, xxvi–xxxvi.

Opportunities for teachers to engage in professional learning and development can have a
substantial impact on student learning. For example, in literacy studies, substantial effect
sizes were reported by Phillips, McNaughton, and MacDonald (2001) (ES = 0.48) and by
Timperley (2006) (ES = 0.89). These gains equate to more than two years' progress in one
year. In writing, English and Bareta (2006) reported an overall effect size of 1.3 over two
years, which similarly equates to about two years' progress in one year.

   This synthesis provides a theoretical framework for thinking about what is known,
together with the associated empirical basis. Conclusions are clustered around three themes:

1 The context of professional learning and development
2 The content of professional learning and development
3 Activities to promote professional learning.

What is known to be effective, however, is not always what is practised. For example, it
is generally accepted that listening to inspiring speakers or attending one-off workshops
rarely changes teacher practice sufficiently to impact on student outcomes. Yet, this type
of activity is the predominant model of professional development.

The context of professional learning and development

Seven contextual elements were identified as important for promoting professional
learning in ways that impacted positively and substantively on a range of student
outcomes. They are:

Extended time for opportunities to learn was necessary, but not sufficient

- Learning opportunities typically occurred over an extended period of time and involved frequent contact with a provider.
- How time was used was more important than the exact nature of the provision (for example, release from teaching duties).

External expertise was typically necessary, but not sufficient

- Engagement of external expertise was a feature of nearly all the interventions in the core studies, with funding frequently used for this purpose.

Teachers' engagement in learning was more important than initial volunteering

- Neither who initiated the professional learning opportunities nor whether they were voluntary or compulsory was associated with particular outcomes for students. What was more important was that teachers engaged in the learning process at some point.

Prevailing discourses challenged if appropriate

- Where prevailing discourses were problematic, they were typically based on assumptions that some groups of students could not learn as well as others and/or emphasised limited curriculum goals.

Opportunities to participate in a professional community of practice were more important than place

- Effective communities provided teachers with opportunities to process new understandings and challenge problematic beliefs, with a focus on analysing the impact of teaching on student learning.

Consistency with wider trends in policy and research

- Approaches promoted were typically consistent with current research findings, recommendations of professional bodies (e.g. national subject associations), and/or current policy.

Active school leadership

- School-based interventions had leaders who provided one or more of the following conditions:
  - Actively organised a supportive environment to promote professional learning opportunities and the implementation of new practices in classrooms;
  - Focused on developing a learning culture within the school and were learners along with the teachers;
  - Provided alternative visions and targets for student outcomes and monitored whether these were met;
  - Created the conditions for distributing leadership by developing the leadership of others.

The content of professional learning and development

Without content on which to base deeper understandings and extend teaching skills there is no foundation for change.

Content included discipline knowledge and the interrelationship between such fundamentals as new curricula, pedagogy, and assessment information; knowledge of students, including their developmental progressions through particular curricula, and their culture; linguistic and cultural resources; and theoretical frameworks and conceptual tools.

Skills of teacher inquiry included analysis of the teacher's own practice and new possibilities in relation to a standard of practice; the ways in which practice impacted on diverse student learners, and new possibilities for greater impact; and methods of inquiring into the adequacy and improvement of practice.

Different aspects integrated

- Integration of theory and practice was a key feature.

- Theory provided the basis for making curricular and pedagogical decisions. Teachers were assisted to translate theory into classroom practice.

- Integration of pedagogical content knowledge, of assessment information, and of how students learn particular curricula was a feature of most curriculum-based interventions documented in the core studies but was given different emphasis in different curricula.

- Greater emphasis on curriculum content knowledge was evident in mathematics, science, and writing.

Clear links between teaching and learning and/or student–teacher relationships established

- All interventions in the core studies were underpinned by an assumption that student learning and teacher–student relationships were strongly influenced by what teachers did in their classrooms.

Assessment used to focus teaching and enhance self-regulation

- Approximately half the interventions in the core studies included assessment for one or more of the following purposes:
  - Providing a catalyst for initial and ongoing engagement;
  - Identifying professional learning needs;
  - Identifying student learning needs through assessment of their understandings and skills in order to focus teaching;
  - Inquiring into the effectiveness of practice with particular students for the purpose of confirming or refining practice.

Sustainability

- Sustainability was dependent on teachers acquiring both of the following:

- In-depth understanding of theory, which served as a tool to assist instructional decision making;
- The skills of inquiry to judge the impact of teaching on learning and to identify next teaching steps.

Activities to promote professional learning

To support professional learning, it was important that teachers were able to engage in multiple and aligned opportunities that supported them to learn and apply new understandings and skills. Key features of effective activities are:

Purposes and activities aligned

- A clear alignment between the intended learning goals and the activities was evident.

A variety of activities

- Teachers were provided with a variety of ways to understand the content. (Listening to experts was not in itself sufficient to change practice.)

Content conveyed through the activity was more important than any particular activity

- Every type of activity that was associated with positive outcomes was also associated with low or no impact.

Professional instruction sequenced

- Typical sequences involved a rationale or catalyst to engage, instruction in key theoretical principles, and then opportunities to translate theory into practice and deepen understanding of theory.

Understandings discussed and negotiated

- Professional development pedagogies shared a focus on providing opportunities for teachers to discuss and negotiate the meaning of concepts taught.
- Understanding of new theories was sometimes developed through engaging teachers' existing theories.

Student perspective maintained

- A variety of activities served to develop teachers' understanding of the relationship between their teaching and student learning.

Professionalism

How does reflective teaching contribute to society?

17

The readings in this chapter are concerned with teacher professionalism and society.

Archer begins (Reading 17.1) with an analysis of how education systems develop and change over time in response to an evolving interplay of pressures and constraints. Teachers, of course, play a part in this.

We then have a group of readings on how the profession thinks about, and develops, itself. Menter et al. (17.2) discuss a range of approaches to teacher education and shows how these relate to educational purposes and aspirations. The General Teaching Council for Northern Ireland (GTCNI) (17.3) provide an illustration of national competences, based on reflective practice. Debate within the Republic of Ireland is conveyed by Sahlberg, Furlong and Munn (17.4), an international panel advising on the importance of combining theory and practice in teaching. Power (17.5) brings us back to the day-to-day challenges of teaching in her representations of the 'distressed', 'oppressed' and 'imaginative' professional.

Reading 17.6 from the Council of Europe's Memorandum on Teaching and Learning about Human Rights in Schools is included as a reminder of the fundamental role of education in democracies. Even on a frustrating day, this reading should affirm the significance of teaching as a vocation.

The final reading concerns the ways in which education policy is formed. Bowe, Ball and Gold (17.7) begin with an analysis of the contexts of macro-political influence, text construction by government agencies and actual practice in LAs, schools and classrooms. They show how policymaking is open to shaping and challenge at each stage.

What influence can individuals, such as teachers, have over social structures, such as the education system? What influence should they have? How should the teaching profession develop itself?

The parallel chapter of *Reflective Teaching in Schools* begins with a review of professions and professionalism. The aims of education in relation to social development are then discussed. Wealth creation, cultural reproduction and social justice are identified as particular goals. In a section on 'classroom teaching and society' the chapter highlights the value issues which reflective teachers face when they recognise the ways in which their actions contribute to the future identities and life-chances of pupils. Reflective teaching is then related to the democratic process and to the importance of teachers contributing their professional voice to policy debates and public decision-making on educational topics.

Of course, there is list of suggested 'Key Readings', and more support is available from reflectiveteaching.co.uk.

Reading 17.1

Thinking about educational systems
Margaret Archer

> This reading comes from the introduction to Margaret Archer's analysis of the ways in which educational systems form, develop and change through time. She argues that such systems reflect the priorities and conceptions of those who have power. However, such power is likely to be contested and, in any event, those in a position to make policy must also relate their ambitions to the constraints of practical realities.
>
> To what extent can you relate Archer's model, as expressed here, to the recent history of changing educational policy?
>
> *Edited from:* Archer, M. (1979) *The Social Origins of Educational Systems*. London: Sage Publications, 1–3.

How do educational systems develop and change?

This question can be broken down into three subsidiary ones: Who gets education? What happens to them during it? Where do they go to after it? These enquiries about inputs, processes and outputs subsume a whole range of issues, many of which have often been discussed independently. They embrace problems about educational opportunity, selection and discrimination, about the management and transmission of knowledge and values and about social placement, stratification and mobility. At the same time they raise the two most general problems of all, namely those about the effects of society upon education and about the consequences of education for society.

The fundamental question here is, 'Why does education have the particular inputs, processes and outputs which characterize it at any given time?' The basic answer is held to be very simple. Education has the characteristics it does because of the goals pursued by those who control it. A second question asks, 'Why do these particular inputs, processes and outputs change over time?' The basic answer given here is equally simple. Change occurs because new educational goals are pursued by those who have the power to modify previous practices. As we shall see, these answers are of a deceptive simplicity. They are insisted upon now, at the beginning because, however complex our final formulations turn out to be, education is fundamentally about what people have wanted of it and have been able to do to it.

The real answers are more complicated but they supplement rather than contradict the above. It is important never to lose sight of the fact that the complex theories we develop to account for education and educational change are theories about the educational activities of people. This very basic point is underlined for two reasons. Firstly, because however fundamental, much of the literature in fact contradicts it and embodies implicit beliefs in hidden hands, evolutionary mechanisms, and spontaneous adjustments to social change. There education is still seen as mysteriously adapting to social requirements and responding to demands of society not of people. Secondly, and for the present purposes much more importantly, our theories will be *about* the educational activities of people even though they will not explain educational development strictly *in terms* of people alone.

The basic answers are too simple because they beg more questions than they solve. To say that education derives its characteristic features from the aims of those who control it immediately raises problems concerning the identification of controlling groups, the bases and processes upon which control rests, the methods and channels through which it is exerted, the extensiveness of control, the reactions of others to this control, and their educational consequences. Similarly, where change is concerned, it is not explained until an account has been given of why educational goals change, who does the changing, and how they impose the changes they seek. To confront these problems is to recognise that their solution depends upon analyzing complex forms of social interaction. Furthermore, the nature of education is rarely, if ever, the practical realization of an ideal form of instruction as envisaged by a particular group. Instead, most of the time most of the forms that education takes are the political products of power struggles. They bear the marks of concession to allies and compromise with opponents. Thus to understand the nature of education at any time we need to know not only who won the struggle for control, but also how: not mere who lost, but also how badly they lost.

Secondly, the basic answers are deceptively simple because they convey the impression that education and educational change can be explained by reference to group goals and balances of power alone. It is a false impression because there are other factors which constrain both the goal formation and goal attainment of even the most powerful group – that is the group most free to impose its definition of instruction and to mould education to its purposes. The point is that no group, not even for that matter the whole of society acting in accord, has a blank sheet of paper on which to design national education. Conceptions of education are of necessity limited by the existing availability of skills and resources. Another way of stating this is to say that cultural and structural factors constrain educational planning and its execution. Since this is the case, then explanations of education and educational change will be partly in terms of such factors.

Moreover, only the minimal logical constraints have been mentioned so far: in practice educational action is also affected by a variable set of cultural and structural factors which make up its environment. Educational systems, rarities before the eighteenth century, emerged within complex social structures and cultures and this context conditioned the conception and conduct of action of those seeking educational development. Among other things the social distribution of resources and values and the patterning of vested interests in the existing form of education were crucially important factors. Once a given form of education exists it exerts an influence on future educational change. Alternative educational plans are, to some extent, reactions to it (they represent desires to change inputs, transform processes, or alter the end products); attempts to change it are affected by it (by the degree to which it monopolizes educational skills and resources); and change is change of it (which means dismantling, transforming, or in some way grappling with it).

Reading 17.2

Teacher education and professionalism
Ian Menter, Moira Hulme, Dely Elliot and Jon Lewin

> This reading is derived from a literature review on the contribution that teacher education can make to the quality of educational experience and personal development of young people in the twenty-first century. Commissioned by the Scottish Government, it identifies four models of teacher education: the *effective* teacher, the *reflective* teacher, the *enquiring* teacher and the *transformative* teacher. Each of these has an important rationale. In practice, most forms of provision for initial training and continuing professional development, whether school- or university-led, seek to combine these elements.
>
> How would you characterise the teacher education programme which you experienced or are experiencing?
>
> *Edited from:* Menter, I, Hulme, M., Elliot, D and Lewin, J. (2010) *Teacher Education in the 21st Century.* Edinburgh: The Scottish Government, 21–5.

Four conceptions of teacher professionalism underlie policy and research literature on teacher education.

The effective teacher

This model has emerged as the dominant one in much official government discourse across the developed world over the last thirty years. It is closely associated with an economically led view of education. The emphases are on technical accomplishment and measurement for an age of accountability (Mahony and Hextall, 2000). Such an approach may be aligned with a nationally prescribed curriculum and a national assessment system, which extends down to the earliest stages of schooling.

This particular aspect of education in the UK has seen considerable recent variation in policy across the four nations, with the effective teacher model being most fully adopted in England. In Scotland, there has not been a national curriculum as such and, with *Curriculum for Excellence,* introduced from 2010, there is even more scope for professional autonomy. In Wales and Northern Ireland there has been much relaxation of the *National Curriculum* since devolution, especially in the earlier years of schooling.

In contrast to the politically driven 'effective teacher' model, the other three approaches emerged more from within the teaching profession and teacher education itself. The notion of teaching as a reflective activity emerged strongly in the UK, partly in response to the growing influence of the effective teacher model, which was seen by some as restricting teacher professionalism, rather than enhancing it (Stronach et al., 2002; Hartley, 2002).

The reflective teacher

The philosophical roots of the reflective teaching model lie in the work of the American educator John Dewey. Early in the twentieth century he developed an approach to teaching based on teachers becoming active decision-makers. Similar ideas were later developed by Donald Schön who wrote about *The Reflective Practitioner* (1983), stressing the significance of values and of theory informing decision-making.

In the UK, such ideas were developed in a very practical way by Andrew Pollard and his collaborators who from the late 1980s onwards, produced a series of books on 'reflective teaching' (e.g. Pollard and Tann, 1987). At the centre of this model was a cyclical approach to planning, making provision, acting, collecting evidence, analysing the evidence, evaluating, reflecting and then planning next steps. Built into such a model is a commitment to personal professional development through practice.

The model took a firm hold in teacher education institutions across the UK during the latter parts of the twentieth century. Indeed, the largest scale studies of initial teacher education undertaken in England by Furlong et al. (2000) found that about 70 per cent of teacher education programmes led from universities and colleges were informed by some version of 'reflective teaching'.

The reflective teaching approach also has significance for experienced teachers. In their Teaching and Learning Research Programme study 'Learning to Learn' Pedder et al. (2005) found that there were opportunities for considerable teacher learning to take place in the classroom context, through, applying research, collaborating with colleagues, or consulting with pupils. However, reflective teaching does not in itself imply a research orientation on the part of the teacher.

The enquiring teacher

In the UK the origins of the notion of 'teacher as researcher' is usually associated with the groundbreaking work of Lawrence Stenhouse (1975), who argued that teachers should indeed take a research approach to their work. He described this as a form of curriculum development.

In this model, teachers are encouraged to undertake systematic enquiry in their own classrooms, develop their practice and share their insights with other professionals. Such ideas have been taken up, developed and enhanced through a range of subsequent initiatives, often associated with university staff working in partnership with teachers and lecturers in schools and colleges.

At various times, such approaches have received 'official' endorsement through funded schemes (see McNamara, 2002; Furlong and Salisbury, 2005; Hulme et al., 2010). Teacher enquiry frequently figures within contemporary approaches to professional development (Campbell et al., 2004; Campbell and Groundwater Smith, 2009) and has been found to 're-energise' teachers (Burns and Haydn, 2002).

Ponte et al. (2004) conducted case studies in the USA, Australia and UK of programmes that aimed to introduce action research in initial teacher education. They concluded that there is a need to introduce student teachers to inquiry-oriented approaches to teaching during initial training in order to provide a firm foundation for career-long professional learning - i.e. to develop a disposition towards thoughtful and critical self-study.

The transformative teacher

The final model incorporates and builds upon elements of the previous two. However its key defining feature is that it brings an 'activist' dimension into the approach to teaching. If the prevalent view of the teacher is someone whose contribution to society is to transmit knowledge and prepare pupils for the existing world, the view here is that teachers' responsibilities go beyond that; they should be contributing to social change and be preparing their pupils to contribute to change in society.

The most cogent articulation of this model is that set out by the Australian teacher educator, Judyth Sachs (2003), who talks of 'teaching as an activist profession'. Those who advocate teaching as a transformative activity will suggest that some challenge to the status quo is not only to be expected but is a necessary part of bringing about a more just education system, where inequalities in society begin to be addressed and where progressive social change can be stimulated (Zeichner, 2009; Cochran-Smith, 2004). In aspiring to achieve greater social justice through education however, those such as Clarke and Drudy (2006) have argued that it is important to consider the influence of teachers' own beliefs and values, which they bring to their work at whatever stage of their career they are at.

The future of teacher professionalism

Eric Hoyle suggested that models of teaching exist at some point on a spectrum between 'restricted' and 'extended' versions of teacher professionalism (Hoyle, 1974). Crudely speaking, the first model depicted above, the effective teacher, rests at the 'restricted' end of the spectrum, where teaching is largely defined in terms of a range of technical skills. The other three models are at various points towards the 'extended' end of the spectrum, where teachers are seen as more autonomous and their own judgement is called upon to a much greater extent (Adams, 2008).

In considering the future of teacher education in the 21st century, Edwards et al. (2002) argued that teachers should be given increased control over the professional knowledge base of teaching, and should be seen as:

> Users and producers of knowledge about teaching, in communities of practice which are constantly refreshed through processes of professional enquiry, in partnerships between practitioners and researchers (p. 125).

Reading 17.3

Teaching: The reflective profession
General Teaching Council for Northern Ireland (GTC NI)

This reading provides an example of a national statement of expected 'standards' or 'competences' for teachers. They often reflect particular priorities from the time of official endorsement, and are often updated as with this illustration. Such statements tend to overlap considerably in relation to professional values, knowledge, understanding, skills and development. Other contemporary examples are provided by Scotland's 2013 Professional Standards (see gtcs.org.uk) or those in Wales, England and the Republic of Ireland. This model combines practical skills with reflective capabilities.

How do you feel about your practice in relation to the issues listed below?

Edited from: General Teaching Council for Northern Ireland (2007) *Teaching: The Reflective Profession.* Belfast: GTCNI, 9, 13–15.

The Council considers that those who are honoured with the title and status of teacher will be knowledgeable, skilful and reflective practitioners who will:

- be concerned with the purposes and consequences of education, as well as what might be called technical proficiency;
- be prepared to experiment with the unfamiliar and learn from their experiences;
- have an approach characterised by open-mindedness and wholeheartedness;
- be committed to professional dialogue in collaboration with colleagues, in school and beyond;
- have working patterns characterised by a process of action, evaluation and revision;
- in keeping with the Council's *Code of Professional Values and Practice,* assume responsibility, as life-long learners, for their ongoing professional development.

Professional competence statements have been set out under broad headings:

Professional values and practice

Teachers should demonstrate that they:

- understand and uphold the core values and commitments enshrined in the Council's *Code of Values and Professional Practice.*

Professional knowledge and understanding

Teachers will have developed knowledge and understanding of:

- contemporary debates about the nature and purposes of education and the social and policy contexts in which the aims of education are defined and implemented.
- the learning area/subject(s) they teach, including the centrality of strategies and initiatives to improve literacy, numeracy and thinking skills, keeping curricular, subject and pedagogical knowledge up-to-date through reflection, self-study and collaboration with colleagues; and in Irish medium and other bilingual contexts, sufficient linguistic and pedagogical knowledge to teach the curriculum.
- how the learning area/subject(s) they teach contribute to the curriculum and be aware of curriculum requirements in preceding and subsequent key stages.
- curriculum development processes, including planning, implementation and evaluation.
- the factors that promote and hinder effective learning, and be aware of the need to provide for the holistic development of the child.
- a range of strategies to promote and maintain positive behaviour, including an acknowledgement of pupil voice, to establish an effective learning environment.
- the need to take account of the significant features of pupils' cultures, languages and faiths and to address the implications for learning arising from these.
- their responsibilities under the Special Educational Needs Code of Practice and know the features of the most common special needs and appropriate strategies to address these.
- strategies for communicating effectively with pupils, parents, colleagues and personnel from relevant child and school support agencies.
- how to use technology effectively, both to aid pupil learning and to support their professional role and how this competence embeds across all of the competences.
- the interrelationship between schools and the communities they serve, and the potential for mutual development and well-being.
- the statutory framework pertaining to education and schooling and their specific responsibilities emanating from it.

Professional skills and application

Regarding planning and leading, teachers will:

- set appropriate learning objectives/outcomes/ intentions, taking account of what pupils know, understand and can do, and the demands of the Northern Ireland Curriculum in terms of knowledge, skills acquisition and progression.

- plan and evaluate lessons that enable all pupils, including those with special educational needs, to meet learning objectives/outcomes/ intentions, showing high expectations and an awareness of potential areas of difficulty.

- when appropriate, deploy, organise and guide the work of other adults to support pupils' learning.

- plan for out-of-school learning, including school visits and field work, where appropriate.

- manage their time and workload effectively and efficiently and maintain a work/life balance.

Regarding teaching and learning, teachers will:

1 create and maintain a safe, interactive and challenging learning environment, with appropriate clarity of purpose for activities.

2 use a range of teaching strategies and resources, including eLearning where appropriate, that enable learning to take place and which maintain pace within lessons and over time.

3 employ strategies that motivate and meet the needs of all pupils, including those with special and additional educational needs and for those not learning in their first language.

4 secure and promote a standard of behaviour that enables all pupils to learn, pre-empting and dealing with inappropriate behaviour in the context of the school policies and what is known about best practice.

5 contribute to the life and development of the school, collaborating with teaching and support staff, parents and external agencies.

Regarding assessment teachers will:

- focus on assessment for learning by monitoring pupils' progress, giving constructive feedback to help pupils reflect on and improve their learning.

- select from a range of assessment strategies to evaluate pupils' learning, and use this information in their planning to help make their teaching more effective.

- assess the levels of pupils' attainment against relevant benchmarking data and understand the relationship between pupil assessment and target setting.

- liaise orally and in written reports in an effective manner with parents or carers on their child's progress and achievements.

Dimensions of development

As teachers progress in their careers they will encounter different challenges and expectations. They grow in confidence, share in the knowledge of colleagues and learn from experience. It can also be anticipated that their practice will become progressively more sophisticated and nuanced. This will be evidenced by:

- greater complexity in teaching, for example, in handling mixed-ability classes, or reluctant learners, or classes marked by significant diversity, or inter-disciplinary work;

- the deployment of a wider range of teaching strategies;

- basing teaching on a wider range of evidence, reading and research;

- extending one's impact beyond the classroom and fuller participation in the life of the school;

- the capacity to exercise autonomy, to innovate, to improvise; and

- a pronounced capacity for self-criticism and self-improvement;

- the ability to impact on colleagues through mentoring and coaching, modelling good practice, contributing to the literature on teaching and learning and the public discussion of professional issues, leading staff development, all based on the capacity to theorise about policy and practice.

Reading 17.4

Combining research and practice in teaching

Pasi Sahlberg, John Furlong and Pamela Munn

This report, commissioned by the Irish Government, highlights an international pattern linking high performance of national systems with recruitment of capable teachers and research-informed teacher education. Such training is often provided from university bases in association with partnership schools, but it can also be located in 'teaching schools' in association with partnership universities. Either way, provision must be made to develop educational understanding in, and of, practice.

Considering a teacher education programme you know well, how does it combine research and practice, evidence and experience, theory and application?

Edited from: Sahlberg, P., Furlong, J. and Munn, P. (2012) *Report of the International Review Panel on the Structure of Initial Teacher Education Provision in Ireland: Review conducted on behalf of the Department of Education and Skills.* Dublin: Higher Education Authority of Ireland, 5, 14–15.

Initial teacher education is probably the single most important factor in having a well-performing public education system. Evidence from the OECD countries is consistent with this notion. Singapore, Korea, Canada and Finland, countries that the OECD labels as having 'strong performing' education systems, have systematically invested in enhancing the initial education of their teachers. In all of these education systems, teachers are educated in academic universities where theory and practice are combined to form a foundation for teaching that is on a par with other academic professions. In all of these high performing education systems, teaching is also perceived by young people as an attractive career choice which makes admission to teacher education highly competitive and intellectually demanding.

Ireland has several advantages in its current system of teachers and teacher education that distinguish the Irish education system from many others. Most importantly, among young Irish people, to be a teacher is a popular choice that carries strong social prestige unlike in most other countries in Europe. Teacher education is widely accessible throughout Ireland and numerous initial teacher education programmes are serving diverse needs of communities and regions in the State. Finally, due to Ireland's economic and social structures, education has a central role to play in the future strategies of the nation. This brings teachers and how they are educated to the core of the implementation of national programmes for sustainable economic growth and prosperity.

One of the priorities of the European Union is to improve teacher quality and teacher education. It has made a number of proposals on areas such as: teachers' knowledge, attitudes and pedagogic skills; coordinated, coherent, and adequately resourced teacher education; reflective practice and research among teachers; the status and recognition of the teaching profession and the professionalisation of teaching. The EU proposals indicate that ITE needs to be upgraded in many countries and that transition from teacher education to school needs to be made smoother through effective mentoring, induction and school leadership.

The EU aspirations have been actualised in Finland which is highly acclaimed for its education system due especially to the quality of its teachers. There is a rigorous selection process for entry to teacher education and the competition for places adds to the attraction of teaching. ITE is research-based and extends to five years leading to a Masters level award. On being employed, teachers assume professional responsibility for curriculum planning, student assessment and school improvement, enjoying a high level of autonomy in their work and high status in society.

In Singapore, the National Institute of Education (NIE) is the sole provider of ITE. Evidence-based and research-informed learning underpins NIE's programmes. NIE's strategic plan for 2007–2012 sets out its ambition to be an institute of distinction, excelling in teacher education and teacher research. It has formed partnerships with other universities in Asia and also in Europe and the USA for the purpose of research collaboration and staff and student exchanges.

It has been found that in high-performing education systems, such as Canada, South Korea, Finland and Singapore, policy on teacher education is a national priority. Teachers are educated in academic universities where theory and practice are combined to form a foundation for teaching that is on a par with other academic professions. Teacher education is research-based and internationalisation is high on the agenda. Also, in these systems, teaching is perceived by young people as an attractive career choice which makes admission to teacher education highly competitive and intellectually demanding.

The main international trends in initial teacher education are the following.

First, teaching is increasingly viewed as a high status profession similar to the work of lawyers, doctors and engineers. Teachers have similar access to Masters and Doctoral studies and thereby to a career path in academic universities and research institutions as well as in schools and classrooms.

Second, as a consequence of the former trend, teacher education is increasingly relying on research knowledge on the one hand and focusing on preparing teachers to use and do research on the other. Research-based teacher education expands conventional teacher competences so that teachers are able to use educational research as part of their work in school. They diagnose their own teaching and learning by using educational research knowledge and methodologies to find the best methods of work, and understand their professional development through critically reflecting on their own thinking and behaviour.

Third, many teacher education programmes are having a more systematic focus on linking theory and practice during the initial preparation of teachers. In some countries, practical learning is also becoming an integral part of Masters' degree studies for ITE, similar to the way in which doctors or lawyers practise during their studies. School placements are giving way to clinical learning in special teacher training schools or carefully assigned regular schools where highly trained master teachers supervise the learning of student teachers. These features are seen as contributing to a continual spiral of improvement in pupils' learning which is the key objective of high quality ITE and continuous professional development.

Reading 17.5

The imaginative professional

Sally Power

The objective of this reading is to suggest that the best way of confronting the contemporary challenges of professional life is to develop something called a 'professional imagination'. Borrowing from the sociology of C. Wright Mills (Reading 5.1), it argues that this will enable professionals to better understand their experiences, position and circumstances. Without such an imagination, professionals will be 'doomed to stumble from one crisis to another'.

How do you see the future of the teaching profession, and your role in it?

Edited from: Power, S. (2008) 'The imaginative professional', in Cunningham, B. (ed.) *Exploring Professionalism.* London: IOE Press, 144–60.

In confronting contemporary challenges, two perspectives on professionals are commonly found – those of the 'distressed' and the 'oppressed', but the perspective of the 'imaginative professional' is also available.

The distressed professional: A therapeutic perspective

The therapeutic perspective presents the contemporary professional as distressed – either because of their own shortcomings, those of their colleagues and/or those of the organisation within which they work.

The therapeutic perspective is the approach we commonly take when thinking about the everyday failures and frustrations of our working days. For example, we may feel unable to cope with myriad requests and think it is because we are insufficiently organised or not competent enough with new technologies. May be we feel we are suffering from 'burnout' whereby our initial enthusiasm and commitment has waned into disillusionment and cynicism.

We also often explain away our professional troubles as resulting not from our own inadequacies but from having to work with inadequate fellow professionals. For example, we can feel overburdened because we have to cover for colleagues.

In addition to blaming ourselves and our colleagues, we may also feel distressed because of poor practices in the organisations in which we work. For example, research has highlighted factors such as lack of participation in decision-making and poor management style as contributing to high levels of stress among professionals.

The identification of 'unhealthy' interpersonal relations at work as the cause of professional distress is highlighted in the mushrooming interest in workplace 'bullying'.

www. C

Evidence from the UK National Workplace Bullying Advice Line cited by the dedicated resource centre BullyOnLine (www.bullyonline.org) suggests that bullying is rife in professionals' workplaces. Teachers are the largest group of callers to the Advice Line (accounting for 20% of callers), followed by healthcare employees (12% of callers) and social workers (10% of callers).

Bullying behaviour from managers is seen to contribute to high levels of professional stress. Health and Safety executive surveys (HSE, 2007) reveal that professionals working in education and health have the highest prevalence rates of work-related stress. Occupations within these fields that were the most stressful were health and social services managers (3.37%) and teaching professionals (2.61%).

Therapeutic remedies to alleviate distress

If we attribute the distress which professionals experience to their own failings, the shortcomings of their colleagues or their organisation, it makes sense to put in place a range of remedies targeted at these problems.

For example, incompetence with new technologies can be dealt with through ongoing staff development. The difficulties of combining complicated domestic lives with work responsibilities can be addressed through stress counselling. The problem of 'dead wood' can be tackled through rigorous appraisal and performance reviews. In terms of organisational malpractices, there are many self-help resources designed to promote personal well-being in the workplace. Some organisations, such as my own university, have put in place a network of 'dignity advisors'. These individuals are trained to provide advice and guidance to reduce the distress caused by workplace bullying.

While these strategies may provide some beneficial effects for some individuals, it is unlikely that they will significantly alter the work lives of professionals. This is because the way in which the problem is defined takes too narrow a perspective – one which focuses on the individual and their immediate milieu. Clearly, something else is going on that requires a broader overview of the contexts in which professionals work.

The oppressed professional: A deterministic perspective

At times of crisis, professionals, just like other workers, experience intensification of work and deskilling.

Larson (1980), writing over twenty years ago, outlined the processes through which educated labour became proleratiarianised – drawing attention to the intensification experienced by even such elevated professionals as doctors. Lawn and Ozga (1988) and Apple (1988) have identified similar processes in the working lives of teachers.

Since the late 1980s, professionals have experienced a whole range of further changes which have impacted on their work. At an international level, there are claims that we are in a new era of social history – couched variously in terms of globalization, post-modernity, post-Fordism and/or the 'information age'. All of these aspects have impacted on the lives of professionals in different ways. For example, the growth of post-Fordism has allegedly taken us beyond models in which 'one size fits all' to one in which professionals are required to offer flexible and personalised services. The 'information age' has allegedly eroded the exclusivity of the knowledge based upon which professionals gain their status – we're all experts now. In the UK, and other nations too, the introduction of quasi-markets into the public sector has allegedly transformed the relationship between professional and client to one of professional and consumer. The rise of new public management and, more recently, the audit culture have brought about new management practices which would have been unrecognisable in the early decades of the post-war welfare state.

Contemporary accounts of the pressures on professionalism may be informed by various theories, but their representations of professionals as beset by forces outside their control are similar. For example, Shore and Wright (2000: 63) use a Foucauldian analysis to show how higher education professionals have been redefined through the audit culture'. Similarly Ball (2001: 211) critiques what he sees as a new mode of social regulation in education 'that bites deeply and immediately into the practice of state professionals – reforming and 're-forming' meaning and identity.'

Resisting oppressive practices

Unlike the therapeutic approach, there is no straightforward remedy to relieve the oppressed professional. Because the sources of oppression are located in the wider orbit – not just the national but the international orbit – individual professionals can do little or nothing to alleviate their conditions. There may, from a Marxist perspective, be the possibility of change through concerted collective struggle (it is unclear what remedy post-structuralist perspectives offer), but this is difficult for the professional. Indeed, here their supposedly elevated status undermines their capacity for collective and radical resistance.

The tension between upholding professional ethics and resisting through collective action is illustrated by those professional associations which refuse to strike. In this sense, appeals to professional altruism become a means of social control rather than social advancement.

The imaginative professional: A sociological perspective

The approaches outlined above are partial and flawed. What is needed is a perspective which encompasses both the immediate orbit *and* the transcending forces. There can be few more compelling accounts of how such an approach can be developed than the 'sociological imagination' proposed by C. Wright Mills (see also Reading 5.1).

Mills (1959: 11) uses the term 'sociological imagination' to refer to the capacity to 'understand the larger historical scene in terms of its meaning for the inner life and external career of a variety of individuals'. In order to do this, he argues, it is essential that we distinguish between 'the personal troubles of milieu' and 'the public issues of social structure'.

Troubles, he outlines, 'occur within the character of the individual and within the range of his immediate relations with others … a trouble is a private matter' (ibid: 14–15). Issues, on the other hand, 'have to do with matters that transcend these local environments of the individual and the range of his inner life. They have to do with the organization of many such milieux into the institutions of a historical society as a whole … an issue is a public matter' (ibid: 15).

In order to illustrate the importance of this distinction, Wright Mills provides a number of examples, including unemployment and divorce. In relation to unemployment, when only one person in a city of 100,000 men is unemployed, it is quite likely that their inability to find work can be explained through their own personal attributes. However, when a significant minority of people are unemployed, it is no longer adequate to account for their lack of work solely in terms of individual failings. Their unemployment is more appropriately explained through reference to the public realm of the labour market and economic structures. The same holds true for marriage. Even though marital breakdown is experienced as an intensely private crisis, the frequency with which it occurs suggests that it is also a public issue. It is, therefore, just as important to look at what is happening in the broader social structure and at the institutions of family and marriage for an explanation of high divorce rates as it is to focus only on the incompatibility of particular couples.

Thus, as people's lives unfold they experience a whole range of difficulties. These difficulties are 'personal' in that they are very real and intensely experienced by the individual in terms of private loss and failure. But they might also need to be understood as more than personal troubles, as public issues that have arisen because of wider changes in society. As Wright Mills argues, 'The individual can understand his own experiences and gauge his own fate *only* by locating himself within his period' (ibid: 12, my emphasis)

It should hopefully be clear by now that Wright Mills' analytical framework for developing a sociological imagination can usefully be applied to understanding the difficulties which professionals encounter in their daily lives and in their careers. If we go back to our distressed professional, it is clear that if they are the only one in their organisation who is experiencing difficulties, then it would indeed be appropriate to offer them personal support. However, if though a significant number of professionals feel that they are stressed or cannot cope, this may point up a public issue.

Thinking about such issues enables us to grasp some of the linkage between our own personal troubles and society's public issues. In short, it will help us to become an imaginative professional who is able to draw on creative and articulate responses to change, rather than experiencing feelings of hopelessness or defensive reaction.

Reading 17.6

Teaching and learning about human rights in schools

Council of Europe

This beginning of this reading reflects its legal origins as a Statute of the Council of Europe, but it goes on to list six areas of for practical action in schools which are intended to develop children and young people's awareness of human rights. This reading clearly represents the long-standing concern that education should promote social justice and, given the complexity and diversity of the contemporary societies, it is not surprising that this should be an important issue for the European Union.

How can teaching and learning about human rights and social justice be sustained in your school?

Edited from: Committee of Ministers of the Council of Europe, (1985) *Recommendation No. R (85) 7, Memorandum on Teaching and Learning about Human Rights in Schools.* Strasbourg: Council of Europe, Appendix.

The recommendation

The Committee of Ministers, under the terms of Article 15.b of the Statute of the Council of Europe:

considering that the aim of the Council of Europe is to achieve a greater unity between its members for the purpose of safeguarding and realising the ideals and principles which are their common heritage;

reaffirming the human rights undertakings embodied in the United Nations Universal Declaration of Human Rights, the Convention for the Protection of Human Rights and Fundamental Freedoms and the European Social Charter; and

having regard to the commitments to human rights education made by member states at international and European conferences in the last decade;

recommends that the governments of member states, having regard to their national education systems and to the legislative basis for them:

encourage teaching and learning about human rights in schools in line with the suggestions contained in the appendix hereto;

draw the attention of persons and bodies concerned with school education to the text of this recommendation.

Human rights in the school curriculum

The understanding and experience of human rights is an important element of the preparation of all young people for life in a democratic and pluralistic society. It is part of social and political education, and it involves intercultural and international understanding.

Concepts associated with human rights can, and should, be acquired from an early stage. For example, the non-violent resolution of a conflict and respect for other people can already be experienced within the life of a pre-school or primary class.

Opportunities to introduce young people to more abstract notions of human rights, such as those involving an understanding of philosophical, political and legal concepts, will occur in the secondary school, in particular in such subjects as history, geography, social studies, moral and religious education, language and literature, current affairs and economics.

Human rights inevitably involve the domain of politics. Teaching about human rights should, therefore, always have international agreements and covenants as a point of reference, and teachers should take care to avoid imposing their personal convictions on their pupils and involving them in ideological struggles.

Skills

The skills associated with understanding and supporting human rights include:

intellectual skills, in particular:

- skills associated with written and oral expression, including the ability to listen and discuss, and to defend one's opinions';
- skills involving judgment, such as: the collection and examination of material from various sources, including the mass media, and the ability to analyze it and to arrive at fair and balanced conclusions: the identification of bias, prejudice, stereotypes and discrimination.

social skills, in particular:

- recognising and accepting differences; establishing positive and non-oppressive personal relationships: resolving conflict in a non-violent way; taking responsibility; participating in decisions; understanding the use of the mechanisms for the protection of human rights at local regional, European and world levels.

Knowledge to be acquired in the study of human rights
The study of human rights in schools will be approached in different ways according to age and circumstances of the pupil and the particular situations of schools and according to age and circumstances of the pupil and the particular situations of schools and education systems. Topics to be covered in learning about human rights could include:

- the main categories of human rights, duties, obligations and responsibilities;
- the various forms of injustice, inequality and discrimination, including sexism and racism;

- people, movements and key events, both successes and failures, in the historical and continuing struggle for human rights;
- the main international declarations and conventions on human rights such as the Universal Declaration of Human Rights and the Convention for the Protection of Human Rights

Rights and Fundamental Freedoms

The emphasis in teaching and learning about human rights should be positive. Pupils may be led to feelings of powerlessness and discouragement when confronted with many examples of violation and negations of human rights. Instances of progress and success should be used.

The study of human rights in schools should lead to an understanding of, and sympathy for, the concepts of justice, equality, freedom, peace, dignity, rights and democracy. Such understanding should be both cognitive and based on experience and feelings. Schools should, thus, provide opportunities for pupils to experience affective involvement in human rights and to express their feelings through drama, art, music, creative writing and audio-visual media.

The climate of the school

Democracy is best learned in a democratic setting where participation is encouraged, where views can be expressed openly and discussed, where there is freedom of expression for pupils and teachers, and where there is fairness and justice. An appropriate climate is, therefore, an essential complement to effective learning about human rights.

Schools should encourage participation in their activities by parents and other members of the community. It may well be appropriate for schools to work with non governmental organisations which can provide information, case-studies and first-hand experience of successful campaigns for human rights and dignity.

Schools and teachers should attempt to be positive towards all their pupils, and recognise that all their achievements are important – whether they be academic, artistic, musical, sporting or practical.

The training of teachers

The initial training of teachers should prepare them for their future contribution to teaching about human rights in their schools. For example, future teachers should:

- be encouraged to take an interest in national and world affairs;
- have the chance of studying or working in a foreign country or a different environment;
- be taught to identify and combat all forms of discrimination in schools and society and be encouraged to confront and overcome their own prejudices.

Future and practising teachers should be encouraged to familiarise themselves with:

- the main international declarations and conventions on human rights;
- the working and achievements of the international organisations which deal with the protection and promotion of human rights, for example through visits and study tours.

All teachers need, and should be given the opportunity, to update their knowledge and to learn new methods through in-service training. This could include the study of good practice in teaching about human rights, as well as the development of appropriate methods and materials.

International Human Rights Day
Schools and teacher training establishments should be encouraged to observe International Human Rights Day (10 December).

Reading 17.7

Three contexts of policymaking
Richard Bowe and Stephen Ball, with Ann Gold

> The authors of this reading provide a framework for thinking about the policymaking process. They describe policy as a 'discourse' and as 'a set of claims about how the world should be and might be' and see it as contested by different social groups. Three contexts in which this takes place are identified, including the context of practice in which practitioners mediate, interpret and recreate the meaning of policy texts.
>
> How does the analysis relate to the latest policies to affect schools in your country?
>
> *Edited from:* Bowe, R. and Ball, S. with Gold. A. (1992) *Reforming Education and Changing Schools.* London: Routledge, 13–23.

We approach policy as a discourse, constituted of possibilities and impossibilities, tied to knowledge on the one hand (the analysis of problems and identification of remedies and goals) and practice on the other (specification of methods for achieving goals and implementation). We see it as a set of claims about how the world should and might be, a matter of the 'authoritative allocation of values'. Policies are thus the operational statements of values, statements of 'prescriptive intent'. They are also, as we conceive it, essentially contested in and between the arenas of formation and 'implementation'.

We envisage three primary policy contexts, each context consisting of a number of arenas of action, some public, some private. These are: the context of influence, the context of text production, and the context of practice (see Figure 17.6.1).

The first context, the *context of influence*, is where public policy is normally initiated. It is here that policy discourses are constructed. It is here that interested parties struggle to influence the definition and social purposes of education, what it means to be educated. The private arenas of influence are based upon social networks in and around the political parties, in and around Government and in and around the legislative process. Here key policy concepts are established (e.g. market forces, National Curriculum, opting out, budgetary devolution), they acquire currency and credence and provide a discourse and

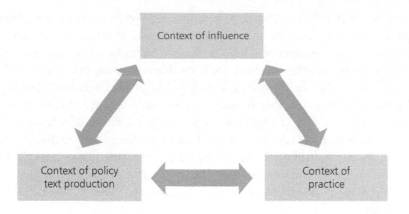

Figure 17.6.1
Three contexts of
policymaking

lexicon for policy initiation. This kind of discourse forming is sometimes given support, sometimes challenged by wider claims to influence in the public arenas of action, particularly in and through the mass media. In addition there are a set of more formal public arenas; committees, national bodies, representative groups which can be sites for the articulation of influence. Clearly in trying to understand the education policy-making of the last three Conservative Governments it is important to be aware of the considerable 'capture' of influence by the New Right think tanks that operated in and around the Conservative Party. But it is also vital to appreciate the ebb and flow in the fortunes of and the changes in personnel of the DES, and to recognize the increasing 'ministerialization' of policy initiation. As we noted earlier, this contrasts starkly with the virtual exclusion of union and local authority representatives from arenas of influence and the much diminished and discredited contribution from the educational establishment.

This context of influence has a symbiotic but none the less uneasy relation to the second context, the *context of policy text production*. Because while influence is often related to the articulation of narrow interests and dogmatic ideologies, policy texts are normally articulated in the language of general public good. Their appeal is based upon claims to popular (and populist) commonsense and political reason. Policy texts therefore *represent* policy. These representations can take various forms: most obviously 'official' legal texts and policy documents; also formally and informally produced commentaries which offer to 'make sense of' the 'official' texts, again the media is important here; also the speeches by and public performances of relevant politicians and officials; and 'official' videos are another recently popular medium of representation. Many of those towards whom policy is aimed rely on these secondhand accounts as their main source of information and understanding of policy as intended. But two key points have to be made about these ensembles of texts which represent policy. First, the ensembles and the individual texts are not necessarily internally coherent or clear. The expression of policy is fraught with the possibility of misunderstanding, texts are generalized, written in relation to idealizations of the 'real world', and can never be exhaustive, they cannot cover all eventualities. The texts can often be contradictory, they use key terms differently, and they are reactive as well as expository (that is to say, the representation of policy changes in the light of events and circumstances and feedback from arenas of practice). Policy is not done and finished at the legislative moment, it evolves in and through the texts that represent it, texts have to be read in relation to the time and the particular site of their production. They also have to be read with and against one another – intertextuality is important. Second, the texts themselves are the outcome of struggle and compromise. The control of the representation of policy is problematic. Control over the timing of the publication of texts is important. A potent and immediate example of struggle in arenas of text production is that which goes on in relation to National Curriculum working party reports. Groups of actors working within different sites of text production are in competition for control of the representation of policy. Most of these struggles go on behind closed doors but occasional glimpses of the dynamics of conflict are possible. What is at stake are attempts to control the meaning of policy through its representation.

Policies then are textual interventions but they also carry with them material constraints and possibilities. The responses to these texts have 'real' consequences. These consequences are experienced within the third main context, the *context of practice*, the arena of practice to which policy refers, to which it is addressed.

The key point is that policy is not simply received and implemented within this arena rather it is subject to interpretation and then 'recreated'.

Practitioners do not confront policy texts as naive readers, they come with histories, with experience, with values and purposes of their own, they have vested interests in the meaning of policy. Policies will be interpreted differently as the histories, experiences, values, purposes and interests which make up any arena differ. The simple point is that policy writers cannot control the meanings of their texts. Parts of texts will be rejected, selected out, ignored, deliberately misunderstood, responses may be frivolous, etc. Furthermore, yet again, interpretation is a matter of struggle. Different interpretations will be in contest, as they relate to different interests, one or other interpretation will predominate although deviant or minority readings may be important.

The policy process is one of complexity, it is one of policy-making and remaking. It is often difficult, if not impossible to control or predict the effects of policy, or indeed to be clear about what those effects are, what they mean, when they happen. Clearly, however interpretations are not infinite, clearly also, as noted already, different material consequences derive from different interpretations in action. Practitioners will be influenced by the discursive context within which policies emerge. Some will have an eye to personal or localized advantage, material or otherwise, which may stem from particular readings of policy texts. But to reiterate, the meanings of texts are rarely unequivocal. Novel or creative readings can sometimes bring their own rewards.

List of figures

Bibliography

ACCAC (2003) *Aiming for Excellence in Key Stage 3: Raising Standards in Literacy and Numeracy.* Cardiff: Welsh Assembly Government.

—(2004) *Review of the School Curriculum and Assessment Arrangements 5–16.* Cardiff: Welsh Assembly Government.

Adams, P. (2008) 'Considering 'best practice': The social construction of teacher activity and pupil learning as performance', *Cambridge Journal of Education*, 38 (3), 375–92.

Alexander, R. J. (1998) 'Basic cores and choices: towards a new primary curriculum', *Education 3–13*, 26 (2), 60–9.

—(2001) *Culture and Pedagogy.* London: Blackwell.

—(2008) *Essays on Pedagogy.* London: Routledge.

Alexander, R. J., Rose, J. and Woodhead, C. (1992) *Curriculum Organization and Classroom Practice in Primary Schools: A Discussion Paper.* London: HMSO

Althusser, L. (1971) *Lenin and Philosophy and Other Essays.* New York: Monthly Review Press.

Apple, M. (1989) *Teachers and Texts.* New York: Routledge and Kegan Paul.

—(1988) 'Work, class and teaching'. In J. Ozga (ed.) *Schoolwork: Approaches to the Labour Process of Teaching.* Milton Keynes: Open University Press.

Archer, M. (1979) *The Social Origins of Educational Systems.* London: SAGE Publications.

Arnold, M. (1874) *High Schools and Universities in Germany.* London: Macmillan.

Aronowitz, S. and Giroux, H. (1986) *Education Under Siege.* London: Routledge and Kegan Paul.

Assessment Reform Group (1999) *Assessment for Learning: Beyond the Black Box.* Cambridge: University of Cambridge, Faculty of Education.

—(2002) *Testing, Motivation and Learning.* Cambridge: University of Cambridge, Faculty of Education.

Bailey, B. (1990) 'Technical education and secondary schooling'. In Summerfield, P. and Evans, E. J. (eds) *Technical Education and the State since 1850.* Manchester: Manchester University Press.

Bain, A. (1879) *Education as a Science.* London: Kegan Paul, Trench and Trubner.

Baker, D. P. and LeTendre, G. K. (2005) *National Differences, Global Similarities: World Culture and the Future of Schooling.* Palo Alto, CA: Stanford University Press.

Bakhtin, M. (1986) *Speech Genres and Other Essays.* Austin, TX: University of Texas Press.

Ball, S. (1981a) *Beachside Comprehensive.* Cambridge: Cambridge University Press.

—(1981b) Initial encounters in the classroom and the process of establishment. In Woods, P. F. (ed.) *Pupil Strategies.* London: Croom Helm.

—(2001) 'Performativities and fabrications in the education economy'. In Gleeson, D. and Husbands, C. (eds) *The Performing School: Managing, Teaching and Learning in a Performance Culture.* London: RoutledgeFalmer.

—(2003) *The More Things Change: Educational Research, Social Class and 'Interlocking' Inequalities.* Professorial Inaugural Lecture, Institute of Education, University of London.

Ball, S., Vincent, C. and Kemp, S. (2003) *Class Identity, Class Fractions and Child Care Markets: middle class mechanisms of social advantage.* ESRC Child Care Project, Working Paper 5. London: Institute of Education.

Bandura, A. 1994. *Self-efficacy: The Exercise of Control.* New York: W. H. Freeman.

Barnes, C., Mercer, G. and Shakespeare, T. (1999) *Exploring Disability: A Sociological Introduction.* Cambridge: Cambridge University Press.

Barnes, D. and Todd, F. (1995) *Communication and Learning in Small Groups.* London: Routledge.

Barron, B. and Darling-Hammond, L. (2010) 'Prospects and challenges for inquiry-based approaches to learning'. In Dumont, H., Istance, D. and Benavides, F. (eds) *The Nature of Learning: Using Research to Inspire Practice.* Paris: OECD.

Barrs, M. and Cork, V. (2001) *The Reader in the Writer: The Links between the Study of Literature and Writing Development at Key Stage 2.* London: The Centre for Literacy in Primary Education.

Bayliss, V. (1998) *Redefining School.* London: Royal Society of Arts.

Bennett, T. (2012) *Teacher: Mastering the Art and Craft of Teaching.* London: Continuum.

Bereiter, C., and Scardamalia, M. (1987) *The Psychology of Written Composition.* Hillsdale, NJ: Lawrence Erlbaum Associates.

Berliner, D. (1990) 'What's all the fuss about instructional time?'. In Ben-Peretz, M. and Bromme, R. (eds) *The Nature of Time in Schools.* New York: Teacher College Press.

—(2001)' Learning about and learning from expert teachers', *International Journal of Educational Research*, 35, 463–82.

—(2004) 'Describing the behaviour and documenting the accomplishments of expert teachers', *Bulletin of Science, Technology and Society*, 24 (3), 200–12.

Bernstein, B. (1971) *Class, Codes and Control*, Vol. 1. London: Routledge and Kegan Paul.

—(2000) *Pedagogy, Symbolic Control and Identity: Theory, Research, Critique.* Oxford: Rowman and Littlefield.

Bibby, T. (2010) *Education: An 'Impossible Profession'? Psychoanalytic Explorations of Learning and Classrooms.* London: Routledge.

Black, P., Gardner, J. and Wiliam, D. (2008) Joint memorandum on reliability of assessments. Submitted to the House of Commons, Children, Schools and Families Committee: Testing and Assessment. Third Report of Session 2007–2008. Vol. II. HC169–II. Norwich: The Stationery Office.

Black, P. and Wiliam, D. (1998) *Inside the Black Box – Raising Standards Through Classroom Assessment.* London: Kings' College School of Education.

—(1998) 'Assessment and Classroom Learning', *Assessment in Education*, 5 (1), 7–74.

Black, P., Harrison, C., Lee, C., Marshall, B. and Wiliam, D. (2003) *Assessment for Learning: Putting it into Practice.* Maidenhead: Open University Press.

Blackledge, A. (1994) 'Language, culture and story in the bilingual primary school'. In Blackledge, A. (ed.) *Teaching Bilingual Children.* Trentham Books: Stoke-on-Trent.

Bloom, B. S. (1976) *Human Characteristics and School Learning.* New York: McGraw-Hill.

Bluebond-Langner, M. (1978) *The Private Worlds of Dying Children.* Princeton, NJ: Princeton University Press.

Blundell, R., Dearden, L., Goodman, A. and Reed, H. (2000) 'The returns to higher education in Britain: evidence from a British cohort', *Economic Journal*, 110, 82–99.

Bourdieu, P. (1986) 'Forms of Capital'. In J. Richardson (ed.) *Handbook of Theory and Research for the Sociology of Education.* New York: Greenwood Press.

Bovens, M. (2005) 'Public accountability'. In Ferlie, E. (ed.), *The Oxford Handbook of Public Management.* Oxford: Oxford University Press.

Bowles, S. and Gintis, H. (1976) *Schooling in Capitalist America.* New York: Basic Books.

Bowles, S., Gintis, H. and Osborne, M. (2001) 'The determinants of individual earnings: a behavioural approach', *Journal of Economic Literature*, XXXIX, December, 1136–76.

Bransford, J. D., Brown, A. L. and Cocking, R. R. (eds) (1999) *How People Learn: Brain, Mind, Experience and School.* Washington, DC: National Academy Press.

Britton, J. (1982) *Prospect and Retrospect: Selected Essays of James Britton*, ed. Pradl, G. London: Heinemann.

Broadfoot, P. (1996) *Education, Assessment and Society*. Buckingham: Open University Press.

—(2007) *Assessment Policy and Practice: The 21ˢᵗ Century Challenge for Educational Assessment*. London: Continuum.

Broekaerts, M. (2010) 'The crucial role of motivation and emotion in classroom learning'. In Dumont, H., Istance, D. and Benavides, F. (eds) *The Nature of Learning: Using Research to Inspire Practice*. Paris: OECD.

Bronfenbrenner, U. (1993) 'Ecological models of human development', *International Encyclopedia of Education*. Vol. 3. Oxford: Elsevier.

Brophy, J. E. and Good, T. L. (1986) 'Teacher behaviour and student achievement'. In Wittrock, M. C (ed.) *Handbook of Research on Teaching*. New York: Macmillan.

Bruner, J. (1960) *The Process of Education*. Cambridge, MA: Harvard University Press.

—(1966) *Towards a Theory of Instruction*. Cambridge, MA: Harvard University Press.

—(1972) *The Relevance of Education*. London: George Allen and Unwin.

—(1983) *Child Talk*. London: Oxford University Press.

—(1996) *The Culture of Education*, Cambridge, MA: Harvard University Press.

—(2000) 'Reading for possible worlds'. In Shanahan, T. and Rodriguez-Brown, F. B. (eds) *4th Yearbook of the National Reading Conference*. Chicago: National Reading Conference.

—(2006) *In Search of Pedagogy Volume II: The Selected Works of Jerome S. Bruner*. New York: Routledge.

Burbules, N. and Hansen, D. (1997) *Teaching and its Predicaments*. Oxford: Westview Press.

Burns, B. and Haydn T. (2002) 'Engaging teachers in research: inspiration versus the daily grind', *Pedagogy, Culture and Society*, 10 (2), 301–21.

Butler, T. and Robson, G. (2001) 'Social capital, gentrification and neighbourhood change in London: a comparison of three south London neighbourhoods', *Urban Studies*, 38 (12), 2145–62.

Butt, G. (2010) *Making Assessment Matter*. London: Continuum.

Calderhead, J. (1994) 'Can the complexities of teaching be accounted for in terms of competences? Contrasting views of professional practice from research and policy'. Mimeo produced for an ESRC symposium on teacher competence.

Campbell, A. and Groundwater-Smith, S. (eds) (2009) *Connecting Inquiry and Professional Learning in Education: International Perspectives and Practical Solutions*. Abingdon: Routledge.

Campbell, A., McNamara, O. and Gilroy, P. (2004) *Practitioner Research and Professional Development in Education*. London: SAGE.

Card, D. 1999. 'The causal effects of education on earnings'. In Ashenfelter, O. and Card, D. (eds) *Handbook of Labour Economics*. Vol. 3. Amsterdam: North-Holland.

Carr, M. (2001) *Assessment in Early Childhood Settings*. London: Paul Chapman.

Carr, M. and Claxton, G. (2004) 'Tracking the development of learning dispositions'. In Daniels, H. and Edwards, A. (eds) *The RoutledgeFalmer Reader in Psychology of Education*. London: RoutledgeFalmer.

Carroll, J. B. (1963) 'A model of school learning', *Teacher College Record, 64,* 723–33.

Castells, M. (2004) *The Power of Identity*. Malden, MA: Blackwell Publishing.

Central Advisory Council for Education (England) (1967) *Children and their Primary Schools*. The Plowden Report. HMSO: London.

Chaplain, R., (2003) *Teaching Without Disruption in the Primary School*. New York: Routledge.

Chevalier, A. and Walker I. (2002) 'Further estimates of the returns to education in the UK'. In Walker, I. and Westergard-Nielsen, W. (eds) *The Returns to Education Across Europe*. Cheltenham: Edward Elgar.

Clarke, M. and Drudy, S. (2006) 'Teaching for diversity, social justice and global awareness', *European Journal of Teacher Education*, 29 (3), 371–86.

Clarke, S. (1998) *Targeting Assessment in the Primary Schools*. London: Hodder and Stoughton

Claxton, G. (1999) *Wise Up: The Challenge of Lifelong Learning*, Stoke-on-Trent: Network Press.

Clegg, D. and Billington, S. (1994) *The Effective Primary Classroom: Management and Organisation of Teaching and Learning*. London: David Fulton.

Cochran-Smith, M. (2004) *Walking the Road – Race, Diversity and Social Justice in Teacher Education*. New York: Teachers' College Press.

Cole, M. (1996), *Cultural Psychology: A Once and Future Discipline*. Cambridge, MA: Harvard University Press.

Collarbone, P (2009) *Creating Tomorrow Planning, Developing and Sustaining Change in Education and Other Public Services*. London: Continuum.

Coolahan, J. (2002) 'Teacher education and the teacher career in an era of lifelong learning', *OECD Education Working Papers*, No.2. Paris: OECD.

Cooley, C. H. (1902) *Human Nature and the Social Order*. New York: Charles Scribner's Sons.

Cornelius-White, J. (2007) 'Learner-centred teacher-student relationships are effective: a meta-analysis', *Review of Educational Research*, 77 (1), 113–43.

Côté, J. E. (2005) 'Emerging adulthood as an institutionalized moratorium: risks and benefits to identity formation'. In Arnett, J. J. and Tanner, J. (eds) *Emerging adults in America: Coming of Age in the 21st Century*. Washington DC: American Psychological Association.

Cowley, S. (2010) *Getting the Buggers to Behave*. London: Continuum.

Crozier, G. and Reay, D. (eds), (2005), *Activating Participation: Parents and Teachers Working Towards Partnership*. Stoke-on-Trent: Trentham.

Cummins, J. and Swain, M. (1986) *Bilingualism in Education*. Harlow: Longman.

Damasio, A. R. (1999) *The Feeling of What Happens*. New York: Harcourt Brace.

Daniels, N., Kennedy, B. and Kawachi, I. (2000) 'Justice is good for our health', *Boston Review*, February/March.

Davie, R., Bulter, N. and Goldsein, H. (eds) (1972) *From Birth to Seven*. Harlow: Longman.

Day, C., Sammons, P., Hopkins, D., Harris, A., Leithwood, K., Gu, Q., Brown, E., Ahtardou, E. and Kington, A. (2009) *The Impact of School Leadership on Pupil Outcomes*. DCSF Research Report 108. London: DCSF.

Day, C., Sammons, P., Stobart, G., Kington, A. and Gu, Q. (2007) *Teachers Matter: Connecting Work, Lives and Effectiveness*. Maidenhead: Open University Press.

De Corte, E. (2010) 'Historical developments in the understanding of learning'. In Dumont, H., Istance, D. and Benavides, F. (eds) *The Nature of Learning: Using Research to Inspire Practice*. Paris: OECD.

Dean, J. (1995) *Teaching History at Key Stage 2*. Cambridge: Chris Kington Publishing.

Dearden, L., McIntosh, S.,Vignoles, A. and Myck, M. (2002) 'The returns to academic and vocational qualifications in the UK', *Bulletin of Economic Research*, 54 (3), 249–74.

Denbo, S. (1988) *Improving Minority Student Achievement: Focus on the Classroom*. Washington, DC: Mid-Atlantic Equity Center Series.

Department for Children, Schools and Families (2008) *The Assessment for Learning Strategy*. Nottingham: DCSF Publications.

—(2009) *Breaking the Link between Disadvantage and Low Attainment*. Nottingham: DCSF.

Department for Education and Employment (1999) *All Our Futures: Creativity, Culture and Education*. National Advisory Committee on Creative and Cultural Education. Sudbury: DfEE.

Department for Education and Science (1978) *Primary Education in England: A Survey by HM Inspector of Schools*. London: HMSO.

—(1978) *Primary Education in England*. London: HMSO.

—(1985) *The Curriculum from 5 – 16*, Curriculum Matters 2, An HMI Series. London: HMSO.

—(1988) *National Curriculum: Task Group on Assessment and Testing: a report*. London: DES.

—(1997) *Excellence in Schools*. London: HMSO.

Department for Education and Skills (2004) *Curricular Target Setting*. London: DfES.

Department of Health (2001) *Seeking Consent: Working With Children*. London: DoH.

Devine, F. (1998) 'Class analysis and the stability of class relations', *Sociology*, 32 (1) 23–42.

Dewey, J. (1916) *Democracy and Education*. New York: Macmillan.

—(1933) *How We Think: A Restatement of the Relation of Reflective Thinking to the Educative Process*. Chicago: Henry Regnery.

Doll, B., Zucker, S. and Brehm, K. (2004) *Resilient Classrooms: Creating Healthy Environments for Learning*. New York: Guilford Press.

Douglas, J. (1964) *The Home and School*. London: Macgibbon and Kee.

Doyle, W. (1977) 'Learning the classroom environment: an ecological analysis', *Journal of Teacher Education*, XXVIII (6), 51–4.

Drummond, M. J. (2008) 'Assessment and values: a close and necessary relationship'. In Swaffield, S. (ed.) *Unlocking Assessment: Understanding for Reflection and Application*. Abingdon: Routledge.

Dumont, H., Istance, D. and Benavides, F. (2010) 'Executive summary'. In *The Nature of Learning: Using Research to Inspire Practice*. Paris: OECD.

Dunifon, R. and Duncan, G. 1997. Long-run effects of motivation on labor-market success, *Social Psychology Quarterly*, 61 (1), 33–48.

Dunne, M., Humphreys, S., Sebba, J., Dyson, A., Gallannaugh, F. and Muijs, D. (2007) *Effective Teaching and Learning for Pupils in Low Attaining Groups*. Research Report 011. London: DfES.

Dunne, P. (1993) *Back to the Rough Ground*. Notre Dame, IN: University of Notre Dame Press

Dweck, C. S., (1986) 'Motivational processes affecting learning'. In *American Psychologist*, October, 1040–6.

—(2006) *Mindset. The New Psychology of Success*. New York: Ballantine.

Eaude, T. (2012) *How Do Expert Primary Class-teachers Really Work?* Knutsford: Critical Publishing.

Eccles, J. S., Wigfield, A. and Schiefele, U. (1997) 'Motivation to succeed'. In Eisenberg, N. (ed.) *Handbook of Child Psychology*. New York: Wiley.

Edmunds, R. (1979) 'Effective schools for the urban poor'. *Educational Leadership*, 37 (3) 15–27

Edwards, A. (2012) *New Technology and Education*. London: Continuum.

Elder, G. H. (1974) *Children of the Great Depression*. Boulder, Colorado: Westview Press.

Ellis E. S., Worthington L. A. and Larking M. J. (1994) 'Research synthesis on effective teaching principles and the design of quality tools for educators'. Technical report No. 5 for the National Centre to Improve the Tools of Educators, University of Oregon.

Emery, H. (2011) 'A Strategy for Pedagogical Development: Teachers Reflecting On and Improving their Classroom Practice and Pupils. Knowledge and Understanding'. Unpublished report. London: DCSF.

Epstein, A. (1978) *Ethos and Identity*. London: Tavistock.

Estyn (2002) *Excellent Schools: A Vision for Schools in Wales in 21st Century*. Cardiff: Estyn.

Facer, K. (2009) *Towards an Area-Based Curriculum: Insights and Directions from the Research*. London: RSA.

Feinstein, L. (2003) 'Inequality in the Early Cognitive Development of British Children in the 1970 Cohort', *Economica*, 70, 73–97.

Feinstein L., Duckworth K., Sabtes R., (eds) (2008) *Education and the Family: Passing Success Across the Generations*. Oxford: Routledge.

Feinstein, L., Vorhaus, J., and Sabates, R. (2008) *Foresight Mental Capital and Wellbeing Project. Learning Through Life: Future Challenges*. London: The Government Office for Science.

Filer, A. and Pollard, A. (2000) *The Social World of Pupil Assessment*. London: Continuum.

Fisher, E. (1993) 'Distinctive features of pupil-pupil talk and their relationship to learning'. *Language and Education*, 7 (4) 239–58.

Fisher, R. (2013) *Teaching Thinking: Philosophical Enquiry in the Classroom*. London: Bloomsbury.

Flinders, K. and Flinders, E. (2000) 'Long term, summative assessment and evaluation'. In Hopkins, J., Telfer, S. and Butt, G. (eds) *Assessment in Practice*. Sheffield: Geographical Association.

Foucault, M. (1988) *The Final Foucault*. Cambridge, MA: MIT Press.

—(1991) *Remarks on Marx*. New York: Semiotext(e).

France, A. (2007) *Understanding Youth in Late Modernity*. Milton Keynes: Open University Press.

Fuller, A. and Unwin, L. (2004) 'Expansive learning environments: integrating organizational and personal development'. In Rainbird, H., Fuller, A. and Munro, A. (eds) *Workplace Learning in Context*. London: Routledge.

Furco, A. (2010) 'The community as a resource for learning'. In Dumont, H., Istance, D. and Benavides, F. (eds) (2010) *The Nature of Learning: Using Research to Inspire Practice*. Paris: OECD.

Furlong, J. and Salisbury, J. (2005) 'Best Practice Research Scholarships: an evaluation', *Research Papers in Education*, 20 (1), 45–83.

Furlong, J., Barton, L., Miles, S., Whiting, C. and Whitty, G. (2000) *Teacher Education in Transition*. Buckingham: Open University Press.

Future Skills Wales (2003) *Generic Skills Survey, Summary Report*. Cardiff: Welsh Assembly Government.

Galton, M., Simon, B. and Croll, P. (1980) *Inside the Primary Classroom*. Routledge and Kegan Paul: London.

Garmezy, N. (1985) 'Stress resistant children: the search for protective factors'. In Stevenson J. E. (ed.) *Recent Research in Developmental Psychology, Journal of Child Psychology and Psychiatry*.

Geertz, C. (1975) *The Interpretation of Cultures*. London: Hutchinson.

General Teaching Council for England (2011) *Teaching Quality: Policy Papers*. London: GTCE.

General Teaching Council for Northern Ireland (2007) *Teaching: The Reflective Profession*. Belfast: GTCNI.

Gipps, C. (1992) *What We Know About Effective Primary Teaching*. London: Tufnell Press.

Gipps, C. and MacGilchrist, B. (1999) 'Primary school learners'. In Mortimore, P. (ed.) *Understanding Pedagogy and its Impact on Learning*. London: Paul Chapman Publishing.

Glaser, R. (1999) 'Expert knowledge and processes of thinking'. In McCormick, R. and Paechter, C. (eds) *Learning and Knowledge*. London: Paul Chapman Publishing.

Glass, G. V. (1976) 'Primary, secondary and meta-analysis of research', *Education Researcher*, 5 (10), 3–8.

Goldsmith, A., Veum, J. and Darity, W. (1997) 'The impact of psychological and human capital on wages', *Economic Inquiry*, 35 (4), 815–29.

Goleman, D. (1996) *Emotional Intelligence – Why it Matters More than IQ*. London: Bloomsbury.

Grabbe, Y. (2008) *Influence of School Teaching and Quality on Children's Progress in Primary School* (DCSF Research Report 028) London: DCSF.

Greany T. and Rodd J. (2004) *Creating a Learning to Learn School*. Stoke-on-Trent: Network Education Press.

Green, A. (1990) *Education and State Formation*. London: Macmillan.

Green, A. and Janmaat, J. G. (2011) *Education, Opportunity and Social Cohesion*. Centre for Learning and Life Chances in Knowledge Economies and Societies. London: Institute of Education.

—(2011) *Regimes of Social Cohesion: Societies and the Crisis of Globalisation*. London: Palgrave.

Green, A., Preston, J. and Janmaat, J. G. (2006) *Education, Equality and Social Cohesion: A Comparative Analysis*. Basingstoke: Palgrave.

Green, A., Preston, J. and Sabates, R. (2003) 'Education, equality and social cohesion: a distributional approach', *Compare*, 33 (4), 453–70.

Gu, Q. (2007) *Teacher Development: Knowledge and Context.* London: Continuum.

Hacking, I. (2007) 'Making up people'. In Lock, M. and Farquhar, J. (eds) *Beyond the Body Proper: Reading the Anthropology of Material Life.* Durham, NC: Duke University Press.

Hallam, S. (2002) *Ability Grouping in Schools: A Review of the Literature.* London: Institute of Education.

Hammond, C. (2002) *Learning to be Healthy.* Centre for Research on the Wider Benefits of Learning. London: Institute of Education.

Hanson, A. (1994) *Testing, Testing: Social Consequences of the Examined Life.* Berkeley, CA: University of California Press.

Hardy, B. (1977) 'Narrative as a primary act of mind'. In Meek, M., Warlow, A. and Barton, G. *The Cool Web.* London: Bodley Head.

Hargreaves, A. (1998) 'The emotional practice of teaching', *Teaching and Teacher Education,* 14 (8), 835–54.

—(2003) *Teaching in the Knowledge Society.* Maidenhead: Open University Press.

—(2005) 'Educational change takes ages: life, career and generational factors in teachers' emotional responses to educational change', *Teaching and Teacher Education,* 21 (8), 967–83.

—(2007) *The Persistence of Presentism and the Struggle for Lasting Improvement,* Professorial Inaugural Lecture, Institute of Education, University of London.

Hargreaves, A. and Fullan, M. (2012) *Professional Capital: Transforming Teaching in Every School.* Boston: Teachers College Press.

Hargreaves, A. and Shirley, D. (2009) *The Fourth Way: The Inspiring Future of Educational Change.* Thousand Oaks, CA: Corwin.

Hargreaves, D. (1967) *Social Relations in a Secondary School,* London: Routledge.

—(1992) *Report of the Committee on the Curriculum and Organisation of ILEA Secondary Schools.* London: ILEA.

—(2004) *Learning for Life: The Foundations of Lifelong Learning.* Bristol: The Policy Press.

—(2005) *Personalising Learning 5: Mentoring and Coaching, and Workforce Development.* London: Specialist Schools and Academies Trust.

Harlen, W. (1991) 'National Curriculum assessment: increasing the benefit by reducing the burden'. In *Education and Change in the 1990s, Journal of the Educational Research Network of Northern Ireland,* 5, February, 3–19.

—(2008) 'Trusting teachers' judgement'. In Swaffield, S. (ed.) *Unlocking Assessment: Understanding for Reflection and Application.* Abingdon: Routledge.

Harlen W., and Deakin Crick R. (2002) 'A systematic review of the impact of summative assessment and tests on students' motivation for learning', *Research Evidence in Education Library.* London: Institute of Education.

Harlen, W., Gipps, C., Broadfoot, P. and Nuttall, D. (1992) 'Assessment and the improvement of education', *Curriculum Journal,* 3 (3), 217–25

Harrison, C. (2004) *Understanding Reading Development.* London: SAGE.

Hart, S., Dixon, A., Drummond, M. J. and McIntyre, D. (2004) *Learning Without Limits.* Maidenhead: Open University Press.

Hartley, D. (2002) 'Global influences on teacher education in Scotland', *Journal of Education for Teaching,* 28 (3), 251–5.

Hattie, J. (2009) *Visible learning: A Synthesis of Over 800 Meta-Analyses Relating to Achievement.* London: Routledge.

—(2012) *Visible Learning for Teachers: Maximizing Impact on Learning.* Abingdon: Routledge.

Haynes, A. (2010) *The Complete Guide to Lesson Planning and Preparation.* London: Continuum.

Health and Safety Executive (2007) *Work-Related Stress: Research and Statistics.* London: HSE.

Healy, T. and Côté, S. (2001) *The Wellbeing of Nations: The Role of Human and Social Capital.* Paris: OECD.

Heckman, J. and Rubinstein, Y. (2001) 'The importance of noncognitive skills: lessons from the GED testing program', *American Economic Review*, 91, 2.

Heilbronn, R. (2011) 'Practical judgement and evidence-informed practice'. In Heilbronn, R. and Yandell, J. (eds) *Critical Practice in Teacher Education: A Study of Professional Learning*. London: IOE Press.

Helsby, G. (1999) *Changing Teachers' Work: The Reform of Secondary Schooling*. Milton Keynes: Open University Press.

Her Majesty's Inspectors (1980) *A View of the Curriculum*. HMI Series, Matters for Discussion, No. 11. London: HMSO.

—(2003) *Boys' Achievement in Secondary Schools*. London: Ofsted.

Herbart, J. F. (1806) *Allgemeine Pädagogik* (Universal Pedagogy), Göttingen: Books on Demand.

Hinton, C. and Fischer, K. (2010) 'Learning from the developmental and biological perspective'. In Dumont, H., Istance, D. and Benavides, F. (eds) *The Nature of Learning: Using Research to Inspire Practice*. Paris: OECD.

Hobbs, G. (2007) *Investigating Social Class Inequalities in Educational Attainment*. Unpublished PhD thesis, University of London: Institute of Education.

Hodkinson, H. and Hodkinson, P. (2002) *Rescuing Communities of Practice from Accusations of Idealism: A Case Study of Workplace Learning for Secondary School Teachers in England*. London: TLRP.

Hodkinson, H. and Hodkinson, P. (2005) 'Improving schoolteachers, workplace learning', *Research Papers in Education,* 20 (2), 109–31.

Hogan, D., Chan, M., Rahim, R., Kwek, D., Aye, K. M., Loo, S. C., Sheng, Y. and Luo, W. (2013) 'Assessment and the logic of instructional practice in Secondary 3 English and Mathematics classes in Singapore', *Review of Education*, 1 (1), 57–106.

Hogan, D., Chan, M., Rahim, R., Towndrow, P., and Kwek, D. (2012) 'Understanding classroom talk in Secondary 3 Mathematics classes in Singapore'. In Kaur, B. *Reasoning, Communication and Connections in Mathematics: Yearbook 2012*, Association of Mathematics Educators. Singapore: World Scientific.

Hogan, D., Kwek, D., Towndrow, P., Rahim, R., Tan, T. K., Kaur, B., et al. (2012) 'Opaque or transparent? First reflections on visible learning in Singapore'. In Deng, Z. S., Gopinathan, S. and Lee, C. (eds), *Globalization and the Singapore Curriculum: From Policy to Classroom*. London: Springer.

Hogan, D., Towndrow, P., Kwek, D., Rahim, R., Chan, M., Aye, K., et al. (2011) *Core 2 Interim Report*. National Institute of Education, Nanyang Technological University, Singapore.

Hogan, D., Towndrow, P., Kwek, D., Yang, H. J., and Tan, T. K. (2013) *Lesson Planning, Task Design and Task Implementation in Secondary 3 Mathematics and English*, Unpublished research report. National Institute of Education, Nanyang Technological University, Singapore.

Hogan, P. (2003) 'Teaching as a way of life', *Journal of Philosophy of Education*, 37 (2), 207–24.

Hoyle, E. (1974) 'Professionality, professionalism and control in teaching', *London Education Review*, 3 (2), 13–9.

Huberman, M. (1993) *The Lives of Teachers*. New York: Teachers College Press.

Hulme, M., Menter, I., Kelly, D. and Rusby, S. (2010) 'Schools of ambition: bridging professional and institutional boundaries'. In Ravid, R. and Slater, J. J. (eds) *Collaboration in Education*. New York: Routledge.

Huxley, A. (1993) *Writers at Work*. The Paris Review Interviews. New York: Viking Press.

Immordino-Yang, M. H. and Damasio, A (2007) 'We feel, therefore we learn: the relevance of affective and social neuroscience to education', *Mind, Brain and Education*, 1 (1), 3–10.

Ireson, J. (1998) *Innovative Grouping Practices in Secondary Schools*. London: DfEE.

Ireson, J. and Hallam, S. (2001) *Ability Grouping in Education*. London: SAGE.

Iser, W. (1978) *The Act of Reading*. London: Routledge.

Jackson, P. (1968) *Life in Classrooms*. New York: Holt, Rinehart and Winston.

James, M. (2007) *Only Connect! Improving teaching and learning in schools*. Inaugural Professorial Lecture, Institute of Education, University of London.

James, M. and Pollard, A. (eds) (2006) *Improving Teaching and Learning in Schools*. A Commentary by the Teaching and Learning Research Programme. London: TLRP.

—(2012a) *Principles for Effective Pedagogy. International Responses to the UK TLRP*. London: Routledge.

—(2012b) 'TLRP's ten principles for effective pedagogy: rationale, development, evidence, argument and impact', *Research Papers in Education*, 26 (3), 275–328.

James, W. (1890) *Principles of Psychology*, Vol. 1. New York: Henry Holt.

Jones, P. (2009) *Rethinking Childhood: Attitudes in Contemporary Society*. London: Continuum.

Keep, E. and Mayhew, K. (1999) 'The assessment: knowledge, skills and competitiveness', *Oxford Review of Economic Policy*, 15 (1), 1–15.

Kelchtermans, G. (2005) 'Teachers' emotions in educational reforms: self-understanding, vulnerable commitment and micropolitical literacy', *Teaching and Teacher Education*, 21, 995–1006.

Keogh, B. K. and Speece, D. L. (1996) 'Learning disabilities within the context of schooling'. In Speece, D. L. and Keogh, B. K. (eds) (1996) *Research on Classroom Ecologies: Implications for Inclusion of Children with Learning Disabilities*. Mahwah, NJ: Lawrence Erlbaum Associates.

Kerry, T. and Eggleston, J. (1988) *Topic Work in the Primary School*. Routledge: London.

Kershner, R. (2009) 'Learning in inclusive classrooms'. In Hick, P., Kershner, R. and Farrell, P. (eds) *Psychology for Inclusive Education: New Directions in Theory and Practice*. London: Routledge.

Könings, K. D., Brand-Gruwal, S. and Van Merriënboer, J. J. G. (2005) 'Towards more powerful learning environments through combining the perspectives of designers, teachers, and students', *British Journal of Educational Psychology*, 75 (4) 645–60.

Kounin, J. (1970) *Discipline and Group Management in Classrooms*. New York: Holt, Rinehart and Winston.

Kress, G. (2010) *The profound shift of digital literacies*. In Gillen, J. and Barton, D. (eds) *Digital Literacies*. TLRP TEL. London: Institute of Education.

Kulik, J. A. and Kulik, C.-L. C. (1992) 'Meta-analytic findings on grouping programs', *Gifted Child Quarterly*, 36 (2), 73–7.

Kuykendall, C. (1989) *Improving Black Student Achievement*. Washington, DC: The Mid-Atlantic Equity Center Series.

Larson, M. (1980) 'Proletarianization and educated labor', *Theory and Society*, 9, 89–130.

Lave, J. (1996) 'Teaching, as Learning, in Practice', *Mind, Culture and Society*, 3 (3), 149–64.

Lave, J., and Wenger, E. (1991), *Situated Learning: Legitimate Peripheral Participation*. New York: Cambridge University Press.

Lawn, M. and Ozga, J. (1988) 'Work, Class and Teaching'. In J. Ozga (ed.) *Schoolwork: Approaches to the Labour Process of Teaching*. Milton Keynes: Open University Press.

Lawrence, D. (2006) *Enhancing Self-Esteem in the Classroom*. London: Paul Chapman.

Leadbeater, C. (2008) *What's Next? 21 Ideas for 21st Century Learning*. London: The Innovation Unit.

LeDoux, J. (1996) *Emotional Brain*. New York: Simon and Schuster.

Lemke, J. L. (2002) 'Becoming the village: education across lives'. In Wells, G. and Claxton, G. (eds) *Learning for Life in the 21st Century: Sociocultural Perspectives on the Future of Education*. Oxford: Blackwell.

Levine, J. (1990) *Bilingual Learners and the Mainstream Curriculum*. London: Falmer Press.

Loban, W (1976) *Language Development: Kindergarten Through Grade Twelve*. Urbana, IL: National Council of Teachers of English.

Lortie, D. C. (1975) *Schoolteacher: A Sociological Study*. Chicago: University of Chicago Press.

Luria, A. R. (1962) 'On the variability of mental functions in the process of child's development', *Voprosy Psikhologii*, 4, 15–22.

MacBeath J., Kirwan T. et al. (2001) *The Impact of Study Support: A Study into the Effects of Out-Of-School-Hours Learning on the Academic Attainment, Attitudes and Attendance of Secondary School Pupils*, Research Brief 273. London: DfES.

Mahony, P. and Hextall, I. (2000) *Reconstructing Teaching*. London: RoutledgeFalmer.

Male, B. and Waters, M. (2012) *The Primary Curriculum Design Handbook*. London: Continuum.

—(2012) *The Secondary Curriculum Design Handbook*. London: Continuum.

Manguel, A. (1996) *A History of Reading*. London: Harper Collins.

Martin, M. O. and Mullis, I. V. S. (eds) (2012) *Methods and Procedures in TIMSS and PIRLS 2011*. Chestnut Hill, MA: Boston College for the IEA.

Marton, F. and Booth, S. (1997) *Learning and Awareness,* Mahwah, NJ: Lawrence Erlbaum Associates.

Marx, K. (1995) *Capital.* Oxford: Oxford University Press.

Mayer, R. (2010) 'Learning with technology'. In Dumont, H., Istance, D. and Benavides, F. (eds) *The Nature of Learning: Using Research to Inspire Practice*. Paris: OECD.

McKinstery J., and Topping K. J. (2003) 'Cross-age peer tutoring of thinking skills in the high school'. *Educational Psychology in Practice*, 19 (3), 199–217.

McNamara, O. (ed.) (2002) *Becoming an Evidence-Based Practitioner: A Framework for Teacher Researchers*. London: Routledge.

McPherson, A. (1992) *Measuring Added Value in Schools,* National Commission on Education Briefing No. 1. London: National Commission on Education.

Menter, I., Hulme, M., Elliot, D and Lewin, J. (2010) *Teacher Education in the 21st Century*. Edinburgh: Scottish Government.

Mercer, N. (1995) *The Guided Construction of Knowledge: Talk Amongst Teachers and Learners*. Clevedon: Multilingual Matters.

—(2000) *Words and Minds: How We Use Language to Think Together*. London: Routledge.

Mercer, N. and Littleton, K. (2007) *Dialogue and the Development of Children's Thinking: A Socio-cultural Approach*. London: Routledge.

Merrett, F. and Wheldall, K. (1990) *Identifying Troublesome Classroom Behaviour*. London: Paul Chapman.

Merton, R. (1968) *The Self-Fulfilling Prophecy, Social Theory and Social Structure*. London: Collier MacMillan.

Mills, C. W. (1959) *The Sociological Imagination*. New York: Oxford University Press.

Mirazchiyski, P. (2013) *Providing School-Level Reports from International Large-Scale Assessments. Methodological Considerations, Limitations, and Possible Solutions*. Amsterdam: IEA.

Moll, L., Amanti, C., Neff, D. and Gonzalez, N. (1992) 'Funds of knowledge for teaching: using a qualitative approach to connect homes and classrooms'. *Qualitative Issues in Educational Research*, 31 (2), 132–41.

Moore, R. (2004) *Education and Society*. London: Polity Press.

Mortimore, P., Sammons, P., Stoll, L., Lewis, D. and Ecob, R. (1988) *School Matters: The Junior Years*. Open Books: London.

Mortimore, J. and Mortimore, P. (1984) *Secondary School Examinations: Helpful Servant or Dominating Masters?* Bedford Way Papers, No. 18, University of London, Institute of Education.

Mortimore, P. (1993) 'School effectiveness and the management of effective learning and teaching', *School Effectiveness and Improvement,* 4 (3), 290–310.

Mortimore, P and Mortimore, J. (1986) 'Education and social class'. In Rogers, R. (ed.) *Education and Social Class*. London: Falmer Press.

Mourshed, M., Chikioke, C. and Barber, M. (2010) *How the World's Most Improved School Systems Keep Getting Better*. New York: McKinsey and Company.

Muijs, D. and Reynolds, D. (1999) *School Effectiveness and Teacher Effectiveness: Some Preliminary Findings from the Evaluation of the Mathematics Enhancement Programme*. Presented at the American Educational Research Association Conference, Montreal, Quebec, 19 April.

—(2010) *Effective Teaching: Evidence and Practice*. London: SAGE.

Muller, J. (2000) *Reclaiming Knowledge: Social Theory, Curriculum and Education Policy*. London: RoutledgeFalmer.

Munro, R. (1997) 'Ideas of difference: stability, social spaces and the labour of division'. In K. Hetherington and R. Munro (eds) *Ideas of Difference: Social Spaces and the Labour of Division*. Oxford: Blackwell.

Muschamp. Y. (1991) 'Pupil self-assessment', *Practical Issues in Primary Education*, No. 9. Bristol: National Primary Centre (South West)

Newton, P. (2008) *Presentation to the Cambridge Assessment Forum for New Developments in Educational Assessment*. Downing College, Cambridge. 10 December.

Nias, J. (1989) *Primary Teachers Talking: A Study of Teaching at Work*. London: Routledge.

Noddings, N. (2003) *Happiness and Education*. Cambridge: Cambridge University Press.

Nonaka, I. and Takeuchi, H. (1995) *The Knowledge-creating company: How Japanese Companies Create the Dynamics of Innovation*. New York: Oxford University Press.

Nystrand, M. and Gamoran, A. (1991) 'Instructional discourse, student engagement and literature achievement', *Research on the Teaching of English*, 25 (3), 261–72.

Nystrand, M. with Gamoran, A., Kachur, R., Prendergast, C. (1997) *Opening Dialogue: Understanding the Dynamics of Language and Learning in the English Classroom*. New York: Teachers College Press.

OECD (2005) *Teachers Matter: Attracting, Developing and Retaining Effective Teachers*. Paris, OECD.

—(2009) *PISA 2009 Assessment Framework: Key Competencies in Reading, Mathematics and Science*. Paris: OECD.

—(2010a) *PISA 2009 results: What Students Know and Can Do. Student Performances in Reading, Mathematics and Science*. Vol. 1. Paris: OECD.

—(2010b) *Strong Performers and Successful Reformers in Education. Lessons from PISA for the United States*. Paris: OECD.

Office for Public Management with the Innovation Unit (2008) *Teachers as Innovative Professionals*. London: OPM.

Office for Standards in Education (1993) *Curriculum Organization and Classroom Practice in Primary Schools – A Follow Up Report*. London: DfE.

—(2008) *Using Data, Improving Schools*. London: OFSTED.

Office for Standards in Education, Children's Services and Skills (2009a) *Improving Primary Teachers' Subject Knowledge Across the Curriculum*. London: Ofsted.

—(2009b) *Twenty Outstanding Primary Schools: Excelling Against the Odds*. London: Ofsted.

—(2009c) *Twelve Outstanding Secondary Schools: Excelling Against the Odds*. London: Ofsted.

—(2010) *Learning: Creative Approaches that Raise Standards*. London: Ofsted.

Organisation for Economic Cooperation and Development (2009) *Creating Effective Teaching and Learning Environments: First Results from TALIS*. Paris: OECD.

Palincsar, A. S. and Brown, A. L. (1984) *Reciprocal Teaching of Comprehension Fostering and Monitoring Activities: Cognition and Instruction*. Hillsdale, NJ: Lawrence Erlbaum.

Partnership Management Board (2007) *Planning for the Revised Curriculum*. Belfast: CCEA.

Pedder, D., James, M. and MacBeath, J. (2005) 'How teachers value and practise professional learning', *Research Papers in Education*, 20 (3), 209–43.

Perrenoud, P. (1998) From formative evaluation to a controlled regulation of learning processes:

Towards a wider conceptual field. *Assessment in Education: Principles, Policy & Practice* 5 (1), 85–102.

Perrot, E. (1982) *Effective Teaching: A Practical Guide to Improving Your Teaching.* London: Longman.

Piaget, J. (1961) 'A genetic approach to the psychology of thought', *Journal of Educational Psychology*, 52, 151–61.

Pillings, D. and Pringle, M. K. (1978) *Controversial Issues in Child Development.* London: Paul Elek.

Pollard, A. (1985) *The Social World of the Primary School.* London: Cassell.

—(1987) 'Social differentiation in primary schools', *Cambridge Journal of Education*, 17 (3), 158–61.

—(1996) *The Social World of Children's Learning.* London: Cassell.

—(2003) 'Learning through life'. In Watson, D. and Slowey, M. *Higher Education and the Lifecourse.* London: Continuum.

—(2010) *Professional and Pedagogy: a Contemporary Opportunity.* London: TLRP.

Pollard, A. with Filer, A. (1996) *The Social World of Children's Learning: Case Studies of Pupils from Four to Seven.* London: Cassell.

Pollard, A. and Filer, A. (2000) *The Social World of Pupil Assessment: Processes and Contexts of Primary Schooling.* London: Continuum.

Pollard, A. and Tann, S. (1987) *Reflective Teaching in the Primary School.* London: Cassell.

Ponte, P., Beijard, D. and Ax, J. (2004) 'Don't wait till the cows come home: action research and initial teacher education in three different countries', *Teachers and Teaching*, 10 (6), 591–621.

Pradl, G. (1988) 'Learning listening'. In Lightfoot, M. and Martin, N. (eds), *The Word for Teaching is Learning: Essays for James Britton.* Oxford: Heinemann Education.

Preston, J. and Green, A. (2003) *The Macro-Social Benefits of Education, Training and Skills in Comparative Perspective.* Wider Benefits of Learning Research Report No. 9. London: Institute of Education.

Pring, R. (1976) *Knowledge and Schooling.* London: Open Books.

—(2000) *Philosophy of Educational Research.* London: Continuum.

Putnam, R. (1993) 'Prosperous Community: Social Capital and Public Life', *The American Prospect,* 3 (13), 11–8.

Qualifications and Curriculum Authority (2009) *Research into Marking Quality: Studies to Inform Future Work on National Curriculum Assessment.* London: QCA.

Reay, D. and Wiliam, D. (1999) ' "I'll be a nothing": structure, agency and the construction of identity through assessment', *British Educational Research Journal*, 25 (3), 343–54.

Reynolds, D. (1982) 'The search for effective schools', *School Organization,* 2 (3), 215–37.

Richardson, R. (2009) *Holding Together.* Stoke-on-Trent: Trentham Books.

Robertson, S. (1996) 'Teachers' work, restructuring and postfordism: constructing the new "professionalism"'. In Goodson, I. and Hargreaves, A. (eds) *Teachers' Professional Lives.* London: Falmer Press.

—(1997) 'Restructuring teachers' labour: "troubling" post-fordisms'. In Biddle, B. Good, T. and Goodson, I. (eds), *International Handbook of Teachers and Teaching,* Vol. 1. Dordrecht: Kluwer.

Robinson, K. with Aronica, I. (2009) *The Element: How Finding Your Passion Changes* Robinson, K. with Aronica, I. (2009) *The Element: How Finding Your Passion Changes Everything.* New York: Viking Books.

Rogers, C. R. (1951) *Client Centred Therapy.* Boston: Houghton Mifflin.

Rogoff, B. (2003), *The Cultural Nature of Human Development.* New York: Oxford University Press.

Rose J. (2006) *Independent Review of the Teaching of Early Reading: Final Report.* London: DfES.

Rosenblatt, L. (1978) *The Reader, the Text, the Poem: The Transactional Theory of the Literary Work.* Carbondale, IL: Southern Illinois University Press.

Rosenshine, B. and Furst, N. (1973) 'The use of Direct Observation to Study Teaching'. In Travers, R. W. M. (ed.) *Second Handbook of Research on Teaching*. Chicago: Rand McNally.

Rosenthal, R. and Jacobson, L. (1968) *Pygmalion in the Classroom: Teacher Expectation and Pupils' Intellectual Development*. New York: Holt, Rinehart and Winston.

Rotter, J. B. (1966) 'Generalised expectancies for internal versus external control of reinforcement', *Psychological Monographs*, 80 (1), 609.

Rowe, N., Wilkin, A. and Wilson, R. (2012) *Mapping of Seminal Reports on Good Teaching*. Developing the Education Workforce. Slough: NFER.

Rudduck, J. and Flutter, J (2004) *How To Improve Your School: Giving Pupils a Voice*. London: Continuum.

Rudduck, J., Chaplain, R. and Wallace, G. (1996) *School Improvement: What Can Pupils Tell Us?* London: David Fulton.

Rutter, M. (1987) 'Psychological resilience and protective mechanisms', *American Journal of Orthopsychiatry,* 57, 316–31.

Rutter, M., Maughan, B., Mortimore, P and Ouston, J. (1979) *Fifteen Thousand Hours: Secondary Schools and Their Effects on Children*. London: Open Books.

Sachs, J. (2003) *The Activist Teaching Profession*. Buckingham: Open University Press.

Sahlberg, P. (2011) *Finnish Lessons: What Can the World Learn from Educational Change in Finland*. New York: Teachers College Press.

Sammons, P. Hillman, J. and Mortimore, P. (1995) *Key Characteristics of Effective Shcools: A Review of School Effectiveness Research*. London: Institute of Education.

Sammons, P., Sylva, K., Melhuish, E., Siraj-Blatchford, I., Taggart, B., Barreau, S. and Simon, B. (1994) *The State and Educational Change: Essays in the History of Education and Pedagogy*. London: Lawrence and Wishart.

Scheneider, B. and Stern, E. (2010) 'The cognitive perspective on learning'. In Dumont, H., Istance, D. and Benavides, F. (eds) (2010) *The Nature of Learning: Using Research to Inspire Practice*. Paris: OECD.

Schlossberg, N. K., Waters, E. B. and Goodman, J. (1995) *Counselling Adults in Transition: Linking Practice with Theory*. New York: Springer.

Schneider, B., Keesler, V. and Morlock, L. (2010) 'The effects of family on children's learning and socialisation'. In Dumont, H., Istance, D. and Benavides, F. (eds) *The Nature of Learning: Using Research to Inspire Practice*. Paris: OECD.

Schon, D. (1983) *The Reflective Practitioner: How Professionals Think in Action*. London: Temple Smith.

Schoon, I. and Bynner, J. (2003) 'Risk and resilience in the life course: Implications for interventions and social policies', *Journal of Youth Studies*, 6 (1), 21–31.

Schuller, T., Preston, J., Hammond, C., Brassett-Grundy, A. and Bynner, J. (2004) *The Benefits of Learning: The Impact of Education on Health, Family Life and Social Capital*. Falmer: Routledge.

Scottish Government (2011) *Principles of assessment in Curriculum for Excellence, Building the Curriculum 5*. A Framework for Assessment. Edinburgh: Scottish Government.

Sedden, T. (2001) 'Revisiting inequality and education; a reminder of class; a retrieval of politics; a rethinking of governance', *Melbourne Studies in Education*, 42 (2), 131–44.

Sennett, R. (2008) *The Craftsman*. London: Allen Lane.

Sfard, A. (1998) 'On two metaphors for learning and the dangers of choosing just one', *Educational Researcher*, 27 (2), 4–13.

Sharples, J., Slavin, R., Chambers, B. and Sharp, C. (2011) *Effective Classroom Strategies for Closing the Gap in Educational Achievement for Children and Young People Living in Poverty, Including White Working-Class Boys*. Schools and Communities Research Review 4. London: C4EO.

Shavelson, R. J. (1976) 'Self-concept: Validation of construct interpretations', *Review of Educational Research*, 46 (3), 407–41.

Shore, C., and Wright, S., (2000) 'Coercive Accountability: The rise of audit culture in higher education'. In Strathern, M. (ed.) *Audit Cultures: Anthropological Studies in Accountability, Ethics, and the Academy*. London: Routledge.

Shulman, L. S. (1986) 'Those who understand: knowledge growth in teaching', *Educational Researcher*, February, 9–10.

—(2004) *The Wisdom of Practice – Essays on Teaching, Learning and Learning to Teach*. San Francisco: Jossey Bass.

Siegler, R. S. (1996) *Emerging Minds: The Process of Change in Children's Thinking*. New York: Oxford University Press.

Simon, B. (1981) 'Why no pedagogy in England?'. In Simon, B. and Taylor, W. (eds) *Education in the Eighties: The Central Issues*. London: Batsford.

—(1983) 'The study of education as a university subject'. *Studies in Higher Education*, 8 (1), 1–13.

Siraj-Blatchford, I., Shepherd, D. L., Melhuish, E., Taggart, B., Sammons, P. and Sylva, K. (2011) *Effective Primary Pedagogical Strategies in English and Mathematics in Key Stage 2: a Study of Year 5 Classroom Practice Drawn from the EPPSE 3–16 Longitudinal Study*. Research Report 129. London: DfE.

Skinner, B. F. (1954) 'The science of learning and the art of teaching', *Harvard Educational Review*, 24, 86–97.

Slavin, R. (1987) 'Ability grouping and student achievement in elementary schools: A best evidence synthesis', *Review of educational research,* 57 (3), 293–336.

—(1990) 'Achievement effects of ability grouping in secondary schools: A best evidence synthesis', *Review of Educational Research*, 60, 471–90.

—(2010) 'Cooperative learning: what makes group-work work?'. In Dumont, H., Istance, D. and Benavides, F. (eds) *The Nature of Learning: Using Research to Inspire Practice*. Paris: OECD.

Smith, A. (1998) *Accelerated Learning in Practice*. Stafford: Network Educational Press.

Smith, D. and Tomlinson, S. (1989) *The School Effect: A Study of Multi-racial Comprehensives*. London: Policy Studies Institute.

Spendlove, D. (2009) *Putting Assessment for Learning into Practice*. London: Continuum.

Steegmuller, F. (1982) *The Letters of Gustave Flaubert*. Cambridge, MA: Harvard University Press.

Steer, A. (2005) *Learning Behaviour*. The Report of the Practitioners' Group on School Behaviour and Discipline. London: DfES.

—(2009) *Learning Behaviour: Lessons Learned*. A Review of Behaviour Standards and Practices in Our Schools. London: DCSF.

Stenhouse, L. (1975) *An Introduction to Curriculum Research and Development*. Oxford: Heinemann.

Sternberg, R. J. and Horvath, J. A. (1995) 'A prototype view of expert teaching', *Educational Researcher,* 24 (6), 9–17.

Stobart, G. (2008) *Testing Times: The Uses and Abuses of Assessment*. London: Routledge.

Stones, E. (1979) *Psychopedagogy: Psychological Theory and the Practice of Teaching*. London: Methuen.

Stronach, I. et al. (2002) 'Towards an uncertain politics of professionalism: teacher and nurse identities in flux', *Journal of Education Policy*, 27 (2), 109–38.

Sturman, L. (2012) 'Making best use of international comparison data', *Research Intelligence*, 119, Autumn/Winter, 16–7.

Swaffield, S. (2011) 'Getting to the heart of authentic Assessment for Learning', *Assessment in Education: Principles, Policy and Practice,* 18 (4), 441–3

Swann, M., Peacock, A., Hart, S. and Drummond, M. J. (2012) *Creating Learning Without Limits*. Maidenhead: Open University Press.

Teaching and Learning in 2020 Review Group (2006) *2020 Vision.* Nottingham: DfES.

Tharp, R. and Gallimore, R. (1988) *Rousing Minds to Life: Teaching, Learning and Schooling in Social Context.* New York: Cambridge University Press.

The Royal Society (2011) *Brain Waves Module 2: Neuroscience: implications for education and lifelong learning.* Report of a Working Group. London: The Royal Society.

Thomas, A. and Pattison, J. (2007) *How Children Learn at Home* London: Continuum.

Thomas, G. and Davis, P. (1997) 'Special needs: objective reality or personal construction? Judging reading difficulty after the Code', *Educational Research,* 39 (3), 263–70.

Thomas, G. and Loxley, A. (2007) *Deconstructing Special Education and Constructing Inclusion.* Maidenhead: Open University Press.

Thomas, L. (2010) *Engaging the Local: The RSA Area Based Curriculum.* London: Royal Society of Arts.

Thompson, M., and Wiliam, D., 2007. Tight but loose: A conceptual framework for scaling up school reforms. Paper presented at a Symposium entitled 'Tight but loose: Scaling up teacher professional development in diverse contexts' at the annual conference of the American Educational Research Association, April 9–11, in Chicago, IL.

Thorne, B. (1993) *Gender Play: Girls and Boys in School.* Buckingham, Open University Press.

Timperley, H., Wilson, A., Barrar H. and Fung, I. (2007) *Teacher Professional Learning and Development: Best Evidence Synthesis Iteration.* Wellington. New Zealand: Ministry of Education.

Tizard, B., Blatchford, D., Burke, J., Farquhar, C. and Plewis, I. (1988) *Young Children at School in the Inner City.* Hove: Lawrence Erlbaum.

Tomasello, M., Carpenter, M., Call, J., Behne, T. and Moll, H. (2005) 'Understanding and sharing of intentions: the origins of cultural cognition', *Behavioural and Brain Sciences*, 2 (8), 675–735.

Turner-Bisset, R. (2000) 'Reconstructing the primary curriculum: integration revisited', *Education 3–13*, 28 (1), 3–8

Turney, A. H. (1931) 'The status of ability grouping', *Educational Administration and Supervision,* 17 (2), 110–27.

Twiselton. S. (2006) 'The problem with English: the exploration and development of student teachers' English subject knowledge in primary classrooms', *Literacy,* 40 (2), 88–96.

Unwin, L (2009) *Sensuality, Sustainability and Social Justice: Vocational Education in Changing Times.* Professorial Inaugural Lecture, Institute of Education, University of London

—(2004) 'Growing beans with Thoreau: rescuing skills and vocational education from the UK's deficit approach', *Oxford Review of Education*, 30 (1), 147–60.

Van Manen, M. (1991) *The Tact of Teaching.* Alberta: The Althouse Press.

—(1995) 'On the epistemology of reflective practice', *Teachers and Teaching: Theory and Practice*, 1 (1) 33–50.

—(1999) 'The language of pedagogy and the primacy of student experience'. In Louhjran, J. (ed.) *Researching Teaching: Methodologies and Practices for Understanding Pedagogy.* London: Falmer Press.

Vincent, C. (2001) 'Parental agency and social class', *Journal of Education Policy*, 16 (4), 347–64.

Vygotsky, L. S. (1978) *Mind in Society: the Development of Higher Mental Processes.* Cambridge, MA: Harvard University Press.

Wang, M. C. (1983) 'Development and consequences of students' sense of personal control'. In Levine, J. M. and Wang, M. C. (eds) *Teacher and Student Perceptions: Implications for Learning.* Hillsdale, NJ: Erlbaum Associates.

Warhurst, C., Grugulis, I. and Keep, E. (2004) (eds) *The Skills That Matter.* Basingstoke: Palgrave.

Watkins, C. (2011) *Managing Classroom Behaviour.* London: ATL.

Watkins, C. and Mortimore, P. (1999) 'Pedagogy: what do we know?'. In Mortimore, P. (ed.) *Pedagogy and its Impact on Learning.* London: Paul Chapman Publishing.

Wells, G. (2001), *Action, Talk, and Text: Learning and Teaching Through Inquiry*. New York: Teachers College Press.

—(2008) 'Dialogue, inquiry and the construction of learning communities'. In Linguard, B., Nixon, J. and Ranson, S. (eds) *Transforming Learning in Schools and Communities*. London: Continuum.

Welsh Assembly Government (2008) *Skills Framework for 3 to 19–year-olds in Wales*. Cardiff: Welsh Assembly Government.

Wenger, E. (1998) *Communities of Practice: Learning, Meaning, and Identity*. Cambridge: Cambridge University Press.

Wertsch, J. V. (1979) 'From social interaction to higher psychological process; a clarification and application of Vygotsky's theory', *Human Cognition,* 2 (1), 15–18.

Whipple, G. M. (1919) *Classes for Gifted Children*. Bloomington, IL: Public School Publishing.

White, J. (2007) *What Schools Are For and Why?* Impact Paper. London: Philosophy of Education Society of Great Britain.

Wiliam, D. (2007) *Assessment for Learning: Why, What and How?* Inaugural lecture, Institute of Education, University of London.

—(2008) Keeping learning on track: Formative assessment and the regulation of learning. In, *Second Handbook of Mathematics Teaching and Learning*, ed. F. K. Lester Jr., Greenwich, CT: Information Age.

—(2010) 'The role of formative assessment in effective learning environments'. In Dumont, H., Istance, D. and Benavides, F. (eds) (2010) *The Nature of Learning: Using Research to Inspire Practice*. Paris: OECD

Wilkinson, R. (1996). *Unhealthy societies: The Afflictions of Inequality*. London: Routledge.

Wilkinson, R. and Pickett, K. (2009) *The Sprit Level: Why More Equal Societies Almost Always Do Better*. London: Allen Lane.

Williams, F. (1992) 'Somewhere over the rainbow: universality and diversity in social policy'. In N. Manning and R. Page (eds) *Social Policy Review*. Canterbury: Social Policy Association.

Williamson, S. (2006) *A New Shape for Schooling: Deep Support*. London: Specialist Schools and Academies Trust.

Willis, P. (1977) *Learning to Labour*. New York: Columbia University Press.

Wilson, J. (2000) *Key Issues in Education and Teaching*. Cassell: London.

Wolf, A. (2002) *Does Education Matter?* London: Penguin.

Wood, D. J., Bruner, J. S. and Ross, G. (1976) 'The role of tutoring in problem solving', *Journal of Child Psychology and Psychiatry,* 17 (2), 89–100.

Woods, P., Jeffrey, B., Troman, G. and Boyle, M. (1997) *Restructuring Schools, Reconstructing Teachers*. Maidenhead: Open University Press.

Wortham, S. (2006) *Learning Identity: The Joint Emergence of Social Identification and Academic Learning*. Cambridge: Cambridge University Press.

Wragg, E. (1997) *The Cubic Curriculum*. Routledge: London.

Young, M. (1971) *Knowledge and Control: New Directions for the Sociology of Education*. London: Collier Macmillan.

—(1998) *The Curriculum of the Future*. London: Falmer.

—(2007) *Bringing Knowledge Back In: From Social Constructivism to Social Realism in the Sociology of Education*. London: Routledge.

Zeichner, K. (2009) *Teacher Education and the Struggle for Social Justice*. London, Routledge.

Zeichner, K. and Gore, J. M. (1990) 'Teacher socialization'. In Houston, W. R. (ed.) *Handbook of Research on Teacher Education*. New York: Macmillan.

Permissions

We are grateful to the authors and publishers listed below for permission to reproduce the following extracts:

1.1 'Being a teacher in times of change', by Qing Gu, edited from *Teacher Development: Knowledge and Context* (2007), reproduced by permission of Bloomsbury Publishing.

1.2 'Being a learner through years of schooling', by Andrew Pollard and Ann Filer, edited from *The Social World of Children's Learning* (1997), reproduced by permission of Bloomsbury Publishing.

1.3 'How pupils want to learn', by Jean Rudduck and Julia Flutter, edited from *How to Improve Your School: Giving Pupils a Voice* (2004), reproduced by permission of Julia Flutter and Bloomsbury Publishing.

1.4 'Learning without limits', by Mandy Swann, Alison Peacock, Susan Hart and Mary Jane Drummond, edited from *Creating Learning Without Limits* (2012), reproduced by permission of Mandy Swann and McGraw Hill.

1.5 'Assumptions about children and young people', by Phil Jones, edited from *Rethinking Childhood: Attitudes in Contemporary Society* (2009), reproduced by permission of Bloomsbury Publishing.

1.6 'Learning through life', by Leon Feinstein, John Vorhaus and Ricado Sabates, edited from *Learning Through Life: Future Challenges*, Foresight Mental Capital and Wellbeing Project (2008), Crown copyright, reproduced under Open Government Licence.

2.1 'The science of learning and the art of teaching', by Burrhus Skinner, edited from 'The science of learning and the art of teaching', *Harvard Education Review,* 24, (1954), reproduced by permission of Harvard Education Review.

2.2 'The genetic approach to the psychology of thought', by Jean Piaget, edited from 'A genetic approach to the psychology of thought', *British Journal of Educational Psychology, Vol. 52* (1961).

2.3 'Mind in society and the ZPD', by Lev Vygotsky, edited from *Mind in Society: The Development of Higher Psychological Processes* (1978), reproduced by permission of Harvard University Press.

2.4 'Learning, development and schooling', by Gordon Wells, edited from 'Dialogue, inquiry and the construction of learning communities', in Linguard, B., Nixon, J. and Ranson, S. (eds) *Transforming Learning in Schools and Communities* (2008), reproduced by permission of Bloomsbury Publishing.

2.5 'Neuroscience and education', edited from *Neuroscience: Implications for Education and Lifelong Learning, Brain Waves Module 2,* Report of a Working Group (2011), reproduced by permission of Working Group members and of The Royal Society.

2.6 'Motivational processes affecting learning', by Carol Dweck, edited from 'Motivational processes affecting learning', *American Psychologist, October* (1986), reproduced by permission of American Psychological Association.

2.7 'Why thinking should be taught', by Robert Fisher, edited from *Teaching Thinking*.

Philosophical Enquiry in the Classroom (2008), reproduced by permission of Robert Fisher and Bloomsbury Publishing.

2.8   'Learning how to learn', by Mary James, edited from *Only Connect! Improving Teaching and Learning in Schools*. A Professorial Inaugural Lecture (2008), reproduced by permission of Mary James and IOE Press.

2.9   'Learning and the development of resilience', by Guy Claxton, edited from *Wise Up: The Challenge of Lifelong Learning* (1999), reproduced by permission of Guy Claxton and Bloomsbury Publishing.

2.10   'Informal Learning', by Alan Thomas and Harriet Pattison, edited from *How Children Learn at Home* (2007), reproduced by permission of Bloomsbury Publishing.

3.1   'Thinking and reflective experience', by John Dewey, edited from *How We Think: A Restatement of the Relation of Reflective Thinking to the Educative Process* (1933), and *Democracy and Education* (1916) published by Henry Regnery and Macmillan.

3.2   'Reflection-in-action', by Donald Schon, edited from The *Reflective Practitioner: How Professionals Think in Action* (1983), reproduced by permission of Perseus Books.

3.3   'The teacher as researcher', by Lawrence Stenhouse, edited from *An Introduction to Curriculum Research and Development* (1975), reproduced by permission of Heinemann.

3.4   'Action research and the development of practice', by Richard Pring, edited from *The Philosophy of Educational Research* (2004), reproduced by permission of Bloomsbury Publishing.

3.5   'Competence and the complexities of teaching', by James Calderhead, edited from 'Can the complexities of teaching be accounted for in terms of competences? Contrasting views of professional practice from research and policy', *mimeo produced for an ESRC symposium on teacher competence* (1994), reproduced by permission of James Calderhead.

3.6   'Practical judgement and evidence-informed practice', by Ruth Heilbronn, edited from 'The nature of practice-based knowledge and understanding', in Heilbronn, R. and Yandell, J. (eds) *Critical Practice in Teacher Education: A Study of Professional Learning* (2010), reproduced by permission of Ruth Heilbronn and IOE Press.

3.7   'Learning in communities of practice', by Heather Hodkinson and Phil Hodkinson, edited from ' (2002), *Rescuing communities of practice from accusations of idealism: a case study of workplace learning for secondary school teachers in England,* reproduced by permission of the Teaching and Learning Research Programme.

4.1   'Brain, mind, experinece and school: a US review', by John Bransford, Ann Brown and Rodney Cocking, edited from *How People Learn: Brain, Mind, Experience, and School* (1999), reproduced by permission of National Academies Press.

4.2   'A tale of two pedagogies: teaching and learning in Singapore', by David Hogan, Phillip Towndrow, Dennis Kwek, Ridzuan Rahim, Melvin Chan and Serena Luo, commissioned for this volume (2013) and reproduced by permission of David Hogan.

4.3   'What the world can learn from educational change in Finland', by Pasi Sahlberg, edited from *Finnish Lessons: What the World Can Learn from Educational Change in Finland?* (2012), reproduced by permission of Teachers' College Press.

4.4   'The nature of learning: an OECD stocktake', by Hanna Dumont, David Istance and Francisco Benavides, edited from *The Nature of Learning. Using Research to Inspire Practice* (2011), reproduced by permission of OECD.

4.5   'Good teaching': a UK review', by Naomi Rowe, Anne Wilkin and Rebekah Wilson, edited from *Mapping of Seminal Reports on Good Teaching* (2012), reproduced by permission of the National Foundation for Educational Research.

4.6   'Visible learning: a global synthesis', by John Hattie, edited from *Visible Learning. A Synthesis of Meta-Analyses Relating to Achievement* (2009), reproduced by permission of Taylor & Francis.

5.1   'The sociological imagination', by C. Wright Mills, edited from *The Sociological Imagination* (1959), reproduced by permission of Oxford University Press.

5.2   'Regimes of social cohesion', by Andy Green and Jan Janmaat, edited from *Education, Opportunity and Social Cohesion.* Centre for Learning and Life Chances in Knowledge Economies and Societies (2009), reproduced by permission of Andy Green, Jan Janmaat and LLAKES.

5.3   'Schooling, social class and privilege', by Stephen Ball, edited from *The More Things Change: Educational Research, Social Class and 'Interlocking' Inequalities.* Professorial Inaugural Lecture (2004), reproduced by permission of Stephen Ball and IOE Press.

5.4   'Disadvantage and low attainment', by Department for Children, Schools and Families, edited from *Breaking the Link between Disadvantage and Low Attainment* (2009), Crown copyright, reproduced under Open Government Licence.

5.5   'Accountability in teaching', by the General Teaching Council for England, *Teaching Quality: Policy Papers* (2011), Crown copyright, reproduced under Open Government Licence.

6.1   'Life in classrooms', by Philip Jackson, edited from *Life in Classrooms* (1968) reproduced by permission of Teachers College, Columbia University.

6.2   'We feel, therefore we learn', by Mary Helen Immordino-Yang and Antonio Damasio, edited from 'We feel, therefore we learn'. The relevance of affective social neuroscience to education, *Mind, Brain, and Education.* 1 (1) (2007), reproduced by permission of the American Educational Research Association.

6.3   'Teachers, pupils and the working consensus', by Andrew Pollard, edited from *The Social World of the Primary School* (1985), reproduced by permission of Andrew Pollard and Bloomsbury Publishing.

6.4   'Classroom rules, routines and rituals', by Roland Chaplain, edited from *Teaching Without Disruption in the Primary School* (2003), reproduced by permission of Roland Chaplain and Taylor & Francis.

6.5   'Teacher expectations and pupil achievement', by Caroline Gipps and Barbara MacGilchrist, edited from 'Primary school learners', in Mortimore, P. (ed.) *Understanding Pedagogy and its Impact on Learning* (1999), reproduced by permission of SAGE Publications.

6.6   'What is self-esteem?', by Dennis Lawrence, edited from *Enhancing Self-Esteem in the Classroom* (1987), reproduced by permission of SAGE Publications.

7.1   'Learning the classroom environment', by Walter Doyle, edited from 'Learning the classroom environment: an ecological analysis', *Journal of Teacher Education,* 28 (6) 51–5 (1977), reproduced by permission of Corwin Press.

7.2   'The big picture on behaviour', by Chris Watkins, edited from *Pupil Behaviour: Advice, Guidance and Protection* (2011), reproduced by permission of Chris Watkins and the Association of Teachers and Lecturers.

7.3   'Virtues of great teachers: justice, courage, patience, wisdom and compassion', by Tom Bennett, edited from *Teacher: Mastering the Art and Craft of Teaching* (2012), reproduced by permission of Bloomsbury Publishing.

7.4   'Ten strategies for managing behaviour', by Sue Cowley, edited from *Getting the Buggars to Behave* (2010), reproduced by permission of Bloomsbury Publishing.

7.5   'Discipline and group management in classrooms', by Jacob Kounin, edited from *Discipline and Group Management in Classrooms* (1970).

7.6   'Positive teaching in the classroom', by Frank Merrett and Kevin Wheldall, edited from *Effective Classroom Behaviour Management* (1990), reproduced by permission of SAGE Publications.

8.1   'Environments as contexts of development', by Urie Bronfenbrenner, edited from 'Ecological models of human development', *International Encyclopedia of Education,* Vol. 3 (1993).

8.2 'Designs for learning environments', by John Bransford, Ann Brown and Rodney Cocking, edited from *How People Learn. Brain, Mind, Experience and School* (1999), reproduced by permission of National Academies Press.

8.3 'Classroom layout, resources and display', by David Clegg and Shirley Billington, edited from *The Effective Primary Classroom: Management and Organisation of Teaching and Learning* (1994), reproduced by permission of David Clegg and Taylor & Francis.

8.4 'Instructional time – and where it goes', by David Berliner, edited from Ben-Peretz, M. and Bromme, R. (eds), *The Nature of Time in Schools* (1990), reproduced by permission of Teachers' College Press.

8.5 'Environment, affordance and new technology', by Anthony Edwards, edited from *New Technology and Education* (2012), reproduced by permission of Bloomsbury Publishing.

8.6 'The profound shift of digital literacies', by Guther Kress, in Gillen, J. and Barton, D. (eds) *Digital Literacies* (2010), reproduced by permission on Gunter Kress and TLRP TEL.

8.7 'Direct and interactive whole-class instruction', by Daniel Muijs and David Reynolds, edited from *Effective Teaching: Evidence and Practice* (2010), reproduced by permission of Daniel Muijs and SAGE Publications.

9.1 'Designing the school curriculum', by Brian Male and Mick Waters, edited from *The Secondary Curriculum Design Handbook* (2012), reproduced by permission of Bloomsbury Publishing.

9.2 'Powerful knowledge', by Michael Young, edited from *Powerful Knowledge in Education* (2013), commissioned for this volume and reproduced by permission of Michael Young.

9.3 'Teaching a subject', by John Wilson, edited from 'Key Issues in Education and Teaching' (2000), reproduced by permission of Bloomsbury Publishing.

9.4 'Aspects of children's learning', by Central Advisory Committee on Education, edited from *Children and their Primary Schools* (1965), Plowden Report, Crown copyright, reproduced under Open Government Licence.

9.5 'The spiral curriculum', by Jerome Bruner, edited from 'The meaning of educational reform', *Journal of the National Association of Montesori Teachers* (1991), reproduced by permission of National Association of Montessori Teachers.

9.6 'Vocational education matters', by Lorna Unwin, edited from *Sensuality, Sustainability and Social Justice Vocational Education in Changing Times* (2009), reproduced by permission of Lorna Unwin and IOE Press.

9.7 'A perspective on teacher knowledge', by Lee Shulman, edited from 'Those who understand: knowledge growth in teaching', *Educational Researcher,* February (1986), reproduced by permission of the American Educational Research Association.

10.1 'Characteristics of the curriculum', by Her Majesty's Inspectors, edited from *The Curriculum from 5 to 16*, Curriculum Matters 2, An HMI Series (1985), Crown copyright, reproduced under Open Government Licence.

10.2 'Implementing a Revised Curriculum', by the Partnership Management Board of Northern Ireland, edited from *Planning for the Revised Curriculum* (2007), Crown copyright, reproduced under Open Government Licence.

10.3 'Constructing an integrated curriculum', by Rosie Turner-Bissett, edited from 'Reconstructing the primary curriculum', *Education 3–13: International Journal of Primary, Elementary and Early Years Education*, 28 (1) (2000), reproduced by permission of Taylor & Francis.

10.4 'An area-based curriculum', by Louise Thomas, edited from *The RSA Area Based Curriculum: Engaging the Local* (2010), reproduced by permission of Louise Thomas and the Royal Society of Arts.

10.5 'A skills framework for 3 to 19-year-olds', by the Welsh Assembly Government, edited from *Skills Framework for 3 to 19–year-olds in Wales* (2008), Crown copyright, reproduced under Open Government Licence.

10.6   'Progression and differentiation', by Anthony Haynes, edited from *The Complete Guide to Lesson Planning and Preparation* (2010), reproduced by permission of Anthony Haynes and Bloomsbury Publishing.

10.7   'Personalised pedagogies for the future', by the Teaching and Learning in 2020 Review Group, edited from *2020 Vision* (2006), Crown copyright, reproduced under Open Government Licence.

11.1   'Folk pedagogy', by Jerome Bruner, edited from *The Culture of Education* (1996), reproduced by permission of Harvard University Press.

11.2   'What is pedagogy and why is it important?', by the General Teaching Council for England, edited from *Professionalism and Pedagogy: A Contemporary Opportunity* (2010), a TLRP Commentary, reproduced by permission of the Teaching and Learning Research Programme.

11.3   'Why no pedagogy in England?', by Brian Simon, edited from 'Why no pedagogy in England?' in B. Simon and W. Taylor (eds) *Education in the Eighties: The Central Issues* (1981), reproduced by permission of Anova Books.

11.4   'Student experiences of teachers and of pedagogy', by Max van Manen, edited from 'The language of pedagogy and the primacy of student experience', in J. Loughran (ed.) *Researching Teaching: Methodologies and practices for understanding pedagogy* (1999), reproduced by permission of Taylor & Francis.

11.5   'Teaching as the assistance of performance', by Roland Tharp and Ronald Gallimore, edited from *Rousing Minds to Life: Teaching, Learning and Schooling in Social Context* (1988), reproduced by permission of Cambridge University Press.

11.6   'Talking and thinking together', by Neil Mercer and Karen Littleton, edited from 'Dialogue and the development of children's thinking: a socio-cultural approach (2007), reproduced by permission of Neil Mercer and Taylor & Francis.

12.1   'Engaging students, through taking them seriously', by Martin Nystrand, edited from *Opening Dialogue: Understanding the Dynamics of Language and Learning in the English Classroom* (1997), reproduced by permission of Teachers' College Press.

12.2   'Using questions in classroom discussion', by Elizabeth Perrot, edited from *Effective teaching: A Practical Guide to Improving Your Teaching* (1982), reproduced by permission of Pearson.

12.3   'The nature of pedagogic repertoire', by Robin Alexander, edited from *Essays on Pedagogy* (2008), reproduced by permission of Robin Alexander and Taylor & Francis.

12.4   'Why is reading so important?', by Colin Harrison, edited from 'Understanding Reading Development' (2004), reproduced by permission of Colin Harrison and SAGE Publications.

12.5   'The development of literacy through reading, listening, discussing and writing', by Myra Barrs and Valerie Cork, edited from *The Reader in the Writer: The link between the study of literature and writing development at Key Stage 2* (2001), reproduced by permission of Centre for Language in Primary Education.

12.6   'From "knowledge telling" to "knowledge transforming"', by Carl Bereiter and Marlene Scardamalia, edited from *The Psychology of Written Composition* (1987), reproduced by permission of Taylor & Francis US.

12.7   'Language, culture and story in the bilingual school', by Adrian Blackledge, edited from *Teaching Bilingual Children* (1994), reproduced by permission of IOE Press.

13.1   'Assessment purposes and principles', by Wynne Harlen, Caroline Gipps, Patricia Broadfoot and Desmond Nuttall, edited from 'Assessment and the improvement of education', *Curriculum Journal, Vol 3., No. 3.* (1992), reproduced by permission of Wynne Harlen and Taylor & Francis.

13.2   'Assessment for learning', by Assessment Reform Group, edited from 'Assessment for Learning: Beyond the Black Box' (1999), reproduced by permission of the Assessment Reform Group.

13.3 'Feedback and learning', by David Spendlove, edited from *Putting Assessment for Learning into Practice* (2009), reproduced by permission of Bloomsbury Publishing.

13.4 'Pupil self-assessment', by Yolande Muschamp, edited from *Practical Issues in Primary Education*, No. 9, (1991), Bristol, National Primary Centre (South West) reproduced by permission of Yolande Muschamp and NPC SW.

13.5 'Authentic assessment for learning', by Sue Swaffield, edited from *'Assessment in Education: Principles, Policy and Practice'*, 18 (4) (2011), reproduced by permission of Sue Swaffield and Taylor & Francis.

13.6 'Creating learner identities through assessment', by Gordon Stobart, edited from *Testing Times: The Uses and Abuses of Assessment* (2008), reproduced by permission of Gordon Stobart and Taylor & Francis.

14.1 'Assessment: Why, who, what, when and how?', by Patricia Broadfoot, edited from *An Introduction to Assessment* (2007), reproduced by permission of Patricia Broadfoot and Bloomsbury Publishing.

14.2 'Principles of assessment in the Curriculum for Excellence', by The Scottish Government, edited from *Principles of assessment in Curriculum for Excellence, Building the Curriculum 5. A Framework for Assessment* (2011), Crown copyright, reproduced under Open Government Licence.

14.3 'Target setting in schools', by Graham Butt, edited from *Making Assessment Matter* (2011), reproduced by permission of Bloomsbury Publishing.

14.4 'How schools can use performance data', by Ofsted, edited from *Using Data, Improving Schools* (2008), Crown copyright, reproduced under Open Government Licence.

14.5 'The reliability, validity and impact of assessment', by Warwick Mansell, Mary James and the Assessment Reform Group, edited from *Assessment in schools. Fit for purpose?* (2008), A TLRP Commentary, reproduced by permission of Warwick Mansell, Mary James, ARG and the Teaching and Learning Research Programme.

14.6 'Making best use of international comparison', by Linda Sturman, edited from 'Making best use of international comparison data', *Research Intelligence,* 119, Autumn/Winter (2012), reproduced by permission of Linda Sturman, NFER and the British Educational Research Association.

14.7 'The myth of objective assessment', by Ann Filer and Andrew Pollard, edited from *The Social World of Pupil Assessment* (2000), reproduced by permission of Ann Filer, Andrew Pollard and Bloomsbury Publishing.

15.1 'Principles for equality and diversity', by Robin Richardson, edited from *Holding Together* (2009), reproduced by permission of IOE Press.

15.2 'Social differentiation in schools', by Andrew Pollard, edited from 'Social differentiation in primary schools', *Cambridge Journal of Education*, 17 (3) (1987), reproduced by permission of Andrew Pollard and Taylor & Francis.

15.3 'Difference or diversity?', by Gary Thomas and Andrew Loxley, edited from *Deconstructing Special Education and Constructing Inclusion* (2007), reproduced by permission of Gary Thomas, Andrew Loxley and McGraw Hill.

15.4 'Ability grouping in schools', by Sue Hallam, edited from *Ability Grouping in Schools* (2002), reproduced by permission of Sue Hallam and IOE Press.

15.5 'How to promote cooperative classroom relationships', by Barrie Thorne, edited from *Gender Play: Girls and Boys in School* (1993), reprinted by permission of Rutgers University Press.

15.6 'Learning in inclusive classrooms', by Ruth Kershner, edited from Hick, P., Kershner, R. and Farrell, P. (eds) *Psychology for Inclusive Education: New Directions in Theory and Practice* (2009), reproduced by permission of Ruth Kershner and Taylor & Francis.

16.1 'Contemporary change and professional development', by Pat Collarbone, edited from

Creating Tomorrow: Planning, Developing and Sustaining Change in Public Services (2009), reproduced by permission of Bloomsbury Publishing.

16.2   'Contemporary change and professional inertia', by Andy Hargreaves, edited from *The Persistence of Presentism and the Struggle for Lasting Improvement* (2008), Inaugural Professorial Lecture, reproduced by permission of Andy Hargreaves and IOE Press.

16.3   'The development of expertise', by Tony Eaude, edited from *How do Expert Primary Classteachers Really Work?* (2012), reproduced by permission of Tony Eaude and Critical Publishing.

16.4   'Improving teacher expertise', by Dylan Wiliam, edited from *Assessment for Learning: Why, What and How?* (2009), Inaugural Professorial Lecture, Institute of Education, University of London, reproduced by permission of Dylan Wiliam and IOE Press.

16.5   'Mind frames for visible learning', by John Hattie, edited from *Visible Learning for Teachers* (2012), reproduced by permission of Taylor & Francis.

16.6   'Teacher professional learning and development', by Helen Timperley, Aaron Wilson, Heather Barrar and Irene Fung, edited from *Teacher Professional Learning and Development*, Best Evidence Synthesis (2007), Crown copyright, reproduced by permission of the New Zealand Ministry of Education.

17.1   'Thinking about education systems', by Margaret Archer, edited from *The Social Origins of Educational Systems* (1979), reproduced by permission of SAGE Publications.

17.2   'Teacher education and professionalism', by Ian Menter, Moira Hulme, Dely Eliot and Jon Lewin, edited from *Teacher Education in the 21st Century* (2010), Crown copyright, reproduced with permission of Ian Menter and under Open Government Licence.

17.3   'Teaching: the reflective profession', by General Teaching Council for Northern Ireland, edited from *Teaching: The Reflective Profession* (2007), Crown copyright, reproduced with permission of GTC NI and under Open Government Licence.

17.4   'Combining research and practice in teaching', by Pasi Sahlberg, John Furlong and Pamela Munn, edited from *Report of the International Review Panel on the Structure of Initial Teacher Education Provision in Ireland* (2012). Review conducted on behalf of the Department of Education and Skills and reproduced under licence by permission of the Government of Ireland.

17.5   'The imaginative professional', by Sally Power, edited from 'The imaginative professional', in Cunningham, B. (ed.) *Exploring Professionalism* (2008), reproduced by permission of Sally Power and IOE Press.

17.6   'Memorandum on teaching and learning about human rights in schools', by Council of Europe, edited from 'Memorandum on teaching and learning about human rights in schools', *Committee of Ministers of the Council of Europe* (1985), *Appendix to Recommendation No. R (85) 7, Memorandum on teaching and learning about human rights in schools, Directorate of Human Rights, Council of Europe, Strasbourg* (1985), reproduced by permission of the Council of Europe.

17.7   'Three contexts of policy making', by Richard Bowe and Stephen Ball, with Ann Gold, edited from *Reforming Education and Changing Schools.* (1992), reproduced by permission of Taylor & Francis.

Index

This index categorises reflective schools, classrooms, teachers, pupils, teaching and learning, and related concepts under different headings; it covers Chapters 1–17 but not personal names. An 'f' after a page number indicates a figure.

The reflective teaching series

This book is one of the *Reflective Teaching Series* – applying principles of reflective practice in early years, schools, further, higher and adult education.

The *Reflective Teaching Series* supports improvements in outcomes for learners through:

- The development of high quality, principled expertise in teaching;
- Partnership between those involved in the academic study and the practice of education.

With adaptions for early years, schools, further, higher and adult education, the series endorses the aspirations of the Teaching Councils of Scotland, Wales, Northern Ireland and the Republic of Ireland. As they put it:

> We view teaching as a complex profession which requires high standards of competence, professional skills and commitment. We consider that high quality teaching is necessary to deliver high standards of learning for our students. We believe that quality teaching is achieved when teachers commit themselves to lifelong learning and ongoing reflection on their professional practice; when they have excellent knowledge of the curriculum which they are expected to teach; when they have deep and detailed understanding of how pupils learn; and when they have the confidence to apply and vary their pedagogical skills to meet the needs of learners in different and sometimes challenging contexts.
>
> We require that teachers are suitably qualified, both academically and professionally, and that they have appropriate values and a commitment to maintaining and improving their professional practice as they progress throughout their careers. *(Joint Statement, April 2013)*

The series is supported by a website, **reflectiveteaching.co.uk**. For each book, this site is being developed to offer a range of resources including reflective activities, research briefings, advice on further reading and additional chapters. The site also offers generic resources such as a compendium of educational terms, links to other useful websites, and a conceptual framework for 'Deepening Expertise'. The latter will also showcase some of the UK's best educational research.

The series is coordinated through meetings of the volume and series editors: Paul Ashwin, Jennifer Colwell, Maggie Gregson, Yvonne Hillier, Amy Pollard and Andrew Pollard. Each volume has an editorial team of contributors whose collective expertise and experience enable research and practice to be reviewed and applied in relation to early years, school, further, adult, vocational and higher education.

The Pollard Partnership

The series is the first product of the Pollard Partnership, a collaboration between Andrew and Amy Pollard to enable the long-term development of this series and to maximise the beneficial use of research and evidence on public life, policymaking and professional practice.

In the long term, we may undertake activities in a range of policy areas. This initiative focuses on education – building on Andrew's longstanding publishing record, research and professional engagement. In this arena, we seek to support teacher professionals in deepening their expertise and in developing policy contexts in which evidence-informed judgement can flourish.

In relation to education and when appropriate, Amy will act as custodian of Andrew's literary legacy. As Andrew's daughter, she is in a unique position to safeguard the value commitment of his work – and will engage with education professionals and associations as appropriate to ensure that future outputs, including **reflectiveteaching.co.uk**, are under-pinned by the necessary expertise.

Amy Pollard specialises in the application of social science to policy and practice and has worked on education projects at Demos (demos.co.uk), the Overseas Development Institute (odi.org.uk) and Anthropology Matters (anthropologymatters.com). She is currently Deputy Director of Involve (involve.org.uk), the public engagement charity. With a PhD in social anthropology, she has worked in charities, think tanks, government and international agencies for over ten years. She was co-founder and chair of Beyond 2015 (beyond2015.org), a major civil society campaign bringing together over 400 civil society groups from more than 80 countries.

Andrew Pollard taught in schools for ten years before entering teacher education and developing a career in educational research. His research interests include learner perspectives, teaching-learning processes, the role of curriculum, pedagogy and assessment, and the development of evidence-informed classroom practice. He has been a Professor of Education at the universities of Bristol, Cambridge, London and West of England. He was Director of the ESRC Teaching and Learning Research Programme (tlrp.org), the UK Strategic Forum for Research in Education (sfre.ac.uk) and of ESCalate (escalate.ac.uk), the Education Subject Centre of the UK's Higher Education Academy. He is Chairman of William Pollard & Co. Ltd. (pollardsprint.co.uk), a print and communications company, founded in 1781.